Mobil
Travel Guide®

Coastal
Southeast
2007

Georgia

North Carolina

South Carolina

ExxonMobil
Travel Publications

Acknowledgements

We gratefully acknowledge the help of our representatives for their efficient and perceptive inspections of the lodging and dining establishments listed; the establishments' proprietors for their cooperation in showing their facilities and providing information about them; and the many users of previous editions who have taken the time to share their experiences. Mobil Travel Guide is also grateful to all the talented writers who contributed entries to this book.

www.mobiltravelguide.com

Front cover photo: Cape Hatteras Lighthouse by Shutterstock, Charleston, South Carolina by SuperStock, Skyline of Atlanta by Digital Vision

ISBN: 0-7627-4253-4 or 978-0-7627-4253-0

ISSN: 1550-1930

Manufactured in the United States of America.

10 9 8 7 6 5 4 3 2 1

Contents

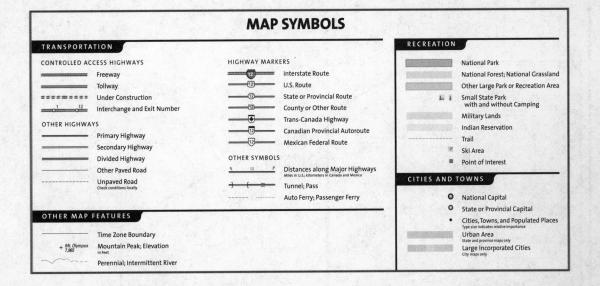

MAP SYMBOLS

TRANSPORTATION

CONTROLLED ACCESS HIGHWAYS

Freeway
Tollway
Under Construction
Interchange and Exit Number

OTHER HIGHWAYS

Primary Highway
Secondary Highway
Divided Highway
Other Paved Road
Unpaved Road
Check conditions locally

HIGHWAY MARKERS

Interstate Route
U.S. Route
State or Provincial Route
County or Other Route
Trans-Canada Highway
Canadian Provincial Autoroute
Mexican Federal Route

OTHER SYMBOLS

Distances along Major Highways
Miles in U.S.; kilometers in Canada and Mexico
Tunnel; Pass
Auto Ferry; Passenger Ferry

OTHER MAP FEATURES

Time Zone Boundary
Mt. Olympus 7,965 Mountain Peak; Elevation
in Feet
Perennial; Intermittent River

RECREATION

National Park
National Forest; National Grassland
Other Large Park or Recreation Area
Small State Park
with and without Camping
Military Lands
Indian Reservation
Trail
Ski Area
Point of Interest

CITIES AND TOWNS

National Capital
State or Provincial Capital
Cities, Towns, and Populated Places
Type size indicates relative importance
Urban Area
State and province maps only
Large Incorporated Cities
City maps only

PACIFIC OCEAN

ALASKA

ARCTIC OCEAN

HAWAII

PACIFIC OCEAN

MEXICO

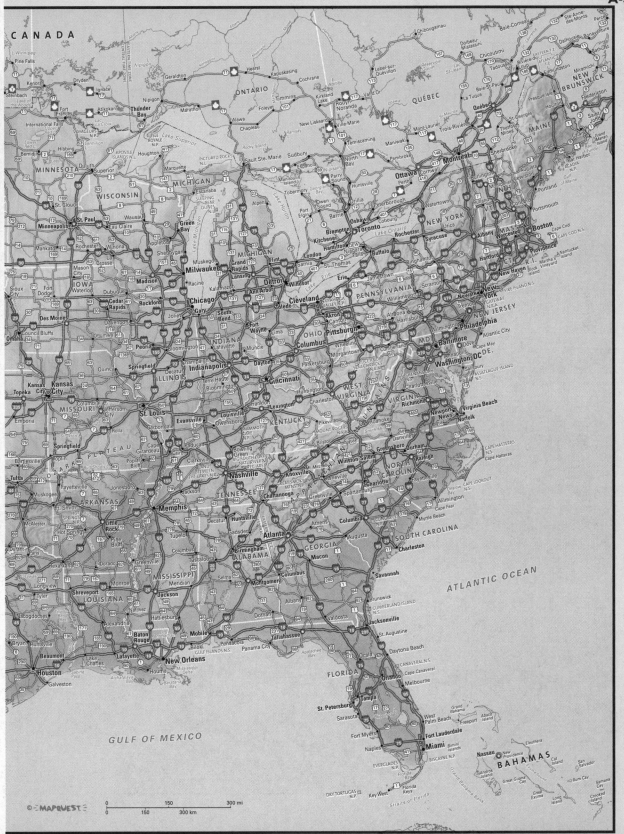

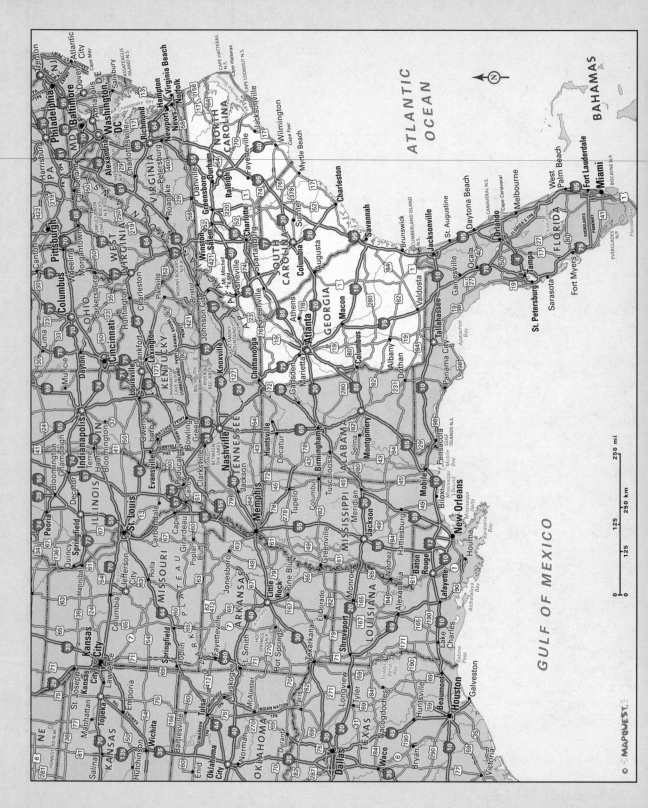

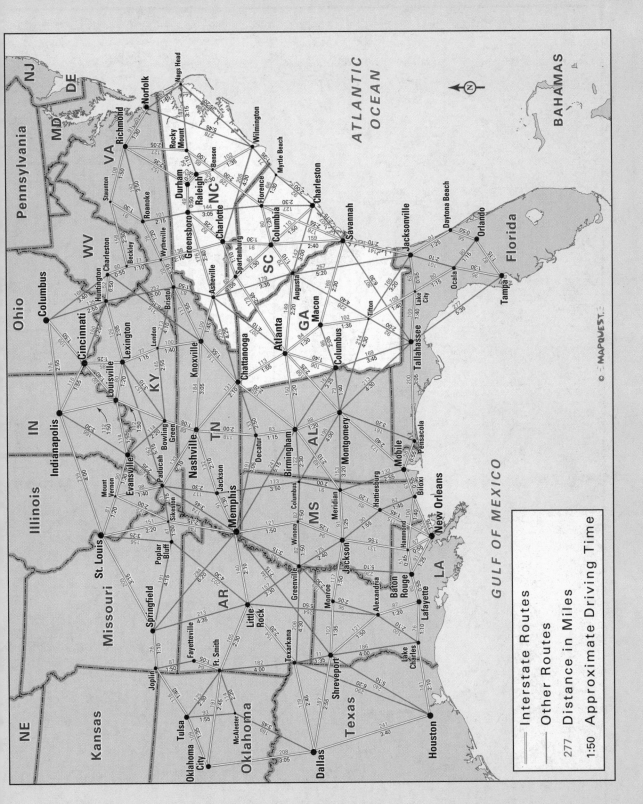

North & South Carolina

MI 25 50
KM 25 50

N

Map of North & South Carolina. Grid references A–F (vertical) and 1–5 (horizontal).

Major cities and places shown include:

Knoxville, Kingsport, Bristol, Johnson City, Boone, Winston-Salem, Mount Airy, Asheville, Black Mountain, Hickory, Statesville, Salisbury, Kannapolis, Concord, Charlotte, Gastonia, Shelby, Spartanburg, Greenville, Anderson, Clemson, Seneca, Rock Hill, Monroe, Rockingham, Gaffney, York, Lancaster, Chester, Cheraw, Union, Newberry, Columbia, Sumter, Camden, Darlington, Hartsville, Florence, Gainesville, Athens, Atlanta, Macon, Warner Robins, Augusta, Aiken, Orangeburg, Barnwell, Walterboro, Summerville, Goose Creek, N. Charleston, Charleston, Savannah, Hilton Head Island, Beaufort.

States labeled: KY., VA., TENN., N. Car. (North Carolina), S.C. (South Carolina), GA. (Georgia).

National forests and parks: Great Smoky Mountains Natl. Park, Pisgah Natl. For., Nantahala Natl. For., Cherokee Natl. For., Chattahoochee Natl. For., Sumter Natl. For., Francis Marion area.

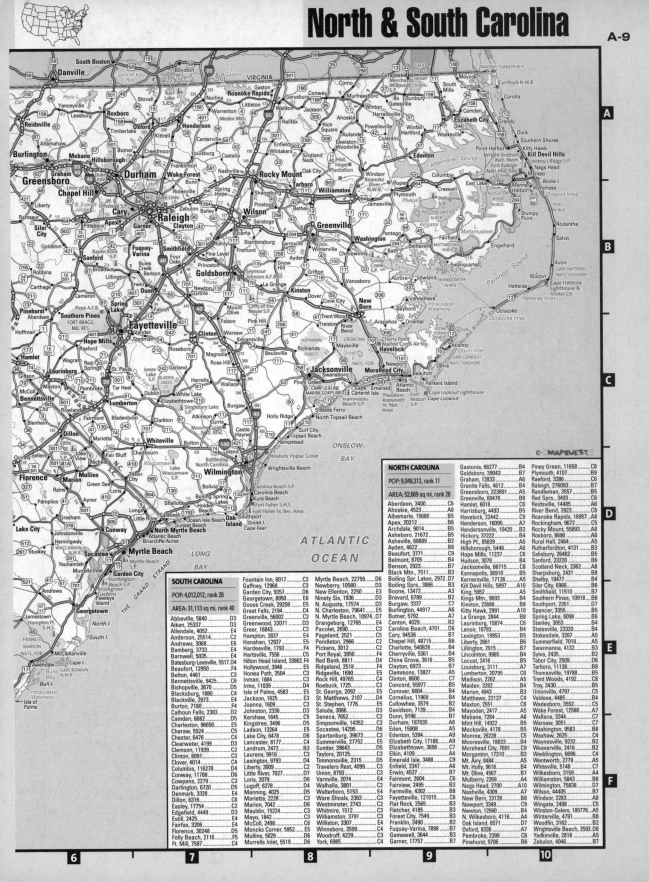

© MapQuest

NORTH CAROLINA

POP: 8,049,313, rank 11

AREA: 52,669 sq mi, rank 28

SOUTH CAROLINA

POP: 4,012,012, rank 26

AREA: 31,113 sq mi, rank 40

Georgia

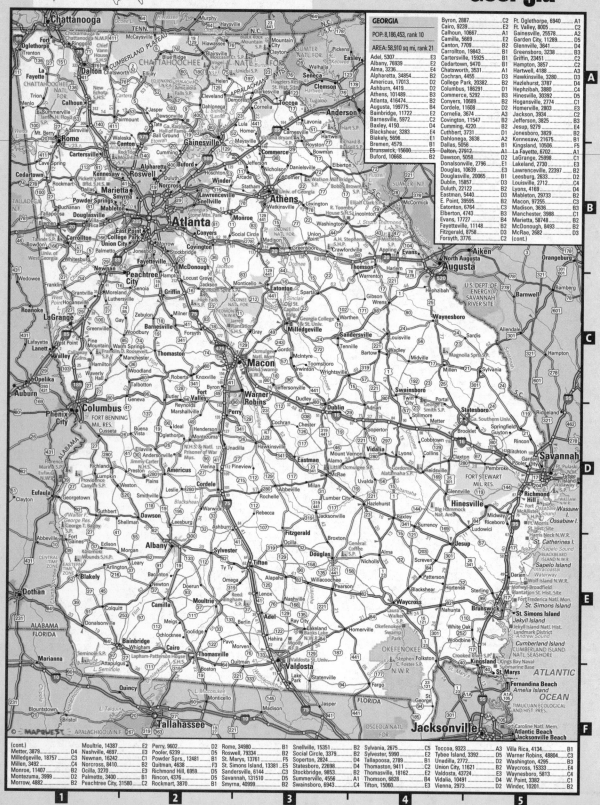

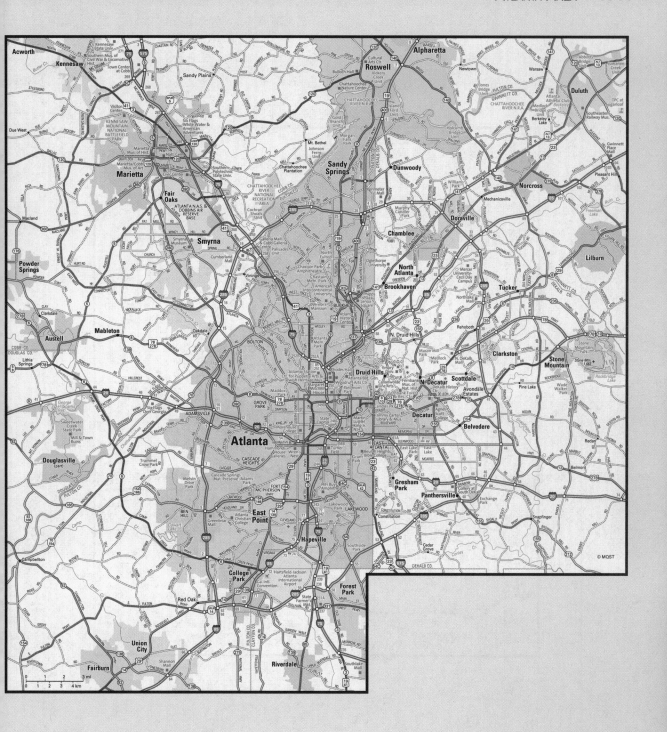

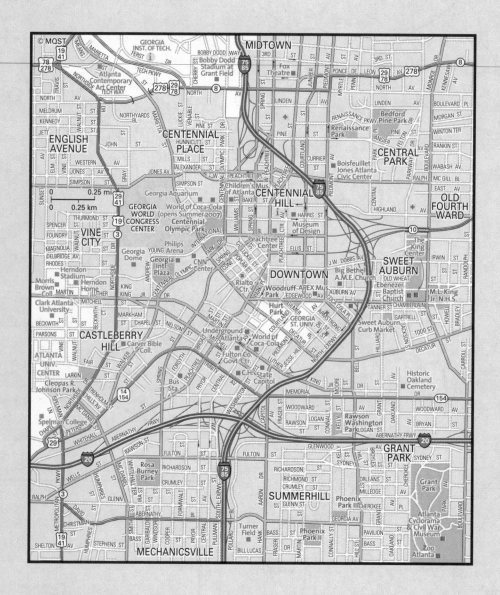

This is a MapQuest intercity distance chart. Distances are in miles. To convert miles to kilometers, multiply the distance in miles by 1.609.

Example: New York, NY to Boston, MA = 215 miles or 346 kilometers (215 × 1.609).

The chart is a symmetric distance matrix. The row cities (top to bottom) are: Wichita, KS; Washington, DC; Vancouver, BC; Toronto, ON; Tampa, FL; Seattle, WA; San Francisco, CA; San Diego, CA; San Antonio, TX; Salt Lake City, UT; St. Louis, MO; Richmond, VA; Reno, NV; Rapid City, SD; Portland, OR; Portland, ME; Pittsburgh, PA; Phoenix, AZ; Philadelphia, PA; Orlando, FL; Omaha, NE; Oklahoma City, OK; New York, NY; New Orleans, LA; Nashville, TN; Montréal, QC; Minneapolis, MN; Milwaukee, WI; Miami, FL; Memphis, TN; Louisville, KY; Los Angeles, CA; Little Rock, AR; Las Vegas, NV; Kansas City, MO; Jackson, MS; Indianapolis, IN; Houston, TX; El Paso, TX; Detroit, MI; Des Moines, IA; Denver, CO; Dallas, TX; Cleveland, OH; Cincinnati, OH; Chicago, IL; Cheyenne, WY; Charlotte, NC; Charleston, WV; Charleston, SC; Burlington, VT; Buffalo, NY; Boston, MA; Boise, ID; Bismarck, ND; Birmingham, AL; Billings, MT; Baltimore, MD; Atlanta, GA; Albuquerque, NM.

The column cities (left to right) are: Albuquerque, NM; Atlanta, GA; Baltimore, MD; Billings, MT; Birmingham, AL; Bismarck, ND; Boise, ID; Boston, MA; Buffalo, NY; Burlington, VT; Charleston, SC; Charleston, WV; Charlotte, NC; Cheyenne, WY; Chicago, IL; Cincinnati, OH; Cleveland, OH; Dallas, TX; Denver, CO; Des Moines, IA; Detroit, MI; El Paso, TX; Houston, TX; Indianapolis, IN; Jackson, MS; Kansas City, MO; Las Vegas, NV; Little Rock, AR; Los Angeles, CA; Louisville, KY; Memphis, TN; Miami, FL; Milwaukee, WI; Minneapolis, MN; Montréal, QC; Nashville, TN; New Orleans, LA; New York, NY; Oklahoma City, OK; Omaha, NE; Orlando, FL; Philadelphia, PA; Phoenix, AZ; Pittsburgh, PA; Portland, ME; Portland, OR; Rapid City, SD; Reno, NV; Richmond, VA; St. Louis, MO; Salt Lake City, UT; San Antonio, TX; San Diego, CA; San Francisco, CA; Seattle, WA; Tampa, FL; Toronto, ON; Vancouver, BC; Washington, DC; Wichita, KS.

© MapQuest.com, Inc.

A Word to Our Readers

Travelers are on the roads in great numbers these days. They're exploring the country on day trips, weekend getaways, business trips, and extended family vacations, visiting major cities and small towns along the way. Because time is precious and the travel industry is ever-changing, having accurate, reliable travel information at your fingertips is critical. Mobil Travel Guide has been providing invaluable insight to travelers for more than 45 years, and we are committed to continuing this service well into the future.

The Mobil Corporation (known as Exxon Mobil Corporation since a 1999 merger) began producing the Mobil Travel Guide books in 1958, following the introduction of the US interstate highway system in 1956. The first edition covered only five Southwestern states. Since then, our books have become the premier travel guides in North America, covering all 50 states and Canada.

Since its founding, Mobil Travel Guide has served as an advocate for travelers seeking knowledge about hotels, restaurants, and places to visit. Based on an objective process, we make recommendations to our customers that we believe will enhance the quality and value of their travel experiences. Our trusted Mobil One- to Five-Star rating system is the oldest and most respected lodging and restaurant inspection and rating program in North America. Most hoteliers, restaurateurs, and industry observers favorably regard the rigor of our inspection program and understand the prestige and benefits that come with receiving a Mobil Star rating.

The Mobil Travel Guide process of rating each establishment includes:

☼ Unannounced facility inspections

☼ Incognito service evaluations for Mobil Four-Star and Mobil Five-Star properties

☼ A review of unsolicited comments from the general public

☼ Senior management oversight

For each property, more than 450 attributes, including cleanliness, physical facilities, and employee attitude and courtesy, are measured and evaluated to produce a mathematically derived score, which is then blended with the other elements to form an overall score. These quantifiable scores allow comparative analysis among properties and form the basis that we use to assign our Mobil One- to Five-Star ratings.

This process focuses largely on guest expectations, guest experience, and consistency of service, not just physical facilities and amenities. It is fundamentally a relative rating system that rewards those properties that continually strive for and achieve excellence each year. Indeed, the very best properties are consistently raising the bar for those that wish to compete with them. These properties proactively respond to consumers' needs even in today's uncertain times.

Only facilities that meet Mobil Travel Guide's standards earn the privilege of being listed in the guide. Deteriorating, poorly managed establishments are deleted. A Mobil Travel Guide listing constitutes a positive quality recommendation; every listing is an accolade, a recognition of achievement. Our Mobil One- to Five-Star rating system highlights its level of service. Extensive in-house research is constantly underway to determine new additions to our lists.

☼ The Mobil Five-Star Award indicates that a property is one of the very best in the country and consistently provides gracious and courteous service, superlative quality in its facility, and a unique ambience. The lodgings and restaurants at the Mobil Five-Star level consistently and proactively respond to consumers' needs and continue their commitment to excellence, doing so with grace and perseverance.

☼ Also highly regarded is the Mobil Four-Star Award, which honors properties for outstanding achievement in overall facility and for providing very strong service levels in all areas. These award winners provide a distinctive experience for the ever-demanding and sophisticated consumer.

⊙ The Mobil Three-Star Award recognizes an excellent property that provides full services and amenities. This category ranges from exceptional hotels with limited services to elegant restaurants with a less-formal atmosphere.

⊙ A Mobil Two-Star property is a clean and comfortable establishment that has expanded amenities or a distinctive environment. A Mobil Two-Star property is an excellent place to stay or dine.

⊙ A Mobil One-Star property is limited in its amenities and services but focuses on providing a value experience while meeting travelers' expectations. The property can be expected to be clean, comfortable, and convenient.

Allow us to emphasize that we do not charge establishments for inclusion in our guides. We have no relationship with any of the businesses and attractions we list and act only as a consumer advocate. In essence, we do the investigative legwork so that you won't have to.

Keep in mind, too, that the hospitality business is ever-changing. Restaurants and lodgings—particularly small chains and stand-alone establish-ments—change management or even go out of business with surprising quickness. Although we make every effort to double-check information during our annual updates, we nevertheless recommend that you call ahead to make sure the place you've selected is still open and offers all the amenities you're looking for. We've provided phone numbers; when available, we also list fax numbers and Web site addresses.

We hope that your travels are enjoyable and relaxing and that our books help you get the most out of every trip you take. If any aspect of your accommodation, dining, or sightseeing experience motivates you to comment, please drop us a line. We depend a great deal on our readers' remarks, so you can be assured that we will read your comments and assimilate them into our research. General comments about our books are also welcome. You can write to us at Mobil Travel Guide, 7373 N Cicero Ave, Lincolnwood, IL 60712, or send an e-mail to info@ mobiltravelguide.com.

Take your Mobil Travel Guide books along on every trip you take. We're confident that you'll be pleased with their convenience, ease of use, and breadth of dependable coverage.

Happy travels!

How to Use This Book

The Mobil Travel Guide Regional Travel Planners are designed for ease of use. Each state has its own chapter, beginning with a general introduction that provides a geographical and historical orientation to the state and gives basic statewide tourist information, from climate to calendar highlights to seatbelt laws. The remainder of each chapter is devoted to travel destinations within the state—mainly cities and towns, but also national parks and tourist areas—which, like the states, are arranged in alphabetical order.

The following sections explain the wealth of information you'll find about those travel destinations: information about the area, things to see and do there, and where to stay and eat.

Maps and Map Coordinates

At the front of this book in the full-color section, we have provided state maps as well as maps of selected larger cities to help you find your way around once you leave the highway. You'll find a key to the map symbols on the Contents page at the beginning of the map section.

Next to most cities and towns throughout the book, you'll find a set of map coordinates, such as C-2. These coordinates reference the maps at the front of this book and help you find the location you're looking for quickly and easily.

Destination Information

Because many travel destinations are close to other cities and towns where travelers might find additional attractions, accommodations, and restaurants, we've included cross-references to those cities and towns when it makes sense to do so. We also list addresses, phone numbers, and Web sites for travel information resources—usually the local chamber of commerce or office of tourism—as well as pertinent statistics and, in many cases, a brief introduction to the area.

Information about airports, ground transportation, and suburbs is included for large cities.

Driving Tours and Walking Tours

The driving tours that we include for many states are usually day trips that make for interesting side excursions, although they can be longer. They offer you a way to get off the beaten path and visit an area that travelers often overlook. These trips frequently cover areas of natural beauty or historical significance.

Each walking tour focuses on a particularly interesting area of a city or town. Again, these tours can provide a break from everyday tourist attractions. The tours often include places to stop for meals or snacks.

What to See and Do

Mobil Travel Guide offers information about nearly 20,000 museums, art galleries, amusement parks, historic sites, national and state parks, ski areas, and many other types of attractions. A white star on a black background ★ signals that the attraction is a must-see—one of the best in the area. Because municipal parks, public tennis courts, swimming pools, and small educational institutions are common to most towns, they generally are not mentioned.

Following an attraction's description, you'll find the months, days, and, in some cases, hours of operation; the address/directions, telephone number, and Web site (if there is one); and the admission price category. The following are the ranges we use for admission fees, based on one adult:

- ✪ **FREE**
- ✪ **$** = Up to $5
- ✪ **$$** = $5.01-$10
- ✪ **$$$** = $10.01-$15
- ✪ **$$$$** = Over $15

Special Events

Special events are either annual events that last only a short time, such as festivals and fairs, or longer, seasonal events such as horse racing, theater, and summer concerts. Our Special Events listings also include infrequently occurring occasions that mark certain dates or events, such as a centennial or other commemorative celebration.

Listings

Lodgings, spas, and restaurants are usually listed under the city or town in which they're located. Make sure to check the related cities and towns that appear right beneath a city's heading for additional options, especially if you're traveling to a major metropolitan area that includes many suburbs. If a property is located in a town that doesn't have its own heading, the listing appears under the town nearest it, with the address and town given immediately after the establishment's name. In large cities, lodgings located within 5 miles of major commercial airports may be listed under a separate "Airport Area" heading that follows the city section.

LODGINGS

Travelers have different wants and needs when it comes to accommodations. To help you pinpoint properties that meet your particular needs, Mobil Travel Guide classifies each lodging by type according to the following characteristics.

Mobil Rated Lodgings

- **Limited-Service Hotel.** A limited-service hotel is traditionally a Mobil One-Star or Mobil Two-Star property. At a Mobil One-Star hotel, guests can expect to find a clean, comfortable property that commonly serves a complimentary continental breakfast. A Mobil Two-Star hotel is also clean and comfortable but has expanded amenities, such as a full-service restaurant, business center, and fitness center. These services may have limited staffing and/or restricted hours of use.

- **Full-Service Hotel.** A full-service hotel traditionally enjoys a Mobil Three-Star, Mobil Four-Star, or Mobil Five-Star rating. Guests can expect these hotels to offer at least one full-service restaurant in addition to amenities such as valet parking, luggage assistance, 24-hour room service, concierge service, laundry and/or dry-cleaning services, and turndown service.

- **Full-Service Resort.** A resort is traditionally a full-service hotel that is geared toward recreation and represents a vacation and holiday destination. A resort's guest rooms are typically furnished to accommodate longer stays. The property may offer a full-service spa, golf, tennis, and fitness facilities or other leisure activities. Resorts are expected to offer a full-service restaurant and expanded amenities, such as luggage assistance, room service, meal plans, concierge service, and turndown service.

- **Full-Service Inn.** An inn is traditionally a Mobil Three-Star, Mobil Four-Star, or Mobil Five-Star property. Inns are similar to bed-and-breakfasts (see below) but offer a wider range of services, most significantly a full-service restaurant that serves at least breakfast and dinner.

Specialty Lodgings

Mobil Travel Guide recognizes the unique and individualized nature of many different types of lodging establishments, including bed-and-breakfasts, limited-service inns, and guest ranches. For that reason, we have chosen to place our stamp of approval on the properties that fall into these two categories in lieu of applying our traditional Mobil Star ratings.

- **B&B/Limited-Service Inn.** A bed-and-breakfast (B&B) or limited-service inn is traditionally an owner-occupied home or residence found in a residential area or vacation destination. It may be a structure of historic significance. Rooms are often individually decorated, but telephones, televisions, and private bathrooms may not be available in every room. A B&B typically serves only breakfast to its overnight guests, which is included in the room rate. Cocktails and refreshments may be served in the late afternoon or evening.

- **Guest Ranch.** A guest ranch is traditionally a rustic, Western-themed property that specializes in stays of three or more days. Horseback riding is often a feature, with stables and trails found on the property. Facilities can range from clean, comfortable establishments to more luxurious facilities.

Mobil Star Rating Definitions for Lodgings

- ★ ★ ★ ★ ★ : A Mobil Five-Star lodging provides consistently superlative service in an exceptionally distinctive luxury environment, with expanded services. Attention to detail is evident throughout the hotel, resort, or inn, from bed linens to staff uniforms.

○ ★ ★ ★ ★ : A Mobil Four-Star lodging provides a luxury experience with expanded amenities in a distinctive environment. Services may include, but are not limited to, automatic turndown service, 24-hour room service, and valet parking.

○ ★ ★ ★ : A Mobil Three-Star lodging is well appointed, with a full-service restaurant and expanded amenities, such as a fitness center, golf course, tennis courts, 24-hour room service, and optional turndown service.

○ ★ ★ : A Mobil Two-Star lodging is considered a clean, comfortable, and reliable establishment that has expanded amenities, such as a full-service restaurant on the premises.

○ ★ : A Mobil One-Star lodging is a limited-service hotel, motel, or inn that is considered a clean, comfortable, and reliable establishment.

Information Found in the Lodging Listings

Each lodging listing gives the name, address/location (when no street address is available), neighborhood and/or directions from downtown (in major cities), phone number(s), fax number, total number of guest rooms, and seasons open (if not year-round). Also included are details on business, luxury, recreational, and dining facilities at the property or nearby. A key to the symbols at the end of each listing can be found on the page following the "A Word to Our Readers" section.

For every property, we also provide pricing information. Because lodging rates change frequently, we list a pricing category rather than specific prices. The pricing categories break down as follows:

○ **$** = Up to $150

○ **$$** = $151-$250

○ **$$$** = $251-$350

○ **$$$$** = $351 and up

All prices quoted are in effect at the time of publication; however, prices cannot be guaranteed. In some locations, short-term price variations may exist because of special events, holidays, or seasonality. Certain resorts have complicated rate structures that vary with the time of year; always confirm rates when making your plans.

Because most lodgings offer the following features and services, information about them does not appear in the listings:

○ Year-round operation

○ Bathroom with tub and/or shower in each room

○ Cable television in each room

○ In-room telephones

○ Cots and cribs available

○ Daily maid service

○ Elevators

○ Major credit cards accepted

SPAS

Mobil Travel Guide is pleased to announce its newest category: hotel and resort spas. Until now, hotel and resort spas have not been formally rated or inspected by any organization. Every spa selected for inclusion in this book underwent a rigorous inspection process similar to the one Mobil Travel Guide has been applying to lodgings and restaurants for more than four decades. After spending a year and a half researching more than 300 spas and performing exhaustive incognito inspections of more than 200 properties, we narrowed our list to the 48 best spas in the United States and Canada.

Mobil Travel Guide's spa ratings are based on objective evaluations of more than 450 attributes. Approximately half of these criteria assess basic expectations, such as staff courtesy, the technical proficiency and skill of the employees, and whether the facility is maintained properly and hygienically. Several standards address issues that impact a guest's physical comfort and convenience, as well as the staff's ability to impart a sense of personalized service and anticipate clients' needs. Additional criteria measure the spa's ability to create a completely calming ambience.

The Mobil Star ratings focus on much more than the facilities available at a spa and the treatments it offers. Each Mobil Star rating is a cumulative score achieved from multiple inspections that reflects the spa management's attention to detail and commitment to consumers' needs.

Mobil Star Rating Definitions for Spas

✪ ★ ★ ★ ★ ★ : A Mobil Five-Star spa provides consistently superlative service in an exceptionally distinctive luxury environment with extensive amenities. The staff at a Mobil Five-Star spa provides extraordinary service above and beyond the traditional spa experience, allowing guests to achieve the highest level of relaxation and pampering. A Mobil Five-Star spa offers an extensive array of treatments, often incorporating international themes and products. Attention to detail is evident throughout the spa, from arrival to departure.

✪ ★ ★ ★ ★ : A Mobil Four-Star spa provides a luxurious experience with expanded amenities in an elegant and serene environment. Throughout the spa facility, guests experience personalized service. Amenities might include, but are not limited to, single-sex relaxation rooms where guests wait for their treatments, plunge pools and whirlpools in both men's and women's locker rooms, and an array of treatments, including at a minimum a selection of massages, body therapies, facials, and a variety of salon services.

✪ ★ ★ ★ : A Mobil Three-Star spa is physically well appointed and has a full complement of staff to ensure that guests' needs are met. It has some expanded amenities, such as, but not limited to, a well-equipped fitness center, separate men's and women's locker rooms, a sauna or steam room, and a designated relaxation area. It also offers a menu of services that at a minimum includes massages, facial treatments, and at least one other type of body treatment, such as scrubs or wraps.

RESTAURANTS

All Mobil Star rated dining establishments listed in this book have a full kitchen and offer seating at tables; most offer table service.

Mobil Star Rating Definitions for Restaurants

✪ ★ ★ ★ ★ ★ : A Mobil Five-Star restaurant offers one of few flawless dining experiences in the country. These establishments consistently provide their guests with exceptional food, superlative service, elegant décor, and exquisite presentations of each detail surrounding a meal.

✪ ★ ★ ★ ★ : A Mobil Four-Star restaurant provides professional service, distinctive presentations, and wonderful food.

✪ ★ ★ ★ : A Mobil Three-Star restaurant has good food, warm and skillful service, and enjoyable décor.

✪ ★ ★ : A Mobil Two-Star restaurant serves fresh food in a clean setting with efficient service. Value is considered in this category, as is family friendliness.

✪ ★ : A Mobil One-Star restaurant provides a distinctive experience through culinary specialty, local flair, or individual atmosphere.

Information Found in the Restaurant Listings

Each restaurant listing gives the cuisine type, street address (or directions if no address is available), phone and fax numbers, Web site (if available), meals served, days of operation (if not open daily year-round), and pricing category. Information about appropriate attire is provided, although it's always a good idea to call ahead and ask if you're unsure; the meaning of "casual" or "business casual" varies widely in different parts of the country. We also indicate whether the restaurant has a bar, whether a children's menu is offered, and whether outdoor seating is available. If reservations are recommended, we note that fact in the listing. When valet parking is available, it is noted in the description. In many cases, self-parking is available at the restaurant or nearby.

Because menu prices can fluctuate, we list a pricing category rather than specific prices. The pricing categories are defined as follows, per diner, and assume that you order an appetizer or dessert, an entrée, and one drink:

✪ **$** = $15 and under

✪ **$$** = $16-$35

✪ **$$$** = $36-$85

✪ **$$$$** = $86 and up

Again, all prices quoted are in effect at the time of publication, but prices cannot be guaranteed.

SPECIAL INFORMATION FOR TRAVELERS WITH DISABILITIES

The Mobil Travel Guide ♿ symbol indicates that an establishment is not at least partially accessible to people with mobility problems. When the ♿ symbol follows a listing, the establishment is not equipped with facilities to accommodate people using wheelchairs or crutches or otherwise needing easy access to doorways and rest rooms. Travelers with severe mobility problems or with hearing or visual impairments may or may not find the facilities they need. Always phone ahead to make sure hat an establishment can meet your needs.

Understanding the Symbols

What to See and Do

★	=	One of the top attractions in the area
$	=	Up to $5
$$	=	$5.01 to $10
$$$	=	$10.01 to $15
$$$$	=	Over $15

Lodgings

$	=	Up to $150
$$	=	$151 to $250
$$$	=	$251 to $350
$$$$	=	Over $350

Restaurants

$	=	Up to $15
$$	=	$16 to $35
$$$	=	$36 to $85
$$$$	=	Over $85

Lodging Star Definitions

★★★★★ A Mobil Five-Star lodging establishment provides consistently superlative service in an exceptionally distinctive luxury environment with expanded services. Attention to detail is evident throughout the hotel/resort/inn from the bed linens to the staff uniforms.

★★★★ A Mobil Four-Star lodging establishment is a hotel/resort/inn that provides a luxury experience with expanded amenities in a distinctive environment. Services may include, but are not limited to, automatic turndown service, 24-hour room service, and valet parking.

★★★ A Mobil Three-Star lodging establishment is a hotel/resort/inn that is well appointed, with a full-service restaurant and expanded amenities, such as, but not limited to, a fitness center, golf course, tennis courts, 24-hour room service, and optional turndown service.

★★ A Mobil Two-Star lodging establishment is a hotel/resort/inn that is considered a clean, comfortable, and reliable establishment, but also has expanded amenities, such as a full-service restaurant on the premises.

★ A Mobil One-Star lodging establishment is a limited-service hotel or inn that is considered a clean, comfortable, and reliable establishment.

Restaurant Star Definitions

★★★★★ A Mobil Five-Star restaurant is one of few flawless dining experiences in the country. These restaurants consistently provide their guests with exceptional food, superlative service, elegant décor, and exquisite presentations of each detail surrounding the meal.

★★★★ A Mobil Four-Star restaurant provides professional service, distinctive presentations, and wonderful food.

★★★ A Mobil Three-Star restaurant has good food, warm and skillful service, and enjoyable décor.

★★ A Mobil Two-Star restaurant serves fresh food in a clean setting with efficient service. Value is considered in this category, as is family friendliness.

★ A Mobil One-Star restaurant provides a distinctive experience through culinary specialty, local flair, or individual atmosphere.

Symbols at End of Listings

- Facilities for people with disabilities not available
- Pets allowed
- Ski in/ski out access
- Golf on premises
- Tennis court(s) on premises
- Indoor or outdoor pool
- Fitness room
- Major commercial airport within 5 miles
- Business center

Making the Most of Your Trip

A few hardy souls might look back with fondness on a trip during which the car broke down, leaving them stranded for three days, or a vacation that cost twice what it was supposed to. For most travelers, though, the best trips are those that are safe, smooth, and within budget. To help you make your trip the best it can be, we've assembled a few tips and resources.

Saving Money

ON LODGING

Many hotels and motels offer discounts—for senior citizens, business travelers, families, you name it. It never hurts to ask—politely, that is. Sometimes, especially in the late afternoon, desk clerks are instructed to fill beds, and you might be offered a lower rate or a nicer room to entice you to stay. Simply ask the reservation agent for the best rate available. Also, make sure to try both the toll-free number and the local number. You may be able to get a lower rate from one than from the other.

Timing your trip right can cut your lodging costs as well. Look for bargains on stays over multiple nights, in the off-season, and on weekdays or weekends, depending on the location. Many hotels in major metropolitan areas, for example, have special weekend packages that offer leisure travelers considerable savings on rooms; they may include breakfast, cocktails, and/or dinner discounts.

Another way to save money is to choose accommodations that give you more than just a standard room. Rooms with kitchen facilities enable you to cook some meals yourself, reducing your restaurant costs. A suite might save money for two couples traveling together. Even hotel luxury levels can provide good value, as many include breakfast or cocktails in the price of a room.

State and city taxes, as well as special room taxes, can increase your room rate by as much as 25 percent per day. We are unable to include information about taxes in our listings, but we strongly urge you to ask about taxes when making reservations so that you understand the total cost of your lodgings before you book them.

Watch out for telephone-usage charges that hotels frequently impose on long-distance, credit-card, and other calls. Before phoning from your room, read the information given to you at check-in, and then be sure to review your bill carefully when checking out. You won't be expected to pay for charges that the hotel didn't spell out. Consider using your cell phone if you have one; or, if public telephones are available in the hotel lobby, your cost savings may outweigh the inconvenience of using them.

Here are some additional ways to save on lodgings:

- Stay in B&B accommodations. They're generally less expensive than standard hotel rooms, and the complimentary breakfast cuts down on food costs.

- If you're traveling with children, find lodgings at which kids stay free.

- When visiting a major city, stay just outside the city limits; these rooms are usually less expensive than those in downtown locations.

- Consider visiting national parks during the low season, when prices of lodgings near the parks drop by 25 percent or more.

- When calling a hotel, ask whether it is running any special promotions or if any discounts are available; many times reservationists are told not to volunteer these deals unless they're specifically asked about them.

- Check for hotel packages; some offer nightly rates that include a rental car or discounts on major attractions.

ON DINING

There are several ways to get a less expensive meal at an expensive restaurant. Early-bird dinners are popular in many parts of the country and offer considerable savings. If you're interested in visiting a Mobil Four- or Five-Star establishment, consider going at lunchtime. Although the prices are probably still relatively high at midday, they may be half of those at dinner, and you'll experience the same ambience, service, and cuisine.

ON ENTERTAINMENT

Although many national parks, monuments, seashores, historic sites, and recreation areas may be visited free of charge, others charge an entrance fee and/or a usage fee for special services and facilities. If you plan to make several visits to national recreation areas, consider one of the following money-saving programs offered by the National Park Service:

○ **National Parks Pass.** This annual pass is good for entrance to any national park that charges an entrance fee. If the park charges a per-vehicle fee, the pass holder and any accompanying passengers in a private noncommercial vehicle may enter. If the park charges a per-person fee, the pass applies to the holder's spouse, children, and parents as well as the holder. It is valid for entrance fees only; it does not cover parking, camping, or other fees. You can purchase a National Parks Pass in person at any national park where an entrance fee is charged; by mail from the National Park Foundation, PO Box 34108, Washington, DC 20043-4108; by calling toll-free 888/467-2757; or at www.nationalparks .org. The cost is $50.

○ **Golden Eagle Sticker.** When affixed to a National Parks Pass, this hologram sticker, available to people who are between 17 and 61 years of age, extends coverage to sites managed by the US Fish and Wildlife Service, the US Forest Service, and the Bureau of Land Management. It is good until the National Parks Pass to which it is affixed expires and does not cover usage fees. You can purchase one at the National Park Service, the Fish and Wildlife Service, or the Bureau of Land Management fee stations. The cost is $15.

○ **Golden Age Passport.** Available to citizens and permanent US residents 62 and older, this passport is a lifetime entrance permit to fee-charging national recreation areas. The fee exemption extends to those accompanying the permit holder in a private noncommercial vehicle or, in the case of walk-in facilities, to the holder's spouse and children. The passport also entitles the holder to a 50 percent discount on federal usage fees charged in park areas, but not on con-

cessions. Golden Age Passports must be obtained in person and are available at most National Park Service units that charge an entrance fee. The applicant must show proof of age, such as a driver's license or birth certificate (Medicare cards are not acceptable proof). The cost is $10.

○ **Golden Access Passport.** Issued to citizens and permanent US residents who are physically disabled or visually impaired, this passport is a free lifetime entrance permit to fee-charging national recreation areas. The fee exemption extends to those accompanying the permit holder in a private noncommercial vehicle or, in the case of walk-in facilities, to the holder's spouse and children. The passport also entitles the holder to a 50 percent discount on usage fees charged in park areas, but not on concessions. Golden Access Passports must be obtained in person and are available at most National Park Service units that charge an entrance fee. Proof of eligibility to receive federal benefits (under programs such as Disability Retirement, Compensation for Military Service-Connected Disability, and the Coal Mine Safety and Health Act) is required, or an affidavit must be signed attesting to eligibility.

A money-saving move in several large cities is to purchase a **CityPass.** If you plan to visit several museums and other major attractions, CityPass is a terrific option because it gets you into several sites for one substantially reduced price. Currently, CityPass is available in Boston, Chicago, Hollywood, New York, Philadelphia, San Francisco, Seattle, southern California (which includes Disneyland, SeaWorld, and the San Diego Zoo), and Toronto. For more information or to buy one, call toll-free 888/330-5008 or visit www. citypass.net. You can also buy a CityPass from any participating CityPass attraction.

Here are some additional ways to save on entertainment and shopping:

○ Check with your hotel's concierge for various coupons and special offers; they often have two-for-one tickets for area attractions and coupons for discounts at area stores and restaurants.

○ Purchase same-day concert or theater tickets for half-price through the local cheap-tickets outlet, such as TKTS in New York or Hot Tix in Chicago.

✪ Visit museums on their free or "by donation" days, when you can pay what you wish rather than a specific admission fee.

✪ Save receipts from purchases in Canada; visitors to Canada can get a rebate on federal taxes and some provincial sales taxes.

ON TRANSPORTATION

Transportation is a big part of any vacation budget. Here are some ways to reduce your costs:

✪ If you're renting a car, shop early over the Internet; you can book a car during the low season for less, even if you'll be using it in the high season.

✪ Rental car discounts are often available if you rent for one week or longer and reserve in advance.

✪ Get the best gas mileage out of your vehicle by making sure that it's properly tuned up and keeping your tires properly inflated.

✪ Travel at moderate speeds on the open road; higher speeds require more gasoline.

✪ Fill the tank before you return your rental car; rental companies charge to refill the tank and do so at prices of up to 50 percent more than at local gas stations.

✪ Make a checklist of travel essentials and purchase them before you leave; don't get stuck buying expensive sunscreen at your hotel or overpriced film at the airport.

FOR SENIOR CITIZENS

Always call ahead to ask if a discount is being offered, and be sure to carry proof of age. Additional information for mature travelers is available from the American Association of Retired Persons (AARP), 601 E St NW, Washington, DC 20049; phone 202/434-2277; www.aarp.org.

Tipping

Tips are expressions of appreciation for good service. However, you are never obligated to tip if you receive poor service.

IN HOTELS

✪ Door attendants usually get $1 for hailing a cab.

✪ Bell staff expect $2 per bag.

✪ Concierges are tipped according to the service they perform. Tipping is not mandatory when you've asked for suggestions on sightseeing or restaurants or for help in making dining reservations. However, a tip of $5 is appropriate when a concierge books you a table at a restaurant known to be difficult to get into. For obtaining theater or sporting event tickets, $5 to $10 is expected.

✪ Maids should be tipped $1 to $2 per day. Hand your tip directly to the maid, or leave it with a note saying that the money has been left expressly for the maid.

IN RESTAURANTS

Before tipping, carefully review your check for any gratuity or service charge that is already included in your bill. If you're in doubt, ask your server.

✪ Coffee shop and counter service waitstaff usually receive 15 percent of the bill, before sales tax.

✪ In full-service restaurants, tip 18 percent of the bill, before sales tax.

✪ In fine restaurants, where gratuities are shared among a larger staff, 18 to 20 percent is appropriate.

✪ In most cases, the maitre d' is tipped only if the service has been extraordinary, and only on the way out. At upscale properties in major metropolitan areas, $20 is the minimum.

✪ If there is a wine steward, tip $20 for exemplary service and beyond, or more if the wine was decanted or the bottle was very expensive.

✪ Tip $1 to $2 per coat at the coat check.

AT AIRPORTS

Curbside luggage handlers expect $1 per bag. Car-rental shuttle drivers who help with your luggage appreciate a $1 or $2 tip.

Staying Safe

The best way to deal with emergencies is to avoid them in the first place. However, unforeseen situations do happen, so you should be prepared for them.

IN YOUR CAR

Before you head out on a road trip, make sure that your car has been serviced and is in good working order. Change the oil, check the battery and belts, make sure that your windshield washer fluid is full and your tires are properly inflated (which can also improve your gas mileage). Other inspections recommended by the vehicle's manufacturer should also be made.

Next, be sure you have the tools and equipment needed to deal with a routine breakdown:

- Jack
- Spare tire
- Lug wrench
- Repair kit
- Emergency tools
- Jumper cables
- Spare fan belt
- Fuses
- Flares and/or reflectors
- Flashlight
- First-aid kit
- In winter, a windshield scraper and snow shovel

Many emergency supplies are sold in special packages that include the essentials you need to stay safe in the event of a breakdown.

Also bring all appropriate and up-to-date documentation—licenses, registration, and insurance cards—and know what your insurance covers. Bring an extra set of keys, too, just in case.

En route, always buckle up! In most states, wearing a seatbelt is required by law.

If your car does break down, do the following:

- Get out of traffic as soon as possible—pull well off the road.
- Raise the hood and turn on your emergency flashers or tie a white cloth to the roadside door handle or antenna.
- Stay in your car.
- Use flares or reflectors to keep your vehicle from being hit.

IN YOUR HOTEL

Chances are slim that you will encounter a hotel or motel fire, but you can protect yourself by doing the following:

- Once you've checked in, make sure that the smoke detector in your room is working properly.
- Find the property's fire safety instructions, usually posted on the inside of the room door.
- Locate the fire extinguishers and at least two fire exits.
- Never use an elevator in a fire.

For personal security, use the peephole in your room door and make sure that anyone claiming to be a hotel employee can show proper identification. Call the front desk if you feel threatened at any time.

PROTECTING AGAINST THEFT

To guard against theft wherever you go:

- Don't bring anything of more value than you need.
- If you do bring valuables, leave them at your hotel rather than in your car.
- If you bring something very expensive, lock it in a safe. Many hotels put one in each room; others will store your valuables in the hotel's safe.
- Don't carry more money than you need. Use traveler's checks and credit cards or visit cash machines to withdraw more cash when you run out.

For Travelers with Disabilities

To get the kind of service you need and have a right to expect, don't hesitate when making a reservation to question the management about the availability of accessible rooms, parking, entrances, restaurants, lounges, or any other facilities that are important to you, and confirm what is meant by "accessible."

The Mobil Travel Guide 🖼 symbol indicates establishments that are not at least partially accessible to people with special mobility needs (people using wheelchairs or crutches or otherwise needing easy access to buildings and rooms). Further information about these criteria can be found in the earlier section "How to Use This Book."

A thorough listing of published material for travelers with disabilities is available from the Disability Bookshop, Twin Peaks Press, Box 129, Vancouver, WA 98666; phone 360/694-2462; disabilitybookshop.virtualave.net. Another reliable organization is the Society for Accessible Travel & Hospitality (SATH), 347 Fifth Ave, Suite 610, New York, NY 10016; phone 212/447-7284; www.sath.org.

Important Toll-Free Numbers and Online Information

Hotels

Adams Mark...............................800/444-2326
www.adamsmark.com

America's Best Value Inn..................888/315-2378
www.americasbestvalueinn.com

AmericInn 800/634-3444
www.americinn.com

AmeriHost Inn 800/434-5800
www.amerihostinn.com

Amerisuites..............................800/833-1516
www.amerisuites.com

Baymont Inns............................800/621-1429
www.baymontinns.com

Best Inns & Suites 800/237-8466
www.bestinn.com

Best Western 800/780-7234
www.bestwestern.com

Budget Host Inn 800/283-4678
www.budgethost.com

Candlewood Suites 888/226-3539
www.candlewoodsuites.com

Clarion Hotels 800/252-7466
www.choicehotels.com

Comfort Inns and Suites 800/252-7466
www.comfortinn.com

Country Hearth Inns 800/848-5767
www.countryhearth.com

Country Inns & Suites...................800/456-4000
www.countryinns.com

Courtyard by Marriott 800/321-2211
www.courtyard.com

Crowne Plaza Hotels and Resorts...........800/227-6963
www.crowneplaza.com

Days Inn................................800/544-8313
www.daysinn.com

Delta Hotels 800/268-1133
www.deltahotels.com

Destination Hotels & Resorts 800/434-7347
www.destinationhotels.com

Doubletree Hotels.......................800/222-8733
www.doubletree.com

Drury Inn 800/378-7946
www.druryhotels.com

Econolodge 800/553-2666
www.econolodge.com

Embassy Suites 800/362-2779
www.embassysuites.com

ExelInns of America........................800/367-3935
www.exelinns.com

Extended StayAmerica 800/398-7829
www.extendedstayhotels.com

Fairfield Inn by Marriott 800/228-2800
www.fairfieldinn.com

Fairmont Hotels...........................800/441-1414
www.fairmont.com

Four Points by Sheraton................. 888/625-5144
www.fourpoints.com

Four Seasons 800/819-5053
www.fourseasons.com

Hampton Inn..............................800/426-7866
www.hamptoninn.com

Hard Rock Hotels, Resorts, and Casinos 800/473-7625
www.hardrockhotel.com

Harrah's Entertainment 800/427-7247
www.harrahs.com

Hawthorn Suites...........................800/527-1133
www.hawthorn.com

Hilton Hotels and Resorts (US) 800/774-1500
www.hilton.com

Holiday Inn Express.........................800/465-4329
www.hiexpress.com

Holiday Inn Hotels and Resorts..............800/465-4329
www.holiday-inn.com

Homestead Studio Suites............... 888/782-9473
www.extendedstayhotels.com

Homewood Suites..........................800/225-5466
www.homewoodsuites.com

Howard Johnson 800/406-1411
www.hojo.com

Hyatt...................................800/633-7313
www.hyatt.com

Inns of America..........................800/826-0778
www.innsofamerica.com

InterContinental........................ 888/424-6835
www.intercontinental.com

Joie de Vivre.............................800/738-7477
www.jdvhospitality.com

Kimpton Hotels 888/546-7866
www.kimptonhotels.com

Knights Inn 800/843-5644
www.knightsinn.com

La Quinta................................800/531-5900
www.lq.com

Le Meridien 800/543-4300	**Ritz-Carlton** 800/241-3333
www.lemeridien.com	www.ritzcarlton.com
Leading Hotels of the World 800/223-6800	**RockResorts** 888/367-7625
www.lhw.com	www.rockresorts.com
Loews Hotels 800/235-6397	**Rodeway Inn** 800/228-2000
www.loewshotels.com	www.rodeway.com
MainStay Suites 800/660-6246	**Rosewood Hotels & Resorts** 888/767-3966
www.mainstaysuites.com	www.rosewoodhotels.com
Mandarin Oriental 800/526-6566	**Select Inn** 800/641-1000
www.mandarinoriental.com	www.selectinn.com
Marriott Hotels, Resorts, and Suites 800/228-9290	**Sheraton** 888/625-5144
www.marriott.com	www.sheraton.com
Microtel Inns & Suites 800/771-7171	**Shilo Inns** 800/222-2244
www.microtelinn.com	www.shiloinns.com
Millennium & Copthorne Hotels 866/866-8086	**Shoney's Inn** 800/552-4667
www.millenniumhotels.com	www.shoneysinn.com
Motel 6 ....800/466-8356	**Signature/Jameson Inns** 800/822-5252
www.motel6.com	www.jamesoninns.com
Omni Hotels 800/843-6664	**Sleep Inn** 877/424-6423
www.omnihotels.com	www.sleepinn.com
Pan Pacific Hotels and Resorts 800/327-8585	**Small Luxury Hotels of the World** 800/525-4800
www.panpacific.com	www.slh.com
Park Inn & Park Plaza 888/201-1801	**Sofitel** 800/763-4835
www.parkinn.com	www.sofitel.com
The Peninsula Group .... Contact individual hotel	**SpringHill Suites** 888/236-2427
www.peninsula.com	www.springhillsuites.com
Preferred Hotels & Resorts Worldwide 800/323-7500	**St. Regis Luxury Collection** 888/625-5144
www.preferredhotels.com	www.stregis.com
Quality Inn 800/228-5151	**Staybridge Suites** 800/238-8000
www.qualityinn.com	www.staybridge.com
Radisson Hotels 800/333-3333	**Summit International** 800/457-4000
www.radisson.com	www.summithotelsandresorts.com
Raffles International Hotels and Resorts 800/637-9477	**Super 8 Motels** 800/800-8000
www.raffles.com	www.super8.com
Ramada Plazas, Limiteds, and Inns 800/272-6232	**The Sutton Place Hotels** 866/378-8866
www.ramada.com	www.suttonplace.com
Red Lion Inns 800/733-5466	**Swissôtel** 800/637-9477
www.redlion.com	www.swissotels.com
Red Roof Inns 800/733-7663	**TownePlace Suites** 888/236-2427
www.redroof.com	www.towneplace.com
Regent International 800/545-4000	**Travelodge** 800/578-7878
www.regenthotels.com	www.travelodge.com
Relais & Chateaux 800/735-2478	**Vagabond Inns** 800/522-1555
www.relaischateaux.com	www.vagabondinn.com
Renaissance Hotels 888/236-2427	**W Hotels** 888/625-5144
www.renaissancehotels.com	www.whotels.com
Residence Inn 800/331-3131	**Wellesley Inn and Suites** 800/444-8888
www.residenceinn.com	www.wellesleyinnandsuites.com

WestCoast Hotels 800/325-4000
www.westcoasthotels.com
Westin Hotels & Resorts 800/937-8461
www.westinhotels.com
Wingate Inns 800/228-1000
www.thewingateinns.com
Woodfin Suite Hotels.........................800/966-3346
www.woodfinsuitehotels.com
WorldHotels 800/223-5652
www.worldhotels.com
Wyndham Hotels & Resorts 800/996-3426
www.wyndham.com

Airlines

Air Canada. 888/247-2262
www.aircanada.com
AirTran 800/247-8726
www.airtran.com
Alaska Airlines 800/252-7522
www.alaskaair.com
American Airlines...........................800/433-7300
www.aa.com
ATA. 800/435-9282
www.ata.com
Continental Airlines.........................800/523-3273
www.continental.com
Delta Air Lines..............................800/221-1212
www.delta.com
Frontier Airlines 800/432-1359
www.frontierairlines.com
Hawaiian Airlines...........................800/367-5320
www.hawaiianairlines.com
Jet Blue Airlines 800/538-2583
www.jetblue.com

Midwest Airlines............................800/452-2022
www.midwestairlines.com
Northwest Airlines...........................800/225-2525
www.nwa.com
Southwest Airlines..........................800/435-9792
www.southwest.com
Spirit Airlines...............................800/772-7117
www.spiritair.com
United Airlines..............................800/241-6522
www.united.com
US Airways 800/428-4322
www.usairways.com

Car Rentals

Advantage..................................800/777-5500
www.arac.com
Alamo 800/327-9633
www.alamo.com
Avis 800/831-2847
www.avis.com
Budget 800/527-0700
www.budget.com
Dollar 800/800-4000
www.dollar.com
Enterprise 800/325-8007
www.enterprise.com
Hertz.......................................800/654-3131
www.hertz.com
National 800/227-7368
www.nationalcar.com
Payless.....................................800/729-5377
www.paylesscarrental.com
Rent-A-Wreck.com 800/535-1391
www.rentawreck.com
Thrifty......................................800/847-4389
www.thrifty.com

Meet The Stars

Mobil Travel Guide 2007 *Five-Star* Award Winners

CALIFORNIA
Lodgings
The Beverly Hills Hotel, *Beverly Hills*
Chateau du Sureau, *Oakhurst*
Four Seasons Hotel San Francisco,
  San Francisco
Hotel Bel-Air, *Los Angeles*
The Peninsula Beverly Hills, *Beverly Hills*
Raffles L'Ermitage Beverly Hills, *Beverly Hills*
St. Regis Monarch Beach Resort & Spa, *Dana
  Point*
St. Regis San Francisco, *San Francisco*
The Ritz-Carlton, San Francisco, *San Francisco*

Restaurants
The Dining Room, *San Francisco*
The French Laundry, *Yountville*

COLORADO
Lodgings
The Broadmoor, *Colorado Springs*
The Little Nell, *Aspen*

CONNECTICUT
Lodging
The Mayflower Inn, *Washington*

DISTRICT OF COLUMBIA
Lodging
Four Seasons Hotel Washington, DC
  Washington

FLORIDA
Lodgings
Four Seasons Resort Palm Beach, *Palm Beach*
The Ritz-Carlton Naples, *Naples*
The Ritz-Carlton, Palm Beach, *Manalapan*

GEORGIA
Lodgings
Four Seasons Hotel Atlanta, *Atlanta*

The Lodge at Sea Island Golf Club,
  St. Simons Island

Restaurants
The Dining Room, *Atlanta*
Seeger's, *Atlanta*

HAWAII
Lodging
Four Seasons Resort Maui, *Wailea, Maui*

ILLINOIS
Lodgings
Four Seasons Hotel Chicago, *Chicago*
The Peninsula Chicago, *Chicago*
The Ritz-Carlton, A Four Seasons Hotel, *Chicago*

Restaurants
Alinea, *Chicago*
Charlie Trotter's, *Chicago*

MAINE
Restaurant
The White Barn Inn, *Kennebunkport*

MASSACHUSETTS
Lodgings
Blantyre, *Lenox*
Four Seasons Hotel Boston, *Boston*

NEVADA
Lodging
Tower Suites at Wynn, *Las Vegas*

Restaurants
Alex, *Las Vegas*
Joel Robuchon at the Mansion, *Las Vegas*

NEW YORK
Lodgings
Four Seasons, Hotel New York, *New York*
Mandarin Oriental, *New York*
The Point, *Saranac Lake*

The Ritz-Carlton New York, Central Park,
  New York
The St. Regis, *New York*

Restaurants
Alain Ducasse, *New York*
Jean Georges, *New York*
Masa, *New York*
per se, *New York*

NORTH CAROLINA
Lodging
The Fearrington House Country Inn, *Pittsboro*

PENNSYLVANIA
Restaurant
Le Bec-Fin, *Philadelphia*

SOUTH CAROLINA
Lodging
Woodlands Resort & Inn, *Summerville*

Restaurant
Dining Room at the Woodlands, *Summerville*

TENNESSEE
Lodging
The Hermitage, *Nashville*

TEXAS
Lodging
The Mansion on Turtle Creek, *Dallas*

VERMONT
Lodging
Twin Farms, *Barnard*

VIRGINIA
Lodgings
The Inn at Little Washington, *Washington*
The Jefferson Hotel, *Richmond*

Restaurant
The Inn at Little Washington, *Washington*

Mobil Travel Guide has been rating establishments with its Mobil One- to Five-Star system since 1958. Each establishment awarded the Mobil Five-Star rating is one of the best in the country. Detailed information on each award winner can be found in the corresponding regional edition listed on the back cover of this book.

Four- and Five-Star Establishments in Coastal Southeast

Georgia

★ ★ ★ ★ ★ Lodgings

Four Seasons Hotel Atlanta, *Atlanta*

The Lodge at Sea Island Golf Club, *St. Simons Island*

★ ★ ★ ★ Lodgings

The Ritz-Carlton, Buckhead, *Atlanta*

The Ritz-Carlton Lodge, Reynolds Plantation,
  Greensboro

★ ★ ★ ★ Spa

The Ritz-Carlton Spa, The Ritz-Carlton Lodge,
Reynolds Plantation,
  Greensboro

★ ★ ★ ★ ★ Restaurants

The Dining Room, *Atlanta*

Seeger's, *Atlanta*

★ ★ ★ ★ Restaurants

Bacchanalia, *Atlanta*

Park 75 at the Four Seasons, *Atlanta*

North Carolina

★ ★ ★ ★ ★ Lodging

The Fearrington House Country Inn, *Pittsboro*

★ ★ ★ ★ Lodgings

The Carolina Hotel, *Pinehurst*

Inn on Biltmore Estate, *Asheville*

Richmond Hill Inn, *Asheville*

★ ★ ★ ★ Spa

The Spa at Pinehurst, The Carolina at Pinehurst,
  Pinehurst

★ ★ ★ ★ Restaurants

Carolina CrossRoads, *Chapel Hill*

The Fearrington House Restaurant, *Pittsboro*

South Carolina

★ ★ ★ ★ ★ Lodging

Woodlands Resort & Inn, *Summerville*

★ ★ ★ ★ Lodgings

Charleston Place, *Charleston*

The Inn at Palmetto Bluff, *Hilton Head Island*

The Sanctuary at Kiawah Island, *Kiawah Island*

★ ★ ★ ★ ★ Restaurant

The Dining Room at the Woodlands, *Summerville*

★ ★ ★ ★ Restaurants

Charleston Grill, *Charleston*

Ocean Room at the Sanctuary, *Kiawah Island*

Peninsula Grill, *Charleston*

★ ★ ★ ★ Spa

The Spa at Sanctuary, *Kiawah Islandt*

Georgia

Georgia, beloved for its antebellum gentility and then devastated by General William Tecumseh Sherman's march to the sea, is now a vibrant, busy state typifying the economic growth of the New South. Founded with philanthropic and military aims, the only colony where rum and slavery were forbidden, the state nevertheless had the dubious honor of accepting the last shipment of slaves to this country. It boasts Savannah, one of the oldest planned cities in the US, and Atlanta, one of the newest of the South's great cities, rebuilt atop Civil War ashes.

The Georgia Colony was founded by James Oglethorpe on behalf of a private group of English trustees and was named for King George II of England. Georgia's barrier islands not only sheltered the fledgling colony, they provided a bulwark on the Spanish Main for English forts to oppose Spanish Florida and helped end the centuries-old struggle for domination among Spanish, French, and English along the South Atlantic Coast.

Today a year-round vacation mecca, the Golden Isles were at times Native American hunting lands, vast sea island plantations, fishing communities isolated after the Civil War, and rich men's private preserves. The Colony trustees brought English artisans to found strong colonies at Savannah, Brunswick, and Darien, where Scottish Highlanders introduced golf to the New World. The Cherokee made early peace with Oglethorpe and remained within the state to set up the Republic of the Cherokee Nation a century later. Gradually, however, all Native American lands of both Creek and Cherokee were ceded; the Cherokees were banished and their lands, including the capital, distributed by lottery.

Population: 8,186,453

Area: 59,441 square miles

Elevation: 0-4,784 feet

Peak: Brasstown Bald Mountain (between Towns and Union counties)

Entered Union: Fourth of original 13 states (January 1, 1788)

Capital: Atlanta

Motto: Wisdom, justice, and moderation

Flower: Cherokee Rose

Bird: Brown Thrasher

Tree: Live Oak

Fair: October in Macon

Time Zone: Eastern

Web Site: www.georgia.org

Fun Fact: Georgia is the nation's largest producer of peanuts, pecans, and peaches.

From their settlements at Savannah, Brunswick, and the coastal islands, Georgia colonists followed the rivers (many of them flowing north) to found inland ports such as Augusta. Colonial boundaries were extended to the Mississippi River by the state of Georgia, but the unfortunate manipulations of land speculators in the legislature deeded all of Mississippi, Alabama, Tennessee, and more for sale as the Yazoo Tract for 1 1/2 cents an acre. Though repudiated by a subsequent legislature and declared unconstitutional by the Supreme Court, the lands were gone forever, and Georgia no longer extended from the Mississippi to the sea. It is, however, still the largest state east of the Mississippi.

Georgia's lot in the Civil War was a harsh one from the time Sherman opened his campaign in Georgia on May 4, 1864, until he achieved the Union objective of splitting the South from the Mississippi to the sea. Reconstruction ushered in the reign of carpetbaggers and a long, slow recovery.

Calendar Highlights

FEBRUARY

Georgia Heritage Festival *(Savannah). Contact the Historic Savannah Foundation, phone 912/233-7787.* Walking tours, open house at historic sites, crafts show, waterfront festival, parade, concerts, Georgia Day.

MARCH

Augusta Invitational Rowing Regatta *(Augusta). Augusta Riverfront Marina.*

Auto racing *(Atlanta). Atlanta Motor Speedway. Phone 770/946-4211.* NASCAR Winston Cup, Busch Grand National, IMSA, and ARCA events.

Cherry Blossom Festival *(Macon). Phone 770/860-4188.* Historic tours, concerts, fireworks, hot air balloons, sporting events, and parade.

APRIL

Masters Golf Tournament *(Augusta). Augusta National Golf Course. Phone 706/667-6700.*

Spring Tour of Homes *(Athens). Contact Fire Hall #2; phone 706/353-1801 or 706/353-1820.* Held by Athens-Clarke Heritage Foundation.

MAY

Seafood Festival *(Savannah). Contact the Savannah Waterfront Association, phone 912/234-0295.* Waterfront. Restaurants offer samples; entertainment, arts and crafts.

SEPTEMBER

Georgia State Fair *(Macon). Central City Park. Phone 478/746-7184.* Grandstand shows, midway, exhibit buildings.

US 10K Classic and Family Sports Festival *(Marietta). Phone 770/432-0100.*

DECEMBER

Christmas in Savannah *(Savannah). Phone toll-free 800/444-CHARM.* Monthlong celebration includes tours of houses, historical presentations, parades, music, caroling, and cultural events.

Georgia boasts many firsts: the *Savannah*, the first steamship to cross the ocean (1819); America's first nuclear-powered merchant ship, the *Savannah* (1959); the first big American gold strike (1828); the cotton gin, invented by Eli Whitney (1793); and the first use of ether as an anesthetic (1842), by Georgia doctor Crawford Long.

Georgia produces peanuts, pecans, cotton, peaches, wood pulp, and paper products. Near Atlanta, a number of national manufacturing and commercial concerns contribute to a diversified economy. Georgia marble is prized the world over.

Georgia boasts many wonders, from its Blue Ridge vacation lands in the north—where Brasstown Bald Mountain rises 4,784 feet—to the deep "trembling earth" of the ancient and mysterious Okefenokee Swamp bordering Florida. Stone Mountain, a giant hunk of rock that rises from the plain near Atlanta, is the world's largest granite exposure. The coastal Golden Isles, set off by the mysterious Marshes of Glynn, support moss-festooned oaks that grow down to the white sand beaches. Visitors still pan for gold in the country's oldest gold mining town, Dahlonega, and find semiprecious stones in the Blue Ridge.

Historical attractions are everywhere, from the world's largest brick fort near Savannah to the late President Franklin D. Roosevelt's "Little White House" at Warm Springs. There is the infamous Confederate prison at Andersonville and the still-lavish splendor of the cottage colony of 60 millionaires of the Jekyll Island Club, now a state-owned resort. The battlefield marking Sherman's campaign before Atlanta and the giant ceremonial mounds of indigenous Native Americans are equally important national shrines.

Tourism is one of Georgia's primary industries. The state's visitor information centers, which are staffed year-round, offer brochures and computerized information to travelers on major highways.

When to Go/Climate

Short winters and mild temperatures are the rule in Georgia. Summers are hot and humid in the southern part of the state; winters can be cold and can include snowfall in the northern regions.

AVERAGE HIGH/LOW TEMPERATURES (°F)

Atlanta

Jan 50/32	**May** 80/59	**Sep** 82/64
Feb 55/35	**Jun** 86/66	**Oct** 73/52
Mar 64/43	**Jul** 88/70	**Nov** 63/43
Apr 73/50	**Aug** 87/69	**Dec** 54/35

Savannah

Jan 60/38	**May** 84/63	**Sep** 85/68
Feb 62/41	**Jun** 89/69	**Oct** 78/57
Mar 70/48	**Jul** 91/72	**Nov** 70/48
Apr 78/55	**Aug** 90/72	**Dec** 62/41

Parks and Recreation

Water-related activities, hiking, riding, various other sports, picnicking, and visitor centers, as well as camping and rental cottages, are available in many of Georgia's state parks. Most parks welcome campers, and there are many comfort stations with hot showers, electric outlets, and laundry. All parks have trailer dump stations, with the exception of Providence Canyon. Camping is limited to two weeks at any one park. Reservations may be made up to 11 months in advance. Parks are open year-round from 7 am-10 pm.

Georgia park vacationers may enjoy cottages at several state parks. These provide complete housekeeping facilities–kitchens with electric ranges and refrigerators, living rooms, one- to three-bedrooms (linens provided), porches, outdoor grills, and picnic tables. They are air-conditioned in summer and heated in winter.

Cottages are available at Amicalola Falls, Black Rock Mountain, Cloudland Canyon, Crooked River, Elijah Clark, Florence Marina, Fort Mountain, Franklin D. Roosevelt, Georgia Veterans Memorial, Hard Labor Creek, Hart, Indian Springs, John Tanner, Little Ocmulgee, Magnolia Springs, Mistletoe, Red Top Mountain, Seminole, Stephen C. Foster, Tugaloo,

Unicoi, Vogel, and Will-A-Way (in Fort Yargo) parks. Phone toll-free 800/864-7275. Cottage reservations can be made up to 11 months in advance; there is a two-day minimum stay at cottages.

Pets are allowed in state parks only if kept on a leash not longer than 6 feet and accompanied by owner at all times. No pets are allowed in cottages, site buildings, or swimming areas. Fees are subject to change.

Detailed information on state parks may be obtained from the Department of Natural Resources, State Parks and Historic Sites, 205 Butler St SE, Suite 1352, Atlanta 30334; phone 404/656-2770.

FISHING AND HUNTING

Georgia's range of fresh and saltwater fishing rivals any other state in variety. There are 26 major reservoirs totaling more than 400,000 acres, and 10 major river systems traverse the state, with thousands of miles of clear, cold-water trout streams and smaller, warm-water streams. Approximately 60,000 small lakes and ponds add to the freshwater total. Some 200 species of freshwater fish are found, 40 of which are considered desirable by game anglers, including largemouth, shoal, striped bass, crappie, and channel catfish. Mountain streams in northern Georgia are a natural source of trout. Fishing in black-water swamp areas in southern Georgia is just as famous for lunker bass and big bream. Coastal waters are good for mackerel, redfish, speckled trout, and giant tarpon; no license is required.

A state fishing license is required for all freshwater fishing; nonresident: season, $24; seven-day permit, $7; one-day permit, $3.50; trout stamp (required to fish in trout waters or to keep trout caught): season, $13. Fees subject to change. For further information on saltwater fishing, contact the Department of Natural Resources, Coastal Resources Division, 1 Conservation Way, Brunswick 31520-8600; phone 912/264-7218. For further information on freshwater fishing, contact the Department of Natural Resources, Wildlife Resources Division, 2123 Hwy 278SE, Social Circle 30279; phone 770/918-6418.

There is hunting from the Blue Ridge in northern Georgia to the piney woods of the south. Nonresident: season, $59; seven-day, $25; one-day, $5.50; big game (deer, wild turkey), $118. Preserve license, $12; bow hunting permit, $25. Wildlife Management Area stamp, $73. Waterfowl stamp, $5.50 (federal stamp also required). Fees are subject to change. For seasons, bag limits, and other details contact the Department of Natural Resources, Wildlife Resources Division, 2111 Hwy 278SE, Social Circle 30279; phone 770/918-6416.

Driving Information

Safety belts are mandatory for all persons in the front seat of a vehicle and all minors anywhere in a vehicle; ages 3 and 4 may use a regulation safety belt; age 2 and under must use an approved safety seat. For further information, phone 404/657-9300.

INTERSTATE HIGHWAY SYSTEM

The following alphabetical listing of Georgia towns in this book shows that these cities are within 10 miles of the indicated interstate highways. Check a highway map for the nearest exit.

Highway Number	Cities/Towns within 10 Miles
Interstate 16	Dublin, Macon, Savannah.
Interstate 20	Atlanta, Augusta, Carrollton, Madison.

GEORGIA'S BLUE RIDGE FOOTHILLS

Less than two hours north of downtown Atlanta, the Blue Ridge Mountains offer a scenic landscape for leisurely driving and sightseeing. The deeper mountains are largely protected within the Chattahoochee National Forest, while the foothills are full of quaint country towns. A 200-mile-loop trip takes drivers to some of the more celebrated destinations, with a wide range of attractions for children and families. From Atlanta, head north on Highway 400 (a toll road) and drive about 50 miles toward Dahlonega; Highway 19 leads you the rest of the way into town.

Named from the Cherokee word *talonega* (yellow), Dahlonega (dah-LON-ah-ga) was the site of the nation's first gold rush in the 1830s. In 1838, the federal government built a branch of the US Mint in Dahlonega, stamping the town's name on $6 million worth of gold coins before the operation was shut down at the onset of the Civil War. The story is told at the Dahlonega Gold Museum (phone 706/864-2257), housed within the old courthouse building in the center of the town square. This is the oldest building in northern Georgia. In the surrounding square, you'll find a colorful assortment of shops, restaurants, cafs, and an old-fashioned general store that sells penny candy. Stop by the visitor center for local maps and guides, including information about gold mine tours right outside of town. Before taking a tour, try your hand at the small (but fruitful!) gold-panning station beside the visitor center. On the south side of the square, the landmark Smith House (84 South Chestatee St; phone 706/864-2348 or toll-free 800/852-9577), which reportedly was built above a gold mine, has been serving all-you-can-eat family-style Southern meals for more than 80 years; they also offer overnight lodging.

From Dahlonega, follow Highway 19 north to Highway 129 east for about 25 miles to Cleveland. Cleveland found its way onto the national map in the 1970s as the birthplace of Cabbage Patch dolls, which still "grow" here in a "hospital" outside of town. Tours offer visitors the chance to witness the dolls being pulled from a cabbage patch twinkling with Christmas lights.

For more family fun, proceed to Helen by heading north on Highway 75. Helen was just a modest mountain town until local promoters were inspired to remake it as a Bavarian village. The villagers took to wearing dirndls and lederhosen, serving bratwurst and Heineken, observing Oktoberfest, and filling the air with accordion music. A museum in the castle on Main Street (phone 706/878-3140) tells the full story. A scenic stretch of the Chattahoochee River cuts through the busy tourist town, and local outfitters shuttle people upstream for leisurely float trips back down.

Return south on Highway 75 and turn east at the old Indian mound onto Highway 17, which rolls through a quieter stretch of the scenic foothills to Clarkesville. A small village here holds antique shops and a couple of cafés. Clarkesville is only 2 miles from the Highway 441/365 expressway that leads south back to Atlanta. Continuing south, the highway merges into I-985 around Gainesville for a speedy return to the city. **(Approximately 200 miles)**

Interstate 75	Adel, Atlanta, Calhoun, Cartersville, Cordele, Dalton, Forsyth, Macon, Marietta, Perry, Tifton, Valdosta.
Interstate 85	Atlanta, Buford, Commerce, La Grange, Norcross.
Interstate 95	Brunswick, Darien, Jekyll Island, Savannah, St. Simons Island.

Additional Visitor Information

For visitor information, including brochures and other materials, contact the Department of Industry, Trade, and Tourism, PO Box 1776, Atlanta 30301-1776; phone 404/656-3590 or toll-free 800/VISIT-GA. Visitor centers are located in Augusta, Columbus, Kingsland, Lavonia, Plains, Ringgold, Savannah, Sylvania, Tallapoosa, Valdosta, and West Point. Information is available 8:30 am-5:30 pm.

Adel (E-3)

See also Tifton, Valdosta

Population 5,307
Elevation 240 ft
Area Code 229
Zip 31620
Information Adel-Cook County Chamber of Commerce, 100 S Hutchinson Ave, PO Box 461; phone 229/896-2281
Web Site www.adelga.net

What to See and Do

Reed Bingham State Park. *542 Reed Bingham Rd, Adel (31620). 6 miles W off Hwy 37.* Phone 229/896-3551. *www.reedbinghamstatepark.org.* Less than 6 miles from busy I-75, this park includes a 375-acre lake that provides opportunities for fishing (bass, crappie, catfish, and bream), boating (three ramps), and water-skiing. You'll also find the Coastal Plain and Gopher Tortoise nature trails and a huge population of black and turkey vultures, which come here to roost in winter. Best viewing is in the morning or late afternoon. Picnicking, camping, playground. For more information, contact the Park Office, Rte 2, Box 394B-1. (Daily 7 am-10 pm)

Limited-Service Hotels

★ ★ **DAYS INN.** *1200 W 4th St, Adel (30121).*

Phone 229/896-4574; toll-free 800/329-7466; fax 229/896-4575. *www.daysinn.com.* 78 rooms, 2 story. Pets accepted, some restrictions; fee. Check-in 2 pm, check-out 11 am. Restaurant. Outdoor pool. **$**

★ **SUPER 8.** *1103 W 4th St; I-75 exit 39, Adel (31620).* Phone 229/896-2244; toll-free 800/446-4656; fax 229/896-2245. *www.super8.com.* 69 rooms, 2 story. Pets accepted, some restrictions; fee. Check-in 2 pm, check-out 11 am. Outdoor pool. **$**

Albany (E-2)

See also Americus, Cordele

Founded 1836
Population 76,939
Elevation 208 ft
Area Code 229
Information Convention and Visitors Bureau, 225 W Broad Ave, 31701; phone 229/434-8700
Web Site www.albanyga.com

Albany lies in a semitropical setting of oaks and pines located in the Plantation Trace region of the state. Colonel Nelson Tift, a Connecticut Yankee, led a party up the Flint River from Apalachicola, Florida, and constructed the first log buildings in Albany. Settlers followed when the Native Americans were moved to western lands. Paper-shell pecans grown in surrounding Dougherty County have made this the "pecan capital of the world." Surrounded by numerous plantations, the area is also well known for quail hunting.

What to See and Do

Albany Museum of Art. *311 Meadowlark Dr, Albany (31707).* Phone 229/439-8400. *www.albanymuseum. com.* This small museum holds an average of 15 permanent and changing exhibits of works by national and regional artists. The collection of sub-Saharan African art is particularly strong. (Tues-Fri 10 am-5 pm, Sat-Sun noon-5 pm; closed holidays) **$**

Lake Chehaw. *Lee County on Philema Rd, Albany. 2 miles NE off Hwy 91.* At the confluence of the Kinchafoonee and Muckalee creeks and the Flint River. Water-skiing, fishing, and boating.

The Parks at Chehaw. *105 Chehaw Park Rd, Albany (31701). 2 1/2 miles NE on Hwy 91.* Phone 229/430-

5275.www.parksatchehaw.org. This 800-acre park invites visitors to commune with nature. The creeks, streams, and cypress swamps are home to all sorts of wildlife, including deer, beavers, tortoises, alligators, and all sorts of birds, and the nature trails throughout the park allow visitors to see the animals up close. An old-style locomotive takes visitors on a 20-minute train ride through a restored area. Also here are a BMX track, a children's play park, and a wild animal park designed by famed naturalist Jim Fowler. Housing 40 animals in natural habitats, the park has the only cheetah population in Georgia. Kids love the petting zoo; there's also an amphitheater where special programs and demonstrations are held. Tent and RV camping (dump station), picnicking. (Daily 9 am-5 pm; closed Jan 1, Thanksgiving, Dec 25) **$**

Thronateeska Heritage Center. *100 W Roosevelt Ave, Albany (31701). Phone 229/432-6955; fax 229/435-1572. www.heritagecenter.org.* This complex of former railroad buildings houses exhibits as well as a hands-on Science Discovery Center for children. Also here is the Wetherbee Planetarium. (Thurs-Sat noon-4 pm; closed holidays) **$$**

Special Event

Fall on the Flint Festival. Entertainment, parade, exhibits, athletic contests. Last weekend in Sept.

Limited-Service Hotels

★ **COMFORT SUITES.** *1400 Dawson Rd, Albany (31707). Phone 229/888-3939; toll-free 800/228-5150; fax 229/435-4431. www.comfortsuites.com.* 62 rooms, 2 story. Complimentary continental breakfast. Check-in 2 pm, check-out noon. Fitness room. Outdoor pool. Airport transportation available. **$**

★ **HAMPTON INN.** *806 N Westover Blvd, Albany (31707). Phone 229/883-3300; toll-free 800/426-7866; fax 229/435-4092. www.hamptoninn.com.* 82 rooms, 2 story. Complimentary continental breakfast. Check-in 2 pm, check-out noon. High-speed Internet access. Outdoor pool. **$**

★ ★ **QUALITY INN.** *1500 Dawson Rd, Albany (31706). Phone 229/435-7721; toll-free 888/462-7721; fax 229/439-9386. www.merryacres.com.* 108 rooms. Complimentary continental breakfast. Check-out

noon. High-speed Internet access. Restaurant, bar. Fitness room. Outdoor pool, children's pool. **$**

★ **RAMADA INN.** *2505 N Slappey Blvd, Albany (31701). Phone 229/883-3211; toll-free 800/525-6685; fax 229/439-2806. www.ramada-albany.com.* 158 rooms, 2 story. Pets accepted; fee. Check-in 3 pm, check-out noon. Restaurant, bar. Outdoor pool, children's pool. Airport transportation available. **$**

★ **REGENCY INN.** *911 E Oglethorpe Expy, Albany (31705). Phone 229/883-1650; fax 229/883-1163.* 151 rooms, 4 story. Complimentary full breakfast. Check-in 3 pm, check-out noon. Outdoor pool. Airport transportation available. **$**

Alpharetta (B-2)

Population 34,854
Web Site www.alpharetta.ga.us

Full-Service Hotel

★ ★ ★ **MARRIOTT ALPHARETTA.** *5750 Windward Pkwy, Alpharetta (30005). Phone 770/754-9600; toll-free 800/228-9290; fax 770/754-9629. www.marriott.com.* 318 rooms, 8 story. Check-in 3 pm, check-out noon. High-speed Internet access, wireless Internet access. Restaurant, bar. Fitness room. Indoor pool, outdoor pool, whirlpool. Airport transportation available. Business center. **$$**

Restaurants

★ ★ ★ **RAY'S KILLER CREEK.** *1700 Mansell Rd, Alpharetta (30004). Phone 770/649-0064; fax 770/649-1391. www.raysrestaurants.com.* Located just off Route 400, this serene restaurant features an outdoor waterfall and stream with gardens and flowers, putting diners at ease before they even step through the front door. The dining room is also welcoming with high wooden ceilings, an open display kitchen, intimate booths, and tiered seating with views of the porch and a pond fed by Foe Killer Creek. The menu features steak, seafood, and other dishes such as cashew-crusted salmon salad and hickory rotisserie chicken. Diners can enjoy live jazz music and a nightcap in the bar

Wednesday through Saturday, and the Sunday brunch should not be missed. Steak menu. Lunch, dinner, Sun brunch. Bar. Children's menu. Business casual attire. Reservations recommended. Valet parking. Outdoor seating. **$$$**

★ ★ **VINNY'S ON WINDWARD.** *5355 Windward Pkwy, Alpharetta (30004). Phone 770/772-4644; fax 770/772-4244. www.knowwheretogogh.com.* The décor in this lively Italian restaurant is traditional with red brick walls, arched entrances and windows, high ceilings with exposed pipes, featured artwork from a popular Atlanta gallery, and antique wood tabletops in the dining room. An open display kitchen invites diners to watch the chefs at work. Or diners could head outside to the terrace area for a quiet evening. There are many wines, both Italian and California, to pair with the inventive menu, or diners can try a glass of Italian grappa. Italian menu. Lunch, dinner. Bar. Children's menu. Business casual attire. Reservations recommended. Valet parking. Outdoor seating. **$$$**

Americus (D-2)

See also Albany, Andersonville, Cordele, Lumpkin

Founded 1832
Population 17,013
Area Code 229
Zip 31709
Information Americus-Sumter County Chamber of Commerce, Tourism Division, 400 Lamar St, Box 724; phone 229/924-2646 or toll-free 888/278-6837
Web Site www.americus-sumterchamber.com

Americus is at the center of an area once known as the "granary of the Creek nations," so called because Native Americans favored this area for the cultivation of maize. The town was named, it is said, either for Americus Vespucius or for the settlers themselves, who were referred to as "merry cusses" because of their happy-go-lucky ways. The town flourished in the 1890s. Many Victorian and Gothic Revival buildings remain from that period.

Today, peanuts, corn, cotton, small grain, and pecans are grown, and bauxite and kaolin are mined in the area. Americus is also a manufacturing center, producing lumber commodities, metal lighting equipment, heating products, and textiles. The town's livestock sales are second in volume in the state. Plains, nine

miles west via Hwy 280, is the hometown of the 39th president, Jimmy Carter.

What to See and Do

Americus Historic Driving Tour. *Phone 229/928-605.* Tour features 38 houses of various architectural styles, including Victorian, Greek Revival, and Classical Revival. Contact the Tourism Council.

Georgia Southwestern State College. *800 Wheatley St, Americus (31709). 2 miles E of junction Hwys 19, 280.* (1906) (2,600 students) Campus (187 acres) with lake. Also here is

> **Carter Display.** *800 Wheatley St, Americus (31709).* Focusing on former President Jimmy Carter and First Lady Rosalynn Carter; photographs, memorabilia; located in James Earl Carter Library. (Daily except during school breaks, holidays) **FREE**

⭐ **Jimmy Carter National Historic Site.** *300 N Bond St,* Plains (31780). *10 miles W on Hwy 280. Phone 229/824-4104; fax 229/824-3441. www.nps.gov/jica.* The visitor center is located in Plains High School, where Jimmy and Rosalynn Carter attended grammar and high school. The school now functions as a museum, with an orientation film, campaign memorabilia, and exhibits on Carter's life and career. Also here is the Plains Depot Museum, the oldest building in town (1888), which served as Carter's campaign headquarters in 1976. (Daily 9 am-5 pm; closed Jan 1, Thanksgiving, Dec 25) **FREE**

Limited-Service Hotel

★ ★ **WINDSOR HOTEL.** *125 W Lamar St, Americus (31709). Phone 229/924-1555; toll-free 888/297-9567; fax 229/928-0533. www.windsor-americus. com.* Built right before the turn of the century, this wonderful country escape has beautiful architecture and design and is located near local antique shops and shopping. Guests will appreciate the rich history that is evident here. Period-style rooms with 12-foot ceilings and ceiling fans. 53 rooms, 3 story. Check-out noon. Restaurant, bar. **$**

Specialty Lodging

1906 PATHWAY INN BED & BREAKFAST. *501 S Lee St, Americus (31709). Phone 229/928-2078; toll-free 800/889-1466. www.1906pathwayinn.com.* For a small-town getaway, this English colonial bed-and-breakfast offers guests relaxation, Southern style. The Old South charm here is warm and inviting. 5 rooms, 2 story. Pets accepted, some restrictions; fee. Complimentary full breakfast. Check-in 4-6 pm, check-out 11 am. **$**

Restaurant

★ ★ ★ **GRAND DINING ROOM.** *125 W Lamar St, Americus (31709). Phone 229/924-1555. www.windsor-americus.com.* Located in the Windsor Hotel (see), this restaurant offers traditional Southern favorites along with cuisine from different regions of the country. Charming Victorian settings complete the elegant and intimate dining experience. American menu. Lunch, dinner. Bar. **$$**

Andersonville (D-2)

See also Americus, Cordele, Perry

Population 331
Elevation 390 ft
Area Code 229
Zip 31711
Web Site www.maconcountyga.org

What to See and Do

Andersonville National Historic Site. *Hwy 49 N, Andersonville. Phone 229/924-0343; fax 229/928-9640. www.nps.gov/ande.* Camp Sumter, a Confederate military prison, was built in early 1864 on a 26-acre tract by soldiers and slaves requisitioned from nearby plantations. The lofty pines that grew in the sandy soil were cut and used to form a stockade. Built to accommodate 10,000 men, the prison at one time held as many as 33,000. Overcrowding, inadequate food, insufficient medicines, and a breakdown of the prisoner exchange system resulted in a high death rate. The site is now a memorial to all prisoners of war throughout history. Included on the grounds are escape tunnels and wells dug by prisoners, Confederate earthworks, three reconstructed sections of stockade wall, and state monuments. (Daily 8 am-5 pm) **FREE** Here are

Andersonville National Cemetery. *US Hwy 49 N, Andersonville. 1/2 miles N of prison site. Phone 229/924-0343.* Graves of more than 17,000 Union soldiers and veterans of US military are in striking contrast to the landscaped grounds. The initial interments were Union soldiers who died in the prison camp. Dedicated as a national cemetery on August 17, 1865.

National Prisoner of War Museum. *Andersonville National Historic Site, Hwy 49 N, Andersonville. Phone 229/924-0343; fax 229/928-9640.* Exhibits, interpretive programs, and interactive videos depict the role of military prisoners in the nation's history. (Daily 8:30 am-5 pm; closed Jan 1, Thanksgiving, Dec 25) **FREE**

Providence Spring. The spring, which bubbled up from the ground after a heavy rain, was said to be in answer to the prisoners' prayers during the summer of 1864.

Civil War Village of Andersonville. *114 Church St, Andersonville. Phone 229/924-2558.* Restored village from the days of the Civil War. Welcome center, pioneer farm, museum (fee), antique shops. (Daily, times and days vary; closed Dec 25) **$**

Special Event

Andersonville Historic Fair. *114 Church St, Andersonville. Phone 229/924-2558.* Civil War reenactments, old time craftsmen, antique dealers; RV campsites. Contact Andersonville Historic Fair, PO Box 6; 229/924-2558. Memorial Day weekend and the first weekend in Oct.

Athens (B-3)

See also Commerce, Madison, Washington, Winder

Founded 1801
Population 45,734
Elevation 775 ft
Area Code 706
Information Convention and Visitors Bureau, 300 N Thomas St, 30601; phone toll-free 800/653-0603; or Athens Welcome Center, 280 E Dougherty St, 30601; phone 706/353-1820
Web Site www.visitathensga.com

Georgia's "Classic City" is the site of the University of Georgia, chartered in 1785. Diversified industry produces nonwoven fabrics, textiles, clocks, electronic components, precision parts, chemicals, and animal feed. Lyman Hall, a signer of the Declaration of Independence, proposed the University, and Abraham Baldwin, the acknowledged founding father, wrote the charter. Although allotted 10,000 acres by the legislature in 1784, it was another 17 years before Josiah Meigs, Baldwin's successor and first official president, erected a few log buildings, called it Franklin College, and held classes under the tolerant eyes of curious Cherokees.

Athens was incorporated in 1806. Its setting on a hill beside the Oconee River is enhanced by towering oaks and elms, white-blossomed magnolias, old-fashioned boxwood gardens, and many well-preserved and still-occupied antebellum houses.

What to See and Do

Double-barreled cannon. *College and Hancock aves, Athens. City Hall lawn.* (1863) A unique Civil War weapon cast at Athens's foundry. Believed to be the only double-barreled cannon in the world.

Historic houses. Phone 706/353-1870. For tour information, contact Athens Welcome Center in Church-Waddel-Brumby House (see) or contact the Athens Convention and Visitors Bureau.

Church-Waddel-Brumby House. *280 E Dougherty St, Athens (30601). Phone 706/353-1820.* (Circa 1820) Restored Federal-style house thought to be the oldest residence in Athens. Houses **Athens Welcome Center,** which has information on self-guided tours of other historic houses and buildings (Mon-Sat 10 am-6 pm, Sun from noon). **FREE**

Founders Memorial Garden. *325 S Lumpkin St, Athens. On University of Georgia campus. Phone 706/542-1365.* Memorial to founders of Ladies' Garden Club of Athens, the first garden club in the US.

Other historic houses. Includes Ross Crane House (Sigma Alpha Epsilon fraternity) (1842), 247 Pulaski St; Lucy Cobb Institute (1858), 200 N Milledge Ave; Joseph Henry Lumpkin House (1841), 248 Prince Ave; Old Franklin Hotel (1845), 480 E Broad St; Governor Wilson Lumpkin House (1842), South campus, University of Georgia. University of Georgia, N campus, also has numerous pre-1860 buildings.

Taylor-Grady House. *634 Prince Ave, Athens (30601). Phone 706/549-8688.*(1839) Restored Greek Revival mansion surrounded by 13 columns said to symbolize 13 original states; period furniture. (Mon-Thurs; closed holidays) **$$**

University president's house. *570 Prince Ave, Athens.* (Circa 1855) Greek Revival mansion surrounded on three sides by massive Corinthian columns. Extensive gardens and picket fences complement classic design. Private residence.

Sandy Creek Nature Center. *205 Old Commerce Rd, Athens. 1/2 mile N of Athens bypass, off Hwy 441. Phone 706/613-3615. www.sandycreeknaturecenter.com.* Approximately 200 acres of woods, fields, and marsh-land; includes a live animal exhibit, a 180-year-old cabin, nature trails. (Tues-Sat; closed Thanksgiving, Dec 25) **FREE** Also here is

ENSAT Center. *205 Old Commerce Rd, Athens (30607). Phone 706/613-3615.* Model of sustainable "green" architecture with ecological exhibits. (Tues-Sat) **FREE**

Sandy Creek Park. *400 Bob Holman Rd, Athens (30607). N on Hwy 441. Phone 706/613-3631; fax 706/613-3612. www.sandycreekpark.com.* Swimming (beach), fishing, boating; hiking, tennis, basketball, picnicking, playgrounds, primitive camping. Walk-ways. (Tues-Sun) **$**

Tree That Owns Itself. *Dearing and Finley sts, Athens (30601).* White oak, descendant of original tree, stands on a plot deeded to it.

University of Georgia. *College Station and River rds, Athens. Phone 706/542-3000. www.uga.edu.* (1785) (32,000 students) Consisting of 14 schools and colleges, the main campus extends more than 2 miles south from the Arch (1858), College Ave, and Broad St. Nearby are farms managed by the College of Agriculture, a forestry preserve, and University Research Park. Historic buildings include Demosthenian Hall (1824); chapel (1832), housing an oil painting (17 by 23 1/2 feet) of the interior of St. Peter's Basilica; Old College (1806), oldest building, designed after Connecticut Hall at Yale; Waddel Hall (1821); and Phi Kappa Hall (1834). Also on campus are

Butts-Mehre Heritage Museum. *1 Selig Cir, Athens. Third and fourth floors of Butts-Mehre Heritage Hall, Lumpkin St and Pinecrest Dr. Phone 706/542-9036.* Exhibits, videos, and trophy cases display Georgia sports memorabilia. (Mon-Fri, Sat afternoons) **FREE**

Georgia Museum of Art. *90 Carlton St, Athens (30602). Phone 706/542-4662; fax 706/542-1051. www.uga.edu/gamuseum.* Contains more than 8,000 pieces, including Eva Underhill Holbrook

Collection; traveling and special exhibits. (Tues-Sun; closed holidays, week of Dec 25) **FREE**

State Botanical Garden. *2450 S Milledge Ave, Athens (30605). Phone 706/542-1244. www.uga.edu/botgarden.* Approximately 300 acres with natural trails, wildlife, and special collections. Gardens (daily); conservatory/visitors center (daily); Callaway Building (Mon-Fri). **FREE**

Special Events

Crackerland Tennis Tournament. *Dan Magill Tennis Complex, University of Georgia, Athens.* Juniors, late July-early Aug. Seniors, mid-Aug.

North Georgia Folk Festival. *Sandy Creek Park, 293 Hoyt St, Athens (30601). Phone 706/208-0985. www.uga.edu/folkdance/folkfest.htm.* This annual music festival showcases several different types of music that have roots in the region. Genres include bluegrass, gospel, and more. Early Oct. **$$**

Spring Tour of Homes. *489 Prince Ave, Athens. Phone 706/353-1801;* Celebration of Athens architecture held by the Athens-Clarke Heritage Foundation. Phone 706/353-1801 or 706/353-1820. Last weekend in Apr.

Limited-Service Hotels

★ **BEST WESTERN COLONIAL INN.** *170 N Milledge Ave, Athens (30601). Phone 706/546-7311; toll-free 800/592-9401; fax 706/546-7959. www.bestwestern.com.* 70 rooms, 2 story. Pets accepted; fee. Complimentary continental breakfast. Check-in 2 pm, check-out 11 am. Outdoor pool. **$**

★★ **HOLIDAY INN ATHENS.** *197 E Broad St, Athens (30603). Phone 706/549-4433; toll-free 800/862-8436; fax 706/548-3031. www.holiday-inn.com.* A large property with a small property feel, this hotel offers expanded amenities and services and a friendly staff. It's located adjacent to the University of Georgia in the heart of downtown. Numerous shops and restaurants are within walking distance. 307 rooms, 6 story. Pets accepted. Check-in 3 pm, check-out 11 am. High-speed Internet access, wireless Internet access. Restaurant, bar. Fitness room. Indoor pool, whirlpool. Airport transportation available. Business center. **$**

★ **HOLIDAY INN EXPRESS ATHENS.** *513 W Broad St, Athens (30601). Phone 706/546-8122; toll-*

free 800/465-4329; fax 706/546-1722. www.chiexpress.com.* This spacious motel is located within walking distance of downtown. There are numerous hotels, motels, and restaurants nearby, and the University of Georgia is a couple blocks west—convenient for visiting families or campus tour visits. 160 rooms, 5 story. Complimentary continental breakfast. Check-in 3 pm, check-out 11 am. High-speed Internet access. Fitness room. Outdoor pool. Airport transportation available. Business center. **$**

Specialty Lodging

RIVENDELL BED AND BREAKFAST. *3581 S Barnett Shoals Rd, Watkinsville (30677). Phone 706/769-4522; fax 706/769-4393.* 5 rooms, 2 story. Children over 10 years only. Complimentary full breakfast. Check-in 5 pm. Check-out 11 am. **$**

Restaurants

★★ **HARRY BISSETT'S NEW ORLEANS CAFE & OYSTER BAR.** *279 E Broad St, Athens (30601). Phone 706/353-7065; fax 706/549-7802. www.harrybissetts.net.* A popular hangout for local University of Georgia students, this old bank building on the main street of downtown Athens has retained its historic charm with the pressed-tin ceilings and brickwork of its original 1895 structure. Fresh seafood is flown in every day, and the barbecued shrimp is a favorite here. Cajun/Creole menu. Lunch, dinner. Closed holidays. Bar. Business casual attire. Reservations recommended. Outdoor seating. **$$**

★ **THE VARSITY.** *1000 W Broad St, Athens (30601). Phone 706/548-6325; fax 706/548-2820. www.thevarsity.com.* Just a few blocks west of the city center and the University of Georgia, this local favorite is reminiscent of an old-fashioned diner/drive-in. Formica tables, an ordering counter, sports pictures and a menu board on the walls, and a red and white color scheme all add to the relaxed atmosphere. Affordable prices along with the floats, hamburgers, and slushes keep guests coming back. American menu. Lunch, dinner. Closed Easter, Thanksgiving, Dec 25. Casual attire. Outdoor seating. **$**

Atlanta (B-2)

See also Atlanta Hartsfield Airport Area, Buford, Cartersville, Marietta, Norcross, Roswell, Winder

Founded 1837
Population 416,474
Elevation 1,050 ft
Area Code 404
Information Convention and Visitors Bureau, 233 Peachtree St NE, Suite 2000, 30303; phone 404/521-6600 or toll-free 800/285-2682
Web Site www.atlanta.net
Suburbs Marietta, Norcross. (See individual alphabetical listings.)

When Atlanta was just 27 years old, 90 percent of its houses and buildings were razed by Union armies after a 117-day siege. Rebuilt by railroads in the 20th century, the city gives an overall impression of modernism.

Standing Peachtree, a Creek settlement, occupied Atlanta's site until 1813. Lieutenant George R. Gilmer led 22 recruits to build a fort here because of difficulties among the Creek and Cherokee. This became the first white settlement and grew into an important trading post.

After Georgia's secession from the Union on January 19, 1861, the city became a manufacturing, storage, supply, and transportation center for the Confederate forces. This made Atlanta the target and last real barrier on General William Tecumseh Sherman's "March to the Sea." Although Atlanta had quartered 60,000 Confederate wounded, it was untouched by actual battle until Sherman began the fierce fighting of the Atlanta Campaign on May 7, 1864, with the engagement at Tunnel Hill, just over the Tennessee line. Despairing of capturing the city by battle, Sherman undertook a siege.

Guns were brought in, and Atlanta civilians got a foretaste of 20th-century warfare as the population and defenders alike were subjected to continuous bombardment by the Union's heaviest artillery. People took refuge in cellars, trenches, and dugouts. Those who could escaped southward by wagon, foot, or train until Union forces seized the railroad 20 miles south at Jonesboro on September 1. General Hood evacuated Atlanta that same night, and the mayor surrendered the city the next day, September 2. Although the terms of surrender promised protection of life and property, Sherman ordered the city evacuated. All but 400 of the 3,600 houses and commercial buildings were destroyed in the subsequent burning.

Many citizens had returned to the city by January of 1865. By June, steps had been taken to reorganize business and repair wrecked railroad facilities. In 1866, Atlanta was made federal headquarters for area reconstruction. During the Reconstruction Convention of 1867-1868 called by General John Pope in Atlanta, the city offered facilities for the state government if it should be chosen the capital. The convention accepted this proposition, and Atlanta became the capital on April 20, 1868.

Atlanta's recovery and expansion as a rail center was begun by 1872, when two more railroads met here. Today, hundreds of manufacturers produce a wide variety of commodities.

Metropolitan Atlanta's population of 2.8 million is as devoted to cultural activities (such as its famed Alliance Theatre) as it is to its many golf courses and its major sports teams. Today Peachtree Street considers itself the South's main street and is more Fifth Avenue than Scarlett O'Hara's beloved lane. Skyscrapers, museums, luxury shops, and hotels rub shoulders along this concourse where Coca-Cola was first served; there are few peach blossoms left.

There are 29 colleges and universities in Atlanta. Georgia Institute of Technology, home of "a rambling wreck from Georgia Tech and a hell of an engineer," is one of the nation's top technological institutes. Other schools include Georgia State, Emory, and Oglethorpe universities. Atlanta University Center is an affiliation of six institutions of higher learning: Atlanta University, Spelman, Morehouse, Clark, and Morris Brown colleges, and the Interdenominational Theological Center.

Additional Visitor Information

For additional accommodations, see ATLANTA HARTSFIELD AIRPORT AREA, which follows ATLANTA.

For information, contact the Convention and Visitors Bureau, 233 Peachtree St NE, Suite 2000, 30303; phone 404/222-6688. Welcome centers are located at Underground Atlanta, Peachtree Center Mall, Lenox Square Mall, and Atlanta Hartsfield Airport.

Martin Luther King, Jr., Historic District

"Free at last, free at last, thank God Almighty we are free at last."
- Reverend Martin Luther King, Jr. (1929-1968)

East of downtown Atlanta is a small neighborhood named Sweet Auburn. Established in the late 19th century, the neighborhood was once known as "the richest Negro street in the world." Martin Luther King, Jr., was born in Sweet Auburn on January 15, 1929. Since his death and entombment here, much of the neighborhood has been declared a National Historic District.

The best way to approach the district from downtown Atlanta is to start at the central Five Points MARTA station. Go north on Peachtree Street, the city's main artery, to pick up Auburn Avenue on the far side of the small brown-bagger's Woodruff Park. Follow Auburn Street east to the King Center, about a mile. On the way you will pass many landmarks that shed light on the community. The modern Auburn Avenue Research Library (101 Auburn) maintains a special collection on African-American history and heritage. The APEX Museum (135 Auburn) has an exhibit on the development of the neighborhood, including a short video, along with displays of African art. The Southern Christian Leadership Conference continues to work for social change out of its offices in the Prince Hall Masonic Building (332 Auburn Avenue). The Ebenezer Baptist Church (407 Auburn) is the heart of the community. This 1922 sanctuary where Dr. King,

his father, and his grandfather preached grew so popular with visitors that the congregation needed to build a much larger sanctuary across the street and now maintains the original 750-seat building for special services. Adjacent to the small sanctuary is the King Center for Nonviolent Social Change (449 Auburn), where the crypt of Martin Luther King, Jr., remains set behind an eternal flame in a reflecting pond in the plaza, visible 24 hours a day. The Center, founded by Dr. King's widow, Coretta Scott King, and now directed by his son Dexter King, maintains exhibits displaying personal effects and mementos, including exhibits on Mahatma Gandhi, who inspired King's dedication to nonviolence. Across the street at the Martin Luther King, Jr., Historic Site visitor center (450 Auburn), the National Park Service has displays about the Nobel Peace Prize winner and screens a 30-minute film with historical footage from the Civil Rights era. The National Park Service also leads guided walking tours of the district.

Martin Luther King, Jr., was born in an upstairs bedroom in a two-story Victorian house at 501 Auburn Avenue. His father, Reverend Martin Luther King, and mother, the former Alberta Williams, had been married in the house three years earlier, and all three of their children where born here. The nine-room Queen Anne style house has been restored and furnished to reflect the time when "M. L." (as he was known) was growing up

Public Transportation

Buses and subway trains (MARTA); phone 404/848-4711; www.itsmarta.com.

What to See and Do

A. G. Rhodes Memorial Hall. *1516 Peachtree St NW, Atlanta (30309). Phone 404/885-7800. www.georgia-trust.org/rhodes.html.* (1903) An outstanding example of Victorian Romanesque architecture. The Georgia Trust offices are housed here; the first floor is a museum. (Mon-Fri 11 am-4 pm, Sun noon-3 pm; closed holidays) **$**

Atlanta Botanical Garden. *1345 Piedmont Ave, Atlanta (30309). Phone 404/876-5859. www.*

atlantabotanicalgarden.org. Features 15 acres of outdoor gardens: Japanese, rose, perennial, and others. The Fuqua Conservatory has tropical, desert, and rare plants from around the world; there's also a special exhibit area for carnivorous plants. (Apr-Sept: Tues-Sun 9 am-7 pm, Oct-Mar: Tues-Sun 9 am-5 pm; closed Jan 1, Dec 25) **$$$**

Atlanta Braves (MLB). *Turner Field, 775 Hank Aaron Dr, Atlanta (30302). Phone 404/522-7630. www.atlantabraves.com.* Professional baseball team.

Atlanta Cyclorama. *Grant Park, 800 Cherokee Ave SE, Atlanta (30315). Phone 404/658-7625.* This theater in the round tells the story of the 1864 Battle for Atlanta as the studio revolves around a massive painting and diorama completed in 1885. (Daily 9 am-4:30 pm) **$$**

Atlanta Falcons (NFL). *Georgia Dome,1 Georgia Dome Dr, Atlanta. Phone 770/965-3115. www.atlantafalcons. com.* Professional football team.

Atlanta Hawks (NBA). *Philips Arena,1 Philips Dr, Atlanta (30303). Phone 404/827-3865. www.hawks.com.* Professional basketball team.

Atlanta History Center. *130 W Paces Ferry Rd, Atlanta (30305). Phone 404/814-4000. www.atlantahistorycenter.com.* The center consists of five major structures and 33 acres of woodlands and gardens. (Mon-Sat 10 am-5:30 pm, Sun noon-5:30 pm; closed holidays) **$$$** On-site are

> **Atlanta History Museum.** *130 W Paces Ferry Rd, Atlanta (30305).* Historical exhibits relating to Atlanta, the Civil War, Southern folk life, and African Americans. (Mon-Sat 10 am-5:50 pm, Sun noon-5:30 pm; closed holidays)

> **McElreath Hall.** *130 W Paces Ferry Rd, Atlanta (30305).* Research library, archives, and Cherokee Garden Library with gardening and horticulture research collection (Mon-Fri; closed holidays) Special events.

> **Swan House.** *130 W Paces Ferry Rd, Atlanta (30305).* (1928) A classically styled mansion preserved as an example of early 20th-century architecture and decorative arts. Mansion is part of spacious landscaped grounds that includes terraces with cascading fountains, formal boxwood garden, and Victorian playhouse. On premises is the Philip Trammell Shutze Collection of Decorative Arts. (Daily; closed holidays) Guided tours.

> **Tullie Smith Farm.** *130 W Paces Ferry Rd, Atlanta (30305).* Guided tours of 1840 plantation-style farmhouse, herb gardens, pioneer log cabin, and other outbuildings; craft demonstrations.

Atlanta Thrashers (NHL). *Philips Arena,1 Philips Dr, Atlanta (30303). Phone 404/878-3300; toll-free 866/715-1500. www.atlantathrashers.com.* Professional hockey team.

Centennial Olympic Park. *265 Luckie St NW, Atlanta (30303). Bounded by Marietta Ave, Techwood Dr, and Baker St. www.centennialpark.com.* This 21-acre park was constructed for the 1996 Summer Olympics and serves as Atlanta's downtown centerpiece. It features the Fountain of Rings (where water shoots up in the shape of Olympic rings), an amphitheater and Great Lawn for festivals and concerts, a visitor center, and

a memorial to the two people killed in the bombing here during the Games. (Daily 7 am-11 pm)

CNN Studio Tour. *1 CNN Ctr, Atlanta (30348). At Centennial Park Dr and Marietta St. Phone 404/827-2300; toll-free 877/426-6868. www.atlantanation.com/ cnntour.html.* Tour the studio, view a re-creation of the main control room, visit an interactive exhibit of top news stories, or learn the secrets of map-pointing only TV weather forecasters know. (45-minute tours leave every 20 minutes; reservations recommended; no children under 4 years permitted). (Daily 9 am-5 pm; closed Easter, Thanksgiving, Dec 25) **$$**

Fernbank Museum of Natural History. *767 Clifton Rd NE, Atlanta (30307). Phone 404/929-6300. www. fernbank.edu.* This monumental four-story modern museum houses exhibits on the Earth's formation, the dinosaur era, the first European settlers in North America, and more. An IMAX theater shows nature-themed films on its giant screen and hosts "Martinis & IMAX" every Friday night. (Mon-Sat 10 am-5 pm, Sun noon-5 pm; closed Thanksgiving, Dec 25) **$$$**

Fernbank Science Center. *156 Heaton Park Dr NE, Atlanta (30307). Phone 678/874-7102. www. fernbanksciencecenter.org.* The center includes an exhibit hall, an observatory, a planetarium (**$**), and a science library; the grounds also contain a 65-acre forest area with marked trails. (Mon-Wed 8:30 am-5 pm, Thurs-Fri 8:30 am-10 pm, Sat 10 am-5 pm, Sun 1-5 pm; closed holidays) **FREE**

Fort McPherson. *Lee St, Atlanta. Hwy 29, approximately 3 miles SW via I-75 and Lakewood Frwy. Phone 404/464-0486. www.mcpherson.army.mil.* A military reservation since May 4, 1889. Historical tours (Mon-Fri, by appointment). **FREE**

Fox Theatre. *660 Peachtree St NE, Atlanta (30308). Phone 404/881-2100. www.foxtheatre.org.* (1929) The "Fabulous Fox," one of the most lavish movie theaters in the world, was conceived as a Shriners' temple with a more than 4,000-seat auditorium. Guests in the theater sit in an Arabian courtyard under an azure-painted sky with hundreds of 11-watt bulbs fixed in crystals, twinkling like stars. With 3,622 pipes, the colossal organ is the second-largest theater organ in the United States. The theater also features the world's largest Moller organ console and three elaborate ballrooms. The restored theater's ornate architecture combines exotic Moorish and Egyptian details. Hosts performances of the Atlanta Ballet, Broadway shows, a summer film festival, a full spectrum of concerts, theatrical events, trade shows, and conventions. Tours (Mon, Wed-Thurs 10 am; Sat 10 am and 11 am). **$$**

Georgia State Farmers' Market. *16 Forest Pkwy, Forest Park (30297). 10 miles S on I-75. agr.state.ga.us/html/ atlanta_farmers_market.html.* Owned and operated by the state and covering 146 acres, this is one of the largest farmers' markets of its kind in the Southeast. (Tues-Sat; closed Dec 25) **FREE**

Jimmy Carter Library and Museum. *441 Freedom Pkway, Atlanta (30307). Phone 404/865-7101. www. jimmycarterlibrary.org.* This museum has exhibits on life in the White House, major events during the Carter administration, and the life of President Carter. It includes a full-scale replica of the Oval Office. (Museum: Mon-Sat 9 am-4:45 pm, Sun noon-4:45 pm; library: Mon-Fri 8:30 am-4:30 pm; closed Jan 1, Thanksgiving, Dec 25) **$$**

Margaret Mitchell House. *990 Peachtree Street Ne,* Atlanta (30309). *At 10th St. Phone 404/249-7015. www. gwtw.org.* Home of the famous Atlanta native, author of *Gone with the Wind,* written here in a cramped basement apartment. The museum displays a portrait of Scarlett O'Hara from the movie; the original door from Tara, Scarlett's home; and a great collection of movie posters. Hour-long guided tours. (Daily 9:30 am-5:30 pm; closed Jan 1, Thanksgiving, Dec 24-25) **$$$**

⭐ **Martin Luther King, Jr. National Historic Site.** *450 Auburn Ave, Atlanta. Phone 404/331-5190. www. nps.gov/malu.* A two-block area in memory of the famed leader of the Civil Rights movement and winner of the Nobel Peace Prize. Features include the Freedom Hall Complex, Chapel of All Faiths, King Library and Archives, and the reflecting pool; films and slides on Dr. King's life and work may be viewed in the screening room (fee). The National Park Service operates an information center. Guided tours of King's boyhood home are conducted by park rangers. (Daily 9 am-5 pm, until 6 pm Memorial Day weekend-Labor Day; closed Jan 1, Thanksgiving, Dec 25) **FREE** At the site are

Ebenezer Baptist Church. *450 Auburn Ave NE, Atlanta (30312). Phone 404/688-7263.* Dr. King was co-pastor at Ebenezer from 1960-1968. Next door to the church is his gravesite with an eternal flame. (Mon-Sat 9 am-5 pm, Sun 1-5 pm) **DONATION**

King Birthplace. *501 Auburn Ave, Atlanta. Phone 404/331-3920.* **FREE**

Parks. Atlanta parks offer dogwood blooms in spring and varied recreational facilities, including golf, swimming, and picnic areas.

Chastain Memorial Park. *135 W Wieuca Rd, Atlanta (30327). Between Powers Ferry Rd and Lake Forrest Dr.* Swimming, tennis, golf, picnicking, amphitheater. Fees for various activities.

Grant Park. *800 Cherokee Ave SE, Atlanta (30315).* Many miles of walks and roads; visible traces of breastworks built for defense of Atlanta; cyclorama depicting the Battle of Atlanta; Atlanta Zoo with a variety of species. Swimming, tennis, picnicking, park (daily). Zoo (daily; closed Jan 1, Thanksgiving, Dec 25).

Piedmont Park. *Piedmont Ave NE and 14th St, Atlanta Off of Monroe Dr on Park Dr. Phone 404/875-7275.* Swimming (fee), lake; tennis (fee); picnicking.

Robert W. Woodruff Arts Center. *1280 Peachtree St NE, Atlanta. www.woodruffcenter.org/wac.* Largest arts complex in the Southeast. Headquarters of Atlanta College of Art and

Alliance Theatre Company. *1280 Peachtree St NE, Atlanta (30309). At the Woodruff Arts Center. Phone 404/733-5000.* This regional theater company presents six mainstage productions, three studio theater productions, and two children's theater productions annually. (Sept-May)

High Museum of Art. *1280 Peachtree St NE, Atlanta. Phone 404/733-4444.* African sculpture; European, American, and contemporary painting and sculpture; decorative art; photography. Rotating exhibits. (Tues-Sat 10 am-5 pm, Sun from noon; closed holidays) **$$$**

Symphony Hall. *1280 Peachtree St, Atlanta (30309). Phone 404/733-5000.* The largest auditorium in the Arts Center. It's the permanent home of the Atlanta Symphony Orchestra, Chorus, and Youth Orchestra; performances (Sept-May and mid-June-mid-Aug).

Six Flags Over Georgia. *7561 Six Flags Pkwy, Austell (30168). 12 miles W of downtown via I-20, exit 47 Six Flags Pkwy, just beyond Atlanta city limits. Phone 770/948-9290. www.sixflags.com/parks/overgeorgia.* A family theme park featuring Georgia's history under the flags of England, France, Spain, the Confederacy, Georgia, and the US. More than 100 rides, shows, and attractions, including the Georgia Cyclone roller coaster, modeled after Coney Island's famous Cyclone;

the Ninja roller coaster with five upside-down turns; water rides; children's activities; and live shows. (Mid-May-early Sept, daily; early Mar-mid-May and early Sept-Oct, weekends only) **$$$$**

State Capitol. *1 Capitol Sq, Atlanta. Phone 404/656-2844. www.cr.nps.gov/nr/travel/atlanta/geo.htm.* (1884-1889) The dome, topped with native gold, is 237 feet high. Inside are historical flags, statues, and portraits. Tours 10 am, 11 am, 1 pm, and 2 pm. (Mon-Fri 8 am-5:30 pm) **FREE** On the fourth floor is

> **Georgia Capitol Museum.** *431 State Capitol, Atlanta (30334). Phone 404/651-6996.* Exhibits of wildlife, snakes, fish, rocks, minerals, and fossils. Dioramas of Georgia industry (Mon-Fri 8 am-5:30 pm) **FREE**

⭐ **Stone Mountain Park.** *Hwy 78 E, Stone Mountian (30087). 19 miles E on Hwy 78. Phone 770/498-5690. www.stonemountainpark.com.* This 3,200-acre park surrounds the world's largest granite monolith, which rises 825 feet from the plain. A monument to the Confederacy, the deep relief carving on the mountain's face depicts three figures: General Robert E. Lee, General "Stonewall" Jackson, and Confederate President Jefferson Davis. It was first undertaken by Gutzon Borglum after World War I, continued by Augustus Lukeman, and completed by Walker Hancock. The top of the mountain is accessible by foot or cable car (fee). Surrounding the sculpture are **Memorial Hall,** a Civil War museum with commentary in seven languages about the mountain and its carving; an **antebellum plantation** featuring 19 buildings restored and furnished with 18th- and 19th-century heirlooms, formal and kitchen gardens, cookhouse, slave quarters, country store, and other outbuildings; **Antique Auto and Music Museum** housing cars dating from 1899 and an antique mechanical music collection; **riverboat** *Scarlett O'Hara,* providing scenic trips around a 363-acre lake; **scenic railroad** with full-size replicas of Civil War trains that make a 5-mile trip around the base of the mountain. Also, a laser show is projected onto the north face of the mountain in 50-minute productions (mid-May-Labor Day, nightly; Apr-mid-May and after Labor Day-Oct, Sat) and a 732-bell carillon plays concerts (Wed-Sun). In addition, the park has 10 miles of nature trails where wild and domestic animals live on 20 wooded acres; beach with bathhouse, fishing, boat rentals; tennis courts, 36-hole golf course, miniature golf, ice skating, picnicking, snack bars, three restaurants, inn, and campground with tent and trailer sites

(hookups, dump station). (Daily 6 am-midnight; attractions open at 10 am; closed Dec 25) **$$$$**

Theater of the Stars. *660 Peachtree Street NE, Atlanta. Phone 404/252-8960. www.theaterofthestars.com.* Nine Broadway musicals with professional casts, most staged at the Fox Theatre (see). Late June-early Nov.

⭐ **Underground Atlanta.** *50 Upper Alabama St SW # 7, Atlanta (30303). Bounded by Wall, Central, Peachtree sts and Martin Luther King, Jr. Dr. Phone 404/523-2311. www.underground-atlanta.com.* A "festival marketplace" featuring shops, pushcart peddlers, restaurants and nightclubs, street entertainers, and various attractions. The six-block area was created in the 1920s when several viaducts were built over existing streets at second-story level to move traffic above multiple rail crossings. Merchants moved their shops to the second floors, relegating the first floors to oblivion for nearly half a century. Today's visitors descend onto the cobblestone streets of a Victorian city in perpetual night. On lower Alabama Street, the shops are housed in the original, once-forgotten storefronts. Underground Atlanta was first "discovered" in the late 1960s and flourished as a center of nightlife before being closed down in 1981 due to a combination of crime and subway construction. The "rediscovered" Underground combines the original below-ground streets with above-ground plazas, promenades, fountains, more shops and restaurants, and a 138-foot light tower. (Shopping Mon-Sat 10 am-9 pm, Sun 11 am-6 pm; open later in summer; restaurant and club hours may vary; closed Dec 25) Highlighted here is

> **The World of Coca-Cola.** *55 Martin Luther King Jr. Dr SW, Atlanta (30303). Between Central Ave and Washington St, S of the New Georgia Railroad Depot. Phone 404/676-5151.* A square block of interactive displays and exhibits trace history of Coca-Cola from its introduction in 1886 at Jacob's Pharmacy Soda Fountain on Atlanta's Peachtree St to present; world's largest collection of Coca-Cola memorabilia; movies; old-fashioned soda fountain. (Sept-May: Mon-Sat 9 am-5 pm, Sun 11 am-5 pm; June-Aug: Mon-Sat 9 am-6 pm, Sun 11 am-5 pm; closed holidays) **$$**

William Breman Jewish Heritage Museum. *1440 Spring St NW, Atlanta (30309). Phone 404/873-1661. www.thebreman.org.* The largest Jewish heritage museum in the Southeast houses a Holocaust gallery and heritage gallery, which tells the story of Atlanta's Jewish community from the first German immigrants in 1845. (Sun-Fri) **$**

Wren's Nest. *1050 Ralph D. Abernathy Blvd SW, Atlanta. Phone 404/753-7735.* Eccentric Victorian house of Joel Chandler Harris, journalist and transcriber of "Uncle Remus" stories. Original family furnishings, books, photographs. Ongoing restoration. (Tues-Sun; closed holidays) Group tours (25+) Tues-Sat (reservations required); individual tours Tues, Thurs, Sat. **$$$**

Yellow River Game Ranch. *4525 Hwy 78, Lilburn. Approximately 17 miles E. Phone 770/972-6643; fax 770/985-0150. www.yellowrivergameranch.com.* A 24-acre animal preserve on the Yellow River where more than 600 animals roam free in a natural wooded area. Visitors can pet, feed, and photograph the animals. Some of the animals at the park include deer, bears, cougars, and buffalo. (Daily, 9:30 am-6 pm; closed Jan 1, Thanksgiving, Dec 24-25) **$$**

Zoo Atlanta. *Grant Park, 800 Cherokee Ave SE, Atlanta (30315). Phone 404/624-5600. www.zooatlanta.org.* Features natural habitat settings and is known for its primate center, aviary, and representative Southeastern habitats exhibits. The giant panda exhibit is a major draw as well. (Daily 9:30 am-4:30 pm; closed Jan 1, Thanksgiving, Dec 25) **$$$$**

Special Events

Atlanta Dogwood Festival. *20 Executive Park Dr NE #2019, Atlanta. Phone 404/817-6642. www.dogwood. org.* This springtime festival in celebration of the blooming of Atlanta's dogwood trees features an artist market, a Frisbee dog contest, a Kids Village full of activities, and live music. Early Apr.

Atlanta Motor Speedway. *1500 S Hwy 41, Hampton (30228). S on I-75, exit 77, and then approximately 15 miles S on Hwy 19/41. Phone 770/946-4211. www. atlantamotorspeedway.com.* NASCAR Winston Cup, Busch Grand National, IMSA, and ARCA auto racing events.

Atlanta Steeplechase. *Kingston Downs,Hwy 20 At Mile Marker 1, Kingston (30145). At Seven Branches Farm. Phone 404/237-7436; fax 404/237-2006. www. atlantasteeplechase.org.* Gates open at 9 am; post time 1:30 pm. Second Sat in Apr.

Georgia Renaissance Festival. *6905 Virlyn B. Smith, Atlanta. Approximately 20 miles S on I-85, exit 12. Phone 770/964-8575. www.garenfest.com.* Hundreds of costumed characters, authentic crafts, games, and food in a re-created 16th-century English village. Seven weekends, mid-Apr-early June.

US 10K Classic and Family Festival. *Cobb Pkwy and Akers Mill Rd SE, Atlanta (30303). Phone 770/432-0100. www.us10k.org.* The US 10K Classic raises money for children's charities and is host to several different race categories: running, walking, wheelchair racing, in-line skating, and cycling. There is also plenty to do for individuals and families not racing including a pre-race pizza and pasta dinner, celebrity autograph sessions, a childrens activity area, and finish line celebration. Labor Day weekend.

Limited-Service Hotels

★ **DAYS INN.** *6840 Shannon Pkwy, Union City (30291). Phone 770/306-6067; toll-free 800/329-7466; fax 770/306-6062. www.daysinn.com.* 90 rooms, 2 story. Pets accepted; fee. Complimentary continental breakfast. Check-in 2 pm, check-out noon. Outdoor pool. **$**
🐾 ⛱

★ ★ **EMBASSY SUITES BUCKHEAD.** *3285 Peachtree Rd NE, Atlanta (30305). Phone 404/261-7733; toll-free 800/362-2779; fax 404/261-6857. www. embassysuites.com.* This atrium-style hotel accommodates guests looking to stay in the prestigious Bucktown neighborhood. The spacious guest suites feature kitchenettes, hair dryers, and irons. 317 rooms, 16 story, all suites. Complimentary full breakfast. Check-in 3 pm, check-out noon. Restaurant, bar. Fitness room. Indoor pool, outdoor pool, whirlpool. Airport transportation available. **$$**
🧍 ⛱

★ ★ **EMBASSY SUITES HOTEL AT CENTENNIAL OLYMPIC PARK.** *267 Marietta St, Atlanta (30313). Phone 404/223-2300; toll-free 800/362-2779; fax 404/223-0925. www.embassysuites.com.* This hotel occupies a prime spot across from Centennial Olympic Park. At night, sit on the balcony and watch the dazzling light display at the Olympic Rings Fountain. Suites offer large bedrooms and living rooms with comfortable couches. 321 rooms, all suites. Complimentary full breakfast. Check-in 3 pm, check-out 11 am. Wireless Internet access. Two restaurants, bar. Fitness room. Outdoor pool, whirlpool. Business center. **$$**
🧍 ⛱ 🧍

★ ★ **EMORY INN.** *1641 Clifton Rd, Atlanta (30329). Phone 404/712-6000; toll-free 800/933-6679; fax 404/712-6701. www.emoryconferencecenter.com.* Located at Emory University and just minutes from downtown Atlanta and Buckhead, this hotel features spacious country French-style guest rooms, a garden courtyard with pool and whirlpool, and a café. It can be tricky to find—look for the sign for the conference center, which is down the hill from the inn. Guests can enjoy nearby shopping, sporting events, and theaters. 105 rooms, 2 story. Check-in 3 pm, check-out noon. Restaurant. Outdoor pool, whirlpool. Business center. **$**

★ ★ ★ **GEORGIA TECH HOTEL AND CON-FERENCE CENTER.** *800 Spring St NW, Atlanta (30308). Phone 404/347-9440; toll-free 800/706-2899; fax 404/347-9088. www.gatechhotel.com.* This newly opened hotel in Midtown offers state-of-the-art conveniences to a clientele of mostly business travelers. From T-1 Internet lines to flat-screen televisions, the urban-style guest rooms are as contemporary as they are easy on the eye. This hotel is a great choice if you're planning a group meeting or conference, as the facilities for these types of gatherings are top-notch. 252 rooms. Check-in 3 pm, check-out noon. High-speed Internet access, wireless Internet access. Restaurant, two bars. Fitness room. Indoor pool, whirlpool. Airport transportation available. Business center. **$**

★ **HAMPTON INN.** *3398 Piedmont Rd NE, Atlanta (30305). Phone 404/233-5656; toll-free 888/537-1091; fax 404/237-4688. www.hamptoninn.com.* 154 rooms, 6 story. Complimentary continental breakfast. Check-in 3 pm, check-out noon. Outdoor pool. **$**

★ **HOLIDAY INN EXPRESS.** *505 Pharr Rd, Atlanta (30305). Phone 404/262-7880; toll-free 800/465-4329; fax 404/262-3734. www.hiexpress.com.* Located in the fashionable Buckhead district, this hotel is great for extended stays and families. With a fully stocked kitchen and separate living area in each suite, guests will feel like they never left home. 87 rooms, 3 story, all suites. Complimentary continental breakfast. Check-in 3 pm, check-out 11 am. Fitness room. Outdoor pool, whirlpool. **$**

Full-Service Hotels

★ ★ ★ **ATLANTA MARRIOTT MARQUIS.** *265 NE Peachtree Center Ave, Atlanta (30303). Phone 770/521-0000; toll-free 800/228-9290; fax 770/586-6299. www.marriott.com.* This polished convention hotel tickles and awes guests with its 50-story atrium and exciting and unlimited view of the city. Guests will delight in the elegantly appointed guest rooms and 120,000 square feet of meeting space. Pleasures also can be found with the first-class comforts this hotel has to offer. 1,675 rooms, 50 story. Check-in 4 pm, check-out noon. High-speed Internet access. Four restaurants, two bars. Fitness room. Indoor pool, outdoor pool, whirlpool. Business center. **$$**

★ ★ ★ **CROWNE PLAZA.** *3377 Peachtree Rd, Atlanta (30326). Phone 404/264-1111; toll-free 800/227-6963; fax 404/233-7061. www.crowneplaza.com.* Set in the prestigious Buckhead section of the city, this newly renovated hotel with boutique-style décor is conveniently close to shopping, dining, and nightlife on Atlanta's renowned Peachtree Street. Unwind after a day of exploring the city in the outdoor pool or fitness room, or enjoy dinner at the hotels Mediterranean restaurant. A MARTA Rail Station is adjacent to the hotel, and attractions such Six Flags over Georgia and the CNN Center are also nearby. 291 rooms, 11 story. Pets accepted, some restrictions; fee. Check-in 4 pm, check-out noon. High-speed Internet access, wireless Internet access. Restaurant, bar. Fitness room. Outdoor pool. **$$**

★ ★ ★ ★ **FOUR SEASONS HOTEL AT-LANTA.** *75 14th St, Atlanta (30309). Phone 404/881-9898; toll-free 800/332-3442; fax 404/873-4692. www.fourseasons.com.* The Four Seasons Hotel is Atlanta's premier address. This Neoclassical granite tower reigns over Midtown, where world-class culture, flourishing businesses, and enticing stores line the streets. Well-suited for both business and leisure travelers, this hotel offers its guests the finest accommodations and flawless, intuitive service. Neutral tones and polished woods set a relaxed elegance in the rooms and suites, while striking views of downtown or midtown Atlanta inspire occupants. Visitors swoon over the luxurious amenities, from plush furnishings to sensational beds, and in-room massage and spa therapies ensure pure relaxation. The state-of-the-art fitness center is complete with an indoor pool and sun terrace, perfect for exercise or repose. Park 75's fresh approach to American cuisine earns praise from locals and hotel guests alike, and its ficus-lined terrace is a pleasing alternative. 244 rooms, 19 story. Pets accepted, some restrictions. Complimentary continental breakfast. Check-in 3 pm, check-out noon. High-speed Internet access. Three restaurants, bar. Fitness room. Indoor pool, whirlpool. Business center. **$$$**

★ ★ ★ **GRAND HYATT ATLANTA.** *3300 Peachtree Rd NE, Atlanta (30305). Phone 404/365-8100; toll-free 800/233-1234; fax 404/233-5686. www.grandatlanta. hyatt.com.* Perched in the heart of Buckhead, Atlanta's well-known fashionable district, this elegant hotel offers impeccable service and handsomely appointed accommodations. 438 rooms, 25 story. Pets accepted, some restrictions; fee. Check-in 3 pm, check-out noon. High-speed Internet access, wireless Internet access. Restaurant, bar. Fitness room. Outdoor pool. Business center. **$$**

★ ★ ★ **HILTON ATLANTA AIRPORT AND TOWERS.** *1031 Virginia Ave, Atlanta (30354). Phone 404/767-9000; toll-free 800/411-8065; fax 404/768-0185. www.atlantaairport.hilton.com.* This hotel is conveniently located near the airport as well as near many of Atlanta's attractions like the zoo, Stone Mountain, and Six Flags. Guests will enjoy the complimentary 24-hour transportation to the airport and MARTA station, as well as the Olympus Gym, pools, Jacuzzi, and 24-hour room service. 504 rooms, 17 story. Pets accepted; fee. Check-in 3 pm, check-out noon. Restaurant, bar. Fitness room. Indoor pool, outdoor pool, whirlpool. Tennis. Business center. **$$**

★ ★ ★ **HILTON ATLANTA AND TOWERS.** *255 Courtland St NE, Atlanta (30303). Phone 404/659-2000; toll-free 800/445-8667; fax 404/221-6368. www. hilton.com.* From the fitness center, jogging track, and basketball and tennis courts to the pool and billiard room, this hotel is guaranteed to restore the senses. 1,224 rooms, 30 story. Check-in 3 pm, check-out 11 am. High-speed Internet access, wireless Internet access. Five restaurants, three bars. Fitness room (fee). Outdoor pool. Tennis. Business center. **$$**

★ ★ ★ **HYATT REGENCY ATLANTA.** *265 Peachtree St NE, Atlanta (30303). Phone 404/577-1234; toll-free 800/233-1234; fax 404/588-4137. www.hyatt-regencyatlanta.com.* Located in the hustle and bustle of downtown, this 23-story atrium hotel successfully combines the convenience of a downtown hotel with superb accommodations and first-class amenities. Minutes away are the Atlanta Market Center, Georgia Dome, Underground Atlanta, and Centennial Olympic Park. 1,260 rooms, 23 story. Check-in 3 pm, check-out noon. High-speed Internet access, wire-

less Internet access. Two restaurants, two bars. Fitness room. Outdoor pool. Business center. **$$**

★ ★ ★ **INTERCONTINENTAL BUCKHEAD.** *3315 Peachtree Rd NE, Atlanta (30326). Phone 404/946-9000; toll-free 877/422-8254; fax 770/604-5247. www.intercontinental.com.* 422 rooms. Pets accepted; fee. Complimentary continental breakfast. Check-in 3 pm, check-out noon. High-speed Internet access, wireless Internet access. Restaurant, bar. Fitness room. Outdoor pool, whirlpool. Business center. **$$$**

★ ★ ★ **JW MARRIOTT HOTEL BUCKHEAD ATLANTA.** *3300 Lenox Rd NE, Atlanta (30326). Phone 404/262-3344; toll-free 800/228-9290; fax 404/262-8689. www.jwmarriottbuckhead.com.* The JW Marriott Hotel Lenox treats its visitors to a privileged address in the heart of Atlanta's fashionable Buckhead neighborhood. This sleek hotel is an obvious choice for business and leisure travelers with its excellent amenities, fine service, and stylish setting. Its location adjacent to the premium shops of Lenox Mall makes it a hit with shopaholics, and many of the city's major attractions are just a short distance away. Business travelers appreciate the little extras here, from the full-service business center with secretarial services to the high-speed Internet access in all rooms. A fitness center and indoor pool attract those who like to fit in a workout on the road, while a restaurant, coffee shop, lounge, and room service cater to appetites at all hours. 371 rooms, 25 story. Check-in 4 pm, check-out noon. High-speed Internet access. Restaurant, bar. Fitness room. Indoor pool, whirlpool. Business center. **$$$**

★ ★ ★ **MARRIOTT DOWNTOWN ATLANTA.** *160 Spring St NW, Atlanta (30303). Phone 404/688-8600; toll-free 877/999-3223; fax 404/524-5543. www. marriott.com.* Ideal for business travelers who also look to enjoy a bit of the city, this contemporary hotel with intimate, yet open spaces offers ample meeting space, a friendly staff and a location that affords guests the opportunity to savor all that Atlanta has to see and do. 312 rooms, 9 story. Pets accepted, some restrictions; fee. Check-in 3 pm, check-out noon. High-speed Internet access. Restaurant, bar. Fitness room. Outdoor pool. Business center. **$$**

★ ★ ★ **OMNI HOTEL AT CNN CENTER.** *100 CNN Center NW, Atlanta (30335). Phone 404/659-*

0000; toll-free 800/843-6664; fax 404/818-4322. www.
omnihotels.com. Located in downtown Atlanta and
conveniently connected to the CNN Center and the
Georgia World Congress Center, this well-appointed
hotel offers guests spacious rooms, flawless service,
and an attention to detail to ensure guests' standards
are met and surpassed. Take a stroll through Centennial Olympic Park located across the street or enjoy
the 50,000-square-foot, state-of-the-art Turner Athletic Club. 1,067 rooms, 15 story. Pets accepted, some
restrictions; fee. Check-in 3 pm, check-out noon.
High-speed Internet access, wireless Internet access.
Restaurant, bar. Fitness room. Outdoor pool, whirl-
pool. Business center. **$$**

★ ★ ★ **THE RITZ-CARLTON, ATLANTA.** 181
Peachtree St NE, Atlanta (30303). Phone 404/659-0400;
toll-free 800/241-3333; fax 404/688-4900. www.ritzcarl-
ton.com. The Ritz-Carlton is the shining star of down-
town Atlanta. This cosmopolitan hotel enjoys a prime
location in the heart of the city, making it convenient
to businesses, government offices, and sporting arenas.
The guest accommodations are handsomely appointed
with traditional furnishings, fabrics, and artwork. Bay
windows draw attention to striking views of the city
skyline. Many suites have kitchenettes, and some even
feature baby grand pianos. Twice-daily housekeeping
and the Ritz-Carlton's signature Technology Butler
Service pamper guests. Diners develop a soft spot for
the clubby atmosphere of the Atlanta Grill, with its
sophisticated updates on Southern cooking. 444 rooms,
25 story. Pets accepted, some restrictions; fee. Check-
in 3 pm, check-out noon. High-speed Internet access.
Restaurant, bar. Fitness room. Business center. **$$$**

★ ★ ★ ★ **THE RITZ-CARLTON, BUCKHEAD.**
3434 Peachtree Rd NE, Atlanta (30326). Phone
404/237-2700; toll-free 800/241-3333; fax 404/239-
0078. www.ritzcarlton.com. The Ritz-Carton Buckhead
is unquestionably the grande dame of Atlanta. This
gracious hotel, nestled in the fashionable uptown
neighborhood, has long been the favorite of the social
set. Southern grace and Ritz-Carlton standards blend
here, resulting in a warm and luxurious experience.
The guest rooms enchant with European furnishings, antiques, and sublime amenities. Bay windows
showcase lovely views of the wooded locale or the
downtown skyline. Attentive and exceptional service
ensures that all guests are cosseted. The fitness center
appeals to athletic-minded visitors, and the indoor
pool with sundeck adds a relaxing touch. Afternoon

tea in the Lobby Lounge is a Georgia tradition, especially after a day of perusing the area's world-famous
stores, and The Café is a popular gathering place to
enjoy casual fare. The pièce-de-résistance, however, is
The Dining Room (see), where award-winning French
cuisine infused with Asian flavors delights the senses.
553 rooms, 22 story. Pets accepted, some restrictions;
fee. Check-in noon, check-out noon. Two restaurants,
bar. Fitness room. Indoor pool, whirlpool. Airport
transportation available. Business center. **$$$**

★ ★ ★ **SHERATON ATLANTA HOTEL.** 165
Courtland St, Atlanta (30303). Phone 404/659-6500;
toll-free 800/325-3535; fax 404/524-1259. www.
sheratonatlantahotel.com. With all its dining options
and other conveniences, this hotel is a home-away-
from-home for business and leisure travelers alike.
760 rooms, 12 story. Pets accepted, some restrictions.
Check-in 3 pm, check-out noon. High-speed Internet
access, wireless Internet access. Four restaurants, bar.
Fitness room. Indoor pool, outdoor pool, whirlpool.
Business center. **$$**

★ ★ ★ **W ATLANTA AT PERIMETER CENTER.**
111 Perimeter Ctr W, Atlanta (30346). Phone 770/396-
6800; toll-free 800/683-6100; fax 770/399-5514. www.
whotels.com. Located in the Perimeter Center Office
Complex and conveniently within walking distance to
numerous restaurants, cinemas, and all the delights of
downtown Atlanta. This refreshing hotel offers guests
unsurpassed sophisticated elegance combined with a
twist of all the comforts of home. From the signature
pillow-top beds and divine linens to the exquisitely
appointed guest rooms, this hotel makes for a truly
memorable stay. 275 rooms, 12 story. Pets accepted,
some restrictions; fee. Check-in 3 pm, check-out noon.
High-speed Internet access. Restaurant, bar. Fitness
room. Outdoor pool, whirlpool. Business center. **$$$**

★ ★ ★ **THE WESTIN BUCKHEAD ATLANTA.**
3391 Peachtree Rd NE, Atlanta (30326). Phone
404/365-0065; toll-free 800/253-1397; fax 404/365-
8787. www.westin.com/buckhead. Located in the
elegant and scenic Buckhead area and adjacent to
Lenox Square Mall, this graceful 22-story hotel is a
landmark and a delight to stay in. All of the guest
rooms are spacious and handsomely appointed with
Biedermeier-style furnishings. The fitness center
is state-of-the-art and the lap pool sparkling and
inviting. Nearby attractions include Zoo Atlanta, the

Fernbank-Musuem of Natural History, and the Jimmy Carter Presidential Center. Just 15 minutes away is the birthplace of Dr. Martin Luther King, Jr. 365 rooms, 22 story. Pets accepted, some restrictions. Check-in 3 pm, check-out noon. High-speed Internet access, wireless Internet access. Restaurant, two bars. Fitness room. Indoor pool. Business center. **$$$**

★ ★ ★ **THE WESTIN PEACHTREE PLAZA.** *210 Peachtree St NW, Atlanta (30303). Phone 404/659-1400; toll-free 800/228-3000; fax 404/589-7424. www.westin.com/peachtree.* As if the superb service, relaxing ambience, and spacious guest rooms with views of downtown weren't enough, this hotel surpasses others by offering special touches such as the "heavenly bed." Guests can dine at either of the delectable restaurants, enjoy a workout in the health club and fitness center, or just relax at the indoor pool. 1,068 rooms, 73 story. Pets accepted, some restrictions. Check-in 3 pm, check-out noon. High-speed Internet access. Two restaurants, two bars. Fitness room. Indoor pool. Business center. **$$**

★ ★ ★ **WYNDHAM PEACHTREE CONFERENCE CENTER HOTEL.** *2443 Hwy 54 W, Peachtree City (30269). Phone 770/487-2000; fax 770/487-8599. www.wyndham.com.* 250 rooms, 4 story. Check-in 3 pm, check-out 11 am. High-speed Internet access, wireless Internet access. Two restaurants, bar. Fitness room, fitness classes available. Indoor pool, outdoor pool, whirlpool. Tennis. Airport transportation available. Business center. **$**

Specialty Lodgings

ANSLEY INN. *253 15th St, Atlanta (30309). Phone 404/872-9000; toll-free 800/446-5416; fax 404/892-2318. www.ansleyinn.com.* A turn-of-the-century English Tudor house built in 1907, the Ansley Inn provides the comforts of home in the heart of Midtown. Set on a quiet, tree-lined street, it is within walking distance of the High Museum of Art, the Margaret Mitchell House, and the Atlanta Botanical Gardens. Large fireplaces; crystal chandeliers; and Chippendale, Queen Anne, and Empire furnishings pay homage to the period, while four-poster beds and Oriental rugs create a warm ambience in the guest rooms. 22 rooms, 3 story. Complimentary full breakfast. Check-in 3 pm, check-out 11 am. High-speed Internet access, wireless Internet access. **$$**

GASLIGHT INN BED & BREAKFAST. *1001 St. Charles Ave NE, Atlanta (30306). Phone 404/875-1001; fax 404/876-1001. www.gaslightinn.com.* Located in the Virginia Highlands area, with easy access to MARTA, the freeway, and plentiful shopping and dining, this popular bed-and-breakfast is full of warmth. The proprietor knows it well, having used it as a private residence until turning it into a B&B. Gaslights and private alcoves characterize this early-1900s home, where guests can enjoy meals in the flower garden or on the front porch. 8 rooms, 2 story. Complimentary full breakfast. Check-in 3 pm, check-out noon. High-speed Internet access, wireless Internet access. **$$**

KING-KEITH HOUSE BED & BREAKFAST. *889 Edgewood Ave NE, Atlanta (30307). Phone 404/688-7330; toll-free 800/728-3879; fax 404/584-8408. www.kingkeith.com.* 6 rooms, 3 story. Check-in 3 pm. Check-out 11 am. **$**

LAUREL HILL BED & BREAKFAST. *1992 McLendon St, Atlanta (30307). Phone 404/377-3217; fax 404/377-0756. www.laurelhillbandb.com.* 6 rooms. Pets accepted; fee. No children allowed. Complimentary full breakfast. Check-in 3-6 pm, check-out 11 am. Wireless Internet access. **$**

SERENBE BED & BREAKFAST. *10950 Hutcheson Ferry Rd, Palmetto (30268). Phone 770/463-2610; fax 770/463-4472. www.serenbe.com.* A cheerful place to bring the kids, this inn, built in 1901, is located on a farm where guests can feed the animals, go on a hayride, or have a marshmallow roast. Guests can enjoy canoe rides and the majestic waterfalls. 7 rooms, 2 story. Complimentary full breakfast. Check-in 3 pm, check-out 11 am. Outdoor pool, whirlpool. **$**

SHELLMONT INN. *Piedmont and 6th sts, Atlanta (30308). Phone 404/872-9290; fax 404/872-5379. www.shellmont.com.* Located in midtown Atlanta's theater and cultural district, this beautifully restored Victorian masterpiece is filled with antiques, Oriental rugs, Tiffany windows, and artwork. Guests here will enjoy an intimate setting. 6 rooms, 2 story. Children under 12 in carriage house only. Complimentary full breakfast. Check-in 3 pm, check-out 11 am. **$$**

SUGAR MAGNOLIA. *804 Edgewood Ave NE, Atlanta (30307). Phone 404/222-0226; fax 404/681-1067. www.sugarmagnoliabb.com.* Nestled in Atlanta's historic Inman Park neighborhood, this elegant Victorian bed-and-breakfast was built in 1892. With six fireplaces, a grand staircase, and beveled windows, the beauty of the architecture is immense. Guest suites are cozy and inviting with period furnishing. 4 rooms, 2 story. Complimentary full breakfast. Check-in 2 pm, check-out noon. **$**

🄳

Restaurants

★ ★ ★ **ANTHONY'S.** *3109 Piedmont Rd NE, Atlanta (30305). Phone 404/262-7379; fax 404/261-6009. www.anthonysfinedining.com.* This centrally located Buckhead restaurant is set back from the road on a 3-acre wooded lot in a plantation home that dates to 1797. The house was originally built in Washington, Georgia, and it was moved 116 miles to its present location. It took more than three years to take apart the house and then reconstruct it—brick by brick, board by board. There are twelve different dining rooms, and the main dining room has seven working fireplaces. The American menu (with Southern influences) has some classics, like veal Anthony (scallopine stuffed with lobster) and pumpkin seed- and coriander-crusted grouper. Anthony's is the perfect choice for special occasion or group dining. American menu. Dinner. Closed Sun; holidays; also week from Dec 25-Jan 1. Bar. Business casual attire. Reservations recommended. Valet parking. **$$$**

★ ★ ★ **ARIA.** *490 E Paces Ferry Rd, Atlanta (30305). Phone 404/233-7673; fax 404/262-5208. www.aria-atl.com.* This cozy space, once a private citizens library, in the upscale Buckhead neighborhood has been transformed into a shrine of industrial chic. White walls, metal curtains, leather square-backed booths, votive candles, and an eclectic chandelier are all part of the scheme to lure diners in for chef Gerry Klaskala's Southern-inspired, American cuisine. There is also a private table in the wine cellar downstairs, but you'll have to call way ahead—it is usually booked three months in advance. American menu. Dinner. Closed Sun. Bar. Business casual attire. Reservations recommended. Valet parking. Outdoor seating. **$$$**

★ ★ ★ **ATLANTA FISH MARKET.** *265 Pharr Rd, Atlanta (30305). Phone 404/262-3165; fax 404/601-1315. www.buckheadrestaurants.com.* Slightly tucked away from the bustle of the Buckhead section (but easily spotted with its giant outdoor fish statue), this large, family-friendly seafood restaurant is a favorite among locals. The restaurant features several airy, comfortable dining rooms and menus printed twice daily to ensure that entrées are fresher than fresh. Diners can even choose their dinner and its preparation: charbroiled, steamed, or sautéed, and then they could watch it being prepared through the open display kitchen. Seafood menu. Lunch, dinner. Bar. Children's menu. Casual attire. Reservations recommended. Valet parking. Outdoor seating. **$$**

★ ★ ★ **AU PIED DE COCHON.** *3315 Peachtree Rd NW, Atlanta (30326). Phone 404/946-9070; toll-free 888/424-6835; fax 404/946-9001. www.aupieddecochonatlanta.com.* This popular, 24-hour French brasserie restaurant is located in the posh Intercontinental Buckhead (see) near Lenox Square Mall and Phipps Plaza. The restaurant is named after the historic French restaurant, and its name means "At the pig's feet." Diners will find pig decorations throughout the restaurant—the feet of the tables are even pig's feet. The rest of the décor is truly eclectic with 350 hand-painted Mexican panels adorning the walls; Italian hand-blown glass chandeliers add to the striking interior. Jazz is played five nights a week, and the same menu is available throughout the day. There is also a raw bar featuring fish flown in daily from around the world. This is a great choice for a delicious meal at any time of the day or night. French menu. Breakfast, lunch, dinner, late-night, Sun brunch. Bar. Children's menu. Casual attire. Reservations recommended. Valet parking. Outdoor seating. **$$$**

★ ★ **BABETTE'S CAFE.** *573 N Highland Ave, Atlanta (30307). Phone 404/523-9121; fax 404/523-7909. www.babettescafe.com.* This rustic European restaurant is located in a cream-colored stucco house between Atlanta's Inman Park and Poncey Highlands neighborhoods. The décor is a mix of farmhouse and bistro and features flower boxes, pale gold faux painted walls, lace curtains, lamp chandeliers, a fireplace, and antique kitchen utensils on the walls. The menu features items from France, Italy, Spain, and the Mediterranean. A nice brunch is offered on Sundays. International menu. Dinner, Sun brunch. Closed Mon. Bar. Children's menu. Casual attire. Reservations recommended. Valet parking. Outdoor seating. **$$**

★ ★ ★ ★ **BACCHANALIA.** *1198 Howell Mill Rd, Suite 100, Atlanta (30318). Phone 404/365-0410; fax 404/365-8020. www.starprovisions.com.* Bacchanalia feels like it just tumbled out of New York City's or

London's SoHo. Set in a rehabilitated factory complex, this urban dining room has an edgy, sleek, industrial-chic feel to it. The dramatic vaulted ceiling and exposed brick-trimmed factory windows of the dining room are the perfect accents to the long, low-lit, sexy bar and glass-enclosed kitchen of this former meat-packing plant. The vibrant seasonal menu changes daily and offers carefully composed upscale American fare that focuses on organic and small-farm produce. Plates are presented with little fuss but lots of flavor and enthusiasm. The wine list, selected by the chef, includes a thoughtful collection of food-friendly, half-bottle choices. American menu. Dinner. Bar. Business casual attire. Reservations recommended. Outdoor seating. **$$$$**

★ ★ **BASIL'S MEDITERRANEAN CAFE.** *2985 Grandview Ave, Atlanta (30305). Phone 404/233-9755; fax 404/233-8042.* The attraction of this quaint Buckhead cottage-turned-café is twofold: first, the atmosphere is that of a laid-back elegance thats hard to find in the hustle and bustle of downtown Atlanta. The other draw is the fact that, in contrast to some places that call themselves Mediterranean when in fact they serve nouveau Italian or Greek food, the food here really is Mediterranean. Influences for the menu are drawn from Spain, Italy, Greece, and Turkey, while the service remains friendly and familiar. Try the "mesa" appetizer, loaded up with stuffed grape leaves, tabouleh, and house-made hummus and babaghanouj, or the Greek shrimp sautéed with white wine and feta cheese. Flower boxes line the outdoor seating area, making it the perfect dining spot on warm nights. Mediterranean menu. Lunch, dinner, Sun brunch. Bar. Children's menu. Casual attire. Reservations recommended. Outdoor seating. **$$**

★ ★ ★ **BLUEPOINTE.** *3455 Peachtree Rd, Atlanta (30326). Phone 404/237-9070; fax 404/237-2387. www.buckheadrestaurants.com.* This popular restaurant is located in the Pennacle office building next to Lenox Square Mall and near lodging and entertainment. The ultramodern décor, featuring chrome railings, eclectic tile floors, an open display kitchen, oversized windows, and blue velvet and leather booths, perfectly complements the inventive cuisine prepared by executive chef Doug Turbush. The sushi bar is a nice option for business lunches. Pacific-Rim/Pan-Asian, seafood menu. Lunch, dinner. Bar. Children's menu. Business casual attire. Reservations recommended. Valet parking. **$$$**

★ ★ ★ **BONE.** *3130 Piedmont Rd NE, Atlanta (30305). Phone 404/237-2663; fax 404/233-5704. www.bonesrestaurant.com.* This clubby restaurant located in the busy section of Buckhead has a decidedly masculine décor and steaks and sides to match. Dark paneling and caricature pictures decorate the bar area, while pictures of Atlanta history are featured in the dining room, and oil paitings of varied dogs surround the back room. The wine gallery room is brick and runs along the wine cellar room. The huge portions and high prices attract a power lunch crowd that likes to smoke cigars. They have their own steak sauce and shortbread cookies that they give away to their best customers—they're worth the return trips. Steak menu. Lunch, dinner. Bar. Business casual attire. Reservations recommended. Valet parking. **$$$**

★ ★ ★ **BRASSERIE LE COZE.** *3393 Peachtree Rd, Atlanta (30326). Phone 404/266-1440; fax 404/266-1436.* Despite its location in the Lenox Square Mall, this bistro-style restaurant is no food-court offering. Its one of the best French restaurants in Atlanta, owned and operated by the same team of Le Bernardin (see) in New York. The menu is a mix of traditional items with a blend of Asian-inspired dishes. For the purist, however, there are still the moules (mussels) marniere, the roasted skate wing, and warm Valrhona chocolate souffle cake for dessert. Don't miss the special events on Bastille Day and the Beaujolais Nouveau wine tasting. French menu. Lunch, dinner. Closed Sun. Bar. Reservations recommended. Valet parking. Outdoor seating. **$$$**

★ ★ ★ **THE CAFE.** *3434 Peachtree Rd NE, Atlanta (30326). Phone 404/237-2700; toll-free 800/241-3333; fax 404/239-0078. www.ritzcarlton.com.* Chef Christophe LeMetayer takes cues from his native France for the menu in this all-day restaurant of the Ritz-Carlton, Buckhead hotel (see). The hotel is located in the upscale community of Buckhead and is within walking distance to Lenox Square and Phipps Plaza shopping malls. The restaurant's dining room is decorated with mahogany walls, blue brocade chairs, large windows, and antique oil paintings. The relaxed mood is set with live piano music, and the room is tiered so diners could enjoy views of the outdoor patio. Sunday brunch is a particular treat, offering more than 100 delectable items. French menu. Breakfast, lunch, dinner, Sun brunch. Bar. Children's menu. Business casual attire. Reservations recommended. Valet parking. Outdoor seating. **$$**

★ ★ ★ **CANOE.** *4199 Paces Ferry Rd NW, Atlanta (30339). Phone 770/432-2663; fax 770/433-2542. www.canoeatl.com.* Situated on the banks of the Chattahoochee River amidst rambling gardens, this casual but sophisticated restaurant serves delicious American cuisine prepared by executive chef Carvel Grant Gould. The eclectic menu ranges from slow roasted beef short ribs to seared Georgia Mountain Trout. The atmosphere is the perfect complement to the cuisine with a canoe-like ceiling, wrought iron paddle table legs, overstuffed chairs, art by local artists, and a brick display kitchen with a copper hood. After a meal here, you'll be so relaxed, you won't want to leave. American menu. Lunch, dinner, Sun brunch. Bar. Business casual attire. Reservations recommended. Valet parking. Outdoor seating. **$$$**

★ ★ **CARBO'S CAFE.** *3717 Roswell Rd NE, Atlanta (30342). Phone 404/231-4433; fax 404/237-6826. www.carbos-cafe.com.* This fine dining restaurant, located in posh Buckhead, was established in 1980 and continues to satisfy diners with its elegant service and sophisticated menu. The décor is traditional with special touches such as a handpainted 60s mural in the bar and an outside gazebo bar area with a dance floor. Nightly piano music adds to the atmosphere for special-occasion dinners. Specialties include broiled Caribbean lobster tail, she crab soup, Dover sole, and herb grilled Australian rack of spring lamb. American menu. Dinner. Closed Sun-Mon. Bar. Business casual attire. Reservations recommended. Valet parking. Outdoor seating. **$$**

★ ★ ★ **CHOPS.** *70 W Paces Ferry Rd, Atlanta (30305). Phone 404/262-2675; fax 404/240-6645. www.buckheadrestaurants.com.* Chops is located in the posh community of Buckhead, near Lenox Square Mall and Phipps Plaza. This place is really two restaurants in one: upstairs, power diners chomp on delicious prime-aged beef in a clubby steakhouse atmosphere—dark mahogany paneling, black leather booths with burgundy seats, and an open display kitchen; downstairs is the Lobster Bar, where romantic diners sit in white stuccco grottos and savor delicate seafood creations. Steak menu. Lunch, dinner. Bar. Business casual attire. Reservations recommended. Valet parking. **$$$**

★ ★ ★ **CITY GRILL.** *50 Hurt Plz, Atlanta (30303). Phone 404/524-2489; fax 404/529-9474. www. citygrillatlanta.com.* Located in an office building that was built in 1912 and was once the Federal Reserve Bank, this sophisticated restaurant features regional American cuisine in an elegant club-like environment. The interior features vaulted ceilings; intricate gold molding; Italian marble tile and chandeliers; large,

drape-covered windows; and a hand-painted garden mural. American menu. Lunch, dinner. Closed Sun. Bar. Children's menu. Business casual attire. Reservations recommended. Valet parking. **$$$**

★ **THE COLONNADE.** *1879 Cheshire Bridge Rd, Atlanta (30324). Phone 404/874-5642.* American menu. Lunch, dinner. Bar. Casual attire. Valet parking. Outdoor seating. No credit cards accepted. **$$**

★ **COWTIPPERS.** *1600 Piedmont Ave, Atlanta (30324). Phone 404/874-3751; fax 404/875-1666. www. cowtippersatlanta.com.* With a rustic cowboy theme, this no-frills, neighborhood restaurnat features an expansive menu with beef and fish specialties. Imaginative details are found throughout the restaurant, including tables painted in cowhide patterns, tin ceilings above the bar, and open-beam ceilings in the dining area. American menu. Lunch, dinner. Bar. Children's menu. Casual attire. Outdoor seating. **$$**

★ ★ **DAILEY'S.** *17 International Blvd, Atlanta (30303). Phone 404/681-3303; fax 404/681-6643. www. daileysrestaurant.com.* Beyond the restored warehouse exterior of this restaurant, patrons enter through a villa-style hallway into one of Atlanta's favorite special-occasion gathering spots. The downstairs features an intimate jazz and cigar bar with leather couches, while the large, spacious dining room upstairs features imaginative American fare and impeccable service. American menu. Lunch, dinner. Closed holidays. Bar. Casual attire. **$$**

★ ★ **DANTE'S DOWN THE HATCH.** *3380 Peachtree Rd NE, Atlanta (30326). Phone 404/266-1600; fax 404/266-2229. www.dantesdownthehatch. com.* Dante's décor is quite unique—this popular museum-like fondue restaurant houses nautical antiques and the hull of a Viking ship built inside the dining room. Cabin-style booths and a pond with turtles and alligators add to the unique experience. The dining room is divided into 13 dining areas surrounding the ship, and the menu is translated into 61 different languages. The restaurant uses Australian beef, and all food is chemical free. Only the best oils—with no fat or cholesterol—from health food stores is used. The owner is always present to greet diners, and Jimmy Carter frequently visits and sits on the balcony. An acoustic guitarist entertains on Mondays, and jazz is offered the rest of the week. Fondue menu. Dinner. Bar. Business casual attire. Reservations recommended. **$$**

★ ★ ★ ★ ★ **THE DINING ROOM.** *3434 Peachtree Rd NE, Atlanta (30326). Phone 404/237-2700; toll-free 800/241-3333; fax 404/239-0078. www.ritzcarlton.com.* If you're looking for a luxurious spot for fine, divine dining in posh Buckhead, head over to The Ritz-Carlton, Buckhead (see) and beg for a table at The Dining Room, the hotel's magnificent venue for sophisticated French fare. The room is opulent, decorated ornately in European style. Deep, tufted banquettes are cloaked in plush Victorian green silk, the walls are decorated with muted sage-toned chinoisserie fabric, and Frette linens top spacious tables. Vintage wall sconces give the room a soft glow, and grand oil paintings add an old-world elegance. The menu is an exercise in pleasure and wonder. Not a note is off as the chef employs subtle Asian touches to accent stunning regional ingredients. After dessert and a spectacular cheese course, it's time for petit fours, which arrive in a mobile cart in numbers. Loosen your belt. This is luxury at its finest, served to perfection. French menu. Dinner. Closed Sun-Mon. Jacket required. Reservations recommended. Valet parking. **$$$$**

★ ★ **DISH.** *870 N Highland Ave NE, Atlanta (30306). Phone 404/897-3463; fax 404/874-2886. www.dish-atlanta.com.* American menu. Dinner, late-night. Bar. Casual attire. Reservations recommended. Outdoor seating. **$$**

★ **DUSTY'S BARBECUE.** *1815 Briarcliff Rd, Atlanta (30329). Phone 404/320-6264; fax 404/320-1343. www.dustys.com.* Located near Emory University, this popular spot is decorated with all manner of pig paraphernalia and red-and-white checked oilcloth tablecloths, but the draw is the tangy, down-home barbecue. Ask for the "sizzling sauce" if you want a more fiery experience. Locals rave about the blackberry cobbler. There is a drive-up window for diners on the go. American, barbecue menu. Lunch, dinner. Children's menu. Casual attire. Outdoor seating. **$**

★ ★ **FIRE OF BRAZIL CHURRASCARIA.** *118 Perimeter Center W, Atlanta (30346). Phone 770/551-4367; fax 770/551-9652. www.fireofbrazil.com.* This unique Brazilian steakhouse is perfect for diners who are looking for a totally new experience. The main focus here is grilled meatsbeef, pork, lamb, chicken, and sausagewhich are brought to each table and carved to the guests liking. The meats are accompanied by a huge 150-item buffet. Brazilian steak menu. Lunch, dinner. Bar. Casual attire. Reservations recommended. Outdoor seating. **$$$**

★ **FLYING BISCUIT CAFE.** *1655 McLendon Ave, Atlanta (30307). Phone 404/687-8888; fax 404/687-8838. www.flyingbiscuit.com.* Dependably filling breakfast entrees are served all day in this bright and eclectic Candler Park restaurant. The café also has a variety of vegetarian offerings and a bakery for take-home goodies. American menu. Breakfast, lunch, dinner. Children's menu. Casual attire. Reservations recommended. **$$**

★ ★ ★ **THE FOOD STUDIO.** *887 W Marietta St, Studio K 102, Atlanta (30318). Phone 404/815-6677; fax 404/815-4811. www.thefoodstudio.com.* Inside a century-old renovated factory building lies this tucked-away oasis of eclectic dining. With dishes such as seared sea scallops with edamame succotash and smoked tomato vinaigrette, and an organic heirloom tomato salad with grilled cornbread and lemon mayonnaise, this restaurant celebrates the wide array of regional flavors found across America. The dining room is located in the upstairs loft of the building, with soft, dim lighting and crisp white-on-white tablecloths, while the downstairs area is designed for take-out diners. American menu. Dinner. Bar. Business casual attire. Reservations recommended. Valet parking. Outdoor seating. **$$$**

★ ★ **FRITTI.** *309 N Highland Ave, Atlanta (30307). Phone 404/880-9559; fax 404/880-0462. www.frittirestaurant.com.* Traditional brick-oven pizza is the specialty here, although Fritti also offers Tuscan-style, wood-roasted meats and fish. Located a few blocks from the Virginia-Highland section of the city, this upscale eatery is a great place to stop for lunch or dinner after a stroll through the neighborhood. Italian menu. Lunch, dinner. Bar. Children's menu. Casual attire. Reservations recommended. Valet parking. Outdoor seating. **$$**

★ **GEORGIA GRILLE.** *2290 Peachtree Rd, Atlanta (30309). Phone 404/352-3517; fax 404/841-9964. www.georgiagrille.com.* Serving Southwestern fare in a friendly environment since 1990, this restaurant was named for and inspired by the art of Georgia O'Keeffe. Small oil paintings are featured throughout the dining room on pale gold walls, as are hand-painted tables topped with butcher paper, and an antique cake cooler. Southwestern menu. Dinner, brunch. Closed Mon. Bar. Children's menu. Casual attire. Reservations recommended. **$$$**

★ **HAVELI.** *225 Spring St, Atlanta (30303). Phone 404/522-4545; fax 404/522-4526.* This traditional Indian restaurant is located in the heart of downtown, convenient to hotels and offices. Lunch and dinner is served in the large, open dining room, which is decorated with gold walls accented with border paper, elephant sculptures, Indian art, green marble tables, and rattan chairs. Indian menu. Lunch, dinner. Bar. Casual attire. Reservations recommended. **$$**

★ ★ **HORSERADISH GRILL.** *4320 Powers Ferry Rd, Atlanta (30342). Phone 404/255-7277; fax 404/847-0603. www.horseradishgrill.com.* For classic Southern food with a modern twist, Atlanta's oldest continuously operating restaurant has kept locals coming back again and again for years. Originally a country inn, the restaurant gets its herbs fresh from an outdoor patch and specializes in variations on old favorites, such as the rosemary-grilled lamb chop with dijon-mint jelly glaze and fried green tomatoes with melted goat cheese and spicy pecans. American menu. Lunch, dinner, Sun brunch. Bar. Children's menu. Business casual attire. Reservations recommended. Valet parking. Outdoor seating. **$$**

★ ★ **HSU'S GOURMET CHINESE.** *192 Peachtree Center Ave, Atlanta (30303). Phone 404/659-2788; fax 404/577-3456. www.hsus.com.* This informal Chinese restaurant is located downtown. Korean-born chef Charlie Shan specializes in Hong Kong and Szechwan cuisine. Succulent Peking duck can be ordered without any advance warning; the whole fish and spicy noodles are superb. Chinese menu. Lunch, dinner. Bar. Children's menu. Casual attire. Reservations recommended. **$$**

★ ★ **IMPERIAL FEZ.** *2285 Peachtree Rd NE, Atlanta (30309). Phone 404/351-0870; fax 404/351-1272. www.imperialfez.com.* When you step into this authentic Moroccan restaurant decorated with tapestry-covered walls and low tables with low-backed seating on one side and pillows on the floor for the other side, you remove your shoes. You are offered the menu (the prixe fixe meal consists of soup, salad, appetizer, main course, dessert, and mint tea), then you are presented with a bath towel—your napkin—to drape over your left shoulder. Next, an urn of water is brought to wash your hands. When your food is presented, you are asked whether you would like to eat with your right hand (customary) or with silverware. After eating, the urn is brought back so you can wash your hand, and then the waitstaff sprinkles your hand with rose water to refresh it. The entire dining experience last 2 1/2 to 3 hours, and the nightly entertainment is belly dancers. This is a truly unique dining experience that should not be missed. Mediterranean, Moroccan

menu. Dinner. Children's menu. Casual attire. Reservations recommended. Valet parking. **$$**

★ ★ ★ **JOEL.** *3290 Northside Pkwy, Atlanta (30327). Phone 404/233-3500; fax 404/467-9450. www.joelrestaurant.com.* International menu. Lunch, dinner. Closed Sun. Bar. Business casual attire. Reservations recommended. Valet parking. Outdoor seating. **$$$**

★ ★ ★ **KYMA.** *3085 Piedmont Rd, Atlanta (30305). Phone 404/262-0702; fax 404/841-9924. www.buckheadrestaurants.com.* True to its name, the atmosphere at Kyma, meaning "wave" in Greek, brings to mind the crisp, clean seascape colors of the Greek Islands—deep blue and pure white. Enjoy a glass of wine and appetizers on the year-round patio, and then head inside to sit under the uniquely painted constellations that adorn the ceilings. This Buckhead restaurant specializes in classic Greek dishes, especially fresh seafood, and be sure to take a look at the wall mosaic in the entry—a unique piece of traditional Greek art made from bits of broken plates. The restaurant also offers a seasonal tasting menu, cooking classes, and a food and wine festival one Wednesday each month—don't miss it. Greek menu. Dinner. Closed Sun. Bar. Business casual attire. Reservations recommended. Valet parking. Outdoor seating. **$$$**

★ ★ ★ **LA GROTTA.** *2637 Peachtree Rd NE, Atlanta (30305). Phone 404/231-1368; fax 404/231-1274. www.lagrottaatlanta.com.* There are two outposts of this upscale Italian restaurant (this one in Buckhead and a sister property in Dunwoody). The professional service and tempting menu cannot be beat. Homemade pastas (such as goat cheese ravioli) and delicious entres (such as grilled salmon) are sure to satisfy. More exotic items like snails and octopus are also available. With its traditional Italian décor featuring fruit scene paintings, dark burgundy walls, and tabletop oil lamps, diners come here for special occasion and romantic meals. Diners can also choose to dine alfresco surrounded by ivy and flowers on the patio. Italian menu. Dinner. Closed Sun; also last week in June and first week in July. Bar. Business casual attire. Reservations recommended. Valet parking. Outdoor seating. **$$$**

★ ★ **LOMBARDI'S.** *94 Pryor St, Atlanta (30303). Phone 404/522-6568; fax 404/577-4457. www.lombardis.com.* Set in the same location in Underground Atlanta for more than 15 years, tourists and government employees tend to dominate the clientele here, since the proximity to both downtown attractions and government buildings is convenient. The menu is comprised of traditional Italian dishes with modern flair, as well as an array of desserts, all made in-house. Italian menu. Lunch, dinner. Bar. Casual attire. Reservations recommended. **$$**

★ **MARY MAC'S TEA ROOM.** *224 Ponce de Leon Ave NE, Atlanta (30308). Phone 404/876-1800; fax 404/881-6003. www.marymacs.com.* This informal neighborhood café, located in Midtown Atlanta, first opened in 1945. It's off-white walls are covered with pictures of dignitaries, politicians, and celebrities that have stopped in for some home cookin'. Mary Mac's offers traditional "meat and three" meals and super-sweet iced tea. This is a great place to go for homestyle Southern cooking. American, Southern menu. Lunch, dinner. Bar. Children's menu. Casual attire. Reservations recommended. **$**

★★★ **MCKENDRICK'S.** *4505 Ashford Dunwoody Ave, Atlanta (30346). Phone 770/512-8888; fax 770/379-1470. www.mckendricks.com.* This popular upscale steak house restaurant is located near the Perimeter Shopping Mall and is a great place for groups or business dinners. The atmosphere is clubby and dark with wood paneled booths, plants, large wine cabinets, and a porch room with window seats. Large martinis and appetizers add to the enjoyment. Steak menu. Lunch, dinner. Bar. Business casual attire. Reservations recommended. Valet parking. **$$$**

★★ **MCKINNON'S LOUISIANE.** *3209 Maple Dr, Atlanta (30305). Phone 404/237-1313; fax 404/237-2026. www.mckinnons.com.* Fresh seafood and French-Creole/Cajun cuisine are the big draw at this two-in-one Buckhead restaurant. If you're looking for a formal meal, head toward the right after you enter. You'll be led to a formal dining room decorated with dark paneling, mirrors, and stain glass. If you veer toward the left, you'll think you landed on Bourbon Street in New Orleans. This room, the Grill Room, is decorated with painted booths and chairs, oilcloth-covered tables, Christmas lights, masks, and hanging fish. There's also piano bar music in this room on Wednesday, Friday, and Saturday. Cajun/Creole menu. Dinner. Bar. Business casual attire. Reservations recommended. **$$**

★★ **NAKATO JAPANESE RESTAURANT.** *1776 Cheshire Bridge Rd NE, Atlanta (30324). Phone 404/873-6582; fax 404/874-7897. www.nakatorestaurant. com.* Traditional sushi forms the basis for a meal at this understated Japanese restaurant in the Cheshire Bridge section of town. Beautiful flower arrangements decorate the dining room, and the service is attentive and friendly. Relax in the comfortable lounge with sofas and a TV before dinner, and try to snag a seat with window views of the Japanese gardens. Japanese menu. Dinner. Bar. Children's menu. Casual attire. Reservations recommended. Valet parking. **$$**

★★★ **NAVA.** *3060 Peachtree Rd, Atlanta (30305). Phone 404/240-1984; fax 404/240-1831. www. buckheadrestaurants.com.* The captivating and dramatic Southwestern décor here (terra-cotta stone floor, hand-carved archway over lounge, log ceiling beams, cow hide-covered bar seats, and Southwest trinkets), complements the food, which is full of bold flavors, vibrant colors, and exotic textures. You'll find this popular restaurant in an office building in Buckhead, near Lenox Square Mall and Phipps Plaza. Take a seat at the cozy bar while you wait for a seattry to be seated on the outdoor patio for a view of the groomed gardens and decorative pool. Southwestern menu. Lunch, dinner. Bar. Casual attire. Reservations recommended. Valet parking. Outdoor seating. **$$$**

★★ **NICKIEMOTO'S.** *990 Piedmont Ave, Atlanta (30309). Phone 404/253-2010; fax 404/253-2014.* Located in Midtown Atlanta in the restaurant and business district, this ultramodern pan-Asian restaurant features a sushi bar and a display kitchen. For diners looking for entertainment during dinner, there is a popular drag show on Monday nights. Pan-Asian menu. Lunch, dinner. Bar. Casual attire. Reservations recommended. Valet parking. Outdoor seating. **$$**

★★★ **NIKOLAI'S ROOF.** *255 Courtland St, Atlanta (30303). Phone 404/221-6362; toll-free 800/445-8667; fax 404/221-6811. www.nikolaisroof. com.* Located atop the downtown Hilton in the heart of Atlanta, this French-Russian restaurant serves a stunning panoramic view along with its chilled vodka and Russian classics like borscht and piroshkis. The restaurant also offers the largest single malt collection in the city. Diners can choose from an eight-course prix fixe dinner and an a la carte menu created by the chef. Wine pairings from the award-winning wine list are also offered. The elegant red and gold décor here makes you feel like royalty, and the staff pampers you like royalty—a wonder dining experience. International menu. Dinner. Closed Sun. Bar. Children's menu. Business casual attire. Reservations recommended. Valet parking. **$$$**

★ **NINO'S ITALIAN RESTAURANT.** *1931 Cheshire Bridge Rd NE, Atlanta (30324). Phone 404/874-6505; fax 404/874-3596. www.ninosatlanta. com.* This Italian favorite is located on a main road in Atlanta's Cheshire Bridge area. It features an outdoor seating area and is a great place for special-occasion dinners. Italian menu. Dinner. Bar. Casual attire. Reservations recommended. Outdoor seating. **$$$**

★ ★ ★ **PANO'S & PAUL'S.** *1232 W Paces Ferry Rd, Atlanta (30327). Phone 404/261-3662; fax 404/261-4512. www.buckheadrestaurants.com.* Don't let the location of this restaurant fool you. Although it is located in a strip mall, it is just down the street from the Governor's Mansion in an affluent neighborhood in Buckhead. Locals say this upscale restaurant defines fine dining for the area. It's décor is elegant with elaborate floral arrangements, rich gold walls and ceilings, and burgundy velvet chairs. Executive Chef Gary Donlick's American/Continental menu includes the famous fried lobster tail and other contemporary specialties. An extensive wine list, weekend piano music, and friendly service complete the experience. American, Continental menu. Dinner. Closed Sun. Bar. Business casual attire. Reservations recommended. **$$$**

★ ★ ★ ★ **PARK 75 AT THE FOUR SEASONS.** *75 14th St NE, Atlanta (30309). Phone 404/253-3840; toll-free 800/332-3442; fax 404/873-4692. www.fourseasons.com.* Located in the Four Seasons Hotel, Atlanta (see), Park 75 is a bright and airy restaurant, a classic choice for tranquil and comfortable fine dining. The serene, pale-yellow dining room is warmed by iron candelabras, custom lighting, and oversized watercolor murals, while the ficus tree-lined Terrace takes its calm from the open air. Although the dining room is soft and soothing, the food is bright and bold. The cross-cultural American menu lives by the seasons, offering a wonderful selection of the finest local vegetables, meats, and fish, sparked to life with classic techniques and a jolt of original style. The signature Park 75 surf and turf, for example, twists the classic by combining butter-braised Maine lobster with milk-fed veal filet and foie gras. A well-conceived wine list is mostly American, although it also offers many boutique and international selections. For a special treat, reserve the chefs table and enjoy an eight-course menu with wines to match. After dinner Wednesday through Saturday, enjoy live piano music and a nightcap at the lounge bar. American menu. Breakfast, lunch, dinner. Bar. Children's menu. Business casual attire. Reservations recommended. Valet parking. **$$$$**

★ ★ **PETITE AUBERGE.** *2935 N Druid Hill Rd, Atlanta (30329). Phone 404/634-6268; fax 404/636-3306. www.petiteauberge.com.* Offering old-world European charm and classic Continental-style haute cuisine, the staff of European chefs prepare dishes in the classical philosophy of French cooking at this family-owned restaurant. The restaurant is located in a strip mall northeast of the city, and is decorated in a classic manner with burgundy walls, black booths, half sheers on the windows, lamps on the windowsills, crystal chandeliers, and a large black-and-white village scene. Continental, French menu. Lunch, dinner. Closed Sun. Bar. Business casual attire. Reservations recommended. Outdoor seating. **$$**

★ ★ **PHILIPPE'S BISTRO.** *10 Kings Cir, Atlanta (30305). Phone 404/231-4113; fax 404/231-4710.* Award-winning Belgian chef-owner Philippe Haddad has made this restaurant one of the Buckhead neighborhood's most popular dinner destinations. The menu offers specialties from Haddad's native country alongside more familiar, yet innovative, upscale fare. Brunch is also a special treat here, offering, of course, authentic Belgian waffles, as well as other tantalizing dishes. French menu. Dinner, brunch. Closed Mon; also week of July 4 and one week in Jan. Bar. Business casual attire. Reservations recommended. Outdoor seating. **$$$**

★ **PITTYPAT'S PORCH.** *25 International Blvd, Atlanta (30303). Phone 404/525-8228; fax 404/524-0471. www.pittypatrestaurant.com/.* This charming American restaurant offers Southern comfort food along with a comfortable atmosphere. Antiques line the lobby, a balcony overlooks the dining room, live piano music is offered every night, and rocking chairs are strategically placed for some time to kick back and relax with a Mint Julep, Pittypat's Pitch, or an Ankle Breaker (and you get to take the glass home). American menu. Dinner. Bar. Children's menu. Casual attire. Reservations recommended. **$$$**

★ ★ **PLEASANT PEASANT.** *555 Peachtree St, Atlanta (30308). Phone 404/874-3223; fax 404/897-2051. www.thepeasantrestaurants.com.* In an old building, slightly off the beaten path of Peachtree Street, this inviting restaurant is a local favorite for relaxed dining. It specializies in unique dishes such as lobster sliders and pecan-crusted salmon. Continental menu. Lunch, brunch. Bar. Casual attire. Valet parking. Outdoor seating. **$$**

★ ★ ★ **PRICCI.** *500 Pharr Rd, Atlanta (30305). Phone 404/237-2941; fax 404/261-0058. www.buckheadrestaurants.com.* There's a certain glitz to this see-and-be-seen upscale Italian restaurant. The décor is ultramodern with mirrored walls above burgundy leather booths, Art Deco lights and posters, and a display kitchen. Among the menu highlights are the pastas and any entrée with veal. The wine list has an extensive selection of regional Italian labels. Pricci is located in Buckhead, near entertainment, shopping, and lodging. Italian menu. Lunch, dinner. Bar. Business casual attire. Reservations recommended. Valet parking. **$$$**

★ ★ ★ **PRIME.** *3393 Peachtree Rd NE, Atlanta (30326). Phone 404/812-0555; fax 404/812-0225. www. heretoserverestaurants.com.* This modern restaurant redefines the term "surf and turf" by including sushi as part of the surf portion. Floor-to-ceiling windows, an open kitchen, and its location in the upscale Lenox Square Mall make it an exciting alternative to the traditional steakhouse. Diners can relax and enjoy their meals, created by Master Chef Tom Catherall, in the beautifully decorated dining room which features cherry wood-paneled walls and cobalt blue lamps over the sushi bar. Seafood, steak, sushi menu. Lunch, dinner. Bar. Children's menu. Business casual attire. Reservations recommended. Valet parking. **$$**

★ ★ ★ **QUINONES AT BACCHANALIA.** *1190 Howell Mill Rd, Atlanta (30318). Phone 404/365-0410. www.starprovisions.com.* Quinones at Bacchanalia's cozy dining area—11 tables, with room for only 36 guests—is set in a subdued and quiet atmosphere. Housed in a former meatpacking building that dates to the 1920s, the restaurant features décor that is both elegant and understated. Pressed Irish linens and oil lamps grace the top of each table, and complementing paintings adorn the walls. A ten-course prix-fixe menu is offered, and new creations are added to the Contemporary American menu daily. Enjoyable food, professional service, and tasteful décor make this a great choice for a romantic or special-occasion dinner. Contemporary American menu. Dinner. Closed Sun-Mon; holidays. Business casual attire. Reservations recommended. **$$$$**

★ ★ ★ **RATHBUN.** *112 Krog St, Atlanta (30307). Phone 404/524-8280; fax 404/524-8580. www. rathbunsrestaurant.com.* This polished but not overdone American cuisine restaurant is located in Inman Park on the east side of Atlanta. The building was formerly a potbelly stove factory (Atlanta Stove Works), and is nestled among rehabbed buildings and condos. The décor is modern industrial with exposed brick walls, a white and gray color scheme with subtle fuchsia accents, an impressive bar area, and real dried flowers on each table. There is also a large, heated, year-round outdoor patio. A local favorite, this attractive restaurant is the perfect place for that special-occasion meal. American menu. Dinner. Closed Sun; holidays. Bar. Business casual attire. Reservations recommended. Valet parking. Outdoor seating. **$$$**

★ ★ **RAY'S ON THE RIVER.** *6700 Powers Ferry Rd, Atlanta (30339). Phone 770/955-1187; fax 770/612-2465. www.raysrestaurants.com.* Just from looking at the menu of this river-view restaurant, it's clear that this place is serious about seafood. The lobster is flown in from Maine, wild Copper River Salmon from Alaska, and an oyster bar will please your palate. Selections of steak, chicken, and pork are also available. The décor is simple with wood chairs, white tablecloths, and large picture windows with views of more than 3 acres of gardens and the river. Don't be surprised to see Pricilla the goose—she comes up from the Chattahoochee River each day to see what's for dinner. Lunch and Sunday brunch are offered, and there is live music Thursday through Saturday evenings. Seafood menu. Lunch, dinner, Sun brunch. Bar. Children's menu. Business casual attire. Outdoor seating. **$$**

★ ★ ★ **RESTAURANT EUGENE.** *2277 Peachtree Rd, Atlanta (30309). Phone 404/355-0321; fax 404/355-0322. www.restauranteugene.com.* American menu. Dinner. Bar. Business casual attire. Reservations recommended. Valet parking. Outdoor seating. **$$$**

★ ★ ★ **THE RIVER ROOM.** *4403 Northside Pkwy, Atlanta (30327). Phone 404/233-5455; fax 404/233-3073. www.riverroom.com.* If you only have time to experience a handful of restaurants in Atlanta, this popular favorite should be one of them. Like sitting outside so you can people-watch as you dine? Done. Theres a spacious fountainside patio that looks out onto a very charming, European-looking square. Jazz fan? Come on a Friday night to the tavern lounge and listen to some of the citys best musicians. Self-proclaimed food connoisseur? The menu here is extensive yet unpretentious, with Southern-infused choices such as feta-stuffed free-range chicken served with couscous and chili-fried onion rings, and baked lobster with a cornbread stuffing. American menu. Lunch, dinner, Sun brunch. Bar. Business casual attire. Reservations recommended. Valet parking. Outdoor seating. **$$**

★ **ROCK BOTTOM.** *3242 Peachtree Rd, Atlanta (30305). Phone 404/264-0253; fax 404/264-9109. www. gordonbiersch.com.* If youve been running around Buckhead for half the day and need to recharge with food, drink, and a little relaxation, this is the place. Flop into a cushy booth, order up one of their specialty brews (six regular brews—brewed on-site—and two beers that change according to season), and peruse their menu chock-full of options, including pizza, pasta, salads, sandwiches, and more. The décor features faux terra-cotta walls, oak paneling, floral-backed red leather seats, multiple TVs, and the vats where they process the beer. Guests can dine at the bar of the display kitchen to watch their pizza being cooked in the open oven. American menu. Lunch, dinner, late-night. Bar. Children's menu. Casual attire. Reservations recommended. Outdoor seating. **$$**

★ ★ ★ **RUTH'S CHRIS STEAK HOUSE.** *5788 Roswell Rd, Atlanta (30328). Phone 404/255-0035; fax 404/255-3111. www.ruthschrisatlanta.com.* This Atlanta outpost of the popular steakhouse chain is located on a busy road between Buckhead and the Perimeter area of Atlanta. The U.S. prime-aged, hand-cut, Midwestern, corn-fed beef, has given this restaurant the name "The Home of Serious Steak." The décor is traditional with mahogany wainscoting green walls and pictures of the Sandy Springs era of 1920. The menu offers generous side dishes, and the service is professional. Steak menu. Dinner. Bar. Business casual attire. Reservations recommended. Valet parking. **$$$**

★ ★ ★ ★ ★ **SEEGER'S.** *111 W Paces Ferry Rd, Atlanta (30305). Phone 404/846-9779; fax 404/846-9217. www.seegers.com.* Giving Atlanta locals a taste of culinary excitement, Seeger's is a deliciously indulgent and comfortably adventurous place to dine. You'll feel swept away the second you enter the 1938 whitewashed brick cottage and take a seat in Seeger's dining room, furnished with contemporary style and modest grace and accented in colors of dark golds and blues. Well-spaced tables are set with Riedel crystal, Bernardaud china, and Christofle silver; smooth damask linens and fresh flowers in precious glass bud vases dress the tabletops. The dining room has only 11 sought-after tables and offers diners the option of sitting in the private upstairs dining room or on the main floor, where brocade-patterned settees and cherry-wood paneled walls add warmth to the stylish space. The Wine Room, which is located downstairs, features white-painted brick walls, an accented gray faux wall, and a crystal chandelier from Milano; flowers and soft lighting complete the mood. The impeccably prepared menu changes daily and showcases both the pristine ingredients of the season and the wellspring of talent and dedication in the kitchen. Presentations are exciting and entertaining, making incredible use of garnishes and unique presentation pieces. Chef Seeger's exceptional prowess in the kitchen glows brightly in each course, from bread through dessert. The wine selections are incredibly diverse and will match any ingredient the chef may

be featuring on an evening. Throughout the meal, the staff is consistently smooth and complimentary, applying a degree of Southern charm and warmth to each interaction. Seeger's is a sublime experience that will call you back to Atlanta, if only for dinner. International menu. Dinner. Closed Sun-Mon. Bar. Jacket required. Reservations recommended. Valet parking. Outdoor seating. **$$$$**

★ ★ **SOHO CAFE.** *4300 Paces Ferry Rd, Ste 107, Atlanta (30339). Phone 770/801-0069; fax 770/801-0093. www.sohoatlanta.com.* This ultramodern American restaurant is located in a small strip mall on the outskirts of Buckhead. A local favorite, SoHo features outdoor seating, modern art, and a display kitchen near the bar area. American menu. Lunch, dinner. Closed Sun; holidays. Bar. Children's menu. Business casual attire. Reservations recommended. Outdoor seating. **$$**

★ ★ ★ **SOTTO SOTTO.** *313 N Highland Ave, Atlanta (30307). Phone 404/523-6678; fax 404/880-0462. www.sottosottorestaurant.com.* Located right next door to its sister restaurant, Fritti (see), this dining spot is consistently rated one of the best Italian restaurants in Atlanta. The dishes here prove that simplicity is the best way to highlight the best ingredients. Diners can see and smell the magic happening in the open kitchen, which is also visible from the street outside. Italian menu. Dinner. Closed Sun. Bar. Business casual attire. Reservations recommended. Valet parking. Outdoor seating. **$$**

★ ★ **SOUTH CITY KITCHEN.** *1144 Crescent Ave, Atlanta (30309). Phone 404/873-7358; fax 404/873-0317. www.southcitykitchen.com.* Southern cooking is the specialty at this Midtown Atlanta restaurant. The ultramodern décor features pale yellow walls, modern art, large windows with a patio view, a display kitchen, and a balcony overlooking the dining room. American menu. Lunch, dinner, Sun brunch. Bar. Children's menu. Business casual attire. Reservations recommended. Outdoor seating. **$$$**
🄳

★ **TAQUERIA SUNDOWN CAFE.** *2165 Cheshire Bridge Rd, Atlanta (30324). Phone 404/321-1118; fax 404/321-1118. www.sundowncafe.com.* Located in the Cheshire Bridge section of Atlanta, this ultramodern Southwestern restaurant is a good value and a great spot for groups. Southwestern menu. Lunch, dinner. Closed Sun. Bar. Casual attire. Outdoor seating. **$$**

★ ★ **THAI CHILI.** *2169 Briarcliff Rd NE, Atlanta (30329). Phone 404/315-6750; fax 404/315-9367. www. thaichilicuisine.com.* Located in the BriarVista Shopping Center for more than a decade, this Thai restaurant is a local favorite and is popular with families. The main dining room is decorated in black and red and the tables have bowls with pink roses carved out of soap. There is also a "kantok" room where diners sit on the floor on cushions and are served family style on a large table. Thai menu. Lunch, dinner. Children's menu. Casual attire. Reservations recommended. **$$**

★ ★ **TOULOUSE.** *2293 Peachtree Rd NE, Atlanta (30309). Phone 404/351-9533; fax 404/351-2299. www. toulouserestaurant.com.* Locals rave about the awesome wine list here, and with more than 60 wines by the glass, as well as occasional wine tastings, it's no wonder. As you enter this romantic French restaurant, you'll be hit by the aroma of all things tasty coming from the wood-burning oven in the open kitchen, and although the atmosphere is that of a laid-back bistro, the menu is anything but dull. Make sure you check out their seasonal menu, which in the past has included intriguing options like strawberry soup and seared flounder with andouille sausage. The outdoor deck is the perfect place to dine on warm evenings. French menu. Dinner. Bar. Business casual attire. Reservations recommended. Outdoor seating. **$$**

★ **THE VARSITY.** *61 North Ave, Atlanta (30308). Phone 404/881-1706; fax 404/874-3989. www. thevarsity.com.* The Varsity has been serving Atlanta its famous chilidogs, onion rings, and fried apple pies since 1928. Servers shout orders like Naked Dog, Walk the Dog, Jo-Ree, and Bag of Rags while avoiding collisions with each other in almost choreographed confusion. It's a show all to itself. American menu. Lunch, dinner, late-night. Children's menu. Casual attire. Outdoor seating. No credit cards accepted. **$**

★ ★ **VENI VIDI VICI.** *41 14th St, Atlanta (30309). Phone 404/875-8424; fax 404/875-6533. www. buckheadrestaurants.com.* The first Buckhead Group restaurant located outside of Buckhead, this upscale Midtown (in the theater and arts district, near Piedmont Park) trattoria serves some of the best Italian food in town. The lunch and dinner menus are organized into small antipasti, perfect for tasting many different things; homemade pastas; and entrées. Its décor is traditional Italian—gold faux painted walls, display kitchen, white tablecloths, and meats, herbs, and garlic hang from a chandelier in the middle of the room. The outdoor seating area is a great option for warm nights. Italian menu. Lunch, dinner. Bar. Business casual attire. Reservations recommended. Valet parking. Outdoor seating. **$$$**

★ ★ ★ **VILLA CHRISTINA.** *4000 Summit Blvd, Atlanta (30319). Phone 404/303-0133; fax 404/303-0118. www.villachristina.com.* Italian menu. Lunch, dinner. Closed Sun. Bar. Business casual attire. Reservations recommended. Valet parking. Outdoor seating. **$$$**

★ ★ **THE VININGS INN.** *3011 Paces Mill Rd, Atlanta (30339). Phone 770/438-2282. www.viningsinn. com.* Featuring a range of dining areas, including the Sunroom, Bear Room, and the Attic Bar, this restaurant is great for anything from drinks and appetizers, to a romantic dinner for two, to a large family gathering. Originally a residence from the 1850s, the restaurant has become a destination for an upscale yet relaxed dining experience. American menu. Lunch, dinner. Bar. Children's menu. Business casual attire. Reservations recommended. Outdoor seating. **$$**

★ ★ ★ **WISTERIA.** *471 Highland Ave, Atlanta (30307). Phone 404/525-5363; fax 404/525-3313. www. wisteria-atlanta.com.* Soft wood tones and light green colors, wine displays, and fresh flowers on the tables make for a pleasant setting at this casual, comfortable restaurant located two and a half blocks west of downtown Decatur. Popular dishes such as fried catfish with hush puppies and Country Captain stew are served with Southern hospitality. American menu. Dinner. Closed Mon; holidays. Bar. Children's menu. Reservations recommended. Valet parking. **$$**

★ **ZOCALO.** *187 10th St, Atlanta (30309). Phone 404/249-7576; fax 404/879-0162. www. zocalocreativemex.com.* Famous for its margaritas and selection of more than 100 types of tequila, this Mexican hot spot is located just a block from Peachtree. Colorful painted tables and chairs, antique signs and pictures, and old-fashioned chandeliers give the dining area a desert saloon feel, while roll-down windows let in refreshing breezes. Mexican menu. Lunch, dinner, Sun brunch. Bar. Children's menu. Casual attire. Valet parking. Outdoor seating. **$$**

Atlanta Hartsfield Airport Area (B-2)

See also Atlanta

Information Phone 404/530-7300 or toll-free 800/897-1910.
Web Site www.atlanta-airport.com.
Lost and Found Phone 404/530-2100, ext. 100
Weather Phone 770/486-8834
Cash machines Concourse A
Airlines Aeromexico, Air Canada, Air France, Air Jamaica, AirTran Airways, American Airlines, American West, ASA, British Airways, ComAir, Continental, Corporate, Delta, Frontier Airlines, Hooters Air, jetBlue Airways, Korean Air, Lufthansa, Midwest Airlines, Northwest, South African Airways, United, USAir.

Limited-Service Hotel

★ ★ **COURTYARD BY MARRIOTT.** *2050 Sullivan Rd, College Park (30337). Phone 770/997-2220; toll-free 800/321-2221; fax 770/994-9743. www.marriott.com.* 144 rooms, 3 story. Check-in 3 pm, check-out noon. High-speed Internet access. Restaurant, bar. Fitness room. Indoor pool, whirlpool. Airport transportation available. Business center. **$**
✈ 🐾 🛏 🏃

Full-Service Hotel

★ ★ ★ **HILTON ATLANTA AIRPORT AND TOWERS.** *1031 Virginia Ave, Atlanta (30354). Phone 404/767-9000; toll-free 800/411-8065; fax 404/768-0185. www.atlantaairport.hilton.com.* This hotel is conveniently located near the airport as well as near many of Atlanta's attractions like the zoo, Stone Mountain, and Six Flags. Guests will enjoy the complimentary 24-hour transportation to the airport and MARTA station, as well as the Olympus Gym, pools, Jacuzzi, and 24-hour room service. 504 rooms, 17 story. Pets accepted; fee. Check-in 3 pm, check-out noon. Restaurant, bar. Fitness room. Indoor pool, outdoor pool, whirlpool. Tennis. Business center. **$$**
🐾 🐾 🏃 🛏 🏃 🏃

Augusta (B-4)

Founded 1736
Population 44,639
Elevation 414 ft
Area Code 706
Information Metropolitan Convention and Visitors Bureau, 1450 Greene St, Suite 110, 30901; phone 706/823-6600 or toll-free 800/726-0243.
Web Site www.augustaga.org

Augusta was the second town marked off for settlement by General James E. Oglethorpe. Today it is as famed for golf as for its red Georgia clay bricks. The city has been a military outpost and upriver trading town, the leading 18th-century tobacco center, a river shipping point for cotton, the powder works for the Confederacy, an industrial center for the New South, and a winter resort.

During the Revolution, the town changed hands several times, but Fort Augusta, renamed Fort Cornwallis by its British captors, was finally surrendered to "Lighthorse Harry" Lee's Continentals on June 5, 1781.

The Civil War played havoc with many of the wealthy families who had contributed to the Confederate cause. To help revive their depleted bank accounts, some Summerville residents opened their houses to paying guests. Attracted by Augusta's mild winter climate, northern visitors began an annual migration in increasing numbers, and by the turn of the 20th century, Augusta had become a popular winter resort. Many wealthy northerners built winter residences here in the 1920s. Golf courses and country clubs added to the lure. The Masters Tournament attracts the interest of golfers worldwide.

Augusta's many firsts include the state's first medical academy (chartered 1828); the first and oldest newspaper in the South to be published continuously, the *Augusta Chronicle* (1785); the first steamboat to be launched in southern waters (1790), invented and built by William Longstreet; and the experimental site for one of Eli Whitney's early cotton gins.

Augusta lies at the head of navigation on the Savannah River. Its importance as a cotton market, and a producer of cotton textiles, kaolin tiles, and brick has been enhanced by diversified manufacturing, processing of cottonseed, farm products, and fertilizers. Fort Gordon, an army base southwest of the city, also contributes to the area's economy. With the Medical College of Georgia, Augusta is a leading medical center in the Southeast.

What to See and Do

Augusta Museum of History. *560 Reynolds St, Augusta (30901). Phone 706/722-8454; fax 706/724-5192. www. augustamuseum.org.* (1802) Historical collections. (Tues-Sat 10 am-5 pm, Sun 1-5 pm; closed holidays) **$**

Augusta State University. *2500 Walton Way, Augusta (30904). Between Katharine St and Arsenal Ave. Phone 706/737-1444; toll-free 800/344-373. www.aug.edu.* (1925) (5,000 students) Site of Augusta Arsenal (1826-1955), of which portions are preserved.

Confederate Powder Works Chimney. *1717 Goodrich St, Augusta (30904). Phone 706/724-0436.* A memorial honoring war dead, this brick chimney is all that remains of what was once the second-largest powder factory in the world.

Cotton Exchange. *32 8th St, Augusta (30901). Phone 706/738-6990.www.augustacottonexchange.com.* Handsome brick building, built in 1886. (Daily) **FREE**

Gertrude Herbert Institute of Art. *506 Telfair St, Augusta (30901). Phone 706/722-5495; fax 706/722-3670. www.ghia.org.* Old Ware's Folly Mansion (1818) houses changing exhibits; works by local artists. (Tues-Fri 10 am-5 pm; closed holidays) **DONATION**

Harris House. *1822 Broad St, Augusta (30904). Phone 706/737-2820. www.augustamuseum.org.* (Circa 1795) House of Ezekiel Harris, tobacco merchant. Period furnishings. Tours (Sat afternoons or by appointment) **$**

Meadow Garden. *1320 Independence Dr, Augusta (30901). Phone 706/724-4174. www.downtownaugusta. com/meadowgarden/meadowgarden.htm.* House (1791-1804) of George Walton, signer of the Declaration of Independence. Period furnishings. Guided tours (Mon-Fri 10 am-4 pm; also Sat by appointment). **$$**

Morris Museum of Art. *1 10th St, Augusta (30901). Phone 706/724-7501; fax 706/724-7612. www.themorris.org.* This museum houses a collection of paintings by Southern artists depicting landscapes, portraits, and Civil War scenes; it also has small folk-art collection. Free admission Sun. (Tues-Sat 10 am-5 pm, Sun noon-5 pm) **$**

National Science Center's Fort Discovery. *1 7th St, Augusta (30901). Phone 706/821-0211; toll-free 800/325-5445. www.nationalsciencecenter.org.* An innovative hands-on science, communications, and technology center with 250 interactive exhibits; high-tech theater; KidScape for children ages 3-7. Also here are a Teacher Resource Center, traveling exhibits, and a science store. (Mon-Sat 10 am-5 pm, Sun noon-5 pm; closed holidays) **$$**

Riverwalk. Augusta's high Savannah River levee has been lavishly restored as a promenade for strollers, skaters, and cyclists, linking the city's major attractions.

St. Paul's Episcopal Church. *605 Reynolds St, Augusta (30901). Phone 706/724-2485; fax 706/724-0904. www. saintpauls.org.* (1750) A granite Celtic cross in the churchyard marks the site of a fort and the spot where Augusta began, established by James Oglethorpe in 1736 in honor of Princess Augusta. Oglethorpe Park, a recreational area on the Savannah River, is located behind the church; picnicking.

Special Events

Augusta Invitational Rowing Regatta. *At Augusta Riverfront Marina.* Mid-late July.

Augusta Opera. *1301 Greene St, Suite 100, Augusta (30901). Phone 706/826-4710; fax 706/826-4732. www. augustaopera.com.* In addition to several opera performances, the Augusta Opera also provides several community outreach programs to further promote this art form. Mid-Sept-mid-May. **$$$$**

Augusta Symphony Orchestra. *Sacred Heart Cultural Center, 1301 Greene St, Suite 200, Augusta (30901). Phone 706/826-4705; fax 706/826-4735. www.augustasymphony.org.* The Augusta Symphonys season is always packed full with concerts and events designed to please all types of audiences. Choose from traditional orchestra concerts, pops performances featuring world famous guest artists, and smaller and more intimate chamber concerts. The Symphony also sponsors community outreach programs intended to attract both children and adult participation. Mid-Sept-mid-May.

Masters Golf Tournament. *Augusta National Golf Course, 2604 Washington Rd, Augusta (30904). Phone 706/667-6000. www.masters.org.* The Masters is one of four major golfing tournaments held each year. It is held every year at Augusta National Golf Club. In addition to a cash award, the winner is presented with the famous green sportcoat, highly coveted among professional golfers. First full week in Apr.

Limited-Service Hotels

★ ★ **AUGUSTA MARRIOTT HOTEL AND SUITES.** *2 10th St, Augusta (30901). Phone 706/722-8900; toll-free 800/333-3333; fax 706/823-6513. www.radisson.com.* Offering Southern charm along with warm hospitality and outstanding accommodations, this hotel promises a very comfortable and relaxing stay. Elegantly appointed guest rooms are spacious and well equipped with everything from workstations to makeup mirrors and offer views of the beautiful Savannah River, downtown Augusta, and the scenic Riverwalk. The hotel's superb location allows guests to be just minutes from restaurants, antique shops, art galleries, and museums. 237 rooms, 11 story. Pets accepted, some restrictions. Check-in 4 pm, check-out noon. Restaurant, bar. Fitness room. Outdoor pool. **$**

★ ★ **AUGUSTA TOWERS HOTEL AND CONVENTION CENTER.** *2651 Perimeter Pkwy, Augusta (30909). Phone 706/855-8100; fax 706/860-1720.* The serene and airy atrium lobby is filled with towering palm trees and beautifully lush plants. Relax in the elegantly appointed guest rooms. Enjoy extra amenities like the indoor and outdoor pools, sauna, whirlpool, and fitness center. 179 rooms. Pets accepted; fee. Check-in 3 pm, check-out noon. Restaurant, bar. Fitness room. Indoor pool, outdoor pool, whirlpool. Airport transportation available. **$$$**

★ ★ **COURTYARD BY MARRIOTT.** *1045 Stevens Creek Rd, Augusta (30907). Phone 706/737-3737; toll-free 800/321-2211; fax 706/738-7851. www.courtyard.com.* Located on Augusta's north side, this hotel designed for business travelers features a business center, and large desks and high-speed Internet access in each room. After a busy day, head to the distinguished Augusta National Golf Club nearby, or relax in the outdoor pool or whirlpool. 130 rooms, 2 story. Check-in 3 pm, check-out noon. High-speed Internet access. Fitness room. Outdoor pool, whirlpool. Business center. **$**

Specialty Lodgings

1810 WEST INN. *254 N Seymour Dr, Thomson (30824). Phone 706/595-3156; toll-free 800/515-1810; fax 706/595-8266. www.1810westinn.com.* 11 rooms, 2 story. Children over 12 years only. Complimentary continental breakfast. Check-in 3 pm, check-out 11 am. Restored farmhouse (1810); antiques. **$**

AZALEA INN. *312 Greene St, Augusta (30901). Phone 706/724-3454; toll-free 877/292-5324; fax 706/724-1033. www.theazaleainn.com.* This enchanting bed-and-breakfast is perfect for a romantic getaway. Located near Augusta's Riverwalk, antiques shops, and brick-lined plazas. 21 rooms, 3 story. Complimentary continental breakfast. Check-in 3-6 pm, check-out 11 am. **$**

ROSEMARY HALL & LOOKAWAY HALL. *804 Carolina Avenue, North Augusta (29841). Phone 803/278-6222; toll-free 800/531-5578; fax 803/278-4877. www.businessatlanta.com/alpharetta.* This historic inn combines two restored Greek Revival homes, one that dates from 1898 and the other from 1902. Located just 1 1/2 miles from downtown Augusta, the inn is situated around natural gardens, and the rooms are filled with antique furnishings. 23 rooms, 2 story. Pets accepted, some restrictions; fee, Children over 12 years only. Complimentary full breakfast. Check-in 3 pm. Check-out 11 am. **$**

Restaurants

★ ★ ★ **CALVERTS.** *475 Highland Ave, Augusta (30909). Phone 706/738-4514; fax 706/312-2121.* Established in 1977, this restaurant in the Surrey Center maintains its position on the top of local favorites. American menu. Dinner. Closed Sun. Bar. Children's menu. Business casual attire. Reservations recommended. **$$$**

★ ★ ★ **LA MAISON RESTAURANT & VERITAS WINE &TAPAS.** *404 Telfair St, Augusta (30901). Phone 706/722-4805; fax 706/722-1753. www.lamaison-telfair.com.* This fine dining restaurant in a Southern Revival home is the epitome of Southern hospitality. In between preparing his game specialties (such as lamb, buffalo, pheasant, and quail), the chef makes sure to stop by every table to say hello. International menu. Dinner. Closed Sun. Bar. Business casual attire. Reservations recommended. Outdoor seating. **$$**

Bainbridge (E-2)

See also Tallahassee, Thomasville

Founded 1829
Population 11,722
Elevation 135 ft
Area Code 229
Zip 31717
Information Bainbridge-Decatur County Chamber of Commerce, PO Box 755, 31718; phone 229/246-4774 or toll-free 800/243-4774

Web Site www.bainbridgegachamber.com

On the banks of 37,500-acre Lake Seminole, Bainbridge is Georgia's first inland port. It is a town of giant water oaks and live oaks on the Flint River. Andrew Jackson's troops built an earthworks defense (Fort Hughes) near the present town during the Indian Wars (1817-1821). The town was later named in honor of William Bainbridge, commander of the frigate *Constitution*. The forests were so rich in this area that Bainbridge was known as the wealthiest town in the state when fortunes were made in lumbering in the early 20th century.

What to See and Do

Earl May Boat Basin and Park. *Bainbridge. W Shotwell St at bypass. Phone 229/246-4774.* This 600-acre park on Lake Seminole has exhibits of turn-of-the-century steam engines and locomotives. Beach swimming; boating (ramps). Volleyball court; playing fields. Camping (hookups). Visitor center (Mon-Fri; closed holidays).

Seminole State Park. *7870 State Park Dr, Donalsonville (39845). 23 miles W on Hwy 253. Phone 229/861-3137. www.gastateparks.org.* Lake Seminole, shallow by Georgia standards, holds a greater number of fish species than any other lake in the state. Swimming beach, boating, water-skiing, fishing; miniature golf, picnicking, concession; camping, cottages. (Daily 7 am-10 pm) **$**

Special Events

Decatur County Fall Festival and Fair. *Phone 229/246-4774.* Carnival, rides, exhibits, livestock show. Mid-Oct.

Riverside Arts Festival. *119 W Water St, Bainbridge. Phone 229/246-4774.* Arts festival featuring a different state each year. First week in March.

Limited-Service Hotels

★ ★ **CHARTER HOUSE INN.** *1401 Tallahassee Hwy, Bainbridge (31717). Phone 229/246-8550; toll-free 800/768-8550; fax 229/246-0260. www.thecharterhouseinn.com.* 124 rooms, 2 story. Check-out noon. Restaurant, bar. Outdoor pool. **$**
🅓 🏊

★ **SUPER 8.** *751 W Shotwell St, Bainbridge (31717). Phone 229/246-0015; toll-free 800/800-8000; fax 229/246-0015. www.super8.com.* 53 rooms, 2 story.

Complimentary continental breakfast. Check-in 2 pm, check-out 11 am. Outdoor pool, whirlpool. **$**
🏊

Blakely (E-1)

See also Dothan

Founded 1826
Population 5,696
Elevation 275 ft
Area Code 229
Zip 31723
Information Chamber of Commerce, 214 Court Square, PO Box 189; phone 229/723-3741
Web Site www.blakelyearlychamber.com

Named for US Navy Captain Johnston Blakeley, a hero of the War of 1812, this is an important peanut producing area.

What to See and Do

Coheelee Creek Covered Bridge. *Old River Rd, Blakely. Old River Rd, 9 miles SW via Hwy 62.* This 96-foot-long bridge is the southernmost standing covered bridge in the US, built in 1891.

Courthouse Square. *Phone 229/723-3741.* On the grounds stands what may be the world's only monument honoring the peanut. And the South's last remaining wooden Confederate flagpole, erected in 1861.

Kolomoki Mounds State Historic Park. *205 Indian Mounds Rd, Blakely (39823). 6 miles N off Hwy 27. Phone 229/724-2150. www.gastateparks.org.* Native American mounds, temple mound, and some excavation indicate a settlement here between AD 800 and AD 1200. Swimming pool, fishing, boating (ramps, dock) on Kolomoki Lake; miniature golf, hiking trails, picnicking, camping. For more information, contact the Superintendent, Rte 1, Box 114. (Daily 7 am-10 pm) In the park is

Indian Museum. *205 Indian Mounds Rd, Blakely (39823). Phone 229/724-2150.* Exhibits explain artifacts and civilization of Kolomoki, Weeden Island, and Swift Creek cultures. Entry into excavated burial mound. Video presentation (fee). (Daily 8 am-5 pm; closed Jan 1, Thanksgiving, Dec 25) **$**

Full-Service Inn

★ ★ ★ **TARRER INN.** *155 S Cuthbert St, Colquitt (39837). Phone 229/758-2888; toll-free 888/282-7737; fax 229/758-2825. www.tarrerinn.com.* Recently restored to its natural and timeless beauty, this charming bed-and-breakfast takes guests back to an era of grand style. Guest rooms are exquisitely decorated with beautiful antiques, and there are three fine dining rooms for ultimate dining pleasure. 12 rooms, 3 story. Complimentary full breakfast. Check-in 3 pm. Check-out 11 am. Restaurant. **$**

Braselton

Web Site www.braselton.net

Special Event

Road Atlanta. *5300 Winder Hwy, Braselton (30517). 8 miles S via Hwy 53. Phone 770/967-6143; toll-free 800/849-7223. www.roadatlanta.com.* Sports car and motorcycle racing. Also street-driving and road-racing training programs. Mar-Nov.

Restaurant

★ ★ ★ **CHATEAU ELAN'S LE CLOS.** *100 Rue Charlemagne Dr, Braselton (30517). Phone 678/425-0900. www.chateauelan.com.* French menu. Dinner. Closed Mon-Wed. Business casual attire. Reservations recommended. **$$$**

Brunswick (E-5)

See also Darien, Jekyll Island, Sea Island, St. Simons Island

Settled 1771
Population 15,600
Elevation 10 ft
Area Code 912
Information Brunswick-Golden Isles Visitors Bureau, 4 Glynn Ave, 31520; phone 912/265-0620 or toll-free 800/933-2627
Web Site www.brunswick-georgia.com

Brunswick, on the southern third of Georgia's seacoast, separated from the Golden Isles by the Marshes of Glynn and the Intracoastal Waterway, was laid out in 1771 by the Colonial Council of the Royal Province of Georgia. Named to honor George II of the House of Brunswick (Hanover), it later became the seat of Glynn County, named in honor of John Glynn, member of the British Parliament and sympathizer with the colonists' struggle for independence.

Gateway to St. Simons Island, Jekyll Island, and Sea Island (see all), Brunswick is also a manufacturing and seafood processing town. Among its principal products are pulp, paper, lumber machinery, lumber products, and processed seafood. Its harbor is a full oceangoing seaport, as well as a home port to coastal fishing and shrimping fleets. Brunswick is known as one of the shrimp capitals of the world. Its natural beauty is enhanced by plantings of palms and flowering shrubs along main avenues, contrasting with moss-covered ancient oaks in spacious parks.

What to See and Do

James Oglethorpe Monument. *Queens Sq, E side of Newcastle St.* Honors the founder of Georgia.

Lover's Oak. *Albany and Prince sts, Brunswick.* Giant oak said to be more than 900 years old; the trunk, at a point 3 feet above ground, measures 13 feet in diameter.

Marshes of Glynn. Marshes separate Brunswick from St. Simons Island, Sea Island, Little St. Simons Island, and Jekyll Island (see all). Traversed by causeways connecting with Hwy 17, the vast saltwater marshes are bisected by several rivers and the Intracoastal Waterway. Of them Sidney Lanier wrote "Oh, like to the greatness of God is the greatness within the range of the marshes, the liberal marshes of Glynn." Marshes of Glynn Overlook Park has picnic facilities, view of marshes.

Limited-Service Hotels

★ ★ **BEST WESTERN BRUNSWICK INN.** *5323 New Jesup Hwy, exit 36 B, Brunswick (31523). Phone 912/264-0144; fax 912/262-0992. www.bestwestern. com.* 145 rooms, 2 story. Pets accepted; restrictions. Complimentary continental breakfast. Check-in 3 pm, check-out 11 am. Restaurant. Outdoor pool. **$**
🐾 🏊

★ **EMBASSY SUITES.** *500 Mall Blvd, Brunswick (31525). Phone 912/264-6100; toll-free 800/432-3229;*

fax 912/267-1615. www.embassysuites.com. The Southern ambience and convenient location of this property will make it perfect for all guests. The property is attached to the Glynn Place Mall and features complimentary full breakfast, an outdoor pool, exercise room, and meeting facilities. 130 rooms, 5 story, all suites. Pets accepted, some restrictions; fee. Complimentary continental breakfast. Check-in 3 pm, check-out noon. Airport transportation available. **$$**

★ **JAMESON INN.** *661 Scranton Rd, Brunswick (31520). Phone 912/267-0800; toll-free 800/526-3766; fax 912/265-1922. www.jamesoninns.com.* 62 rooms, 2 story. Pets accepted. Complimentary continental breakfast. Check-in 3 pm, check-out 11 am. Fitness room. Outdoor pool. **$**

★ **QUALITY INN.** *125 Venture Dr, Brunswick (31525). Phone 912/265-4600; toll-free 877/424-6423; fax 912/265-8268. www.qualityinn.com.* 83 rooms, 2 story. Complimentary continental breakfast. Check-in 1 pm, check-out 11 am. Outdoor pool. **$**

Restaurants

★ **CAPTAIN JOE'S.** *5296 New Jesup Hwy (Hwy 341), Brunswick (31523). Phone 912/264-8771; fax 912/265-6759.* Seafood, steak menu. Lunch, dinner. Closed Thanksgiving, Dec 24-25. Children's menu. Casual attire. **$$**

★ ★ **MATTEO'S ITALIAN RESTAURANT.** *5448 New Jesup Hwy, Brunswick (31523). Phone 912/267-0248.* Italian, pizza menu. Lunch, dinner. Closed Sun; holidays. Children's menu. Casual attire. **$**

★ **NEW CHINA.** *3202 Glynn Ave, Brunswick (31520). Phone 912/265-6722.* Chinese menu. Lunch, dinner. Closed Thanksgiving, Dec 25. Casual attire. **$**

Buford (B-2)

See also Atlanta, Gainesville, Norcross

Population 10,668
Elevation 1,187 ft
Area Code 770
Zip 30518
Information Gwinnett Convention and Visitors Bureau, 6500 Sugarloaf Pkwy, Suite 200, Duluth 30097; phone 770/623-3600
Web Site www.gcvb.org

What to See and Do

Chateau Elan Winery and Resort. *100 Tour de France, Braselton (30517). 11 1/2 miles NW on I-85, exit 126. Phone 678/425-0900; toll-free 800/233-9463. www. chateauelanatlanta.com.* Winery tours and tastings begin Mon-Sat at 11 am, Sun at noon; closed Dec 25. Two 18-hole public golf courses (**$$$$**); golf academy. Equestrian center, tennis center, 7 miles of bike trails. Restaurants, hotel (see Full-Service Resorts). **FREE**

Lake Lanier Islands. *7000 Holiday Rd, Buford (30518). N of town. Phone 770/932-7200.* A 1,200-acre, year-round resort. Swimming, water-skiing, beach, and water park with wave pool, ten water slides, and other attractions, fishing, boating (ramps, rentals); horseback riding, two 18-hole golf courses, tennis, picnicking, two hotels, resort (see), cottages, tent and trailer camping (hookups). Special events are held May-Oct. Fees for some activities. Contact 6950 Holiday Rd, Lake Lanier Islands, 30518.

Limited-Service Hotel

★ **DAYS INN.** *4267 Buford Dr, Buford (30180). Phone 770/932-0111; fax 770/945-3261.* 40 rooms, 2 story. Check-out 11 am. **$**

Full-Service Resorts

★ ★ ★ **CHATEAU ELAN WINERY AND RESORT.** *100 Rue Charlemagne, Braselton (30517). Phone 678/425-0900; toll-free 800/233-9463; fax 678/425-6000. www.chateauelanatlanta.com.* Escape to the French countryside without ever leaving Georgias Southern hospitality behind when visiting the Chteau lan Winery and Resort. Just 40 minutes north of Atlanta, this delightful resort feels a continent away from the big city's hustle and bustle with its charming manor house and lush vineyards. Winemaking is a source of great pride here, and the eight restaurants perfectly complement the property's excellent product. European influences are discovered throughout the resort, from the classic styling of the elegant accommodations to the tranquil spa. Guests fill their days with a wide variety of activities; golf is a favored pursuit, with three courses and an academy, and the equestrian center is considered one of the states best. 310 rooms, 5 story. Check-in 3 pm, check-out noon.

Restaurant, bar. Children's activity center. Fitness room. Two indoor pools, two outdoor pools, whirlpools. Golf, 63 holes. Tennis. Airport transportation available. Business center. **$$**

★ ★ ★ **EMERALD POINTE RESORT.** *7000 Holiday Rd, Lake Lanier Islands (30518). Phone 770/945-8787; toll-free 800/768-5253; fax 770/932-5471. www.lakelanierislands.com.* Best known for its championship golf course, here guests will find a fun-filled experience. Set on a hillside surrounded by hardwood trees and Lake Sidney Lanier, the islandlike setting has swimming, boating, and more. This is a favorite Southern retreat. 224 rooms, 4 story. Check-in 3 pm, check-out noon. Restaurant, bar. Children's activity center. Fitness room. Beach. Outdoor pool, children's pool, whirlpool. Golf. Business center. **$**

★ ★ ★ **RENAISSANCE PINEISLE RESORT AND GOLF CLUB.** *9000 Holiday Rd, Buford (30518). Phone 770/945-8921; toll-free 800/372-7409; fax 770/945-0351. www.renaissancehotels.com.* Sparkling waters and grand forests are the setting at this beautiful resort overlooking Lake Lanier. With championship golf, tennis, seven tempting restaurants, and 22,000 square feet of meeting space, guests can enjoy all there is to offer. 250 rooms, 5 story. Check-in 4 pm. Check-out 11 am. Restaurant, bar. Children's activity center. Fitness room. Beach. Indoor pool, outdoor pool, whirlpool. Golf. Tennis. Business center. **$**

Full-Service Inn

★ ★ ★ **WHITWORTH INN.** *6593 McEver Rd, Flowery Branch (30542). Phone 770/967-2386; fax 770/967-2649. www.whitworthinn.com.* Bask in the tranquility of this beautifully landscaped bed and breakfast located 40 miles north of Atlanta. Guests will enjoy the country setting of this quiet, intimate hideaway and leave relaxed and renewed. 10 rooms, 3 story. Complimentary full breakfast. Check-in 3 pm. Check-out 11 am. **$**

Restaurant

★ ★ **BREEZES.** *9000 Holiday Rd, Lake Lanier Islands, Buford (30518). Phone 770/945-8921; fax 770/945-1024. www.pineisle.com.* This casual restaurant serves satisfying American food. In season, an all-you-can-eat lobster boil is served on Friday nights. American menu. Breakfast, lunch, dinner, Sun brunch. Bar. Valet parking. **$$**

Calhoun (A-1)

See also Chatsworth, Dalton, Rome

Population 10,667
Elevation 715 ft
Area Code 706
Zip 30701
Information Gordon County Chamber of Commerce, 300 S Wall St; phone 706/625-3200 or toll-free 800/887-3811
Web Site www.cityofcalhoun-ga.com

Once called Oothcaloga, "place of the beaver dams," the name was changed in 1850 to honor John Caldwell Calhoun, Secretary of State to President John Tyler. Although the town was directly in the path of General Sherman's 1864 "March to the Sea," Calhoun was not destroyed. Now, Calhoun is the seat of Gordon County and center of a dairy, beef cattle, and poultry raising area. The town has a major carpet industry and several major manufacturing companies that provide a wide range of products.

What to See and Do

New Echota State Historic Site. *1211 Chatsworth Hwy NE, Calhoun (30701). 1/2 mile E of I-75, exit 317, on Hwy 225. Phone 706/624-1321. gastateparks.org/info/echota/.* Tavern (1805), an 1830s log store, and a museum orientation center. Citizens of Calhoun bought the 200-acre site in the early 1950s and donated it to the state. After establishing a government in 1817, the legislature of the Cherokee Indian Nation in 1825 established a capital surrounding the site of their Council House. The written form of the Cherokee language, created by the brilliant Sequoyah, had been developed by 1821, and the print shop was built in 1827. The first issue of the Cherokee newspaper, the *Cherokee Phoenix,* was printed in this shop in 1828 in both Cherokee and English; the paper continued publication until 1834. Samuel A. Worcester, a most able missionary, arrived from Boston in 1827 and built a house, which is the only original building still standing. The Vann Tavern, built by Cherokees at another location, was moved to the park as part of the restoration. The Cherokee Nation had a legislative hall, a supreme court house, a mission, and several other buildings at New Echota. At the height of Cherokee prosperity, gold was found in Cherokee territory, which then included parts of

Georgia, North Carolina, Alabama, and Tennessee. In 1835, after a long legal battle, the Cherokees were forced to sell their territory and move to Oklahoma. In the winter of 1838-1839, the Cherokees were driven to their new location over the "Trail of Tears," one-fourth of them dying en route. Many hid out in the Great Smoky Mountains; their descendants now form the Eastern Cherokees. The buildings of the restored New Echota are furnished authentically and are a dramatic reconstruction of a remarkable episode in Native American history. (Tues-Sat 9 am-5 pm, Sun 2-5:30 pm; closed Jan 1, Thanksgiving, Dec 25) **$**

Resaca Confederate Cemetery. *5 miles N on I-75, Resaca exit (320). Phone toll-free 800/887-3811.* Site of the Civil War battle that opened the way to Atlanta for General Sherman. Civil War markers and cemetery on the Civil War Discovery Trail. (Daily) **FREE**

Limited-Service Hotels

★ **JAMESON INN.** *189 Jameson St SE, Calhoun (30701). Phone 706/629-8133; toll-free 800/526-3766; fax 706/629-7985. www.jamesoninns.com.* This Colonial-style inn prides itself on service, comfort, and affordability. Guests suites are large with a separate sitting area. It's also located near local parks and lakes. 59 rooms, 2 story. Pets accepted; restrictions, fee. Complimentary continental breakfast. Check-in 2 pm, check-out 11 am. Fitness room. Outdoor pool. **$**

★ ★ **QUALITY INN.** *915 Hwy 53 E, Calhoun (30701). Phone 706/629-9501; toll-free 800/225-4686; fax 706/629-9501. www.qualityinn.com.* 100 rooms, 2 story. Pets accepted, some restrictions; fee. Complimentary continental breakfast. Check-in 1 pm, check-out 11 am. Restaurant, bar. Fitness room. Outdoor pool. **$**

Full-Service Hotel

★ ★ ★ **BARNSLEY GARDENS.** *597 Barnsley Gardens Rd, Adairsville (30103). Phone 770/773-7480; fax 770/773-1779. www.slh.com/barnsley.* 70 rooms, 1 story. Pets accepted; fee. Check-in 3 pm, check-out noon. Restaurant, bar. Fitness room. Indoor pool, outdoor pool, whirlpool. Airport transportation available. Business center. **$$**

Restaurant

★ **PENGS PAVILLION.** *1120 S Wall St, Calhoun (30701). Phone 706/629-1453.* Chinese menu. Lunch, dinner. Closed Sun; holidays. **$**

Carrollton (B-1)

Population 19,843
Elevation 1,116 ft
Area Code 770
Zip 30117
Information Carroll County Chamber of Commerce, 200 Northside Dr; phone 770/832-2446
Web Site www.carroll-ga.org

Carrollton was named in honor of Charles Carroll, one of the signers of the Declaration of Independence. The town serves as a regional retail, service, manufacturing, and health care center for several counties in western Georgia and eastern Alabama. Carrollton is home to Southwire, one of the nation's largest privately owned rod and cable manufacturing companies. The world's largest tape and record manufacturing plant, owned by Sony, is located here as well.

What to See and Do

John Tanner State Park. *354 Tanner Beach Rd, Carrollton. 6 miles W off Hwy 16. Phone 770/830-2222.* Two lakes offer the longest beach in the state park system. Swimming, fishing, boating (rentals); picnicking, camping, motel.

University of West Georgia. *1601 Maple St, Carrollton (30118). Phone 678/839-5000. www.westga.edu.* (1933) (7,500 students) A unit of the state university system. On campus are the John F. Kennedy Memorial Chapel and

> **Thomas Bonner House.** *1600 Maple St, Carrollton (30118). Phone 678/839-6464.* (Circa 1840) Restored plantation house, campus information center. (Mon-Fri; closed holidays, school breaks)

Limited-Service Hotel

★ **SUPER 8.** *128 Hwy 61 Connector, Villa Rica (30180). Phone 770/459-8000; fax 770/459-8413.* 64 rooms, 2 story. Complimentary continental breakfast. Check-out 11 am. Outdoor pool. **$**

Restaurant

★ **MAPLE STREET MANSION.** *401 Maple St, Carrollton (30117). Phone 770/834-2657; fax 770/834-3812. www.maplestreetmansion.com.* This turn-of-the-century mansion has been turned into a charming restaurant and banquet site. Some Carrollton residents insist the house is haunted by several spirits. American menu. Lunch Lunch weekdays, dinner, late-night. Closed Sun-Mon; Jan 1, Dec 24-25. Bar. **$$**

Cartersville (B-1)

See also Atlanta, Marietta, Rome

Founded 1832
Population 15,925
Elevation 787 ft
Area Code 770
Zip 30120
Information Cartersville/Bartow County Convention and Visitors Bureau, PO Box 200397; phone 770/387-1357 or toll-free 800/733-2280
Web Site www.notatlanta.org

Cartersville is in the center of an area rich in minerals. Its economy is based on textile manufacturing, plastics, the quarrying of limestone, and the mining of ocher, barite, and manganese. An Anheuser-Busch brewery also contributes to the economy.

What to See and Do

Allatoona Lake. *513 Allatoona Dam Rd SE, Cartersville. Headquarters is 3 miles N on I-75, exit 125, then E on Hwy 20, then 4 miles S on Spur 20. Phone 770/382-4700.* (US Army Corps of Engineers) Swimming, water-skiing, fishing, boating (ramps); hiking trails, overlook, picnicking, camping (fee). Contact Park Ranger, PO Box 487.

Etowah Indian Mounds Historic Site and Archaeological Area. *813 Indian Mounds Rd SW, Cartersville (30120). 3 miles S, off Hwys 113, 61. Phone 770/387-3747.* The most impressive of more than 100 settlements in the Etowah Valley, this village was occupied from A.D. 1000-1500. It was the home of several thousand people of a relatively advanced culture. Six earthen pyramids grouped around two public squares, the largest of which occupies several acres, served as funeral mounds, bases for temples, and the residences of the chiefs. Museum displays artifacts from the excavations; crafts, foods, way of life of the Etowah; painted white

marble mortuary. (Tues-Sat 9 am-5 pm, Sun 2 pm-5:30 pm; closed Jan 1, Thanksgiving, Dec 25) **$**

Red Top Mountain State Lodge Park. *50 Lodge Rd SE, Cartersville (30121). 2 miles E of I-75, exit 285. Phone 770/975-0055; fax 770/975-4228. www.gastateparks. org/info/redtop/.* Swimming, water-skiing, boating (ramps, dock, marina); trails, miniature golf, picnicking, concession. Restaurant. Lodge. Camping, cottages.

William Weinman Mineral Museum. *51 Mineral Museum Dr, Cartersville (30184). I-75 exit 293. Phone 770/386-0576; fax 770/386-0600. www. weinmanmuseum.org.* Displays of cut gemstones, minerals, and rocks from Georgia and around the world; mine tunnel with waterfall. (Mon-Sat 10 am-5 pm; closed holidays) **$**

Limited-Service Hotels

★ **COMFORT INN.** *28 Hwy 20 Spur SE, Cartersville (30121). Phone 770/387-1800; toll-free 800/228-5150; fax 678/535-0007. www.comfortinn.com.* 60 rooms, 2 story. Pets accepted; restrictions, fee. Complimentary continental breakfast. Check-in noon, check-out 11 am. Outdoor pool. **$**

★ **DAYS INN.** *5618 Hwy 20 SE, Cartersville (30121). Phone 770/382-1824; toll-free 800/329-7466; fax 770/606-9312. www.daysinn.com.* 52 rooms, 2 story. Complimentary continental breakfast. Check-in 11 am, check-out 11 am. Outdoor pool. **$**

★ ★ **HOLIDAY INN.** *2336 Hwy 411 NE, Cartersville (30184). Phone 770/386-0830; toll-free 800/465-4329; fax 770/386-0867. www.holiday-inn.com.* 144 rooms, 2 story. Pets accepted. Check-out noon. Restaurant, bar. Outdoor pool, whirlpool. **$**

Chatsworth (A-1)

See also Calhoun, Dalton; also see Chattanooga, TN

Population 3,531
Elevation 750 ft
Area Code 706
Zip 30705
Information Chatsworth-Murray County Chamber of Commerce, 126 N Third Ave; phone 706/695-6060
Web Site www.murraycountychamber.org

Murray County has a strong carpet industry. Almost a third of the land is forest and mountains. Opportunities for fishing, hunting, camping, backpacking, and mountain biking abound in the surrounding Cohutta Wilderness and woodlands. A Ranger District office of the Chattahoochee National Forest is located in Chatsworth. Talcum, a mineral that most people know only as a comfort to the skin, was once mined here in large quantities.

What to See and Do

Carters Lake. *181 Fort Mountain Park Rd, Chatsworth. 15 miles S, off Hwy 411. Phone 706/334-2248.* Swimming, fishing, boating (ramps); hiking trails, overlooks, camping (mid-Apr-late Oct; fee). Contact Resource Manager's office at dam site.

Fort Mountain State Park. *181 Fort Mountain Rd, Chatsworth. 7 miles E via Hwy 52. Phone 706/695-2621.* A mountain park with ruins of a prehistoric stone wall; observation tower. Swimming, fishing, paddleboats (rentals); self-guided nature trail, picnicking, cabins, camping.

Vann House State Historic Site. *82 Hwy 225 N, Chatsworth (30705). 3 miles W on Hwy 52-A at junction Hwy 225. Phone 706/695-2598. www.gastateparks. org/info/chiefvann.* (1804) This brick house was the showplace of the Cherokee Nation. James Vann was half Scottish, half Cherokee. His chief contribution to the tribe was his help in establishing the nearby Moravian Mission for the education of the young Cherokees. The three-story house, with foot-thick brick walls, is modified Georgian in style; partly furnished. (Tues-Sun; closed Jan 1, Thanksgiving, Dec 25) **$**

Special Event

Appalachian Wagon Train. *Murray County Saddle Club,, Chatsworth (30705). 1 mile E via Hwy 76. Phone 706/695-6060.* Horse and mule shows, trail rides, square dancing, parade. Early July.

Limited-Service Hotel

★ ★ **COHUTTA LODGE & CONFERENCE CENTER.** *500 Cochise Trail, Chatsworth (30705). Phone 706/695-9601; fax 706/695-0913. www. cohuttalodge.com.* 61 rooms, 3 story. Check-in 3 pm, check-out 11 am. Restaurant. Indoor pool. Tennis. **$**

Restaurant

★ **COHUTTA DINING ROOM.** *500 Cochise Trail, Chatsworth (30705). Phone 706/695-9601; fax 706/695-0913. www.cohuttalodge.com.* American menu. Breakfast, lunch, dinner. **$$**

Chickamauga and Chattanooga National Military Park (A-1)

See also Dalton

Web Site www.nps.gov/chch
9 miles S of Chattanooga, TN on Hwy 27.

Established in 1890, this is the oldest and largest national military park in the United States. The two-day battle fought at Chickamauga was one of the Civil War's fiercest, with 36,000 casualties, and was the greatest success of Confederate armies in the West. However, the inability of General Braxton Bragg to follow up the success of September 19 and 20, 1863, and his defeat two months later on Missionary Ridge at Chattanooga, Tennessee, meant the loss of a strategic railway center and opened the gateway to a Union advance into the Deep South.

General Bragg had evacuated Chattanooga on September 9, to maintain rail communications southward after Union Commander Rosecrans had abruptly crossed the Tennessee River southwest of the city. However, with the arrival of reinforcements from Lee's army in the east giving him a numerical advantage, Bragg turned back north to surprise Rosecrans' scattered forces. On September 18, the two armies stumbled into each other on the west bank of Chickamauga Creek.

By the morning of September 19, Union troops attacked and were driven back in heavy fighting. Confederate troops broke the Union line the morning of the 20th, sweeping the entire right wing and part of the center from the field. Union troops on the left, with the aid of reserve corps and all under the command of General George H. Thomas, took up new positions on Snodgrass Hill, holding up under terrific assaults by Confederates until the Union Army was able to retreat in good order to Chattanooga. Thomas earned the nickname "Rock of Chickamauga."

Highway 27 extends more than 3 miles through the 5,400-acre Chickamauga Battlefield, where the battle has been commemorated by markers, monuments, tablets, and artillery pieces. Woods and fields are kept as close as possible to the way they were in wartime, and some old buildings lend added atmosphere.

Chickamauga Battlefield is but one of 17 areas forming the National Military Park. Other major areas (all in Tennessee) are Point Park on Lookout Mountain, the Reservations on Missionary Ridge, Signal Point on Signal Mountain, and Orchard Knob in Chattanooga—totaling nearly 3,000 acres.

The Chickamauga visitor center, on Highway 27 at the north entrance to the battlefield, is the logical starting point for auto tours. The center has the Fuller Collection of American Military Shoulder Arms, consisting of 355 weapons, as well as a 26-minute multimedia program (fee) describing the Battle of Chickamauga. Visitor center (daily; closed Dec 25). Park (daily). The National Park Service also offers guided tours, walks, evening programs, and musket/cannon firing demonstrations (June-August). For further information, contact PO Box 2128, Fort Oglethorpe 30742; phone 706/866-9241.

Clayton (A-3)

See also Hiawassee, Toccoa

Population 2,019
Elevation 1,925 ft
Area Code 706
Zip 30525
Information Rabun County Chamber of Commerce, Box 750; phone 706/782-4812; a Rabun County Welcome Center is located on Hwy 441 N; phone 706/782-5113 or 706/782-4812
Web Site co.clayton.ga.us

Located in the mountainous and forested northeast corner of Georgia, Clayton offers visitors a wide variety of activities, including hiking, mountain climbing, camping, boating, fishing, hunting, skiing, and whitewater rafting. A ranger district office of the Chattahoochee National Forest (see DAHLONEGA) is located in Clayton.

What to See and Do

Chattooga Wild and Scenic River. *8 miles SE via Hwy 76.* Originating in the mountains of North Carolina, the Chattooga tumbles southward 57 miles to its terminus, Lake Tugaloo, between Georgia and South Carolina. Designated a Wild and Scenic River by Congress in 1974, the Chattooga is one of the few remaining free-flowing streams in the Southeast. The scenery along the river is spectacular, with gorges, waterfalls, and unusual rock formations.

Foxfire Museum and Center. *200 Foxfire Ln, Clayton. In Mountain City. Phone 706/746-5828. www.foxfire. org.* Located in replica of log cabin, the museum contains artifacts and crafts of early Appalachian life, including the inner workings of an old gristmill. (Mon-Sat 8:30 am-4:30 pm; closed holidays) **$**

Raft trips. Southeastern Expeditions. *50 Executive Park S, Suite 5016, Atlanta (30329). Phone 404/329-0433; toll-free 800/868-7238.* Whitewater raft trips on the Chattooga River in northeast Georgia. Full-day tours. (Mar-Oct) **$$$$**

Special Event

Homemakers' Harvest Festival. *7 miles N on Hwy, 23, 441 in Dillard.* Mountain arts and crafts. Fri-Sat in Oct.

Restaurant

★ **CAFE NAPOLI.** *7750 Forsyth, Clayton (63105). Phone 314/863-5731; fax 314/863-2835. www. cafenapoli.com.* Twinkling fairy lights, pink tablecloths, and an intimate mood add to the great people-watching atmosphere (Clayton's big hitters often dine here). The menu is also a treat, with southern Italian specialties and a great wine list. Italian menu. Lunch, dinner. Closed holidays. Bar. Valet parking. **$$$**

Columbus (D-1)

See also Lumpkin, Pine Mountain

Founded 1827
Population 185,781
Elevation 250 ft
Area Code 706

Information Tourist Division, Convention and Visitors Bureau, 900 Front Ave, PO Box 2768, 31901; phone 706/322-1613 or toll-free 800/999-1613; or the Georgia Welcome Center, 1751 Williams Rd; 24-hour visitor information hotline; phone 706/322-3181 **Web Site** www.visitcolumbusga.com

Power from the falls of the Chattahoochee River feeds the industries of this dynamic city. With a 9-foot-deep navigable channel to the Gulf of Mexico, it is at the head of navigation on the Chattahoochee. Originally a settlement of the Creek Indians, the site was chosen as a border stronghold by Governor Forsyth in 1828. The city reached a peak of frenzied manufacturing and commerce between 1861 and 1864, when it supplied the Confederate Army with shoes, caps, swords, and pistols.

The Columbus Iron Works (1853) supplied Columbus and the surrounding area with cast-iron products, farming equipment, steam engines, and industrial and building supplies. It was a major supplier of cannons for the Confederate States during the Civil War. Reconstruction created havoc for a time, but by 1874 Columbus's industries were more numerous and varied than before the war: from 1880-1920 a commercial ice-making machine was produced in the town, and by the beginning of World War II, Columbus was a great iron-working center and the second largest producer of cotton in the South.

Much of the original city plan of 1827 is still evident, with streets 99- to 164-feet wide flanked by magnificent trees. Dogwood and wisteria add color in the spring. The atmosphere is exemplified by the brick-lined streets and gaslights in the 28-block historic district and by the Victorian gardens, gazebos, and open-air amphitheaters on the Chattahoochee Promenade along the banks of the river.

What to See and Do

Columbus Convention and Trade Center. *801 Front Ave, Columbus (31901). Phone 706/327-4522.* Converted from the historic Columbus Iron Works. Exhibit space, banquet facilities, outdoor amphitheater.

The Columbus Museum. *1251 Wynnton Rd, Columbus (31906). Phone 706/748-2562.www.columbusmuseum. com.* Features Chattahoochee Legacy, a regional history gallery with re-created period settings; fine and decorative arts galleries; and Transformations, a youth-oriented participatory gallery. (Tues-Wed, Fri-Sat 10 am-5 pm; Thurs until 9 pm; Sun 1-5 pm; closed holidays) **FREE**

Fort Benning. *I-185S, Columbus (31905). Phone 706/545-2958. www.benningmwr.com.* Largest infantry post in the US, established during World War I, the fort was named for Confederate General Henry L. Benning of Columbus. Infantry school; demonstrations of Airborne 5000 at jump tower (Mon mornings). **FREE** Here is

> **National Infantry Museum.** *Bldg 396, Baltzell Ave, Fort Benning (31905). Phone 706/545-2958.* Exhibits of US infantry weapons, uniforms, equipment from the Revolutionary War to the Gulf War; experimental and developmental weapons; collection of foreign weapons and equipment. (Daily Mon-Fri 10 am-4:30 pm, Sat-Sun 12:30-4:30 pm; closed holidays) **FREE**

Port Columbus Civil War Naval Museum Center. *1002 Victory Dr, Columbus (31902). Phone 706/327-9798. www.portcolumbus.org.* Salvaged remains of Confederate gunboats *Jackson* and *Chattahoochee;* relics, ship models, uniforms, paintings, and other exhibits on Confederate naval operations. (Daily 9 am-5 pm; closed Dec 25) **$**

Springer Opera House. *103 10th St, Columbus (31901). At 1st Ave. Phone 706/324-5714; fax 706/324-4461. www.springeroperahouse.org.* (1871) Restored Victorian theater in which many famous performers have appeared, including Shakespearean actor Edwin Booth; museum. Guided tours.

Special Event

Riverfest Weekend. *708 Broadway, Columbus (31906). At the riverfront. Phone 706/324-7417; fax 706/323-7979. www.columbusriverfest.com.* Riverfest Weekend features two main entertainment areas: the Folklife Village with a juried arts and crafts show, folk art, Native American exhibits, and living history demonstrations and the Salisbury Fair with a food court, live entertainment, antique cars, and a carnival. Late Apr.

Limited-Service Hotels

★ **BEST WESTERN COLUMBUS.** *3443 Macon Rd, Columbus (31907). Phone 706/568-3300; toll-free 800/780-7234; fax 706/563-2388. www.bestwestern. com.* 66 rooms, 3 story. Complimentary continental breakfast. Check-in 2 pm, check-out noon. Fitness room. Outdoor pool. **$**

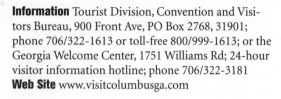

★ ★ **FOUR POINTS BY SHERATON.** *5351 Sidney Simons Blvd, Columbus (31904). Phone 706/327-6868; fax 706/327-0041. www.starwood.com.* 178 rooms, 5 story. Check-out noon. Restaurant, bar. Outdoor pool, whirlpool. Airport transportation available. **$**

★ **LA QUINTA INN.** *3201 Macon Rd, Columbus (31906). Phone 706/568-1740; toll-free 800/687-6667; fax 706/569-7434. www.laquinta.com.* 122 rooms, 2 story. Pets accepted. Complimentary continental breakfast. Check-out noon. Outdoor pool. **$**

Full-Service Hotel

★ ★ ★ **MARRIOTT.** *800 Front Ave, Columbus (31901). Phone 706/324-1800; fax 706/576-4413.* Situated among the scenic downtown historical business district, this hotel caters to corporate travelers and families alike. Leave the worrying behind because this hotel offers the ultimate in services and makes for a welcoming retreat. Relax and enjoy the warm and friendly service, spacious guest rooms, and outdoor pool. Step outside and enjoy, within walking distance, a stroll along the Chattahoochee River and Riverwalk. 177 rooms, 6 story. Check-in 3 pm, check-out noon. Restaurant, bar. Outdoor pool. Airport transportation available. **$**

Restaurants

★ ★ ★ **BLUDAU'S GOETCHIUS HOUSE.** *405 Broadway, Columbus (31901). Phone 706/324-4863; fax 706/324-0438. www.goetchiushouse.com.* This classic Southern restaurant is situated in a restored antebellum mansion overlooking the river. A special Chateaubriand is the favorite entée. Mint juleps are served in the speakeasy downstairs. American menu. Dinner. Closed Sun, holidays. Bar. Outdoor seating. **$$**

★ **COUNTRY'S NORTH.** *6298 Veterans Pkwy, Columbus (31909). Phone 706/660-1415; fax 706/660-1615. www.countrysbarbecue.com.* American menu. Lunch, dinner. Closed holidays. Children's menu. Outdoor seating. **$**

Commerce (B-3)

See also Athens, Gainesville, Toccoa

Population 5,292
Elevation 931 ft
Area Code 706
Zip 30529
Web Site www.commercega.org

What to See and Do

Crawford W. Long Medical Museum. *28 College St, Jefferson (30549). 10 miles SW via Hwy 15, on College St in Jefferson or 5 miles S on I-85, exit 50. Phone 706/367-5307. www.crawfordlong.org.* Museum contains diorama of Dr. Long's first use of ether as an anesthetic in surgery, an enormous breakthrough in medicine. Also here are documents, artifacts, and history of anesthesia exhibit. Entrance is in Jackson County Historical Society building, which has other exhibits on local history. A third building has an 1840s doctor's office, an apothecary shop, a 19th-century general store exhibit, and an herb garden. (Tues-Sat 10 am-5 pm; closed holidays) **DONATION**

Limited-Service Hotel

★ **HOWARD JOHNSON.** *148 Eisenhower Dr, Commerce (30529). Phone 706/335-5581; fax 706/335-7889. www.hojo.com.* 120 rooms, 2 story. Pets accepted; fee. Complimentary continental breakfast. Check-out noon. Outdoor pool, children's pool. **$**

Cordele (D-2)

See also Albany, Americus, Andersonville, Perry

Founded 1888
Population 11,608
Elevation 319 ft
Area Code 229
Zip 31015
Information Cordele-Crisp Tourism Commission, 302 E 16th Ave, PO Box 158; phone 229/273-3526
Web Site www.cordele-crisp-chamber.com

Watermelons, sweet potatoes, soybeans, pecans, cotton, peanuts, corn, and cantaloupes are produced in Crisp County, of which Cordele is the seat. The local state farmers' market sells more watermelons than any other market in the state; Cordele residents thus refer to their city as the "Watermelon Capital of the World." Garment making and the manufacture of enormous baling presses for scrap metals, agricultural implements, air conditioners, foundry products, mobile homes, livestock feed, fiberglass items, steel fittings, and several other industries are locally important.

What to See and Do

Georgia Veterans Memorial State Park. *2459-A Hwy 280 W, Cordele. 9 miles W via Hwy 280. Phone 229/276-2371.* Swimming pool, water-skiing, fishing, boating; golf, picnicking, concession, camping, cabins. Museum; model airplane field with historic aircraft.

Special Event

Watermelon Festival. *302 E 16th Ave, Cordele (31015). Phone 229/273-1668; fax 229/273-5132.* Parade; watermelon-eating, seed-spitting, and largest watermelon contests; fishing rodeo; Miss Heart of Georgia contest; arts and crafts; entertainment. mid-June to early July.

Limited-Service Hotel

★ **COMFORT INN.** *1601 16th Ave E, Cordele (31015). Phone 229/273-2371; toll-free 800/228-5150; fax 229/273-8351. www.comfortinn.com.* 59 rooms, 2 story. Complimentary continental breakfast. Check-in 2 pm, check-out 11 am. Outdoor pool. **$**

Restaurants

★ ★ **DAPHNE LODGE.** *US 280 W, Cordele (31015). Phone 229/273-2596.* American menu. Dinner. Closed Sun-Mon; holidays. **$$**

★ **OLDE INN.** *2536 Hwy 280 W, Cordele (31015). Phone 229/273-1229.* Late 1800s building with original fireplace. American menu. Dinner. Closed Sun-Mon; July 4, Thanksgiving, Dec 25. Children's menu. **$$**

Cumberland Island (E-5)

See also Brunswick, Jekyll Island, St. Simons Island

Web site www.nps.gov/cuis

What to See and Do

Cumberland Island National Seashore. *Off the coast, NE of St. Marys. Phone 912/882-4335. www.nps. gov/cuis.* Cumberland Island National Seashore, off the coast of Georgia, is an island 16 miles long and 1 1/2 to 3 miles wide. It is accessible by passenger tour boat, which operates year-round. Mainland departures are from St. Marys (fee); reservations by phone are necessary.

A visit to the island is a walking experience, and there are no restaurants or shops. The island's western side is fringed with salt marsh, and white sand beaches face the Atlantic Ocean. The interior is forested primarily by live oak; interspersed are freshwater marshes and sloughs. Activities include viewing the scenery and wildlife, swimming, and exploring historical areas led by a ranger. Native Americans, Spanish, and English have all lived on the island; most structures date from the pre-Civil War plantation era, though there are turn-of-the-century buildings built by the Thomas Carnegie family. Camping (daily); reservations by phone necessary. Ferry (mid-Mar-Sept, daily; winter, Mon, Thurs-Sun; closed Dec 25) For further information, contact the Superintendent, PO Box 806, St. Marys 31558.

Full-Service Inn

★ ★ ★ **THE GREYFIELD INN.** *Cumberland Island. Mailing address: 8 Second St, Fernandina Beach, FL (32035). Phone 904/261-6408. www.greyfieldinn.com.* To truly get away from it all, escape to the historic Greyfield Inn, built in 1900. Accessible by private ferry from Fernandina Beach, Florida, this inn is a tranquil place to enjoy Cumberland Island's natural beauty and abundant wildlife, including wild horses and many species of birds. The mansion's veranda comes complete with rocking chairs for whiling away the afternoon, while elegant cuisine is offered in the inn's candlelit dining room in the evenings. Furnished with family heirlooms and antiques, the guest rooms and suites vary widely; note that not all have private baths. Room rates include breakfast, picnic lunch, gourmet dinner (jacket required, so pack appropriately), and snacks throughout the day, as well as unlimited use of the inn's sporting, fishing, and beach equipment. A two-night minimum stay is required. 17 rooms, 4 story. Children over 6 years only. Check-out noon. Restaurant, bar. Fitness room. **$$$$**

Dahlonega (A-2)

See also Gainesville

Settled 1833
Population 3,638
Elevation 1,454 ft
Area Code 706
Zip 30533
Information Dahlonega-Lumpkin County Chamber of Commerce, 13 S Park St; phone 706/864-3711
Web Site www.dahlonega.org

Gold fever struck this area in 1828, 20 years before the Sutter's Mill discovery in California. Dahlonega, derived from the Cherokee word for the color yellow, yielded so much ore that the federal government established a local mint which produced $6,115,569 in gold coins from 1838 to 1861. Dahlonega is the seat of Lumpkin County, where tourism, manufacturing, higher education, and agribusiness are the major sources of employment. A US Forest Service Visitor Center is located in Dahlonega.

What to See and Do

Amicalola Falls State Park. *418 Amicalola Falls Lodge Rd, Dawsonville (30534). 20 miles W off Hwy 52. Phone 706/265-8888.* Highest waterfall in the eastern US (729 feet). Trout fishing, hiking trails, picnicking, concession, restaurant, camping, cabins, lodge.

Chattahoochee National Forest. *1755 Cleveland Hwy, Dahlonega. Phone 770/297-3000. www.fs.fed.us/conf.* This vast forest (748,608 acres) includes Georgia's Blue Ridge Mountains toward the north, which have elevations ranging from 1,000 to nearly 5,000 feet. Because the forest ranges from the Piedmont to mountainous areas, the Chattahoochee has a diversity of trees and wildlife. There are 25 developed camping areas, 24 picnicking areas, ten wilderness areas, and six swimming beaches. For the Chattahoochee-Oconee National Forest Recreation Area directory, contact the US Forest Service, 508 Oak St NW, Gainesville 30501. In the forest are

Anna Ruby Falls. *Off Hwy 356, 6 miles N of Helen.* Approximately 1,570 acres surrounding a double waterfall, with drops of 50 and 153 feet. This scenic area is enhanced by laurel, wild azaleas, dogwood, and rhododendron. Visitor center. **$**

Appalachian National Scenic Trail. *799 Washington St, Dahlonega (25425). Phone 304/535-6331.* Thirteen lean-tos are maintained along the 76 miles marked southern portion of the trail. Following the crest of the Blue Ridge divide, the trail begins outside Dahlonega and continues for over 2,000 miles to Mount Katahdin, Maine.

Track Rock Gap. *1881 Hwy 515, Dahlonega (30514). Off Hwy 76, 8 miles SW of Young Harris.* Well-preserved rock carvings of ancient Indian origin; figures resemble animal and bird tracks, crosses, circles, and human footprints.

Consolidated Gold Mines. *185 Consolidated Gold Mine Rd, Dahlonega. At junction GA 52, US 19 and GA 9. Phone 706/864-8473.* Underground mine tour (35-40 minutes) through tunnel network; displays of original equipment used. Instructors available for gold panning. (Daily 10 am-5 pm; closed Thanksgiving, Dec 25) **$$$**

Crisson's Gold Mine. *2736 Morrison Moore Pkwy E, Dahlonega . 2 1/2 miles N via US 19 to end of Wimpy Mill Rd, then 1 mile E. Phone 706/864-6363.* Gold and gem panning; indoor panning (winter). Demonstration of working stamp mill, more than 100 years old. Gift shop. (Daily 10 am-6 pm; closed Dec 25) **$$**

Dahlonega Courthouse Gold Museum State Historic Site. *1 Public Sq, Dahlonega (30533). In old Lumpkin County Courthouse (1836). Phone 706/864-2257.* Exhibits on first major gold rush; display of gold coins minted in Dahlonega. Film shown every half hour. (Mon-Sat 9 am-5 pm, Sun from 10 am; closed Jan 1, Thanksgiving, Dec 25) **$**

Lake Winfield Scott. *1881 Hwy 515, Dahlonega. 15 miles N on Hwy 19, 129, then 4 miles SW on Hwy 180. Phone 706/745-6928.* A US Forest Service Recreation Area with an 18-acre lake in the Blue Ridge Mountains. Swimming, bathhouse, fishing; picnicking, campsites (fee). (May-Oct) For more information, contact the Ranger District Office, Box 9, Blairsville 30512.

North Georgia College and State University. *Hwy 60, College Cir, Dahlonega (30597). College Ave. Phone 706/864-1400. www.ngcsu.edu.* (1873) (4,000 students) Part of the state university system, North Georgia College's administration building, Price Memorial, was built on the foundation of the old US Branch Mint; unique gold steeple. Liberal arts and military college.

Vogel State Park. *7485 Vogel State Park Rd, Blairsville (30512). 25 miles N of Dahlonega, 11 miles S of Blairsville on Hwy 19/129. Phone 706/745-2628.* Rugged area in the heart of north Georgia's mountains. At the foot of Blood and Slaughter Mountains, 22-acre Lake Trahlyta has swimming, bathhouse, fishing, paddleboats; picnicking, grills, playground, camping, 35 furnished cabins. **$**

Special Events

Gold Panning Competition. *Phone 706/864-3711; toll-free 800/231-5543. www.dahlonega.org.* Consolidated gold mine. Third weekend in Apr.

Gold Rush Days. *Phone 706/864-3711; toll-free 800/231-5543. www.dahlonega.org.* A celebration remembering the Gold Rush of 1828, Gold Rush Days draws visitors to the mountains to view more than 300 related exhibits and participate in family activities. Third weekend in Oct.

Limited-Service Hotel

★ **SUPER 8.** *20 Mountain Dr, Dahlonega (30533). Phone 706/864-4343; toll-free 800/800-8000; fax 706/864-4343. www.super8.com.* 60 rooms, 2 story. Check-in 2 pm, check-out 11 am. Outdoor pool. **$**
☲

Full-Service Resort

★ ★ **FORREST HILLS MOUNTAIN RESORT.** *135 Forrest Hills Dr, Dahlonega (30533). Phone 770/534-3244; toll-free 800/654-6313; fax 706/864-0757. www.foresths.com.* 30 rooms. Pets accepted; fee. Check-in 3 pm, check-out 11 am. Restaurant. Outdoor pool. Tennis. Business center. Surrounded by north Georgia mountain forest. **$**
🍴 ☲ 🎿 🏃

Specialty Lodging

THE SMITH HOUSE. *84 S Chestatee St, Dahlonega (30533). Phone 706/867-7000; toll-free 800/852-9577;* *fax 706/864-7564. www.smithhouse.com.* 16 rooms, 2 story. Complimentary continental breakfast. Check-in 2 pm, check-out 11 am. Restaurant. Outdoor pool. **$**
☲

Restaurant

★ ★ **SMITH HOUSE.** *84 S Chestatee St, Dahlonega (30533). Phone 706/867-7000; toll-free 800/852-9577; fax 706/864-7564. www.smithhouse.com.* American menu. Lunch, dinner. Closed Mon. **$**
☲

Dalton (A-1)

See also Calhoun, Chatsworth, Chickamauga and Chattanooga National Military Park

Founded 1837
Population 27,912
Elevation 759 ft
Area Code 706
Information Welcome Center, 2211 Dug Gap Battle Rd, PO Box 2046, 30722-2046; phone 706/270-9960 or toll-free 800/331-3258
Web Site www.daltoncvb.com

Once a part of the Cherokee Nation, Dalton was involved in fierce battles and skirmishes in the Civil War as Union forces advanced on Atlanta. Today, Dalton has more than 100 carpet outlets and manufactures a large portion of the world's carpets. Dalton also produces other tufted textiles, chemicals, latex, thread, and yarn.

What to See and Do

Crown Garden and Archives. *715 Chattanooga Ave, Dalton. 2 miles N via I-75 and Hwy 41, Walnut Ave exit. Phone 706/278-0217.* Headquarters of the Whitfield-Murray Historical Society. Genealogical library; changing exhibits include Civil War items; permanent exhibit on the history of bedspread tufting in the area. (Tues-Fri 10 am-5 pm; closed holidays) **DONATION**

Special Event

Prater's Mill Country Fair. *452 Varnell School St, Dalton. Phone 706/694-6455.* 10 miles NE on Hwy 2. Food, late 1800s entertainment; canoeing on Coahulla Creek, pony rides, exhibits; Three-story gristmill in operation. Mother's Day weekend and Columbus Day weekend.

Limited-Service Hotels

★ ★ **BEST WESTERN INN OF DALTON.** *2106 Chattanooga Rd, Dalton (30720). Phone 706/226-5022; toll-free 800/780-7234; fax 706/226-5022. www.bestwestern.com.* 99 rooms, 2 story. Pets accepted; fee. Check-out noon. Restaurant, bar. Outdoor pool. **$**

★ ★ **HOLIDAY INN.** *515 Holiday Dr, Dalton (30720). Phone 706/278-0500; fax 706/278-7082.* 199 rooms, 2 story. Pets accepted; fee. Check-out noon. Restaurant, bar. Fitness room. Outdoor pool, children's pool. **$**

Restaurant

★ ★ **DALTON DEPOT.** *110 Depot St, Dalton (30720). Phone 706/226-3160; toll-free 888/235-7963; fax 706/275-9721.* American menu. Lunch, dinner. Closed Sun; holidays. Bar. Children's menu. **$$**

Darien (E-5)

See also Brunswick, Jekyll Island, Sea Island, St. Simons Island

Founded 1736
Population 1,719
Elevation 20 ft
Area Code 912
Zip 31305
Information McIntosh Chamber of Commerce, 105 Fort King George Dr, PO Box 1497; phone 912/437-6684
Web Site www.mcintoshcounty.com

James Oglethorpe recruited Scottish Highlanders to protect Georgia's frontier on the Altamaha River in 1736. Calling their town Darien, they guarded Savannah from Spanish and native attack and carved out large plantations from the south Georgia wilderness. After 1800, Darien thrived as a great timber port until the early 20th century. Today, shrimp boats dock in the river over which Darien Scots once kept watch.

What to See and Do

Fort King George State Historic Site. *14 Fort King George Dr, Darien (31305). 1 1/2 miles E of Hwy 17 on Fort King George Dr. Phone 912/437-4770; fax 912/437-5479.* (1721) South Carolina scouts built this fort near an abandoned Native American village and Spanish mission to block Spanish and French expansion into Georgia, thereby establishing the foundation for the later English Colony of Georgia. The fort and its blockhouse have been entirely reconstructed to original form. The museum interprets the periods of Native American, Spanish, and British occupations; the settlement of Darien; and Georgia's timber industry. (Tues-Sat 9 am-5 pm, Sun 2-5:30 pm; closed Jan 1, Thanksgiving, Dec 25) **$**

Hofwyl-Broadfield Plantation State Historic Site. *5556 Hwy 17 N, Brunswick (31525). 6 miles S on Hwy 17. Phone 912/264-7333. gastateparks.org/info/hofwyl/.* (1807) The evolution of this working rice plantation (1807-1973) is depicted through tours of the 1851 plantation house, museum, and trails. Tours (Tues-Sat 9 am-5 pm, Sun 2-5:30 pm; closed Jan 1, Thanksgiving, Dec 25). **$**

Special Event

Blessing of the Fleet Festival. *At Darien Bridge. Phone 912/437-6684. www.mcintoshcounty.com.* Elaborately decorated boats parade down the river as clerics of several denominations stand on the bridge and bless them as they pass. While the Sunday morning boat parade is the highlight of the weekend, activities begin the Friday before with a street parade, fish fry, and art festival. Weekend in Mar, Apr, or May.

Doraville

Restaurant

★ **SEOUL GARDEN KOREAN RESTAURANT.** *5938 Buford Hwy, Doraville (30340). Phone 770/452-0123; fax 770/452-7735.* Korean menu. Lunch, dinner. Casual attire. Reservations recommended. **$**

Douglas (E-3)

Founded 1858
Population 10,639
Elevation 259 ft
Area Code 912
Zip 31533
Information Chamber of Commerce, 211 S Gaskin Ave, PO Box 2470, 31534; phone 912/384-1873
Web Site www.douglasga.org

The town's central location between I-75 and I-95 has helped Douglas develop into a leading trade and distribution center for the southeast. A number of *Fortune* 500 companies operate within Coffee County.

What to See and Do

General Coffee State Park. *46 John Coffee Rd, Nicholls (31554). 6 miles E on Hwy 32. Phone 912/384-7082.* A 1,510-acre park on the Seventeen-Mile River in Coffee County. Swimming pool, fishing; nature trails, picnicking, playgrounds, camping, lodging.

Dublin (B-2)

Population 15,857
Elevation 228 ft
Area Code 478
Information Dublin-Laurens County Chamber of Commerce, 1200 Bellevue Ave, PO Box 818, 31040; phone 478/272-5546
Web Site www.dublin-georgia.com

The seat of Laurens County, Dublin sits on land once occupied by Creek Indians. Area industries manufacture a wide range of goods, including textiles, carpeting, missile control systems, and computer components. The first aluminum extrusion plant in the US is located here. Agricultural products include soybeans, wheat, grain, peanuts, corn, cotton, and tobacco.

What to See and Do

Dublin-Laurens Museum. *311 Academy Ave, Dublin. Bellevue and Academy at Church. Phone 478/272-9242.* Local history museum featuring Native American artifacts, art, textiles, and relics from early settlers. (Tues-Fri 1-4:30 pm; closed Jan 1, Thanksgiving, Dec 25) **FREE**

Fish Trap Cut. *Oconee River, Hwy 19.* Believed to have been built between 1000 BC and AD 1500, this large rectangular mound, smaller round mound, and canal may have been used as an aboriginal fish trap.

Historic buildings. Greek Revival and Victorian houses can be found along Bellevue Ave.

Special Event

St. Patrick's Festival. Includes parade, ball, contests, golf tournaments, arts and crafts show, square dancing, and entertainment. Mar.

Limited-Service Hotel

★ **HOLIDAY INN EXPRESS.** *2192 Hwy 441 S, Dublin (31021). Phone 478/272-7862; toll-free 800/465-4329; fax 478/272-1077. www.holiday-inn.com.* 124 rooms, 2 story. Pets accepted, some restrictions. Complimentary full breakfast. Check-in 3 pm, check-out noon. Restaurant, bar. Fitness room. Outdoor pool. Airport transportation available. **$**

Eatonton (C-3)

See also Madison, Milledgeville

Population 6,764
Area Code 706
Zip 31024
Information Eatonton-Putnam Chamber of Commerce, 105 Washington Ave, PO Box 4088; phone 706/485-7701 or 706/485-4875
Web Site www.eatonton.com

In the early 19th century, large tracts of land in this area were acquired and put under cultivation; by the mid-1800s, the town of Eatonton had become a center of planter culture, that archetypal romantic concept of cotton fields, mansions, wealth, and Southern grace. Joel Chandler Harris was born in Eatonton in 1848. He successfully immortalized the traditional ways of the Old South by creating the character "Uncle Remus" to retell the "Br'er Rabbit" and "Br'er Fox" folk tales heard on the plantation.

Eatonton is also the hometown of Alice Walker, author of *The Color Purple*, an acclaimed depiction of the South of a different time. Eatonton, the seat of Putnam County, is known as the largest dairy producer in the state.

What to See and Do

Alice Walker: A Driving Tour. *105 Washington Ave, Eatonton (31024). Phone 706/485-7701.* Driving tour past the author's birthplace, church, and house where she grew up. Contact the Chamber of Commerce for brochure and information.

Lake Oconee. *125 Wallace Dam Rd, Eatonton (31024). Lawrence Shoals Recreation Area. Off Hwy 16 (see MADISON). Lake Sinclair. S on Hwy 441 (see MILLEDGEVILLE). Phone 706/485-8704.* Both are

Georgia Power Company projects created by the impoundment of the Oconee River.

Rock Eagle Effigy. *350 Rock Eagle Rd, Eatonton (31024). 7 miles N on Hwy 441, located in Rock Eagle 4-H Center. Phone 706/484-2800.* This 8-foot-high mound of milky white quartz is shaped like a great prone bird, wings spread, head turned eastward, 102 feet from head to tail and 120 feet wingtip to wingtip. Archaeologists estimate the monument is more than 5,000 years old and was probably used by Native Americans for religious ceremonies. It may be viewed from an observation tower. **FREE**

Uncle Remus Museum. *214 S Oak St, Eatonton. 3 blocks S of courthouse on Hwy 441 in Turner Park. Phone 706/485-6856. www.uncleremus.com/museum.html.* Log cabin made from two original slave cabins. Reconstruction of cabin fireplace; shadow boxes with illustrations of 12 tales; mementos of era, first editions; diorama of old plantation; other relics. (June-Aug, daily 10 am-5 pm, Sun from 2 pm; rest of year, Wed-Mon) **$**

Special Event

Putnam County Dairy Festival. Parade, dairy and farming-related contests, arts and crafts fair, entertainment. First Sat in June.

Forsyth (C-2)

See also Macon

Population 3,776
Elevation 705 ft
Area Code 478
Zip 31029
Information Forsyth-Monroe County Chamber of Commerce, 267 Tift College Dr, PO Box 811; phone 478/994-9239
Web Site www.forsyth-monroechamber.com

What to See and Do

Jarrell Plantation State Historic Site. *711 Jarrell Plantation Rd, Forsyth (31046). 18 miles E of I-75 exit 185 on Hwy 18 E, then N on Jarrell Plantation Rd. Phone 478/986-5172.* This authentic plantation has 20 historic buildings dating from 1847 to 1940, including a plain-style plantation house, sawmill, gristmill, and blacksmith shop. Farm animals; seasonal demonstrations. (Tues-Sat 9 am-5 pm, Sun 2-5:30 pm; closed Jan 1, Thanksgiving, Dec 25) **$**

The Whistle Stop Cafe. *443 McCrackin St, Forsyth. I-75, exit 186, then 8 miles E to Juliette. Phone 478/994-3670.* Town of Juliette, GA was where the movie *Fried Green Tomatoes* was filmed. Cafe and other stores along McCrackin St. Cafe (Mon-Sat and Sun afternoons).

Limited-Service Hotels

★ **BEST WESTERN HILLTOP INN.** *951 Hwy 42 N, Forsyth (31029). Phone 478/994-9260; toll-free 800/780-7234; fax 478/994-1280. www.bestwestern.com.* 120 rooms, 2 story. Check-out noon. Outdoor pool, children's pool. **$**

★ ★ **HOLIDAY INN.** *480 Holiday Cir, Forsyth (31029). Phone 478/994-5691; toll-free 800/465-4329; fax 478/994-3254. www.holiday-inn.com.* 120 rooms, 2 story. Pets accepted, some restrictions; fee. Check-out noon. Restaurant, bar. Fitness room. Outdoor pool, children's pool. Business center. Chapel on premises. **$**

Restaurant

★ **WHISTLE STOP CAFE.** *443 McCrackin St, Juliette (31046). Phone 478/992-8886.* Film site of *Fried Green Tomatoes.* Breakfast, lunch. Closed holidays. **$**

Fort Frederica National Monument (E-5)

See also Brunswick, Jekyll Island, Sea Island, St. Simons Island

Web Site www.nps.com/fofr

12 miles NE of Brunswick via St. Simons/Sea Island Causeway toll.

Fort Frederica marked the southern boundary of British Colonial North America. It was carefully planned by the trustees in London in 1736 and included the town of Frederica, named after Frederick, Prince of Wales.

Having picked the site of the fort on a bluff commanding the Frederica River, General James

Oglethorpe returned to England and helped select families to build and settle it. Forty-four men and 72 women and children landed at St. Simons Island on March 16, 1736. In 1738, a regiment of 650 British soldiers arrived. The fort was then strengthened with "tabby" (a kind of cement made of lime, oyster shells, sand, and water), and the whole town was enclosed with earth and timber works from 10 to 13 feet high that included towers and a moat.

Oglethorpe used Fort Frederica as a command post for his invasion of Florida. He built other forts on St. Simons and other islands and attacked Spanish outposts to the south. In July 1742, Spaniards launched an attack on Fort Frederica, but Oglethorpe repulsed this with an ambush at Bloody Marsh, ending Spanish attempts to gain control of Georgia.

Frederica flourished as a military town until after the peace of 1748. With the withdrawal of the regiment the following year, the shopkeepers and tradesmen at Frederica had to move elsewhere. The town did not long survive these losses. Archaeological excavations have exposed some of it, and stabilization work has been done by the National Park Service. Outdoor exhibits make it easy to visualize the town as it was, and the visitor center has exhibits, touch computers, and a film dealing with its life and history. Self-guided audio tour (fee). (Daily; closed Dec 25) Contact the Superintendent, Rte 9, Box 286-C, St. Simons Island, 31522; phone 912/638-3639. Golden Age Passport (see MAKING THE MOST OF YOUR TRIP). Entrance per vehicle **$**

Fort McAllister Historic Park(D-5)

See also Savannah

Web Site gastateparks.org/info/ftmcallister

25 miles S of Savannah, via Hwy 144 from I-95 or Hwy 17; 10 miles E of Richmond Hill off Hwy 17. Phone 912/727-2339. fortmcallister.org.

This Confederate fort built for the defense of Savannah stands on the left bank of the Great Ogeechee River, commanding the river's mouth. Fort McAllister's fall on December 13, 1864, marked the end of Sherman's march to the sea, opening communications between the Union Army and the fleet and rendering further defense of Savannah hopeless.

Prior to this, McAllister had proved that its type of massive earthwork fortifications could stand up against the heaviest naval ordnance. It protected the blockade-running ship *Nashville* from pursuit by Union gunboats in July and November 1862. It successfully resisted the attacks of *Monitor*-type ironclads of the Union Navy in 1863. The USS *Montauk* shelled the fort with the heaviest shells ever fired by a naval vessel against a shore work up to that time. The fort sustained only one casualty. There were huge holes in its parapets, but the damage was minor. Its gun emplacements were separated by large "traverses," several used to house powder magazines. The fort that seemed to be "carved out of solid earth" was termed "a truly formidable work" by a Union naval officer in 1864. General Sherman called the capture of the fort and overpowering its garrison "the handsomest thing I have seen in this war." Union losses were 24 killed, 110 wounded (mostly by mines outside the fort); the Confederate garrison of 230 men had 70 casualties—16 killed and 54 wounded—in the 15-minute battle.

The earthworks have been restored to approximate conditions of 1863-1864. A museum containing mementos of the *Nashville* and the fort was completed in 1963 and opened on the centennial of the great bombardment. (Tues-Sat, also Sun afternoon; closed Thanksgiving, Dec 25; fee) Fort McAllister has a campground and day-use facilities (fee); boating (ramps, dock). Contact the Superintendent, 3894 Fort McAllister Rd, Richmond Hill 31324. Phone 912/727-2339. **$**

Fort Pulaski National Monument (D-5)

See also Savannah

Web Site www.nps.gov/fopu

15 miles E of Savannah off Hwy 800.

A unit of the Department of the Interior's National Park Service, Fort Pulaski National Monument was established by President Coolidge in 1924. The site, named in honor of Revolutionary war hero Casimir Pulaski, commemorates an international turning point in the history of fortification and artillery. It was here on April 11, 1862, that newly developed rifled cannons easily overtook a masonry fortification. After centuries of use throughout the world, both masonry forts and smooth-bore cannons were obsolete.

Most visitors begin the tour at the visitor center, which contains a small museum, an information desk, and a bookstore featuring more than 300 items on the Civil War and other site-related and regional subjects.

Restored to its mid-19th-century appearance, the fort contains several rooms, or casemates, depicting garrison life during its Confederate (1861-1862) and Union (1862-1875) occupations. This exhibit includes an officer's quarters and mess, medical dispensary, chapel, quartermaster's office, supply room, and enlisted men's quarters. Other displays include several examples of smooth-bore and rifled artillery and carriages. While self-guided tours are available year-round, ranger-conducted programs and demonstrations are presented daily in the summer.

There are three major trails in the monument. The nature trail is a 1/4 mile paved loop through several historic sites. The picnic trail is a 1/2-mile paved trail from the visitor center to the picnic and recreation area, which borders the vast salt marshes and forested hammocks of the Savannah River estuary. The third trail follows the historic dike originally surveyed by Robert E. Lee. A walk on any segment of the trail provides excellent opportunities to see a wide variety of plants and wildlife, as well as scenic views of the fort.

Fishing, boating, and other water-related activities are offered at the park. The north channel shoreline and the bridge approaches at the south channel are the best fishing locations. A boat ramp and fishing dock just off Hwy 80 at Lazaretto Creek provide more opportunities for fishing. All facilities are open daily except Dec 25. For more information, phone 912/ 786-5787.

Gainesville (A-2)

See also Buford, Commerce, Dahlonega, Toccoa

Population 25,578
Elevation 1,249 ft
Area Code 770
Information Gainesville/Hall County Convention and Visitors Bureau, 830 Green St, 30501; phone 770/536-5209
Web Site www.gainesvillehallcvb.org

On the shore of 38,000-acre Lake Sidney Lanier, Gainesville is a poultry producing and marketing center with a variety of industries. It is also the headquarters for the Chattahoochee National Forest (see DAHLONEGA). Contact the Forest Supervisor, US Forest Service, 508 Oak St, 30501; phone 770/536-0541.

What to See and Do

Brenau University. *500 Washington St SE, Gainesville (30501). Phone 770/534-6299; toll-free 800/252-5119. www.brenau.edu.* (1878) (2,000 students) Liberal arts residential college for women with coed evening and weekend programs; off-campus, graduate, and undergraduate divisions. On campus is Brenau Academy, a four-year preparatory high school for girls. Pearce Auditorium (1897) has fine acoustics, stained-glass windows, and ceiling frescoes. Trustee Library has displays of American art.

Green Street Historical District. A broad street with Victorian and Classical Revival houses dating from the late 19th and early 20th centuries. Here is

Green Street Station. *311 Green St SE, Gainesville. Phone 770/536-0889.* Home of Georgia Mountains Historical and Cultural Trust. Houses historical and arts and crafts exhibits of northeast Georgia, as well as the Mark Trail Memorial Exhibit. (Tues-Fri; closed holidays) **$**

Lake Lanier Islands. *6950 Holiday Rd, Gainesville (30518). W edge of town.* (see BUFORD).

North Geogia Premium Outlets. *800 Hwy 400 S, Dawsonville (30534). Off Hwy 400, 23 miles NE on Hwy 53. Phone 706/216-3609. www.premiumoutlets.com.* An outlet mall with about 140 stores, including Coach, Crate & Barrel, and Hugo Boss. (Mon-Sat 10 am-9 pm, Sun 11 am-7 pm)

Special Event

Road Atlanta. *5300 Winder Hwy, Braselton (30517). 8 miles S via Hwy 53. Phone 770/967-6143; toll-free 800/849-7223. www.roadatlanta.com.* Sports car and motorcycle racing. Also street-driving and road-racing training programs. Mar-Nov.

Limited-Service Hotels

★ ★ **BEST WESTERN LANIER CENTRE.** *400 E Butler Pkwy, Gainesville (30501). Phone 770/531-0907; toll-free 800/782-8966; fax 770/531-0788. www. bestwestern.com.* 122 rooms, 4 story. Check-out noon.

Restaurant, bar. Fitness room. Outdoor pool. **$**

★ ★ **QUALITY INN & SUITES.** *726 Jesse Jewell Pkwy, Gainesville (30504). Phone 770/536-4451; toll-free 800/228-5151; fax 770/538-2880. www.choicehotels.com.* 132 rooms, 3 story. Pets accepted, some restrictions. Check-out noon. Restaurant, bar. Outdoor pool. **$**

Restaurants

★ **POOR RICHARD'S.** *1702 Park Hill Dr, Gainesville (30501). Phone 770/532-0499; fax 770/532-3193. www.prgainesville.com.* Steak menu. Dinner. Closed Sun. Bar. Children's menu. Casual attire. **$$**

★ ★ **RUDOLPH'S.** *700 Green St, Gainesville (30501). Phone 770/534-2226; fax 770/536-8261. www. rudolphsdining.com.* Located on the city's most historic street, this American restaurant, open since 1976, offers pleasing renditions of traditional preparations of filet mignon, veal, and seafood. The live jazz band creates a lively atmosphere on Friday and Saturday nights. American, Continental menu. Lunch, dinner, Sun brunch. Bar. Children's menu. Business casual attire. Reservations recommended. **$$**

Golden Isles (E-5)

See also Brunswick, Jekyll Island, Sea Island, St. Simons Island

Web Site www.bgivb.com

2744 Hwy 17 S, Brunswick (31523).

Four barrier subtropical islands off Georgia's coast at Brunswick. Best known of the group are Sea Island (see), St. Simons Island (see), and Jekyll Island (see), all of which may be reached by road. Others are Cumberland, Little St. Simons Island, Ossabaw, St. Catherine's, and Sapelo, reachable only by water.

Native Americans hunted on these islands for giant turtles, waterfowl, deer, and other animals. Spaniards established a chain of missions, which existed for about a century, the largest on St. Simons. The French made halfhearted efforts to settle on the islands. James Oglethorpe built Fort Frederica (see) on St. Simons in 1736 and later defeated Spanish forces attempting to recapture the island.

Now the Golden Isles are resort areas, offering beautiful scenery, swimming, a wide variety of sports facilities, and accommodations.

Greensboro (B-3)

Population 3,238
Web Site www.greeneccoc.org

Full-Service Resort

★ ★ ★ ★ **THE RITZ-CARLTON LODGE, REYNOLDS PLANTATION.** *One Lake Oconee Trail, Greensboro (30642). Phone 706/467-0600; fax 706/467-7124. www.ritzcarlton.com.* The Ritz-Carlton Lodge has one of the most enviable resort locations in the South. Just over an hour from Atlanta, this sprawling resort on the 8,000-acre Reynolds Plantation overlooks the sparkling water of Lake Oconee, Georgia's second largest lake. While imparting first-class service and modern-day conveniences, this fantastic resort mimics the grand style of the Great Camps that populated the Adirondacks during the early 20th century. Like a wealthy relative's lake home, The Ritz-Carlton Lodge welcomes you with its gracious style and magnificent setting. You can fill your days with endless activities, and the lake provides a wealth of opportunities from fishing and boating to swimming and water-skiing. Golf is a major attraction here, and with 81 holes designed by legends like Jack Nicklaus, Rees Jones, Tom Fazio, and Bob Cupp, it is no wonder. The Gun Club entertains with its skeet and trap shooting, five-stand shooting pavilion, and sporting clay course. After an active day, retire to one of the exceedingly comfortable guest rooms. Dominated by a rich blend of American and European design principles, the accommodations are sophisticated without pretension and welcome the entire family. 251 rooms. Check-in 3 pm, check-out noon. High-speed Internet access. Restaurant, bar. Children's activity center. Fitness room, spa. Indoor pool, outdoor pool, children's pool, whirlpool. Golf, 81 holes. Business center. **$$$**

Spa

★ ★ ★ ★ **THE SPA AT THE RITZ-CARLTON LODGE, REYNOLDS PLANTATION.** *1 Lake Oconee Trail, Greensboro (30642). Phone 706/467-0600; toll-free 800/241-3333. www.ritzcarlton.com.* The 26,000-square-foot spa is the shining star at Reynolds Plantation. The facility is superbly designed with the spa visitor in mind. Private spaces that inspire reflection and relaxation can be found throughout, from the outdoor terraces with lake views to the indoor pool with lounges and a towering stone fireplace. This dynamic facility pays tribute to the Creek Indians, the first inhabitants of the Lake Oconee area. Everything from the architecture to the philosophy and the treatments reflects the spa's dedication to Native American healing traditions. The seasonally inspired body buffs and polishes pay special attention to the skin's varying needs throughout the year. The winter body buff tackles dry skin with its blend of evening primrose, eucalyptus, and rosewood, while the summer body glow uses lemongrass, grapefruit seed, and sassafras root to achieve a healthy skin tone. Thistle and Peru balsam are used in the spring scrub, while the fall's sweet orange, patchouli, pumpkin seeds, and sea salt help soothe sun-exposed skin and awaken the senses. Wood, fire, earth, metal, and water are each represented by a different type of clay in the five-element body wrap that concludes with a luxurious bath; select the clay that best suits your needs. The Oconee mud wrap uses indigenous mud along with wild yam, elderberry, juniper, and sage to hydrate skin. The resort's wellness center caters to health and sports enthusiasts with its advanced cardiovascular equipment, indoor lap pool, health screenings, and consultations with counselors who will design an exercise program to help you achieve higher levels of fitness.

Hamilton

Web Site www.harris-county.com/hamiltonga

Restaurant

★ ★ ★ OAK TREE VICTORIAN RESTAURANT.
Hwy 27, Hamilton (31811). Phone 706/628-4218; fax 706/628-5478. www.victoriangrill.com. Owned by Joyce and Robert Cusic, this restaurant highlights French and Italian specialties. The Victorian setting makes for an elegant dining experience. French menu. Dinner. Closed Sun; holidays. **$$**

Hampton

What to See and Do

Atlanta Motor Speedway Camping. *1500 N Hwy 41, Hampton (30228). Phone 770/946-4211.* The best place to camp for the Atlanta Motor Speedway is at the track itself. Unreserved camping spots for tents and RVs are available for $40, payable on-site. Camping spaces in the general RV area measure 20 feet by 40 feet. The spaces in the tent/pop-up area near the lake are 15 feet by 30 feet. Reserved spaces are available in four locations around the speedway. A 20-foot-by-40-foot space for tents and pop-ups costs $100. A 25-foot-by-45-foot RV space costs $125. No hook-ups. Call the speedway ticket office well in advance of race days for reservations. Campers can stake out more than one space as long as all sites are paid for. Grills and contained fires are allowed. If a barrel fire is used, the barrel must be removed from the property after the event. Dump stations. Restrooms, showers.

Atlanta Motor Speedway Track Tours. *Atlanta Motor Speedway, 1500 N Hwy 41, Hampton (30228). Phone 770/946-4211. www.atlantamotorspeedway.com.* Official track tours take groups to the Petty Garden, a luxury suite, the garages, Victory Lane, and two laps in the Speedway van. (Mon-Sat 9 am-4:30 pm; Sun 1-4:30 pm; not offered during Race Weeks) **$**

Special Event

Atlanta Motor Speedway. *1500 S Hwy 41, Hampton (30228). S on I-75, exit 77, and then approximately 15 miles S on Hwy 19/41. Phone 770/946-4211. www.atlantamotorspeedway.com.* NASCAR Winston Cup, Busch Grand National, IMSA, and ARCA auto racing events.

Helen (A-2)

See also Toccoa

Population 430
Elevation 1,446 ft
Area Code 706
Zip 30545
Information Helen/White County Convention and Visitors Bureau, 726 Brucken St, PO Box 730; phone 706/878-2181 or toll-free 800/858-8027
Web Site www.helenga.org

The natural setting of the mountains and the Chattahoochee River helped create the atmosphere for this logging town, transformed into a charming alpine village. Helen was reborn in 1969 when the citizens, with the help of a local artist, decided to improve the town's appearance.

The result is the relaxed atmosphere of a small Bavarian town. Quaint cobblestone streets, gift shops with an international flavor, crafters, restaurants, and festivals—a bit of the Old World in the heart of the mountains of northeast Georgia.

What to See and Do

Anna Ruby Falls. *In Chattahoochee National Forest.* (see DAHLONEGA).

Babyland General Hospital. *73 W Underwood St, Cleveland (30528). 9 miles SW via GA 75 N, on US 129. Phone 706/865-2171; fax 706/219-1699. www. cabbagepatchkids.com.* Authentic turn-of-the-century hospital, home of the original "Cabbage Patch Kids"—soft-sculptured "babies" created by artist Xavier Roberts. (Mon-Sat 9 am-5 pm, Sun 10 am-5 pm; closed holidays) **FREE**

Nacoochee Indian Mound. *1 mile SE on Hwy 17.* Located in former center of the Cherokee Nation.

Richard B. Russell Scenic Highway. *5 miles N of Helen.* Highway winds around mountainsides, offering spectacular scenic views.

Stovall Covered Bridge over Chickamauga Creek. *7 miles E on Hwy 255.* The smallest covered bridge in Georgia.

Unicoi State Park. *1788 Hwy 356 N, Helen. 2 miles NE on Hwy 356. Phone 706/878-2201.* A 1,081-acre park adjacent to Anna Ruby Falls. Swimming beach, fishing, paddleboat (rentals), canoeing (rentals); nature and hiking trails, picnicking, camping, cottages, lodge/ conference center, restaurant, craft shop. Programs on natural resources, folk culture. Standard hours, fees. Contact Director of Sales, PO Box 849.

Special Events

Fasching Karnival. *726 Brucken Strasse, Helen.* German Mardi Gras. Jan-Feb.

Helen to the Atlantic Balloon Race & Festival. *Hwy 75, Helen (30545). Phone 706/878-2271.www.helenballoon. com.* The weekend begins with a Friday morning lift-off for about 25 balloons participating in the Helen to the Atlantic race, which ends anywhere along I-95. After those balloons take off, several more stay in Helen for local flights or special activities—visitors can help with inflation, be a part of a chase crew, or even take a tethered balloon ride. First weekend in June.

Oktoberfest. *726 Brucken Strasse, Helen. Phone 706/878-1908. www.helenga.org/oktoberfest.html.* German music and beer festival; one of the longest running Oktoberfests in the country. Sept-Oct. **$$**

Volksmarch. *1074 Edelweiss Strasse, Helen. Phone 706/878-1908.* Bavarian walk in the forest. Third weekend in Apr.

Limited-Service Hotels

★ ★ **CASTLE INN.** *8287 Main St, Helen (30545). Phone 706/878-3140; toll-free 877/878-3140; fax 706/878-2470. www.castleinn-helen.com.* 12 rooms, 2 story. Check-in 3 pm, check-out 11 am. Restaurant. **$**

★ **COMFORT INN.** *101 Edelweiss Strasse, Helen (30545). Phone 706/878-8000; toll-free 800/443-6488; fax 706/878-1231. www.comfortinn.com.* 60 rooms, 2 story. Complimentary continental breakfast. Check-out 11 am. Outdoor pool. **$**
🏊

★ ★ **UNICOI LODGE AND CONFERANCE CENTER.** *1788 Hwy 356, Helen (30545). Phone 706/878-2201; toll-free 800/573-9659; fax 706/878-1897. www.unicoilodge.com.* 100 rooms, 3 story. Check-in 4 pm, check-out 11 am. Restaurant. Tennis. Access to all facilities of state park. **$**
🎿

Restaurant

★ ★ **HOFBRAUHAUS.** *1 Main St, Helen (30545). Phone 706/878-2248; fax 706/878-1202. www. riverfronthotel.com.* German menu. Dinner. Closed Dec 25. Bar. Children's menu. **$$**

Hiawassee (A-2)

See also Clayton

Population 808
Elevation 1,980 ft
Area Code 706
Web Site www.mountaintopga.com

A picturesque mountain town in the heart of Georgia's "Little Switzerland," Hiawassee is on Lake Chatuge, surrounded by Chattahoochee National Forest (see DAHLONEGA). Its backdrop is a range of the Blue Ridge Mountains topped by Brasstown Bald Mountain, Georgia's highest peak. Rock hunting, including hunting for the highly prized amethyst crystal, is a favorite activity in surrounding Towns County. Mountaineers of northern Georgia gather from 26 surrounding counties to participate in a fair, the rule of which is "everybody can bring something."

What to See and Do

Brasstown Bald Mountain-Visitor Information Center. *2941 St Hwy 180, Hiawassee (30546). S on Hwy 17, 75, then W on Hwy 180, then N on Hwy180 spur. Phone 706/896-2556.* At 4,784 feet, this is Georgia's highest peak. Observation deck affords a view of four states. Visitor center has interpretive programs presented in mountain-top theater and exhibit hall. Parking/shuttle fee. (June-Oct, daily; late Apr-May, weekends only, weather permitting) **FREE**

Lake Chatuge. *Hwy 76 W, Hiawassee (30546). W edge of town. Phone 706/896-2835.* This approximately 7,000-acre TVA lake provides opportunities for fishing, boating, and camping.

Special Events

Georgia Mountain Fair. *1311 Music Hall Rd, Hiawassee (30546). Phone 706/896-4191. www. georgia-mountain-fair.com.* Individual accomplishment and "friendlier living" is the theme of this gathering of mountain farm people; arts and crafts, farm produce, flowers, minerals, Native American relics; board splitting, soap and hominy making, quilting; general store, still, farm museum, midway, music hall; entertainment, parade. Camping, beach, and tennis courts at Georgia Mountain Fairgrounds and Towns County Recreation Park. Twelve days in late July.

Georgia Mountain Fall Festival. *1311 Music Hall Rd, Hiawassee (30546). Phone 706/896-4191. www. georgia-mountain-fair.com/falsched.html.* At the fairgrounds. Ten days in mid-Oct. **$$**

Full-Service Resort

★ ★ ★ **BRASSTOWN VALLEY RESORT.** *6321 Hwy 76, Young Harris (30582). Phone 706/379-9900; toll-free 800/201-3205; fax 706/379-9999. www. brasstownvalley.com.* Guests get lost in the views from this mountain lodge as they take in the beautiful Blue Ridge Mountain countryside. This resort offers a rustic feel with many modern touches and with plenty to see and do. 102 rooms, 5 story. Check-in 4 pm, check-out noon. Restaurant, bar. Children's activity center. Fitness room. Indoor pool, outdoor pool, whirlpool. Golf. Tennis. Business center. **$**

Indian Springs State Park (C-2)

Web Site gastateparks.org/info/indspr/
5 miles SE of Jackson on Hwy 42.

Called "the oldest state park in the United States," this was originally a gathering place for Creek Native Americans, who valued sulphur springs for curative powers. General William McIntosh, a Creek, headed the encampment in this area in 1800. In 1821, McIntosh signed a treaty ceding most of the Creek lands between the Flint and Ocmulgee rivers and north to the Chattahoochee. In 1825, he relinquished the rest of the Creek land in Georgia.The state disposed of all Native American lands except 10 acres called Indian Springs Reserve. Butts County citizens bought an adjoining 513 acres, donating it to the state for a park with a mineral spring, a 105-acre lake, and a museum (summer only). Swimming beach, fishing, boating (rentals); nature trails, picnicking, camping, cottages. Standard hours, fees. Contact Superintendent, 678 Lake Clark Rd, Flovilla 30216; phone 770/504-2277.

Jekyll Island (E-5)

See also Brunswick, Darien, Golden Isles, Sea Island, St. Simons Island

Population 1,500
Elevation 5 ft
Area Code 912
Information Jekyll Island Convention and Visitors Bureau, PO Box 13186, 31527; phone 912/635-3636 or toll-free 800/841-6586
Web Site www.jekyllisland.com

Connected to the mainland by a causeway, Jekyll Island, the smallest of Georgia's coastal islands (see GOLDEN ISLES) with 5,600 acres of highlands and

10,000 acres of marshland, was favored by Native Americans for hunting and fishing. Spanish missionaries arrived in the late 16th and early 17th centuries and established a mission. In 1734, during an expedition southward, General James Oglethorpe passed by the island and named it for his friend and financial supporter, Sir Joseph Jekyll. Later, William Horton, one of Oglethorpe's officers, established a plantation on the island.

Horton's land grant passed to several owners before the island was sold to Christophe du Bignon, a Frenchman who was escaping the French Revolution. It remained in the du Bignon family as a plantation for almost a century. In 1858, the slave ship *Wanderer* arrived at the island and unloaded the last major cargo of slaves ever to land in the US. In 1886, John Eugene du Bignon sold the island to a group of wealthy businessmen from the northeast, who formed the Jekyll Island Club.

Club members who wintered at Jekyll in exclusive privacy from early January to early April included J. P. Morgan, William Rockefeller, Edwin Gould, Joseph Pulitzer, and R. T. Crane, Jr. Some built fabulous "cottages," many of which are still standing. But by World War II, the club had been abandoned for economic and social reasons, and in 1947, the island was sold to the state. The Jekyll Island Authority was created to conserve beaches and manage the island while maintaining it as a year-round resort.

What to See and Do

Horton House. *NW side of the island.* Ruins of former house (1742) of William Horton, sent from St. Simons as captain by General James Oglethorpe. On Jekyll, he established an outpost and plantation. Horton became major of all British forces at Fort Frederica after Oglethorpe's return to England. This house was later occupied by the du Bignon family as part of their plantation.

Jekyll Island Club Historic District. *901 Jekyll Island Causeway, Jekyll Island (31527).* Once one of the nation's most exclusive resorts, this restored district is a memorable example of turn-of-the-century wealth. Exhibition buildings and shops are open daily (closed Jan 1, Dec 25). Tours are available (daily, fee; tickets, information at the visitor center, the former Jekyll Island Club stables) for Mistletoe Cottage (1900), Indian Mound (or Rockefeller) Cottage (1892), du Bignon Cottage (1884), and the Faith Chapel (1904).

Period rooms and changing exhibits can be viewed in several houses.

Public facilities. Beachfront bathhouses, pier fishing, charter boats for offshore and inlet fishing, sightseeing cruises, nature center; bicycle trails, rentals, golf, driving range, miniature golf, 13 clay tennis courts, pro shop. Picnicking on E shore; shopping center. Camping at N end. Some fees.

Summer Waves. *210 S Riverview Dr, Jekyll Island. Phone 912/635-2074.* Water park (11 acres) featuring wave pool, enclosed speed slide, serpentine slides, tubing river, children's pool; picnicking, concessions. (Late May-early Sept, daily, times vary by day) **$$$$**

Special Event

Beach Music Festival. *901 Jekyll Pkwy, Jekyll Island. Phone 912/635-3636. www.jekyllfest.com.* Music groups perform all afternoon on the famous beach. Late Aug. **$$$**

Limited-Service Hotel

★ ★ **HOLIDAY INN.** *200 S Beachview Dr, Jekyll Island (31527). Phone 912/635-3311; toll-free 800/753-5955; fax 912/635-3919. www.holiday-inn.com.* 198 rooms, 4 story. Pets accepted; fee. Check-in 4 pm, check-out 11 am. Restaurant, bar. Fitness room. Beach. Outdoor pool, children's pool. **$**

🐾 🏃 ⛲

Full-Service Resort

★ ★ ★ **JEKYLL ISLAND CLUB HOTEL.** *371 Riverview Dr, Jekyll Island (31527). Phone 912/635-2600; toll-free 800/535-9547; fax 912/635-2818. www.jekyllclub.com.* Once a popular and exclusive retreat for the nation's wealthy elite, this gorgeous hotel on Georgia's historic Jekyll Island will leave guests feeling pampered and entertained. With golf, fishing, water sports, shopping, and more, it's simply a piece of heaven on earth. 157 rooms, 4 story. Check-in 4 pm, check-out noon. Restaurant, bar. Children's activity center. Beach. Outdoor pool. Golf. Tennis. Airport transportation available. **$$**

⛲ 🏃 ⛳

Restaurants

★ ★ **BLACKBEARD'S.** *200 N Beachview Dr, Jekyll Island (31527). Phone 912/635-3522; fax 912/635-4144.* American menu. Lunch, dinner. Closed Dec 25. Bar.

Children's menu. Casual attire. Outdoor seating. **$$**

★ ★ ★ **GRAND DINING ROOM.** *371 River-view Dr, Jekyll Island (31527). Phone 912/635-2600; fax 912/635-2818. www.jekyllclub.com.* The formal dining room of this historic resort is as grand as its name suggest. A dramatic colonnade leads to a large fireplace, lined by plushly upholstered chairs. The low-country cooking features local fish and seafood. American menu. Breakfast, lunch, dinner, Sun brunch. Children's menu. Jacket required (dinner). Reservations recommended. Valet parking. **$$$**

★ **LATITUDE 31.** *1 Pier Rd, Jekyll Island (31527). Phone 912/635-3800. www.latitude-31.com.* American menu. Lunch Tues-Sat, dinner. Closed Mon; holidays. Bar. Children's menu. Casual attire. Outdoor seating. **$$**

★ **ZACHRY'S SEAFOOD.** *44 Beachview Dr, Jekyll Island (31527). Phone 912/635-3128; fax 912/635-9889.* Seafood menu. Lunch, dinner. Closed Dec 25, Children's menu. Casual attire. **$$**

Kennesaw Mountain National Battlefield Park (B-2)

See also Atlanta, Marietta

Web Site www.nps.gov/kemo

Approximately 3 miles NW of Marietta off Hwy 41 or I-75, exit 116. Phone 770/427-4686; fax 770/528-8399. www.nps.gov/kemo.

At Kennesaw Mountain in June of 1864, General William Tecumseh Sherman executed the last of a series of flanking maneuvers that were started 100 miles to the north on May 7. The Battle of Kennesaw Mountain stalled but did not halt General Sherman's invasion of Georgia. Kennesaw Mountain National Battlefield Park commemorates the 1864 Atlanta campaign.

In a series of flanking maneuvers and minor battles in May and June, Sherman's 100,000-man Union Army forced the 65,000-man Confederate Army, under the command of General Joseph E. Johnston, back from Dalton to the vicinity of Kennesaw Mountain 20 miles north of Atlanta. On June 19, Johnston took position and dug in, anchoring his right flank on the steep mountain slopes and extending his left flank several miles to the south. He trusted that strong fortifications and rugged terrain would make up for the disparity in numbers.

The Confederates abandoned their positions after a heavy day's fighting and occupied strong points between Kennesaw and Lost mountains. Sherman first tried to march around to an area just south of the Confederate position, but Johnston shifted 11,000 troops to counter the maneuver. In fierce fighting at Kolb's Farm on June 22, Confederate attacks were repulsed, but Sherman was temporarily stymied.

Although the Confederate entrenchments seemed strong, Sherman suspected that they were weakly held. A sharp frontal attack, he decided, might break through and destroy Johnston's entire army. On the morning of June 27, after a heavy artillery bombardment, Sherman struck the Confederate line at two places simultaneously. At Pigeon Hill, 5,500 attackers were quickly driven under cover by sheets of Southern bullets. Two miles to the south, 8,000 Union infantrymen stormed up Cheatham Hill and for a few minutes engaged the Confederates in hand-to-hand combat on top of their earthworks. Casualties were so severe that the location was nicknamed "Dead Angle." By noon, both attacks had failed. Sherman had lost 3,000 men, Johnston only 500.

Sherman reverted to his flanking strategy, and on July 2, the Confederates withdrew, eventually to Atlanta. The siege and fall of Atlanta soon followed. Sherman then began his devastating "March to the Sea."

The visitor center, on Hwy 41 and Stilesboro Road, north of Kennesaw Mountain, has exhibits, an audiovisual program, and information (daily; closed Dec 25). A road leads to the top of Kennesaw Mountain (daily: Mon-Fri, drive or walk; Sat-Sun, bus leaves every half hour, Feb-Nov, or walk—no driving). (The Cheatham Hill area, in the south-central section of the park, has the same hours as the Kennesaw Mountain road; closed Dec 25).

Park (daily; closed Dec 25). Self-guided tours. For additional information, contact Park Ranger, 900 Kennesaw Mountain Dr, Kennesaw 30152-4854; phone 770/427-4686. **FREE**

La Grange (C-1)

See also Pine Mountain

Settled 1828
Population 25,998
Elevation 772 ft
Area Code 706
Zip 30240
Information La Grange-Troup County Chamber of Commerce, 111 Bull St, Box 636, 30241-0636; phone 706/884-8671
Web Site www.lagrangechamber.com

La Grange is said to be the only town in the Confederacy that organized its own female military company. Legend has it that La Grange was so loyal to the Confederacy that every man marched off to battle. A women's home guard was named for Nancy Hart, Revolutionary heroine. When the defenseless city was about to be invaded by Wilson's Raiders, the Nancy Harts marched out to the fray. The Union colonel, named La Grange, was so affected by this female defense that he marched on without burning the city.

What to See and Do

Bellevue. *204 Ben Hill St, La Grange (30240). Phone 706/884-1832.* (1852-1853) Greek Revival house of US senator Benjamin Harvey Hill; period furnishings. (Tues-Sat 10 am-noon, 2-5 pm; closed holidays) **$$**

Chattahoochee Valley Art Museum. *112 Lafayette Pkwy, Hogansville (30240). Phone 706/882-3267.* Art museum housed in remodeled 1800s jail. Changing exhibits by local, national, and international artists. (Tues-Fri 9 am-5 pm, Sat from 11 am; closed holidays) **FREE**

West Point Lake. *500 Resource Management Dr, West Point (31833). W on Hwy 109. Phone 706/645-2937.* Approximately 26,000 acres with 525 miles of shoreline. Swimming, fishing, boating; hunting, camping (fee).

Limited-Service Hotel

★ **BEST WESTERN LAFAYETTE GARDEN INN.** *1513 Lafayette Pkwy, La Grange (30240). Phone 706/884-6175; fax 706/884-1106. www. lafayettegardeninn.com.* 143 rooms, 2 story. Check-in 2 pm, check-out 11 am. Fitness room. Outdoor pool. **$**

Lookout Mountain

Web Site www.lookoutmtnattractions.com

Specialty Lodging

CHANTICLEER INN. *1300 Mockingbird Ln, Lookout Mountain (30750). Phone 706/820-2015; fax 706/820-7976. www.stayatchanticleer.com.* 17 rooms. Complimentary continental breakfast. Check-in 3 pm, check-out 11 am. High-speed Internet access. Outdoor pool. **$**

Lumpkin (D-1)

See also Americus, Columbus

Population 1,250
Elevation 593 ft
Area Code 229
Zip 31815

What to See and Do

Lake Walter F. George. *Rte 1 Hwy 39, Lumpkin. Approximately 18 miles W via Hwy 39C, or approximately 30 miles SW via Hwy 27. Phone 229/768-2516.* This 45,000-acre lake, stretching south along the border of Georgia and Alabama, was created by the damming of the Chattahoochee River. Fishing is good for bass, bream, crappie, and catfish, and the lake's 640-mile shoreline provides countless hidden coves and inlets. Various state parks are situated on the lake's border, including

> **Florence Marina State Park.** *Rte 1 Hwy 39, Omaha. Phone 229/838-4244.* More than 140 acres at the northern end of Lake Walter F. George. Swimming pool, fishing, boating, johnboat rentals (fee); 18-hole miniature golf (fee), tennis, camping, cottages. Contact Manager, Rte 1, Box 36, Omaha 31821.

Providence Canyon State Conservation Park. *Rte 1, Lumpkin (31815). 7 miles W via Hwy 39C. Phone 229/838-6202.* Georgia's "Little Grand Canyon" has spectacular erosion gullies up to 150 feet deep. Hiking, picnicking, interpretive center (daily). Contact Superintendent, Rte 1, Box 158.

Westville. *Martin Luther King Blvd, Lumpkin. Phone 229/838-6310; toll-free 888/733-1850. www.westville.*

org. Living history village featuring buildings (circa 1850); decorative arts and work skills of early Georgia. Demonstrations by craftsworkers include quilting, weaving, candlemaking, potterymaking, blacksmithing, and basket weaving; syrup making in season. (Tues-Sat, 10 am-5 pm; closed Jan 1, Thanksgiving, Dec 25; also early Jan) **$$**

Special Event

Westville events. *Phone 229/838-6310. www.westville. org.* Westville has many varied events throughout the year. Of special interest are the Spring Festival (early Apr), the May Day celebration (early May), Independence Day (July 4), "Fair of 1850" (late Oct-early Nov), and a variety of Christmas activities (Dec).

Macon (C-3)

See also Forsyth, Milledgeville, Ocmulgee National Monument, Perry

Founded 1823
Population 97,255
Elevation 325 ft
Area Code 478
Information Macon-Bibb County Convention and Visitors Bureau, Terminal Station, 200 Cherry St, PO Box 6354, 31208; phone 478/743-3401 or toll-free 800/768-3401
Web Site www.maconga.org

Macon began as a trading post. It served as a fort and rallying point for troops in the War of 1812; later it became a river landing for shipping to the seacoast by oar-propelled flat-bottom boats; then Macon became a major regional cotton market. Having launched *The Pioneer*, a forerunner of all Southern river steamers, Macon was not content to remain just a port. In 1838, a railroad linked Macon with Forsyth; five years later it was connected by rail to Savannah. In 1848, a third line, the Southwestern, connected Macon with the fertile southwest section of the state. The town had become a major railroad center.

Macon's role in the Civil War was to manufacture and distribute quartermaster supplies and ordnance. Harnesses, small weapons, cannons, and shots were produced, and the city harbored $1.5 million in Confederate gold. In 1864, refugees poured in from devastated northern Georgia. In July and November,

Union forces were twice repulsed. The city finally surrendered to Wilson's Raiders in April 1865.

Sidney Lanier was born and lived here, practicing law before turning to poetry. Macon is also the hometown of rock' n' roll singer Little Richard and soul singer Otis Redding.

What to See and Do

Around Town Tours of Historic Macon. *200 Cherry St, Macon (31201). Phone 478/743-3401; toll-free 800/768-3401.* Operated by the Middle Georgia Historical Society. Guides available (fee) for private tours of city or bus tours.

City Hall. *700 Poplar St, Macon. Phone 478/751-7170.* (1836) Main entrance of Classical Revival building is flanked by panels depicting history of Macon area. Building was state capitol Nov 18, 1864-Mar 11, 1865, during the last session of the Georgia General Assembly under the Confederate States of America. Tours. (Mon-Fri 8:30 am-5:30 pm; closed holidays) **FREE**

Georgia Music Hall of Fame. *200 Martin Luther King, Jr Blvd, Macon (31201). Phone 478/751-3334; toll-free 888/427-6257. www.gamusichall.com.* Georgia's musical heritage is explored through different exhibits such as the Soda Fountain playing songs of the 1950s, the Jazz Club, Gospel Chapel, and Rhythm & Blues Revue. Videos can be selected for viewing in the Gretsch Theater. (Mon-Sat 9 am-5 pm, Sun from 1 pm; closed holidays) **$$**

Georgia Sports Hall of Fame. *301 Cherry St, Macon (31201). Phone 478/752-1585. www.gshf.org.* Built to resemble a classic ballpark, the Hall houses exhibits on Georgia's famous athletes and professional and college teams. (Mon-Sat 9 am-5 pm, Sun from 1 pm) **$$**

Grand Opera House. *639 Mulberry St, Macon (31201). Phone 478/301-5300. www.mercer.edu/thegrand.* Originally the Academy of Music (1884), theater was restored in 1970.

Hay House. *934 Georgia Ave, Macon (31201). Phone 478/742-8155; fax 478/745-4277. www.hayhouse.org.* (1855-1859) An Italian Renaissance Revival villa with 24 rooms; elaborate ornamental plaster, woodwork, stained glass; ornate period furnishings, and objets d'art. (Mon-Sat 10 am-5 pm, Sun from 1 pm; closed holidays) **$$**

Lake Tobesofkee. *6600 Moseley Dixon Rd, Macon. 3 miles W via I-475, exit Hwy 74. Phone 478/474-8770.*

A 1,750-acre lake and a 650-acre park. Swimming, water-skiing, fishing, boating (launch); nature trails, tennis, picnicking, camping (hookups). (Daily)

Macon Historic District. *Downtown. Phone toll-free 800/768-3401.* District comprises nearly all of old Macon; 48 buildings and houses have been cited for architectural excellence and listed on National Register of Historic Places; an additional 575 structures have been noted for architectural significance. Walking and driving tours noted on Heritage Tour Markers. For tour maps, contact the Convention and Visitors Bureau.

Macon Museum of Arts and Sciences & Mark Smith Planetarium. *4182 Forsyth Rd, Macon (31210). Phone 478/477-3232. www.masmacon.com.* Three galleries with permanent and changing art and science exhibits; displays of live amphibians, birds, reptiles, and small mammals; nature trails; observatory. Planetarium shows. (Mon 9 am-8 pm, Tues-Sat 9 am-5 pm, Sun from 1 pm; closed Jan 1, Dec 25) **$$**

Mercer University. *1400 Coleman Ave, Macon (31207). Phone 478/301-2715; toll-free 800/637-2378. www. mercer.edu.* (1833) (6,100 students) Founded as Mercer Institute in Penfield, moved to Macon in 1871. Liberal arts, business, law, engineering, and medicine are offered at Macon campus; also campus in Atlanta.

Old Cannonball House & Macon-Confederate Museum. *856 Mulberry St, Macon (31201). Phone 478/745-5982; fax 478/745-5944. www.cannonballhouse.org.* (1853) Greek Revival house struck by Union cannonball in 1864. Museum contains Civil War relics and Macon historical items. (Mon-Sat 10 am-5 pm; closed Jan 1, Thanksgiving, Dec 25) **$**

Sidney Lanier Cottage. *935 High St, Macon (31201). Phone 478/743-3851.* (1840) Gothic Revival house was birthplace of the nationally known poet; period furnishings. Headquarters of Middle Georgia Historical Society. (Mon-Fri 9 am-4 pm, and Sat 9:30 am-12:30 pm; closed holidays) **$**

Sidney's Tours of Historic Macon. *200 Cherry St, Macon. Phone 478/743-3401; toll-free 800/768-3401.* Operated by the Macon-Bibb County Convention and Visitors Bureau. Examples of Greek Revival architecture, Victorian cottages, Italianate mansions, antebellum houses; statues, monuments, other landmarks left standing by General Sherman on his "March to the Sea." (Mon-Sat; no tours holidays) **$$$$**

Tubman African-American Museum. *340 Walnut St, Macon (31201). Phone 478/743-8544. www. tubmanmuseum.com.* Features African-American art, African artifacts, and traveling exhibits on the history and culture of African-American people. Resource center, workshops, and tours (by appointment). (Mon-Fri 9 am-5 pm, Sat from 10 am, Sun from 2 pm; closed holidays) **$**

Wesleyan College. *4760 Forsyth Rd, Macon (31210). On Hwy 41. Phone 478/477-1110; toll-free 800/447-6610. www.wesleyancollege.edu.* (1836) (700 women) This four-year liberal arts college was chartered to grant degrees to women. Campus tours by appointment.

Special Events

Cherry Blossom Festival. *794 Cherry St, Macon. Phone 478/751-7429; fax 478/751-7408. www.cherryblossom. com.* Historic tours, concerts, fireworks, hot air balloons, sporting events, parade. Mid-Mar.

Georgia State Fair. *Central City Park, 1 Riverside Dr, Macon (31208). Phone 478/746-7184. www. georgiastatefair.org.* Entertainment stages, midway, exhibit buildings. Late-Sept.

Limited-Service Hotels

★ ★ **BEST WESTERN RIVERSIDE INN.** *2400 Riverside Dr, Macon (31204). Phone 478/743-6311; toll-free 888/454-4565; fax 478/743-9420. www.bestwestern. com.* 122 rooms, 2 story. Check-in 2 pm, check-out 11 am. Restaurant, bar. Outdoor pool. **$**

★ **HOLIDAY INN EXPRESS.** *2720 Riverside Dr, Macon (31204). Phone 478/743-1482; toll-free 800/465-4329; fax 478/745-3967. www.holiday-inn.com.* 93 rooms, 6 story. Pets accepted; fee. Complimentary continental breakfast. Check-out noon. Outdoor pool. **$**

Full-Service Hotel

★ ★ ★ **CROWNE PLAZA.** *108 1st St, Macon (31201). Phone 478/746-1461; toll-free 800/227-6963; fax 478/738-2460. www.crowneplaza.com.* Located in the heart of historic downtown, this elegant hotel welcomes guests with gracious accommodations and first-class leisure activities. From the outdoor pool with sauna and sundeck, to the nightclub that entices guests to dance the night away, this hotel offers an oasis of comfort. 298 rooms, 16 story. Pets accepted. Check-in 4 pm, check-out 11 am. Restaurant, bar. Fitness room. Outdoor pool. Airport transportation available. **$**

Madison (B-3)

See also Athens, Eatonton

Population 3,636
Elevation 667 ft
Area Code 706
Zip 30650
Information Welcome Center, 115 E Jefferson, PO Box 826; phone 706/342-4454 or toll-free 800/709-7406
Web Site www.madisonga.org

General Sherman spared Madison on his Civil War "March to the Sea." The result is a contemporary city with a wealth of well-preserved antebellum and Victorian residences. Several movies have been filmed in the town to take advantage of the 19th-century atmosphere.

What to See and Do

Lake Oconee. *125 Wallace Dam Rd, Madison (31024). E on I-20. Phone 706/485-8704.* This lake, approximately 19,000 acres with 374 miles of shoreline, was created by the impoundment of the Oconee River. Around the lake, visitors can beach, swim, fish, boat (marinas), picnic, and camp.

Madison-Morgan Cultural Center. *434 S Main St, Madison (30650). Phone 706/342-4743; fax 706/342-1154. www.uncleremus.org/madmorg.* Romanesque Revival school building (1895) with art galleries, restored schoolroom, museum of local history, original auditorium, and ongoing schedule of performances. (Tues-Sat 10 am-5 pm, Sun from 2 pm; closed holidays) **$$**

Special Events

Holiday Tour of Homes. Historic private homes. First weekend in Dec.

Spring Tour of Homes. Historic houses, scenic gardens, period furnishings, and antiques. Apr-May.

Limited-Service Hotel

★ **BEST WESTERN.** *10111 Alcovy Rd, Covington (30014). Phone 770/787-4900; fax 770/385-9805.* 50 rooms, 2 story. Pets accepted; fee. Complimentary continental breakfast. Check-out noon. Fitness room. Outdoor pool. **$**

Specialty Lodging

BRADY INN BED AND BREAKFAST. *250 N 2nd St, Madison (30650). Phone 706/342-4400. www. bradyinn.com.* Restored Victorian cottage in historic downtown. 7 rooms. Complimentary full breakfast. Check-in 3-6 pm. Check-out 11 am. **$**

Marietta (B-2)

See also Atlanta, Cartersville, Norcross

Founded 1834
Population 58,748
Elevation 1,128 ft
Area Code 770
Information Cobb County Convention and Visitors Bureau, One Galleria Pkwy, Atlanta, 30339; phone toll-free 800/451-3480
Web Site www.cobbcvb.com

What to See and Do

White Water. *250 N Cobb Pkwy, Marietta (30062). Phone 770/948-9290.* Water theme park with 40 rides; body flumes, rapids ride, wave pool, float. (Memorial Day-Labor Day, daily; May, weekends) **$$$$** Adjacent is

> **American Adventures.** *250 Cobb Pkwy N, Marietta (30062). Phone 770/948-9290.* Children's amusement park with over a dozen rides. (Daily; closed holidays) Fee for various activities. **$$$$**

Limited-Service Hotels

★ **HAMPTON INN ATLANTA-MARIETTA.** *455 Franklin Rd SE, Marietta (30067). Phone 770/425-9977; toll-free 800/426-7866; fax 770/427-2545. www. hamptoninnmarietta.com.* This 2-4-story hotel is located near several restaurants and is just off Interstate 75 in a suburban business park. Both business and leisure travelers will appreciate the numerous amenities such as the outdoor pool and children's pool, the business center, fitness room, Internet access, and complimentary breakfast. 139 rooms, 4 story. Complimentary full breakfast. Check-in 3 pm, check-out noon. High-speed Internet access, wireless Internet access. Fitness room. Outdoor pool, children's pool. Airport transportation available. Business center. **$**

★★ **HOLIDAY INN.** 2265 Kingston Ct SE, Marietta (30067). Phone 770/952-7581; toll-free 800/465-4329; fax 770/952-1301. www.holiday-inn.com. 193 rooms, 7 story. Check-in 3 pm, check-out noon. High-speed Internet access, wireless Internet access. Restaurant, bar. Fitness room. Outdoor pool. Airport transportation available. **$**

★ **LA QUINTA INN ATLANTA MARIETTA.** 2170 Delk Rd, Marietta (30067). Phone 770/951-0026; toll-free 800/531-5900; fax 770/952-5372. www.laquinta.com .This family friendly motel is located just off Interstate 75 near an assortment of restaurants. Kids will love the outdoor pool and complimentary breakfast. Feel free to bring Fido along for the trip, too—pets are welcome. 130 rooms, 3 story. Pets accepted. Complimentary continental breakfast. Check-in 1 pm, check-out noon. High-speed Internet access, wireless Internet access. Outdoor pool. Airport transportation available. **$**

Full-Service Hotels

★★★ **HYATT REGENCY SUITES PERIMETER NORTHWEST ATLANTA.** 2999 Windy Hill Rd, Marietta (30067). Phone 770/956-1234; toll-free 800/233-1234; fax 770/956-9479. www.atlantasuites.hyatt.com. Located just 15 minutes from downtown Atlanta and near I-75 just north of the perimeter (I-285), this suburban all-suite property offers an array of amenities for both the business and leisure traveler. Business travelers will appreciate the fitness room, business center, and complimentary Internet access, while leisure travelers will enjoy the outdoor pool, whirlpool, and sundeck. 202 rooms, 7 story, all suites. Pets accepted, some restrictions; fee. Check-in 3 pm, check-out noon. High-speed Internet access, wireless Internet access. Restaurant, bar. Fitness room. Outdoor pool, whirlpool. Airport transportation available. Business center. **$$**

★★★ **MARIETTA CONFERENCE CENTER AND RESORT.** 500 Powder Springs St, Marietta (30064). Phone 770/427-2500; toll-free 888/685-2500; fax 678/819-3224. www.mariettaresort.com. Come enjoy the history of beautiful Marietta while relaxing in luxury suites, dining on delectable cuisine, and enjoying all the first-class amenities this full-service resort offers. Located just a short walk from Marietta Square and overlooking a championship golf course, this resort (former site of the Georgia Military Institute) turns business into pleasure and makes pleasure a way of life. Along with the resort's featured amenities such as an outdoor pool, whirlpool, tennis, and golf, the resort also hosts croquet games on the lawn in the summer. 199 rooms, 6 story. Check-in 3 pm, check-out noon. High-speed Internet access, wireless Internet access. Two restaurants, bar. Fitness room. Outdoor pool, whirlpool. Golf, 18 holes. Tennis. Airport transportation available. Business center. **$**

Specialty Lodging

THE WHITLOCK. 57 Whitlock Ave, Marietta (30064). Phone 770/428-1495; fax 770/919-9620. www.whitlockinn.com. Located just one block west of Marietta Square on a stately tree-lines street, this fully restored Victorian mansion with distinctively different guest rooms provides all the charm one would expect in the South. Guests can enjoy antique shopping and carriage rides as they embrace Southern hospitality. A complimentary full breakfast is offered, and there is also a basket filled with books and magazines in each guest room. 5 rooms, 2 story. Children over 12 years only. Complimentary full breakfast. Check-in 3 pm, check-out 11 am. High-speed Internet access, wireless Internet access. Airport transportation available. **$**

Restaurants

★★ **GRAZIE A BISTRO.** 1000 Whitlock Ave NW, Marietta (30064). Phone 770/499-8585; fax 770/499-8585. www.grazieabistro.com. With live piano and jazz five days a week, side dishes and appetizers built for two to share, and sophisticated villalike surroundings, including a fireplace, it's clear that this bistro is great for a romantic night out. And as if the atmosphere wasn't enough, you might want to make a return trip just to get a better taste of the extensive, diverse menu.

Italian menu. Dinner Wed-Sun, Sun brunch. Bar. Children's menu. Casual attire. Reservations recommended. Outdoor seating. **$$$**

★ **LA STRADA.** *2930 Johnson Ferry Rd NE, Marietta (30062). Phone 770/640-7008. www.lastradainc.com.* Don't be surprised if you're the only non-local dining at this neighborhood restaurant, where returning customers cant stay away from the soft-shell crab and tiramisu. Italian menu. Dinner. Bar. Children's menu. Casual attire. **$$**

★ ★ **SHILLING'S ON THE SQUARE.** *19 N Park Sq NE, Marietta (30060). Phone 770/428-9520; fax 770/428-9918. www.shillingsonthesquare.com.* This old-fashioned building actually houses two restaurants in one: downstairs, diners will find a casual atmosphere with an equally casual menu that includes sandwiches and salads, while the upstairs restaurant features a more formal dining area. Many loyal customers return because of this versatility—accommodating many types of groups and occasions—as well as the varied American menu. A pianist performs Fridays and Saturdays, and a jazz trio on Wednesdays. American menu. Lunch, dinner, brunch. Closed Thanksgiving, Dec 25. Bar. Children's menu. Casual attire. Reservations recommended. **$$$**

Milledgeville (C-3)

See also Eatonton, Macon

Founded 1803
Population 18,757
Elevation 335 ft
Area Code 478
Zip 31061
Information Convention and Visitors Bureau, 200 W Hancock St; phone toll-free 800/653-1804
Web Site www.milledgevillecvb.com

Milledgeville was laid out to be the state capital and served in that capacity from 1804-1868. When the state records were transferred to Milledgeville from Louisville in 1807, wagons were escorted by troops of cavalry from Washington, DC.

Milledgeville's houses typify the development of Southern architecture. The earliest structures had small stoops; houses of the next period had two porches, one above the other; with the third period, the two-story columns became Greek porticos, the second story, a balcony. Later, porches became broad, multicolumned verandas, extending across the front and even around to the sides and back of the house.

What to See and Do

Georgia College & State University. *231 W Hancock St, Milledgeville. Phone 478/445-5004; toll-free 800/342-0471. www.gcsu.edu.* (1889) (5,500 students) Occupies one of four 20-acre plots "reserved for public use" when the city was laid out. The Museum and Archives of Georgia Education is located on campus. Also on campus is

> **Old Governor's Mansion.** *120 S Clarke St, Milledgeville (31061). Phone 478/445-4545.* Greek Revival residence of Georgia governors from 1839-1868. Guided tours. (Tues-Sat 10 am-4 pm, Sun from 2 pm; closed holidays, Thanksgiving weekend, week of Dec 25) **$$**

Historic Guided Trolley Tour. *200 W Hancock, Milledgeville. Phone 478/452-4687.* Includes stops at St. Stephens Episcopal Church and Stetson-Sanford House. Tour departs from the Convention and Visitors Bureau Office, 200 W Hancock. The office also has information on walking tours. Trolley tour (Mon-Fri 10 am, Sat 2 pm). **$$$**

Lake Sinclair. *3069 N Columbia St, Milledgeville. N on Hwy 441, Hwy 24. Phone 478/452-1605.* This 15,330-acre lake with 417 miles of shoreline was created by the impoundment of the Oconee River. It offers fishing, boating (marinas), and camping.

Limited-Service Hotel

★ **DAYS INN.** *2551 N Columbia St, Milledgeville (31061). Phone 478/453-8471; toll-free 800/329-7466; fax 478/453-8482. www.daysinn.com.* 100 rooms, 2 story. Complimentary continental breakfast. Checkout 11 am. Fitness room. Outdoor pool, children's pool, whirlpool. Tennis. **$**
🧍 🛏 🎿

Norcross (B-2)

See also Atlanta, Buford, Marietta, Winder

Population 8,410
Elevation 1,057 ft
Area Code 770
Information City of Norcross, 65 Lawrenceville St, 30071; phone 770/448-2122
Web Site www.gcvb.org

Norcross, a suburb of Atlanta, is approximately 20 miles northeast of the city. Citizens have preserved many old residences; there is a 112-acre historic district here with a restored downtown square.

Special Event

BellSouth Golf Classic. *Tournament Players Club at Sugarloaf, 2595 Sugarloaf Club Dr, Duluth (30097). Phone 770/436-2643. www.bellsouthclassic.com.* Jack Nicklaus, Phil Mickelson, and Tiger Woods are just three of the famous faces who have participated in—and won—The BellSouth Classic, a PGA event. More than 125,000 fans attend the tournament each year, as the course has several mounds for easy viewing, making it ideal for spectators. Late Mar-early Apr.

Limited-Service Hotels

★ **COMFORT INN AND SUITES.** *5985 Oakbrook Pkwy, Norcross (30093). Phone 770/662-8175; toll-free 877/424-6423; fax 770/840-1183. www.comfortinn.com.* 115 rooms, 3 story. Pets accepted; restrictions, fee. Complimentary continental breakfast. Check-in 3 pm, check-out 11 am. Outdoor pool, whirlpool. **$**

★ **HOMEWOOD SUITES.** *10775 Davis Dr, Alpharetta (30004). Phone 770/998-1622; toll-free 800/225-5466; fax 770/998-7834. www. homewoodsuites.com.* 112 rooms, 6 story, all suites. Pets accepted; restrictions, fee. Complimentary full breakfast. Check-in 3 pm, check-out noon. High-speed Internet access, wireless Internet access. Fitness room. Outdoor pool. Business center. **$**

★ **LA QUINTA INN.** *5945 Oakbrook Pkwy, Norcross (30093). Phone 770/368-9400; fax 770/441-9396.* 247 rooms, 3 story. Pets accepted, some restrictions; fee. Complimentary full breakfast. Check-in 3 pm, check-out 11 am. Outdoor pool, whirlpool. **$**

Full-Service Hotels

★ ★ ★ **HILTON ATLANTA NORTHEAST.** *5993 Peachtree Industrial Blvd, Norcross (30092). Phone 770/447-4747; toll-free 800/445-8667; fax 678/533-2888. www.hilton.com.* This hotel ensures that even the most discerning guest will find pleasure in being offered a relaxing stay amid spacious and recently designed guest rooms, as well as a warm and friendly staff catering to a guest's every desire. 272 rooms, 10 story. Pets accepted, some restrictions; fee. Check-in 3 pm, check-out noon. High-speed Internet access, wireless Internet access. Restaurant, bar. Fitness room. Indoor pool, outdoor pool, whirlpool. Airport transportation available. Business center. **$**

★ ★ **HOLIDAY INN.** *6050 Peachtree Industrial Blvd NW, Norcross (30071). Phone 770/448-4400; fax 770/840-8008. www.hisatlanta.com.* 244 rooms, 8 story. Check-in 3 pm, check-out noon. High-speed Internet access, wireless Internet access. Restaurant, bar. Fitness room. Indoor pool, outdoor pool, whirlpool. Business center. **$**

★ ★ ★ **MARRIOTT ATLANTA GWINNETT PLACE.** *1775 Pleasant Hill Rd, Duluth (30096). Phone 770/923-1775; toll-free 800/228-9290; fax 770/923-0017. www.marriott.com/atlgp.* Located on 11 landscaped acres in the heart of Gwinnett County in the northeastern suburb of Atlanta, this hotel offers a very relaxing stay. Enjoy the spacious guest rooms, indoor and outdoor pool, whirlpool, and health club, or relax in the Buttons Lounge offering live entertainment on the weekends. 426 rooms, 17 story. Check-in 4 pm, check-out noon. High-speed Internet access, wireless Internet access. Two restaurants, two bars. Fitness room. Indoor pool, outdoor pool, whirlpool. Business center. **$$**

★ ★ ★ **MARRIOTT ATLANTA NORCROSS-PEACHTREE CORNERS.** *475 Technology Pkwy, Norcross (30092). Phone 770/263-8558; toll-free 800/228-9290; fax 770/263-0766. www.marriott.com.* Located in Technology Park, this well-appointed 218-room hotel is a business traveler's delight. With a well-equipped business center and 4,000 square feet of meeting space, the hotel and its staff ensure that every meeting is a success. 222 rooms, 6 story. Check-in 3 pm, check-out noon. High-speed Internet access, wireless Internet access. Restaurant, bar. Fitness room. Indoor pool, whirlpool. Business center. **$**

Restaurants

★ ★ **DOMINICK'S.** *95 S Peachtree St, Norcross (30071). Phone 770/449-1611; fax 770/449-0096. www. dominickslittleitaly.com.* Italian menu. Lunch Mon-Fri, dinner. Closed Sun; Dec 25. Bar. Children's menu. **$$**

★ ★ ★ **HI LIFE.** *3380 Holcomb Bridge Rd, Norcross (30092). Phone 770/409-0101; fax 770/409-1160. www. atlantahilife.com.* This American restaurant has a sleek, modern design. The creative food is fresh and flavorful; of particular note is a four-course lobster tasting menu. American menu. Lunch Mon-Fri, dinner. Closed Sun; Jan 1, Thanksgiving, Dec 25. Bar. Children's menu. Business casual attire. Reservations recommended. Outdoor seating. **$$**

★ ★ **SIA'S.** *10305 Medlock Bridge Rd, Duluth (30097). Phone 770/497-9727. www.siasrestaurant.com.* American, Asian, Southwestern menu. Lunch, dinner. Closed Sun. Bar. Children's menu. Business casual attire. Reservations recommended. Outdoor seating. **$$$**

★ **ZAPATA.** *5975 Peachtree Pkwy, Norcross (30092). Phone 770/248-0052.* Serving traditional Mexican food and featuring live music on Fridays and Saturdays, this colorfully decorated restaurant offers friendly service and more moderate portions—perfect for diners who want to try a few new things. Mexican menu. Lunch, dinner. Bar. Casual attire. **$**

Ocmulgee National Monument (C-3)

See also Macon

Web Site www.nps.gov/ocmu

2 miles E of Macon on Hwy 80, Alt 129.

Ocmulgee, the most scientifically excavated of the South's major Native American sites, shows evidence of 12,000 years of settlement, including six successive occupations from at least 10,000 BC to 1825. The major remains consist of nine ceremonial mounds, a funeral mound, and a restored ceremonial earth lodge of the early Mississippian Period (AD 900 to 1100).

Exhibits and dioramas in the museum depict this sequence: Paleo-Indian Period, from more than 12,000 years ago, when Ice Age hunters trailing mammoth and other now-extinct game arrived using stone-tipped spears. During the Archaic Period, after the Ice Age ended, hunter-gathering people hunted small game and supplemented their diet with mussels, fish, seeds, berries, and nuts. They made polished stone tools and camped along the streams. By 2000 BC, crude pottery was fashioned. During the Woodland Period (beginning 1000 BC), some plants were cul-

tivated, villages were larger, and mounds were being built. Pottery was stamped with elaborate designs carved into wooden paddles. The Early Mississippian Period began about AD 900, when invaders brought cultivated corn, beans, squash, and tobacco to the Macon Plateau. They built a large town with burial and temple mounds and circular, earth-covered council chambers. This ceremonial center declined around AD 1100. Late Mississippian Period villagers of the Lamar Culture combined elements of the Mississippian and older Woodland ways of life. They may have been direct ancestors of the historic Creek who lived here when Europeans first settled Georgia. The Creek soon became involved in the struggle between France, Spain, and England for possession of the New World.

Exhibits and dioramas in the museum show the Native American from earliest origins to his removal to Oklahoma in the early 1800s. Great Temple Mound, more than 40 feet high, is the largest in the park. An audio program is conducted in the restored earthlodge, which was the Mississippian council chamber. (Daily; closed Jan 1, Dec 25) For information, contact the Superintendent, 1207 Emery Hwy, Macon 31217; phone 912/752-8257.

Okefenokee Swamp (E-4)

See also Waycross

Web Site www.okefenokee.com

Phone 912/283-0583. www.okefenokee.com. Information Refuge Manager, Rte 2, Box 3330, Folkston 31537; phone 912/496-7836. One of the largest preserved freshwater wetlands in the US, the Okefenokee Swamp encompasses more than 700 square miles, stretching an average of 25 miles in width and 35 miles in length. The swamp's southern border is beyond the Florida line. Called "land of trembling earth" by Native Americans, its lakes of dark brown water, lush with moss-draped cypress, are headwaters for the Suwannee and St. Marys rivers. The swamp embraces vast marshes, termed "prairies," which comprise 60,000 acres.

What to See and Do

Okefenokee National Wildlife Refuge. *11 mi SW Folkston, Okefenokee Swamp (31537). Phone 912/496-7836.* Occupies more than 90 percent of the swamp region and harbors bears, deer, bobcats, alligators, and aquatic birds. Naturalists have discovered many rare plants on the swamp floor, which has been described as "the most beautiful and fantastic landscape in the world." The cypress stand mile after mile, their dense formations broken by watery "prairies" or covered by deposits of peat on the swamp's floor ranging to 15 feet in thickness. It is possible to cause small trees and shrubs to shake by stamping on the "trembling earth"; these trees take root in the crust of peat beds and never reach the solid bottom. Such forests are interspersed with varied swamp vegetation. The bay, one of the swamp's most distinctive trees, blooms from May-Oct, producing a white flower in contrast to its rich evergreen foliage. Aquatic flowers, such as yellow spatterdock and white water lily, blend with pickerel-weed, golden-club, and swamp iris in the spring. The swamp is also the home of the sandhill crane and round-tailed muskrat. (Hours vary with season) **$**

Okefenokee Swamp Park. *5700 Okefenokee Swamp Park Rd, Waycross. Phone 912/283-0583.* This park, located on Cowhouse Island, has serpentarium and reptile shows. Guided boat tours (fee); canoe rentals. Cypress boardwalk into swamp to 90-foot-high observation tower. Picnicking. Interpretive centers. (Daily) No overnight facilities. Camping available at nearby Laura S. Walker State Park (see WAYCROSS). **$$$$**

Stephen C. Foster State Park. *Hwy 177, Fargo. Phone 912/637-5274.* Park offers access to Billy's Lake, Minnie's Lake, and Big Water (daily during daylight hours without a guide). Fishing, boating (rentals, basin, dock, ramp), canoeing (rentals), sightseeing boat tours; nature trails, picnicking, concession, camping, cabins. Museum.

Suwannee Canal Recreation Area. *11 miles SW of Folkston, Okefenokee Swamp (31537). Phone 912/496-7836.* Area provides entry to the Chesser, Grand, Mizell, and Chase prairies, where small lakes and "gator holes" offer some of the nation's finest bird-watching. Area also has restored swamp homestead and guided swamp tours. Boating (ramp, boat, and motor rentals), canoeing, guided boat tours; nature trails, boardwalk (3/4 mile) with observation tower. Picnicking. Visitor center. (Daily sunrise-7:30 pm; closed Dec 25) Fees for some activities.

Wilderness canoeing. *Phone 912/496-3331.* There are seven overnight stops and trips available from two to five days (three-day limit Mar-Apr); wooden platforms for campsites. Mar-May and Oct-early Nov are most popular times. Buy advance reservations (two months) and special permit from the refuge manager. **$$$**

Perry (D-2)

See also Andersonville, Cordele, Macon

Population 9,602
Elevation 337 ft
Area Code 478
Zip 31069
Information Perry Area Convention and Visitors Bureau, 101 General Courtney Hodges Blvd, PO Box 1619; phone 478/988-8000
Web Site www.perryga.com

The blooming wildflowers and trees during March and April have made Perry a favorite stopover place for spring motorists. The town is full of stately houses and historical churches. Perry is known as the "Crossroads of Georgia" because of its location near the geographic center of the state.

What to See and Do

⭐ **The Andersonville Trail.** *A 75-mile loop drive from Perry to Cordele (see). Phone 478/988-8000. www. perryga.com.* Along the drive are American Camellia Society gardens, two state parks, antebellum houses, and Andersonville National Historic Site. Contact the Convention and Visitors Bureau for information.

Massee Lane Gardens. *100 Massee Ln, Fort Valley (31030). 14 miles W on Hwy 127 to Marshallville, then 3 miles N on Hwy 49. Phone 478/967-2722.* Camellia garden (10 acres) reaches height of bloom between Nov-Mar; large greenhouse, Japanese garden, rose garden. Colonial-style headquarters contains more than 300 sculptures of Boehm and other porcelains, other items. Headquarters include the Annabelle Lundy Fetterman Educational Museum, exhibition hall (rare books, porcelain); auditorium with presentation on history of gardens, gift shop. (Mon-Sat 10 am-4:30 pm, Sun from 1 pm). **$**

Special Events

Mossy Creek Barnyard Festival. *Deep Piney Woods, N on I-75, exit 142, 3 miles E. Phone 478/922-8265. www.mossycreekfestival.com.* Semiannual event with craftsmen, artists, entertainment, and demonstrations. Third weekend in Apr and third weekend in Oct.

Old-Fashioned Christmas at the Crossroads. Community Christmas tree, parade, candlelight service. Dec.

Limited-Service Hotels

★ **COMFORT INN.** *1602 Sam Nunn Blvd, Perry (31069). Phone 478/987-7710; toll-free 800/642-7710; fax 478/988-2624. www.comfortinn.com.* 102 rooms, 2 story. Complimentary continental breakfast. Check-out 11 am. Fitness room. Indoor pool, whirlpool. **$**

🏃 🛏

★ ★ **HOLIDAY INN.** *200 Valley Dr, Perry (31069). Phone 478/987-3313; toll-free 800/808-8804; fax 478/988-8269. www.holiday-inn.com.* 203 rooms, 2 story. Check-in 3 pm, check-out noon. Restaurant, bar. Fitness room. Outdoor pool. **$**

🏃 🛏

★ ★ **NEW PERRY HOTEL.** *800 Main St, Perry (31069). Phone 478/987-1000; toll-free 800/877-3779; fax 478/987-4866. www.newperryhotel.com.* 43 rooms, 3 story. Pets accepted; fee. Check-out noon. Restaurant. Outdoor pool. **$**

🐾 🐕 🛏

Pine Mountain (C-1)

See also Columbus, La Grange

Population 1,141
Elevation 860 ft
Area Code 706
Zip 31822
Web Site www.pinemountain.org

What to See and Do

Franklin D. Roosevelt State Park. *2970 Hwy 190, Pine Mountain (Harris County). 5 miles SE off jct Hwy 27, Hwy 190. Phone 706/663-4858.* One of the largest parks in the state system, it has many historic buildings and King's Gap Indian trail. Swimming pool, fishing; hiking, bridle and nature trails, picnicking, camping, cottages.

⭐ **Little White House Historic Site.** *401 Little White House Rd, Warm Springs (31830). Approximately 15 miles E on Hwy 18 and Hwy 194, then 1/2 mile S on Hwy 85 W. Phone 706/655-5870. www.fdr-littlewhite-house.org.* Cottage in which President Franklin D. Roosevelt died on Apr 12, 1945, is preserved as it was on the day he died. On display is original furniture, memorabilia, and the portrait on which Elizabeth Shoumatoff was working when the president was stricken with a massive cerebral hemorrhage. A film

about Roosevelt's life at Warm Springs and in Georgia is shown at the F. D. Roosevelt Museum and Theater. Picnic area, snack bar. (Daily, 9 am-4:45 pm; closed Jan 1, Thanksgiving, Dec 25) **$$**

⭐ **The Gardens at Callaway.** *Hwy 354 and Hwy 18, Pine Mountain. Phone 706/663-2281; toll-free 800/225-5292; fax 706/225-5292. www.callawaygardens.com.* This distinctive public garden and resort, consisting of 14,000 acres of gardens, woodlands, lakes, recreation areas, and wildlife, was conceived by prominent textile industrialist Cason J. Callaway to be "the finest garden on earth since Adam was a boy." Originally the family's weekend vacation spot in the 1930s, Callaway and his wife, Virginia, expanded the area and opened it to the public in 1952. Today Callaway is home to more than 100 varieties of butterflies, 230 varieties of birds, 400 varieties of fruits and vegetables, and thousands of species of plantlife, including the rare plunifolia azalea, indigenous to the area. The complex offers swimming, boating, and other water recreation around 13 lakes, including 175-acre Mountain Creek Lake and the white sand beach of Robin Lake; 23 miles of roads and paths for hiking or jogging, 63 holes of golf (a 9-hole and three 18-hole courses), 10 lighted tennis courts, two indoor racquetball courts, 10 miles of bike trails, skeet and trapshooting ranges, fishing, fly-fishing, picnicking, country store, cottages, villas, and inn (see), restaurants, and 5,000-foot paved and lighted runway and terminal. Also on the garden grounds are

> **Cecil B. Day Butterfly Center.** *Hwy 354 and Hwy 18, Pine Mountain. Phone 706/663-2281.* An 8,000-square-foot, glass-enclosed conservatory housing up to 1,000 free-flying butterflies, as well as ground pheasants, exotic plants, and waterfalls.

> **Ida Cason Callaway Memorial Chapel.** *Hwy 354 and Hwy 18, Pine Mountain (31822). Phone 706/663-2281.* A woodland chapel patterned after rural wayside chapels of the 16th and 17th centuries; organ concerts year-round. **Pioneer log cabin** is an authentic 18th-century structure in which life of early Georgia settlers is demonstrated. **$$$$**

> **John A. Sibley Horticultural Center.** *Hwy 354 and Hwy 18, Pine Mountain. Phone 706/663-2281.* Five acres displaying unique collections of exotic and native plants, seasonal flower beds, and lush green lawns; also sculpture garden and 22-foot waterfall.

> **Mr. Cason's Vegetable Garden.** *Hwy 354 and Hwy 18, Pine Mountain. Phone 706/663-2281.* Vegetable

garden (7 1/2 acres) that produces hundreds of varieties of fruits, vegetables, and herbs; setting for the *Victory Garden South* television show.

Full-Service Resort

★ ★ ★ **MOUNTAIN CREEK INN AT CALLA-WAY GARDENS.** *17800 Hwy 27, Pine Mountain (31822). Phone 706/663-2281; toll-free 800/225-5292; fax 706/663-6812. www.callawaygardens.com.* Offering plenty of outdoor recreational treats, including tennis and a championship golf course, this 14,000-acre property provides a perfect venue to relax, have fun, and play your cares away. A butterly conservatory is also on site. 349 rooms, 3 story. Check-in 4 pm, check-out 11 am. Restaurant, bar. Children's activity center. Fitness room. Beach. Indoor pool, outdoor pool, children's pool. Golf. Tennis. Airport transportation available. Business center. $

🛐 🛌 👭 🏊 🚶

★ ★ **BULLOCH HOUSE.** *47 Bulloch St, Warm Springs (31830). Phone 706/655-9068. www.thebullochhouse.com.* American menu. Lunch, dinner (Fri-Sat). Closed holidays. Children's menu. Outdoor seating. House built 1892; original floors and fireplaces. $

Rome (B-1)

See also Calhoun, Cartersville

Founded 1834
Population 34,980
Elevation 605 ft
Area Code 706
Zip 30161
Information Greater Rome Convention and Visitors Bureau, 402 Civic Center Hill, PO Box 5823, 30162-5823; phone 706/295-5576; or toll-free 800/444-1834
Web Site www.romegeorgia.org

According to legend, five men, seven hills, three rivers, a spring, and a hat were the equation that led to the founding of Rome, Georgia. The seven hills suggested that "Rome" be one of the names drawn from the hat by the five founders, two of whom had discovered the site at the junction of three rivers.

Nobles' Foundry Lathe, one of the few that produced Confederate cannons, is on display on Civic Center Hill and is a reminder of Sherman's occupation. Rome

fell despite the frantic ride of Georgia's Paul Revere, a mail carrier named John E. Wisdom, who rode 67 miles by horse from Gadsden, Alabama, in 11 hours to warn "the Yankees are coming."

What to See and Do

Berry College. *2277 Martha Berry Hwy, Mt. Berry (30149). On Hwy 27. Phone 706/232-5374. www.berry.edu.* (1902) (1,800 students) Campus, forest preserves, and 100 buildings comprise more than 26,000 acres, one of the largest campuses in the world. Old overshot waterwheel is one of the largest in the world. Close to campus is

Oak Hill and the Martha Berry Museum. *24 Veterans Memorial Hwy, Rome (30165). Veterans Memorial Hwy and Hwy 27. Phone 706/291-1883.* Antebellum plantation house of Martha Berry, founder of Berry College. Manicured lawns, formal gardens, and nature trails. Museum is located on grounds of Oak Hill and serves as reception center for visitors. (Mon-Sat 10 am-5 pm) $

Capitoline Wolf Statue. *601 Broad St, Rome. In front of City Hall. Phone 706/295-5576.* Replica of the famous statue of Romulus and Remus in Rome, Italy. Presented by that city as a gift to Rome, Georgia in 1929.

Chieftains Museum. *501 Riverside Pkwy, Rome (30161). N off Hwy 27. Phone 706/291-9494.* Eighteenth-century house of prominent Cherokee leader Major Ridge; artifacts with emphasis on Cherokee history. (Tues-Fri 9 am-3 pm, Sat 10 am-4 pm; closed holidays) $$

The Old Town Clock (1871) and Clocktower Museum. *601 Broad St, Rome. Phone 706/295-5576.* Surmounting 104-foot-high water tower of brick and superstructure of cypress wood, clock face is 9 feet in diameter. Bronze striking bell is 32 inches high, 40 inches in diameter at rim. Tower was built to hold the city's water supply and is located atop one of Rome's seven hills. Now, the water tank houses a museum with artifacts from Rome's history. (Apr-Nov, weekends; also by appointment)

Special Event

Heritage Holidays. River rides, parade, tours, wagon train, music. Third weekend in Oct.

Limited-Service Hotels

★ **DAYS INN.** *840 Turner McCall Blvd, Rome (30161). Phone 706/295-0400; toll-free 800/329-7466.*

www.daysinn.com. 107 rooms, 5 story. Complimentary continental breakfast. Check-out 11 am. Outdoor pool. **$**

★ ★ **HOLIDAY INN.** *20 Hwy 411 E, Rome (30161). Phone 706/295-1100; toll-free 800/465-4329; fax 706/291-7128. www.holiday-inn.com.* 200 rooms, 2 story. Pets accepted; fee. Check-in 3 pm, check-out noon. Restaurant, bar. Fitness room. Indoor pool, outdoor pool, whirlpool. Business center .**$**

Roswell (B-2)

See also Atlanta

Web Site cvb.roswell.ga.us

Limited-Service Hotel

★ ★ **DOUBLETREE HOTEL.** *1075 Holcomb Bridge Rd, Roswell (30076). Phone 770/992-9600; fax 770/993-6539.* 174 rooms, 7 story. Pets accepted; fee. Check-in 3 pm, check-out noon. High-speed Internet access, wireless Internet access. Restaurant, bar. Fitness room. Outdoor pool. **$**

Restaurants

★ ★ ★ **DICK & HARRY'S.** *1570 Holcomb Bridge Rd, Roswell (30076). Phone 770/641-8757; fax 770/641-8884. www.dickandharrys.com.* American menu. Lunch, dinner. Closed Sun; holidays. Bar. Children's menu. Casual attire. Valet parking. Outdoor seating. **$$**

★ **SUBURB-A-NIGHT PIZZA.** *1090 Alpharetta St, Roswell (30075). Phone 770/594-8765.* Pizza. Dinner, late-night. Closed holidays. Bar. **$$**

★ ★ ★ **VAN GOGH'S.** *70 W Crossville Rd, Roswell (30075). Phone 770/993-1156; fax 770/643-0854. www. knowwheretogogh.com.* This out-of-the-way restaurant offers a surprisingly lovely dining experience. The food is eclectic American, while the setting is all old-Southern charm. The combination makes for a fun time. The cozy bar is the perfect place to meet friends before dinner—grab a seat in one of the plush velvet-backed chairs near the fireplace. Then head into the main dining room, dotted with Van Gogh reproductions, for a delicious meal created by chef-

owners Christopher and Michele Sedgwick. The wine cellar offers more than 500 selections from around the world—giving diners numerous pairing options. American menu. Lunch, dinner. Bar. Children's menu. Business casual attire. Reservations recommended. Valet parking. **$$$**

Saint Mary's

Specialty Lodgings

GOODBREAD HOUSE B AND B. *209 Osborne St, Saint Mary's (31558). Phone 912/882-7490. www. goodbreadhouse.com.* Built in 1872 as a hotel. 5 rooms, 2 story. Pets accepted. Complimentary full breakfast. Check-in 2 pm. Check-out noon. **$**

SPENCER HOUSE INN BED & BREAKFAST. *101 E. Briant, Saint Mary's (31558). Phone 912/882-1872; toll-free 888/840-1872; fax 912/882-9427. www. spencerhouseinn.com.* Built in 1872 as a hotel. 14 rooms, 3 story. Complimentary full breakfast. Check-in 3-7 pm. Check-out 11 am. **$$**

Savannah

See also Fort McAllister Historic Park, Fort Pulaski National Monument, Tybee Island

Founded 1733
Population 131,510
Elevation 42 ft
Area Code 912
Information Savannah Area Convention and Visitors Bureau, 301 Martin Luther King Blvd, 31401, 31402; phone 912/944-0455 or toll-free 877/SAVANNAH
Web Site www.savcvb.com

Savannah has a wealth of history and architecture that few American cities can match. Even fewer have managed to preserve the same air of colonial grace and charm. The city's many rich, green parks are blooming legacies of the brilliance of its founder, General James E. Oglethorpe, who landed at Yamacraw Bluff with 120 settlers on February 12, 1733. His plan for the colony was to make the "inner city" spacious, beautiful, and all that a city should be. Bull Street, named for Colonel William Bull, one of Oglethorpe's aides, stretches south from the high bluffs overlooking the

Savannah River and is punctuated by five handsome squares and Forsyth Park.

Savannah then changed its outer garb of wood palisades to a gray "Savannah brick" fort surmounting the bluff. By Revolutionary times wharves served ocean trade, and sailors caroused in seamen's inns. The town had its liberty pole and a patriots' battalion when news of Lexington came. The Declaration of Independence led to Savannah's designation as capital of the new state. By December, however, the British had retaken the city with 2,000 troops, and the royal governor, who had fled earlier, returned. An attempt by American troops to recapture Savannah failed, and more than 1,000 Americans and 700 Frenchmen were killed. General "Mad Anthony" Wayne's forces finally drove the British from Savannah in 1782.

In 1795, tobacco culture and Eli Whitney's cotton gin brought prosperity back to Savannah. Meanwhile, the city's growth followed the orderly pattern laid out by Colonel Bull. By the first decade of the new century, Classical Revival or Regency architecture had superseded Georgian Colonial. Savannah, with new forts protecting the estuary and strengthening Fort Wayne on the bluff, fared better during the War of 1812. Afterward, architect William Jay and master builder Isaiah Davenport added splendid mansions that fronted palm-lined squares. The steamboat *Enterprise* plied upriver from here to Augusta in 1816; three years later, on May 22, 1819, the SS *Savannah* set sail from Savannah for Liverpool to be the first steamer to cross the Atlantic. Savannah had become the leading market and shipping point for cotton, naval stores, and tobacco, and prosperity increased until the Civil War.

Throughout the war, Savannah tried to hold its own. Fort Pulaski (see), which the Confederates took control of even before Secession, was retaken by a Union artillery assault on April 11, 1862, and became a Union military prison. Despite repeated Union naval battering, the Confederates held Fort McAllister (see) until Sherman's "March to the Sea" on December 13, 1864. Although Confederate troops resisted for three days after Sherman demanded Savannah's surrender, Union forces eventually occupied the city, and Confederates were forced to escape to Hutchison Island.

Reconstruction was painful, but 20 years later cotton was king again. Surrounding pine forests produced lumber and resins; the Cotton and Naval Stores Exchange was launched in 1882 while financiers and brokers strode the streets with confidence. By the 20th century, Savannah turned to manufacturing. With more than 200 industries by World War II, the city's prosperity has been measured by the activity of its port, which included shipbuilding booms during both world wars. Extensive developments by the Georgia Port Authority in the past decade have contributed to the city's commercial, industrial, and shipping growth.

Today more than 1,400 historically and architecturally significant buildings have been restored in Savannah's historic district, making it one of the largest urban historic landmark districts in the country. Another area, the Victorian district south of the historic district, offers some of the best examples of post-Civil War Victorian architecture in the country. The city that launched the Girl Scouts of America also plays host to modern Girl Scouts who visit the shrine of founder Juliette Gordon Low.

Additional Visitor Information

Visitor information is also available from the Savannah Area Convention and Visitors Bureau, PO Box 1628, 31402-1628; phone 912/644-6401 or toll-free 877-728-2662.

The Savannah Visitors Center, 301 Martin Luther King Jr. Blvd, is open daily, providing information on area attractions (including a free visitors guide with translations in French, German, Spanish, and Japanese). All guided bus tours depart from the center on a regular basis.

What to See and Do

Andrew Low House. *329 Abercorn St, Savannah (31401). Phone 912/233-6854. www.andrewlowhouse. com.* (Circa 1848) Built for Andrew Low, this was later the residence of Juliette Gordon Low, founder of Girl Scouts of America. Period furnishings. (Mon-Wed, Fri-Sat 10 am-4:30 pm, Sun from noon; closed holidays; also mid-late Dec) **$$**

Christ Episcopal Church. *28 Bull Street, Savannah. Johnson Sq between E St. Julian and E Congress sts. Phone 912/238-0434. www.christchurchsavannah.org.* (1838) The mother church of Georgia, the congregation dates from 1733. Among early rectors were John Wesley and George Whitfield. The present church is the third building erected on this site. (Tues and Fri, limited hours)

City Hall. *Bull and Bay sts, Savannah (31401). Phone 912/651-6410. www.ci.savannah.ga.us.* (1905) A gold dome tops the four-story neoclassic facade of this building, which replaced the original 1799 structure. A tablet outside commemorates sailing of the SS *Savannah;* a model is displayed in the Council Chamber. Another tablet is dedicated to the *John Randolph,* the first iron-sided vessel launched in American waters (1834). (Mon-Fri) **FREE**

Colonial Park Cemetery. *E Oglethorpe Ave and Abercorn St, Savannah.* (1753) This was the colony's first and only burial ground for many years; Button Gwinnett, a signer of the Declaration of Independence, is buried in cemetery, as are other distinguished Georgians. Closed since 1853, it has been a city park since 1896.

Congregation Mickve Israel. *20 E Wayne St, Savannah (31401). E side of Monterey Sq. Phone 912/233-1547; toll-free 800/728-6610; fax 912/233-3086. mickveisrael. org.* Only Gothic-style synagogue in US contains Torah scroll brought to America by congregation founders, Portuguese and German Jews who came to Savannah in 1733. Synagogue museum has portraits, religious objects, documents, letters from Presidents Washington, Jefferson, Madison. Guided tours (Mon-Fri 10 am-noon, 2-4 pm). **$**

Davenport House. *119 Habersham St, Savannah (31401). Phone 912/236-8097; fax 912/233-7938. www. davenportsavga.com.*(1815-1820) Built by master builder Isaiah Davenport, this is one of the finest examples of Federal architecture in Savannah. Saved from demolition in 1955 by the Historic Savannah Foundation, it is now restored and furnished with period antiques. Gardens. (Mon-Sat 10 am-4 pm, Sun from 1 pm; closed holidays) **$$**

Factors Walk. *W and E Bay sts, Savannah. Between Bull and E Broad sts.* Named by cotton factors of the 19th century, this row of business houses "on the Bay" is accessible by a network of iron bridgeways over cobblestone ramps.

Georgia Historical Society. *501 Whitaker St, Savannah (31401). Phone 912/651-2128; fax 912/651-2831. www. georgiahistory.com.* Research library and archives for Savannah and Georgia history and genealogy. (Tues-Sat) **$**

Gray Line bus tours. *215 W Boundary St, Savannah (31401). Phone 912/234-8687; toll-free 800/426-2318; fax 912/239-9747. www.grayline.com.* Contact 1115 Louisville Rd, 31415.

Green-Meldrim House. *1 W Macon St, Savannah (31410). Phone 912/233-3845.* Antebellum house used by General Sherman during occupation of Savannah (1864-1865) is now Parish House of St. John's Church. Tours. (Tues and Thurs-Sat, 10 am-3:30 pm; closed holidays, occasionally for parish activities, also last two weeks before Easter) **$**

Historic Savannah Waterfront Area. *John P. Rousakis Riverfront Plaza, Savannah.* Restoration of the riverfront bluff to preserve and stabilize the historic waterfront, including a nine-block brick concourse of parks, studios, museums, shops, restaurants, and pubs.

Juliette Gordon Low Birthplace. *10 E Ogelthorpe Ave, Savannah (31401). Phone 912/233-4501; fax 912/233-4659. www.girlscouts.org/who_we_are/birthplace.* (1818-1821) Restored Regency town house was birthplace, in 1860, of the founder of Girl Scouts of the USA. Many original Gordon family pieces. Garden restored to Victorian period. (Mon-Tues, Thurs-Sat 10 am-4 pm, sun from 11 am; closed holidays) **$$**

Laurel Grove Cemetery (South). *37th and Ogeechee rds, Savannah.* Possibly the oldest black cemetery currently in use; both antebellum slave and free black graves. Buried here is Andrew Bryan (1716-1812), pioneer Baptist preacher.

Owens-Thomas House. *124 Abercorn St, Savannah (31401). Phone 912/233-9743.* (1816-1819) Authentically furnished Regency-style house designed by William Jay. Lafayette was an overnight guest in 1825. Walled garden is designed and planted in 1820s style. (Tues-Sat 10 am-5 pm, Sun from 2 pm; closed holidays, also Jan) **$$**

Savannah History Museum. *303 Martin Luther King, Jr. Blvd, Savannah (31401). Adjacent Savannah Visitor Center. Phone 912/238-1779. www.chsgeorgia.org/shm.* This 19th-century railroad shed was renovated to house historical orientation center. Mural in lobby chronicles major events in Savannah's 250-year history. (Daily; closed Jan 1, Thanksgiving, Dec 25). **$** Here are

> **Auxiliary Theater.** *112 Bryan Ctr, Savannah (90848).* Special audiovisual presentations.

> **Exhibit Hall.** Artifacts, antiques, and memorabilia from Savannah's past; pre-colonial Native American artifacts, Revolutionary and Civil war uniforms and weapons; 1890 *Baldwin* locomotive; replica of the SS *Savannah,* first steamboat to cross the Atlantic.

Main Theater. Orientation film provides an overview of the history of Savannah from 1733-present as seen through the eyes of General James E. Oglethorpe.

Savannah National Wildlife Refuge. *N via Hwy 17 or Hwy 17 A, across the Savannah River in South Carolina. Phone 912/652-4415. www.fws.gov/savannah.*

Ships of the Sea Maritime Museum. *41 Martin Luther King, Jr. Blvd, Savannah (31401). Phone 912/232-1511. www.shipsofthesea.org.* Ship models, figureheads; scrimshaw, sea artifacts; ship's carpenter shop. (Tues-Sun; closed holidays) **$$**

Telfair Museum of Art. *121 Barnard St, Savannah. Phone 912/232-1177. www.telfair.org.* Regency mansion (1818) is one of three surviving buildings in Savannah by William Jay, English architect. Period rooms with family furnishings, silverware, porcelains; Octagon Room. Telfair is the oldest public art museum in the Southeast, with a permanent collection of 18th-, 19th-, and 20th-century American and European paintings and sculpture; prints, silver, decorative arts. Concerts, lectures; tours. (Daily; closed holidays) **$$**

Touring Savannah. *250 Martin Luther King, Jr. Blvd, Savannah. Old Savannah Tours. Phone 912/234-8128.* Various guided bus tours of historic landmark district and other areas. Tours depart from the visitor center (see ADDITIONAL VISITOR INFORMATION) and downtown hotels and inns. (Daily 9 am-4:30 pm; closed St. Patrick's Day, Thanksgiving, Dec 25) **$$$$**

Trustees' Garden Site. *E Broad St, Savannah.* Original site of 10-acre experimental garden modeled in 1733 after the Chelsea Gardens in London by colonists who hoped to produce silk, wine, and drugs. Peach trees planted in garden were responsible for Georgia's peach industry. Fort Wayne occupied the site in 1762. Not of military importance until the Revolution, the fort was named for General "Mad Anthony" Wayne. Strengthened by the British (1779), the Americans rebuilt it during the War of 1812. The massive buttressed brick walls later served as the foundation for a municipal gas company building. The **Pirates' House** (1734), former inn for visiting seamen, has been restored and is a restaurant; Robert Louis Stevenson referred to the inn in *Treasure Island.*

US Customs House. *1-5 E Bay St, Savannah.* (1850) Erected on the site of the colony's first public building. The granite columns' carved capitals were modeled from tobacco leaves. Tablet on Bull St marks the site where John Wesley preached his first Savannah sermon; tablet on Bay St marks the site of Oglethorpe's headquarters.

Wormsloe State Historic Site. *7601 Skidaway Rd, Savannah (31406). 8 miles SE on Skidaway Rd. Phone 912/353-3023.* Remains of early fortified 18th-century tabby house. (Tabby is a kind of cement made from lime, oyster shells, sand, and water.) Visitor center exhibits outline history of site and of Noble Jones family, owners for more than 200 years. (Tues-Sat 9 am-5 pm, Sun 2-5:30 pm) **$**

Special Events

Georgia Heritage Festival. *Phone 912/651-2125. www.georgiahistory.com/GaHeritage.* Walking tours, open house at historic sites, crafts show, waterfront festival, parade, concerts, Georgia Day. Late Jan-mid-Feb.

N. O. G. S. Tour of Hidden Gardens of Savannah. *Phone 912/961-4805. www.gcofsavannahnogstour.org.* Includes eight private walled gardens in historic Savannah, tea at Harper Fowlkes House. Late Apr. **$$$$**

Night in Old Savannah. *Battlefield Park, 300 Martin Luther King Blvd, Savannah. Phone 912/651-3673.* Foods of more than 25 countries; entertainment, including jazz, country, and rhythm and blues. Mid-Apr. **FREE**

Savannah Scottish Games and Highland Gathering. *J.F. Gregory Park, Hwy 144, Richmond Hill. 2 miles E via President St extension. www.savannahscottishgames. com.* The clans gather for a weekend of Highland games, piping, drumming, dancing, and the traditional "Kirkin' o' th' Tartans." Early May. **$$**

Savannah Seafood Festival. *404 E Bay St, Savannah. Waterfront. Phone 912/234-0295.* Restaurants sell samples; entertainment, arts and crafts. Contact Savannah Waterfront Association. First weekend in May.

Savannah Tour of Homes and Gardens. *18 Abercorn St, Savannah (31401). Phone 912/234-8054. www. savannahtourofhomes.org.* Sponsored by Christ Episcopal Church with Historic Savannah Foundation. Day and candlelight tours of more than 30 private houses and gardens. Contact 18 Abercorn St, 31401. Mar.

St. Patrick's Day Parade. *N of Jones St to the river, W of E Broad St, E of Boundary St and the Talmadge Bridge. www.savannahga.gov/cityweb/stpat/parade.* Rivals New York City's in size. Mar. **FREE**

Limited-Service Hotels

★ ★ **COURTYARD BY MARRIOTT.** *6703 Abercorn St, Savannah (31405). Phone 912/354-7878; toll-free 800/321-2211; fax 912/354-1432. www.courtyard.*

com. 144 rooms, 3 story. Check-in 3 pm. Check-out noon. Restaurant, bar. Fitness room. Outdoor pool, whirlpool. **$**

★ ★ **DAYS INN.** *201 W Bay St, Savannah (31401). Phone 912/236-4440; toll-free 877/542-7666; fax 912/232-2725. www.daysinn.com.* 257 rooms, 7 story. Check-in 4 pm. Check-out 11 am. Restaurant. Outdoor pool. **$**

★ **HAMPTON INN.** *201 Stephenson Ave, Savannah (31405). Phone 912/355-4100; fax 912/356-5385. www.hamptoninn.com.* 128 rooms, 2 story. Complimentary continental breakfast. Check-in 3 pm, check-out noon. Outdoor pool. **$**

★ ★ **HOLIDAY INN.** *601 E Bay St, Savannah (31401). Phone 912/238-1200; fax 912/236-2184. www.savannahhotel.com.* Located on scenic Washington Square, in the heart of the Historic District, this elegant hotel welcomes guests with a genuine hospitality and serene ambience that takes guests back to a long-forgotten era. The 145 guest rooms have been renovated with guest comfort in mind. Offering luxurious accommodations charmingly appointed with touches of Savannah's rich history, along with a staff trained to ensure guests every comfort, this hotel makes for a truly delightful stay. 145 rooms, 3 story. Check-in 3 pm, check-out noon. Restaurant, bar. Fitness room. Outdoor pool, whirlpool. **$$$**

Full-Service Hotels

★ ★ **HILTON SAVANNAH DE SOTO.** *17 E Liberty St, Savannah (31401). Phone 912/232-9000; toll-free 800/774-1500; fax 912/232-6018. www.hilton.com.* 246 rooms, 10 story. Check-in 4 pm, check-out noon. Restaurant, bar. Fitness room. Outdoor pool. Airport transportation available. Business center. **$$**

★ ★ ★ **HYATT REGENCY SAVANNAH.** *2 W Bay St, Savannah (31401). Phone 912/238-1234; fax 912/944-3678. www.hyatt.com.* Located in the heart of the historic district and perched along the exquisitely scenic waterfront of Savannah River, this hotel successfully combines superb accommodations, first-class amenities, and an attentive staff to ensure that even the most strenuous guests leave satisfied after experiencing the friendly Southern hospitality. 347 rooms,

7 story. Check-in 3 pm, check-out noon. Restaurant, bar. Fitness room. Indoor pool. Business center. **$**

★ ★ ★ **MARRIOTT SAVANNAH RIVERFRONT.** *100 General McIntosh Blvd, Savannah (31401). Phone 912/233-7722; toll-free 800/932-2198; fax 912/233-3765. www.marriott.com.* Adjacent to the world-renowned River Street and located on the historic Riverfront, this hotel makes for a truly delightful stay. Inside, guests are welcomed with attentive service and handsomely appointed accommodations. A stroll along the hotel's riverwalk will lead guests to all the delights River Street has to offer with its friendly taverns, quaint shops and succulent restaurants. 383 rooms, 8 story. Check-in 4 pm. Check-out 11 am. Restaurant, bar. Fitness room. Indoor pool, outdoor pool, whirlpool. **$$**

Full-Service Resort

★ ★ ★ **THE WESTIN SAVANNAH HARBOR RESORT AND SPA.** *1 Resort Dr, Savannah (31421). Phone 912/201-2000; fax 912/201-2001. www.westin.com.* 403 rooms, 16 story. Check-in 4 pm. Check-out noon. Restaurant, bar. Children's activity center. Fitness room, spa. Outdoor pool, children's pool, whirlpool. Golf. Tennis. Airport transportation available. Business center. **$$**

Full-Service Inns

★ ★ ★ **17 HUNDRED 90 INN & RESTAURANT.** *307 E President St, Savannah (31401). Phone 912/236-7122; toll-free 800/487-1790; fax 912/236-7123. www.17hundred90.com.* 14 rooms. Complimentary continental breakfast. Check-in 2 pm, check-out 11 am. Restaurant. **$$**

★ ★ ★ **EAST BAY INN.** *225 E Bay St, Savannah (31401). Phone 912/238-1225; toll-free 800/500-1225; fax 912/232-2709. www.eastbayinn.com.* Just steps away from the historic waterfront, this romantic inn has many beautiful rooms filled with period furnishings and antiques. Enjoy a cheese and wine reception each evening. 28 rooms, 3 story. Pets accepted; fee. Complimentary continental breakfast. Check-in 3 pm, check-out 11 am. Restaurant. **$$**

★ ★ ★ THE PRESIDENT'S QUARTERS INN.

225 E President St, Savannah (31401). Phone 912/233-1600; toll-free 800/233-1776; fax 912/238-0849. www.presidentsquarters.com. Once a place where diplomats and generals layed their heads, the President's Quarters, now opens its doors to guests. Feel like royalty relaxing in the elegantly appointed parlors, or strolling through their renowned gardens. 19 rooms, 4 story. Complimentary full breakfast. Check-in 2 pm. Check-out 11 am. Restaurant. **$$**
🉐

★ ★ ★ RIVER STREET INN.

124 E Bay St, Savannah (31401). Phone 912/234-6400; toll-free 800/253-4229; fax 912/234-1478.www.riverstreetinn.com. 86 rooms, 5 story. Check-in 4 pm, check-out noon. Restaurant, bar. **$$**

Specialty Lodgings

BALLASTONE INN & TOWNHOUSE.

14 E Oglethorpe Ave, Savannah (31401). Phone 912/236-1484; toll-free 800/822-4553; fax 912/236-4626. www.ballastone.com. Opening as Savannah's first bed-and-breakfast, this inn sets the standard for all bed-and-breakfasts to follow. Set in this 160-year-old mansion, each spacious suite is ensured to make guests feel like they are receiving the royal treatment. 17 rooms, 4 story. Children over 16 years only. Complimentary full breakfast. Check-in 3 pm. Check-out 11 am. **$$**
🉐

BED & BREAKFAST INN.

117 W Gordon St, Savannah (31401). Phone 912/238-0518; toll-free 888/238-0518; fax 912/233-2537. www.savannahbnb.com. 15 rooms, 4 story. Complimentary full breakfast. Check-in 3 pm, check-out 11 am. Restored 1853 Federal town house in the Historic District. **$**
🉐

ELIZA THOMPSON HOUSE.

5 W Jones St, Savannah (31401). Phone 912/236-3620; toll-free 800/348-9378; fax 912/238-1920. www.elizathompsonhouse.com. Elegantly restored and recently refurbished, each room offers quiet and comfortable surroundings. The gracious staff on hand is always ready to show off their prized inn and their beautiful city. 25 rooms, 3 story. Complimentary full breakfast. Check-in 3 pm. Check-out 11 am. **$$**
🉐

FOLEY HOUSE INN.

14 W Hull St, Savannah (31401). Phone 912/232-6622; toll-free 800/647-3708; fax 912/231-1218. www.foleyinn.com. To say the staff makes guests feel at home here is an understatement. Located in the heart of historic Savannah, this is a great choice for a romantic getaway. 18 rooms, 4 story. Complimentary full breakfast. Check-in 3 pm, check-out 11 am. **$$**
🉐

THE GASTONIAN.

220 E Gaston St, Savannah (31401). Phone 912/232-2869; toll-free 800/322-6603; fax 912/232-0710. www.gastonian.com. 17 rooms, 4 story. Children over 12 years only. Complimentary full breakfast. Check-in 3 pm. Check-out noon. Whirlpool. **$$$**
🉐

THE KEHOE HOUSE.

123 Habersham St, Savannah (31401). Phone 912/232-1020; toll-free 800/820-1020; fax 912/231-0208. www.kehoehouse.com. Savor the many charms of Savannah at The Kehoe House. This inviting and gracious bed-and-breakfast enjoys a superior location in the heart of the Historic District overlooking Columbia Square. History buffs will relish the many treasures within walking distance from this stunning mansion listed on the National Register of Historic Places. Guests are treated to a unique experience here, where the 13 rooms are individually designed and elegantly appointed. This inn manages to celebrate its history while welcoming the present, with crystal chandeliers, antiques, and period furnishings residing alongside high- speed Internet access and multi-line telephones. The breakfasts here are extraordinary and made to order, while the afternoons invite guests to linger with a cup of tea and a plate of exceptional hors d'oeuvres. 14 rooms, 5 story. Complimentary full breakfast. Check-in 3 pm, check-out 11 am. **$$$$**
🉐

OLDE HARBOUR INN.

508 E Factors Walk, Savannah (31401). Phone 912/234-4100; toll-free 800/553-6533; fax 912/233-5979. www.oldeharbourinn.com. 24 rooms, 3 story. Pets accepted; fee. Complimentary continental breakfast. Check-in 3 pm, check-out 11 am. Built in 1892, originally housed the offices and warehouse of an oil company. **$$**
🉐 🏴

Restaurants

★ ★ 1790 INN & RESTAURANT.

307 E President St, Savannah (31401). Phone 912/236-7122; fax 912/236-7123. www.17hundred90.com. International menu. Lunch, dinner. Bar. Casual attire. **$$$**

★ ★ **BELFORD'S.** *313 W Julian St, Savannah (31401). Phone 912/233-2626; fax 912/233-2621.* American menu. Breakfast, lunch, dinner, Sun brunch. Closed Thanksgiving, Dec 24-25. Bar. Children's menu. Casual attire. Reservations recommended. Outdoor seating. **$$**

★ ★ **BISTRO SAVANNAH.** *309 W Congress St, Savannah (31401). Phone 912/233-6266; fax 912/232-7957.* American menu, Seafood menu. Dinner. Closed Thanksgiving, Dec 25. Bar. Casual attire. **$$$**

★ ★ **CHART HOUSE.** *202 W Bay St, Savannah (31401). Phone 912/234-6686; fax 912/232-4872. www. chart-house.com.* Seafood, steak menu. Dinner. Bar. Children's menu. Casual attire. Outdoor seating. Covered balcony over Savannah River. **$$**

★ ★ ★ **ELIZABETH ON 37TH.** *105 E 37th St, Savannah (31401). Phone 912/236-5547; fax 912/232-1095. www.elizabethon37th.com.* Opened in 1981 by chef Elizabeth Terry and her husband, Michael, this charming restaurant is a birthplace of New Southern cuisine. The interior of the 1900 Greek Revival-style mansion feels like home with brightly painted walls, antique chairs, and warm service. The fresh tastes and authenticity of the cuisine (Terry extensively researched 18th- and 19th-century Savannah cooking) draws admiration from across the country. American menu. Dinner. Closed holidays; last two weeks of Aug. Casual attire. **$$$**
🄳

★ ★ **GARIBALDI'S CAFE.** *315 W Congress St, Savannah (31401). Phone 912/232-7118; fax 912/232-7957.* Seafood menu. Dinner. Closed Dec 25. Bar. Casual attire. Former 1871 Germania firehouse in historic district. **$$$**

★ **JOHNNY HARRIS.** *1651 E Victory Dr, Savannah (31404). Phone 912/354-7810; toll-free 888/547-2823; fax 912/354-6567. www.johnnyharris.com.* This restaurant is Savannah's oldest continuously operating restaurant. American menu. Lunch, dinner. Closed Sun; Jan 1, Dec 25. Bar. Children's menu. Casual attire. **$$**

★ **MOON RIVER BREWING CO.** *21 W Bay St, Savannah (31401). Phone 912/447-0943; fax 912/447-0944. www.moonriverbrewing.com.* American menu. Lunch, dinner. Bar. Children's menu. Casual attire. **$$**

★ ★ **MRS. WILKES' DINING ROOM.** *107 W Jones St, Savannah (31401). Phone 912/232-5997; fax 912/233-8970. www.mrswilkes.com.* American menu. Lunch. Closed Sat-Sun; holidays. Casual attire. **$**

★ ★ **OLDE PINK HOUSE.** *23 Abercorn St, Savannah (31401). Phone 912/232-4286; fax 912/231-1934.* This is the only restaurant in town located in a historic mansion (dating from the 18th century). The seven candlelit dining rooms are furnished with period pieces and artwork. American menu. Dinner. Bar. Children's menu. Casual attire. **$$**
🄳

★ ★ **RIVER HOUSE.** *125 W River St, Savannah (31401). Phone 912/234-1900; toll-free 800/317-1912; fax 912/234-7007. www.riverhouseseafood.com.* Seafood menu. Lunch, dinner. Closed Thanksgiving, Dec 25. Bar. Children's menu. Casual attire. **$$**

Sea Island (E-5)

See also Brunswick, Darien, Fort Frederica National Monument, Golden Isles, Jekyll Island, St. Simons Island

Population 750
Elevation 11 ft
Area Code 912
Zip 31561
Web Site www.seaisland.com

Full-Service Hotel

★ ★ ★ ★ ★ **THE LODGE AT SEA ISLAND GOLF CLUB.** *100 Retreat Ave, St. Simons Island (31522). Phone 912/638-3611; toll-free 866/465-3536; fax 912/638-5159. www.seaisland.com.* Generations of privileged travelers have made Sea Island their vacation destination. Marrying the romance of the Old South with the grand tradition of old-world Europe, this scenic island allows guests to time-travel to a bygone era of refinement and splendor, where round-the-clock personal butlers attend to every need and the strains of a bagpipe signal the end of the day. The Lodge's guest rooms are a delightful interpretation of a genteel manor house, with teak furnishings, antiques from around the globe, wood floors graced by priceless carpets, and ample amenities. Created in the spirit of European sporting estates, this resort is a playground for the elite with plentiful country pursuits. The centuries old Shooting School is a source of great pride; tennis and equestrian facilities are first-rate; and avid golfers are thrilled by the three championship golf courses just steps from the Atlantic Ocean. The accommodations have private balconies if relaxing with a good book is more your style. From sensational spa treatments to exquisite meals, this resort is dedicated to excellence. 40 rooms, 3 story.

Complimentary continental breakfast. Check-in 3 pm, check-out noon. High-speed Internet access, wireless Internet access. Three restaurants, two bars. Fitness room, fitness classes available, spa. Beach. Whirlpool. Golf, 36 holes. Tennis. Business center. **$$$$**

Full-Service Resort

★ ★ ★ **THE CLOISTER.** *100 Hudson Pl, Sea Island (31561). Phone 912/638-3611; toll-free 800/732-4752; fax 912/634-3964. www.cloister.com.* The Cloister is the jewel in the crown of Sea Island's resorts. This elegant retreat is an American classic, catering to vacationing couples and families for nearly 75 years. Exclusive, though unpretentious, The Cloister feels like a private club. The accommodations are the last word in coastal elegance, where traditional furnishings are enlivened with pastel colors and lively prints. This resort is the embodiment of the sporting life, offering everything from boating, tennis, and golf to shooting, equestrian activities, and a spa. For those who need a little R and R, the resort's 5-mile stretch of sandy beach is the answer to the overscheduled day. After a long day of sunning or sporting, the four restaurants entice with sophisticated Southern cuisine, seafood, and beef. 212 rooms, 3 story. Complimentary continental breakfast. Check-in 3 pm, check-out noon. Restaurant, bar. Children's activity center. Fitness room, spa. Beach. Outdoor pool, whirlpool. Golf, 54 holes. Tennis. Airport transportation available. Business center. **$$$$**

Smyrna (B-2)

Population 40,999
Web Site www.ci.smyrna.ga.us

Restaurant

★ **OLD SOUTH BAR-B-Q.** *601 Burbank Cir, Smyrna (30080). Phone 770/435-4215. www.oldsouthbbq. com.* Barbecue menu. Lunch, dinner. Casual attire. **$**

St. Simons Island (E-5)

See also Brunswick, Darien, Golden Isles, Jekyll Island, Sea Island

Population 13,381
Elevation 0-30 ft
Area Code 912
Zip 31522
Information St. Simons Visitors Center, 530 B Beachview Dr, Neptune Park; phone toll-free 912/638-9014
Web Site www.gacoast.com

One of Georgia's Golden Isles (see), St. Simons Island has been under five flags: Spain, France, Britain, US, and Confederate States of America. Fragments of each culture remain.

John and Charles Wesley preached under St. Simons' oaks before a church was built at Frederica, and later Aaron Burr spent a month at Hampton's Point after killing Alexander Hamilton in a duel. St. Simons' plantations flourished and were noted for the luxurious and sporting life of planters from about 1800 to the Civil War. Cotton and slavery collapsed after Sherman's forces razed the estates. Former slave quarters remained; inhabitants turned to fishing and garden crops for subsistence as St. Simons was nearly forgotten until the 20th century.

What to See and Do

Gascoigne Bluff. *Where the bridge crosses the Frederica River, SW side of island.* This is a low-wooded, shell-covered bank named for Captain James Gascoigne, commander of HMS *Hawk,* which convoyed the two ships bringing settlers (1736). Great live oaks cut here were used to build first US Navy vessels, including the *Constitution* ("Old Ironsides") (1794). St. Simons Marina is open to the public.

Glynn Art Association. *319 Mallery St, St. Simons Island (31522). Phone 912/638-8770. www.glynnart.org.* Triannual art festivals; monthly exhibitions of works by regional artists, traveling exhibits, lectures, classes (fee). (Tues-Fri 9 am-5 pm, Sat 10 am-4 pm; closed holidays) **FREE**

St. Simons Island Lighthouse Museum. *101 12th St, St. Simons Island (31522). Phone 912/638-4666; fax 912/638-6609. www.saintsimonslighthouse.org.* Housed in restored 1872 lightkeeper's house; exhibits on history of St. Simons lighthouse and Golden Isles. (Mon-Sat 10 am-5 pm, Sun 1:30-5 pm; closed holidays) **$** Includes

St. Simons Lighthouse. *101 12th St, St. Simons Island (31522). S end of island. Phone 912/638-4666; fax 912/638-6609.* The original lighthouse (1810), which was 75 feet high, was destroyed by Confederate troops in 1861 to prevent it from guiding Union invaders onto the island. The present lighthouse, 104 feet high, has been in continuous operation, except during wartime, since 1872. Visitors may climb to the top. **$**

Special Events

Golden Isles Art Festival. *Postell Park, 550 Beachview Dr, St. Simons Island (31522). Phone 912/638-1770. www.glynnart.org.* Juried arts and crafts exhibits, demonstrations, entertainment, food. Early Oct.

Homes and Gardens Tour. *Phone 912/638-3166.* Tour of houses and gardens on St. Simons Island and Sea Island. Varies each year. Mid-Mar.

Sunshine Festival. *Neptune Park, 550 Beachview Dr, St. Simons Island (31522). Phone 912/634-0411.* Juried arts and crafts exhibits; food; fireworks on July 4. Weekend closest to July 4.

Limited-Service Hotel

★ **BEST WESTERN ISLAND INN.** *301 Main St, St. Simons Island (31522). Phone 912/638-7805; toll-free 800/673-6323; fax 912/634-4720. www.bestwestern. com.* This off-the-beaten-track hotel is located in a little gathering of doctors' offices in a quiet area just over the Tottas Causeway. The plantation-style property is surrounded by well-kept grounds, and a gazebo houses a hot tub. Complimentary continental breakfast is offered for a great start to you day. 61 rooms, 2 story. Complimentary continental breakfast. Check-in 3 pm, check-out 11 am. High-speed Internet access, wireless Internet access. Outdoor pool, whirlpool. **$**

Full-Service Resorts

★ ★ ★ **KING AND PRINCE RESORT.** *201 Arnold Rd, St. Simons Island (31522). Phone 912/638-3631; toll-free 800/342-0212; fax 912/638-7699. www. kingandprince.com.* This family friendly, full-service resort is located on the ocean's edge directly on the beach and is within minutes to a quaint shopping village and various restaurants. The historic getaway

was open for business in 1935 as a dance hall. Then in 1941, the main hotel building was open for business. The current property still exudes classic Southern charm. The property offers a variety of accommodations such as ocean front rooms, a 1-bedroom house, and even a 5-bedroom house. Outdoor amenities are abundant, including bike, kayak, and sailboat rentals; pools; a beach; and tennis. 186 rooms, 4 story. Check-in 4 pm, check-out 11 am. High-speed Internet access, wireless Internet access. Two restaurants, two bars. Fitness room. Beach. Indoor pool, outdoor pool, whirlpool. Golf, 18 holes. Tennis. Airport transportation available. Business center. **$$**

★ ★ **SEA PALMS GOLF & TENNIS RESORT.** *5445 Frederica Rd, St. Simons Island (31522). Phone 912/638-3351; toll-free 800/841-6268; fax 912/634-8031. www.seapalms.com.* Ideal for both conference retreats or personal playtimes, the ultra-modern Sea Palms offers spacious rooms with wet bars and mini refrigerators to recover from a hard day at work or at play. Guest rooms are decorated in soothing beige tones, rattan chairs, and the suites have complete kitchens. There's plenty to do around the resort including outdoor pools, tennis and golf courses, bicycle rentals, and playgrounds. 140 rooms, 3 story. Check-in 4 pm, check-out 11 am. Two restaurants, bar. Fitness room. Two outdoor pools. Golf, 27 holes. Tennis. Airport transportation available. Business center. **$$**

Full-Service Inn

★ ★ ★ **THE LODGE ON LITTLE ST. SIMONS ISLAND.** *1000 Hampton Point Dr, St. Simons Island (31522). Phone 912/638-7472; toll-free 888/733-5774; fax 912/634-1811. www.littlestsimonsisland.com.* 13 rooms, 2 story. Check-in 4 pm, check-out 10 am. Restaurant. Fitness room. **$$$$**

Specialty Lodgings

ST. SIMONS INN BY THE LIGHTHOUSE. *609 Beachview Dr, St. Simons Island (31522). Phone 912/638-1101; fax 912/638-0943. www.stsimonsinn. com.* 34 rooms, 3 story. Complimentary continental breakfast. Check-in 3 pm, check-out 11 am. Outdoor pool. **$**

Restaurants

★ **BENNIE'S RED BARN.** *5514 Frederica Rd, St. Simons Island (31522). Phone 912/638-2844; fax 912/634-2440. www.benniesredbarn.com.* Family operated since 1955, this family-friendly eatery features tables set with red and white-checked tablecloths; large picture windows; mounted stuffed animals; and high rafters with spotlights that highlight a large stone fireplace. There are no printed menus here–the servers recite them to the guests. On Thursday through Saturday evenings, guests can enjoy the live music at Ziggys, a nightclub connected to the restaurant. American menu. Dinner. Closed holidays. Bar. Children's menu. Casual attire. Reservations recommended. **$$**
🅳

★ **BROGEN'S SOUTH.** *200 Pier Alley, St. Simons Island (31522). Phone 912/638-1660; fax 912/638-2047. www.brogens.com.* American menu. Lunch, dinner. Closed Sun, Oct-Apr; Jan 1, Easter, Dec 25. Bar. Outdoor seating. **$$**
🅳

★ ★ **CHELSEA.** *1226 Ocean Blvd, St. Simons Island (31522). Phone 912/638-2047; fax 912/638-1183. www.chelsea-ssi.com.* Enjoy a romantic evening at this local favorite on Ocean Boulevard, just minutes from the charming shopping area, lighthouse museum, and various lodgings. The atmosphere is relaxed, and flower planters and a fireplace add to the warm ambience. Seafood menu. Dinner. Bar. Children's menu. Casual attire. Reservations recommended. Outdoor seating. **$$**

★ ★ **J. MAC'S.** *407 Mallory St, St. Simons Island (31522). Phone 912/634-0403; fax 912/638-3757. www.jmacsislandrestaurant.com.* J. Mac's is situated in the heart of the island's quaint shopping and eating district. The tastefully simple décor features brick walls accented with mirrors, blue lamps and candles on the tables, and a bar area with bistro tables set by window views; French posters on the walls add to the ambience. In season, live piano music is featured. French menu. Dinner. Closed Sun; holidays; also four days after Labor Day and four days after Memorial Day. Bar. Children's menu. Reservations recommended. **$$$**

★ **MIYABI SEAFOOD & STEAK.** *202 Retreat Plaza, St. Simons Island (31522). Phone 912/638-0885; fax 912/638-2797.* Japanese menu. Dinner. Closed Thanksgiving, Dec 25; also Super Bowl Sun. Bar. Children's menu. **$$**

Statesboro (D-4)

Settled 1796
Population 22,698
Elevation 258 ft
Area Code 912
Zip 30458
Information Convention and Visitors Bureau, 3 S Main St, PO Box 1516; phone 912/489-1869
Web Site www.visit-statesboro.com

What to See and Do

Georgia Southern University. *Hwy 301 S, Statesboro (30460). Phone 912/681-5611. www.georgiasouthern.edu.* (1906) (14,000 students) On campus are art department gallery (Mon-Fri; closed holidays); museum (daily; closed holidays); planetarium (by appointment); botanical garden (daily); Center for Wildlife Education and Raptor Center (daily; closed Sun June-Aug holidays).

Special Event

Kiwanis Ogeechee Fair. *Kiwanis Community Building, Hwy 67, Statesboro. Phone 912/842-5540.* Sept-Oct.

Full-Service Inn

★ ★ ★ **HISTORIC STATESBORO INN.** *106 S Main St, Statesboro (30458). Phone 912/489-8628; toll-free 800/846-9466; fax 912/489-4785. www.statesboroinn.com.* This country inn boasts an atmosphere and surroundings unmatched in comfort and style. Rich in history, this inn also offers elegant dining featuring a menu of seasonal favorites with Southern flavors. 16 rooms, 2 story. Pets accepted. Complimentary full breakfast. Check-in 1 pm, check-out 11 am. Restaurant. **$**
🅳 🐾

Thomasville (E-2)

See also Bainbridge

Population 18,162
Elevation 285 ft
Area Code 229
Zip 31792
Information Welcome Center, 401 S Broad St, PO Box 1540, 31799; phone 229/227-7099
Web Site www.thomasvillega.com

What to See and Do

Big Oak. *Crawford and Monroe sts, Thomasville. 1 block behind Post Office and Federal Courthouse.* Giant live oak is 68 feet tall, has a limb spread of 162 feet, and a trunk circumference of 24 feet. The approximately 320-year-old tree was enrolled as a member of the National Live Oak Society in 1936.

Lapham-Patterson House State Historic Site. *626 N Dawson St, Thomasville (31792). Phone 229/225-4004. www.gastateparks.org/info/lapham.* (1885) Restored three-story Victorian house features decorative shinglework, elaborate chinoiserie porches, fanciful gables, and cantilevered balconies; built by Chicago merchant as resort cottage. Tours on the hour. (Tues-Sat 9 am-5 pm, Sun 2-5:30 pm; closed Thanksgiving, Dec 25, Jan1; last tour at 4 pm) **$**

Pebble Hill Plantation. *1251 Hwy 319 S, Thomasville (31799). 5 miles SW via Hwy 319. Phone 229/226-2344. www.pebblehill.com.* Historic plantation dates from 1820s; elaborate Greek Revival house furnished with art, antiques, porcelains, crystal, silver, and Native American relics belonging to Hanna family of Ohio, who rebuilt house, guest houses, stables, and garages after a fire in the 1930s. Gardens; livestock. Wagon rides; tours (Tues-Sat 10 am-5 pm, Sun 1-5 pm; closed Thanksgiving, Dec 24-25, Jan 1; must be over 6 years of age). **$$**

Thomas County Museum of History. *725 N Dawson St, Thomasville (31792).* Five buildings on the property include a log house with period furnishings; an 1877 frame house furnished in middle-class fashion of that period; an 1893 Victorian bowling alley; a garage housing historic vehicles; and a 1920s mansion, which houses the main museum. Photographs, period costumes, artifacts. (Closed holidays, also last 2 weeks in Aug) **$**

Thomasville Cultural Center. *600 E Washington St, Thomasville (31799).* A center for visual and performing arts. Facilities include art galleries with permanent and changing exhibits, children's rm, and 550-seat auditorium. Concerts, musicals, children's programs, art classes, and other programs are offered. Galleries, building tours (Mon-Fri 9 am-5 pm, Sat 1-5 pm; closed holidays). **FREE**

Special Event

Rose Festival. *Phone 229/227-7020. www. downtownthomasville.com/RoseFest.* Parade, rose show, arts and crafts. Late Apr.

Limited-Service Hotel

★ **AMERICA'S BEST VALUE INN.** *3538 Hwy 84 E, Cairo (31728). Phone 229/377-4400; fax 229/377-5831. www.daysinn.com.* 34 rooms, 2 story. Check-out 11 am. Outdoor pool. **$**
🏊

Full-Service Resort

★ ★ ★ **MELHANA THE GRAND PLANTA-TION.** *301 Showboat Ln, Thomasville (31792). Phone 229/226-2290; toll-free 888/920-3030; fax 229/226-4585. www.melhana.com.* Built on the grounds of a historic plantation,this resort has an indoor pool, tennis courts, horseback riding, as well as a wide assortment of leisure activities. Explore the vast grounds by day and enjoy gourmet dining in the dining room each evening. 30 rooms, 2 story. Complimentary full breakfast. Check-in 3 pm, check-out 11 am. Restaurant, bar. Children's activity center. Fitness room. Indoor pool. Tennis. Airport transportation available. Business center. **$$**
🏃 🏊 🎿 🚶

Specialty Lodgings

1884 PAXTON HOUSE INN. *445 Remington Ave, Thomasville (31792). Phone 229/226-5197; fax 229/226-9903. www.1884paxtonhouseinn.com.* Stroll from this Victorian mansion and see the rich history and beauty of Thomasville. Marvel in the beauty and grace of the old inn as worries are rocked away on the spacious veranda. 4 rooms, 2 story. Children over 12 years only. Complimentary full breakfast. Check-in 3-6 pm. Check-out 11 am. Indoor pool. **$$**
🐾 🏊

SERENDIPITY COTTAGE. *339 E Jefferson St, Thomasville (31792). Phone 229/226-8111; toll-free 800/383-7377; fax 229/226-2656. www. serendipitycottage.com.* 4 rooms, 2 story. Children over 12 years only. Complimentary full breakfast. Check-in 4 pm, check-out 11 am. **$**
🐾

Restaurant

★ ★ **PLAZA RESTAURANT.** *217 S Broad St, Thomasville (31792). Phone 229/226-5153; fax 229/226-2458.* Greek, American menu. Breakfast, lunch, dinner Mon-Sat. Closed holidays. Bar. Children's menu. **$$**

Tifton (E-3)

See also Adel

Population 15,060
Elevation 357 ft
Information Tifton-Tift County Chamber of Commerce, 100 Central Ave, PO Box 165, 31793; phone 229/382-6200
Web Site www.tiftontourism.com

What to See and Do

Georgia Agrirama, 19th-Century Living History Museum. *I-75 exit 20 and 8th St, Tifton (31793). Phone 229/386-3344; toll-free 800/767-1875.www. agrirama.com.* Operating exhibits include farms and farmhouses, one-room school, gristmill, newspaper office, blacksmith shop, church, cotton gin, sawmill, turpentine still, country store, drugstore, variety works, and more from 1870 to 1910. A logging train runs year-round. Costumed interpreters. (Tues-Sat 9 am-5 pm; closed holidays) **$$**

Limited-Service Hotel

★ **QUALITY INN.** *1104 King Rd, Tifton (31794). Phone 229/382-4410; fax 229/382-3967.* 91 rooms, 2 story. Pets accepted, some restrictions; fee. Complimentary continental breakfast. Check-out 11 am. Bar. Indoor pool, whirlpool. **$**

Restaurant

★ **CHARLES SEAFOOD RESTAURANT.** *701 W 7th St (Hwy 82), Tifton (31794). Phone 229/382-9696; fax 229/387-7413.* American menu, Seafood menu. Lunch, dinner. Closed Sun; July 4, Dec 25. **$$**

Toccoa (A-3)

See also Clayton, Commerce, Gainesville, Helen

Population 9,323
Elevation 1,017 ft
Area Code 706
Zip 30577
Information Toccoa-Stephens County Chamber of Commerce, 160 N Alexander St, PO Box 577; 706/886-2132
Web Site www.toccoagachamber.com

What to See and Do

Hartwell Lake. *5625 Anderson Hwy, Hartwell (30643). 6 miles E on Hwy 123 to the lake; continue approximately 21 miles E on the same road to access Twin Lakes campground, follow signs. Phone 706/376-4788.* This 56,000-acre reservoir with 962 miles of shoreline was created by a dam on the Savannah River. Swimming, water-skiing, fishing, boating (ramps, marinas); picnicking. Numerous campsites (Mar-Nov; fee) surround the lake. Reservoir (daily).

Toccoa Falls College. *Falls Rd, Toccoa Falls (30598). NW edge of town off Hwy 17 A. Phone 706/886-6831; toll-free 888/785-5624. www.toccoafalls.edu.* (1907) (911 students) On Nov 6, 1977, a 40-year-old earthen dam above the college collapsed, spewing tons of water over the 186-foot Toccoa Falls and inundating the campus—one of the worst such disasters in Georgia history. There is no longer a lake or dam above the falls. Toccoa Falls is open to the public (daily; closed Dec 25). **FREE**

Traveler's Rest State Historic Site. *11 Stage Coach Private Dr, Toccoa (30577). 6 miles NE off Hwy 123. Phone 706/886-2256.* Plantation house (circa 1840) built on land granted in 1785 to Jesse Walton, a Revolutionary soldier and political leader. Two-story structure covers 6,000 square feet. Later owned and enlarged by Devereaux Jarrett, it served as a stagecoach inn and post office. Museum (Thurs-Sat 9 am-5 pm, Sun 2-5:30pm; closed holidays). **$**

Limited-Service Hotel

★ **DAYS INN.** *1101 S Big A Rd, Toccoa (30577). Phone 706/886-9461; toll-free 800/329-7466; fax 706/886-0907. www.daysinn.com.* 78 rooms, 2 story. Complimentary continental breakfast. Check-in 11 am, check-out 11 am. Outdoor pool. **$**

Tybee Island (D-5)

See also Savannah

Population 3,392
Elevation 17 ft
Area Code 912
Zip 31328
Information Savannah Area Convention and Visitors Bureau, 101 E Bay St; phone toll-free 877/SAVANNAH
Web Site www.tybeeisland.com

A popular year-round Georgia resort has evolved on this V-shaped sandbar fronting the Atlantic for nearly 4 miles and the Savannah River for more than 2 miles. The beach runs the entire length of the island; its north end is marked by old coastal defenses, a museum, and a lighthouse at the tip. Reached by a causeway from Savannah and Hwy 80, the beach has a boardwalk, fishing pier, amusements, hotels, motels, and vacation cottages.

What to See and Do

Tybee Museum and Lighthouse. *30 Meddin Dr, Tybee Island. N end of island. Phone 912/786-5801; fax 912/786-6538. www.tybeelighthouse.org.* Museum is housed in a coastal artillery battery built in 1898. Battery Garland is one of six gun emplacements that made up Fort Screven. Museum traces history of Tybee from colonial times to 1945; exhibits on Martello Tower, Civil War, Fort Screven; doll and gun collections. The lighthouse is one of the oldest active lighthouses in the US; visitors may climb to the top for a scenic view of Tybee and historic Fort Screven. Exhibits and gift shop in 1880s lighthouse keeper's cottage. (Wed-Mon; closed holidays; also March 17). **$$**

Valdosta (E-3)

See also Adel

Settled 1860
Population 43,724
Elevation 229 ft
Area Code 229
Information Chamber of Commerce, 416 N Ashley St, 31603-1964; phone 229/247-8100
Web Site www.valdostachamber.com

When local citizens discovered that surveyors had left the town off the railroad right-of-way, they lost no time moving the town 4 miles east of the original community (then called Troupville). Named for Val de Aosta (Vale of Beauty), the governor's estate, Valdosta later became a rail center with seven branch lines of three systems. One of the state's most prosperous small cities, Valdosta's products include timber, tobacco, and cattle. Agriculture, tourism, Valdosta State University, and Moody Air Force Base, 12 miles to the north, also contribute to the economy. Valdosta is in the center of a large wooded area with many lakes nearby.

What to See and Do

Barber House. *416 N Ashley St, Valdosta. Phone 229/247-8100.* (1915) Restored neo-Classical house serves as offices for Valdosta-Lowndes County Chamber of Commerce; elaborate woodwork, original light fixtures and furniture. Self-guided tours. (Mon-Fri, 8:30 am-5 pm) **FREE**

Converse Dalton Ferrell House. *305 N Patterson St, Valdosta. Phone 229/244-8575.* (1902) Neo-Classical house with wide two-story porch that wraps around front and two sides. Interior has 20-foot ceilings, 14-foot high pocket doors, golden-oak woodwork, some original light fixtures. (By appointment only) Contact the Convention and Visitors Center.

The Crescent (Valdosta Garden Center). *904 N Patterson St, Valdosta. Phone 229/244-6747.*(1898) Neo-Classical house named for the dramatic two-story, crescent-shaped porch supported by 13 columns. House includes grand staircase, second-floor bathroom with gold-leaf tiles and fireplace, and ballroom on third floor. In garden are chapel and octagonal school house. (Mon-Fri 2-5 pm; also by appointment) **DONATION**

Lowndes County Historical Society Museum. *305 W Central Ave, Valdosta. Phone 229/247-4780.* Originally a Carnegie library, now contains collection of artifacts from Civil War to present; genealogical library. (Mon-Fri 10 am-5 pm; closed holidays) **FREE**

Limited-Service Hotels

★ ★ **BEST WESTERN KING OF THE ROAD.** *1403 N St. Augustine Rd, Valdosta (31602). Phone 229/244-7600; toll-free 800/780-7234; fax 229/245-1734. www.bestwestern.com.* 137 rooms, 3 story. Pets accepted, some restrictions. Complimentary continental breakfast. Check-out 11 am. Restaurant, bar. Outdoor pool. Airport transportation available. **$**

★ **COMFORT INN.** *2101 W Hill Ave, Valdosta (31601). Phone 229/242-1212; toll-free 800/228-5150; fax 229/242-2639. www.comfortinn.com.* 138 rooms, 2 story. Complimentary continental breakfast. Check-out noon. Bar. Outdoor pool. Airport transportation available. Business center. **$**

★ **HAMPTON INN.** *1705 Gornto Rd, Valdosta (31601). Phone 229/244-8800; toll-free 800/426-7866;*

fax 229/244-6602. www.hamptoninn.com. 102 rooms, 2 story. Complimentary continental breakfast. Check-out noon. Outdoor pool. **$**

★ **LA QUINTA INN AND SUITES.** *1800 Club House Dr, Valdosta (31601). Phone 229/247-7755; toll-free 800/531-5900; fax 229/245-1359. www.laquinta. com.* 121 rooms, 2 story. Complimentary continental breakfast. Check-out noon. Outdoor pool, whirlpool. Business center. **$**

Restaurants

★ ★ **CHARLIE TRIPPER'S.** *4479 N Valdosta Rd, Valdosta (31602). Phone 229/247-0366; fax 229/244-5367. www.charlie-trippers.com.* American menu. Dinner. Closed Sun-Mon; holidays. Bar. **$$$**

★ ★ **MOM & DAD'S.** *3840 N Valdosta Rd, Valdosta (31602). Phone 229/333-0848; fax 229/247-8167.* Italian menu. Dinner. Closed Sun-Mon; holidays. Bar. Children's menu. **$$**

Washington (B-3)

See also Athens

Settled 1769
Population 4,295
Elevation 618 ft
Area Code 706
Zip 30673
Information Washington-Wilkes Chamber of Commerce, 25 East Sq, Box 661; phone 706/678-2013
Web Site www.washingtonwilkes.org

The first city incorporated in the name of George Washington, it was the site of the Confederacy's last cabinet meeting (May 5, 1865) and the home of the South's first woman newspaper editor (Sarah Hillhouse of *The Monitor,* who printed editorials about the weather). Natives refer to this town as "Washington-Wilkes" (it is in Wilkes County) to distinguish it from the nation's capital.

Settlers first built a stockade called Heard's Fort. Elijah Clark led them in resistance to British troops, enabling patriots to hold Wilkes County when the rest of Georgia fell in 1779 (Kettle Creek Battleground). The last Confederate cabinet meeting convened in the Heard Building with President Davis and 14 officials on May 5, 1865. On June 4, Union soldiers seized $100,000 of the $500,000 in gold remaining in the Confederate Treasury. Legend persists that the rest of the gold (not recovered when Davis was captured at Irwinville) is buried in or near Washington.

What to See and Do

Alexander H. Stephens State Park. *456 Alexander St N, Crawfordville (30631). 19 miles SW on GA 47 to Crawfordville, then 1/2 mile N. Phone 706/456-2602.* In 1,190-acre park is Liberty Hall (Circa 1830), restored house of A. H. Stephens, Vice President of the Confederacy; Confederate Museum (Tues-Sat, also Sun afternoons; closed Thanksgiving, Dec 25; fee). Fishing, boating, rentals; nature trails, picnicking, camping. Contact Superintendent, PO Box 283, Crawfordville 30631.

Callaway Plantation. *2160 Lexington Rd, Washington (30673). 5 miles W on Hwy 78. Phone 706/678-7060.* This complete working plantation complex includes a red brick Greek Revival mansion (1869); a gray frame "Federal plainstyle" house (circa 1790) with period furnishings; a hewn log kitchen (circa 1785) with utensils; and agricultural equipment. RV parking (hookups). (Tues-Sat 10 am-5 pm, Sun 12:30-3:30 pm; closed holidays) **$**

Courthouse Square. On square are historic markers noting last cabinet meeting of Confederacy; inscription of first land-grant record; capstone from cotton factory (1811); World War II Memorial; Hill House (circa 1784), first property owned by a woman in NE Georgia; and a Vietnam Memorial.

Elijah Clark State Park. *2959 McCormick Hwy, Washington. 23 miles NE on Hwy 378, on the western shore of Clark Hill Lake. Phone 706/359-3458.* The park includes a log cabin museum with colonial life demonstrations, as well as opportunities for swimming beach, water-skiing, fishing, and boating (ramp). Nature trails, picnicking, camping, cottages.

J. Strom Thurmond Dam and Lake. *Lincolnton. 16 miles NE on Hwy 378 to Lincolnton, then S on Hwy 47, E on Hwy 150. Phone toll-free 800/533-3478.* Swimming, fishing, boating (ramps); hiking, picnicking, camping (year-round; fee). For more information, contact the Resource Manager's Office (E end of dam), Thurmond Lake, Rte 1, Box 12, Clarks Hill, SC 29821.

Kettle Creek Battleground. *8 miles SW on Kettle Creek, off Hwy 44.* Marker indicates site of a decisive battle of Revolutionary War.

Robert Toombs House State Historic Site. *216 E Robert Toombs Ave, Washington (30673). Phone 706/678-2226; fax 706/678-7515.* (1797) Restored residence of unreconstructed Confederate statesman and soldier. Frame Federal-era house with Greek Revival portico; period furniture, exhibits, video. Contact the Superintendent, PO Box 605. (Tues-Sat 9 am-5 pm, Sun from 2 pm; closed holidays) **$**

Washington-Wilkes Historical Museum. *308 E Robert Toombs Ave, Washington (30673). Phone 706/678-2105.* Located in white frame, antebellum house (circa 1836), the museum includes period furnishings, Civil War mementos, Native American items, earthenware. (Tues-Sat 10 am-5 pm, also Sun 12:30-3:30 pm; closed Jan 1, Thanksgiving, Dec 25) **$**

Limited-Service Hotel

★ **JAMESON INN.** *115 Ann Denard Dr, Washington (30673). Phone 706/678-7925; fax 706/678-7962.* 43 rooms, 2 story. Complimentary continental breakfast. Check-out 11 am. **$**

Waycross (E-4)

See also Okefenokee Swamp

Settled 1818
Population 15,333
Elevation 135 ft
Area Code 912
Zip 31501
Information Tourism and Conference Bureau, 315 Plant Ave Suite B, 31501; phone 912/283-3742
Web Site www.okefenokeetourism.com

The name Waycross reflects the town's strategic location at the intersection of nine railroads and five highways. Situated at the edge of the Okefenokee Swamp, the town's early settlers put up blockhouses to protect themselves from local Native Americans. The production of naval stores and the marketing of furs were of prime importance before Okefenokee became a national wildlife refuge. Today the economy of Waycross is based on a diversity of industries, including timber, railroad, mobile homes, and tourism.

What to See and Do

Laura S. Walker State Park. *5653 Laura Walker Rd, Waycross. 9 miles SE via Hwy 82 and Hwy 177. Phone 912/287-4900.* Within the park is a 106-acre lake.

Swimming pool, water-skiing, fishing, boating; golfing, picnicking, playground, camping.

Okefenokee Heritage Center. *1460 N Augusta Ave, Waycross (31503). Phone 912/285-4260.* Exhibits on Okefenokee area history; art gallery with changing exhibits; social science room with exhibit on Native Americans of southern Georgia; 1912 train depot and railroad cars; turn-of-the-century print shop; nature trails; Power House building; 1840s pioneer house. (Tues-Sat 10 am-5 pm, Sun from 1 pm; closed holidays) **$**

Southern Forest World. *1440 N Augusta Ave, Waycross (31503).* Exhibits, with audiovisual displays, detail development and history of forestry in the South; logging locomotive, 38-foot model of a loblolly pine, giant cypress tree. Nature trails. (Tues-Sat; closed holidays) **$**

Special Event

Pogofest. Parade, exhibits, barbecue. Apr.

Limited-Service Hotel

★ ★ **HOLIDAY INN.** *1725 Memorial Dr, Waycross (31501). Phone 912/283-4490; toll-free 800/465-4329; fax 912/283-4490. www.holiday-inn.com.* 148 rooms, 2 story. Pets accepted; fee. Complimentary full breakfast. Check-out noon. Restaurant, bar. Fitness room. Outdoor pool. Airport transportation available. **$**
⬛🧍⬛

Winder (B-2)

See also Athens, Atlanta, Norcross

Population 10,201
Elevation 984 ft
Area Code 770
Zip 30680
Information Barrow County Chamber of Commerce, 6 Porter St, PO Box 456; phone 770/867-9444
Web Site www.barrowchamber.com

What to See and Do

Fort Yargo State Park. *210 S Broad St, Winder (30680). 1 mile S via Hwy 81. Phone 770/867-3489.* The park is named for a fort of hand-hewn pine logs built during Native American uprisings in the 1790s. Swimming, beach, fishing, boating, and canoeing (rentals); nature trails, picnicking, camping.

At the north end is

> **Will-A-Way Recreation Area.** *Phone 770/867-6123.* Designed to benefit disabled persons. Swimming pool, fishing, boating; nature trails, picnicking, camping area for disabled and special chairs for water access.

Limited-Service Hotel

★ **DEER ACRES INN.** *802 N Broad St, Monroe (30656). Phone 770/267-3666; fax 770/267-7189.* 45 rooms, 2 story. Complimentary continental breakfast. Check-in 11 am, check-out 11 am. Outdoor pool. **$**

North Carolina

North Carolina, besides being a wonderful place for a vacation, is a cross-section of America—a state of magnificent variety with three distinctive regions: the coast, the heartland, and the mountains. Its elevation ranges from sea level to 6,684 feet atop Mount Mitchell in the Black Mountain Range of the Appalachians. It has descendants of English, German, Scottish, Irish, and African immigrants. It has Quakers, Moravians, Episcopalians, and Calvinists. It produces two-thirds of our flue-cured tobacco, as well as cotton, peanuts, and vegetables on its farms. Fabrics, furniture, and many other products are made in its factories. It also has one of the finest state university systems in the nation with campuses at Chapel Hill, Raleigh, Greensboro, Charlotte, Asheville, and Wilmington.

Population: 6,628,637
Area: 48,843 square miles
Elevation: 0-6,684 feet
Peak: Mount Mitchell (Yancey County)
Entered Union: Twelfth of original 13 states (November 21, 1789)
Capital: Raleigh
Motto: To be rather than to seem
Nickname: Tar Heel State, Old North State
Flower: American Dogwood
Bird: Cardinal
Tree: Pine
Fair: October in Raleigh
Time Zone: Eastern
Web Site: www.visitnc.com
Fun Facts: North Carolina is the largest producer of sweet potatoes in the country.

In 1585, the first English settlement was unsuccessfully started on Roanoke Island. Another attempt at settlement was made in 1587—but the colony disappeared, leaving only the crudely scratched word "CROATOAN" on a tree—perhaps referring to the Croatan Indians who may have killed the colonists or absorbed them into their own culture, leaving behind one of history's great mysteries. Here, in the Great Smoky Mountains, the Cherokees lived before the government drove them westward to Oklahoma over the Trail of Tears, on which one-third of them died. Descendants of many members of this tribe, who hid in the inaccessible rocky coves and forests, still live here. Some "mountain people," isolated, independent, still singing songs dating back to Elizabethan England, also live here. Few North Carolinians owned slaves, very few owned many, and, early on, the state accepted free blacks (in 1860 there were 30,463) as a part of the community.

Citizens take pride in being called "Tar Heels." During the Civil War, North Carolinians returning from the front were taunted by a troop from another state who had "retreated" a good deal earlier. The Carolinians declared that Jefferson Davis had decided to bring up all the tar from North Carolina to use on the heels of the other regiment to make them "stick better in the next fight." General Lee, hearing of the incident, said, "God bless the Tar Heel boys."

Individualist and democratic from the beginning, this state refused to ratify the Constitution until the Bill of Rights had been added. In 1860 its western citizens strongly supported the Union. It did not join the Confederate States of America until after Fort Sumter had been fired upon and Lincoln had called for volunteers. Its independence was then challenged, and it furnished one-fifth of the soldiers of

Calendar Highlights

APRIL

Greater Greensboro Chrysler Classic Golf Tournament *(Greensboro). For more information, contact the Convention and Visitors Bureau, phone 336/379-1570.* Top golfers compete for more than $1.8 million on the PGA circuit.

North Carolina Azalea Festival *(Wilmington). Phone 910/794-4650.* Garden and home tours, horse show, celebrity entertainers, pageants, parade, and a street fair.

Springfest *(Charlotte).* Three-day festival in uptown offers food and live entertainment.

MAY

Artsplosure Spring and Arts Festival *(Raleigh). Moore Square and City Market. Phone 919/832-8699.* Citywide celebration of the arts. Showcase for regional dance, music, and theater performances by nationally known artists; outdoor arts and crafts show; children's activities.

Gliding Spectacular *(Nags Head, Outer Banks). Phone toll-free 877/FLY-THIS.* Hang-gliding competition, novice through advanced. Spectacular flying and fun events.

JUNE

Rogallo Kite Festival *(Nags Head, Outer Banks). Phone toll-free 877/FLY-THIS.* Competition for homebuilt kites; stunt kite performances, demonstrations; kite auction.

"Singing on the Mountain" *(Linville). Phone toll-free 800/468-7325.* On the slopes of Grandfather Mountain. All-day program of modern and traditional gospel music featuring top groups and nationally known speakers. Concessions or bring your own food.

JULY

Mountain Dance and Folk Festival *(Asheville). Civic Center. Phone 828/257-4530 or toll-free 800/257-1300.* Folk songs and ballads. Finest of its kind for devotees of the five-string banjo, gut-string fiddle, clogging, and smooth dancing.

SEPTEMBER

Bull Durham Blues Festival *(Durham). Historic Durham Athletic Park. Phone 919/683-1709.* Celebrates the blues with performances held at the location where *Bull Durham* was filmed.

CenterFest *(Durham). Phone 919/560-2787.* Downtown. Two-day event with more than 250 artists and craftsmen; musicians, jugglers, and clowns; continuous entertainment from three stages.

OCTOBER

Southern Highland Craft Guild Fair *(Asheville). Civic Center. Phone 828/298-7928.* More than 175 craftsmen from nine Southern states exhibit and demonstrate their skills. Folk and contemporary entertainment daily.

State Fair *(Raleigh). State Fairgrounds. Phone 919/733-2145 or 919/821-7400.*

---

the Southern armies even though its population was only one-ninth of the Confederacy's. Eighty-four engagements (most of them small) were fought on its soil. Jealous of its rights, North Carolina resisted the authority of Confederate Army officers from Virginia and loudly protested many of the policies of Jefferson Davis, but its 125,000 men fought furiously, and 40,000 of them died for what they believed was right. For years after the Civil War, North Carolina was a poverty-stricken state, although it suffered less from the inroads of carpetbaggers than many of its neighbors did.

The state seems designed for vacationers. Beautiful mountains and flowering plants, lake and ocean swimming and boating, hunting and fishing, superb golf courses, old towns, festivals, pageantry, and parks are a few of the state's many attractions.

When to Go/Climate

North Carolina has the most varied climate of any state on the East Coast. Subtropical temperatures on the coast are contrasted by a medium continental climate in the western mountain areas. Fall is hurricane season along the coast; winter in the western mountains can be snowy and cold. Fall foliage is magnificent in September and October; March and April are marked by blooming dogwood and azaleas.

AVERAGE HIGH/LOW TEMPERATURES (°F)

Cape Hatteras National Seashore

Jan 52/37	**May** 74/60	**Sep** 81/68
Feb 53/38	**Jun** 81/68	**Oct** 72/58
Mar 60/44	**Jul** 85/72	**Nov** 65/49
Apr 67/51	**Aug** 85/72	**Dec** 57/41

Raleigh

Jan 49/29	**May** 79/55	**Sep** 81/61
Feb 53/31	**Jun** 85/64	**Oct** 72/48
Mar 62/39	**Jul** 88/68	**Nov** 63/40
Apr 72/46	**Aug** 87/68	**Dec** 53/32

Parks and Recreation

Water-related activities, hiking, riding, various other sports, picnicking, and visitor centers, as well as camping, are available in many of North Carolina's parks. Parks are open daily: June-Aug, 8 am-9 pm; Apr-May and Sept to 8 pm; Mar and Oct to 7 pm; Nov-Feb to 6 pm. Most parks have picnicking and hiking. Swimming ($3; 6-12, $2; under 3, free) and concessions open Memorial Day-Labor Day. Admission and parking free (excluding reservoirs; $4); canoe and boat rentals ($3/hour for the first hour, $1/hour thereafter); fishing. Campgrounds: open all year, limited facilities in winter; family of six for $12/day; hookups $5 more; primitive sites $8/day; youth group tent camping $1/person ($8 minimum). Senior citizen discounts offered. Dogs on leash only. Campgrounds are on first come, first served basis; reservations are allowed for minimum of seven days, maximum of 14 days.

Information, including a comprehensive brochure, may be obtained from the Division of Parks and Recreation, Department of Environment, Health, and Natural Resources, 1615 MSC Raleigh 27699-1615; phone 919/733-7275 or 919/733-4181.

FISHING AND HUNTING

Nonresident fishing license: $30; daily license: $10; three-day license: $15. Nonresident six-day license: $25; basic hunting license: $40. Nonresident trapping license: $100. Waterfowl stamp (mandatory): $10.

For latest regulations, contact License Section, Wildlife Resources Commission, Archdale Building, 512 N Salisbury St, Raleigh 27604-1188; phone 919/662-4370.

Driving Information

Safety belts are mandatory for all persons in the front seat of a vehicle. Children under 6 years anywhere in a vehicle must be in an approved child passenger restraint system; ages 3-6 may use a regulation safety belt; children under 3 years must use an approved child passenger restraint system. For further information, phone 919/733-7952.

INTERSTATE HIGHWAY SYSTEM

The following alphabetical listing of North Carolina towns listed in this book shows that these cities are within 10 miles of the indicated interstate highways. Check a highway map for the nearest exit.

Highway Number	Cities/Towns within 10 Miles
Interstate 26	Asheville, Hendersonville, Tryon.
Interstate 40	Asheville, Burlington, Durham, Greensboro, Hickory, Maggie Valley, Marion, Morganton, Raleigh, Statesville, Waynesville, Wilmington, Winston-Salem.
Interstate 77	Charlotte, Cornelius, Statesville.
Interstate 85	Burlington, Charlotte, Concord, Durham, Gastonia, Greensboro, Henderson, High Point, Lexington, Salisbury.
Interstate 95	Dunn, Fayetteville, Lumberton, Roanoke Rapids, Rocky Mount, Smithfield, Wilson.

Additional Visitor Information

The North Carolina Gazetteer, by William S. Powell (University of North Carolina Press, Chapel Hill, 1968) lists more than 20,000 entries that will enable the reader to find any place in the state, as well as

THE OUTER BANKS

North Carolina has two coasts: the mainland coast, which runs along a wide expanse of tidal rivers, estuaries, and marshlands; and the Atlantic coast, which follows a series of barrier islands with shifting dunes, exotic wildlife, and live oaks misshapen by fierce winds (hurricane season runs from June through November). From Nags Head to Morehead City, a 75-mile stretch of these narrow barrier islands are protected as the Cape Hatteras National Seashore, constituting the largest stretch of undeveloped coastline on the Eastern Seaboard. A scenic drive from the Virginia state line to Morehead City takes drivers along the 200 miles of highway linking these islands. Start on Highway 168 at the Virginia border, 22 miles south of Norfolk. Highway 168 proceeds south and then merges with Highway 158 in Barco. Continue south across the Wright Memorial Bridge to the Outer Banks. Your first stop will be in Kitty Hawk, home to the Wright Brothers National Memorial (phone 919/441-7430). The memorial commemorates the first powered airplane flight, which took place on December 17, 1903, off the Highway 158 bypass south of town. Also in Kitty Hawk, a National Park Service ranger station distributes maps of the national seashore, marking places to hike, bike, and camp. Pick up the Highway 12 "Beach Road" by jogging east off the central highway to reach the popular resort of Nags Head, 6 miles south of Kitty Hawk. The most developed of the Outer Bank towns, Nags Head offers a wide range of lodging and dining choices for visitors. The

beach road and bypass merge a few miles south of Nags Head at Whalebone Junction. Just east on Highway 64, a 5-mile detour takes you to the Fort Raleigh National Historic Site on Roanoke Island (phone 252/473-5772), where they tell the story of the "Lost Colony" of Roanoke, the first English settlement in North America. The colony at Roanoke was founded in 1585, but within a few years, the colonists had disappeared without a trace, creating one of our nations greatest unsolved mysteries. South of Whalebone, Highway 12 becomes the central route south along the islands. The route leads 50 miles south past pristine beaches and old fishing villages and around Cape Hatteras. (Another visitor center is west of the cape around Buxton.) A ferry transports cars across the narrow inlet between Hatteras Island and Ocracoke Island, where the highway resumes for another 14 miles south to Ocracoke. Downtown Ocracoke makes a pleasant stop for a stroll. You'll find many fine restaurants, cafés, and inns, and bike rentals abound near the small harbor. There's a visitor center across from the ferry landing. From the dock, ferries take two different routes east across the Pamlico Sound: one ferry heads north to Swan Quarter, while the other travels south to Cedar Island. Either route is about 50 miles from Highway 17, the old Atlantic Coast Highway, which can lead you back north toward Virginia or south toward South Carolina. Reservations are recommended for either ferry route (phone toll-free 800/BY-FERRY). **(Approximately 200 miles)**

information about size, history, and derivation of name. The Travel and Tourism Division, 301 N Wilmington, Raleigh 27601, phone toll-free 800/VISIT-NC, has free travel information, including brochures.

North Carolina Welcome Center locations are I-85 N, Box 156, Norlina 27563; I-85 S, Box 830, Kings Mountain 28086; I-95 N, Box 52, Roanoke Rapids 27870; I-40, Box 809, Waynesville 28786; I-95 S, Box 518, Rowland 28383; I-26, Box 249, Columbus 28722; I-77 N, Box 1066, Dobson 27017; and I-77 S, Box 410724, Charlotte 28241-0724.

Albemarle (B-5)

See also Concord

Founded 1857
Population 15,680
Elevation 455 ft
Area Code 704
Zip 28001
Information Stanly County Chamber of Commerce, 116 E North St, PO Box 909, 28002; phone 704/982-8116
Web Site www.stanleychamber.org

Albemarle is in the gently rolling hills of the Uwharrie Mountains, in the Piedmont section of the state. It manufactures textiles, aircraft tires, automotive parts, and aluminum.

What to See and Do

Cotton Patch Gold Mine. *41697 Gurley Rd, Albemarle. 3 miles W off Hwy 740.* Phone 704/463-5797. Prospecting; concessions, picnic facilities. Camping (hookups). (Wed-Sun) **$$$**

Morrow Mountain State Park. *740 Morrow Mt Rd, Albemarle. 7 miles E off Hwy 740.* Phone 704/982-4402. Approximately 4,700 acres of hilly forested terrain, touched on two sides by Lake Tillery. Swimming pool, bathhouse, fishing, boating (rentals, launching). Natural history museum. Nature trails, hiking, riding. Picnic facilities, concessions. Camping (no hookups); six cabins, families only (Mar-Nov; advance reservations required).

Stanly Museum and Visitor Center. *245 E Main St, Albemarle.* Phone 704/986-3777. Originally built as a three-room log cabin in the 1850s, the Snuggs House has been enlarged and houses period artifacts. Research room. (Tues-Sat; also weekends by appointment; closed holidays) Also on lot is Marks House, town's oldest building (1850s) once used as residence/law office. **FREE**

Town Creek Indian Mound State\Historic Site. *509 Town Creek Mound Rd, Albemarle . 11 miles S on Hwy 52, then 12 miles E on Hwy 731 to Town Creek Mound Rd.* Phone 910/439-6802. Reconstructed 14th-century Native American ceremonial center with stockade, temples, and mortuary. Visitor center, audiovisual shows, exhibits (Tues-Sun; closed holidays in winter). Picnic area. **FREE**

Asheboro (B-5)

See also Greensboro, High Point, Lexington

Founded 1779
Population 21,672
Elevation 844 ft
Area Code 336
Zip 27203
Information Asheboro-Randolph Chamber of Commerce, 317 E Dixie Dr, PO Box 4774; phone 336/626-2626
Web Site chamber.asheboro.com

Situated in the agriculturally and industrially rich Piedmont and the timber-covered Uwharrie Mountains, Asheboro has served as the seat of Randolph County for over a century. Planked roads, covered bridges, and the waters of the Deep and Uwharrie rivers provided the impetus for industrial development late in the 19th century. Asheboro is in the heart of North Carolina's pottery-making country.

What to See and Do

North Carolina Z|oological Park. *4401 Zoo Pkwy, Asheboro (27205). 6 miles S on Hwy 159.* Phone toll-free 800/488-0444. www.nczoo.org. The nation's first natural habitat zoo. North American region exhibits span more than 200 acres; African habitats cover more than 300 acres and feature nine outdoor exhibits; Forest Aviary. (Apr-Sept: daily 9 am-5 pm; Oct-Mar: daily 9 am-4 pm; closed Dec 25) **$$**

Seagrove Area Potteries. *Seagrove (27341). 10 miles S on Hwy 73/74.* Phone 336/626-0364. More than 80 artists practice traditional hand-turning of pottery. Shops. **FREE**

Special Event

Asheboro Fall Festival. *Downtown Asheboro.* Phone 336/629-0399. Arts, crafts, food, parade, music, entertainment. First weekend in Oct.

Asheville (B-2)

See also Brevard, Burnsville, Hendersonville, Maggie Valley, Waynesville

Settled 1794
Population 68,889
Elevation 2,134 ft
Area Code 828
Information Convention and Visitors Bureau, 36 Montford, 28802-1010; phone 828/258-6101 or toll-free 800/257-1300
Web Site www.exploreasheville.com

Thomas Wolfe came from Asheville, the seat of Buncombe County, as did the expression "bunkum" (nonsense). A local congressman, when asked why he had been so evasive during a masterful oration in which he said nothing, replied, "I did it for Buncombe." Wolfe wrote often of his hill-rimmed home, shrewdly observant of the people and life of Asheville.

Angels in Asheville

Asheville, the capital of North Carolina's beautiful mountain region, is best known for the glamorous Biltmore Estate south of town. By comparison, downtown Asheville seems rather homespun. In fact, its most notorious landmark, the house where the novelist Thomas Wolfe grew up, is positively down at the heels, preserved that way to remain true to its description in Wolfe's most famous novel, *Look Homeward, Angel*, a thinly disguised portrait of Asheville.

The heart of downtown Asheville is Pack Square, at the intersection of Broadway and Patton Avenue. Around the square lie City Hall; the county courthouse; a library; and Pack Place (phone 828/257-4500), the citys education, art, and science center. Pack Place contains a variety of museums, performing arts venues, galleries, and shops. Children favor the health museum here, which features a talking transparent woman and a skeletal cyclist, as well as the mineral and gem museum. The YMI Cultural Center highlights African-American history.

The southwest corner of the square bears the statue of an angel, looking homeward, marking the spot where the angel appears in Wolfe's famous story.

This was also the site of the stonecutting shop once run by Wolfe's father. Head two blocks north to Walnut Street, turn east on Walnut, then north again on Spruce to find the house where Thomas Wolfe lived from 1900-1920, known locally as the "Old Kentucky Home." Wolfe fans recognize the ordinary white frame house, however, as the "Dixieland" boardinghouse so vividly described in his most famous novel. The house is now officially designated the Thomas Wolfe National Historic Site (48 Spruce Street, phone 828/253-8304), and the visitor center screens a film about the author's life.

Return to Broadway and head back south toward Pack Square to find Bean Street, on Broadway at College, for a cup of coffee. Go east on College a block to the T. S. Morrison Emporium (39 North Lexington), which continues to ply its trade in penny candy, toys, tools, and housewares—just as it has since it opened in 1891. For more entertainment, head back to Broadway, which turns into Biltmore Avenue south of Pack Square. Hear nationally known musicians at the Be Here Now club (5 Biltmore Avenue) or take in an art flick at the Fine Arts Cinema across the street.

Asheville is a vacation headquarters in the Blue Ridge Mountains, as well as a marketing and industrial city. It is the North Carolina city closest to the Great Smoky Mountains National Park (see) and attracts many of the park's visitors with its annual mountain fetes, local handicrafts, and summer theaters. It is the headquarters for the Uwharrie National Forest, Pisgah National Forest (see BREVARD), Nantahala National Forest (see FRANKLIN), and Croatan National Forest (see NEW BERN). The Blue Ridge Parkway brings many travelers to Asheville on their way south from the Shenandoah Valley of Virginia.

For further information about Croatan, Nantahala, Pisgah, and Uwharrie national forests, contact the US Forest Service, phone 828/257-4202.

What to See and Do

Asheville Community Theatre. *35 E Walnut St, Asheville. Phone 828/254-1320.* Comedies, musicals, and dramas performed throughout the year. **$$$$**

⭐ **Biltmore Estate.** *1 Approach Rd, Asheville (28801). S on Hwy 25, three blocks N of I-40 exit 50. Phone 828/255-1333; toll-free 800/624-1575. www.biltmore. com.* The 8,000-acre country estate includes 75 acres of formal gardens, numerous varieities of azaleas and roses, and the 250-room chateau (85 rooms are open for viewing), which is the largest house ever built in the New World. George W. Vanderbilt commissioned Richard Morris Hunt to design the house, which was begun in 1890 and finished in 1895. Materials and furnishings were brought from many parts of Europe and Asia; a private railroad was built to transport them to the site. Life here was living in the grand manner. Vanderbilt employed Gifford Pinchot, later governor of Pennsylvania and famous for forestry and conservation achievements, to manage his forests. Biltmore was the site of the first US forestry school. Much of the original estate in now part of Pisgah National Forest. Tours of the estate include gardens, conservatory, and winery facilities; tasting. Four restaurants on grounds. Guidebook (fee) is recommended. (Daily; closed Thanksgiving, Dec 25) **$$$$**

Biltmore Homespun Shops. *111 Grovewood Rd, Asheville (28804). Near Macon Ave, 2 miles NE. Phone 828/253-7651.* At the turn of the century, Mrs. George W. Vanderbilt opened a school to keep alive the skills of hand-dyeing, spinning, and hand-weaving wool into cloth. The business still has the old machinery and handlooms. An antique automobile museum and the North Carolina Homespun Museum are in an 11-acre park adjoining Grove Park Inn Resort. (Apr-Oct, daily; rest of year, Mon-Sat; closed Thanksgiving, Dec 25) **FREE**

Botanical Gardens at Asheville. *151 WT Weaver Blvd, Asheville (28804). On campus of University of North Carolina. Phone 828/252-5190. www.ashevillebotanicalgardens.org.* A 10-acre tract with thousands of flowers, trees, and shrubs native to southern Appalachia; 125-year-old "dog trot" log cabin. (Daily dawn-dusk) Visitor center, gift shop (Mar-mid-Nov daily 9:30 am-4 pm). **FREE**

Chimney Rock Park. *25 miles SE on Hwy 74, just past jct Hwys 64, 9. Phone 828/625-9611; toll-free 800/277-9611. www.chimneyrockpark.com.* The towering granite monolith Chimney Rock affords a 75-mile view; four hiking trails lead to the 404-foot Hickory Nut Falls, Moonshiner's Cave, Devil's Head balancing rock, and Nature's Showerbath. Trails, stairs, and catwalks; picnic areas, playground; nature center; observation lounge with snack bar, gift shop. 26-story elevator shaft through granite. (Daily 8:30 am-6 pm, weather permitting; closed Jan 1, Thanksgiving, Dec 25) **$$$**

Folk Art Center. *382 Blue Ridge Pkwy, Asheville. 5 miles E on US 70, then 1/2 miles N on the Blue Ridge Pkwy to Milepost 382. Phone 828/298-7928.* Home of the Southern Highland Craft Guild. Stone and timber structure; home of Blue Ridge Pkwy info center; craft exhibits, demonstrations, workshops, related programs. (Daily; closed Jan 1, Thanksgiving, Dec 25) **FREE**

Graves of Thomas Wolfe (1900-1938) and O. Henry (William Sydney Porter) (1862-1910). *Riverside Cemetery, 53 Birch St, Asheville (28801). Entrance on birch St off Pearson Dr.*

Mount Mitchell State Park. *Burnsville. 27 miles NE on Blue Ridge Pkwy, then 5 miles N on Hwy 128.* (See LITTLE SWITZERLAND)

Nantahala Outdoor Center. *13077 Hwy 19 W, Bryson City (28713). Phone toll-free 800/232-7238. www.noc.com.* Offers various trips on the Nantahala, French Broad, Ocee, Pigeon, Nolichucky, and Chattooga rivers ranging from 1 1/2 to 6 hours. **$$$$**

Pack Place Education, Arts, and Science Center. *2 S Pack Sq, Asheville (28801). Phone 828/257-4500. www.packplace.org.* This 92,000-square-foot complex features multiple museums and exhibit galleries as well as a state-of-the-art theater. A permanent exhibit entitled "Here Is the Square" relates the history of Asheville. Restaurant (lunch only); gift shop. (Tues-Sat 10 am-5 pm, Sun 1-5 pm; closed Jan 1, Thanksgiving, Dec 24-25) Includes

Asheville Art Museum. *2 S Pack Sq, Asheville (28801). Phone 828/253-3227.* Permanent collection and changing exhibits. (Tues-Sat 10 am-5 pm, Fri until 8 pm, Sun 1-5 pm) **$$**

Colburn Gem and Mineral Museum. *2 S Pack Sq, Asheville (28801). Phone 828/254-7162.* Displays of 1,000 minerals from around the world; includes information on mineral locations in the state. (Tues-Sun) **$**

Diana Wortham Theatre. *2 S Pack Sq, Asheville (28801). Phone 828/257-4530.* This 500-seat theater hosts local, regional, and national companies.

The Health Adventure. *2 S Pack Sq, Asheville (28801). Phone 828/254-6373.* Extensive collection of imaginative, educational exhibits on the human body, including a talking transparent woman, a bicycle-pedaling skeleton, and an opportunity to hear the sound of your own heartbeat. Also on premises is Creative PlaySpace, a special exhibit for young children. **$$**

YMI Cultural Center. *39 S Market St, Asheville (28801). Phone 828/252-4614.* Galleries featuring permanent and rotating exhibts of African-American art. (Tues-Sun) **$**

Thomas Wolfe Memorial. *52 N Market, Asheville. Phone 828/253-8304.* The state maintains the Wolfe boardinghouse as a literary shrine, restored and furnished to appear as it did in 1916. In Asheville it is known as the "Old Kentucky Home." In *Look Homeward, Angel* it was referred to as "Dixieland"; Asheville was "Altamont." Visitor center with exhibit. (Tues-Sun; closed holidays) **$**

Western North Carolina Nature Center. *75 Gashes Creek Rd, Asheville. 3 miles E on Hwy 81. Phone*

828/298-5600. Live animals, children's petting barn-yard, natural history exhibits, nature trail, educational programs. (Daily) **$$**

Wolf Laurel Ski Resort. *Valley View Cir, Mars Hill. 27 miles N off Hwy 23. Phone 828/689-4111; toll-free 800/817-4111. www.skiwolflaurel.com.* Quad, double chair lifts, tow rope; patrol, school, rentals; snow making; restaurant, lodge. Longest run 3/4 mile; vertical drop 700 feet. (Mid-Dec-mid-Mar, daily) **$$$$**

Zebulon B. Vance Birthplace State Historic Site. *911 Reems Creek Rd, Weaverville (28787). 9 miles N on Hwy 19/23, exit New-Stock Rd, then 6 miles N on Reems Creek Rd. Phone 828/645-6706.* Log house (reconstructed 1961) and outbuildings on site where Civil War governor of North Carolina grew up. Honors Vance family, which was deeply involved with early history of state. Visitor center, exhibits. Picnic area. (Apr-Oct, Mon-Fri; rest of year, Tues-Fri) **FREE**

Special Events

Mountain Dance and Folk Festival. *2 S Pack Sq, Asheville (28801). Phone 828/257-4530.* Diana Wortham Theater. Folk songs and ballads. Finest of its kind for devotees of the five-string banjo, gut-string fiddle, clogging, and smooth dancing.

Shakespeare in the Park. *246 Cumberland Ave, Asheville (22880). Phone 828/254-4540.* Montford Park Players. Weekends early June-late Aug.

Shindig-on-the-Green. *College and Spruce sts, Asheville. In front of County Plaza. Phone 828/258-6109.* Mountain fiddling, dulcimer players, singing, square dancing. Sat evenings, July-Labor Day, except the last weekend in July.

Southern Highland Craft Guild Fair. *Civic Center, 87 Haywood St, Asheville (28801). Just off I-240. Phone 828/298-7928.* More than 175 craftsmen from nine Southern states exhibit and demonstrate their skills. Folk and contemporary entertainment daily. Mid-July and mid-Oct.

World Gee Haw Whimmy Diddle Competition. *Folk Art Center, 382 Blue Ridge Pkwy, Asheville (28805). Phone 828/298-7928.* Competitions, demonstrations, storytelling, music, dance. Third weekend in Sept.

Limited-Service Hotels

★ ★ **BEST WESTERN BILTMORE.** *22 Woodfin St, Asheville (28801). Phone 828/253-1851; toll-free*

888/854-6897; fax 828/252-9205. www.bestwestern. com/ashevillebiltmore. 154 rooms, 5 story. Pets accepted; fee. Complimentary continental breakfast. Check-in 3 pm, check-out noon. Restaurant. Fitness room. Outdoor pool. **$**
🕴 🏊

★ **COMFORT INN.** *890 Brevard Rd, Asheville (28806). Phone 828/665-4000; toll-free 800/228-5150; fax 828/665-9082. www.choicehotels.com.* 125 rooms, 5 story, all suites. Pets accepted; fee. Complimentary continental breakfast. Check-in 3 pm, check-out noon. Fitness room. Outdoor pool, whirlpool. Airport transportation available. **$**
🐾 🕴 🏊

★ **DAYS INN.** *1435 Tunnel Rd, Asheville (28805). Phone 828/298-4000; fax 828/210-0197. www.daysinn. com.* 84 rooms, 3 story. Pets accepted, some restrictions; fee. Complimentary continental breakfast. Check-in 3 pm, check-out noon. Outdoor pool. **$**
🅱 🐾 🏊

★ ★ **DOUBLETREE HOTEL.** *115 Hendersonville Rd, Asheville (28803). Phone 828/274-1800; fax 828/274-1802. www.biltmoreasheville.doubletree.com.* 160 rooms, 5 story. Check-in 3 pm, check-out 11 am. Restaurant, bar. Fitness room. Outdoor pool, whirlpool. **$**
🕴 🏊

★ **FOREST MANOR INN.** *866 Hendersonville Rd, Asheville (28803). Phone 828/274-3531; toll-free 800/866-3531; fax 828/274-3531. www.forestmanorinn. com.* 21 rooms. Closed Jan-Apr 1. Complimentary continental breakfast. Check-in 2:30 pm, check-out 11 am. Outdoor pool. On 4 wooded acres. **$**
🅱 🏊

Full-Service Hotels

★ ★ ★ **HAYWOOD PARK HOTEL & PROMENADE.** *1 Battery Park Ave, Asheville (28801). Phone 828/252-2522; toll-free 800/228-2522; fax 828/253-0481. www.haywoodpark.com.* This all-suite hotel has been elegantly furnished and decorated with polished brass, warm oak, and Spanish marble. There are 33 rooms available, each with fine furnishings, a wet bar, and a bathroom that features either a garden tub or Jacuzzi. 33 rooms, 4 story. Check-in 2 pm, check-out noon. High-speed Internet access. Restaurant, bar. Fitness room. **$$**
🕴

★ ★ ★ ★ **INN ON BILTMORE ESTATE.** *1 Antler Hill Rd, Asheville (28803). Phone 828/225-1660; toll-*

free 866/336-1240; fax 828/225-1629. www.biltmore.com. The Inn on Biltmore Estate provides guests with world-class accommodations in the heart of an American landmark. This gracious hotel is uniquely situated within the historic Vanderbilt Biltmore Estate, offering guests the chance to gambol the grounds that Vanderbilt and his illustrious guests once roamed. While ensconced in the resplendent accommodations, guests can easily imagine what it was like to visit this American aristocrat. Set against the backdrop of the smoky Blue Ridge Mountains, the property is rife with recreational opportunities, from carriage and horseback rides to river float trips on the French Broad River with a view of the estate. The hotels distinguished character extends to its dining establishments. The Dining Room showcases refined regional cooking; afternoon tea is a daily tradition; and the Lobby Lounge is ideal for informal meals. 213 rooms, 7 story. Check-in 4 pm, check-out 11 am. Restaurant, bar. Fitness room. Outdoor pool, whirlpool. Airport transportation available. **$$$**

★ ★ ★ **RENAISSANCE HOTEL.** 31 Woodfin St, Asheville (28801). Phone 828/252-8211; fax 828/236-9616. www.renaissancehotels.com. This property is centrally located around the area's attractions. Visitors will find plenty of shopping in the local mall, a farmers' market, and other complexes in the area. Also nearby are art galleries, a civic center, and more. 281 rooms, 12 story. Check-in 3 pm, check-out noon. High-speed Internet access. Restaurant, bar. Fitness room. Outdoor pool. Business center. **$**

Full-Service Resort

★ ★ ★ **THE GROVE PARK INN RESORT & SPA.** 290 Macon Ave, Asheville (28804). Phone 828/252-2711; fax 828/252-6102. Since 1913, health enthusiasts and those seeking respite from the everyday have made their way to the historic Grove Park Inn. This spectacular destination, set in the shadow of Asheville's Blue Ridge Mountains, is the ultimate year-round resort. Light-filled and spacious, the guest rooms pay homage to the Arts & Crafts aesthetic with Mission-style furnishings and decorative accents. Active-minded travelers choose from the 18-hole Donald Ross-designed golf course, a superb tennis facility, and a state-of-the-art fitness center, while relaxation-seekers head for the 40,000-square-foot, grotto-like spa. The spa, crafted out of natural rock, is a delight for the senses with cascading waterfalls and golden sunlight streaming in through the skylights. From hydro bath treatments to flotation body masques, it exceeds the expectations of its well-traveled visitors. 510 rooms, 10 story. Check-in 4 pm, check-out 11 am. Six restaurants, two bars. Children's activity center. Fitness room, spa. Indoor pool, outdoor pool, whirlpool. Golf, 18 holes. Tennis. Business center. **$$$**

Full-Service Inn

★ ★ ★ **RICHMOND HILL INN.** 87 Richmond Hill Dr, Asheville (28806). Phone 828/252-7313; toll-free 888/742-4554; fax 828/252-8726. www.richmond-hillinn.com. Visitors retreat to Richmond Hill Inn for quiet reflection and repose. Once the private home of an influential politician, this Victorian estate now welcomes guests seeking a break from quotidian concerns. The Queen Anne-style mansion and croquet cottages are magically set among 6 acres of formal gardens, meandering brooks, and a 9-foot waterfall. Tranquility is paramount here; strolling the grounds often leads to the discovery of a favorite hidden corner. Located on the upper floors of the mansion and in the cottages, the rooms and suites reflect the traditions of the late 19th century. Guests enjoy delicious country breakfasts before heading out to explore Asheville's historic treasures or traverse its great outdoors, and a lovely afternoon tea awaits their return. Gabrielle's décor is firmly rooted in the Victorian era, but the kitchen proudly embraces modern times with its sensational continental menu. 36 rooms, 3 story. Complimentary full breakfast. Check-in 3 pm, check-out 11 am. Restaurant. Fitness room. **$$$**

Specialty Lodgings

ALBEMARLE INN. 86 Edgemont Rd, Asheville (28801). Phone 828/255-0027; toll-free 800/621-7435; fax 828/236-3397. www.albemarleinn.com. This dramatic, majestic home, with enormous white pillars and beautiful, well-manicured gardens, offers guests an elegant and luxurious experience. Rooms are thoughtfully decorated and feature 360-thread count lace sheets, Egyptian cotton towels, and clawfoot tubs. The dining area features wicker tables set with crisp white tablecloths, lillies, and floral place mats and napkins. Complimentary wine and hors d'oeuvres are served nightly on the veranda in summer, and around the fireplace in winter. 11 rooms, 3 story. Children over 12 years only. Complimentary full breakfast. Check-in 3 pm, check-out 11 am. **$$**

APPLEWOOD MANOR INN. *62 Cumberland Cir, Asheville (28801). Phone 828/254-2244; toll-free 800/442-2197; fax 828/254-0899. www.applewoodmanor.com.* 4 rooms, 2 story. Children over 12 years only. Complimentary full breakfast. Check-in 3 pm. Check-out 11 am. Colonial turn-of-the-century home built in 1910; antiques. **$**

THE BEAUFORT HOUSE VICTORIAN INN. *61 N Liberty St, Asheville (28801). Phone 828/254-8334; toll-free 800/261-2221. www.beauforthouse.com.* Experience Victorian afternoon tea, gourmet breakfasts, and elegant guest rooms in the former home of Charleton Heston. The mansion is surrounded by 2 acres of beautifully landscaped grounds complete with 5,000 flowers. 11 rooms, 4 story. Children over 10 years only. Complimentary full breakfast. Check-in 4 pm. Check-out 11 am. **$**

CEDAR CREST VICTORIAN INN. *674 Biltmore Ave, Asheville (28803). Phone 828/252-1389; toll-free 800/252-0310. www.cedarcrestinn.com* Dating from 1891, the luxurious mansion that has been transformed into this romantic inn is listed on the National Register of Historic Places. Of particular note is the ornate woodwork on the first floor and the Victorian gardens, lush with dogwood and rhododendrons. 12 rooms, 3 story. Children over 10 years only. Complimentary full breakfast. Check-in 3 pm, check-out 11 am. **$$**

LION AND THE ROSE. *276 Montford Ave, Asheville (28801). Phone 828/255-7673; toll-free 800/546-6988; fax 828/285-89810. www.lion-rose.com.* This elegantly restored Georgian mansion is nestled in beautifully landscaped gardens. The innkeepers' personal attention and impeccable attention to detail add to its quaint romantic feel. For those who appreciate antiques, this inn will not disappoint. 5 rooms, 3 story. Children over 12 years only. Complimentary full breakfast. Check-in 3 pm, check-out 11 am. **$$**

THE OLD REYNOLDS MANSION. *100 Reynolds Heights, Asheville (28804). Phone 828/254-0496; toll-free 800/709-0496; fax 828/254-8229. www.oldreynoldsmansion.com.* 10 rooms, 3 story. Closed Sun-Thurs in Nov-June. Complimentary full breakfast. Check-in 3 pm, check-out 11 am. Outdoor pool. Antebellum mansion (1855) on hill overlooking mountains, verandas. **$**

OWL'S NEST. *2630 Smokey Park Hwy, Candler (28715). Phone 828/665-8325; toll-free 800/665-8868; fax 828/667-2539. www.engadineinn.com.* Located just outside of Asheville, this inn was built in 1885 and has been restored to its original Victorian grandeur. The wraparound porches and mountain views are exquisite, and dining by the fireplace is cozy and relaxing. 5 rooms, 3 story. Children over 12 years only. Complimentary full breakfast. Check-in 3 pm, check-out 11 am. **$**

Restaurants

★ ★ ★ **FLYING FROG CAFE.** *1 Battery Park Ave, Asheville (28801). Phone 828/254-9411; fax 828/225-4858. www.flyingfrogcafe.com.* International menu. Dinner. Closed Tues. Bar. Casual attire. **$$**

★ ★ ★ **GABRIELLE'S.** *87 Richmond Hill Dr, Asheville (28806). Phone 828/252-7313; toll-free 800/545-9238; fax 828/252-8726. www.richmondhillinn.com.* Every meal at Gabrielle's is an extraordinary dining experience. Savor the American cuisine in one of Gabrielle's two elegant dining rooms. While the formal service mirrors the elegance of a bygone era, the food combines old and new into a sumptuous culinary and visual experience. Only the finest ingredients, grown locally, are used to create the seasonally changing menu. American menu. Dinner. Closed Jan; Tues. Business casual attire. Reservations recommended. Valet parking. Outdoor seating. **$$$**

★ ★ **GREENERY.** *148 Tunnel Rd, Asheville (28803). Phone 828/253-2809; fax 828/254-0645. www.greenery-restaurant.com.* American menu. Dinner. Closed Jan 1. Bar. Children's menu. Casual attire. **$$**

★ ★ ★ **HORIZONS.** *290 Macon Ave, Asheville (28804). Phone 828/252-2711; toll-free 800/438-5800; fax 828/252-6442. www.groveparkinn.com.* Located in the Grove Park Inn, this restaurant has sweeping views, elegant décor, and innovative classic cuisine. An extensive wine list will provide a wonderful accompaniment to any meal. International menu. Dinner. Bar. Jacket required. Reservations recommended. Valet parking. **$$$$**

★ ★ **LA PAZ.** *10 Biltmore Plz, Asheville (28803). Phone 828/277-8779; fax 828/277-1974. www.lapaz.com.* Mexican menu. Lunch, dinner. Bar. Children's menu. Casual attire. Outdoor seating. **$$**

★ ★ **THE MARKET PLACE RESTAURANT & WINE BAR.** *20 Wall St, Asheville (28801). Phone 828/252-4162; fax 828/253-3120. www.marketplace-*

restaurant.com. American, French menu. Dinner. Closed Sun; Jan-Feb, Sun in Mar-Sept, Nov-Dec; holidays. Bar. Casual attire. Outdoor seating. **$$$**

Banner Elk (A-3)

See also Blowing Rock, Boone, Linville

Population 811
Elevation 3,739 ft
Area Code 828
Zip 28604
Information Chamber of Commerce, PO Box 335; phone 828/898-5605
Web Site www.avery.com

What to See and Do

Grandfather Mountain. *2050 Blowing Rock Hwy, Banner Elk (28646). 3 miles N via Hwy 221.* (see LINVILLE).

Ski Beech. *1007 Beech Mountain Pkwy, Banner Elk (28604). 3 miles N on Hwy 184. Phone 828/387-2011; toll-free 800/438-2093. www.skibeech.com.* Quad chairlift, six double chair lifts, J-bar, rope tow; patrol, school, rentals; snowmaking, ice skating; restaurant, cafeteria; nursery, shopping. Vertical drop 830 feet. Night skiing. (Mid-Nov-mid-Mar, daily) **$$$$**

Sugar Mountain. *1009 Sugar Mountain Dr, Banner Elk. Off Hwy 184. Phone 828/898-4521. www.skisugar.com.* Triple, four double chair lifts, three surface lifts; patrol, school, rentals, snowmaking; children's program; lodging, cafeteria; nursery. Vertical drop 1,200 feet. (Mid-Nov-mid-Mar, daily)

Specialty Lodging

ARCHER'S MOUNTAIN. *2489 Beech Mountain Pkwy, Banner Elk (28604). Phone 828/898-9004; toll-free 888/827-6155; fax 828/898-9007. www.archersinn.com.* Nestled high on the side of Beech Mountain, this rustic inn features wood-burning fireplaces and porches complete with mountain views and rocking chairs. Enjoy breakfast, lunch, or dinner (or all three) at the inns restaurant and take a break from the bustle of the world below. 15 rooms, 2 story. Complimentary full breakfast. Check-in 3 pm, check-out 11 am. Restaurant. **$**

Restaurant

★ ★ **JACKALOPE'S VIEW.** *2489 Beech Mountain Pkwy, Banner Elk (28604). Phone 828/898-9004; toll-free 888/827-6155; fax 828/898-9007. www.archersinn. com.* American menu. Dinner. Closed Mon; Dec 25. Bar. Casual attire. Outdoor seating. **$$$**

Beaufort (C-9)

See also Morehead City

Population 3,771
Elevation 7 ft
Area Code 252
Zip 28516
Information Crystal Coast Visitors Center, 3409 Arendell St, PO Box 1406, Morehead City 28557; phone 252/726-8148 or toll-free 800/SUNNY-NC
Web Site www.crystalcoastnc.org

Beaufort, dating from the colonial era, is a seaport with more than 125 historic houses and sites.

What to See and Do

Beaufort Historic Site. *138 Turner St, Beaufort (28516). Phone 252/728-5225. www.historicbeaufort. com.* Old burying ground, 1829 restored old jail, restored houses (1767-1830), courthouse (circa 1796), apothecary shop, art gallery, and gift shop. Obtain additional information and a self-guided walking tour map from the Safrit Historical Center, 138 Turner St, PO Box 363. (Mon-Sat; closed holidays) **$$$**

Cape Lookout National Seashore. *131 Charles St, Harkers Island (28531). Phone 252/728-2250. www.nps. gov/calo.* This unit of the National Park System, on the outer banks of North Carolina, extends 55 miles south from Ocracoke Inlet and includes unspoiled barrier islands. There are no roads or bridges; access is by boat only (fee). Catch a ferry from Beaufort, Harkers Island, Davis, Atlantic, or Ocracoke (Apr-Nov). Excellent fishing and shell collecting; primitive camping; interpretive programs (seasonal). The lighthouse (1859) at Cape Lookout is still operational. Visitor center (daily 8:30 am-4:30 pm; closed Jan 1, Dec 25).

North Carolina Maritime Museum and Watercraft Center. *315 Front St, Beaufort . Phone 252/728-7317.* Natural and maritime history exhibits, field trips; special programs in maritime and coastal natural history. (Daily; closed Jan 1, Thanksgiving, Dec 25) **FREE**

Special Events

Beaufort by the Sea Music Festival. Late Apr.

Old Homes Tour and Antiques Show. *138 Turner St, Beaufort (28516). Phone 252/728-5225.* Private homes and historic public buildings; Carteret County Militia; bus tours and tours of old burying ground; historical crafts. Sponsored by the Beaufort Historical Association, Inc., PO Box 1709. Last weekend in June.

Specialty Lodgings

PECAN TREE INN. *116 Queen St, Beaufort (28516). Phone 252/728-6733. www.pecantree.com.* 7 rooms, 2 story. Children over 10 years only. Complimentary continental breakfast. Check-in 3 pm, check-out 11 am. Restaurant. **$**
🅳

THE CEDARS INN. *305 Front St, Beaufort (28516). Phone 252/728-7036; fax 252/728-1685. www.cedarsinn.com.* 11 rooms, 2 story. Children over 10 years only. Complimentary full breakfast. Check-in 3 pm, check-out 11 am. Restaurant. Beach. **$**
🅳

Belhaven (B-9)

Population 1,968

Specialty Lodging

RIVER FOREST MANOR. *738 E Main St, Belhaven (27810). Phone 252/943-2151; toll-free 800/346-2151; fax 252/943-6628. www.riverforestmanor.com.* 9 rooms, 2 story. Complimentary continental breakfast. Check-in 1 pm, check-out 11 am. Restaurant. Outdoor pool, whirlpool. Tennis. Airport transportation available. View of river. Golf carts available for touring town. **$**
🌊 🎿

Restaurant

★ ★ **RIVER FOREST MANOR.** *738 E Main St, Belhaven (27810). Phone 252/943-2151; fax 252/943-6628. www.riverforestmanor.com.* American menu. Dinner, Sun brunch. Bar. **$$**

Blowing Rock (A-3)

See also Banner Elk, Boone, Linville

Founded 1889
Population 1,418
Elevation 4,000 ft
Area Code 828
Zip 28605
Information Chamber of Commerce, PO Box 406; phone 828/295-7851 or toll-free 800/295-7851
Web Site www.blowingrock.com

On the Blue Ridge Parkway, Blowing Rock was named, based on Native American folklore, for the cliff near town where lightweight objects thrown outward are swept back to their origin by the wind. It has been a resort area for more than 100 years; a wide variety of recreational facilities and shops can be found nearby.

What to See and Do

Appalachian Ski Mountain. *940 Ski Mt Rd, Blowing Rock. 3 miles N on Hwy 321, near Blue Ridge Pkwy intersection. Phone 828/295-7828; toll-free 800/322-2373. www.appskimtn.com.* Two quad, double chair lift, rope tow, handle-pull tow; patrol; French-Swiss Ski College, Ski-Wee children's program; equipment rentals; snowmaking; restaurant; eight runs, longest run 2,700 feet, vertical drop 400 feet. (Dec-mid-Mar; closed Dec 24 evening-Dec 25) Night skiing (all slopes lighted); half-day and twilight rates. **$$$$**

Blowing Rock. *432 Rock Rd, Blowing Rock. 2 miles SE on Hwy 321. Phone 828/295-7111.* Cliff (4,000 feet) hangs over Johns River Gorge 2,000-3,000 feet below. Scenic views of Grandfather, Grandmother, Table Rock, and Hawksbill mountains. Observation deck. Gift shop. (Daily) **$$**

Julian Price Memorial Park. *Blue Ridge Pkwy, Blowing Rock. SW via Hwy 221 and Blue Ridge Pkwy. Phone 828/963-5911.* Boating (hand-powered only, rentals). Picnicking. Camping (trailer facilities, no hookups; June-Oct only; fee). Amphitheater; evening interpretive programs (May-Oct). Park open year-round (weather permitting). **FREE**

Moses H. Cone Memorial Park. *Blue Ridge Pkwy, Blowing Rock. On Blue Ridge Pkwy. Phone 828/295-7591.* Former summer estate of textile magnate. Bridle paths, two lakes, 25 miles of hiking and cross-country skiing trails. (May-Oct, daily) **FREE**

Parkway Craft Center. *Blue Ridge Pkwy, Blowing Rock. Blue Ridge Pkwy mile post 294.* Phone 828/295-7938. Demonstrations of weaving, wood carving, pottery, jewelry making, other crafts. (May-Oct, daily) Handcrafted items for sale. **FREE**

Mystery Hill. *129 Mystery Hill Ln, Blowing Rock (28605). N on Hwy 321.* Phone 828/264-2792. Educational exhibits explore science, optical illusion, and natural phenomena. Features Mystery House, Hall of Mystery, and BubbleRama. Gift shop. (Daily; closed Thanksgiving, Dec 25) **$$**

Tweetsie Railroad. *296 Tweetsie Railroad, Blowing Rock. 4 miles N on Hwy 321.* Phone 828/264-9061. *www.tweetsierailroad.com.* A 3-mile excursion, with mock holdup and raid, on old narrow-gauge railroad; Western town with variety show at Tweetsie Palace; country fair, petting zoo; craft village; chair lift to Mouse Mountain Picnic Area. (May-Oct, limited hours) **$$$$**

Special Event

Tour of Homes. Phone 828/295-7851. Fourth Fri in July.

Limited-Service Hotels

★ **ALPINE VILLAGE INN.** *297 Sunset Dr, Blowing Rock (28605).* Phone 828/295-7206. *www.alpine-village-inn.com.* 17 rooms. Pets accepted; fee. Check-in 2 pm, check-out 11 am. **$**
🐾

★ **BLOWING ROCK INN.** *788 N Main St, Blowing Rock (28605).* Phone 828/295-7921; fax 828/295-9948. *www.blowingrockinn.com.* 24 rooms. Closed mid-Dec-Mar. Check-in 2 pm, check-out 11 am. **$**
🅳

★ **CLIFF DWELLERS INN.** *116 Lakeview Terrace, Blowing Rock (28605).* Phone 828/295-3121; toll-free 800/322-7380; fax 828/295-3121. *www.cliffdwellers.com.* 21 rooms, 3 story. Check-in 3 pm, check-out 11 am. View of mountains. **$**
🅳

Full-Service Resorts

★ ★ **CHETOLA RESORT AT BLOWING ROCK.** *N Main St, Blowing Rock (28605).* Phone 828/295-5500; toll-free 800/243-8652; fax 828/295-5529. *www.chetola.com.* This Blue Ridge Mountains retreat, bordered on one side by a national forest, leaves guests wanting for nothing. The Highlands Sports and Recreation Center, conference center, professional tennis courts, and other amenities are all located within the resort's 78-acre property. 104 rooms, 3 story. Check-in 3 pm, check-out 11 am. High-speed Internet access, wireless Internet access. Three restaurants, bar. Children's activity center. Fitness room, fitness classes available. Indoor pool, whirlpool. Tennis. Business center. **$$**
🧍 🛏 🎿 🏃

★ ★ ★ **HOUND EARS CLUB.** *328 Shulls Mills Rd, Blowing Rock (28607).* Phone 828/963-4321; fax 828/963-8030. *www.houndears.com.* Set atop the Blue Ridge Mountains, this small, secluded resort is a relaxing respite. The golf course was designed by George Cobb, and the views are breathtaking. 28 rooms, 2 story. Check-in 3 pm, check-out 11 am. Two restaurants, three bars. Children's activity center. Fitness room, fitness classes available. Outdoor pool. Golf, 18 holes. Tennis. **$$**
🧍 🛏 🏌 🎿

Full-Service Inn

★ ★ ★ **CRIPPEN'S COUNTRY INN.** *239 Sunset Dr, Blowing Rock (28605).* Phone 828/295-3487; toll-free 877/295-3487; fax 828/295-0388. *www.crippens.com.* 8 rooms, 3 story. Children over 12 permitted. Complimentary continental breakfast. Check-in 3 pm, check-out 11 am. High-speed Internet access, wireless Internet access. Restaurant. Bar. Business center. **$**
🅳 🏃

Specialty Lodgings

INN AT RAGGED GARDENS. *203 Sunset, Blowing Rock (28605).* Phone 828/295-9703. *www.ragged-gardens.com.* The historic vacation village of Blowing Rock in the Appalachian high country is home to this elegant 19th-century inn. Original stone pillars and floors, period furnishings, individually decorated rooms, and a full acre of beautifully landscaped property beckon. 11 rooms, 3 story. Children over 12 years only. Complimentary full breakfast. Check-in 3 pm, check-out 11 am. **$$**
🅳

MAPLE LODGE. *152 Sunset Dr, Blowing Rock (28605).* Phone 828/295-3331; fax 828/295-9986. *www.maplelodge.net.* 11 rooms, 2 story. Closed Jan-Feb. Children over 12 years only. Complimentary full breakfast. Check-in 3 pm, check-out 11 am. **$$**
🅳

Restaurants

★ ★ **BEST CELLAR.** *202 Sunset Dr, Blowing Rock (28605). Phone 828/295-3466; fax 828/295-4772.* International/Fusion menu. Dinner. Bar. Casual attire. Reservations recommended. Valet parking. Outdoor seating. **$$$**

★ ★ ★ **CRIPPEN'S.** *239 Sunset Dr, Blowing Rock (28605). Phone 828/295-3487; toll-free 877/295-3487; fax 828/295-0388. www.crippens.com.* This spacious, cozy dining room is located in the Crippens Country Inn (see). American menu. Dinner. Closed holidays; also Super Bowl Sun. Bar. Children's menu. Business casual attire. Reservations recommended. Outdoor seating. **$$$**

Boone (A-3)

See also Banner Elk, Blowing Rock, Jefferson, Linville

Settled 1772
Population 13,472
Elevation 3,266 ft
Area Code 828
Zip 28607
Information Convention and Visitors Bureau, 208 Howard St, 28607-4032; phone 828/262-3516 or toll-free 800/852-9506; or North Carolina High Country Host, 1700 Blowing Rock Rd; phone 828/264-1299 or toll-free 800/438-7500
Web Site www.visitboonenc.com

Boone, the seat of Watauga County, was named for Daniel Boone, who had a cabin and hunted here in the 1760s. This "Heart of the High Country" sprawls over a long valley, which provides a natural pass through the hills. Watauga County boasts several industrial firms providing its economic base, in addition to tourism, agriculture, and Appalachian State University. Mountain crafts are featured in a variety of craft fairs, festivals, and shops.

What to See and Do

Appalachian State University. *287 River St, Boone (28608). Atop Blue Ridge Mountains. Phone 828/262-2000. www.appstate.edu.* (1899) (13,000 students) Offers 90 undergraduate and 12 graduate majors. Dark Sky Observatory. (See also SPECIAL EVENTS) Opposite is

Appalachian Cultural Museum. *University Hall Dr, Blowing Rock (28605). Phone 828/262-3117.* This regional museum presents an overview of the Blue Ridge area. Exhibits include Native American artifacts, plus exhibit on Daniel Boone, mountain music, and the environment. (Tues-Sat 10 am-5 pm, Sun 1-5 pm) **$**

Daniel Boone Native Gardens. *651 Horn in the West Dr, Boone (28607). 1 mile E off Hwy 421, adjacent to Daniel Boone Amphitheatre. Phone 828/264-6390.* (see SPECIAL EVENTS) **$**

Special Events

An Appalachian Summer. *Appalachian State University, 287 River St, Boone (28608). Phone toll-free 800/841-2787.* Concerts, drama, art exhibits.

Horn in the West. *Daniel Boone Amphitheatre, Boone. 1 mile E off Hwy 421. Phone 828/264-2120.* Outdoor drama depicts Daniel Boone and settlers of the mountains during the Revolutionary War. Tues-Sun evenings. Mid-June-mid-Aug.

Limited-Service Hotel

★ **HOLIDAY INN EXPRESS.** *1943 Blowing Rock Rd, Boone (28607). Phone 828/264-2451; toll-free 800/465-4329; fax 828/265-3861. www.holiday-inn.com.* 138 rooms, 2 story. Complimentary continental breakfast. Check-in 3 pm, check-out 11 am. Fitness room. Outdoor pool. **$**

Specialty Lodging

LOVILL HOUSE INN. *404 Old Bristol Rd, Boone (28607). Phone 828/264-4204; toll-free 800/849-9466. www.lovillhouseinn.com.* Captain E. F. Lovill, a Civil War hero and state senator, built this traditional farmhouse in 1875. The 11-acre, wooded property offers a charming wraparound porch with plenty of rocking chairs. 6 rooms, 2 story. Closed Mar; two weeks in Sept. Children over 12 years only. Complimentary full breakfast. Check-in 3 pm, check-out 11 am. **$$**

Restaurants

★ **DAN'L BOONE INN.** *130 Hardin St, Boone (28607). Phone 828/264-8657. www.danlbooneinn.com.* American menu. Breakfast, lunch, dinner. Casual attire. No credit cards accepted. **$**

★ ★ **MAKOTO.** *2124 Blowing Rock Rd, Boone (28607). Phone 828/264-7976; fax 828/262-0579. www. makotos-boone.com.* Japanese menu. Lunch, dinner. Bar. Children's menu. Casual attire. Outdoor seating. **$$**

Brevard (B-2)

See also Asheville, Hendersonville

Settled 1861
Population 6,789
Elevation 2,230 ft
Area Code 828
Zip 28712
Information Chamber of Commerce, 35 W Main St, PO Box 589; phone 828/883-3700 or toll-free 800/648-4523
Web Site www.brevardnc.com

An industrial and mountain resort center near the entrance to Pisgah National Forest, Brevard has several industries, including Sterling Diagnostic Imaging, Inc, Coats American Company, and the Ecusta division of P. H. Glatfelter.

What to See and Do

Mount Pisgah. *Blue Ridge Pkwy, Hwy 276 to within 1 mile of the summit; a trail takes visitors the rest of the way.* 5,749 feet.

Pisgah National Forest. *160A Zillicoa St, Asheville (28802). Phone 828/257-4200. www.cs.unca.edu/nfsnc.* A 499,816-acre, four-district forest. The Cradle of Forestry Visitor Center (summer, daily; fee) is at the site of the first forestry school in the US. The forest surrounds Mount Mitchell State Park (see LITTLE SWITZERLAND), which contains the highest point in the US east of the Mississippi (6,684 feet). Linville Gorge Wilderness is 10,975 acres of precipitous cliffs and cascading falls (permit required May-Oct for overnight camping; contact the Grandfather Ranger District in MARION). Wiseman's View looks into Linville Gorge. Shining Rock Wilderness contains 18,500 acres of rugged alpine scenery. The forest shares with Cherokee National Forest in Tennessee the 6,286-foot Roan Mountain, with its purple rhododendron and stands of spruce and fir. Swimming; good fishing for trout, bass, and perch; hunting for deer, bears, and small game; miles of hiking and riding trails; picnic sites; campgrounds (fee).

Special Events

Festival of the Arts. *349 Andante Ln, Brevard (28712). Phone 828/884-2787.* Music, crafts, art, sporting events. Second week in July.

Summer Festival of Music. *Brevard Music Center. Whittington-Pfhol Auditorium, 349 Andante Ln, Brevard (28712). Phone 828/884-2011.* More than 50 programs presented, including symphonic, choral, chamber, recital; musical comedy and operatic performances; guest artists. Late June-early Aug. Mon-Sat evenings, Sun afternoons.

Twilight Tour on Main. *Main St, Brevard (28712). Phone 828/884-3278.* Horse and buggy rides, entertainment, refreshments. First Sat in Dec.

Limited-Service Hotel

★ **HOLIDAY INN EXPRESS HOTEL & SUITES.** *1570 Asheville Hwy, Brevard (28712). Phone 828/862-8900; fax 828/862-8909. www.brevardexpress. com.* 63 rooms. Check-in 3 pm, check-out 11 am. Outdoor pool. **$**
⌨

Bryson City (B-2)

See also Cherokee, Fontana Dam, Franklin, Great Smoky Mountains National Park, Robbinsville, Waynesville

Population 1,411
Elevation 1,736 ft
Area Code 828
Zip 28713
2 Chamber of Commerce, PO Box 509-W; phone 828/488-3681 or toll-free 800/867-9246
Web Site www.greatsmokies.com

At the confluence of the Little Tennessee and Tuckasegee rivers, Bryson City is also at the entrance to Great Smoky Mountains National Park. Fontana Lake, part of the TVA system, is nearby. Industries include textiles.

What to See and Do

Great Smoky Mountains Railway. *119 Front St, Dillsboro (28725). Phone toll-free 800/872-4681. www. gsmr.com.* Half-day rail excursions to Nantahala Gorge aboard diesel or steam locomotives. One-hour layover; view whitewater sports. Special excursions throughout the year (fees and dates vary). (Mar-Nov) **$$$$**

Whitewater rafting. Rolling Thunder River Company. *10 miles W on Hwy 19 S/74 W, at Nantahala Gorge. Phone 828/488-2030; toll-free 800/344-5838. www.rollingthunderriverco.com.* Guided raft, canoe, and kayak trips through the Smoky Mountains; day and overnight. Reservations recommended. For information and fees, contact Box 88, Almond 28702. (Apr-Oct)

Specialty Lodging

THE CHALET INN. *285 Lone Oak Dr, Whittier (28789). Phone 828/586-0251; toll-free 800/789-8024. www.chaletinn.com.* 6 rooms, 2 story. Children over 12 years only. Complimentary full breakfast. Check-in 3-8 pm, check-out 10:30 am. European ambience in the Blue Ridge Mountains. **$**

FOLKESTONE INN BED & BREAKFAST. *101 Folkestone Rd, Bryson City (28713). Phone 828/488-2730; toll-free 888/812-3385; fax 828/488-0722. www.folkestoneinn.com.* 10 rooms, 3 story. Pets accepted. Children over 10 years only. Complimentary full breakfast. Check-in 3 pm, check-out 11 am. Built in 1926; restored country farmhouse. **$**
🐾

Burlington (A-6)

See also Greensboro, High Point

Settled Circa 1700
Population 44,917
Elevation 656 ft
Area Code 336
Information Burlington/Alamance County Convention and Visitors Bureau, PO Drawer 519, 27216; phone 336/570-1444 or toll-free 800/637-3804
Web Site www.burlington-area-nc.org

In 1837, E. M. Holt converted his father's gristmill on Alamance Creek into a textile mill. The Alamance Mill produced the first commercially dyed plaids south of the Potomac, changing the face of the textile industry in the South.

What to See and Do

Alamance Battleground State Historic Site. *5803 S NC Hwy 62, Burlington (27215). 6 miles SW on Hwy 62. Phone 336/227-4785.* On May 16, 1771, a two-hour battle was fought here between the colonial militia under Royal Governor Tryon and about 2,000 rebellious "Regulators." The latter were defeated. Restored log house; visitor center, exhibits, audiovisual presentation; picnic area. (Mon-Sat; closed holidays) **FREE**

Alamance County Historical Museum. *4777 S Hwy 62, Burlington (27215). 5 miles S on Hwy 62. Phone 336/226-8254.* 19th-century house-museum depicts life of textile pioneer E. M. Holt. Period rooms, audiovisual presentations. Rotating exhibits feature antique clothing and toys, Native American artifacts, traditional pottery and local history pieces. Docent-guided tours. (Tues-Sun) **FREE**

Dentzel Menagerie Carousel. *7300 MacArthur Blvd, Burlington (27216). In City Park. Phone 336/222-5033.* (Circa 1910) Rare hand-carved carousel; restored. (Apr-late Aug, Tues-Sun; late Aug-Oct, weekends) **$**

Lake Cammack Park and Marina. *4790 Union Ridge Rd, Burlington (27217). Phone 336/421-3872.* An 800-acre city reservoir. Water-skiing, fishing, boating. Picnic area, playground. (Fri-Wed; days vary winter) **$$**

Special Events

Antiques Fair. Three-day event where antiques are sold and auctioned. Mar.

The Sword of Peace Summer Outdoor Drama. *301 Drama Rd, Snow Camp (27349). 18 miles SW via I-85, Liberty 49 S exit, then Hwy 49S and Hwy 1005 to Snow Camp. Phone toll-free 800/726-5115.* Repertory outdoor theater (evenings) and summer arts festival; 150-year-old and 200-year-old buildings converted into museums, craft gallery, and cane mill. Late June-late Aug. Thurs-Sat. Contact PO Box 535, Snow Camp 27349.

Limited-Service Hotel

★ **COMFORT INN.** *2701 Kirkpatrick Rd, Burlington (27215). Phone 336/584-4447; fax 336/585-1300.* 116 rooms, 4 story. Complimentary continental breakfast. Check-in 3 pm, check-out noon. Fitness room. Outdoor pool, whirlpool. **$**
🧍 🏊

Burnsville (B-3)

See also Asheville, Little Switzerland

Population 1,482
Elevation 2,814 ft
Area Code 828

Zip 28714
Information Yancey County Chamber of Commerce, 106 W Main St; phone 828/682-7413 or toll-free 800/948-1632
Web Site www.yanceychamber.com

A Ranger District office of the Pisgah National Forest (see BREVARD) is located here.

Special Events

Mount Mitchell Crafts Fair. *Town Sq, Burnsville.* First Fri and Sat in Aug.

Old Time Days. *Town Sq, Burnsville.* Late Sept.

Specialty Lodging

NU WRAY INN. *102 Town, Burnsville (28714).Phone 828/682-2329; toll-free 800/368-9729; fax 828/682-1113. www.nuwrayinn.com.* 26 rooms, 3 story. Pets accepted, some restrictions. Check-in 3 pm, check-out 11 am. Restaurant. **$**

Buxton (B-10)

See also Cape Hatteras National Seashore, Ocracoke

Population 3,250
Elevation 10 ft
Area Code 252
Zip 27920
Web Site www.outerbanks.org

This town is on Hatteras Island, part of the Outer Banks (see). It is surrounded by Cape Hatteras National Seashore (see).

Limited-Service Hotel

★ **COMFORT INN.** *Hwy 12 and Old Lighthouse Rd, Buxton (27920). Phone 252/995-6100; toll-free 800/424-6423; fax 252/995-5444. www.choicehotels. com.* 60 rooms, 2 story. Complimentary continental breakfast. Check-in 3 pm, check-out 11 am. Beach. Outdoor pool. **$**
🛏

Restaurant

★ **TIDES.** *Hwy 12, Buxton (27920). Phone 252/995-5988.* American menu. Breakfast, dinner. Closed Dec-Mar. **$$**

Cape Hatteras National Seashore

(B-10)

See also Buxton, Fort Raleigh National Historic Site, Hatteras, Kill Devil Hills, Nags Head, Ocracoke

Web Site www.nps.gov/caha

Enter from Cedar Island or Swan Quarter toll ferry. Reservations recommended. Free ferry from Ocracoke Island to Hatteras Island.

This thin strand stretches for 75 miles along the Outer Banks (see), threaded between the windy, pounding Atlantic and the shallow Pamlico Sound. Nags Head (see) is the northern limit of the recreational area, which has three sections (separated by inlets): Bodie (pronounced *body*, Hatteras (largest of the barrier islands), and Ocracoke (see), the most picturesque. Bounded on three sides by the park, but separate from it, are the villages of Rodanthe, Waves, Salvo, Avon, Buxton, Frisco, Hatteras, and Ocracoke. Although the area is noted for long expanses of sand beaches, wildflowers bloom most of the year. There are also stands of yaupon (holly), loblolly pine, and live oak. Several freshwater ponds are found on Bodie, Hatteras, and Ocracoke Islands. Many migratory and nonmigratory waterfowl winter here, including gadwalls, greater snow and Canada geese, loons, grebes, and herons.

There is an information station at Whalebone Junction (Memorial Day-Labor Day, daily), south of Nags Head. Near Bodie Island Lighthouse is a bird observation platform, a nature trail, and a visitor center (Good Friday-Columbus Day, daily) with natural history exhibits. There are also visitor centers with history exhibits at Ocracoke (same hours), Bodie Island Lighthouse (same hours), and the Cape Hatteras Lighthouse at Buxton (daily; closed Dec 25).

Sportfishing, boating, sailing, swimming (recommended only at protected beaches); picnicking and camping (fee), also waterfowl hunting in season under regulation.For further information, contact the Superintendent, Rte 1, Box 675, Manteo 27954; or phone the Hatteras Island Visitor Center, 252/995-4474.

Cashiers (C-2)

See also Franklin, Highlands

Population 196
Elevation 3,486 ft
Area Code 828
Zip 28717
Information Cashiers Area Chamber of Commerce, 202 Hwy 64 W, PO Box 238; phone 828/743-5191
Web Site www.cashiersnorthcarolina.com

High in the Blue Ridge Mountains, this well-known summer resort area offers scenic drives on twisting mountain roads, hiking trails, views, waterfalls, lake sports, fishing, and other recreational activities.

What to See and Do

Fairfield Sapphire Valley Ski Area. *4350 Hwy 64 W, Sapphire (28774). 3 miles E on Hwy 64. Phone 828/743-3441. www.skisapphire.com.* Chair lift, rope tow; patrol, school, snowmaking. Longest run 1,600 feet, vertical drop 200 feet. (Mid-Dec-mid-Mar, daily) Night skiing. Evenings, half-day rates. Other seasons: swimming, fishing, boating; hiking, horseback riding; golf, tennis; recreation center. Restaurants, inn. **$$$$**

Lake Thorpe. *5 miles N on Hwy 107.* Fishing, swimming, water-skiing. Boats may be rented at Glenville (on the lake) or launched from here.

Full-Service Resort

★ ★ ★ **HIGH HAMPTON INN AND COUNTRY CLUB.** *Hwy 107 S, Cashiers (28717). Phone 828/743-2411; toll-free 800/334-2551; fax 828/743-5991. www.highhamptoninn.com.* Nestled in the Blue Ridge Mountains, this 1,400-acre property boasts a private lake and a quiet, wooded landscape. Guests of the inn, private cottages, or colony homes stay busy with the inn's scenic golf course, six clay tennis courts, and hiking trails. 120 rooms, 3 story. Closed mid-Nov-Apr. Check-in 3 pm, check-out 1 pm. Two restaurants, bar. Children's activity center. Fitness room. Beach. Golf, 18 holes. Tennis. Airport transportation available. Business center. **$$**

Full-Service Inn

★ ★ ★ **THE GREYSTONE.** *Greystone Ln, Lake Toxaway (28747). Phone 828/966-4700; toll-free 800/824-5766; fax 828/862-5689. www.greystoneinn.com.* The main building of this historic inn was built in 1915 and welcomed Fords and Rockefellers to the natural beauty of the picturesque lake. Restored in 1985, the inn still pampers with individually decorated rooms, a full-service spa, and outdoor recreation. 33 rooms, 3 story. Complimentary full breakfast. Check-in 3 pm, check-out noon. Restaurant. Children's activity center. Fitness room. Beach. Outdoor pool. Golf. Tennis. **$$$**

Specialty Lodging

INNISFREE VICTORIAN INN. *108 Innisfree Dr, Glenville (28736). Phone 828/743-2946. www.innisfreeinn.com.* This inn and neighboring garden house is a wonderful place to visit whatever the season. The large, wraparound veranda is shaded by oak trees and faces Lake Glenville and the surrounding Blue Ridge Mountains. 10 rooms, 2 story. No children allowed. Complimentary full breakfast. Check-in 3-10 pm, check-out 11 am. **$$**

Chapel Hill (B-6)

See also Durham, Raleigh

Founded 1793
Population 48,715
Elevation 487 ft
Area Code 919
Information Chapel Hill-Carrboro Chamber of Commerce, 104 S Estes Dr, PO Box 2897, 27515; phone 919/967-7075
Web Site www.carolinachamber.org

The community of Chapel Hill is centered around the University of North Carolina, the oldest state university in the US. This school has been a leader in American education for more than 170 years and is now part of a "research triangle," together with Duke University at Durham and North Carolina State University at Raleigh. Despite heavy losses of faculty and students to the Civil War, the school remained open until the years of Reconstruction, 1870-1875. During the next decade, the university was reborn.

What to See and Do

Chapel of the Cross. *304 E Franklin St, Chapel Hill (27514). Adjacent to Morehead Planetarium. Phone 919/929-2193.* (1842-1848) Antebellum Gothic Revival Episcopal church. (Sun-Fri)

Horace Williams House. *610 E Rosemary St, Chapel Hill (27514). Phone 919/942-7818. www.chapelhill-preservation.com.* Historic house is home to the Chapel Hill Preservation Society; changing art exhibits, chamber music concerts. Guided tours. (Tues-Fri, also Sun afternoons; closed holidays and the first two weeks in Aug) **FREE**

North Carolina Botanical Garden. *15501 Old Mason Farm Rd, Chapel Hill . Phone 919/962-0522. www.ncbg.unc.edu.* Approximately 600 acres; variety of trees and plants of the southeastern US; wildflower areas, herb gardens. Nature trails. (Daily). **FREE**

University of North Carolina at Chapel Hill. *250 E Franklin St, Chapel Hill (27514). Phone 919/962-1630. www.unc.edu.* (1795) (Approximately 27,000 students) This institution, the first state university in the country, is on a 720-acre campus and has more than 200 buildings. On campus are

Coker Arboretum. *Cameron Ave and Raleigh St, Chapel Hill (27599). Phone 919/962-0522.* Covers 5 acres. Extensive collection of ornamental plants and shrubs.

Davie Poplar. *N of Old Well.* Ancient ivy-covered tree named for the "father of the university," William Richardson Davie; more than 200 years old.

Kenan Stadium. *Chapel Hill (27617). University of North Carolina at Chapel Hill, behind Bell Tower.* (1927) Seats 52,000; in a wooded natural bowl.

Memorial Hall. *Cameron Ave and South Rd, Chapel Hill (27514). Opposite New West.* (1930) White columns front this structure dedicated to war dead, honored alumni, and university benefactors. James K. Polk, class of 1818, has a commemorative tablet here. He graduated first in his class and became the 11th President of the US.

Morehead-Patterson Memorial Bell Tower. *Stadium Dr and South Rd, Chapel Hill (27514).* (1930) A 172-foot Italian Renaissance campanile; concert chimes. The 12 bells range in weight from 300 pounds to almost 2 tons. Popular tunes are rung daily.

Morehead Planetarium. *250 E Franklin St, Chapel Hill (27514). Phone 919/549-6863.* Offers indoor star-gazing, art gallery with permanent and changing exhibits, scientific exhibits; rare Zeiss instrument. Shows (daily; closed Dec 24-25). Rose garden has mammoth sundial showing time around the world. **$**

Old East. *Chapel Hill . E of Old Well.* Oldest state university building in the country; cornerstone laid in 1793. Matched by Old West (1823). Still being used as a residence hall.

Old Well. *Cameron Ave, Chapel Hill. In the center of campus.* Long the unofficial symbol of the university, this well was the only source of water here for nearly a century. The present "Greek temple" structure dates from 1897

Paul Green Theater. *South and Country Club rds, Chapel Hill (27514). Phone 919/962-7529.* (1978) PlayMakers Repertory Company. Named for one of the first dramatic arts students at the university. Green is known as the father of American outdoor drama. (Oct-May)

PlayMakers Theater. *Country Club and South rds, Chapel Hill (27514).* (1851) Greek Revival temple was designed as a combination library and ballroom.

South (Main) Building. *Cameron Ave and Raleigh St, Chapel Hill (27514). Opposite Old Well.* Cornerstone laid in 1798, but the building was not completed until 1814, during which time the boys lived inside the roofless walls in little huts. Future President James K. Polk lived here from 1814-1818.

Wilson Library. *South Rd and Stadium Dr, Chapel Hill (27514). Phone 919/962-0114.* Houses special collections. Includes North Carolina Collection Gallery; historic rooms, texts, and artifacts. Also here is the Southern Historical Collection, featuring manuscripts, rare books, and photographs (daily). Phone 919/962-0114.

Limited-Service Hotels

★ **BEST WESTERN UNIVERSITY INN.** *1310 Raleigh Rd, Chapel Hill (27517). Phone 919/932-3000; fax 919/968-6513. www.bestwestern.com.* This upscale motel sits on beautifully landscaped grounds and is located 1 mile from UNC-CH campus. Restaurant and Franklin Street for boutique shopping are also nearby. 84 rooms, 1 story. Complimentary continental breakfast. Check-in 3 pm, check-out 11 am. High-speed Internet access, wireless Internet access. Outdoor pool. **$**

★ **HAMPTON INN CHAPEL HILL.** *1740 Fordham Blvd, Chapel Hill (27514). Phone 919/968-3000; toll-free 800/426-7866; fax 919/929-0322. www.hamptoninn.com.* This Hampton Inn is located across the street from shopping and dining and between the Chapel Hill UNC and Duke campuses. The rooms feature pillowtop matresses, preprogrammed radios, and laptop tables. 121 rooms, 2 story. Complimentary continental breakfast. Check-in 3 pm, check-out noon. High-speed Internet access, wireless Internet access. Outdoor pool. Business center. **$**
🛏️ 🏃

★ ★ **HOLIDAY INN CHAPEL HILL.** *1301 N Fordham Blvd, Chapel Hill (27514). Phone 919/929-2171; toll-free 888/452-5765; fax 919/929-5736. www.hichapelhill.com.* If you're looking for a fun place to stay in Chapel Hill, look no further than this hotel. This property has what is called "Home of the Sports Experience." The lobby is painted in UNC colors, the front desk staff dress in referee uniforms, all types of sports equipment are displayed on the outside walls leading to the rooms, and the floors have blue foot prints with tar on the heel—for the UNC Tar Heels. Oh, and they offer hot chocolate and popcorn six nights a week—what else do you need? 134 rooms, 2 story. Pets accepted; fee. Check-in 3 pm, check-out noon. Wireless Internet access. Restaurant, bar. Fitness room. Outdoor pool. Business center. **$**
🐾 🏃 🛏️ 🏃

Full-Service Hotels

★ ★ ★ **THE CAROLINA INN.** *211 Pittsboro St, Chapel Hill (27516). Phone 919/933-2001; toll-free 800/962-8519; fax 919/918-2760. www.carolinainn.com.* Guests can enjoy the quiet village setting of Chapel Hill from this inn, which provides excellent accommodations. Set in the middle of the University of North Carolina Campus and around the corner from the Chapel Hill Medical Center, it is a short distance to art galleries, museums, charming shops, and fine restaurants. The entrance alludes to a feeling of Southern grandeur, and the red brick building has a Georgian Revival theme. Inside the inn, hardwood floors, oriental rugs, mahogany tables, palms, and fresh flowers add to the setting. 184 rooms, 3 story. Check-in 3 pm, check-out noon. High-speed Internet access, wireless Internet access. Restaurant, bar. Fitness room. Business center. **$$**
🏃 🏃

★ ★ ★ **SHERATON HOTEL.** *1 Europa Dr, Chapel Hill (27517). Phone 919/968-4900; toll-free 800/325-*
3535; fax 919/968-3520. www.sheratonchapelhill.com.* This ultramodern hotel is located on the main road connecting the Chapel Hill-UNC campus and Durham-Duke campus, and it is a short distance to Interstate 85 and the Research Triangle. The wraparound open lobby features marble floors and floor-to-ceiling windows looking out to the pool and water fountain. 168 rooms, 4 story. Check-in 3 pm, check-out noon. High-speed Internet access. Restaurant, bar. Fitness room. Outdoor pool. Business center. **$**
🏃 🛏️ 🏃

★ ★ ★ **SIENA HOTEL.** *1505 E Franklin St, Chapel Hill (27514). Phone 919/929-4000; toll-free 800/223-7379; fax 919/968-8527. www.sienahotel.com.* Southern hospitality and grand European styling make the Siena Hotel a favorite in Chapel Hill. This elegant hotel is a gracious home-away-from-home with its welcoming service and lavish ambience. The guest rooms and suites are tastefully appointed with fine Italian furnishings, rich fabrics, and unique decorative objects, while modern amenities ensure the highest levels of comfort. Guest privileges at the UNC golf course and nearby fitness center and spa are extended to hotel occupants, and business travelers appreciate the many thoughtful amenities created especially for them. Dining is of special note here, where Il Palio Ristorante charms visitors throughout the day with its bountiful breakfasts and delicious northern Italian-influenced lunch and dinner selections. 79 rooms, 4 story. Pets accepted. Check-in 4 pm, check-out noon. High-speed Internet access. Restaurant, bar. Business center. **$$**
🐾 🏃

Restaurants

★ **ALLEN & SON BARBEQUE.** *6203 Milhouse Rd, Chapel Hill (27514). Phone 919/942-7576; fax 919/942-7576.* This local's favorite barbecue restaurant is located in the country, about 10 miles outside of Chapel Hill. Families like the children's menu, outdoor seating, and no-frills décor which features pale gold walls with mounted deer heads, green-and-white checkered oilcloths, and wooden chairs. American menu. Lunch, dinner. Closed Sun-Mon; two weeks in summer, two weeks around Christmas. Children's menu. Casual attire. Outdoor seating. **$**

★ ★ ★ **AURORA.** *1350 Raleigh Rd, Chapel Hill (27514). Phone 919/942-2400; fax 919/929-5927. www.aurorarestaurant.com.* Northern Italian cuisine is featured at this quaint Chapel Hill restaurant. Aurora is located minutes from I-40 and just 1 mile from the UNC campus. The décor has a neat appearance featuring hardwood floors, light painted walls, white tablecloths, and a display kitchen so you could watch the chef prepare your meal. The glowing embers of the hickory/oak-burning fire adds to the meal preparation and the decor. Italian menu. Dinner, brunch. Bar. Children's menu. Business casual attire. Reservations recommended. Outdoor seating. **$$$**

★ ★ ★ **CAROLINA CROSSROADS.** *211 Pittsboro St, Chapel Hill (27516). Phone 919/933-2001; toll-free 800/962-8519; fax 919/962-3400. www.carolinainn. com.* Set in the historic Carolina Inn, the Carolina Crossroads restaurant is a picture-perfect example of Southern hospitality. The dining room seems primed for an elegant evening soiree, with hardwood floors, mahogany chairs, crystal chandeliers, oil paintings, blue-and-white floral tapestry chairs, and dramatic fabric drapes. The menu often strikes delicious notes, with regional dishes incorporating local, seasonal ingredients prepared in a progressive American style. You'll find everything from a classic North Carolina pulled pork sandwich (a necessary food group in these parts) to more ladylike dishes like salmon with grilled acorn squash in white-wine butter sauce, part of the chef's nightly six-course tasting menu. For a chance to feel like Scarlet O'Hara, settle in for afternoon tea or cocktails at the restaurants old-world bar, complete with cozy, tufted leather chairs and a blazing fireplace. American menu. Breakfast, lunch, dinner. Bar. Children's menu. Business casual attire. Reservations recommended. Valet parking. Outdoor seating. **$$$**

★ ★ ★ **IL PALIO.** *1505 E Franklin St, Chapel Hill (27514). Phone 919/929-4000; toll-free 800/223-7379; fax 919/968-8527. www.sienahotel.com.* Situated in the Siena Hotel, this Italian restaurant offers guests a fine-dining experience. Il Palio is decorated with Italian artwork, large credenzas, mahogany chairs, and crisp white tablecloths—vased pink lilies are the finishing touch. French doors divide the cozy garden room from the main dining area. The restaurant features nightly live piano or guitar music to complement your meal, and the friendly wine steward will help in selecting the right wine for the occassion. Italian menu. Breakfast, lunch, dinner. Bar. Children's menu. Business casual attire. Reservations recommended. Valet parking. **$$$**

★ ★ **LA RESIDENCE.** *202 W Rosemary St, Chapel Hill (27516). Phone 919/967-2506; fax 919/967-2504. www.laresidencedining.com.* This popular Chapel Hill campus hangout has heated/air-cooled outdoor seating, an enclosed tent area in the back, and a bar. It's not all about late-night partying though, there is a romantic dining room for endulging in the American-French cuisine. American, French menu. Dinner. Bar. Business casual attire. Reservations recommended. Outdoor seating. **$$$**

★ **SPANKY'S.** *101 E Franklin St, Chapel Hill (27514). Phone 919/967-2678; fax 919/928-9335. www.spankys-restaurant.com.* This casual American grille restaurant is located across the street from the UNC Campus, and it's down the street from the UNC Medical Center. Many boutique shops line both sides of the street. The décor and atmosphere are relaxed with brick walls, large windows, wooden tables, and four television sets for the college sports crowd. American menu. Lunch, dinner. Bar. Children's menu. Casual attire. **$$**

★ **SQUID'S.** *1201 N Fordham Blvd, Chapel Hill (27514). Phone 919/942-8757; fax 919/929-0780. www. squidsrestaurant.com.* This steak and seafood restaurant is located on a busy street that runs between Chapel Hill and Durham. Its décor is cheery and inviting with pale yellow walls and metal fish and tropical art on the walls. A large aquarium with tropical fish divides the lobby from the dining room. Seafood, steak menu. Dinner. Bar. Children's menu. Casual attire. Outdoor seating. **$$**

Charlotte (B-4)

See also Concord, Cornelius, Gastonia, Gaffney

Settled 1748
Population 540,828
Elevation 700 ft
Area Code 704
Information Convention and Visitors Bureau, 330 S Tryon St, 28202; phone 704/334-2282 or toll-free 800/722-1994
Web Site www.visitcharlotte.com

The Carolinas' largest metropolis, Charlotte grew quickly as a regional retail, financial, and distribution center and became the nation's leader in the textile industry. General Cornwallis occupied the town for a short time in 1780, but met such determined resistance that he called it a "hornet's nest," a name that has been applied with pride on the city seal and by several local groups. Gold was discovered here in 1799, and the region around Charlotte was the nation's major gold producer until the California gold rush in 1848. There

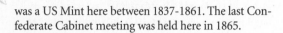

was a US Mint here between 1837-1861. The last Confederate Cabinet meeting was held here in 1865.

Chiefly agricultural and dependent on slave labor in antebellum days, the region took eagerly to industry after Appomattox. Abundant water power for electricity from the Catawba River has been a principal reason for its rapid growth. Today, Charlotte is among the largest banking centers in the country.

Public Transportation

Airport. Information 704/359-4013; lost and found 704/359-4012.
Buses Charlotte Transit System, phone 704/336-3366

What to See and Do

Carolina Panthers (NFL). *Bank of America Stadium, 800 S Mint St, Charlotte (28202). Phone 704/358-7000. www.panthers.com.*

Charlotte Bobcats (NBA). *Charlotte Arena, 333 E Trade St, Charlotte (28217). Phone 704/262-2287. www.nba.com/bobcats.* New professional basketball team.

Charlotte Coliseum. *100 Paul Buck Blvd, Charlotte. Phone 704/372-3600.* This 23,000-seat arena hosts various sport events as well as family shows and concerts.

The Charlotte Museum of History and Hezekiah Alexander Homesite. *3500 Shamrock Dr, Charlotte (28215). Phone 704/568-1774. www.charlottemuseum.org.* Includes the Hezekiah Alexander House (1774), the oldest dwelling still standing in Mecklenburg County; two-story springhouse; working log kitchen. Tours (fee). Admission free Sun. (Tues-Sat 10 am-5 pm, Sun 1-5 pm; open Mon in summer; closed holidays) **$$**

Charlotte Sting (WNBA). *Charlotte Coliseum, 100 Paul Buck Blvd, Charlotte (28217). www.wnba.com/sting.* Women's professional basketball team.

Discovery Place. *301 N Tryon St, Charlotte (28202). Phone 704/372-6261; toll-free 800/935-0553. www.discoveryplace.org.* Discovery Place is a hands-on science museum that gives kids (and adults who like to play) a chance to learn about electricity, weather, rocks, minerals, and other scientific wonders. Visit the aquarium, science circus, life center, rain forest, collections gallery, and OMNIMAX theater, as well as major traveling exhibits. (Daily; closed Thanksgiving, Dec 24-25) **$$**

James K. Polk Memorial State Historic Site. *12032 Lancaster Hwy, Pineville (28134). Phone 704/889-7145.* *www.polk.nchistoricsites.org.* Replica of log cabin and outbuildings at the birthplace of the 11th President of the United States. Visitor center with exhibits, film. Guided tour. (Tues-Sat) **FREE**

Latta Plantation Center and Nature Preserve. *5226 Sample Rd, Huntersville (28078). 12 miles NW via I-77, exit 16B (Sunset Rd W), right at Beattie's Ford Rd, 5 miles, then left at Sample Rd. Phone 704/875-1391. www.lattaplantation.org.* A more than 1,200-acre nature preserve on Mount Island Lake. Interpretive center, Carolina Raptor Center, Audubon bird sanctuary, equestrian center (fees apply for some). Bridle paths, hiking trails, fishing, picnicking, canoe access. (Daily) **FREE** Also here are

Historic Latta Plantation. *5225 Sample Rd, Huntersville (28078). Phone 704/875-2312.* (Circa 1800) Restored Federal-style plantation house, original smokehouse; barns, farm animals; kitchen garden, cotton field. (Memorial Day-Labor Day, daily; rest of the year, Tues-Sun; closed holidays) **$**

Mint Museum of Art. *2730 Randolph Rd, Charlotte (28207). Phone 704/337-2000.* The first Branch of the US Mint operated in the building from 1837 to 1861 and 1867-1913, and in 1933 it was chartered as an art museum. Collections include European and American art from Renaissance to contemporary, fine pottery and porcelain, maps, period costumes, pre-Columbian and African artifacts, and an exhibition of coins. (Tues-Sun; closed holidays) **$$**

Mint Museum of Craft and Design. *220 N Tryon St, Charlotte. Phone 704/337-2000.* (Tues-Sun; closed holidays) **$$**

Levine Museum of the New South. *200 E Seventh St, Charlotte (28202). Phone 704/333-1887. www.museumofthenewsouth.org.* The museum chronicles the history of the post-Civil War South with an ever-changing series of exhibits featuring industry, ideas, people, and historical eras such as the civil rights movement. (Tues-Sat 10 am-5 pm, Sun noon-5 pm) **$$**

Nature Museum. *1658 Sterling Rd, Charlotte . Phone 704/372-6261.* Live animal room, nature trail, puppet theater, earth science hall. (Daily; closed Thanksgiving, Dec 25) **$**

Ovens Auditorium. *2700 E Independence Blvd, Charlotte . 5 miles E on Hwy 74. Phone 704/372-3600.* Shows by touring Broadway companies (fall-late spring), musicals, symphony.

Paramount's Carowinds. *14523 Carowinds Blvd, Charlotte (28273). I-77, exit 90, at state line. Phone 704/588-2600; toll-free 800/888-4386. www.carowinds. com.* This 100-acre family theme park has more than 40 rides, shows, and attractions including the 12-acre water entertainment complex WaterWorks; Nickelodeon Central children's area; Drop Zone stunt tower; and rollercoasters. The 13,000-seat Paladium Amphitheater hosts special events. (June-late Aug: daily; Mar-May and Sept-Oct: weekends) **$$$$**

Spirit Square Center for the Arts and Education. *130 Tryon St, Charlotte . Phone 704/333-4686.* Exhibitions by well-known contemporary artists; studio art classes (fee); performances (fee).

University of North Carolina at Charlotte. *9201 University Blvd, Charlotte . NE off I-85. Phone 704/547-4286.*(1946) (15,000 students) Beautiful landscaping and blooming plants (Mar-Nov); rhododendron garden (blooms Apr-May); ornamental garden, public greenhouse with rainforest and orchid collection. Sculpture garden. Rare book room and panoramic view of campus, 10th floor of library (Mon-Fri; closed holidays). Walking tour guide and map.

Special Events

Auto racing. *Lowe's Motor Speedway, 5555 Concord Pkwy, Charlotte. Phone 704/455-3200.* Coca-Cola 600 Winston Cup stock car race (Memorial Day weekend); CUAW GM 500 (Oct); Spring AutoFair car show and flea market (mid-Apr); Fall AutoFair (mid-Sept-Oct).

Center City Fest. *129 W Trade St, Charlotte (28202).* Three-day festival in uptown. Food, live entertainment. Last weekend in Apr.

Festival in the Park. *Freedom Park, 1900 E Blvd, Charlotte (28203). Phone 704/338-1060. www.festivalinthepark.org.* Arts and crafts, entertainment. Late Sept.

Opera. *345 N College St, Charlotte. Phone 704/332-7177. www.operacarolina.org.* Opera Carolina. Oct-Apr.

Symphony. *201 S College St, Charlotte. Phone 704/332-6136.* Charlotte Symphony Orchestra, Inc. Performs year-round.

Theatre Charlotte. *501 Queens Rd, Charlotte. Phone 704/334-9128. www.theatrecharlotte.org.* Classic and Broadway plays. Features six productions a year on alternate months beginning in Sept. Thurs-Sat evenings, Sun.

Limited-Service Hotels

★ ★ **COURTYARD BY MARRIOTT.** *333 W W. T. Harris Blvd, Charlotte (28262). Phone 704/549-4888; toll-free 800/321-2211; fax 704/549-4946. www.marriott.com/cltun.* Situated near Highway 85, as well as the UNC campus, this hotel features guest laundry and high-speed Internet access in the lobby. Varied dining and shopping options are also located nearby. 152 rooms, 4 story. Check-in 3 pm, check-out noon. High-speed Internet access. Laundry services. Fitness room. Outdoor pool, whirlpool.**$**

★ ★ **COURTYARD BY MARRIOTT CHARLOTTE CITY CENTER.** *237 S Tryon St, Charlotte (28202). Phone 704/926-5800; toll-free 800/321-2211; fax 704/926-5801.www.marriott.com/cltup.* This convenient, comfortable hotel occupies the ground level and 12th-15th floors of an interesting building, where a parking structure fills in the remaining floors. Located in the heart of downtown, it is within walking distance to numerous shops, restaurants, businesses, and cultural venues. A courtyard is located on the 12th floor. 181 rooms. Check-in 3 pm, check-out noon. High-speed Internet access. Restaurant, bar. Fitness room. Outdoor pool, whirlpool. Airport transportation available. Business center. **$**

★ ★ **DOUBLETREE HOTEL.** *895 W Trade St, Charlotte (28202). Phone 704/347-0070; toll-free 800/222-8733; fax 704/347-0267. www.doubletree.com.* This property's location makes it convenient for business travelers, as it is just blocks from the convention center, and for leisure travelers, since uptown offers shopping and dining. Guest rooms feature equipped work desks and data ports. 187 rooms, 8 story. Check-in 4 pm, check-out noon. High-speed Internet access, wireless Internet access. Restaurant, bar. Fitness room. Outdoor pool, whirlpool.**$**

★ ★ **EMBASSY SUITES.** *4800 S Tryon St, Charlotte (28217). Phone 704/527-8400; toll-free 800/362-2779; fax 704/527-7035. www.embassy-charlotte.com.* This all-suite hotel offers tons of fitness facilities, including a workout room, an indoor pool, Jacuzzi, and sauna. Each morning guests can enjoy a fully cooked-to-order complimentary breakfast before visiting the attractions in the area. 274 rooms, 8 story, all suites. Complimentary full breakfast. Check-in 3 pm, check-out noon. High-speed Internet access, wireless Internet access. Restaurant, bar. Fitness room. Indoor pool, whirlpool. Airport transportation available. Business center. **$**

★ **LA QUINTA INN AND SUITES CHARLOTTE COLISEUM.** *4900 S Tryon St, Charlotte (28217). Phone 704/523-5599; toll-free 800/687-6667; fax 704/523-5156. www.laquinta.com.* Guests will find good value and comfort at this convenient property. Situated on the west side of Tryon Street, it is only ten minutes south of uptown Charlotte. 131 rooms. Pets accepted. Complimentary continental breakfast. Check-in 3 pm, check-out noon. High-speed Internet access, wireless Internet access. Fitness room. Outdoor pool, whirlpool. Airport transportation available. **$**

★ **RAMADA.** *7900 Nations Ford Rd, Charlotte (28217). Phone 704/522-7110; toll-free 800/272-6232; fax 704/521-9778. www.ramada.com.* 116 rooms, 3 story. Pets accepted, some restrictions; fee. Complimentary continental breakfast. Check-in 3 pm, check-out noon. Outdoor pool. **$**

★ **SUMMERFIELD SUITES.** *4920 S Tryon St, Charlotte (28217). Phone 704/525-2600; toll-free 800/996-3426; fax 704/521-9932. www.wyndham.com.* Centrally located just ten minutes from uptown Charlotte, this hotel is perfect for family vacations. With a relaxed atmosphere, it is well suited for relocation extended stays. 144 rooms, 5 story, all suites. Pets accepted, some restrictions; fee. Complimentary full breakfast. Check-in 3 pm, check-out noon. High-speed Internet access. Fitness room. Outdoor pool. Airport transportation available. Business center. **$**

★★ **WYNDHAM GARDEN HOTEL-CHARLOTTE AIRPORT.** *2600 Yorkmont Rd, Charlotte (28208). Phone 704/357-9100; toll-free 800/996-3426; fax 704/357-9159. www.wyndham.com.* This property, across from the Charlotte Coliseum and 15 minutes from downtown, is great for business travelers. Rooms are comfortable with generous work space, and guests receive a free daily newspaper and complimentary transportation to the nearby airport. Relax amid the pool's gardenlike landscaping. 173 rooms, 3 story. Check-in 3 pm, check-out noon. High-speed Internet access, wireless Internet access. Restaurant, bar. Fitness room. Outdoor pool, whirlpool. Airport transportation available. **$**

Full-Service Hotels

★★★ **CHARLOTTE JW MARRIOTT SOUTH-PARK.** *2200 Rexford Rd, Charlotte (28211). Phone 704/364-8220; toll-free 800/334-0331; fax 704/442-9678. www.theparkhotel.com.* Minutes from Charlottes uptown business district, The Charlotte JW Marriott SouthPark enjoys a quiet location in the elegant enclave of South Park. While the convenient setting and modern amenities make this an obvious choice for business travelers, the nine-hole putting green, Charles Grayson Day Spa, and fitness center with pool are ideal for leisure visitors. The hotel is a perfect base for serious shoppers. The rooms and suites are tastefully appointed with rich colors and traditional furnishings, and the spacious bathrooms enhance the luxurious residential atmosphere. The specialty suites present an appealing alternative with their distinctive flair. The amiable staff provides intuitive service, adding to the seamless experience. Smoky's Grill has a cozy ambience, and its menu of universal favorites pleases all diners. 194 rooms, 6 story. Pets accepted; fee. Check-in 4 pm, check-out 11 am. High-speed Internet access, wireless Internet access. Restaurant, bar. Fitness room. Outdoor pool, whirlpool. Business center. **$**

★★★ **THE DUNHILL HOTEL.** *237 N Tryon St, Charlotte (28202). Phone 704/332-4141; toll-free 800/354-4141; fax 704/376-4117. www.dunhillhotel.com.* 60 rooms, 10 story. Pets accepted; some restrictions, fee. Check-in 3 pm, check-out noon. Restaurant, bar. **$**

★★★ **HILTON CHARLOTTE CENTER CITY.** *222 E 3rd St, Charlotte (28202). Phone 704/377-1500; toll-free 800/445-8667; fax 704/377-4143. www.charlotte.hilton.com.* Perfect for business or pleasure, this hotel is in the financial district near the finest shops and restaurants in the area. Also nearby are beaches, golf courses, and the Carolina Mountains. This property also offers all amenities for guest comfort. 407 rooms, 22 story. Check-in 3 pm, check-out noon. High-speed Internet access, wireless Internet access. Restaurant, bar. Business center. **$$**

★★★ **HILTON UNIVERSITY PLACE.** *8629 J. M. Keynes Dr, Charlotte (28262). Phone 704/547-7444; toll-free 800/445-8667; fax 704/548-1081. www.charlotteuniversity.hilton.com.* Guest rooms and suites that have great views of the university area, guests are sure to be pleased. Relax over dinner at the Lakeside Restaurant or in the Lakeside Lounge, enjoy the pool, or take advantage of the many nearby attractions. 393 rooms, 12 story. Check-in 3 pm, check-out noon. High-speed Internet access, wireless Internet access. Restaurant, bar. Fitness room. Outdoor pool. Business center. **$**

★ ★ ★ **HYATT CHARLOTTE AT SOUTH PARK.**
5501 Carnegie Blvd, Charlotte (28209). Phone 704/554-1234; toll-free 800/233-1234; fax 704/554-8319. www.hyatt.com. Found in the prestigious 90-acre South Park business district, this well-appointed hotel sits across from the South Park shopping mall and is near downtown Charlotte and the Charlotte/Douglas International Airport. Guest will feel welcome in the unique, square-shaped atrium, which provides plenty of natural light and a water fountain. 262 rooms, 7 story. Check-in 3 pm, check-out noon. High-speed Internet access, wireless Internet access. Restaurant, bar. Fitness room. Indoor pool. Airport transportation available. Business center. **$**

★ ★ ★ **MARRIOTT CITY CENTER.** *100 W Trade St, Charlotte (28202). Phone 704/333-9000; toll-free 800/228-9290; fax 704/342-3419. www.marriottcitycenter.com.* Located in the central uptown business district, this hotel is only blocks from the New Charlotte Convention Center and Bank of America Stadium. 438 rooms, 19 story. Check-in 3 pm, check-out noon. High-speed Internet access. Three restaurants, three bars. Fitness room. Indoor pool, whirlpool. Business center. **$$**

★ ★ ★ **OMNI HOTEL.** *132 E Trade St, Charlotte (28202). Phone 704/377-0400; toll-free 800/843-6664; fax 704/347-0649. www.omnihotels.com.* This downtown hotel is located near a science center, performance and cultural center, and other attractions. 374 rooms, 15 story. Pets accepted, some restrictions; fee. Check-in 3 pm, check-out noon. High-speed Internet access, wireless Internet access. Restaurant, bar. Fitness room. Outdoor pool. Business center.**$$**

★ ★ ★ **RENAISSANCE CHARLOTTE SUITES.**
2800 Coliseum Centre Dr, Charlotte (28217). Phone 704/357-1414; toll-free 800/468-3571; fax 704/357-1401. www.renaissancehotels.com. This upscale convention and conference hotel is conveniently located in a business parkjust 15 minutes from downtown, next door to the Coliseum, and near the Charlotte/Douglas International Airport. A good choice for both business and leisure travelers, it offers spacious guest suites with microwaves, refrigerators, wet bars, and sofa sleepers. 275 rooms, 9 story, all suites. Check-in 4 pm, check-out noon. High-speed Internet access, wireless Internet access. Restaurant, bar. Fitness room. Indoor pool, whirlpool. Airport transportation available. Business center. **$$**

★ ★ ★ **THE WESTIN.** *601 S College St, Charlotte (28202). Phone 704/375-2600; toll-free 800/937-8461; fax 704/375-2623. www.westin.com/charlotte.* 700 rooms. Pets accepted. Check-in 3 pm, check-out noon. High-speed Internet access. Restaurant, bar. Fitness room (fee). Indoor pool. Business center. **$$**

Full-Service Resort

★ ★ ★ **THE BALLANTYNE RESORT, A LUXURY COLLECTION HOTEL.** *10000 Ballantyne Commons Pkwy, Charlotte (28277). Phone 704/248-4000; fax 704/248-4005. www.ballantyneresort.com.* Golfers make a beeline for Charlottes' Ballantyne Resort. This elegant resort within the city limits is a paradise for golf enthusiasts, with one of the state's best 18-hole courses and the renowned Dana Rader Golf School. Guests who prefer to spend their time on the tennis courts will delight in the fantastic facility run by a leading pro, while spa-goers will be in bliss with more than 60 different treatments to soothe their troubles away. A continental flair dominates the guest rooms and suites, and lavish touches, such as marble entrances and bathrooms, leave a lasting impression. A natural choice for conferences, this resort is also ideal for quick breaks for couples or family vacations. 250 rooms. Pets accepted; some restrictions. Check-in 3 pm, check-out noon. High-speed Internet access, wireless Internet access. Three restaurants, bar. Fitness room. Indoor pool. Golf, 18 holes. Tennis. Business center. **$$**

Specialty Lodgings

THE DUKE MANSION. *400 Hermitage Rd, Charlotte (28207). Phone 704/714-4400; toll-free 888/202-1009; fax 704/444-2263. www.dukemansion.com.* This gracious Southern estate is a lovely setting for a weekend getaway. The home was once owned by James Buchanan Duke, who is responsible for establishing both Duke Energy and Duke University. Today, acres of gardens surround the well-maintained home, which has treetop rooms as well as standard guest rooms, some with sleeping porches. The mansion also serves as a facility for meetings and retreats. 20 rooms. Complimentary full breakfast. Check-in 3 pm, check-out noon. High-speed Internet access. Fitness room. **$** 🏃

THE MOREHEAD INN. *1122 E Morehead St, Charlotte (28204). Phone 704/376-3357; toll-free 888/667-3432; fax 704/335-1110. www.moreheadinn.com.* 12 rooms. Complimentary full breakfast. Check-in 3 pm, check-out noon. High-speed Internet access, wireless Internet access. **$$**

VAN LANDINGHAM ESTATE. *2010 The Plaza, Charlotte (28205). Phone 704/334-8909; toll-free 888/524-2020; fax 704/940-8830. www.vanlandinghamestate.com.* 9 rooms. Complimentary full breakfast. Check-in noon, check-out noon. High-speed Internet access. **$**

THE VICTORIAN VILLA. *10925 Windy Grove Rd, Charlotte (28278). Phone 704/394-5545; fax 704/394-5525. www.victorianvillainn.com.* 5 rooms. Check-in 4 pm, check-out 11 am. **$$**

Restaurants

★ **AMALFI'S.** *8542 University City Blvd, Charlotte (28213). Phone 704/547-8651; fax 704/547-0303.* Italian menu. Lunch, dinner. Closed Mon; week of July 4. Children's menu. Casual attire. Outdoor seating. **$$**

★ ★ ★ **BISTRO 100.** *100 N Tryon St, Charlotte (28202). Phone 704/344-0515; fax 704/344-4773. www.bistro100restaurant.com.* Good food, enjoyable décor, and warm, skillful service are all found at this French bistro with an American twist. Fresh flowers top each table, and guests can enjoy views of Trade and College streets from the floor-to-ceiling windows. The décor is fresh and contemporary and so is the cuisine. French menu. Lunch, dinner, Sun brunch. Closed Jan 1, Dec 25. Bar. Children's menu. Business casual attire. Reservations recommended. Valet parking. **$$$**

★ ★ ★ **BONTERRA.** *1829 Cleveland Ave, Charlotte (28203). Phone 704/333-9463; fax 704/372-9463. www.bonterradining.com.* American menu. Dinner. Closed Sun. Bar. Business casual attire. Reservations recommended. Valet parking. Outdoor seating. **$$$**

★ **BRIXX PIZZA.** *225 E 6th St, Charlotte (28202). Phone 704/347-2749; fax 704/347-5739. www.brixxpizza.com.* Specialties here include wood-fired pizzas with a variety of toppings; some pasta and salads.

Italian menu. Lunch, dinner. Bar. Children's menu. Casual attire. Outdoor seating. **$$**

★ **FLYING SAUCER DRAFT EMPORIUM.** *9605 N Tryon St, Charlotte (28262). Phone 704/568-7253; fax 704/510-9741. www.beerknurd.com.* This restaurant offers salads, soft pretzels, wings, burgers, and more than 200 beers in bottles and on tap. American menu. Lunch, dinner, late-night. Bar. Casual attire. Outdoor seating. **$$**

★ **FUEL PIZZA CAFE.** *1501 Central Ave, Charlotte (28205). Phone 704/376-3835; fax 704/376-3805. www.fuelpizza.com.* This may be Charlotte's best local chain. The pizza joint in an old filling station offers big slices with a variety of toppings, including veggie-friendly options like spinach and tomato. American menu. Lunch, dinner. Children's menu. Casual attire. Outdoor seating. **$**

★ ★ **FUSE BOX.** *227 W Trade St, Suite 1200, Charlotte (28202). Phone 704/376-8885; fax 704/376-8882.* Just one block west of the major downtown area, Fuse Box is located on the ground level of an office building on the south side of Trade Street. The casual setting, pleasant staff, and convenient location mix well with the fresh creations. Sushi, Thai menu. Lunch, dinner. Closed Sun; holidays. Bar. Casual attire. **$$**

★ ★ ★ **GRILL ROOM.** *10000 Ballantyne Commons Pkwy, Charlotte (28277). Phone 704/248-4000; fax 704/248-4005. www.ballantyneresort.com.* The setting is relaxing and welcoming at the Grill Room, located on the ground level of the Ballantyne Resort (see) on the south side of Charlotte. Bright and elegant, the room features wrought-iron grillwork, fresh flowers on each table, and exquisite views of the golf course. The regional Southern cuisine is fresh and beautifully prepared, and the service comes naturally. Guests can enjoy live music every Tuesday through Saturday. American, Southern menu. Breakfast, lunch, dinner, brunch. Bar. Children's menu. Business casual attire. Reservations recommended. Valet parking. **$$$**

★ ★ **GUYTANO'S.** *6000 Fairview Rd, Charlotte (28287). Phone 704/554-1114.* Italian menu. Lunch, dinner. Closed holidays. Bar. Business casual attire. Reservations recommended. **$$$**

★ ★ **THE KABOB HOUSE.** *6432 E Independence Blvd, Charlotte (28212). Phone 704/531-2500.* Middle Eastern menu. Lunch, dinner. Closed Mon. Casual attire. Reservations recommended. **$$**

★ **KNIFE & FORK.** *2531 N Sharon Amity Rd, Charlotte (28205). Phone 704/568-9711.* This is the closest thing to a New York diner in Charlotte. A good breakfast menu, along with sandwiches, salads, seafood, and a friendly proprietor. American menu. Breakfast, lunch. Children's menu. Casual attire. **$**

★ ★ ★ **LA BIBLIOTHEQUE.** *1901 Roxborough Rd, Charlotte (28211). Phone 704/365-5000; fax 704/365-3081. www.labibliotheque.net.* If guests are looking for the full dining-out experience, this is the place. Included in this experience are the completely knowledgeable servers. Whatever diners order, they're guaranteed it will be served with the same professionalism every time. French menu. Lunch, dinner. Closed Sun; holidays. Bar. Business casual attire. Reservations recommended. Outdoor seating. **$$$**

★ ★ ★ **LAVECCHIA'S SEAFOOD GRILLE.** *225 E 6th St, Charlotte (28202). Phone 704/370-6776. www.lavecchias.com.* Located in the heart of downtown Charlotte, LaVecchia's is a festive spot for lovers of seafaring entrées like sea bass and seared yellowfin tuna. The fish is as fresh as you'll find in Charlotte, which must explain why the restaurant is a local favorite that's packed with a stylish crowd. To complement the oceanic menu—dishes like grilled swordfish, fried trout, and the signature lobster with citrus butter sauce (this one requires a bib)—the restaurant is decked out in a modern, urban, marine-themed design. Aquamarine is a prominent color, metal sculptures of sea creatures hang from the room's cavernous ceilings, and tropical fish-filled aquariums are tucked into the walls. Seafood menu. Dinner. Closed Sun. Bar. Children's menu. Business casual attire. Reservations recommended. Valet parking. Outdoor seating. **$$$**

★ **LUPIE'S CAFE.** *2718 Monroe Rd, Charlotte (28205). Phone 704/374-1232. www.lupiescafe.com.* Hot chili, spaghetti with meat sauce, macaroni and cheese, and banana puddingthe menu is small, but there are so many highlights. Simple, filling, inexpensive fare. American menu. Lunch, dinner. Closed Sun. Closed. Bar. Casual attire. **$**

★ **MAMA FU'S ASIAN HOUSE.** *1600 E Woodlawn, Charlotte (28209). Phone 704/714-5080; fax 704/714-5082. www.mamafus.com.* This chain restaurant specializes in noodle dishes and salads with chicken, beef, shrimp, tofu, or all veggie. Pan-Asian menu. Lunch, dinner. Children's menu. Casual attire. Outdoor seating. **$**

★ ★ ★ **MCNINCH HOUSE.** *511 N Church St, Charlotte (28202). Phone 704/332-6159; fax 704/376-0212. www.mcninchhouserestaurant.com.* The unique setting, attention to detail, and the changing menu

are well-suited for that special-occasion dinner. Situated in a historic building, McNinch House features large bay windows in each room, antiques displayed throughout, and a spacious porch and flower gardens outside. Located in a residential area on the west side of Church Street, it is within walking distance of downtown hotels and businesses. French menu. Dinner. Closed Sun-Mon; holidays. Bar. Jacket required. Reservations recommended. Valet parking. **$$$$**

★ **MERT'S HEART & SOUL.** *214 N College St, Charlotte (28202). Phone 704/342-4222; fax 704/342-4499. www.mertsuptown.com.* The super laid-back atmosphere of this neighborhood favorite is clear the moment you walk through the door—you're greeted by the smells of soul food simmering in the kitchen and eclectic décor in red, purple, and beige. American menu. Lunch, dinner, brunch. Children's menu. Casual attire. Outdoor seating. **$$**

★ ★ ★ **PATOU BISTRO.** *1315 E Blvd, Charlotte (28203). Phone 704/376-2233; fax 704/342-2381. www.patoubistro.com.* With outdoor dining and black-and-white photos displayed throughout, guests will enjoy the atmosphere of a true French bistro. French menu. Lunch, dinner. Closed Sun. Bar. Casual attire. Reservations recommended. Outdoor seating. **$$**

★ **PRESTO BAR AND GRILL.** *445 W Trade St, Charlotte (28202). Phone 704/334-7088; fax 704/334-5338. www.prestobarandgrill.com.* Presto is really a bistro, with a wide-ranging, well-executed menu. Good choices include the salmon club sandwich, chicken marsala, and any of the salads. American menu. Lunch, dinner. Closed Sun. Bar. Casual attire. Reservations recommended. Outdoor seating. **$$**

★ **RAINBOW CAFE.** *201 S College St, Charlotte (28244). Phone 704/372-2256; fax 704/372-2257. www.uptowncateringco.com.* The clean and simple décor of this second-floor eatery can be deceiving, as the lunch hour here is mobbed with hungry business people—sometimes the kitchen turns out up to 300 lunches a day. But don't be intimidated—the restaurant is popular for a reason and worth braving the crowds. American menu. Lunch, dinner. Closed Sat-Sun; holidays. Bar. Children's menu. Casual attire. **$**

★ **RANCH HOUSE.** *5614 Wilkinson Blvd, Charlotte (28208). Phone 704/399-5411. www.ranchhouseofcharlotte.com.* Seafood, steak menu. Dinner. Closed Sun; holidays; also first two weeks in July. Bar. Children's menu. Casual attire. Reservations recommended. **$$**

★ ★ ★ **UPSTREAM.** *6902 Phillips Place Ct, Charlotte (28210). Phone 704/556-7730; fax 704/552-2793. www.upstreamit.com.* Seafood menu. Lunch, dinner, brunch. Bar. Business casual attire. Reservations recommended. Valet parking. Outdoor seating. **$$$**

Cherokee (B-2)

See also Bryson City, Great Smoky Mountains National Park , Maggie Valley, Waynesville

Population 8,519
Elevation 1,991 ft
Area Code 828
Zip 28719
Information Cherokee Travel and Promotion, PO Box 460; phone 828/497-9195 or toll-free 800/438-1601
Web Site www.cherokee-nc.com

This is the capital of the Eastern Band of the Cherokee, who live on the Qualla Reservation at the edge of Great Smoky Mountains National Park (see) and the Blue Ridge Parkway. The reservation is the largest east of the Mississippi. These descendants of members of the tribe who avoided being driven to Oklahoma over the "Trail of Tears" are progressive in their ideas, yet determined to maintain their ancient traditions.

What to See and Do

Cherokee Heritage Museum and Gallery. *Acquoni Rd, Cherokee .* On Hwy 441 and Big Cove Rd. In Saunooke's Village. Phone 828/497-3211. Interpretive center features Cherokee culture and history. Gift shop. (Daily; closed three weeks late Dec-early Jan) **$**

Museum of the Cherokee Indian. *589 Psali Blvd, Cherokee (28719).* On Hwy 441 at Drama Rd. On Cherokee Reservation. Phone 828/497-3481 www.cherokeemuseum.org. Arts and crafts, audiovisual displays, portraits, prehistoric artifacts. (Daily; closed Jan 1, Thanksgiving, Dec 25) **$$**

Oconaluftee Indian Village. *Hwy 441 N, Cherokee .* 1/2 mile N on Hwy 441. Adjacent to Mountainside Theater. Phone 828/497-2111. Replica of Native American village of more than 250 years ago. Includes seven-sided council house, herb garden, craft demonstrations, lectures. Guided tours (Mid-May-late Oct, daily). **$$$**

Santa's Land. *571 Wolftown Rd, Cherokee (28719).* 3 miles E on Hwy 19 N. Phone 828/497-9191. Christmas theme park featuring Santa Claus and helpers; rides;

zoo; entertainment, including magic show; lake with pedal boats; primitive crafts; snack shops, picnic area, play areas; gardens. (Early May-late Oct, daily) **$$$$**

Special Event

Unto These Hills. *Mountainside Theater, Hwy 441 N, Cherokee .* On Hwy 441, 1/2 mile from jct Hwy 19. Phone 828/497-2111. Kermit Hunter drama re-creating the history of the Cherokee Nation from 1540-1838; in natural a amphitheater. Mid-June-late Aug. Mon-Sat evenings.

Limited-Service Hotels

★ ★ **BEST WESTERN GREAT SMOKIES INN.** *441 N and Aquoni Rd, Cherokee (28719). Phone 828/497-2020; toll-free 800/937-8376; fax 828/497-3903. www.bestwestern.com.* 152 rooms, 2 story. Pets accepted; fee. Check-in 2 pm, check-out 11 am. Restaurant. Outdoor pool. **$**
🐾 ⛆

★ **COMFORT INN.** *44 Tsalagi Rd, Cherokee (28719). Phone 828/497-2411; toll-free 800/228-5150; fax 828/497-6555. www.comfortinn.com.* 87 rooms. Complimentary continental breakfast. Check-in 2 pm, check-out 11 am. Outdoor pool, whirlpool. **$**
⛆

★ ★ **HOLIDAY INN.** *Hwy 19 S, Cherokee (28719). Phone 828/497-9181; toll-free 800/465-4329; fax 828/497-5973. www.holiday-inn.com.* 154 rooms, 2 story. Check-in 3 pm, check-out 11 am. Restaurant. Fitness room. Indoor pool, outdoor pool, whirlpool. **$**
🏋 ⛆

Cherryville (B-4)

See also Gastonia, Shelby

Founded 1881
Population 5,361
Elevation 960 ft
Area Code 704
Zip 28021
Information Chamber of Commerce, 301 E Main St, PO Box 305; phone 704/435-3451 or 704/435-4200
Web Site www.gastontourism.com

Customs of Cherryville's original German settlers still live on in this town nestled in the rolling hills of the Piedmont.

Special Event

Shooting in the New Year. Old rite to bring fertility to fruit trees and for good luck in the coming year. Men chant blessings and fire black powder muzzleloaders as they go from home to home. Dec 31-Jan 1.

Concord (B-5)

Population 27,347
Elevation 704 ft
Area Code 704
Zip 28026
Information Chamber of Commerce, 3003 Dale Earnhardt Blvd, PO Box 1029; phone 704/782-4111
Web Site www.cabarruschamber.org

Concord was founded by Scottish-Irish and German-Dutch settlers and received its name when the two factions settled a dispute regarding the location of the county seat. An early textile area in the South, Concord continues to lead in dyeing, finishing, and weaving of hosiery and knitted textiles.

What to See and Do

Apollo Mobile Home and Travel Park. *4275 Morehead Rd, Concord (28027). Phone 704/455-2409.* Shaded areas allow for camping unhampered by the hot Carolina sun at this park located just a few minutes walk from Lowe's Motor Speedway. Sites are rented on a first-come, first-served basis, and there is a three-night minimum. 100 sites, full hook-ups, 30/50-amp service.

Checkered Flag Lightening. *Concord Mills, 8111 Concord Mills Blvd, Concord (28027). Phone 704/979-7223. www.smsonline.com.* Realitsic racing simulators that let visitors feel the sensation of racing at speeds of up to 200 miles per hour.

Concord Mills. *8111 Concord Mills Blvd, Concord (28027). Phone 704/979-3000. www.concordmills.com.* This outlet mall has more than 200 stores, including factory outlets for popular chains such as Banana Republic and Saks Fifth Avenue. It draws more tourists on an annual basis than any other attraction in the Carolinas. It includes a movie theater. (Daily; closed holidays)

Concord Motorsport Park. *7940 Hwy 601 S, Concord (28025). Phone 704/782-4221. www.concordmotorsportpark.com.* The NASCAR Dodge Weekly Series runs Saturday nights from April through October at this 1/2-mile asphalt tri-oval 30 miles northeast of Charlotte, in the heart of NASCAR country. The grandstands seat 8,000, and there are spots for 28 RVs at Turn 3. **$$$$**

Dale Earnhardt Tribute. *Dale Earnhardt Plaza, Dale Earnhardt Blvd and Hwy 3, Kannapolis (28081). At Main and B sts. Phone toll-free 800/848-3740. www.cabarruscvb.com.* The people of Kannapolis have preserved the memory of their favorite son, Dale Earnhardt, in 900 pounds of bronze. The statue is near murals depicting Earnhardts career.

Fleetwood RV Racing Resort at Charlotte, Lowe's Motor Speedway. *5555 Concord Pkwy S, Concord (28027). Phone 704/455-4445. www.lowesmotorspeedway.com.* You cant stay any closer to Lowe's Motor Speedway. The prices are far from dirt cheap, but since nearby hotels raise the rates for Race Week, this is one of the more affordable options near the speedway. Plus, there are shuttles to the races. Lowes officials warn that the full hook-up sites sell out quickly before both the May and October races; book early for the best selection. Generators are allowed but must be turned off from midnight to 7 am, unless there is a medical reason to keep them on. The fee for the sites allows one tent or camping unit and one vehicle per site, a rule speedway officials attribute to fire marshals. 462 sites, full hook-ups. More than 7,000 primitive sites. Water stations (fee), dump stations (fee), restrooms, showers.

NASCAR Silicon Motor Speedway. *Concord Mills, 8111 Concord Mills Blvd, Concord (28027). Phone 704/979-7223. www.smsonline.com.* Realitsic racing simulators that let visitors feel the sensation of racing at speeds of up to 200 miles per hour.

NASCAR Speedpark, Concord Mills. *8461-G1 Concord Mills Blvd, Concord (28027). Phone 704/979-6770. www.nascarspeedpark.com.* A 7-acre race-themed amusement park with five racetracks, a state-of-the-art interatctive arcade, one 18-hole miniature golf course, kiddie rides, Lazer Tag, and a snack bar. (Daily; closed Thanksgiving, Dec 25) **$$$$**

Race Shop Tours. *Phone 704/788-8802. www.raceshoptours.net.* Offers sightseeing tours of 23 race teams in eight stops in one seven-hour area tour. Most teams are based around Charlotte, and this is a way to check them out up close. Rates and itineraries vary, and special bookings may be made in advance. Private tours are also available for an additional charge. **$$$$**

Reed Gold Mine State Historic Site. *9621 Reed Mine Rd, Midland (28107).* 10 miles SE on Hwy 601 and Hwy 200 to Georgeville, then 2 miles S on Hwy 1100. Phone 704/721-4653. When you hear the phrase "There's gold in them thar hills," you probably think "California." But this coast has its own stockpile of the natural wonder. In fact, the Reed Gold Mine State Historic Site boasts the first documented discovery of gold in the United States way back in 1799, long before those California 'forty-niners hit the mines. Stop and check out the underground mine tours, history trail, working machinery, demonstrations, exhibits, visitor center, and film, or enjoy the panning area and see what you find. Picnic areas are available for a pre- or post-tour meal. Panning area (Apr-Oct, daily; fee). (Tues-Sat; closed holidays) **FREE**

Richard Petty Driving Experience. *Lowe's Motor Speedway, 5555 Concord Pkwy S, Concord (28027).* Phone toll-free 800/237-3889. www.1800bepetty.com. Always wanted to rip a stock car around the curves at a NASCAR racetrack? This is the largest of the driving schools that takes fans right out onto the track at Lowe's Motor Speedway. For anywhere between $99 for a ride-along to almost $3,000 for an "advanced racing experience," you can live your dream. **$$$$**

Sam Bass Gallery. *6104 Performance Dr SW, Concord (28027).* Phone 704/455-6915; toll-free 800/556-5464. www.sambass.com. Sam Bass is the first officially licensed artist of NASCAR. His gallery sells NASCAR artwork and is down the road from Lowe's Motor Speedway. (Mon, Thurs-Fri 10 am-5 pm, Sat 10 am-4 pm) **FREE**

Cornelius (B-4)

See also Charlotte, Statesville

Founded 1893
Population 11,969
Elevation 831 ft
Area Code 704
Zip 28031
Information North Mecklenburg Chamber and Visitors Center,19900 W Catawba Ave, PO Box 760; phone 704/892-1922
Web Site www.lakenorman.org

A dispute between two cotton companies in Davidson during the late 1800s led to one of the firms relocating south of the city limits and establishing a new town. Originally called Liverpool, the community changed its name to Cornelius in honor of an investor.

What to See and Do

Lake Norman. *NW of town.* Lake Norman is the state's largest freshwater lake, at 32,510 acres; it was created by the Cowans Ford Dam, a Duke Power project on the Catawba River. There are nine public access areas, with fishing areas and boating access.

Memory Lane Motorsports & Historic Automotive Museum. *769 River Hwy, Mooresville (28117).* Phone 704/662-3673. www.memorylaneautomuseum.com. One-of-a-kind vehicles from race cars to vintage cars and motorcycles are on display at the museum, in addition to toys, memorabilia, and more. (Mon-Sat 9 am-5 pm) **$$**

North Carolina Auto Racing Hall of Fame. *119 Knob Hill Rd, Mooresville (28117).* I-77, exit 36. Phone 704/663-5331. www.ncarhof.com. As Mooresville's official visitors center, the museum offers a large display of more than 35 cars dedicated to all types of auto racing, and provides free race shop guides and maps to fans. Fans can savor racing's greatest moments at the Goodyear Mini-Theater, or marvel at the artistry of some of motorsports top artists. The gift shop is also the official Race City, USA merchandise headquarters, and carries a wide selection of racing memorabilia. (Daily) **$**

Limited-Service Hotels

★ **BEST WESTERN LAKE NORMAN.** *19608 Liverpool Pkwy, Cornelius (28031).* Phone 704/896-0660; toll-free 888/207-0666; fax 704/896-8633. www.bestwesternlakenorman.com. Pets are welcome at this updated hotel, located a short distance from both Lake Norman and Charlotte. A restaurant is adjacent, however, guests can also enjoy area dining and shopping as well. 80 rooms, 4 story. Pets accepted, some restrictions; fee. Complimentary continental breakfast. Check-in 3 pm, check-out 11 am. Fitness room. Outdoor pool, whirlpool. **$**

★ **HAMPTON INN.** *19501 Statesville Rd, Cornelius (28031).* Phone 704/892-9900; toll-free 800/426-7866; fax 704/896-7488. www.hamptoninn.com. Located just off Interstate 77, this hotel features easy access to Lake Norman attractions and the excitement of the NASCAR races at Lowe's Motor Speedway. The surrounding area includes plenty of restaurant options for any taste. 116 rooms, 5 story. Complimentary continental breakfast. Check-in 3 pm, check-out noon. Fitness room. Outdoor pool. **$**

★ ★ **HOLIDAY INN.** *19901 Holiday Ln, Cornelius (28031). Phone 704/892-9120; toll-free 800/465-4329; fax 704/892-3854. www.holiday-inn.com.* Conveniently set between Lake Norman and downtown Charlotte, this hotel features an on-site restaurant and bar, as well as a courtyard pool. Located near Davidson College, this is an ideal spot for visitors to the campus. 116 rooms, 2 story. Pets accepted; fee. Check-in 3 pm, check-out 11 am. Restaurant, bar. Fitness room. Outdoor pool. **$**

Specialty Lodging

DAVIDSON VILLAGE INN. *117 Depot St, Davidson (28036). Phone 704/892-8044; toll-free 800/892-0796; fax 704/896-2184. www.davidsoninn.com.* 18 rooms, 3 story. Complimentary continental breakfast. Check-in 3 pm, check-out 11 am. **$**

Restaurant

★ ★ **KOBE JAPANESE HOUSE OF STEAK & SEAFOOD.** *20465 Chartwell Center Dr, Cornelius (28031). Phone 704/896-7778; fax 704/896-0579.* Japanese menu. Lunch, dinner. Closed Thanksgiving, Dec 25. Bar. Casual attire. Reservations recommended. **$$**

Dunn (B-7)

See also Fayetteville, Goldsboro, Smithfield

Population 9,196
Elevation 213 ft
Area Code 910
Zip 28334
Web Site www.dunnchamber.com

What to See and Do

Bentonville Battleground State Historic Site. *5466 Harper House Rd, Four Oaks. 15 miles E via Hwy 55 to Newton Grove, 3 miles N via Hwy 701 to Hwy 1008, then 3 miles E. Phone 910/594-0789. www.bentonvillebattlefield.nchistoricsites.org.* Biggest battle on North Carolina soil, March 19-21, 1865. It was the last organized attempt to stop General William Tecumseh Sherman after he left Atlanta. A month later, the rebel cause was lost; Lee surrendered at Appomattox April 9; Lincoln was shot April 14; and Johnston surrendered April 26. The restored Harper House was used as a hospital to treat the wounded of both sides.

Reconstructed and original trenches. Picnic area. Visitor center, audiovisual show. (Hours vary; closed Jan 1, Thanksgiving, Dec 24-25) **FREE**

Limited-Service Hotel

★ **JAMESON INN.** *901 Jackson Rd, Dunn (28334). Phone 910/891-5758; toll-free 800/526-3766; fax 910/891-1290. www.jamesoninns.com.* 40 rooms. Pets accepted; some restrictions, fee. Check-in varies, check-out 11 am. Outdoor pool. **$**

Durham (A-6)

See also Chapel Hill, Raleigh

Founded 1853
Population 187,035
Elevation 406 ft
Area Code 919
Information Convention and Visitors Bureau, 101 E Morgan St, 27701; phone toll-free 800/772-2855
Web Site www.durham-nc.com

Durham's sparkle has brought it near-top national ranking in numerous livability studies. Known for excellence in medicine, education, research, and industry, Durham is also a recreational and cultural center in the rolling Piedmont region.

In 1924, an endowment from James B. Duke, head of the American Tobacco Company, helped establish Duke University as a leader among the nation's institutions of higher learning. North Carolina Central University makes its home here. In the 1950s, Durham County was chosen as the site of Research Triangle Park, a planned scientific research center that includes the Environmental Protection Agency, the National Institute for Environmental Health Sciences, IBM Corporation, the Glaxo Wellcome Company, and others. Duke University Medical Center, Durham Regional Hospital, and several other outstanding medical institutions here have earned Durham the title "City of Medicine, USA."

What to See and Do

Bennett Place State Historic Site. *4409 Bennett Memorial Rd, Durham (27705). Just SW of jct I-85 exit 173 and Hwy 70. Phone 919/383-4345.* Site of signing (Apr 26, 1865) of surrender of Confederate General Johnston to Union General Sherman, one of the last and most significant of the Confederate surrenders. Reconstructed Bennett homestead. Picnicking. Visitor center, exhibits, audiovisual show. (Tues-Sat; closed holidays) **FREE**

Duke Homestead State Historic Site. *2828 Duke Homestead Rd, Durham . 1/2 mile N of jct I-85, Guess Rd. Phone 919/477-5498. www.dukehomestead. nchistoricsites.org.* (1852) Ancestral home of the Duke family; first Duke tobacco factory; curing barn; outbuildings; farm crops. Tobacco museum, exhibits, film; furnishings of period. Tours. (Tues-Sat; closed holidays) **FREE**

Duke University. *2138 Campus Dr, Durham (27706). Phone 919/684-3214. www.duke.edu.* (1838) (10,000 students) Situated on 8,000 acres. Includes original Trinity College. The West Campus, occupied since 1930, is the showplace of the university. On campus are

Duke Chapel. *2138 Campus Dr, Durham (27706). Phone 919/681-1704.*Beautiful Gothic-style chapel with a carillon of 50 bells in its 210-foot tower; 5,000-pipe Flentrop organ. (Daily) Chapel Dr to main quadrangle.

Duke Libraries. *2138 Campus Dr, Durham (27706). Phone 919/684-3009.* Most comprehensive in the South, with more than 4 million volumes and 7 million manuscripts. Large Confederate imprint collection; Walt Whitman manuscripts.

Duke Medical Center. *Fulton and Elba sts, Durham (27710). Phone 919/684-8111.* Research and teaching complex. Treats more than 1/2 million patients annually.

Duke's Wallace Wade Stadium. *Whitford and Science Dr, Durham (27708). Phone 919/681-2583.* (33,941 capacity) Home of the Duke Blue Devils. Also the 8,564-seat Cameron Indoor Stadium.

Museum of Art. *Duke University Rd and Anderson St, Durham . E Campus, off W Main St. Phone 919/684-5135.* (Tues-Sun; closed holidays) **FREE**

Sarah P. Duke G ardens. *426 Anderson St, Durham (27705). Main entrance on Anderson St. Phone 919/684-3698.* 55 acres of landscaped gardens, pine forest. Continuous display. (Daily) **FREE**

Historic Stagville Center. *5828 Old Oxford Hwy, Bahama . 7 miles NE via Roxboro Rd and Old Oxford Hwy. Phone 919/620-0120.* State-owned historic property, once part of the Bennehan-Cameron plantation; several historic 18th- and 19th-century plantation

buildings on 71 acres of land. (Tues-Sat; closed holidays) **FREE**

North Carolina Museum of Life and Science. *433 W Murray Ave, Durham. Phone 919/220-5429.* North Carolina wildlife; hands-on science exhibits; aerospace, weather, and geology collections; train ride (fee); farmyard; science park; discovery rooms; Butterfly House. Picnic area. (Daily; closed Jan 1, Thanksgiving, Dec 25) **$$**

West Point on the Eno. *5101 N Roxboro Rd, Durham (27704). I-85, Duke St, exit 3 1/2 miles N. Phone 919/471-1623.* A 371-acre park along the scenic Eno River; restored farmhouse (1850), working gristmill; museum of photography; blacksmith shop. Picnicking, hiking, fishing, boating; environmental programs (fee). Park (daily). Mar-Dec, Sat-Sun). **FREE**

Special Events

American Dance Festival. *715 Broad St, Durham (27705). Page Auditorium and Reynolds Industries Theater, Duke University, West Campus. Phone 919/684-6402.* Six weeks of performances by the finest of both major and emerging modern dance companies from the United States and abroad. June-July.

Bull Durham Blues Festival. *Historic Durham Athletic Park, 409 Blackwell St, Durham (27701). Phone 919/683-1709.* Celebrates the blues with performances held at the location where *Bull Durham* was filmed. Weekend mid-Sept.

CenterFest. *Downtown. Phone 919/560-2722.* Two-day event with over 250 artists and craftsmen; musicians, jugglers, and clowns; continuous entertainment from three stages. Mid-Sept.

Limited-Service Hotels

★ **BEST WESTERN SKYLAND INN.** *5400 Hwy 70, Durham (27705). Phone 919/383-2508; toll-free 800/937-8376; fax 919/383-7316. www.bestwestern. com.* The Best Western Skyland Inn sits on 6 acres in the country and is located 1/2 mile from I-85, 4 miles from Duke, and 10 miles from UNC. 31 rooms, 1 story. Pets accepted; fee. Complimentary continental breakfast. Check-in noon, check-out 11 am. High-speed Internet access, wireless Internet access. Outdoor pool. **$**

★ **COURTYARD BY MARRIOTT DURHAM.** *1815 Front St, Durham (27705). Phone 919/309-1500;*

toll-free 800/321-2211; fax 919/383-8189. www.court-yard.com. This Courtyard by Marriott is conveniently located off I-85 and is within walking distance to a shopping plaza and dining. It is also within 1 mile of the Duke Medical Center, the VA Hospital, and Duke University. 146 rooms, 4 story. Check-in 3 pm, check-out noon. High-speed Internet access. Restaurant. Fitness room. Outdoor pool, whirlpool. Business center. **$**

★ ★ DOUBLETREE GUEST SUITES RA-LEIGH/DURHAM. 2515 Meridian Pkwy, Durham (27709). Phone 919/361-4660; toll-free 800/365-9876; fax 919/361-2256. www.doubletree.com. Close to major airports and adjacent to Research Triangle Park, this ultramodern hotel is conveniently located off Interstate 40. Situated in a parklike setting, guests can enjoy walking trails, volleyball, and basketball offered on-site. The back of the property borders a lake, and paddleboats and bikes are available for a fee. Guest rooms include microwaves; refrigerators; wet bars; and a TV in the living room, bedroom, and bathroom. 203 rooms, 7 story, all suites. Check-in 3 pm, check-out noon. High-speed Internet access. Restaurant, bar. Fitness room. Indoor pool, outdoor pool, whirlpool. Airport transportation available. Business center. **$$**

★ QUALITY INN & SUITES. 3710 Hillsborough Rd, Durham (27705). Phone 919/382-3388; toll-free 877/424-6423; fax 919/382-9298. www.choicehotels.com. This hotel is located minutes from Research Triangle Park, Duke Medical Center, shopping, and dining. Fresh baked cookies are offered every evening and there is a Wednesday night reception with complimentary drinks and snacks. 122 rooms, 3 story. Pets accepted; fee. Complimentary continental breakfast. Check-in 3 pm, check-out noon. High-speed Internet access, wireless Internet access. Fitness room. Outdoor pool. **$**

Full-Service Hotels

★ ★ ★ HILTON DURHAM. 3800 Hillsborough, Durham (27705). Phone 919/383-8033; toll-free 800/445-8667; fax 919/383-0833. www.durham.hilton.com. This traditional Hilton hotel is located just off I-85 and is minutes to Research Triangle Park, RDU Airport, Duke University Medical Center, shopping, and dining. The family-friendly property offers two restaurants, a bar, high-speed and wireless Internet access, an outdoor pool, a fitness room, and a business center. 194 rooms, 6 story. Check-in 3 pm, check-out noon. High-speed Internet access, wireless Internet access. Two restaurants, bar. Fitness room. Outdoor pool, whirlpool. Business center. Credit cards accepted. **$**

★ ★ ★ MARRIOTT DURHAM CIVIC CENTER. 201 Foster St, Durham (27701). Phone 919/768-6000; toll-free 800/228-9290; fax 919/768-6037. www.marriott.com. Located in the heart of downtown, this hotel is near the theater district, Durham Athletic Park, and Duke University. The elegant charm here is enhanced by fountains that flow through the atrium lobby. Guests receive complimentary use of the nearby YMCA or can use the on-site exercise facilities. 189 rooms, 10 story. Check-in 4 pm, check-out noon. High-speed Internet access, wireless Internet access. Restaurant, bar. Fitness room. Business center. **$**

★ ★ ★ MARRIOTT RESEARCH TRIANGLE PARK. 4700 Guardian Dr, Durham (27703). Phone 919/941-6200; toll-free 800/228-9290; fax 919/941-6229. www.marriott.com. Accessible to Interstate 40 and Highway 70, this ultramodern hotel is only five minutes from Research Triangle Park and RDU Airport. North Carolina State, University of North Carolina, and Duke campuses are all close by. 225 rooms, 6 story. Check-in 3 pm, check-out noon. High-speed Internet access, wireless Internet access. Restaurant, bar. Fitness room. Indoor pool, outdoor pool, whirlpool. Airport transportation available. Business center. **$$**

★ ★ ★ MILLENNIUM HOTEL. 2800 Campus Walk Ave, Durham (27705). Phone 919/383-8575; toll-free 866/866-8086; fax 919/383-8495. www.millennium-hotels.com. This hotel is conveniently located near Duke University and Medical Center, with easy access to Interstate 85. The Research Triangle Park and University of North Carolina are also nearby. Relax in the lounge, where mahogany bookshelves, overstuffed sofas, and wing-backed chairs provide the atmosphere of a private club. 316 rooms, 4 story. Pets accepted, some restrictions; fee.Check-in 3 pm, check-out noon. High-speed Internet access. Restaurant, bar. Fitness room. Indoor pool. Airport transportation available. Business center. **$**

★ ★ WASHINGTON DUKE INN & GOLF CLUB. 3001 Cameron Blvd, Durham (27705). Phone 919/490-0999; toll-free 800/443-3853; fax 919/688-

0105. *www.washingtondukeinn.com.* Campus living never looked this elegant, yet the Washington Duke Inn & Golf Club calls 300 acres within the Duke University campus home. Tucked away within the forest and golf club, this elegant resort is Durham's leading hotel. Sophisticated and stylish, this inn has the amenities of a large resort with the charm and ambience of a country-house hotel. The rooms and suites reflect the English country influences, as does the daily afternoon tea. From the classic elegance of the lauded Fairview to the convivial spirit of the Bull Durham Lounge, the dining choices here are terrific, and with a leading golf course just outside the door and privileges at the university's fitness facilities, guests are never at a loss for something to do. 271 rooms, 5 story. Check-in 3 pm, check-out noon. High-speed Internet access, wireless Internet access. Two restaurants, bar. Fitness room. Indoor pool, outdoor pool, children's pool, whirlpool. Golf, 18 holes. Tennis. Business center. **$$$**

Specialty Lodging

ARROWHEAD INN BED & BREAKFAST. *106 Mason Rd, Durham (27712). Phone 919/477-8430; toll-free 800/528-2207; fax 919/471-9538. www.arrowhead-inn.com.* Located about 7 miles from I-85, this circa 1775, manor-style home sits on 6 acres of manicured gardens. A rocking chair porch with tall pillars invite you to come in and stay awhile. The house features original moldings, mantelpieces, and heart-of-pine floors. The guest rooms are decorated with antiques and period furniture, four-poster beds, and fireplaces. The Keeping Room, which runs along the back of the house, features brick floors, paneled walls, bookcases, a fireplace, a TV, and a wet bar, making it a great place to unwind. 9 rooms, 2 story. Complimentary full breakfast. Check-in 3 pm, check-out 11 am. High-speed Internet access, wireless Internet access. **$$**

Restaurants

★ ★ ★ **FAIRVIEW.** *3001 Cameron Blvd, Durham (27706). Phone 919/493-6699; toll-free 800/443-3853; fax 919/681-3514. www.washingtondukeinn.com.* Located in the Washington Duke Inn & Golf Club, this Southern-influenced restaurant has been touted "the most elegant place to dine in the Research Triangle Park." Music from the baby grand piano only adds to the elegance and warmth that diners experience while enjoying a culinary delight. Try for a seat by one of the many windows for a beautiful view of the golf course.

And weather permitting, the terrace is the perfect spot for outdoor dining. American menu. Breakfast, lunch, dinner, Sun brunch. Bar. Children's menu. Business casual attire. Reservations recommended. Valet parking. Outdoor seating. **$$$**

★ ★ ★ **MAGNOLIA GRILL.** *1002 9th St, Durham (27705). Phone 919/286-3609; fax 919/286-2691.* In Magnolia Grill, husband-and-wife chefs/owners Ben and Karen Barker mine an independent streak in Southern cooking. He handles the savories, taking Southern ingredients beyond regional confines in dishes like smoked trout with avocado and red pepper slaw, sea bass carpaccio with Thai crab vinaigrette, fennel-crusted grouper in lobster reduction, and roast pheasant with wild rice risotto. She creates the sweets that take Southern comforts upscale, including shaker pie and upside-down caramel banana cake with bourbon praline ice cream. Lodged in a former health food grocery, Magnolia Grill keeps the vibe casual with wooden floors and artwork on loan from local painters, encouraging neighborhood repeaters as well as special-occasion celebrants. American, Southern menu. Dinner. Closed Sun-Mon; also first week in Jan and last week in July. Bar. Business casual attire. Reservations recommended. **$$$**

★ ★ ★ **PAPA'S GRILLE.** *1821 Hillandale Rd, Durham (27705). Phone 919/383-8502; fax 919/382-9529. www.papasgrille.com.* Guests can watch the chefs at work in the open display kitchen of this restaurant located in a little strip mall near Route 70 and Interstate 85. Bistro tables surround the outside of the room, while dining room tables are set with crisp white tablecloths, dark blue glasses, and candles. Framed Greek scenes and a Greek village and island mural grace the walls. Windows are dressed with lace curtains, giving a romantic touch. Mediterranean menu. Lunch, dinner. Closed Sun; Easter, Dec 25. Bar. Business casual attire. Reservations recommended. **$$**

★ ★ **PARIZADE.** *2200 W Main St, Durham (27705). Phone 919/286-9712; fax 919/416-9706. www.ghgrestaurants.com.* Parizade is located on the ground level of the Wachovia Building, near the Duke campus. The building itself is impressive, and the ultramodern décor is eye catching. Hammered copper panels hang over the open display kitchen, forming an enlarged circle over the pillar tops. A courtyard in the back lures guests in with its little white lights and a cascading waterfall. Mediterranean menu. Lunch, dinner. Closed Dec 25. Bar. Business casual attire. Reservations recommended. Outdoor seating. **$$$**

Edenton (A-9)

See also Chapel Hill, Raleigh

Settled 1658
Population 5,394
Elevation 16 ft
Area Code 252
Zip 27932
Information Chamber of Commerce, 116 E King St, PO Box 245; phone 252/482-3400; or Historic Edenton, 108 N Broad St, PO Box 474, phone 252/482-2637
Web Site www.visitedenton.com

This is one of the oldest communities in North Carolina and was the capital of the colony for more than 22 years. The women of Edenton staged their own Revolutionary tea party on October 25, 1774, signing a resolution protesting British injustice. A bronze teapot, at the west side of the Courthouse Green, commemorates the event.

The seat of Chowan County, Edenton is now an important industrial town and marketing place. It is a charming town with the graciousness of the Old South and many houses and buildings that date back to the 1700s. Joseph Hewes, a signer of the Declaration of Independence, lived here.

What to See and Do

Historic Edenton. *108 N Broad St,* Edenton (27932). *Phone 252/482-2637.* Tour of historic properties, which may be seen individually or as a group; allow 2 1/2 to 3 hours for complete tour. (Daily; closed Jan 1, Dec 24-25) **$$** Also here are

> **Chowan County Courthouse.** *E King and Court sts, Edenton.* (1767) A fine example of Georgian architecture; in continuous use since it was built.

> **Cupola House.** *W Water and S Broad sts, Edenton.* (1758) Considered an outstanding example of Jacobean architecture. Formal garden restored from 1769 map of Edenton.

> **Historic Edenton Visitor Center.** *108 N Broad St, Edenton.* Audiovisual program (free), exhibits, visitor information, gift shop, tickets for guided tours of Historic Edenton.

> **James Iredell House.** *108 N Broad St, Edenton (27932). Phone 252/482-2637.* (1800/1827). Home of early attorney general of North Carolina who

was appointed by George Washington to first US Supreme Court.

St Paul's Episcopal Church. *W Church and Broad sts, Edenton.* (1736). A charming church with many old gravestones in its yard; three colonial governors are buried here.

Merchant's Millpond State Park. *71 Hwy 158 E, Gatesville (27938). 25 miles N on Hwy 32, 5 miles N of Gatesville on Hwy 1403. Phone 252/357-1191. www.ncsparks.net.* This 2,900-acre swamp forest is dominated by massive gum and cypress trees. Pond fishing, canoeing (rentals). Nature trails. Picnicking. Developed and primitive camping. Interpretive program. Contact Superintendent, Rte 1, Box 141-A, Gatesville 27938.

Newbold-White House. *Harvey Point Rd, Hertford. 15 miles N on Hwy 17 Bypass to Hertford, SE on Hwy 1336. Phone 252/426-7567.* (1730) This brick structure was a meeting place for the proprietary government of North Carolina. (Mar-Dec, Tues-Sat) **$**

Other historic buildings. *108 N Broad St, Gatesville (27938). Phone 252/482-2637.* Shown in a guidebook published by the Edenton Woman's Club and sold at the Historic Edenton Visitor Center ($). Since most houses are not open to the public, we suggest calling the Historic Edenton Visitor Center for further information.

Somerset Place State Historic Site. *2572 Lake Shore Rd, Creswell (27928). 18 miles SE via Hwy 32, Hwy 64 to Creswell, then 7 miles S. On Lake Phelps in Pettigrew State Park. Phone 252/797-4560. www.somersetplace. nchistoricsites.org.* Original plantation, one of the largest in North Carolina, encompassed more than 100,000 acres. First primary crop was rice, which gave way to corn and wheat. Mansion and outbuildings built (circa 1830). (Daily; closed holidays) **FREE**

Specialty Lodgings

CAPTAIN'S QUARTERS INN. *202 W Queen St, Edenton (27932). Phone 252/482-8945; toll-free 800/482-8945. www.captainsquartersinn.com.* 8 rooms, 2 story. Children over 8 years only. Complimentary full breakfast. Check-in 4-10 pm. Check-out 11 am. Built in 1907; antiques. **$**

LORDS PROPRIETORS INN. *300 N Broad St, Edenton (27932). Phone 252/482-3641; toll-free 888/394-6622; fax 252/482-2432. www.edentoninn.com.* This inn is actually three separate homes gracing 2 acres of what's known as the South's prettiest town. All 20

rooms are decorated with period antiques and reproductions. The New American dining room is for guests
only and offers an impressive seasonal menu. 20 rooms,
2 story. Check-in 1 pm, check-out 11 am. **$$**

Elizabeth City (A-9)

Settled Circa 1665
Population 17,188
Elevation 18 ft
Area Code 252
Zip 27909
Information Elizabeth City Area Chamber of Com-
merce, 502 E Ehringhaus St, PO Box 426; phone
252/335-4365
Web Site www.discoverec.org

A town with a freshwater harbor on the Pasquotank
River and accessible to the ocean, Elizabeth City
has seen seafaring activity since the middle of the
17th century. In 1793, the town was chartered at the
narrows of the river as Redding and, in 1801, was
renamed Elizabeth City. The Dismal Swamp Canal,
dug in 1793, provided a critical north-south transpor-
tation route and brought prosperity to Elizabeth City.
Shipyards, warehouses, fisheries, tanneries, sawmills,
and other industries flourished along with commis-
sion merchants, artisans, and navigators; trading
occured with Norfolk, the West Indies, New England,
New York, and Charleston.

Although captured in the Civil War, Elizabeth City
sustained minor damage. Today, many antebellum
homes still stand alongside the historic homes and
commercial buildings of the late 19th and early 20th
centuries, a testament to the vitality of the commu-
nity. Wood, agriculture, small specialty industries, and
the US Coast Guard contribute to the area's steady
economic growth. The town also welcomes boating
traffic from the Intracoastal Waterway and is a coveted
location for sportfishing and hunting. It serves as a
gateway to Nags Head and Cape Hatteras National
Seashore (see).

What to See and Do

Dixieland Motorsports Complex. *1522 Northside Rd,
Elizabeth City . Phone 252/771-5151.* The complex
sponsors stock car, go-cart, and motorcycle races.
Stock cars race on Fri, go-carts on Sat, and motor-
cycles on Sun. Apr-late Oct. **$$$**

Fun Junktion. *983 Simpson Ditch Rd, Elizabeth City.
Phone 252/337-6600.* This 133-acre public park features lakes, nature trails, a swimming area, a children's
playground, and picnic facilities.

Historic District. A 30-block area in the city center,
that contains the largest number of antebellum commercial buildings in the state. Tour brochures are
available at the Chamber of Commerce.

Museum of the Albemarle. *501 S Water St,* Elizabeth
City (27909). *Phone 252/335-1453.www.museu-
mofthealbemarle.com.* Regional historical displays;
Native American exhibits; local artifacts, including
decoys, fire engines; changing exhibits. (Daily; closed
state holidays) **FREE**

Special Events

Albemarle Craftsman's Fair. *200 E Ward St, Elizabeth
City (27909).* Late Oct.

Historic Ghostwalk. Historic homes tour with skits.
Late Oct.

Mistletoe Show. Crafts, wood carvings. Second weekend in Nov.

Limited-Service Hotels

★ **HAMPTON INN.** *402 Halstead Blvd, Elizabeth
City (27909). Phone 252/333-1800; toll-free 800/426-
7866; fax 252/333-1801.www.hamptoninn.com.* 100
rooms, 5 story. Complimentary continental breakfast.
Check-in 3 pm, check-out 11 am. Outdoor pool,
whirlpool. **$**

★ **HOLIDAY INN EXPRESS.** *306 S Hughes Blvd,
Elizabeth City (27909). Phone 252/338-8900; toll-free
877/553-2964; fax 252/338-5120.www.hiexpress.com.* 80
rooms, 5 story. Complimentary continental breakfast.
Check-in 3 pm, check-out 11 am. Outdoor pool. **$**

Restaurant

★ **MARINA.** *Camden Causeway, Elizabeth City
(27909). Phone 252/335-7307; fax 252/335-9867.* Seafood, steak menu. Dinner. Closed Mon; Jan 1, Dec 25.
Bar. Children's menu. Casual attire. Outdoor seating. **$**

Fayetteville (C-6)

See also Dunn, Goldsboro

Founded 1739
Population 121,015
Elevation 102 ft
Area Code 910
Information Convention and Visitors Bureau, 245 Person St, 28301; phone 910/483-5311 or toll-free 800/255-8217
Web Site www.visitfayettevillenc.com

In 1783, the towns of Cross Creek and Campbellton merged and were renamed Fayetteville for the Marquis de Lafayette, becoming the first US city to honor him. It was the site of North Carolina's Constitutional Convention in 1787 and the capital of the state from 1789-1793. By 1831 it had become a busy commercial city.

Fayetteville is the state's farthest inland port, at the head of navigation on the Cape Fear River, with an 8-foot-deep channel connecting it to the Intracoastal Waterway. Fayetteville State University (1867) and Methodist College (1956) are located here. In 1985, Fayetteville received the All-America City Award. Today, it's a center for retail, manufacturing, and conventions, as well as the home of Fort Bragg and Pope Air Force Base.

Fayetteville Fun Fact

In Fayetteville, Babe Ruth hit his first professional home run on March 17, 1914.

What to See and Do

Cape Fear Botanical Garden. *536 N Eastern Blvd, Fayetteville. Phone 910/486-0221.www.capefearbg.org.* On 85 acres overlooking Cross Creek and the Cape Fear River. Wildflowers, oaks, native plants. Nature trails. (Mid-Dec-mid-Feb, Mon-Sat; rest of year, daily; closed holidays) **$**

First Presbyterian Church. *Bow and Ann sts, Fayetteville. Phone 910/483-0121.* Classic Southern colonial-style architecture and whale-oil chandeliers. Among contributors to the original building (destroyed by fire in 1831) were James Monroe and John Quincy Adams. Tours (by appointment only).

Fort Bragg and Pope AFB. *200 Maynard St*, Pope AFB (28308). *10 miles NW on Hwy 24. www.bragg.army. mil.* Here are

82nd Airborne Division War Memorial Museum. *Gela and Ardennes sts, Fort Bragg. Phone 910/432-3443.*Weapons, relics of World War I and II, Vietnam, Korea, Desert Storm; history of 82nd airborne division; gift shop. (Tues-Sat; closed Jan 1, Dec 25) **FREE**

John F. Kennedy Special Warfare Museum. *Ardennes and Marion sts, Fort Bragg (28307). Phone 910/432-1533.* Guerrilla warfare weapons. (Tues-Sun; closed holidays) **FREE**

Parachute jumps. *Phone 910/396-6366.*

Museum of the Cape Fear. *801 Arsenal Ave, Fayetteville. Phone 910/486-1330.* Retraces the regional cultural history from prehistoric Indian artifacts through 20th century. A branch of the North Carolina Museum of History. (Tues-Sun; closed holidays) **FREE**

Special Event

Dogwood Festival. *301 Hay St, Fayetteville (28301). Phone 910/323-1934* Late Apr.

Limited-Service Hotels

★ **COMFORT INN.** *1957 Cedar Creek Rd, Fayetteville (28312). Phone 910/323-8333; toll-free 800/621-6596; fax 910/323-3946. www.comfortinn.com.* 120 rooms, 2 story. Complimentary continental breakfast. Check-in 3 pm, check-out noon. Fitness room. Outdoor pool. **$**
🕴 🖼

★ **FAIRFIELD INN.** *562 Cross Creek Mall, Fayetteville (28303). Phone 910/487-1400; toll-free 800/228-2800; fax 910/487-0081. www.fairfieldinn.com.* 135 rooms, 3 story. Complimentary continental breakfast. Check-in 3 pm, check-out noon. Outdoor pool. **$**
🖼

★ **HAMPTON INN.***1922 Cedar Creek Rd, Fayetteville (28312). Phone 910/323-0011 toll-free 800/426-7866; fax 910/323-8764. www.hamptoninn.com.* 121 rooms, 2 story. Complimentary continental breakfast. Check-in 3 pm, check-out noon. Outdoor pool. **$**
🖼

★ ★ **HOLIDAY INN.** *1944 Cedar Creek Rd, Fayetteville (28302). Phone 910/323-1600; toll-free 800/465-4329; fax 910/323-0691.www.holiday-inn.com.* 198

rooms, 2 story. Pets accepted; fee. Check-in 3 pm, check-out noon. Restaurant, bar. Fitness room. Indoor pool. **$**

★ **HOLIDAY INN EXPRESS.** *1706 Skibo Rd, Fayetteville (28303). Phone 910/867-6777; toll-free 800/465-4329; fax 910/864-9541. www.hiexpress.com.* 84 rooms, 4 story. Complimentary continental breakfast. Check-in 2 pm, check-out 11 am. High-speed Internet access. Outdoor pool. **$**

★ **QUALITY INN.** *2035 Eastern Blvd, Fayetteville (28306). Phone 910/485-8135; toll-free 800/828-2346; fax 910/485-8682. www.qaulityinn.com.* 62 rooms, Check-in noon, check-out noon. Restaurant. Outdoor pool. **$**

Restaurants

★ **CANTON STATION.** *301 N McPherson Church Rd, Fayetteville (28303). Phone 910/864-5555.* Lunch, dinner. Bar. Children's menu. Casual attire. **$**

★ ★ **TRIO CAFE.** *201 S McPherson Church Rd, Fayetteville (28303). Phone 910/868-2443; fax 910/868-1128. www.mocafe.net.* Mediterranean menu. Dinner, Sun brunch. Closed holidays. Bar. Outdoor seating. **$$**

Fontana Dam (B-1)

See also Bryson City, Great Smoky Mountains National Park

Founded 1947
Population 130
Elevation 2,900 ft
Area Code 704
Zip 28733
Web Site www.westernncattractions.com/fontana.htm

At the southwest corner of Great Smoky Mountains National Park, this village was originally built for the construction crew that worked on the Fontana Dam project. The 480-foot dam is crossed by the Appalachian Trail. The region is now a resort area, with swimming, fishing, boating, hiking, and horseback riding centering around Fontana Lake, 30 miles long.

Fort Raleigh National Historic Site (A-10)

See also Cape Hatteras National Seashore, Kill Devil Hills, Nags Head, Outer Banks

Web Site www.nps.gov/fora
Off Hwy 64, 3 miles N of Manteo.

The first English colony in America was attempted here on Roanoke Island in 1585. Virginia Dare, born here August 18, 1587, was the first child of English parents born in what is now the United States.

Governor John White left the island for England a few days after Virginia's birth, intending to return shortly with supplies. He was detained by the war with Spain and did not get back until August 1590. The colony had disappeared, leaving behind only the mysterious word "CROATOAN" cut into a tree or post.

What happened to the colonists is unknown, though some believe that the present-day Lumbee Indians of Robeson County descend from them. Fort Raleigh has been excavated, and the fort built by the colonists reconstructed. The Lindsay Warren Visitor Center has relics, an audiovisual program, and exhibits. Park and Visitor Center (daily; closed Dec 25). For further information, contact Fort Raleigh National Historic Site, Rte 1, Box 675, Manteo, 27954; phone 252/473-5772.

Special Event

***The Lost Colony* Outdoor Drama.** *Waterside Theater, Manteo. 3 miles NW of Manteo on Hwy 64/264. Phone toll-free 800/488-5012.* Outdoor drama by Pulitzer Prize winner Paul Green about the first English colony established in the New World, whose curious disappearance remains a mystery to this day. Mid-June-late Aug. Mon-Sat evenings. Reservations recommended. Contact 1409 Hwy 64, Manteo, 27954. **$$$$**

Franklin(B-2)

See also Bryson City, Cashiers, Highlands

Population 3,490
Elevation 2,133 ft
Area Code 828
Zip 28734
Information Chamber of Commerce, 425 Porter St; phone 828/524-3161 or toll-free 800/336-7829
Web Site www.franklin-chamber.com

Home of the Cowee Valley ruby mines, Franklin attracts rock hounds who often find interesting gems in surface mines. Franklin is surrounded by waterfalls, mountain lakes, and streams that offer excellent fishing for trout and bass, as well as boating, tubing, and swimming. Around the county are 420,000 acres of the Nantahala National Forest, which offers hiking trails, camping, and fishing. A Ranger District office is located here. The Appalachian Trail bisects the western part of the county through Standing Indian Wildlife Management area and over Wayah Bald Mountain.

What to See and Do

Franklin Gem and Mineral Museum. *25 Phillips St, Franklin (Macon Co). Phone 828/369-7831. www. fgmm.org.* Gems and minerals; Native American artifacts, fossils; fluorescent mineral display. (May-Oct, Mon-Sat) **FREE**

Gem mines. There are more than a dozen mines in the area, most offering assistance and equipment for beginners. For a complete list of mines contact the Chamber of Commerce.

Macon County Historical Museum. *36 W Main St, Franklin (Macon Co). Phone 828/524-9758. www. maconnchistorical.org.* Artifacts, documents depicting early history of Macon County; genealogical material. (Apr-Oct, Tues-Sat) **FREE**

Nantahala National Forest. *90 Sloan Rd, Franklin (Macon Co) (28734). W of town Phone 828/524-6441.* Nantahala, a Native American name meaning Land of the Noonday Sun, refers to Nantahala Gorge, so deep and narrow that the sun reaches the bottom only at noon. Scenic drives through the southern Appalachians; sparkling waterfalls, including the Whitewater Falls—a series of cascades dropping 411 feet within a distance of 500 feet—and the 17,013-acre Joyce Kilmer-Slickrock Wilderness (see ROBBINSVILLE), with

more than 100 species of trees native to the region are part of this 518,560-acre forest. Hiking, camping (fee); swimming, boating, fishing for bass and trout; hunting for deer, wild boar, turkey, and ruffed grouse. For further information, contact the District Ranger, 100 Otis St, PO Box 2750, Asheville 28802.

Perry's Water Garden. *136 Gibson Aquantic Farm Rd, Franklin (Macon Co) (28734). 8 miles NW on Hwy 28 to Cowee Creek Rd, then E 2 miles to Leatherman Gap Rd. Phone 828/524-3264. www.perryswatergarden.net.* Water park with 4 1/2-acre sunken garden, waterfall, hundreds of water lilies and other flowers, wishing well, trails, picnicking. (Mid-May-Labor Day, daily) **FREE**

Scottish Tartans Museum. *W.C. Burrell Building, 95 E Main St, Franklin . W. C. Burrell Building. Phone 828/524-7472. www.scottishtartans.org.* American extension of Scottish Tartans Society in Edinburgh, Scotland. Exhibits trace heritage of Scottish Tartan and traditional Scottish dress. Research library. Gift shop. (Daily; closed Jan 1, Easter, Dec 25) **$**

Special Events

Macon County Fair. Mid-Sept.

Macon County Gemboree. Jewelry and gem exhibits, ruby mining, field trips. Late July.

Limited-Service Hotel

★ **DAYS INN.** *1320 E Main St, Franklin (28734). Phone 828/524-6491; toll-free 800/329-7466; fax 828/369-9636. www.daysinn.com.* 41 rooms. Pets accepted, some restrictions; fee. Complimentary continental breakfast. Check-in 3 pm, check-out 11 am. Outdoor pool. Scenic view of mountains. **$**

Restaurants

★ ★ **FROG & OWL KITCHEN.** *46 E Main St, Franklin (28734). Phone 828/349-4112; fax 828/349-4112.* French menu. Lunch, dinner. Closed Thanksgiving, Dec 25; children's menu. Casual attire. Reservations recommended. **$$**

★ **GAZEBO CAFE.** *44 Heritage Hollow, Franklin (28734). Phone 828/524-8783; fax 828/369-2725.* American menu. Lunch. Closed holidays; also mid-Nov-mid-Apr. Children's menu. Casual attire. Entire restaurant is outdoors; three different patio levels for dining. **$**

Gastonia (B-4)

See also Charlotte, Cherryville, Shelby

Population 66,277
Elevation 816 ft
Area Code 704
Information Gaston County Department of Tourism, PO Box 2339, 2668; phone 704/867-2170 or toll-free 800/849-9994
Web Site www.gastontourism.com

This is an industrial town in the Piedmont, turning out textiles, textile machinery, and supplies. In addition, Gastonia produces chain saws, plastics, oil seals, lithium, automotive parts, trucks, and truck parts.

What to See and Do

Gaston County Museum of Art and History. *131 W Main St, Dallas. 6 miles N via Hwy 321, Dallas exit. Phone 704/922-7681.* Located in Hoffman Hotel (1852) and Dallas Depot (1901). Sculpture, paintings, Gaston County artifacts and documents, carriage and sleigh collection, textile history exhibit. 19th-century parlors. (Tues-Sat; closed holidays) **FREE**

Lake Wylie. *310 Blutcher Cir, Lake Wylie (29710). S on Hwy 274. Phone 803/831-2101. www.hallmarine.com.* An artificial lake formed by Duke Power Company development; fishing, swimming, water-skiing; marina.

Schiele Museum of Natural History and Planetarium. *1500 E Garrison Blvd, Gastonia (28052). Phone 704/866-6900.. www.schielemuseum.org.* Habitat settings showcasing more than 75,000 mounted birds, mammals, reptiles, fish; rocks and minerals; Native American arts and crafts; forestry exhibits; and 28-acre nature park. Major exhibits on the Southeast and North Carolina, special exhibits and events, films, and a restored mid-1700s pioneer farm with living history programs. Hall of Natural History, Hall of Earth and Man. Also here is Catawba Indian Village, with recreated dwellings from 1500s to 1900s. Planetarium programs (fee). (Daily) **$**

Limited-Service Hotel

★ **HAMPTON INN.** *1859 Remount Rd, Gastonia (28054). Phone 704/866-9090; toll-free 800/426-7866; fax 704/866-7070. www.hamptoninn.com.* Conveniently situated, clean, and comfortable, this is an ideal lodging option for travelers visiting or passing through the Gastonia area. 108 rooms, 5 story. Complimentary continental breakfast. Check-in 3 pm, check-out noon. Outdoor pool. **$**
⌨

Goldsboro (B-7)

See also Dunn, Fayetteville, Smithfield

Population 39,043
Elevation 121 ft
Area Code 919
Information Wayne County Chamber of Commerce, 308 N William St, 27530; phone 919/734-2241
Web Site www.greatergoldsboro.com

Center of the bright-leaf tobacco belt, Goldsboro is also the seat of Wayne County and home of Seymour Johnson Air Force Base. Poultry production and tobacco warehousing and processing are important industries. There are also many food, wood product, and textile plants here.

What to See and Do

Cliffs of the Neuse State Park. *345 A Bark Entrance Rd, Seven Springs (28578). 14 miles SE, off Hwy 111. Phone 919/778-6234.* Over 700 acres on Neuse River. Swimming, bathhouse, fishing, boating (rowboat rentals). Nature trails. Picnicking. Tent and trailer sites (mid-Mar-Nov; fee). Museum, interpretive center.

Governor Charles B. Aycock Birthplace State Historic Site. *264 Governor Avcock Rd, Fremont (27830). 12 miles N, off Hwy 117 just S of Fremont. Phone 919/242-5581.* Mid-1800s farmhouse and outbuildings; audiovisual presentation in one-room school (1893); exhibits in visitor center portray life of the "educational governor." Picnicking. (Mon-Sat; closed holidays) **FREE**

Limited-Service Hotels

★ **HOLIDAY INN EXPRESS.** *909 N Spence Ave, Goldsboro (27534). Phone 919/751-1999; toll-free 800/465-4329; fax 919/751-1506. www.hiexpress.com/goldsboronc.* 122 rooms, 5 story. Pets accepted, some restrictions; fee. Complimentary continental breakfast. Check-in 3 pm, check-out noon. High-speed Internet access. Fitness room. Outdoor pool. Business center. **$**
🐾 🧍 ⌨ 🚶

★ ★ **QUALITY INN.** *708 Corporate Dr, Goldsboro (27534). Phone 919/735-7901; fax 919/735-7901. www. qualityinn.com.* 125 rooms, 2 story. Pets accepted; fee. Complimentary continental breakfast. Check-in 3 pm, check-out noon. High-speed Internet access, wireless Internet access. Restaurant, bar. Fitness room. Outdoor pool. **$**

Great Smoky Mountains National Park (B-1)

See also Bryson City, Cherokee, Fontana Dam, Maggie Valley

Web Site www.nps.gov/grsm

50 miles W of Asheville off Hwy 19.

The Appalachian Mountains, product of a slow up-thrusting of ancient sediments that took place more than 200 million years ago, stand tall and regal in this 800-square-mile area. Red spruce, basswood, eastern hemlock, yellow birch, white ash, cucumber trees, silverbells, Fraser fir, tulip poplar, red maple, and Fraser magnolias tower above hundreds of other species of flowering plants. Perhaps the most spectacular of these are the purple rhododendron, mountain laurel, and flame azalea, in bloom from early June to mid-July.

The moist climate has helped make this a rich wilderness. From early spring to late fall, the "coves" (as the open valleys surrounded by peaks are called) and forest floors are covered with a succession of flowers with colorful variety. Summer brings heavy showers, warm days (although 15° F to 20° F cooler than in the valleys below), and cool nights. Autumn is breathtaking as the deciduous trees change color. Winter brings snow, occasionally heavy, and fog over the mountains. Winter is a very good time to visit the park, but be aware of temporary road closures.

Half in North Carolina and half in Tennessee, with the Appalachian Trail following the state line along the ridge for 70 miles, this is a place to hike. In the lowlands are the cabins, barns, and mills of the mountain people whose ancestors came years ago from England and Scotland. It is also a place to see the descendants of the once mighty Cherokee Nation, whose ancestors hid in the mountains from the soldiers in the winter of 1838-1839 to avoid being driven over the Trail of Tears to Oklahoma. This is the tribe of Sequoyah, the brilliant chief who invented a written alphabet for the Cherokee people.

Stop first at one of the three visitor centers: Oconaluftee Center in North Carolina, 2 miles north of Cherokee on Newfound Gap Road, designated Hwy 441 outside the park (daily; closed Dec 25; phone 423/436-1200); Sugarlands in Tennessee, 2 miles southwest of Gatlinburg (daily; closed Dec 25; phone 423/436-1200); or Cades Cove in Tennessee, 10 miles southwest of Townsend (daily, closed Dec 25; phone 423/436-1200). All have exhibits and information about the park. There are hundreds of miles of foot trails and bridle paths. Camping is popular; ask at any visitor center for locations and regulations. There are developed campgrounds (fee). For reservations at Elkmont, Cades Cove, or Smokemont, phone toll-free 800/365-2267; reservations are not taken for other sites.

The views from Newfound Gap and the observation tower at Clingmans Dome (closed in winter) are spectacular. Cades Cove is an outdoor museum reflecting the life of the original mountain people, about 25 miles west of Sugarlands. It has log cabins and barns. Park naturalists conduct campfire programs and hikes during the summer. There are also self-guided nature trails. LeConte Lodge, reached only by foot or horseback, is an accommodation within the park. Phone 423/429-5704 (late Mar-mid-Nov).

Fishing is permitted with a Tennessee or North Carolina state fishing license. Obtain a list of regulations at the visitor centers and campgrounds. The park is a wildlife sanctuary; any disturbance of plant or animal life is forbidden. Dogs and cats are not permitted on trails but may be brought in if kept on a leash or other physical restrictive controls. Never feed, tease, or frighten bears; always give them a wide berth, as they can inflict serious injury. Watch bears from your car with the windows closed.

For the disabled, there is an all-access trail, the Sugarland Valley Nature Trail, equipped with special interpretive exhibits. Accessibility information is available at the visitor centers. **FREE**

For information, contact the Superintendent, Great Smoky Mountains National Park, 107 Park Headquarters Rd, Gatlinburg, TN 37738; phone 423/436-1200.

Greensboro (A-5)

See also Asheboro, Burlington, High Point, Winston-Salem

Founded 1808
Population 223,891
Elevation 841 ft
Area Code 336
Information Greensboro Area Convention and Visitors Bureau, 317 S Greene St, 27401; phone 336/274-2282 or toll-free 800/344-2282
Web Site www.greensboronc.org

William Sydney Porter (O. Henry) was born and raised near Greensboro, a diversified Piedmont industrial city whose products are typical of North Carolina: textiles, cigarettes, machinery, and electronic components. It was settled by Quakers, Germans, and the Scotch-Irish with a zeal for political, religious, and economic freedom. Men from this region fought in the Revolution and the War of 1812 and turned to the Confederacy in 1861. It was in Greensboro, the rebel supply depot, that Jefferson Davis met General Johnston after Richmond fell in 1865 and agreed on surrender terms. Today it is an educational, manufacturing, and distribution center.

What to See and Do

Charlotte Hawkins Brown Memorial State Historic Site. *6136 Burlington Rd, Sedalia . 10 miles E on I-85 to exit 135, then 1/2 mile W on Hwy 70. Phone 336/449-4846. www.nchistoricsites.org/chb/chb.htm.* North Carolina's first state historic site, honoring the achievements of African-American education in the state. In 1902, C. H. Brown, granddaughter of former slaves, founded Palmer Memorial Institute, which became one of the finest preparatory schools for blacks in the nation. Guided tours of historic campus (several buildings being restored), visitor center, audiovisual program. Picnicking. (Apr-Oct, Tues-Sat; rest of year, Tues-Sun; closed holidays) **FREE**

Greensboro Historical Museum. *130 Summit Ave, Greensboro (27401). Phone 336/373-2043. www.greensborohistory.org.* Housed in an 1892 building in the downtown area, the museum features displays on the Revolutionary War, First Lady Dolly Madison, and writer O. Henry, among others. (Tues-Sat 10 am-5 pm, Sun 2-5 pm; closed holidays) **FREE**

Guilford College. *5800 W Friendly Ave, Greensboro . 2 miles N of I-40. Phone 336/316-2000.* (1837) (1,300 stu-

dents) Oldest coed college in the South. Beautiful wooded 340-acre campus with Georgian-style buildings and a unique solar energy fieldhouse. Quaker archives dating from 1680 (Tues-Fri, by appointment; closed holidays). Official home of Eastern Music Festival (June-Aug).

Guilford Courthouse National Military Park. *2332 New Garden Rd, Greensboro (27410). 6 miles NW and 1/4 mile E off Hwy 220 on New Garden Rd. Phone 336/288-1776. www.nps.gov/guco.* On March 15, 1781, Lord Cornwallis won a costly victory that was one link in a series of events that led to his surrender at Yorktown in October of the same year. After destroying a quarter of the enemy troops, General Nathanael Greene (for whom the city is named) made a successful retreat and then severely hampered the British plan of subduing the Southern colonies. The 220-acre park, established in 1917, has monuments marking important locations and honoring those who fought here; two signers of the Declaration of Independence, John Penn and William Hooper, are also buried here. Self-guided auto tour; walking trails. The visitor center has a museum housing Revolutionary War weapons, other items; 20-minute film. (Daily; closed Jan 1, Dec 25) **FREE**

Hagan-Stone Park. *5920 Hagan Stone Park Rd, Pleasant Garden (27313). 6 miles S on Hwy 421, then 2 miles W on Hagan-Stone Park Rd. Phone 336/674-0472.* Swimming, fishing. Hiking. Picnicking, playground. Camping (hookups, dump station). Park (all year). Some fees. Pets on leash only.

Natural Science Center of Greensboro. *4301 Lawndale Dr, Greensboro (27455). Phone 336/288-3769. www.natsci.org.* Natural science museum with zoo and indoor exhibits including geology, paleontology, aquarium, herpetarium, and science and technology. Check out the 36-foot-tall Tyrannosaurus rex model. Planetarium shows; inquire for schedule. (Mon-Sat 9 am-5 pm, Sun 12:30-5 pm) **$$**

University of North Carolina at Greensboro. *1000 Spring Garden St, Greensboro. Phone 336/334-5243.* (1891) (13,000 students)

Weatherspoon Art Museum. *Spring Garden and Tate St, Greensboro (27402). Anne and Benjamin Cone Building. Phone 336/334-5770.* Permanent collection of over 4,000 contemporary paintings, graphic arts, sculpture. (Tues-Sun; closed school holidays) **FREE**

Special Event

Greater Greensboro Chrysler Classic Golf Tournament. *4600 Forest Oaks Dr, Greensboro (27406). Phone 336/379-1570.* Top golfers compete for more than $3 million on PGA circuit. Late Sept-early Oct.

Limited-Service Hotels

★ **COMFORT INN.** *2001 Veasley St, Greensboro (27407). Phone 336/294-6220; toll-free 800/424-6423; fax 336/291-4463. www.choicehotels.com/hotel/nc411.* 122 rooms, 2 story. Pets accepted; restrictions, fee. Complimentary continental breakfast. Check-in 2 pm, check-out noon. High-speed Internet access, wireless Internet access. Outdoor pool. **$**

★ ★ **EMBASSY SUITES.** *204 Centreport Dr, Greensboro (27409). Phone 336/668-4535; toll-free 800/362-2779; fax 336/668-3901. www.embassy-suitesgreensboro.com.* Visitors can relax in this hotel's seven-story atrium filled with greenery and fountains and illuminated by the sun through skylights. The hotel is conveniently located near shopping, restaurants and other attractions. 219 rooms, 7 story. Complimentary full breakfast. Check-in 3 pm, check-out noon. Restaurant, bar. Fitness room. Indoor pool, whirlpool. Airport transportation available. Business center. **$$**

★ **HAMPTON INN.** *2004 Veasley St, Greensboro (27407). Phone 336/854-8600; toll-free 800/426-7866; fax 336/854-8741. www.hamptoninn.com.* 120 rooms, 2 story. Complimentary continental breakfast. Check-in 3 pm, check-out noon. Outdoor pool. **$**

★ **QUALITY INN.** *120 Seneca Rd, Greensboro (27406). Phone 336/275-9575; toll-free 800/424-6423; fax 336/275-9572. www.qualityinn.com.* 115 rooms, 2 story. Complimentary full breakfast. Check-in 2 pm, check-out 11 am. Wireless Internet access. Outdoor pool, children's pool. **$**

Full-Service Hotels

★ ★ **MARRIOTT GREENSBORO AIRPORT.** *1 Marriott Dr, Greensboro (27409). Phone 336/852-6450; toll-free 800/228-9290; fax 336/665-6522. www.marriott.com.* This hotel is located on the Piedmont Triad International Airport ground, but offers 17 acres of beautiful landscaped grounds with a lake. 299 rooms, 6 story. Check-in 3 pm, check-out noon. Two restaurants, bar. Fitness room. Indoor pool, outdoor pool, whirlpool. Airport transportation available. **$$**

★ ★ **MARRIOTT GREENSBORO DOWN-TOWN** *304 N Greene St, Greensboro (27401). Phone*

336/379-8000; fax 336/275-2810. www.marriott.com. Situated in the historic area of downtown Greensboro, this hotel is within walking distance of shopping, antique shops, water and city parks, fine and casual dining restaurants, and other attractions. 280 rooms, 11 story. Check-in 3 pm, check-out 11 am. Restaurant, bar. Children's activity center. Fitness room. Indoor pool, whirlpool. **$$**

★ ★ ★ **O. HENRY HOTEL.** *624 Green Valley Rd, Greensboro (27408). Phone 336/854-2000; toll-free 877/854-2100; fax 336/854-2223. www.ohenryhotel.com.* 131 rooms. Complimentary full breakfast. Check-in 3 pm, check-out noon. High-speed Internet access. Restaurant, bar. Outdoor pool. Airport transportation available. Business center. **$$**

Full-Service Resort

★ ★ ★ **GRANDOVER RESORT & CONFERENCE CENTER.** *1000 Club Rd, Greensboro (27407). Phone 336/294-1800; toll-free 800/472-6301; fax 336/856-9991. www.grandover.com.* The Grandover Resort & Conference Center simply can't be beaten for its exceptional, award-winning golf, fine dining, stylish accommodations, and good old southern hospitality. This contemporary resort is truly a golfer's dream, with 36 holes awaiting play, along with the Ken Venturi Golf School. A new spa has just been added to the property, perfect for those who need a post-game massage or for others who want to spend the entire day luxuriating at the sparkling facility. Four clay tennis courts and a state-of-the-art fitness center provide other diversions. The rooms and suites are spacious and inviting, with fantastic views over the emerald links, and personalized service adds to the experience. 247 rooms, 11 story. Check-in 4 pm, check-out noon. Restaurant, bar. Fitness room, spa. Indoor pool, outdoor pools, whirlpool. Golf, 36 holes. Tennis. **$$**

Restaurant

★ ★ **GATE CITY CHOP HOUSE.** *106 S Holden St, Greensboro (27407). Phone 336/294-9977; fax 336/294-1048. www.chophouseofnc.com.* Enjoy a drink at the circular oak bar while waiting for seating in one of the five dining areas. American menu. Lunch, dinner. Closed Sun; July 4, Thanksgiving, Dec 24-25. Bar. Casual attire. Outdoor seating. **$$$**

Greenville (B-8)

See also Washington, Williamston

Founded 1786
Population 60,476
Elevation 55 ft
Area Code 252
Information Greenville-Pitt County Convention and Visitors Bureau, 525 S Evans St, PO Box 8027, 27835-8027; phone toll-free 800/537-5564
Web Site www.visitgreenvillenc.com

An educational, cultural, commercial, and medical center, Greenville is one of the towns named for General Nathanael Greene, a hero of the American Revolutionary War.

What to See and Do

East Carolina University. *E 5th St, Greenville (27858). Medical Center campus, W side of town. Phone 252/328-6131. (1907)* (17,600 students) Jenkins Fine Arts Center, ECU Music School, and Gray Art Gallery offer many cultural events to the public.

Greenville Museum of Art. *802 Evans St, Greenville . Phone 252/758-1946.* Collections emphasize North Carolina contemporary fine arts and drawings, also paintings and prints of the period 1900-1945. (Tues-Fri, also Sat afternoons; closed holidays) **DONATION**

River Park North Science and Nature Center. *1000 Mumford Rd, Greenville (27834). 5 miles N on Mumford Rd. Phone 252/329-4560.* A 309-acre park with four lakes and 1.2 miles of Tar River water frontage. Science center near park entrance offers hands-on exhibits. Fishing, boating (ramp; no gas motors), pedal boats. Picnicking. (Tues-Sun; closed holidays) **$**

Limited-Service Hotels

★ **HAMPTON INN.** *3439 S Memorial Dr, Greenville (27834). Phone 252/355-2521; toll-free 800/426-7866; fax 252/355-0262. www.hamptoninn.com.* 121 rooms, 2 story. Complimentary continental breakfast. Check-in 4 pm, check-out noon. Fitness Room. Outdoor pool. **$**

★ **QUALITY INN.** *821 S Memorial Dr, Greenville (27834). Phone 252/758-5544; toll-free 877/424-6423; fax 252/758-1416. www.qualityinn.com.* 114 rooms, 2 story. Complimentary continental breakfast. Check-in

3 pm, check-out noon. Fitness Room. Outdoor pool. Airport transportation available. **$**

Restaurants

★ ★ **BEEF BARN.** *400 St Andrews Dr, Greenville (27834). Phone 252/756-1161; fax 252/756-7655. www. beefbarn.net.* Steak, seafood menu. Lunch, dinner. Closed holidays. Bar. Children's menu. Casual attire. Reservations recommended. **$$**

★ **PARKER'S BAR-B-QUE.** *3109 S Memorial Dr, Greenville (27834). Phone 252/756-2388; fax 252/756-6950.* American menu. Lunch, dinner. Closed Thanksgiving, Dec 25, Children's menu. Casual attire. No credit cards accepted. **$**

Hatteras (B-10)

See also Cape Hatteras National Seashore

Population 1,660
Elevation 2 ft
Area Code 252
Zip 27943
Web Site www.outerbanks.org

This Hatteras Island fishing village on the Outer Banks (see) was settled, it is said, by shipwrecked sailors from Devon, England. The Devon accent is indeed heard here and on the islands of Ocracoke and Manteo. There are ferries south to Ocracoke (see).

Henderson (A-7)

Founded 1840
Population 16,095
Elevation 509 ft
Area Code 252
Zip 27536
Information Vance County Tourism Department, 943K W Andrews Ave; phone 252/438-2222
Web Site www.kerrlake-nc.com

Tobacco has historically been the major crop in Vance County, of which Henderson is the seat. The manufacturing and processing of textiles, hosiery, furniture, food, tobacco, mobile homes, and glass containers are local industries. Tourism helps drive the economy.

What to See and Do

Kerr Reservoir. *6254 Satterwhite Point Rd, Henderson (27536). 6 miles N off I-85. Phone 252/438-7791. www. ncsparks.net.* Part of the development of the Roanoke River basin by the US Army Corps of Engineers. Approximately 800 miles of shoreline and 50,000 acres of water. Swimming, water-skiing, fishing, boating, several private marinas; picnicking, camping (fee). Seven state recreation areas around lake, some open only Apr-Oct. (Daily) State camping areas (water and electric hook-ups in all, except some sites in Bullocksville).

Special Event

Parade of Lights on Water. *Kerr Lake, 269 Glass House Rd, Henderson (27356). Phone 252/438-7791.* Fireworks, entertainment. Fourth of July.

Hendersonville (B-3)

See also Asheville, Brevard, Tryon

Population 10,420
Elevation 2,146 ft
Area Code 828
Information Chamber of Commerce, 330 N King St, 28792; phone 828-692-1413
Web Site www.hendersonvillechamber.org

The county seat of Henderson County, Hendersonville is well-known as a summer resort colony and popular retirement community. Manufacturing, agriculture, and tourism help make up the county's balanced economy.

What to See and Do

⭐ **Carl Sandburg Home National Historic Site.** *81 Carl Sandburg Ln, Flat Rock (28731). 3 miles S on Hwy 25. In Flat Rock. Phone 828/693-4178. www.nps.gov/carl.* The famous poet's 264-acre farm residence, Connemara, is maintained as it was when Sandburg and his family lived here from 1945 until his death in 1967. Tours lasting 30 minutes depart regularly throughout the day. On the grounds are a house and a historic barn for the three breeds of goats that Sandburg raised, as well as a visitor center. (Daily 9 am-5 pm; closed Dec 25) **$**

Holmes State Forest. *Hendersonville . SW on Crab Creek Rd. Phone 828/692-0100.* This managed forest was designed to facilitate a better understanding of the value of forests in our lives. It features "talking trees"

with recorded narration about the site and the forest's history. Picnicking (reservations required). Group camping (reservations required). For reservations or information, contact Rte 4, Box 308. (Mid-Mar-Nov, Tues-Sun) **FREE**

Jump-Off Rock. *5th Ave, 6 miles W.* Panoramic view from atop Jump-Off Mountain.

Special Events

Flat Rock Playhouse. *2661 Greenville Hwy, Flat Rock (28731). 3 1/2 miles S on Hwy 25. Phone 828/693-0731.* Outstanding professional theater since 1939; State Theater of North Carolina since 1961. Vagabond Players offer ten Broadway and London productions in 15 weeks. Mid-May-mid-Dec. Wed-Sat evenings; Thurs, Sat, Sun matinees.

North Carolina Apple Festival. *401 N Main St, Hendersonville (28792). Phone 828/697-4557.* Labor Day weekend.

Limited-Service Hotels

★ **COMFORT INN.** *206 Mitchell Dr, Hendersonville (28792). Phone 828/693-8800; toll-free 800/424-6423; fax 828/693-8800.www.comfortinn.com.*84 rooms, 2 story. Pets accepted; fee. Complimentary continental breakfast. Check-in 3 pm, check-out 11 am. Outdoor pool. **$**
🐾 ⚊

★ **HAMPTON INN.** *155 Sugarloaf Rd, Hendersonville (28792). Phone 828/697-2333; toll-free 800/426-7866; fax 828/693-5280. www.hamptoninn.com/hi/ hendersonville.* 118 rooms, 4 story. Complimentary continental breakfast. Check-in 2 pm, check-out noon. Outdoor pool.**$**
⚊

Full-Service Resort

★ ★ ★ **HIGHLAND LAKE INN.** *Highland Lake Rd, Flat Rock (28731). Phone 828/693-6812 toll-free 800/635-5101; fax 828/696-8951. www.hlinn.com.* 63 rooms, 3 story. Check-in 4 pm, check-out 11 am. High-speed Internet access. Restaurant, bar. Beach. Outdoor pool. Tennis. **$$**
⚊ 🏃

Full-Service Inn

★ ★ **ECHO MOUNTAIN INN.** *2849 Laurel Park Hwy, Hendersonville (28739). Phone 828/693-9626;*

toll-free 800/324-6466; fax 828/693-9626. www. echoinn.com. 45 rooms, 2 story. Complimentary continental breakfast. Check-in 2 pm, check-out 11 am. Outdoor pool.**$**

Specialty Lodgings

LAKE LURE INN. *2771 Memorial Hwy, Lake Lure (28746). Phone 828/625-2525; toll-free 800/277-5873; fax 828/625-9655.* 50 rooms, 3 story. Complimentary continental breakfast. Check-in 3 pm, check-out 11 am. Restaurant, bar. Outdoor pool. **$**

LODGE ON LAKE LURE BED & BREAKFAST. *361 Charlotte Dr, Lake Lure (28746). Phone 828/625-2789; toll-free 800/733-2785; fax 828/625-2421. www. lodgeonlakelure.com.* This inn promises a unique balance of the casual countryside with an elegant bed-and-breakfast. The innkeepers are family and welcome guests to their home for relaxed excursions. The beauty of the lake also adds a wonderful backdrop to this scenic property. 16 rooms, 2 story. Children over 8 years only. Complimentary full breakfast. Check-in 3-8 pm, check-out 11 am. **$$**

THE WAVERLY INN. *783 N Main St, Hendersonville (28792). Phone 828/693-9193; toll-free 800/537-8195; fax 828/692-1010. www.waverlyinn.com.* 15 rooms, 3 story. Complimentary full breakfast. Check-in 1 pm, check-out 11 am. Restored guest house (1898); Victorian décor, upstairs sun porch.**$**

WOODFIELD. *2905 Greenville Hwy, Flat Rock (28731). Phone 828/693-6016; toll-free 800/533-6016; fax 828/693-0437. www.woodfieldinn.com.* 17 rooms, 3 story. Complimentary full breakfast. Check-in 3 pm, check-out 11 am. Tennis. Built in 1852; antiques. **$$**

Restaurants

★ ★ ★ **EXPRESSIONS.** *114 N Main St, Hendersonville (28792). Phone 828/693-8516; fax 828/696-8666.* This delightful restaurant has been a well-loved fixture of simple elegance on Main Street for more than two decades. The upscale cuisine, featuring seafood, beef, duck, quail, pork, and chicken is beautifully and innovatively presented. Guests can choose from a list of more than 200 fine domestic and French wines, and they also can enjoy a comfortable upstairs lounge

that's perfect for unwinding after a busy day. American menu. Lunch, dinner, Sun brunch. Bar. Business casual attire. Reservations recommended. Outdoor seating. **$$$**

★ ★ **SINBAD.** *202 S Washington St, Hendersonville (28739). Phone 828/696-2039. www.sinbadrestaurant. com.* Choose between dining indoors overlooking the beautiful gardens or dining outdoors under the beautiful NC skies. Mediterranean menu. Lunch, dinner. Closed Sun-Mon; also Jan 1, Thanksgiving, Dec 25. Bar. **$$**

Hickory (B-4)

See also Statesville

Population 37,222
Elevation 1,163 ft
Area Code 828
Information Catawba County Chamber of Commerce, 1055 Southgate Corporate Park SW, 28602; phone 828/328-6111
Web Site www.catawbachamber.org

Nationally known brands of furniture and hosiery are produced here, as are ceramics and electronic equipment.

What to See and Do

Arts Center of Catawba Valley. *243 3rd Ave NE, Hickory.* Here are

> **Catawba Science Center.** *243 Third Ave NE, Hickory (28601). Phone 828/322-8169.* Interactive exhibits feature life, earth, medical, and physical sciences. Also changing exhibits. (Tues-Sun; closed holidays) **$**

> **Hickory Museum of Art.** *234 3rd Ave, Hickory (28601). Phone 828/327-8576.* American realist 19th- and 20th-century art, including works by Gilbert Stuart; Hudson River School, Thos. Cole to Homer Martin; American impressionists; European, Oriental, and pre-Columbian pieces; changing exhibits quarterly. (Tues-Sun; closed Easter, Dec 25) **FREE**

Bunker Hill Covered Bridge. *On Hwy 70, approximately 10 miles E. Phone 828/465-0383.* One of only two remaining covered bridges in the state. Built in 1895, it spans Lyle's Creek. Nature trail, picnicking.

Catawba County Museum of History. *21 E 1st St, Newton (28658). 3 miles S, Courthouse Sq. Phone 828/465-0383.* Exhibits include a fire engine (1919), country doctor's office (1920), Waugh Cabin (1839), Barringer Cabin (1759), a blacksmith shop (1870), and an agriculture exhibit. (Tues-Sun; closed holidays) **FREE**

Lake Hickory. *4 miles N.* This 4,100-acre lake with a 105-mile shoreline was created by the Oxford Dam on the Catawba River. It offers boating, fishing, swimming, and marinas.

Lenoir-Rhyne College. *625 7th Ave and 8th St NE, Hickory (28601). Phone 828/328-1741.* (1891) (Approximately 1,700 students) Observatory (Sept-Apr, evenings, weather permitting). Concerts, athletic contests, dramatic productions, art exhibits, convocation programs, and other special events throughout the academic year.

Murray's Mill. *1489 Murrays Mill Rd, Catawba (28609). 10 miles E via I-40. Phone 828/465-0383.* (1890) Overshot waterwheel, working machinery; milling museum and demonstrations. Country store (1890), folk art gallery (1880). (Thurs-Sun; closed holidays) **$**

Special Event

Auto racing. *Hickory Motor Speedway, 3130 Hwy 70 SE, Newton. 4 miles E on Hwy 70. Phone 828/464-3655.* Stock car racing. Mid-Mar-Mid-Nov.

Limited-Service Hotels

★ **COMFORT INN.** *1125 13th Dr SE, Hickory (28602). Phone 828/323-1211; fax 828/322-4395. www.comfortsuites.com.* 116 rooms, 2 story. Complimentary full breakfast. Check-in 3 pm, check-out 11 am. Fitness room. Outdoor pool. **$**

★ **HAMPTON INN.** *1520 13th Ave Dr SE, Hickory (28602). Phone 828/323-1150; toll-free 800/426-7866; fax 828/324-8979. www.hamptoninn.com.* 119 rooms, 2 story. Complimentary continental breakfast. Check-in 3 pm, check-out noon. Outdoor pool. **$**

★ ★ **HOLIDAY INN.** *1385 Lenoir Rhyne Blvd SE, Hickory (28601). Phone 828/323-1000; toll-free 800/366-5010; fax 828/322-4275. www.holiday-inn.com.* 200 rooms, 2 story. Complimentary continental breakfast. Check-in 3 pm, check-out noon. Restaurant, bar. Fitness room. Indoor pool, whirlpool. **$**

Restaurants

★ ★ ★ **1859 CAFE.** *443 2nd Ave SW, Hickory (28602). Phone 828/322-1859; fax 828/322-5697.* International menu. Dinner. Closed Sun; Thanksgiving, Dec 24-25. Bar. Casual attire. Reservations recommended. Outdoor seating. **$$$**

★ ★ ★ **VINTAGE HOUSE.** *271 3rd Ave NW, Hickory (28601). Phone 828/324-1210; fax 828/324-2218.* American menu. Dinner. Closed Sun; first week in June, first week in July. Bar. Casual attire. **$$**

High Point (A-5)

See also Asheboro, Burlington, Greensboro, Lexington, Winston-Salem

Founded 1859
Population 85,839
Elevation 939 ft
Area Code 336
Information Convention and Visitors Bureau, 300 S Main St, PO Box 2273, 27261; phone 336/884-5255 or toll-free 800/720-5255
Web Site www.highpoint.org

Furniture and hosiery are the products that make High Point prosperous. The city rests on the highest point along the North Carolina and Midland Railroad, which the state built in 1853. The plank road (finished in 1854), stretching 130 miles from Salem to Fayetteville, made it a center of trade; mileposts on this road had carved numbers instead of painted ones so travelers could feel their way at night.

What to See and Do

Furniture Discovery Center. *101 W Green Dr, High Point. Phone 336/887-3876.* Nation's only museum of modern-day furniture manufacturing. Hands-on displays; miniatures; hall of fame; special exhibits. (Apr-Oct, daily; rest of year, Tues-Sun; closed holidays) **$$**

Peterson Doll and Miniature Museum. *101 W Green Dr, High Point (27260). Phone 336/885-3655.* Collection of more than 2,000 dolls and related artifacts from around the world, some dating back to the 15th century. (Apr-Oct, daily; Nov-Mar, Tues-Sun; closed holidays) **$**

World's Largest Chest of Drawers. *508 N Hamilton St,* High Point. Building designed to look like a 19th-century dresser; symbolizes the city's position as a furniture center. Built in 1926. **FREE**

Special Events

Day in the Park. *City Lake Park, 602 W Main St, Jamestown (27282). Phone 336/889-2787.* Arts and crafts, rides, entertainment. Mid-Sept.

North Carolina Shakespeare Festival. *High Point Theatre, 220 E Commerce Ave, High Point. Phone 336/841-2273.* Season includes three productions and *A Christmas Carol.* Aug-Oct and Dec.

Limited-Service Hotel

★ ★ **RADISSON HOTEL HIGH POINT.** *135 S Main St, High Point (27260). Phone 336/889-8888; toll-free 800/333-3333; fax 336/885-2737. www.radisson. com/highpointnc.* 252 rooms, 8 story. Pets accepted; fee. Check-in 3 pm, check-out noon. Restaurant, bar. Indoor pool. Airport transportation available. **$**

Specialty Lodging

BOULDIN HOUSE BED AND BREAKFAST. *4332 Archdale Rd, High Point (27263). Phone 336/431-4909; toll-free 800/739-1816; fax 336/431-4914. www. bouldinhouse.com.* 5 rooms. Children over 12 years only. Complimentary full breakfast. Check-in 5-7 pm. Check-out 10:30 am.**$**

Restaurant

★ ★ ★ **J BASUL NOBLE'S.** *101 S Main St, High Point (27260). Phone 336/889-3354; fax 336/889-1424. www.noblesrestaurants.com.* Italian menu. Dinner. Closed Sun; holidays. Bar. Casual attire. Outdoor seating. **$$**

Highlands (C-2)

See also Cashiers, Franklin

Population 909
Elevation 3,835 ft
Area Code 828
Zip 28741
Information Chamber of Commerce, 396 Oak St, PO Box 404; phone 828/526-2112
Web Site www.highlandsinfo.com

Highlands is a summer resort near the Georgia state line. Many unusual plants are part of the primeval rain forest preserve. Completely encircled by Nan-tahala National Forest (see FRANKLIN), the area surrounding the town is called "land of the waterfalls." A Ranger District office is located here.

What to See and Do

Bridal Veil Falls, Dry Falls. *NW of town on Hwy 64, Hwy 28.* Behind Dry Falls the visitor may stand and look through to the Cullasaja River without getting wet. Also here is Lower Cullasaja Falls. The road here was cut from vertical cliffs and overlooks the river 250 feet below.

Highlands Nature Center. *930 Horse Cove Rd, Highlands (28741). E Main St (Horse Cove Rd), 1/2 mile E of jct Hwy 64, Hwy 28.* On grounds of Highlands Biological Station. *Phone 828/526-2623.* Cherokee artifacts, minerals of North Carolina; local flora and fauna, botanical garden; nature trail, hikes; lectures, movies. (Late May-Labor Day, Mon-Sat) **FREE**

Scaly Mountain Ski Area. *Hwy 106, Scaly Mountain. 7 miles S on Hwy 106. Phone 828/526-3737. www. scalymountain.com.* Chair lift, rope tow; patrol, school, rentals; snowmaking; cafeteria. Longest run 600 feet; vertical drop 225 feet. (Mid-Dec-early Mar, daily) Half-day rates. **$$$$**

Limited-Service Hotel

★ **HIGHLANDS SUITE HOTEL.** *200 Main St, Highlands (28741). Phone 828/526-4502; toll-free 877/553-3761; fax 828/526-4840. www.highlandssuitehotel.com.* 29 rooms, 2 story, all suites. Complimentary continental breakfast. Check-in 4 pm, check-out noon. **$**

Full-Service Inn

★ ★ ★ **OLD EDWARDS INN AND SPA.** *445 Main St, Highlands (28741). Phone 828/526-8008; fax 828/526-8301.* 30 rooms. Children over 11 years only. Complimentary continental breakfast. Check-in 4 pm, check-out noon. Wireless Internet access. Restaurant, bar. Spa. Tennis. **$$$$**

Specialty Lodging

HIGHLANDS INN. *4th and E Main sts, Highlands (28741). Phone 828/526-9380; toll-free 800/964-6955; fax 828/526-8810. www.highlandsinn-nc.com.* 37 rooms, 3 story. Closed Dec-Mar. Complimentary full breakfast. Check-in 4 pm, check-out 11 am. Restaurant. **$**

Restaurants

★ ★ ★ **MADISON'S RESTAURANT AND WINE GARDEN.** *445 Main St, Highlands (28741). Phone 828/787-2525; toll-free 866/526-8008; fax 828/526-8301. www.oldedwardsinn.com.* American menu. Breakfast, lunch, dinner. Bar. Children's menu. Business casual attire. Reservations recommended. Valet parking. Outdoor seating. **$$$**

★ ★ **NICK'S.** *108 Min St, Highlands (28741). Phone 828/526-2706; fax 828/526-2150.* American menu. Lunch, dinner. Closed Wed; also Jan-Feb. Children's menu. Casual attire. Reservations recommended. **$$**

★ ★ **ON THE VERANDAH.** *1536 Franklin Rd, Highlands (28741). Phone 828/526-2338; fax 828/526-4132. www.ontheverandah.com.* American menu. Dinner, Sun brunch. Closed Jan-mid-Mar; weekdays in Dec and Mar. Children's menu. Casual attire. Reservations recommended. Outdoor seating. **$$$**

Jacksonville (C-8)

Population 66,715
Elevation 15 ft
Area Code 910
Web Site www.jacksonvillenc.net

This town is on the edge of the New River Marine Base (Camp Lejeune). There is excellent fishing nearby.

Limited-Service Hotels

★ **BEST WESTERN COURTYARD RESORT.** *603 N Marine Blvd, Jacksonville (28540). Phone 910/455-4100; fax 910/455-3023. www.bestwestern. com.* 121 rooms. Complimentary continental breakfast. Check-in 3 pm, check-out noon. Wireless Internet access. Outdoor pool. Fitness room. **$**

★ **HAMPTON INN.** *474 Western Blvd, Jacksonville (28546). Phone 910/347-6500; toll-free 800/426-7866; fax 910/347-6858. www.hamptoninn.com.* 120 rooms, 2 story. Pets accepted, some restrictions; fee. Complimentary continental breakfast. Check-in 2 pm, check-out noon. Outdoor pool. **$**

★ **HOLIDAY INN EXPRESS.** *2115 Hwy 17 N, Jacksonville (28546). Phone 910/347-1900; toll-free 800/465-4329; fax 910/347-7593. www.holiday-inn. com.* 118 rooms, 4 story. Complimentary continental breakfast. Check-in 4 pm, check-out 11 am. High-speed Internet access, wireless Internet access. Outdoor pool. **$**

Jefferson (A-4)

See also Boone, Wilkesboro

Founded 1800
Population 1,422
Elevation 2,960 ft
Area Code 336
Zip 28640
Information Ashe County Chamber of Commerce, PO Box 31, 6 N Jefferson Ave, 28694; phone 336/246-9550
Web Site www.ashechamber.com

What to See and Do

Ashe County Cheese Factory. *106 E Main St, West Jefferson. 2 miles S on Hwy 194. Phone 336/246-2501; toll-free 800/445-1378.* North Carolina's only cheese factory. Viewing of cheese production; samples. (Mon-Sat; closed holidays; also Dec 26) **FREE**

Mount Je|fferson State Park. *1 mile S off Hwy 221. At the summit of Mount Jefferson. Phone 336/246-9653.* A national natural landmark; excellent view of the Blue Ridge Mountains. Approximately 500 acres. Hiking, nature trails. Picnicking. No camping available.

Full-Service Inn

★ ★ ★ **GLENDALE SPRINGS INN.** *7414 Hwy 16, Glendale Springs (28629). Phone 336/982-2103; toll-free 800/287-1206; fax 336/982-4036. www.glendalespringsinn.com.* In a quaint community on the top of the Blue Ridge Mountains, this historic inn is as well known for its dining room as for its accommodations. The property was built in 1892. 9 rooms, 2 story. Complimentary full breakfast. Check-in 2 pm. Check-out 11 am. Restaurant. **$**

Kill Devil Hills (A-10)

*See also Cape Hatteras National Seashore, Fort Raleigh
National Historic Site, Manteo, Nags Head*

Population 5,897
Elevation 20 ft
Area Code 252
Zip 27948
Information Dare County Tourist Bureau, 704 US
64/264, PO Box 399, Manteo 27954; phone 252/473-
2138 or toll-free 800/446-6262.
Web Site www.outerbanks.org

Although the name Kitty Hawk is usually associated
with the Wright Brothers, their early flying experiments took place on and near these dunes on the
Outer Banks (see).

What to See and Do

Wright Brothers National Memorial. *1401 National
Park Dr, Kill Devil Hills (27954). Off Hwy 158, between
mileposts 7 and 8. Phone 252/441-7430.* The field
where the first powered flight took place on December
17, 1903, is marked showing the takeoff point and
landing place. The living quarters and hangar buildings used by the Wrights during their experiments
have been replicated. The visitor center has reproductions of a 1902 glider and a 1903 flyer, with exhibits on the story of their invention. Also 3,000-foot
airstrip. (Daily; closed Dec 25) **$$**

Limited-Service Hotels

★ **BEST WESTERN OCEAN REEF SUITES.**
*107 Virginia Dare Ct, Kill Devil Hills (27948). Phone
252/441-1611; toll-free 800/528-1234; fax 252/441-
1482. www.bestwestern.com.* 71 rooms, 5 story. Check-
in 4 pm, check-out 11 am. Fitness room. Beach.
Outdoor pool, whirlpool. **$$**

★ **COMFORT INN.** *401 N Virginia Dare Trail, Kill
Devil Hills (27948). Phone 252/480-2600; toll-free
800/424-6423; fax 252/480-2873. www.comfortinn.
com.* 119 rooms, 3 story. Complimentary continental
breakfast. Check-in 4 pm, check-out 11 am. Beach.
Outdoor pool. **$**

★ **DAYS INN.** *201 N Virginia Dare Trail, Kill Devil
Hills (27948). Phone 252/441-7211; toll-free 800/329-*
7466; fax 252/441-8080. www.obxlodging.com. 54
rooms. Complimentary continental breakfast. Check-
in 4 pm, check-out 11 am. Beach. Outdoor pool. **$**

★ ★ **RAMADA.** *1701 S Virginia Dare Trail, Kill
Devil Hills (27948). Phone 252/441-2151; toll-free
800/635-1824; fax 252/441-1830. www.ramada.com.*
171 rooms, 5 story. Pets accepted; fee. Check-in 4 pm,
check-out 11 am. High-speed Internet access. Restaurant, bar. Fitness room. Beach. Indoor pool,whirlpool.
Business center. **$$**

Full-Service Resort

★ ★ ★ **THE SANDERLING.** *1461 Duck Rd, Duck
(27949). Phone 252/261-4111; toll-free 800/701-4111;
fax 252/261-1352. www.sanderling.com.* Nestled on the
northern reaches of North Carolina's ruggedly beautiful
Outer Banks, The Sanderling is a resort for those who
want to get away from it all without leaving comfort
behind. From the low-rise cedar-shingled buildings to
the Eco-Center, everything about this resort has been
designed to complement the natural setting. Comprised
of three inns and oceanside villas, The Sanderling of-
fers a stylish, contemporary country atmosphere in its
accommodations. Mornings begin with fresh-baked
goods delivered to the rooms, and days are filled with
a variety of adventures, including those that require
little more than relaxing with a great massage. Miles
of pristine beachfront beckon guests, and the seaside
ambience extends to dining, where a highly intrigu-
ing restaurant is housed within a historic US lifesaving
station. 88 rooms. Check-in 4 pm, check-out 11 am.
Restaurant, bar. Fitness room. Indoor pool, whirlpool.
Tennis. **$$**

Restaurants

★ ★ **FLYING FISH CAFE.** *2003 S Croatan Hwy,
Kill Devil Hills (27948). Phone 252/441-6894; fax
252/480-2073. www.flyingfishcafe.net.* Mediterranean
menu. Dinner. Bar. Children's menu. Casual attire.
Reservations recommended. **$$**

★ **JOLLY ROGER.** *1836 N Virginia Dare Trail, Kill
Devil Hills (27948). Phone 252/441-6530; fax 252/480-
3241.* American menu. Breakfast, lunch, dinner. Bar.
Children's menu. Casual attire. **$$**

★ ★ **PORT O' CALL.** *504 Virginia Dare Trail, Kill
Devil Hills (27948). Phone 252/441-800; fax 252/441-*

5725. www.outerbanksportocall.com. Seafood, steak menu. Dinner. Closed Jan-Mar. Bar. Children's menu. Casual attire. Reservations recommended. **$$**

Kinston (B-8)

See also New Bern

Population 23,688
Elevation 44 ft
Area Code 252
Zip 28501
Web Site www.visitkinston.com

What to See and Do

CSS Neuse **State Historic Site.** *2612 W Vernon Ave, Kinston. Phone 252/522-2091.*Remains of Confederate ironclad gunboat sunk by her crew in 1865 and not raised until 1963. Visitor center relates story of the *Neuse* through an audio show, artifacts recovered from the gunboat, photographs; memorial has exhibits on life of Caswell, first elected governor of the state of North Carolina. Picnicking. (Apr-Sept, Mon-Sat; Oct-Mar, Mon-Fri; closed holidays)

Limited-Service Hotel

★ **HAMPTON INN.** *1382 Hwy 258 S, Kinston (28504). Phone 252/523-1400; toll-free 800/250-5370; fax 252/523-1326.www.hamptoninn.com.* 123 rooms, 4 story. Complimentary continental breakfast. Check-in 3 pm, check-out noon. Outdoor pool.**$**
⊠

Laurinburg (C-6)

See also Pinehurst, Southern Pines

Settled (Circa 1700)
Population 15,874
Elevation 227 ft
Area Code 910
Information Laurinburg-Scotland County Area Chamber of Commerce, 606 Atkinson St, PO Box 1025, 28353; phone 910/276-7420
Web Site www.laurinburgchamber.org

Laurinburg is the seat of Scotland County, named for its early Scottish Highland settlers. Industrial development has expanded this agricultural center's economy.

What to See and Do

St. Andrews Presbyterian College. *1700 Dogwood Mile, Laurinburg (28352).* S city limits. *Phone 910/277-5000.*(1958) (800 students) Contemporary-style buildings on an 800-acre campus around a 70-acre lake. Mosaic-tiled wall depicts story of humankind. On campus are

> **Science Center.** *1700 Dogwood Mile, Laurinburg (28352).* Features interdisciplinary laboratory, guides. (Sept-May and summer session, Mon-Fri; other times by appointment) **FREE**

> **Vardell Art Gallery.** *Vardell Building, 1700 Dogwood Mile, Laurinburg (28352). Phone 910/277-5000.* (Mid-Sept-May, Mon-Fri; closed school holidays) **FREE**

Limited-Service Hotel

★ ★ **COMFORT INN.** *1705 401 Bypass S, Laurinburg (28352). Phone 910/277-7788; toll-free 800/424-6423; fax 910/277-7229. www.comfortinn.com.* Set at the intersection of Highways 401 and 74, this award-winning hotel features cozy rooms and impeccable service. In-room amenities include down pillows and comforters. 80 rooms, 3 story. Complimentary continental breakfast. Check-in 3 pm, check-out noon. High-speed Internet access. Restaurant, bar. Fitness room. Outdoor pool. **$**
⊠ ⊠

Lexington (B-5)

See also Asheboro, High Point, Salisbury, Winston-Salem

Settled 1750
Population 19,953
Elevation 809 ft
Area Code 336
Zip 27292
Information Chamber of Commerce, 16 E Center St, PO Box C, 27293; phone 336/248-5929
Web Site www.visitlexingtonnc.org

In 1775, settlers learned of the battle of Lexington in Massachusetts and decided to name this town for it. Local industry is diversified and includes furniture making, textiles and clothing, food processing, electronics, ceramics, machinery, and fiberglass. Native to the area is traditional pork barbecue, which can be found in many local restaurants.

What to See and Do

Davidson County Historical Museum. *2 S Main St, Lexington (27292). Center of city. Phone 336/242-2035* (1858). Greek Revival building facing the town square; old courtroom houses museum of local history. (Tues-Fri; closed holidays) **FREE**

High Rock Lake. *10 miles SW on Hwy 70 or S on Hwy 8.* Its 300-mile shoreline is a center for water sports in the piedmont.

Linville (A-3)

See also Banner Elk, Blowing Rock, Boone, Little Switzerland

Population 244
Elevation 3,669 ft
Area Code 828
Zip 28646

Linville is in the heart of a ruggedly beautiful resort area. Several miles to the south, just off the Blue Ridge Parkway, is scenic Linville Falls, cascading down the steep Linville Gorge, designated a national wilderness. Visible from vantage points in this area are the mysterious Brown Mountain lights.

What to See and Do

⭐ **Grandfather Mountain.** *2050 Blowing Rock Rd, Linville (28646). 2 miles NE via Hwy 221, 1 mile S of jct Blue Ridge Pkwy and Hwy 221. Phone 828/733-4337. www.grandfather.com.* Highest peak of the Blue Ridge Mountains, with spectacular views, rugged rock formations, 1-mile-high swinging bridge; bald eagles, gold eagles, river otters, deer, cougars, black bears, bear cubs, and others in natural habitats. Hiking trails, picnic areas. Museum with exhibits on local animals, birds, flowers, geology; restaurant, gift shop. (Daily; winter, weather permitting; closed Thanksgiving, Dec 25) **$$$**

Special Events

Grandfather Mountain Highland Games. *Hwy 221 and Grandfather Mt, Linville. MacRae Meadows, on Hwy 221 at Grandfather Mountain. Phone 828/733-2013.* Gathering of members of more than 100 Scottish clans and societies to view or participate in traditional Scottish sports, track-and-field events, mountain marathon; highland dancing, piping, and drumming; ceremonies and pageantry. Mid-July.

Grandfather Mountain Nature Photography Weekend. *2050 Blowing Rock Hwy, Linville (28646). Grandfather Mountain. Phone 828/733-2013.* Nationally known photographers give illustrated lectures; nature photography contest; picnic dinner. Preregistration required. Early June.

"Singing on the Mountain". *On the slopes of Grandfather Mountain.* All-day program of modern and traditional gospel music featuring top groups and nationally known speakers. Concessions or bring your own food. Fourth Sun in June.

Full-Service Resort

★ ★ ★ **THE ESEEOLA LODGE AT LINVILLE GOLF CLUB.** *175 Linville Ave, Linville (28646). Phone 828/733-4311; toll-free 800/742-6717; fax 828/733-3227. www.eseeola.com.* The Eseeola Lodge at Linville Golf Club appeals to the entire family with its array of activities, delicious dining, and comfortable accommodations. Avid golfers hit the historic links, designed by Donald Ross in 1924, and appreciate the services of the clubhouse and pro shop. Eight tennis courts keep tennis players busy; swimmers adore the pool; and the manicured croquet lawn inspires others to give this whimsical game a whirl. A well-equipped playground and day camp capture the attention of younger guests, while their parents enjoy the adult recreational opportunities. Antique and handmade quilts complete a captivating Americana décor in the rooms and suites, and modern amenities ensure comfort. The chef prepares his menu daily based on the freshest ingredients, and the four-course dinner of international dishes with a Southern bent is sure to please. 25 rooms, 2 story. Closed late Oct-mid-May. Complimentary full breakfast. Check-in 3 pm, check-out 11 am. Two restaurants, bar. Children's activity center. Fitness room. Outdoor pool. Golf, 18 holes. Tennis. Business center. **$$$**
🏃 ⛱ 🏌 🏊 🚶

Little Switzerland

(B-3)

See also Burnsville, Linville, Marion, Morganton

Founded 1910
Population 200
Elevation 3,500 ft
Area Code 828
Zip 28749
Information Mitchell County Chamber of Commerce, Rte 1, Box 796, Spruce Pine 28777; phone 704/765-9483 or toll-free 800/227-3912
Web Site www.mitchell-county.com

A restful summer resort amid the high mountains of western North Carolina, Little Switzerland is bisected by the Blue Ridge Parkway.

What to See and Do

Emerald Village. *McKinney Mine Rd and Blue Ridge Pkwy, Little Switzerland. Phone 828/765-6463.* Historical area includes mines; North Carolina Mining Museum; Main Street 1920s Mining Community Museum; Gemstone Mine, where visitors can prospect for gems under shaded flumes (fee; equipment furnished); Mechanical Music Maker Museum; waterfall and scenic overlook; shops and deli. (Daily; closed holidays) **$$**

Mount Mitchell State Park. *20 miles S on Blue Ridge Pkwy, then N on Hwy 128. Adjacent to Pisgah National Forest, a natural national landmark. Phone 828/675-4611.* The road leads to the summit (6,684 feet; the highest point east of the Mississippi River) for incomparable views. Trails. Picnicking, restaurant, refreshment stands. Small-tent camping area. Observation tower, museum.

Museum of North Carolina Minerals. *Hwy 226, Little Switzerland . At jct Blue Ridge Pkwy and Hwy 226. Phone 828/765-2761.* Mineral exhibits of the state. (May-Nov, daily; rest of year, Wed-Sun; closed Jan 1, Thanksgiving, Dec 24-26) **FREE**

Limited-Service Hotel

★ ★ **CHALET SWITZERLAND INN.** *226 A blue Ridge Prky, Little Switzerland (28749). Phone 828/765-2153; toll-free 800/654-4026; fax 828/765-0049. www.switzerlandinn.com.* Named after its Swiss Alps-like view, this inn has welcomed guests since 1910 to a panoramic hideaway of misty mountains and lush valleys where accommodations fill four main buildings and several rustic, individual cottages. Dine inside or out on casual, American cuisine. 73 rooms, 2 story. Closed Nov-mid-Apr. Pets accepted. Complimentary full breakfast. Check-in 3 pm, check-out 11 am. Restaurant, bar. Outdoor pool. Tennis.**$**

Lumberton (C-6)

See also Burnsville, Linville, Marion, Morganton

Founded 1787
Population 20,795
Elevation 137 ft
Area Code 910
Zip 28358
Information Visitors Bureau, 3431 Lackey St, 28358; phone 910/739-9999 or toll-free 800/359-6971
Web Site www.lumberton-nc.com

Lumberton is the county seat of Robeson County and the home of many industries, including one of the largest tobacco marketing centers in the state. Hunting for quail, duck, dove, and rabbit is excellent in the area. Pembroke, to the northwest, is the population center for some 30,000 Lumbee Native Americans, believed by some historians to include descendants of the "lost colonists" (see FORT RALEIGH NATIONAL HISTORIC SITE).

What to See and Do

Jones Lake State Park. *113 Joneslake Dr, Elizabeth Town (28337). 25 miles E on Hwy 41 to Elizabethtown, then 4 miles N on Hwy 242. Phone 910/588-4550.* More than 2,200 acres with swimming, fishing, boating. Interpretive trails. Picnicking. Primitive camping (mid-Mar-Nov).

One-room schoolhouse. Restored early American furnished classroom. (Mon-Fri; closed holidays)

Special Event

Scottish Highland Games. *200 College St, Red Springs (28377). Phone 910/843-5000.* Celebration of Scottish heritage with music, dancing, competitions, childrens events. Late Sept-early Oct.

Limited-Service Hotels

★ **COUNTRY INN & SUITES BY CARLSON.** *3010 Roberts Ave, Lumberton (28358). Phone 910/738-*

2481; toll-free 800/456-4000; fax 910/738-8260. www.
countryinns.com/lumbertonnc. Walking into this hotel
is like walking into someone's home, with its high
ceilings, fireplace, and cozy living area. And, just as at
home, there is a desk in the common area with a computer and printer for guests' use. 53 rooms, 4 story.
Complimentary continental breakfast. Check-in 3 pm,
check-out noon. High-speed Internet access. Fitness
room. Outdoor pool. **$**

★ ★ **HOLIDAY INN.** *101 Wintergreen Dr, Lumber-*
ton (28358). Phone 910/671-1166; toll-free 800/465-
4329; fax 910/671-1166.www.holiday-inn.com. In addition to the new carpeting, furniture, bedspreads, and
drapes installed during a 2003 renovation, the rooms
at this Holiday Inn feature just about everything a
traveler could need, including high-speed Internet access, microwaves, refrigerators, a sofa bed, and coffee
and tea makers. 107 rooms, 2 story. Check-in 3 pm,
check-out noon. High-speed Internet access. Restaurant. Fitness room. Outdoor pool. **$**

Restaurant

★ ★ **JOHN'S.** *4880 Kahn Dr, Lumberton (28358).*
Phone 910/738-4709 ; fax 910/738-6060. Interna-
tional menu. Dinner. Closed Sun-Mon; holidays. Bar.
Children's menu. Casual attire. **$$$**

Maggie Valley(B-2)

See also Asheville, Cherokee, Great Smoky Mountains
National Park, Waynesville

Population 607
Elevation 3,020 ft
Area Code 828
Zip 28751
Information CVB Chamber of Commerce, 2487 Soco
Rd, PO Box 87; phone 828/926-1686 or toll-free
800/785-8259
Web Site www.maggievalley.org

In 1909, Henry Setzer decided the expanding com-
munity of Plott needed a post office. He submitted
the names of his three daughters to the postmaster
general, who selected Maggie, then age 14. Lying in the
shadow of the Great Smoky Mountains National Park
(see), the town is 4 miles from the Soco Gap entrance

to the Blue Ridge Parkway and has become a year-
round resort area.

What to See and Do

Cataloochee Ski Area. *1080 Ski Lodge Rd, Maggie Val-*
ley (28751). 4 miles N via Hwy 19 to Fie Top Rd. Phone
828/926-0285; toll-free 800/768-0285. www.cataloochee.
com. Quad, two double chair lifts, T-bar, rope tow;
patrol, school, rentals; snowmaking; half-day and
twilight rates; cafeteria, bar. Longest run 3,800 feet,
vertical drop 740 feet. (Dec-mid-Mar, daily) **$$$$**

Soco Gardens Zoo. *3578 Soco Rd, Maggie Valley .*
Phone 828/926-1746. A 2 1/2-acre zoo with more than
25 different species of animals, including exotic birds,
alligators, bears, snow leopards, monkeys, jaguars, and
wallabies. Reptile house, poisonous and non-poison-
ous snake shows. Guided tours. Gift shop. (May-Oct,
daily) **$$**

Stompin Ground. *3116 Soco Rd, Maggie Valley. Phone*
828/926-1288. Bluegrass and country music; clogging;
exhibition dancers; square dancing (audience partici-
pation). (May-Oct, nightly) **$$$**

Special Events

Clogging Hall of Fame. *3116 Soco Rd, Maggie Valley*
(28751). Phone 828/926-1288. World-class cloggers
from all across US compete. Oct.

International Folk Festival. *Phone 828/452-2997.*
Premier folk groups from over 10 countries demon-
strate their cultural heritage through lively music and
costumed dance. 11 days in late July.

Limited-Service Hotel

★ **COMFORT INN.** *3282 Soco Rd, Maggie Valley*
(28751). Phone 828/926-9106; toll-free 800/228-5150;
fax 828/926-9106. www.comfortinn.com. 68 rooms, 2
story. Complimentary continental breakfast. Check-in
2 pm, check-out 11 am. Outdoor pool. **$**

Specialty Lodging

CATALOOCHEE SKI AREA. *119 Ranch Dr, Maggie*
Valley (28751). Phone 828/926-0285; toll-free 800/868-
1401; fax 828/926-0354. www.cataloochee.com. This
location offers awesome skiing for beginners and
experts on exciting slopes and winding trails in the
Great Smoky Mountains. Guests can relax in the lodge

with a hot toddy and put their feet up around the crackling circular fireplace. Enjoy a hearty home-cooked meal or picnic on the sun-drenched deck overlooking the slopes. 26 rooms, 2 story. Check-in 3 pm, check-out 11 am. Children's activity center. Whirlpool. Tennis. **$**

Restaurant

★ ★ **J. ARTHUR'S.** *2843 Soco Rd, Maggie Valley (28751). Phone 828/926-1817; fax 828/926-0019. www. jarthurs.com.* Seafood, steak menu. Dinner. Closed Thanksgiving, Dec 25; Sun-Tues in Nov-Apr. Bar. Children's menu. Casual attire. Outdoor seating. Loft dining area. **$$**

Manteo (A-10)

See also Kill Devil Hills, Nags Head

Population 1,052
Elevation 5 ft
Area Code 252
Zip 27954
Information Dare County Tourist Bureau, 704 Hwy 64/264, PO Box 399; phone 252/473-2138 or toll-free 800/446-6262
Web Site www.outerbanks.org

Fishing in the waters off Manteo is excellent. A large sport fishing fleet is available for booking at Oregon Inlet as well as on Roanoke Island.

What to See and Do

Elizabethan Gardens. *1411 National Park Dr, Manteo (27954). 3 miles N on Hwy 64/264. On Roanoke Island. Phone 252/473-3234.* These 10 1/2 acres include Great Lawn, Sunken Garden, Queen's Rose Garden, an herb garden, a 16th-century gazebo with thatched roof, and an ancient garden statuary. Plants bloom all year: spring peak, mid-Apr; summer peak, mid-July; fall peak, mid-Oct; and winter peak, mid-Feb. Gate House Reception Center displays period furniture, English portraits, coat of arms. (Daily; closed Jan 1, Dec 25) **$$**

North Carolina Aquarium on Roanoke Island. *374 Airport Rd, Manteo (27954). 3 miles N via Hwy 64/264, Airport Rd exit. Phone 252/473-3493.* Aquarium and marine-oriented educational and research facility. Public aquaria and exhibits, films and educational programs. (Daily; closed Jan 1, Thanksgiving, Dec 25) **$$**

Roanoke Island Festival Park. *Manteo waterfront, Manteo. Phone 252/475-1500.* Representative 16th-century sailing vessel similar to those that brought the first English colonists to the New World more than 400 years ago. Living history interpretation (summer). Visitor center with exhibits and audiovisual program. (Feb-Dec, daily; closed Thanksgiving, Dec 25) **$$**

Special Event

***The Lost Colony* Outdoor Drama.** *Manteo. Waterside Theater, 3 miles NW of Manteo on Hwy 64/264. Phone toll-free 800/488-5012.* Outdoor drama by Pulitzer Prize winner Paul Green about the first English colony established in the New World, whose curious disappearance remains a mystery to this day. Mid-June-late Aug. Mon-Sat evenings. Reservations recommended. Contact 1409 Hwy 64, Manteo 27954. **$$$$**

Full-Service Inn

★ ★ ★ **TRANQUIL HOUSE INN.** *405 Queen Elizabeth St, Manteo (27954). Phone 252/473-1404; toll-free 800/458-7069; fax 252/473-1526. www.tranquilinn. com.* Built in 1988 in the style of a 19th-century Outer Banks resort, this waterfront property offers continental breakfast and evening wine and cheese with each of its 25 rooms. Elegant dockside dining overlooking Shallowbag Bay can be found at 1587 Restaurant. 25 rooms, 3 story. Complimentary continental breakfast. Check-in 3 pm, check-out 11 am. Restaurant. **$$**

Restaurant

★ ★ **THE WATERFRONT TRELLIS.** *Queen Elizabeth Ave, Manteo (27954). Phone 252/473-1727; fax 252/473-6072.* Fusion, French menu. Lunch, dinner. Closed Thanksgiving, Dec 25. Bar. Children's menu. Casual attire. Reservations recommended. **$$**

Marion (B-3)

See also Little Switzerland, Morganton

Founded 1843
Population 4,943
Elevation 1,395 ft
Area Code 704
Zip 28752
Web Site www.marionnc.org

Permits for the Linville Gorge Wilderness of the Pisgah National Forest (see BREVARD) can be obtained at the Grandfather Ranger District Office (Rte 1, Box 110A; phone 704/652-2144) located here.

What to See and Do

Linville Caverns. *Hwy 221 N, Marion. Beneath Humpback Mountain. Phone toll-free 800/419-0540.* Half-hour guided tours. Gift shop. (Mar-Nov, daily; rest of year, weekends only) **$$**

Morehead City (C-9)

See also Beaufort

Founded 1857
Population 7,691
Elevation 16 ft
Area Code 252
Zip 28557
Information Crystal Coast Visitors Center, 3409 Arendell St, PO Box 1406; phone 252/726-8148 or toll-free 800/SUNNY-NC
Web Site www.sunnync.com

Just across the Intracoastal Waterway from Beaufort, Morehead City is the largest town in Carteret County and a year-round resort town. It is involved in both sport and commercial fishing. The port accommodates oceangoing vessels and charter boats.

What to See and Do

Carteret County Museum of History and Art. *1008 Arendell St, Morehead City. Phone 252/247-7533.* Paintings and artifacts from the 19th century. Includes genealogy research library. (Tues-Sat) **FREE**

Fishing. Onshore and offshore; charter boats available. Gulfstream fishing for marlin, amberjack, dolphin, mackerel, and bluefish.

Fort Macon State Park. *E Fort Macon Rd, Atlantic Beach . 2 miles E of town. On Bogue Banks. Phone 252/726-3775.* This restored fort, built in 1834, was originally used as a harbor defense. Beach (lifeguards in summer), bathhouse (fee); surf fishing; hiking, nature trails. Museum; interpretive program (summer); battle reenactments. Snack bar. **FREE**

Town of Atlantic Beach. *Across the bridge from Morehead.* Swimming, fishing, boating; boardwalk.

Special Events

Atlantic Beach King Mackerel Tournament. *125 W Fort Macon Rd, Atlantic Beach (28512). Phone 252/247-2334.* Mid-Sept.

Big Rock Blue Marlin Tournament. *209 N 35th St, Morehead City (28557). Phone 252/247-3575.* Largest tournament of its kind on the East Coast. Fishing for blue marlin, cash awards, registration required. Six days in early June.

North Carolina Seafood Festival. *Evans and 10th sts, Morehead City. Phone 252/726-6273.* Seafood, arts and crafts, music. First weekend in Oct.

Limited-Service Hotels

★ ★ **BUCCANEER INN.** *2806 Arendell St, Morehead City (28557). Phone 252/726-3115; fax 252/726-3864.* 91 rooms, 3 story. Complimentary full breakfast. Check-in 4 pm, check-out 11 am. Restaurant, bar. Outdoor pool. **$**
🏊

★ **HAMPTON INN.** *4035 Arendell St, Morehead City (28557). Phone 252/240-2300; toll-free 800/426-7866; fax 252/240-2311. www.hamptoninn.com.* 119 rooms, 4 story. Complimentary continental breakfast. Check-in 4 pm, check-out 11 am. Fitness room. Outdoor pool. **$**
🚶 🏊

Full-Service Hotel

★ ★ ★ **SHERATON ATLANTIC BEACH OCEANFRONT HOTEL.** *2717 Fort Macon, Atlantic Beach (28512). Phone 252/240-1155; toll-free 800/624-887; fax 252/240-1452. www.sheratonatlanticbeach.com.* This beachfront hotel features 200 rooms, each with a private balcony. It offers two restaurants, two lounges with entertainment, an indoor and outdoor pool, and more. Golf, tennis, and white-sand beaches are in the area. 200 rooms, 9 story. Check-in 3 pm, check-out noon. Two restaurants, two bars. Fitness room. Beach. Indoor pool, outdoor pool, whirlpool. **$$**
🚶 🏊

Specialty Lodging

EMERALD ISLE INN AND BED & BREAKFAST. *502 Ocean Dr, Emerald Isle (28594). Phone 252/354-3222. www.emeraldisleinn.com.* 4 rooms, 2 story. Complimentary full breakfast. Check-in 3 pm. Check-out 11 am. On Bogue Banks. **$**

HARBOR LIGHT GUEST HOUSE. *332 Live Oak Dr, Cape Carteret (28584). Phone 252/393-6868; toll-free 800/624-8439; fax 252/393-6868.* 9 rooms, 3 story. Children over 16 years only. Complimentary full breakfast. Check-in 3 pm. Check-out 11 am. Overlooks Bogue Sound. **$$**

Restaurants

★ **CAPTAIN BILL'S WATERFRONT.** *701 Evans St, Morehead City (28557). Phone 252/726-2166; fax 252/726-1979.* Seafood menu. Lunch, dinner. Children's menu. Casual attire. Outdoor seating. **$$**

★ **MRS. WILLIS.** *3114 Bridges St, Morehead City (28557). Phone 252/726-3741.* Seafood, steak menu. Lunch, dinner. Bar. Children's menu. Casual attire. **$$**

★ **SANITARY FISH MARKET.** *501 Evans St, Morehead City (28557). Phone 252/247-3111. www.sanitaryfishmarket.com.* Seafood menu. Lunch, dinner. Closed Dec-Jan. Children's menu. Casual attire. **$$**

Morganton (B-3)

See also Little Switzerland, Marion

Population 17,310
Elevation 1,182 ft
Area Code 828
Zip 28655
Information Burke County Travel and Tourism, 102 E Union St, Courthouse Sq; phone 828/433-6793
Web Site www.ci.morganton.nc.us

This is the seat of Burke County and a manufacturing town producing furniture, textiles, shoes, chemicals, electronics, clothing, and other products. In 1893, the county became a haven for the Waldenses, a religious group from the French-Italian Alps that was seeking freedom and space to expand outside their alpine homeland.

What to See and Do

Boat tours. *9066 Hwy 126, New Bern (28761). Phone 828/584-0666.* Tours of Lake James on the 38-foot pontoon *Harbor Queen.* Departs Mountain Harbor Marina. **$$$**

Lake James. *8 miles W on Hwy 126.* **Lake Rhodhiss.** 10 miles E off Hwy 70. Boating, fishing, and swimming.

Special Events

From This Day Forward. *Church St. Valdese. Phone toll-free 800/743-8398.* Outdoor historical drama depicting hardships of the Waldenses and their struggle for religious freedom. Thurs-Sun evenings. Mid-July-mid-Aug.

Historic Morganton Festival. *Downtown, Morganton (28655). Phone 828/438-5280.* Arts, crafts, ethnic foods, band concert. Mid-Sept.

Waldensian Celebration of the Glorious Return. *Main St W, Valdese (28690). Off I-40, exit 112. Phone 828/879-2129.* Commemoration of the end of persecution during the reign of Louis XIV; ethnic games, arts and crafts, dances, food. Mid-Aug.

Limited-Service Hotels

★ ★ **HOLIDAY INN MORGANTON.** *2400 S Sterling St, Morganton (28655). Phone 828/437-0171; toll-free 800/465-4329; fax 828/437-1639. www.holiday-inn.com.* 133 rooms, 2 story. Pets accepted; fee. Check-in 3 pm, check-out noon. Restaurant, bar. Fitness room. Outdoor pool. **$**

★ **SLEEP INN.** *2400 A S Sterling St, Morganton (28655). Phone 828/433-9000; toll-free 800/424-6423; fax 828/438-3674. www.sleepinn.com.* 61 rooms, 2 story. Pets accepted; fee. Complimentary continental breakfast. Check-in 3 pm, check-out 11 am. **$**

Nags Head (A-10)

See also Cape Hatteras National Seashore, Fort Raleigh National Historic Site, Kill Devil Hills, Manteo

Population 2,700
Elevation 10 ft
Area Code 252
Zip 27959
Information Dare County Tourist Bureau, 704 Hwy 64/264, PO Box 399, Manteo 27954; phone 252/473-2138 or toll-free 800/446-6262.
Web Site www.outerbanks.org

This is a year-round fishing and beachcombing town on the Outer Banks (see), just south of Kill Devil Hills (see). There are fishing piers and boats for rent. Swimming is good in summer. A museum is located at Jockey's Ridge State Park, which boasts one of the largest sand dunes on the East Coast.

The soft sand dunes and Atlantic breezes make this a popular area for hang gliding. Offshore, partly buried in the drifting sand, are many wrecks of both old sailing ships and more modern vessels.

Cape Hatteras National Seashore (see) is south of Nags Head.

Special Events

Hang Gliding Spectacular. *Jockeys Ridge State Park, Nags Head (27959). Phone 252/441-4124.* Hang gliding competition, novice through advanced. Spectacular flying and fun events. Mid-May.

Rogallo Kite Festival. *Jockey's Ridge State Park, 3941 S Croatan Hwy, Nags Head (Outer Banks) (2959). Phone 252/441-4124.* Competition for homebuilt kites; stunt kite performances, demonstrations; kite auction. Mid-June.

Limited-Service Hotels

★ **NAGS HEAD INN.** *4701 S Virginia Dare Trail, Nags Head (27959). Phone 252/441-0454; toll-free 800/327-8881; fax 252/441-0454. www.nagsheadinn.com.* 100 rooms, 5 story. Closed Sun after Thanksgiving-Dec 26. Check-in 4 pm, check-out 11 am. Beach. Indoor pool, whirlpool. **$**
⌨

★ **SURF SIDE MOTEL.** *6701 S Virginia Dare Trail, Nags Head (27959). Phone 252/441-2105; toll-free 800/552-7873; fax 252/441-2456. www.surfsideobx.com.* 76 rooms, 5 story. Complimentary continental breakfast. Check-in 3 pm, check-out 11 am. Fitness room. Beach. Indoor pool, outdoor pool, whirlpool. **$**
🧍 ⌨

Specialty Lodging

FIRST COLONY INN. *6720 S Virginia Dare Trail, Nags Head (27959). Phone 252/441-2343; toll-free 800/368-9390. www.firstcolonyinn.com.* This beach-style bed-and-breakfast has welcomed Outer Banks' visitors since 1932 and is on the National Register of Historic Places. Rooms are decorated in English antiques, and the shingled building is wrapped in wide, two-story verandas affording great sunset views. 26 rooms, 3 story. Complimentary full breakfast. Check-in 3 pm, check-out 11 am. Outdoor pool. **$**
⌨

Restaurants

★ ★ **OWENS'.** *7114 S Virginia Dare Trail, Nags Head (27959). Phone 252/441-7309; fax 252/441-4670. www.owensrestaurant.com.* American menu. Dinner. Closed Jan-mid-Mar. Bar. Children's menu. Casual attire. Historic artifacts of the US Lifesaving Service (forerunner of the US Coast Guard) on display; uniforms, log books, photographs. **$$$**

★ ★ **PENGUIN ISLE.** *6708 S Croatan Hwy, Nags Head (27959). Phone 252/441-2637; fax 252/441-2562. www.penguinisle.com.* American menu. Dinner. Closed Dec 24-25; also Jan-Feb. Bar. Children's menu. Casual attire. Reservations recommended. Outdoor seating. **$$**

★ ★ **WINDMILL POINT.** *Hwy 158, Nags Head (27959). Phone 252/441-1535; fax 252/441-1569. www.windmillpointrestaurant.com.* American menu. Dinner, brunch. Bar. Children's menu. Casual attire. **$$$**

New Bern (B-8)

See also Kinston

Settled 1710
Population 23,128
Elevation 15 ft
Area Code 252
Information Visitor Information Center, 314 S Front St, PO Box 1413, 28560; phone 252/637-9400 or toll-free 800/437-5767
Web Site www.visitnewbern.com

The first settlers here, one of North Carolina's earliest towns, were Germans and Swiss seeking political and religious freedom in the New World. The name Bern came from the city in Switzerland. Many Georgian- and Federal-style buildings give New Bern an architectural ambience unique in North Carolina. Many of these homes can be visited during April and October.

Swimming, boating, and freshwater and saltwater fishing can be enjoyed on the Neuse and Trent rivers. A Ranger District Office of the Croatan National Forest is located here.

What to See and Do

Attmore-Oliver House. *512 Pollock St, New Bern. Phone 252/638-8558.* (Circa 1790) This house, headquarters for the New Bern Historical Society, exhibits

18th- and 19th-century furnishings and historical objects, including Civil War artifacts and a doll collection. (Early Apr-mid-Dec, Tues, Thurs, Sat; also by appointment; closed July 4, Thanksgiving, Dec 25) **$**

Croatan National Forest. *160 Zillicoa St, Asheville. SE via Hwy 70. Phone 252/638-5628.* A unique coastal forest (157,724 acres), with many estuaries and waterways; northernmost habitat of the alligator. Pocosins (Native American for "swamp on a hill") have many unusual dwarf and insect-eating plants. Swimming, boating, and fishing in Neuse River; hunting for deer, bear, turkey, quail and migratory waterfowl; picnicking; camping (fee). For further information, contact the Forest Supervisor, 100 Otis St, PO Box 2750, Asheville 28802.

New Bern Firemen's Museum. *408 Hancock St, New Bern. Off Hwy 17, 70 Business. Phone 252/636-4087.* Antique fire-fighting equipment, relics, and pictures; 1927 double-size ladder trucks and engines, 1941 pumper. (Mon-Sat; closed Thanksgiving, Dec 25) **$**

⭐ **Tryon Palace Historic Sites and Gardens.** *610 Pollock St, New Bern. S end of George St, 1 block S of Hwy 17, 70 Business, Hwy 55. Phone toll-free 800/767-1560.* Built from 1767-1770 by Royal Governor, William Tryon, this "most beautiful building in the colonial Americas" burned by accident in 1798 and lay in ruins until being rebuilt between 1952-1959. It served as the colonial and first state capitol. Reconstruction, furnishings, and 18th-century English gardens are beautiful and authentic. Guided tours (Daily; closed Jan 1, Thanksgiving, Dec 24-26). Also self-guided garden tours. Combination ticket available. **$$$$** On grounds are

Dixon-Stevenson House. *610 Pollock St, New Bern (28560).* (Circa 1830) The early Federal architecture, including the interior woodwork and widow's walk, reflects maritime history of the area. Furnished in Federal and Empire antiques.

John Wright Stanly House. *307 George St, New Bern (28560).* (Circa 1780) Georgian-style house furnished with 18th-century American antiques. Elegant interior woodwork. Formal gardens typical of the period.

New Bern Academy. *Hancock and New Sts, New Bern (28560). Phone 252/514-4900.* (Circa 1810) Four blocks from Tryon Palace complex, in the historic residential district. Major surviving landmark of an educational institution founded in the 1760s, the Academy is restored as a self-guided museum of New Bern Civil War history, early education, and local architecture.

Limited-Service Hotels

★ **COMFORT INN.** *218 E Front St, New Bern (28560). Phone 252/636-0022; fax 252/636-0051. www.comforthotels.com.* 100 rooms, 4 story. Complimentary continental breakfast. Check-in 3 pm, check-out 11 am. High-speed Internet access, wireless Internet access. Outdoor pool, whirlpool. **$**

★ **HAMPTON INN.** *200 Hotel Dr, New Bern (28562). Phone 252/637-2111; toll-free 800/448-8288; fax 252/637-2000. www.hamptoninn.com.* 101 rooms, 4 story. Complimentary continental breakfast. Check-in 3 pm, check-out 11 am. Fitness room. Outdoor pool, children's pool. **$**

Full-Service Hotel

★ ★ ★ **SHERATON NEW BERN HOTEL AND MARINA.** *100 Middle St, New Bern (28560). Phone 252/638-3585; toll-free 800/326-3745; fax 252/638-8112. www.sheraton.com/newbern.* With a downtown waterfront location, this hotel offers all the amenities a visitor could want, with 171 rooms, 19 full suites, and 19 mini-suites. Historic paddlewheel rides. Golf, tennis, and beaches are nearby. 171 rooms, 5 story. Pets accepted, some restrictions; fee. Check-in 3 pm, check-out noon. High-speed Internet access. Restaurant, two bars. Fitness room. Outdoor pool. Business center. **$**

Specialty Lodgings

AERIE INN BED & BREAKFAST. *509 Pollock St, New Bern (28562). Phone 252/636-5553; toll-free 800/849-5553; fax 252/514-2157. www.aerieinn.com.* 7 rooms, 2 story. Complimentary full breakfast. Check-in 3 pm, check-out 11 am. Victorian house built in 1880; antiques. One block east of Tryon Palace. **$**

HARMONY HOUSE INN. *215 Pollock St, New Bern (28560). Phone 252/636-3810; toll-free 800/636-3113; fax 252/636-3810. www.harmonyhouseinn.com.* 10 rooms, 2 story. Complimentary full breakfast. Check-in 3-8 pm, check-out 11 am. Airport transportation available. Greek Revival house built in 1850. **$**

MEADOWS INN. *212 Pollock St, New Bern (28560). Phone 252/634-1776; toll-free 877/551-1776; fax 252/634-1776. www.meadowsinn-nc.com.* 8 rooms, 3 story. Complimentary full breakfast. Check-in 3-6 pm, check-out 11 am. Airport transportation available. In a restored house (circa 1848); antiques, canopied beds. **$**

Ocracoke (B-10)

See also Buxton, Cape Hatteras National Seashore

Population 769
Elevation 6 ft
Area Code 252
Zip 27960
Web Site www.ocracoke-nc.com

Settled in the 17th century, Ocracoke was, according to legend, once used as headquarters by the pirate Blackbeard. On the Outer Banks (see), Ocracoke offers excellent fishing and hunting for wildfowl. The lighthouse, built in 1823, is still in use.

One of the visitor centers for Cape Hatteras National Seashore (see) is here.

What to See and Do

Cedar Island to Ocracoke Ferry Service. *Hwy 12, Ocracoke . Phone 252/928-3841; toll-free 800/293-3779.* Winter and summer, daily. Swan Quarter to Ocracoke; All year, daily. Ferries are crowded; there may be a wait. Reservations are recommended; they may be made up to one year in advance.

Ocracoke to Hatteras Ferry. N across Hatteras Inlet.

Limited-Service Hotel

★ **ANCHORAGE INN.** *Hwy 12, Ocracoke (27960). Phone 252/928-1101; fax 252/928-6322. www.the-anchorageinn.com.* 37 rooms, 4 story. Closed Dec-Feb. Pets accepted; fee. Complimentary continental breakfast. Check-in 3 pm, check-out 11 am. Outdoor pool. **$**

Specialty Lodging

OCRACOKE ISLAND INN. *100 Lighthouse Rd, Ocracoke (27960). Phone 252/928-4351; toll-free 877/456-3466; fax 252/928-4352. www.ocracokeislandinn.com.*

29 rooms, 3 story. Check-in 3 pm, check-out noon. Restaurant. Outdoor pool. Built in 1901; antiques. **$$**

Restaurant

★ ★ **BACK PORCH.** *110 Back Rd, Ocracoke (27960). Phone 252/928-6401.* Seafood menu. Dinner. Closed mid-Nov-mid-Apr. Casual attire. Outdoor seating. **$$**

Outer Banks (B-10)

See also Fort Raleigh National Historic Site

Web Site www.outer-banks.com

The Outer Banks are a chain of narrow, sandy islands stretching 175 miles from Cape Lookout to Back Bay, Virginia. Parts of the chain are 30 miles from the mainland. Cape Hatteras is about 75 miles from the southern end. The islands may be reached by bridge from Point Harbor and Manteo or by ferry from Cedar Island and Swan Quarter to Ocracoke (see).

The following Outer Banks areas are included in the Mobil Travel Guide. For information on any of them, see the individual alphabetical listing: Buxton, Cape Hatteras National Seashore, Hatteras, Kill Devil Hills, Nags Head, Ocracoke.

Pilot Mountain (A-5)

Population 1,281
Elevation 1,152 ft
Area Code 336
Zip 27041

What to See and Do

Pilot Mountain State Park. *4 miles S on Hwy 52. Phone 336/325-2355.* More than 3,700 acres; hard-surfaced road up mountain to parking. Foot trail to base of rocky knob; extensive view. Canoeing on the Yadkin River. Nature and riding trails. Picnicking. Camping.

Pinehurst (B-6)

See also Laurinburg, Southern Pines

Founded 1895
Population 9,706
Elevation 529 ft
Area Code 910
Zip 28374
Information Convention and Visitors Bureau, PO Box 2270, Southern Pines 28388; phone 910/692-3330 or toll-free 800/346-5362
Web Site www.homeofgolf.com

A famous year-round resort village, Pinehurst preserves an era steeped both in tradition and golfing excellence. Its New England style was designed over 100 years ago by the firm of Frederick Law Olmsted, which also designed New York's Central Park and landscaped Asheville's Biltmore Estate. Handsome estates and other residences, mostly styled in Georgian Colonial, dot the village. The Pinehurst Resort and Country Club has eight 18-hole golf courses, a 200-acre lake, 24 tennis courts, and other recreational facilities that are open to members as well as to guests staying there.

What to See and Do

Sandhills Horticultural Gardens. *Sandhills Community College, 3395 Airport Road, Pinehurst. Phone 910/695-3882.* The 25 acres include Ebersole Holly Garden; Rose Garden; Conifer Garden; Hillside Garden with bridges, waterfalls, and gazebo; Desmond Native Wetland Trail Garden, a nature conservancy, and bird sanctuary; and Sir Walter Raleigh Garden, a 1-acre formal English garden. Docent-guided group tours (by appointment only). (Daily) **FREE**

Limited-Service Hotel

★ **COMFORT INN.** *9801 Hwy 15-501, Pinehurst (28374). Phone 910/215-5500; toll-free 800/831-0541; fax 910/215-5535. www.comfort.pmcproperties.com.* A golf theme is carried thoughout this property located within a short drive of dining and shopping. The famed Pinehurst golf resort is also nearby. Guest rooms provide a mini-refrigerator and microwave, and the multipurpose room features an inviting fireplace and windows overlooking the pool. 77 rooms, 2 story. Complimentary continental breakfast. Check-in 3 pm, check-out noon. High-speed Internet access, wireless Internet access. Bar. Fitness room. Outdoor pool. **$**

Full-Service Resort

★ ★ ★ ★ **THE CAROLINA HOTEL.** *Carolina Vista Dr, Pinehurst (28374). Phone 910/295-6811; toll-free 800/487-4653; fax 910/235-8466. www.pinehurst.com.* Pinehurst, in the southern Sandhills of North Carolina, is the ultimate destination for those who believe that emerald-green fairways are the paths to heaven. This place is a veritable Mecca for golfers, with eight 18-hole courses designed by the sport's leading names, including Fazio, Jones, Maples, and Ross. The 31 miles of golf contain 780 bunkers and the largest number of golf holes in the world at a single resort. Its no wonder that the finest players converge upon Pinehurst annually for internationally recognized championships; those needing to sharpen their skills head for the highly acclaimed Golf Advantage School. In the center of it all, The Carolina Hotel, a National Historic Landmark, reigns as Pinehurst's finest lodging. This historic Victorian hotel set amid exquisitely manicured lawns provides guests with handsomely furnished accommodations and first-class service. A wraparound porch with hanging ferns and rocking chairs invites guests to relax and watch the world go by. Two of the resort's nine restaurants are located here, while the convenient setting places guests within walking distance of the luxurious spa, the fitness center, and a shopping village. Nongolfers are treated to a wide variety of activities, from tennis and sailing to swimming in the shimmering pool. Horse-and-carriage rides offer tours of the village, as does a complimentary shuttle. 262 rooms, 4 story. Check-in 4 pm, check-out noon. High-speed Internet access. 9 restaurants, bar. Children's activity center. Fitness room, fitness classes available. Spa. Beach. Indoor pool, outdoor pool, children's pool, whirlpool. Golf, 144 holes. Tennis. Airport transportation available. Business center. **$$$**

Full-Service Inn

★ ★ ★ **HOLLY INN.** *155 Cherokee Rd, Pinehurst (28374). Phone 910/295-6811; toll-free 800/487-4653; fax 910/235-8466. www.pinehurst.com.* The Holly Inn was the first hotel built in Pinehurst (dating back to 1895), and it is part of the Pinehurst Resort. The inn has the charm of a traditional classic inn: dark wood paneling, fireplaces, and antiques mixed with traditional furniture. The guest rooms are decorated in a lodge style, with rattan club chairs, and tones of gold, green, and terra cotta. The fine dining 1895 Restaurant features an American/Continental menu with Carolina influences. The Tavern is more casual and serves lunch and dinner. Guests at Holly Inn have access to all the activities of the Carolina Hotel. This is Southern hospitality at its best. 82 rooms, 4 story. Check-in 4 pm, check-out noon. High-speed Internet access. Two restaurants, bar. Fitness room. Outdoor pool. Airport transportation available. Credit cards accepted. **$$**

Specialty Lodging

MAGNOLIA. *65 Magnolia Rd, Pinehurst (28374). Phone 910/295-6900; toll-free 800/526-5562; fax 910/215-0858. www.themagnoliainn.com.* This historical 1896 inn is nestled in the quaint New England-style village of Pinehurst and is within walking distance of the Carolina Hotel, golf courses, tennis, dining, and shopping. The rooms are casually decorated, and there are two rooms with fireplaces. 11 rooms, 3 story. Pets accepted. Complimentary full breakfast. Check-in 4 pm, check-out noon. High-speed Internet access, wireless Internet access. Restaurant, bar. Outdoor pool. **$**

Spa

★ ★ ★ ★ **THE SPA AT PINEHURST.** *1 Carolina Vista Dr, Pinehurst (28374). Phone 910/235-8320. www.pinehurst.com.* Pinehurst is a place of great tradition, where southern hospitality, gracious manners, and world-class recreation have lured sophisticated travelers for decades. Comprised of five different lodging venues, Pinehurst certainly has something to suit your personal style. Grand and historic, the Carolina is the resorts shining star. This Victorian hotel is the picture of elegance, and its rooms and suites reflect the resorts heritage and refinement. The Holly is a charming spot with its Art Nouveau, Queen Anne Revival, and Arts and Crafts influences, and the Manor has a distinctly clubby contemporary appeal. Spacious and stylishly modern, the villas and condominiums are ideal for large groups, families, or those enjoying extended stays at Pinehurst. With five different places to stay, it is no wonder that Pinehurst has a variety of dining experiences available. Nine different restaurants entice diners to enjoy casual suppers or elegant culinary triumphs. Guests who prefer to dress for dinner will enjoy evenings at the celebrated 1895 Room or the Carolina Dining Room, while more casual dining is found at the clubby Ryder Cup Lounge, Tavern, Hackers Bar & Grill, Donald Ross Grill, and at the various clubhouses. Golf and Pinehurst are synonymous, and with eight internationally recognized courses that are home to numerous PGA championships, it is no wonder that golfers make pilgrimages to this legendary resort. Designed by some of the games greatest course architects, the courses present thrilling challenges and rewarding play, and the Golf Advantage School is one of the sports best educational facilities. While it may seem sacra religious to participate in any other activity at Pinehurst, there are plenty of other things to do here, including tennis, swimming, and water sports at the lakefront beach club. Pinehurst is defined by its regal country club ambience, and the Spa at Pinehursts design and spirit echo that feeling. Rich, dark woods are used throughout the facility to create a clubhouse of relaxation. Masculine, yet universally appealing, the spa is elegant and traditional. In addition to relaxation lounges and treatment rooms, the spa also offers salon services with a traditional barber shop for men, and an exercise facility with fitness evaluations, consultations, and classes. One step inside the spa and your concerns over your poor short game will quickly disappear. This spa relaxes with over forty different treatments inspired by nature and the resorts southern location. The body wraps are a celebration of the region, with magnolia mud and mint julep varieties available here. Pine-inspired treatments are also plentiful, from the pine salt body scrub to the exfoliating pine cream of the Pinehurst deluxe body treatment. Eight massage therapies are included on the menu, including a special massage designed for golfers. From soothing magnolia luxury facials to chemical peels, the facials and skin care treatments target dryness, fine lines, and wrinkles with botanical extracts and modern medicine. Nothing beats the relaxing effects of hydrotherapy, and the spas baths and soaks menu features soothing water therapies.

Restaurant

★ ★ ★ **1895.** *155 Cherokee Rd, Pinehurst (28374). Phone 910/235-8434; toll-free 800/487-4653; fax 910/235-8466. www.pinehurst.com.* This charming fine-dining restaurant is located in the historical Holly Inn and is part of the famous Pinehurst Resort. The restaurant features a Continental menu with Carolina influence. Its décor is bold, with moldings of dark heart of pine wood ceiling accenting a skylight cupola. There are intimate booths and tables set with crisp white tablecloths, brocade arm chairs, and black-and-white pictures. American, Continental menu. Dinner. Closed Mon-Tues. Bar. Business casual attire. Reservations recommended. Valet parking. Outdoor seating. **$$$**

Pittsboro (B-6)

Founded 1771
Population 2,236
Area Code 919
Zip 27312
Information Chatham County Chamber of Commerce, 12 East St, PO Box 87, Pittsboro, 27312; phone 919/542-8200, or toll-free 800/468-6242
Web Site www.visitchathamcounty.com

Full-Service Inn

★ ★ ★ ★ **THE FEARRINGTON HOUSE COUNTRY INN.** *2000 Fearrington Village Center, Pittsboro (27312). Phone 919/542-2121; fax 919/542-4202. www.fearrington.com.* The Fearrington House offers just the right mix of country sensibilities and worldly sophistication. Located about 10 miles south of Chapel Hill and part of a charming village of shops, this country house hotel is nestled on family farmland that dates to the 1700s. Its former incarnation as a dairy barn is evident today in the striped Galloway cows that still call the grounds their home. The rooms and suites feature a country theme sprinkled with eclectic items like ecclesiastical doors serving as headboards and pine floors rescued from a workhouse along the Thames. Canopied beds and original art lend a hand in creating a stylish look. Mornings are celebrated with hearty breakfasts, while English afternoon tea curbs midday hunger pangs. Aspiring chefs flock to the hotel's popular cooking school for an insiders look at the kichen. 33 rooms, 2 story. Children over 6 years only. Complimentary full breakfast. Check-in 3 pm, check-out noon. High-speed Internet access. Restaurant, bar. Fitness room. Indoor pool, outdoor pool, whirlpool. Tennis. Business center. Credit cards accepted. **$$$**

Restaurants

★ ★ ★ ★ **THE FEARRINGTON HOUSE RESTAURANT.** *2000 Fearrington Village Center, Pittsboro (27312). Phone 919/542-2121; fax 919/542-4202. www.fearrington.com.* This charming Victorian-style country inn and restaurant (previously the Fearrington family homestead, built in 1927) is located near Chapel Hill, nestled into rolling green farmland dating to the 1700s. Settling in for dinner here is like stepping into a fairy tale. The property is covered with beautiful flower gardens and lush landscapes, and the restaurant is accented with elegant antique furnishings and little touches that may leave you questioning the need for modernity. Fearrington House is a restaurant for special occasions, especially those that call for a soft, intimate, and romantic setting—try to get a seat in the cozy Wine Room. Dinner lives up to the lovely and serene surroundings. The upscale menu is American, with techniques borrowed from France and robust flavors taken from the local region. The thoughtful, seasonal menu is complemented by a deep international wine list that features close to 500 selections from the US, France, and Australia, with a focus on Californian varietals. American, French menu. Dinner. Bar. Jacket required. Reservations recommended. Valet parking. Outdoor seating. **$$$$**

★ **MARKET CAFE.** *2000 Fearrington Village, Pittsboro (27312). Phone 919/542-2121; fax 919/542-4020. www.fearringtonvillage.com.* The Market Café is located in the quaint Fearrington Village, surrounded by boutique shops, the Inn, and the restaurant. The Café has two floors: the first floor is an informal deli offering sandwiches, soups, and baked goods. The second floor has several rooms with a casual décor and features sit-down dining and an American menu. American, other menu. Lunch, brunch. Children's menu. Casual attire. Reservations recommended. Outdoor seating. **$**

Raleigh (B-7)

See also Chapel Hill, Durham, Smithfield

Founded 1792
Population 276,093
Elevation 363 ft
Area Code 919
Information Greater Raleigh Convention and Visitors Bureau, 1 Hannover Sq, 421 Fayetteville St Mall, Suite 1505, PO Box 1879, 27602-1879; phone 919/834-5900 or toll-free 800/849-8499
Web Site www.raleighcvb.org

The capital of North Carolina, Raleigh is also known as a center of education and high-technology research. It still retains the flavor of a relaxed residential town with two centuries of history. Fine residences coexist with apartment houses and modern shopping centers; rural areas with meadows and plowed fields can be found within a few miles.

Named for Sir Walter Raleigh, the town was laid out in 1792, following a resolution by the North Carolina General Assembly that an "unalterable seat of government" should be established within 10 miles of Isaac Hunter's tavern. The founders were able to find a site just 4 miles from the tavern. The site was laid off in a square. Lots within and just outside the city were sold as residences, which helped finance the capitol building and the governor's residence. Both structures were subsequently destroyed (the capitol by fire in 1831, the governor's residence by Union troops during the Civil War). Their replacements remain standing today. Fortunately, many of the lovely homes and gardens of the antebellum period have survived.

Like much of North Carolina, Raleigh was sprinkled with Union sympathizers until Fort Sumter was fired upon. Lincoln's call for volunteers was regarded as an insult, and North Carolina joined the Confederacy. Raleigh surrendered quietly to General Sherman in April 1865. During Reconstruction, carpetbaggers and scalawags controlled the Assembly, voted themselves exorbitant salaries, set up a bar in the capitol, and left permanent nicks in the capitol steps from the whiskey barrels rolled up for the thirsty legislators.

Located within 15 miles of Raleigh is the Research Triangle Park, a 6,800-acre research and development center with more than 50 companies. Complementing these facilities are the resources of three major universities that form the triangle region—North Carolina State University, Duke University in Durham, and the University of North Carolina at Chapel Hill.

What to See and Do

Capital Area Visitor Center. *301 N Blount St, Raleigh. Phone 919/807-7905.* Information center, brochures. Tours may be scheduled to the State Capitol, the North Carolina Executive Mansion, the State Legislative Building, historic sites, and other attractions. (Daily; closed Jan 1, Thanksgiving, Dec 25-26) **FREE**

Carolina Hurricanes (NHL). *1400 Edwards Mill Rd, Raleigh (27612). Phone 919/861-2300.* Raleigh Entertainment and Sports Arena.

Falls Lake State Recreation Area. *13304 Creedmoor Rd, Wake Forest (27587). 12 miles N via Hwy 50. Phone 919/676-1027.* This man-made lake was built as a reservoir and for flood control. Approximately 38,000 acres of land and water offer a swimming beach, water-skiing, fishing, and boating (ramps), as well as opportunities for hiking and picnicking (shelters). There are three state recreation areas in the vicinity. **$$**

J. C. Raulston Arboretum at North Carolina State University. *4415 Beryl Rd, Raleigh. Phone 919/515-3132.* Eight acres of gardens featuring more than 5,000 diverse trees and shrubs from around the world. (Daily)

Mordecai Historic Park. *1 Mimosa St, Raleigh (27604). Mimosa St and Wake Forest Rd. Phone 919/857-4364.* Preserved plantation home (1785 and 1826) with many original furnishings, noted for its neoclassical architecture; early Raleigh office building, St. Mark's chapel, Badger-Iredell Law Office, 1830s herb garden. Also house in which Andrew Johnson, 17th president of the US, was born. Guided tours. (Tues-Sat) **$$**

North Carolina Museum of Art. *2110 Blue Ridge Rd, Raleigh (27607). Phone 919/839-6262.* European and American paintings and sculptures; Egyptian, Greek, Roman, African, and pre-Columbian objects; Judaica collection; changing exhibits. Amphitheatre. Restaurant. (Tues-Sun; closed holidays) **FREE**

North Carolina Museum of History. *5 E Edenton St, Raleigh. Phone 919/807-7900.* Several innovative exhibits convey the state's history. Gift shop. Auditorium. (Tues-Sun) **FREE**

Pullen Park. *520 Ashe Ave, Raleigh. Phone 919/831-6468.* Scenic 72-acre park in the heart of downtown featuring 1911 carousel, train ride, paddle boats, indoor aquatic center, ball fields, tennis courts, playground, and picnic shelters. (Daily) **FREE**

State Capitol. *1 E Edenton St, Raleigh (27601). Capitol Sq. Phone 919/733-4994. www.ncstatecapitol.com.* (1840) A simple, stately Greek Revival-style building. Statues of honored sons and daughters decorate the grounds. The old legislative chambers, in use until 1963, have been restored to their 1840s appearance, as have the old state library room and the state geologist's office. Self-guided tours. (Daily; closed Jan 1, Thanksgiving, late Dec) **FREE**

State Legislative Building. *16 West Jones St, Raleigh (27601). Salisbury and Jones sts. Phone 919/733-7928.* First building constructed to house a state general assembly (1963); designed by Edward Durell Stone in a blend of modern and classical styles. Tours of chambers may include view of legislators at work. (Daily; closed Jan 1, Thanksgiving, Dec 25) **FREE**

William B. Umstead State Park. *8801 Glenwood Ave, Raleigh (27617). Crabtree Creek Section. 10 miles NW on Hwy 70. Phone 919/571-4170.* On 5,480 acres with a 55-acre lake. Fishing, boating. Hiking, riding. Picnicking. Camping (Mar-mid-Dec, Thurs-Sun). Nature study. Reedy Creek

Section, 10 miles NW off I-40. Approximately 1,800 acres. Fishing. Hiking, riding. Picnicking. Nature study.

Special Events

Artsplosure Spring Arts Festival. *Downtown, Raleigh (27601). Moore Sq and City Market. Phone 919/832-8699.* Citywide celebration of the arts. Showcase for regional dance, music, theater performances by nationally known artists; outdoor arts and crafts show; children's activities. Mid-May.

North Carolina State Fair. *State Fairgrounds, 1025 Blue Ridge Blvd, Raleigh (27607). 5 miles W on Hwy 1, then 1 mile W on Hwy 54. Phone 919/733-2145. www.ncstatefair.org.* Midway, concerts, tractor pull, demolition derby, petting zoo. Mid-Oct.

Limited-Service Hotels

★ **CANDLEWOOD SUITES.** *4433 Lead Mine Rd, Raleigh (27612). Phone 919/789-4840; toll-free 888/226-3539; fax 919/789-4841. www.candlewoodsuites.com.* Perfect for a long-term stay, this all-suite property offers full kitchens, comfortable work areas, VCRs, and CD players. Located less than a mile from Interstate 440, it is also near Crabtree Shopping Mall, with its shopping, entertainment, and dining options. 122 rooms, all suites. Pets accepted, some restrictions; fee. Check-in 3 pm, check-out noon. High-speed Internet access. Fitness room. **$**

★ ★ **CLARION HOTEL STATE CAPITAL.** *320 Hillsborough St, Raleigh (27603). Phone 919/832-0501; toll-free 800/424-6423; fax 919/833-1631. www.clarionhotel.com.hotel/nc376.* Ultramodern with spacious guest rooms, this hotel offers a good location and value. Situated in downtown Raleigh, it is in the heart of the government, corporate, and entertainment districts. The 20th-floor restaurant gives way to fantastic views of the city. Microwaves/refrigerators are available upon request. 202 rooms, 19 story. Check-in 3 pm, check-out 11 am. High-speed Internet access. Restaurant, bar. Fitness room. Business center. **$**

★ ★ **COURTYARD BY MARRIOTT RALEIGH NORTH.** *1041 Wake Towne Dr, Raleigh (27609). Phone 919/821-3400; toll-free 800/321-2211; fax 919/821-1209. www.courtyard.com/rduwf.* 153 rooms, 3 story. Check-in 3 pm, check-out noon. High-speed Internet access. Fitness room. Outdoor pool, whirlpool. Business center. **$**

★ **DAYS INN SOUTH-RALEIGH.** *3901 S Wilmington St, Raleigh (27603). Phone 919/772-8900; toll-free 800/325-2525; fax 919/772-1536. www.daysinn.com.* Guests looking for a clean, no-frills place to stay will find this property near Interstate 40 convenient and budget friendly. Shopping malls and dining options are all nearby, and it is within minutes of downtown. 103 rooms, 3 story. Complimentary continental breakfast. Check-in 2 pm, check-out 11 am. High-speed Internet access, wireless Internet access. Outdoor pool. **$**

★ **ECONO LODGE RALEIGH.** *2641 Appliance Court, Raleigh (27604). Phone 919/856-9800; toll-free 800/424-6423; fax 919/856-9898. www.choicehotels.com/hotel/nc487.* Located off Interstate 440 at the Capital Boulevard exit (exit 11), this no-frills property offers a clean, inexpensive nights stay. The first two floors of this building have outdoor access, while the third floor's access is indoors. Many area attractions are nearby. 137 rooms, 3 story. Pets accepted, some restrictions; fee. Complimentary continental breakfast. Check-in 2 pm, check-out 11 am. High-speed Internet access, wireless Internet access. Outdoor pool. **$**

★ ★ **EMBASSY SUITES HOTEL RALEIGH/ CRABTREE VALLEY.** *4700 Creedmoor Rd, Raleigh (27612). Phone 919/881-0000; toll-free 800/362-2779; fax 919/782-7225. www.embassysuites.com.* With a nine-story atrium for guests to relax in, plus a pool, Jacuzzi, and exercise room, this hotel is perfect for vacationers. The property is located off Interstate 440 and near the Crabtree Valley Mall, where visitors will find great shopping, dining, and plenty of entertainment. 225 rooms, 9 story, all suites. Complimentary full breakfast. Check-in 3 pm, check-out noon. High-speed Internet access, wireless Internet access. Restaurant, bar. Fitness room. Indoor pool, whirlpool. Airport transportation available. **$**

★ **HAMPTON INN RALEIGH-CRABTREE VALLEY.** *6209 Glenwood Ave, Raleigh (27612). Phone 919/782-1112; fax 919/782-9119. www.hamptoninn.com.* Situated near the Crabtree Mall and only 8 miles from the RDU Airport, this convenient location is on the main route between Raleigh and Durham, near shopping and dining. Guests can enjoy a complimentary evening manager's reception Monday through Thursday. 141 rooms, 6 story. Complimentary continental breakfast. Check-in 3 pm, check-out noon. High-speed Internet access, wireless Internet access. Fitness room.

Outdoor pool. Airport transportation available. **$**

★ ★ **HOLIDAY INN BROWNSTONE.** *1707 Hillsborough St, Raleigh (27607). Phone 919/828-0811; toll-free 800/331-7919; fax 919/834-0904. www.brownstonehotel. com.* Adjacent to North Carolina University, this property is also located 1 mile from downtown Raleigh and the State Government Complex. Executive-level guest rooms feature Tempur-pedic beds that conform to your body. 187 rooms, 9 story. Check-in 3 pm, check-out 11 am. High-speed Internet access, wireless Internet access. Restaurant, bar. Fitness room. Outdoor pool. **$**

Full-Service Hotels

★ **CANDLEWOOD SUITES.** *1020 Buck Jones Rd, Raleigh (27606). Phone 919/468-4222; toll-free 888/226-3539; fax 919/468-4090. www.candlewoodsuites.com.* Shopping and dining options are close to this all-suite property located near Interstate 40. The theme and furnishings are traditional, and each suite has a kitchen (no stove). The Candlewood Cupboard offers microwavable food, drinks, snacks, and ice cream on the honor systemyou pay for what you take, and there is a gazebo and grill for summer picnics. VCRs and CD players are included in the rooms, with free video and CD rentals. 81 rooms, all suites. Pets accepted, some restrictions; fee. Check-in 3 pm, check-out noon. High-speed Internet access. Fitness room.

★ ★ ★ **MARRIOTT RALEIGH CRABTREE VALLEY.** *4500 Marriott Dr, Raleigh (27612). Phone 919/781-7000; toll-free 800/228-9290; fax 919/781-3059. www.marriott.com/rdunc.* Visitors will stay in one of the comfortable guest rooms at this location on a parklike setting, with attractive gardens and landscaping adjacent to the building. Accessible to Interstate 440 and Highway 70, it is only 15 minutes from Research Triangle Park and RDU Airport and across the street from Crabtree Valley Mall. The décor is ultramodern, with marble floors, an atrium lobby, and a lush tropical garden on the staircase. Nearby activities include tennis facilities and museums of art, history, and natural science. 375 rooms, 6 story. Check-in 3 pm, check-out noon. High-speed Internet access, wireless Internet access. Restaurant, bar. Fitness room. Indoor pool, outdoor pool, whirlpool. Airport transportation available. Business center. **$$**

★ ★ ★ **SHERATON RALEIGH CAPITAL CENTER HOTEL.** *421 S Salisbury St, Raleigh (27601). Phone 919/834-9900; toll-free 800/325-3535; fax 919/833-1217. www.sheratonraleigh.com.* The convention center is right next to this hotel, which is located in the heart of downtown and near the state capitol, dining, museums, and entertainment. Marble floors, high ceilings, and a balcony overlooking the lobby add to the ultramodern design. Guest rooms are attractively decorated in mono tones, with off-white walls, rust duvets, and white pillows. 355 rooms, 17 story. Pets accepted. Check-in 3 pm, check-out noon. High-speed Internet access, wireless Internet access. Restaurant, bar. Fitness room. Indoor pool, whirlpool. Business center. **$**

Restaurants

★ ★ **42 STREET OYSTER BAR & SEAFOOD GRILL.** *508 W Jones St, Raleigh (27603). Phone 919/831-2811; fax 919/831-2917. www.42ndstoysterbar. com.* You'll step back in time when you enter the Oyster Bar—wainscoted walls, antique photographs depicting the good ol' days, and many mounted fish add to the days-gone-by setting. Booths line the room and bistro tables are set in the middle; guests can also choose to dine at the counter. This local favorite is situated in the heart of downtown and features a live band on Thursday through Saturday evenings. Seafood menu. Lunch, dinner. Closed holidays. Bar. Children's menu. Casual attire. Reservations recommended. **$$**

★ **ABYSSINIA ETHIOPIAN RESTAURANT.** *2109-146 Avent Ferry Rd, Raleigh (27606). Phone 919/664-8151.www.abyssiniarestaurantnc.com.*Middle Eastern menu. Dinner. Bar. Casual attire. **$$**

★ ★ ★ **ANGUS BARN.** *9401 Glenwood Ave, Raleigh (27617). Phone 919/787-3505; toll-free 800/277-2270; fax 919/783-5568. www.angusbarn.com.* A variety of barn antiques, including an Amish buggy, greet guests as they pull up to the portico of Angus Barn. Once inside, there are baskets of red delicious apples on barrels and a country store selling some of the restaurants foods and accessories, including homemade pies, salad dressings, and peppermills. The décor is unique and the service is warm and friendly. This is not your average run-of-the-mill steakhouse; it is one of the few restaurants in the country to age its own beef before it is hand cut and then grilled to perfection. A popular and cozy restaurant, it has been serving meat lovers with its thick steaks since 1960, but it also wins bonus points for enormous lobster, fresh seafood, and steakhouse classics like oysters Rockefeller and chateaubriand. Live music is featured on Wednesdays, Fridays, and Saturdays. Seafood, steak menu. Dinner. Bar. Children's menu. Business casual attire. Reservations recommended. Valet parking. **$$$**

★ ★ **CARVERS CREEK.** *2711 Capital, Raleigh (27604). Phone 919/872-2300; fax 919/850-0261. www. carverscreek.com.* Carvers Creek is right off Interstate 440 at the Capital Boulevard exit. With a hunting lodge theme, it features snowshoes, skis, antlers, and moose heads on the walls; an atrium ceiling with hanging plants; and antiques, old barrels, and trunks. Steak menu. Lunch, dinner. Bar. Children's menu. Casual attire. Reservations recommended **$$**

★ **CASA CARBONE RISTORANTE.** *6019-A Glenwood Ave, Raleigh (27612). Phone 919/781-8750; fax 919/781-8751. www.casacarbone.com.* Casa Carbone Ristorante is located in a small strip mall near the Crabtree Shopping Mall and several lodging establishments. Fruit-decorated tablecloths complement the wallpaper trim, and pictures of Italian scenes adorn the walls. Several dining areasone with intimate boothsgive guests a choice. Italian menu. Dinner. Closed Mon; holidays; also Super Bowl Sun. Casual attire. **$$**

★ ★ **IRREGARDLESS CAFE.** *901 W Morgan, Raleigh (27603). Phone 919/833-8898; fax 919/833-2211. www.irregardless.com.* Seafood, vegetarian menu. Lunch, dinner, late-night, Sun brunch. Closed Mon. Bar. Children's menu. Casual attire. **$**

★ **LAS MARGARITAS.** *231 Timber Dr, Garner (27529). Phone 919/662-1030.* Mexican menu. Lunch, dinner. Closed holidays. Bar. Children's menu. Casual attire. **$$**

★ ★ ★ **SECOND EMPIRE.** *330 Hillsborough St, Raleigh (27603). Phone 919/829-3663; fax 919/829-9319. www.second-empire.com.* This restaurant is housed in a renovated Second Empire Victorian home, originally built in 1879. The original heart pine floors; masonry walls, doors, and windows; along with interesting artwork add to the elegant ambience in the upstairs dining room, which offers fine dining. For a more casual dining experience, head downstairs to the Tavern, with its exposed brick walls. American menu. Dinner. Closed Sun. Bar. Business casual attire. Reservations recommended. **$$$**

★ ★ ★ **SIMPSON'S.** *5625 Creedmoor Rd, Raleigh (27612). Phone 919/783-8818; fax 919/783-9070. www. simpsonsrestaurant.com.* Guests can enjoy a romantic, warm atmosphere as they dine by candlelight with soft background music from the pianist (Fri and Sat evenings). The restaurant, fashioned after an old English pub, features mahogany décor and tables set with crisp white tablecloths, fresh flowers, and candles. The owner, Mr. Simpson, gives all the women patrons a beautiful fresh rose every night. Seafood, steak menu. Dinner. Closed Sun; holidays. Bar. Business casual attire. Reservations recommended. **$$$**

★ ★ **VINNIE'S STEAKHOUSE.** *7440 Six Forks Rd, Raleigh (27615). Phone 919/847-7319; fax 919/841-0130. www.vinniessteakhouse.com.* Vinnie's is located north of the city in a bedroom community with strip malls nearby. The décor features dark paneling and dark green-painted walls. Pieces of art and little lamps with shades adorn the walls by the tables. A large temperature-controlled walk-in wine cooler separates the dining room from the bar. Italian, steak menu. Dinner. Closed Sun; Jan 1, July 4, Dec 24-25. Bar. Business casual attire. Reservations recommended. Outdoor seating. Credit cards accepted. **$$$**

★ ★ **WINSTON'S GRILLE.** *6401 Falls of Neuse Rd, Raleigh (27615).Phone 919/790-0700; fax 919/878-8710. www.winstonsgrille.com.* Gas lanterns light the entryway of this eatery located north of the city. Guests can watch the chefs in the open kitchen as they prepare such dishes as Backyard Rotisserie Chicken, an herb-roasted half chicken with homemade mashed potatoes; Winstons Prime Rib, a slow-roast 12-ounce cut; and Marinated Pork Loin, two 4-ounce cuts of marinated pork loin with peppercorn demi-glace and mashed potatoes. American menu. Lunch, dinner, brunch. Closed Thanksgiving, Dec 25 bar. Children's menu. Casual attire. Reservations recommended. Outdoor seating. **$$**

Roanoke Rapids (A-8)

Population 16,957
Elevation 170 ft
Area Code 252
Zip 27870
Information Halifax County Tourism Development Authority, PO Box 144; phone 252/535-1687 or toll-free 800/522-4282
Web Site www.visithalifax.com

What to See and Do

Historic Halifax State Historic Site. *25 Saint David, Halifax . 9 miles SE off Hwy 301 or S on I-95, exit 168. Phone 252/583-7191.* The Halifax Resolves, first formal sanction of American independence, were adopted here on April 12, 1776. Buildings include Owens House (1760), Burgess Law Office, Eagle Tavern (1790), Sally-Billy House, clerk's office, jail, Montfort Archaeology Exhibit Center. Other features are Magazine Spring, garden, and churchyard. Visitor center; audiovisual programs, exhibits. (Apr-Oct, daily; rest of year, Tues-Sun; closed holidays) Historical dramas presented in summer (fee). **FREE**

Lake Gaston. *10 miles W via Hwy 158 and Hwy 1214.* This 34-mile-long, 20,300-acre lake offers opportunities for fishing, boating (ramps), and picnicking.

Roanoke Rapids Lake. *NW edge of town.* Covers 5,000 acres. Launching facilities.

Limited-Service Hotel

★ **BEST WESTERN ROANOKE RAPIDS.** *I-95 N and Hwy 46, Roanoke Rapids (27870). Phone 252/537-1011; toll-free 800/832-8375; fax 252/537-9258. www.bestwestern.com.* 100 rooms, 2 story. Complimentary continental breakfast. Check-in noon, check-out 11 am. Restaurant. Outdoor pool. **$**

Robbinsville (B-2)

See also Bryson City

Population 747
Elevation 2,064 ft
Area Code 828
Zip 28771

A Ranger District Office of the Nantahala National Forest (see FRANKLIN) is located here.

What to See and Do

Joyce Kilmer-Slickrock Wilderness. *13 miles NW via Hwy 129, Hwy 1116 and 1127. Inquire at District Ranger Office (mid-Apr-Oct, weekends and holidays), N off Hwy 129, Phone 828/479-6431.* A 17,013-acre area within Nantahala National Forest (see FRANKLIN). More than 100 species of trees native to region; trails through forest to view prime specimens. Located within the area is the Joyce Kilmer Memorial Forest, a 3,840-acre stand of virgin timber dedicated to the author of the poem *Trees*; and a National Recreation Trail. **FREE**

Rocky Mount (A-8)

See also Wilson

Settled 1840
Population 55,893
Elevation 120 ft
Area Code 252
Information Chamber of Commerce, 100 Coast Line St, 27802; phone 252/446-0323
Web Site www.rockymountchamber.org

This is one of the country's largest bright-leaf tobacco marts. Cotton products in the form of yarn, bolts of fabric, and ready-to-wear clothing flow from the mills. The factories produce fertilizer, furniture, chemicals, metal products, lumber, and pharmaceuticals. Rocky Mount is also the home of Hardee's Food Systems.

What to See and Do

Children's Museum. *225 Church St, Rocky Mount. Phone 252/972-1167.* Hands-on exhibits provide children with experiences of the latest technological advances. (Daily; closed Thanksgiving, Dec 25) **$**

Special Event

Tobacco auctions. Numerous warehouses. Inquire locally. Aug-mid-Nov.

Limited-Service Hotels

★ **HAMPTON INN.** *530 N Winstead Ave, Rocky Mount (27804). Phone 252/937-6333; toll-free 800/426-7866; fax 252/937-4333. www.hamptoninn.com.* 124 rooms, 4 story. Complimentary continental breakfast. Check-in 3 pm, check-out noon. Outdoor pool. **$**

★ ★ **HOLIDAY INN.** *651 Winstead Ave, Rocky Mount (27804). Phone 252/937-6888; toll-free 888/543-2255; fax 252/937-4788. www.holiday-inn.com.* 169 rooms, 4 story. Check-in 3 pm, check-out noon. Restaurant, bar. Fitness room. Outdoor pool. **$**

Salisbury (B-5)

See also Concord, Lexington, Statesville

Founded 1753
Population 26,462
Elevation 746 ft
Area Code 704
Zip 28144
Information Rowan County Convention and Visitors Bureau, PO Box 4044, 28145; phone 704/638-3100 or toll-free 800/332-2343. Visit the visitor information center at 132 E Innes for brochures, maps, and audio tape tours.
Web Site www.visitsalisburync.com.

A trading, cultural, and judicial center since 1753, it is here that Daniel Boone spent his youth and Andrew Jackson studied law. Salisbury's wide, shady streets were twice taken over by military troops. The first time was by Lord Cornwallis during the Revolutionary War, and the Civil War brought General Stoneman. During the Civil War, Salisbury was the site of a Confederate prison for Union soldiers where 5,000 died; they are buried here in the National Cemetery. Among the dead was Robert Livingstone, Union soldier and son of African missionary David Livingstone. Livingstone College was named for the father. Catawba College and Rowan-Cabarrus Community College complete Salisbury's triad of higher learning.

What to See and Do

Dan Nicholas Park. *6800 Bringle Ferry Rd, Salisbury (28146). 2 miles N on I-85, to exit 79, then 6 miles SE. Phone 704/636-0154.* This 330-acre park has lake with fishing, paddleboats (fee). Hiking, nature trail; tennis, miniature golf (fee). Picnicking. Camping hookups (fee). Outdoor theater, two nature museums, petting zoo, carousel, and miniature train ride. Park (all year). **FREE**

Dr. Josephus Hall House. *226 S Jackson, Salisbury. Phone 704/636-0103.* (1820) Large antebellum house set amid giant oaks and century-old boxwoods; contains most of its original Federal and Victorian furnishings. House was used as Union commander's headquarters following Civil War. (Sat-Sun afternoons) **$**

N. C. Transportation Museum. *411 S Salisbury Ave, Spencer. 2 miles NE via I-85. Phone 704/636-2889.* Once the steam locomotive repair facility for Southern Railway, now a transportation museum, railroad yards, and shops. Back shop and 37-stall Bob Julian Roundhouse (1924). Rolling stock includes six engines (steam and diesel); restored luxury private cars; freight cars, trolley, passenger coaches. Train ride (seasonal; fee). Visitor center, two exhibit buildings, audiovisual show. (Apr-Oct, daily; rest of year, Tues-Sun; closed Dec 25) **FREE**

Old Stone House. *Old Stone House Rd, Granite Quarry . 4 miles SE, off Hwy 52. Phone 704/633-5946.* (1766) Built of hand-laid granite with walls 2 feet thick. Restored (1966); authentically furnished; family burial ground opposite. (Apr-Nov, Sat-Sun afternoons) **$$**

Poets and Dreamers Garden. *701 W Monroe St, Salisbury (28144). On campus of Livingstone College.* Formal, Biblical, and Shakespearean gardens; fountain, sundial. Tomb of founder Joseph Charles Price in garden.

Utzman-Chambers House. *116 S Jackson St, Salisbury . In Federal Town House Museum (1819). Phone 704/633-5946.* Period rooms, authentic regional furniture; 19th-century garden. (Thurs-Sun, afternoons; closed holidays, Dec 24) **$**

Waterworks Visual Arts Center. *E Liberty and N Main Sts, Salisbury. Phone 704/636-1882.* Adaptive restoration of former Salisbury Waterworks into arts center. Changing exhibits; studios, classes; courtyard; sensory garden. Guided tours. (Daily; closed holidays) **FREE**

Limited-Service Hotels

★ **HAMPTON INN.** *1001 Klumac Rd, Salisbury (28144). Phone 704/637-8000; toll-free 800/426-7866; fax 704/639-9995. www.hamptoninn.com/hi/salisbury.* The amenities at this business- and leisure-friendly hotel are really what make a stay here worthwhile. With new upgrades like high-speed Internet in the rooms, as well as special bed tables for laptops, and in-room microwaves and refrigerators, every traveler will feel at home here. 121 rooms, 4 story. Pets accepted. Complimentary continental breakfast. Check-in 3 pm, check-out noon. High-speed Internet access. Outdoor pool. **$**

★ ★ **HOLIDAY INN.** *530 Jake Alexander Blvd, Salisbury (28147). Phone 704/637-3100; toll-free 800/465-4329; fax 704/637-9152. www.holiday-inn.com.* With nearby shopping, dining, golfing, and a nightclub, this hotel is ideally located for the leisure traveler. The property also features a game room, open atrium, and a large pavilion area, which is perfect for group events. 181 rooms, 3 story. Pets accepted; fee. Check-in 3 pm, check-out noon. Wireless Internet access. Restaurant, bar. Fitness room. Indoor pool, outdoor pool, whirlpool. **$**

Sanford (B-6)

Population 23,220
Elevation 375 ft
Area Code 919
Zip 27330
Web Site www.sanfordnc.net

What to See and Do

House in the Horseshoe State Historic Site. *324 Alston House Rd, Sanford (27330). 12 miles W on Hwy 42 to Carbonton, then 5 miles S on Hwy 1644. Phone 910/947-2051.* House (circa 1770) was the residence of North Carolina governor Benjamin Williams; site of a Revolutionary War skirmish. (Tues-Sun; closed holidays) **FREE**

Raven Rock State Park. *3009 Raven Rock Rd, Lillington . 18 miles S on Hwy 421. Phone 910/893-4888.* A 2,990-acre park characterized by 152-foot outcrop of rock jutting over Cape Fear River. Fishing. Nature trails, interpretive programs. Picnicking. Primitive camping.

Limited-Service Hotel

★ **QUALITY INN.** *1403 N Horner Blvd, Sanford (27330). Phone 919/774-6411; toll-free 877/424-6423; fax 919/774-7018. www.comfortinnsanfordnc.com.* This clean and recently renovated motel is a great value for bargain seekers. In addition to amenities such as hair dryers, irons and ironing boards, data ports, cable TV, and a fitness center, a complimentary 30-item hot breakfast is offered to guests. 122 rooms, 2 story. Complimentary full breakfast. Check-in 2 pm, check-out noon. Bar. Fitness room. Outdoor pool. **$**

Smithfield (B-7)

See also Dunn, Goldsboro, Raleigh

Population 11,510
Elevation 153 ft
Area Code 919
Zip 27577
Web Site www.smithfield-nc.com

Limited-Service Hotel

★ **COMFORT INN.** *1705 Industrial Park Dr, Selma (27576). Phone 919/965-2150; toll-free 800/228-5150;*
fax 919/965-5200. www.comfortinn.com. 80 rooms, 2 story. Complimentary continental breakfast. Check-in 2 pm, check-out 11 am. Fitness room. Outdoor pool. **$**

Shelby (B-4)

See also Cherryville, Gastonia

Population 19,477
Elevation 853 ft
Area Code 704
Information Cleveland County Economic Development, 311 E Marion St, PO Box 1210, 28151; phone 704/484-4999 or toll-free 800/480-8687
Web Site www.clevelandcounty.com/tourism

Seat of Cleveland County, this town in the Piedmont boasts of diversified industry and agriculture. It is named for Colonel Isaac Shelby, hero of the Battle of Kings Mountain in the Revolutionary War. (See KINGS MOUNTAIN NATIONAL MILITARY PARK, SC.) The town celebrates its heritage and culture with special events, fairs, and historic preservation.

What to See and Do

Central Shelby Historic District Walking Tour. *Courthouse Sq, Shelby (28150). Phone 704/484-3100.* Two-hour self-guided tour encompasses much of original area established in 1841. Features 38 architecturally significant structures circa the 1850s.

South Brunswick Islands (D-8)

See also Southport

Web Site www.sbichamber.com

What to See and Do

South Brunswick Islands. *South Brunswick Islands. www.weblync.com/sbi_chamber.* The South Brunswick Islands offer wide, gently sloping beaches and beautiful scenery. Located just 50 miles from the Gulf Stream, the region has a subtropical climate and mild temperatures. Resort activities are plentiful and include fishing, swimming, tennis, and golf. Shallotte is the hub of the area that includes Holden, Ocean

Isle, and Sunset beaches. The islands are reached by bridges across the Intracoastal Waterway.

Special Events

A Day at the Docks. *Holden Beach. South Brunswick Islands.* Phone 910/754-6644. Arts and crafts, bobble race. Late Mar.

King Classic King Mackerel Tournament. *3238 Pompano St, Holden Beach (28462).* Phone 910/754-6644; toll-free 800/546-4622. Late Aug.

North Carolina Oyster Festival. *Ocean Isle Beach, South Brunswick Islands (28470). In Shallotte.* Phone 910/754-6644. Arts and crafts, music, sports, oyster-shucking contest. Third weekend in Oct.

Limited-Service Hotel

★ **THE WINDS INN AND SUITES.** *310 E 1st St, Ocean Isle Beach (28469).* Phone 910/579-6275; toll-free 800/334-3581; fax 910/579-2884. www.thewinds.com. 86 rooms, 4 story. Complimentary full breakfast. Check-in 4 pm, check-out 11 am. Restaurant, bar. Fitness room. Indoor pool, outdoor pool, whirlpool. Beach. **$**

Southern Pines (B-6)

See also Laurinburg, Pinehurst

Population 10,918
Elevation 512 ft
Area Code 910
Zip 28387
Information Convention and Visitors Bureau, PO Box 2270, 28388; phone 910/692-3330 or toll-free 800/346-5362
Web Site www.homeofgolf.com

The Sandhills, among fine longleaf and loblolly pines, are famed for golf and horses. Known as "sand country," it first gained popularity as a resort in the 1880s, but the enthusiasm for golf in the 1920s fueled Southern Pines' growth as a recreational and resort area. The area is still steeped in tradition and history, with golf and equestrian activities as popular as ever.

What to See and Do

Shaw House. *100 SW Broad St, Southern Pines.* Phone 910/692-2051. Antebellum house of simple and

sturdy style is lightened by unusual mantels of carved cypress. Guided tours (Tues-Sat; closed holidays). Also on the premises are Britt Sanders Cabin and Garner House. **FREE**

Weymouth Woods-Sandhills Nature Preserve. *1024 Fort Bragg Rd, Southern Pines (28387).* 3 miles SE on Indiana Ave, then N on Fort Bragg Rd. Phone 910/692-2167. Excellent examples of Sandhills ecology. Hiking trails along pine-covered "sandridges." Natural history museum. (Daily; closed Dec 25) **FREE**

Special Event

House and Garden Tour. Conducted by Southern Pines Garden Club. Mid-Apr.

Limited-Service Hotels

★ ★ **DAYS INN.** *650 US Hwy 1, Southern Pines (28388).* Phone 910/692-8585; toll-free 800/262-5737; fax 910/692-5213. 162 rooms, 2 story. Pets accepted; fee. Check-in 3 pm, check-out noon. Restaurant, bar. Fitness room. Outdoor pool. **$**

★ **HAMPTON INN.** *1675 Hwy 1 S, Southern Pines (28387).* Phone 910/692-9266; toll-free 800/426-7866; fax 910/692-9298. www.hamptoninn.com. 126 rooms, 2 story. Complimentary continental breakfast. Check-in 2 pm, check-out noon. High-speed Internet access. Outdoor pool. **$**

★ ★ ★ **MID PINES INN AND GOLF CLUB.** *1010 Midland Rd, Southern Pines (28387).* Phone 910/692-2114; toll-free 800/290-2334; fax 910/692-4615. www.pineneedles-midpines.com. Every hole remains where Donald Ross put it in 1921, when he designed the challenging golf course at this stately inn. The large main building houses a restaurant, lounge, and more than 100 nicely appointed rooms. 112 rooms, 3 story. Check-in 2 pm, check-out 11 am. Restaurant, bar. Outdoor pool. Golf, 18 holes. Tennis. **$**

Full-Service Resort

★ ★ ★ **PINE NEEDLES LODGE.** *1005 Midland Rd, Southern Pines (28388).* Phone 910/692-7111; toll-free 800/747-7272; fax 910/692-5349. www.pineneedles-midpines.com. Legendary golfer Peggy Kirk has been welcoming guests and players to Pine Needles for more than three generations. The course is designed by Donald Ross and has been host to two recent US Women's Opens. The rustic lodge and elegant restaurant make for a relaxing golf holiday. 78 rooms, 4 story. Check-in 2 pm, check-out 11 am. Restaurant, bar. Fitness room. Outdoor pool. Golf, 18 holes. Tennis. **$**

🏃 🏊 ⛷ ⛳

Restaurants

★ ★ **LA TERRACE.** *270 SW Broad St, Southern Pines (28387). Phone 910/692-5622; fax 910/692-4603.* French menu. Lunch, dinner. Closed Sun; Jan 1, Dec 25. Outdoor seating. **$$**

★ **SQUIRE'S PUB.** *1720 Hwy 1 S, Southern Pines (28387). Phone 910/695-1161; fax 910/695-3667.* British menu. Lunch, dinner. Closed Sun; Thanksgiving, Dec 24-25. Bar. Children's menu. Five dining areas. **$**

★ **VITO'S RISTORANTE.** *615 SE Broad St, Southern Pines (28387). Phone 910/692-7815.* Italian menu. Dinner. Closed Sun; holidays. **$$**

Southport (D-8)

See also South Brunswick Islands, Wilmington

Founded 1792
Population 2,351
Elevation 22 ft
Area Code 910
Zip 28461
Information Southport-Oak Island Area Chamber of Commerce, 4841 Long Beach Rd SE; phone 910/457-6964 or toll-free 800/457-6964
Web Site www.southport-oakisland.com

Saltwater and freshwater fishing are very good in the vicinity of Cape Fear. Deep-sea charter boats are available at Southport, Long Beach, and Shallotte Point. There is a good yacht harbor facility for small boats and yachts, a municipal pier, three ocean piers, as well as several beaches and golf courses nearby.

Fort Johnston (1764) was the first fort built in North Carolina. With Fort Fisher and Fort Caswell (1825), it guarded the mouth of the Cape Fear River during the Civil War, making it possible for blockade runners to reach Wilmington. Fort Johnston (restored) is the residence of the Commanding Officer of the Sunny Point Military Ocean Terminal.

What to See and Do

Brunswick Town-Fort Anderson State Historic Site. *8884 St Philips Road SE, Southport (28479). 14 miles N on Hwy 133, then 5 miles S on Plantation Rd. Phone 910/371-6613.* Brunswick, founded in 1726, thrived as a major port exporting tar and lumber. Fearing a British attack, its citizens fled when the Revolution began; in 1776 the town was burned by British sailors. Twenty-three foundations have been excavated. Built across part of the town are the Civil War earthworks of Fort Anderson, which held out for 30 days after the fall of Fort Fisher in 1865. Visitor center, exhibits, audiovisual show; marked historical trailside exhibits; nature trail, picnic area. (Tues-Sat; closed holidays) **FREE**

Ferry Service. *Southport to Fort Fisher, Hwy 211 and Ferry Rd, Southport . Phone 910/457-6942; toll-free 800/293-3779.* Approximately 30-minute crossing.

Fort Fisher State Historic Site. *1610 Fort Fisher Blvd S, Kure Beach. 6 miles E via Hwy 421, ferry. Phone 910/458-5538.* The largest earthworks fort in the Confederacy; until the last few months of the Civil War, it kept Wilmington open to blockade runners. Some of the heaviest naval bombardment of land fortifications took place here on Dec 24-25, 1864, and on Jan 13-15, 1865. Tours. Visitor center has exhibits, audiovisual shows. Reconstructed gun emplacement. Picnic area. (Apr-Oct, daily; rest of year, Tues-Sun; closed holidays) **FREE**

Long Beach Scenic Walkway. *SE 19th St, Long Beach. Across Davis Canal. Phone 910/278-5518.* Crosses several important wetland communities; viewing of maritime forests, wetland birds, marsh animals, and seacoast fowl.

Maritime Museum. *116 N Howe St, Southport. Phone 910/457-0003.* Houses memorabilia pertaining to the history of the lower Cape Fear area. (Tues-Sat; closed holidays) **$**

Special Event

US Open King Mackerel Tournament. *606 W West St, Southport (28461).* First weekend in Oct.

Specialty Lodging

LOIS JANE'S RIVERVIEW INN. *106 W Bay St, Southport (28461). Phone 910/457-6701; fax 910/457-6701.* 5 rooms. Complimentary full breakfast. Check-in 2 pm. Check-out 11 am. Built in 1892; antiques. **$**
🅳

Statesville (B-4)

See also Cornelius, Hickory, Salisbury

Founded 1789
Population 23,320
Elevation 923 ft
Area Code 704
Zip 28677
Information Greater Statesville Chamber of Commerce, 115 E Front St, PO Box 1064, 28687; phone 704/873-2892
Web Site www.statesvillechamber.org

Statesville is a community of many small, diversified industries, including furniture, apparel, metalworking, and textiles. Iredell County, of which Statesville is the seat, is known for its dairy and beef cattle.

What to See and Do

Fort Dobbs State Historic Site. *438 Fort Dobbs Rd, Statesville (28625). N via I-40, Hwy 21, State Rd 1930, then 1 1/2 miles W. Phone 704/873-5866.* Named for Royal Governor Arthur Dobbs, the now-vanished fort was built during the French and Indian War to protect settlers. Exhibits, nature trails, excavations. (by appointment only; closed holidays) **FREE**

Lake Norman State Park. *159 Inland Sea Dr, Troutman (28166). 10 miles S via I-77, Hwy 21. Phone 704/528-6350.* On Lake Norman (see CORNELIUS); 1,548 acres. Swimming, fishing, boating (ramp, canoes, paddle boats, rentals). Nature trails. Picnicking. Tent and trailer sites.

Special Events

Carolina Dogwood Festival. *Center St, Statesville (28687).* Apr.

Iredell County Fair. *630 N Main St, Troutman (28166). Phone 704/872-4032.* One week beginning Labor Day.

National Balloon Rally. *115 E Front St, Statesville (28677).* Third weekend in Sept.

Tar Heel Classic Horse Show. Early May.

Limited-Service Hotels

★ **QUALITY INN.** *715 Sullivan Rd, Statesville (28677). Phone 704/878-2721; fax 704/873-6694. www.qualityinn. com.* Families will love the outdoor pool and complimentary continental breakfast each morning at this comfort-able, contemporary hotel, located right off Highway 40. 122 rooms, 2 story. Pets accepted; fee. Complimentary continental breakfast. Check-in 3 pm, check-out 11 am. **$**
🐾 🖼️

★ ★ **HOLIDAY INN.** *1215 Gardner Bagnal Blvd, Statesville (28677). Phone 704/878-9691; toll-free 800/465-4329; fax 704/873-6927. www.holiday-inn.com.* Close to the beautiful Blue Mountain range and a few hours drive from the beach, this conveniently located hotel is just off Highway 77 and gives guests access to shopping and dining in the area. 134 rooms, 2 story. Check-in 3 pm, check-out noon. Restaurant, bar. Fitness room. Outdoor pool. **$**
🧍 🖼️

Tryon (B-3)

See also Hendersonville

Population 1,760
Elevation 1,085 ft
Area Code 828
Zip 28782
Information Polk County Travel and Tourism, Visitor Information, 425 N Trade St; phone 828/859-8300 or toll-free 800/440-7848
Web Site www.nc-mountains.org

On the southern slope of the Blue Ridge Mountains in the "thermal belt," almost at the South Carolina border, Tryon was named for Royal Governor William Tryon, who held office during the Revolution. The Fine Arts Center is the focal point for much of the cultural life of the community.

What to See and Do

Foothills Equestrian Nature Center (FENCE). *3381 Hunting Country Rd, Tryon. Phone 828/859-9021.* Nature preserve (300 acres) has 5 miles of riding and hiking trails; wildlife programs; bird and nature walks. Host to many equestrian events. (Mon-Fri) **FREE**

White Oak Mountain. Scenic drive around the mountain. Turn off onto Houston Rd at Columbus and take dirt road, which winds around mountain.

Special Events

Blue Ridge Barbecue. *Harmon Field Rd, Tryon (28782). Phone 828/859-6236.* Music festival, arts and crafts. Early June.

Steeplechase Races. *3381 Hunting Country Rd, Tryon (28782). Phone toll-free 800/438-3681. Late Apr.*

Full-Service Inn

★ ★ ★ **PINE CREST INN.** *85 Pine Crest Ln, Tryon (28782). Phone 828/859-9135; toll-free 800/633-3001; fax 828/859-9135. www.pinecrestinn.com.* Located in the foothills of the Blue Ridge Mountains, near the Foothills Equestrian Nature Center, this lovely inn is meant to evoke an English country manor. The English innkeepers have restored the hardwood floors, stone fireplaces, and other historic fixtures of the buildings that comprise the inn. 39 rooms, 2 story. Complimentary full breakfast. Check-in 3 pm. Check-out 11 am. Restaurant. **$$$**

Restaurant

★ ★ ★ **PINE CREST INN RESTAURANT.** *85 Pine Crest Ln, Tryon (28782). Phone 828/859-9135; toll-free 800/633-3001; fax 828/859-9136. www. pinecrestinn.com.* Beamed ceilings, a stone fireplace, and heavy pine tables greet visitors at this restaurant with a Colonial-style décor. International/Fusion menu. Breakfast, dinner, Sun brunch. Bar. Children's menu. Business casual attire. Reservations recommended. Outdoor seating. **$$**

Warsaw (C-7)

Population 3,051
Elevation 160 ft
Area Code 910
Zip 28398
Web Site www.townofwarsawnc.com

What to See and Do

Duplin Wine Cellars. *505 N Sycamore St, Rose Hill. 2 miles S via Hwy 117; off I-40 exit 380. Phone 910/289-3888.* Largest winery in state. Videotape, tour, wine tasting, retail outlet. (Mon-Sat; closed holidays) **FREE**

Washington (B-8)

See also Williamston, also see Greenville, SC

Founded 1776
Population 9,583
Elevation 14 ft
Area Code 252
Zip 27889

Information Chamber of Commerce, PO Box 665; phone 252/946-9168
Web Site ci.washington.nc.us

First American village named for the first president, Washington was rebuilt on the ashes left by evacuating Union troops in April 1864. The rebels lost the town in March 1862, and, because it was an important saltwater port, tried to retake it for two years. Evidence of the shelling and burning can be seen in the stone foundations on Water St. Water sports, including sailing, yachting, fishing, and swimming, are popular.

What to See and Do

Bath State Historic Site. *207 Carteret St, Bath . 17 miles E on Hwy 264 and Hwy 92. Phone 252/923-3971.* Oldest incorporated town in state (1705). Buildings include Bonner House (circa 1820), Van Der Veer House (circa 1790) and Palmer-Marsh House (circa 1745). (Apr-Oct, daily; rest of year, daily except Mon; closed holidays). Visitor center, film. Picnic area. **$**

Special Event

Washington Summer Festival. Beach music, street dance, ski show, arts and crafts, children's rides. Last full weekend in July.

Limited-Service Hotel

★ **COMFORT INN.** *1636 Carolina Ave, Washington (27889). Phone 252/946-4444; toll-free 800/228-5150; fax 252/946-2563. www.comfortinn.com.* 56 rooms, 2 story. Complimentary continental breakfast. Check-in 3 pm, check-out 11 am. High-speed Internet access, wireless Internet access. Fitness room. Outdoor pool. **$**
🚶 ⊠

Specialty Lodging

RIVER FOREST MANOR. *738 E Main St, Belhaven (27810). Phone 252/943-2151; toll-free 800/346-2151; fax 252/943-6628. www.riverforestmanor.com.* 9 rooms, 2 story. Complimentary continental breakfast. Check-in 1 pm, check-out 11 am. Restaurant. Outdoor pool, whirlpool. Tennis. Airport transportation available. View of river. Golf carts available for touring town. **$**
⊠ 🎿

Waynesville (B-2)

See also Asheville, Bryson City, Cherokee, Maggie Valley

Population 9,232
Elevation 2,644 ft
Area Code 828
Zip 28786
Information Visitor and Lodging Information, 1233 N Main St, Suite I-40; phone toll-free 800/334-9036
Web Site www.waynesville.com

Popular with tourists, this area offers mountain trails for riding and hiking, superb scenery, and golf and fishing in cool mountain streams. Waynesville is 26 miles from the Cherokee Indian Reservation (see CHEROKEE) and Great Smoky Mountains National Park (see). Maggie Valley (see), about 6 miles northwest, is in a particularly attractive area.

Special Event

International Folk Festival. *Phone 828/452-2997.* Premier folk groups from over 10 countries demonstrate their cultural heritage through lively music and costumed dance. 11 days in late July.

Full-Service Inns

★ ★ ★ **BALSAM MOUNTAIN INN.** *68 Seven Springs Dr, 40, Balsam (28707). Phone 828/456-9498; toll-free 800/224-9498; fax 503/212-9855. www. balsaminn.com.* 50 rooms, 3 story. Pets accepted, some restrictions; fee. Complimentary full breakfast. Check-in 3 pm, check-out 11 am. Restaurant. **$**

★ ★ ★ **THE SWAG COUNTRY INN.** *2300 Swag Rd, Waynesville (28785). Phone 828/926-0430; toll-free 800/789-7672; fax 828/926-2036. www.theswag.com.* The Swag Country Inn entices guests to get back to nature while in the lap of luxury. Situated atop a 5,000-foot mountain and nestled on 250 acres, with a private entrance to Great Smoky Mountain National Park, which is just a few steps away, this country inn enjoys majestic natural surroundings. Discreet and intimate, the inn wraps its guests in a cocoon of rustic elegance. The rooms and suites are distinguished by handcrafted interiors; handmade quilts, woven rugs, and original artwork speak to the mountaineer in all guests. Closed during the winter months, travelers reap the three-season rewards of this advantageous spot. Nature trails beckon adventuresome types, while others head for the redwood sauna and whirlpool. Gourmet comfort food is enjoyed throughout the day, from the picnic baskets and brown-bag lunches thoughtfully provided for day-trippers and hikers to delicious dinners, where the convivial spirit encourages many to forge new friendships. 15 rooms, 2 story. Closed mid-Nov-Apr. Children over 7 only in main building. Complimentary full breakfast. Check-in 3 pm, check-out 11 am. Restaurant (public by reservation). Twenty-eight-person whirlpool. **$$$$**

Specialty Lodging

WINDSONG: A MOUNTAIN INN. *459 Rockcliffe Ln, Clyde (28721). Phone 828/627-1194. www. windsongbb.com.* This hidden treasure in the Smoky Mountains cove offers a fantastic view and resortlike accommodations. Gourmet breakfasts, cozy rooms, and leisurely recreation are just a few of the amenities designed to pamper guests. 5 rooms, 3 story. Children over 12 years only. Complimentary full breakfast. Check-in 3-6 pm, check-out 11 am. Tennis. **$**

YELLOW HOUSE ON PLOT CREEK ROAD. *89 Oakview Dr, Waynesville (28786). Phone 828/452-0991; toll-free 800/563-1236; fax 828/452-1140. www. theyellowhouse.com.* A place best described by its overwhelming beauty and serenity. With a collage of gourmet breakfasts and springtime colors reminiscent of a French countryside, only closer. A fabulous yellow house tucked into the hills at a 3,000-foot elevation, the property has bedrooms that each complement the remarkable landscape. 6 rooms, 3 story. Children over 12 years only. Complimentary full breakfast. Check-in 3-7 pm, check-out 11 am. **$**

Wilkesboro (A-4)

See also Jefferson

Settled 1779
Population 3,159
Elevation 1,042 ft
Area Code 336
Zip 28697
Web Site www.north-wilkesboro.com

What to See and Do

Stone Mountain State Park. *3042 Frank Pkwy, Roar-*

ing Gap (28668). Phone 336/957-8185. A 13,500-acre natural landmark with waterfalls and wooded areas. The mountain, in the center of the park, is a 600-foot dome-shaped granite mass measuring 6 miles in circumference. Three of the South's Civil War heroesRobert E. Lee, Stonewall Jackson, and Jefferson Davisare carved into its north face in the world's largest bas-relief sculpture. The park is popular for mountain climbing. There are 17 miles of designated trout streams. Extensive nature, hiking trails. Picnicking. Developed and primitive camping (dump station). Interpretive program in summer.

Williamston (B-8)

See also Greenville, Washington

Population 5,843
Elevation 80 ft
Area Code 252
Zip 27892
Web Site www.townofwilliamston.com

What to See and Do

Hope Plantation. *138 Hope House Rd, Williamston (27983). Hwy 13 to Windsor, then 4 miles W on Hwy 308.* Phone 252/794-3140. Two-hour guided tour of Georgian plantation house (circa 1800) built by Governor David Stone. Period furnishings; outbuildings; gardens. (Mon-Sat, also Sun afternoons) **$$** Included in admission is

> **King-Bazemore House.** (1763) Tour of this unique Colonial-style house with gambrel roof, dormer windows, and solid brick ends. Period furnishings; outbuildings; gardens.

Limited-Service Hotels

★ **ECONO LODGE.** *100 East Blvd, Williamston (27892).* Phone 252/792-8400; fax 252/809-4800. *www. econolodge.com.* 59 rooms, 2 story. Complimentary continental breakfast. Check-in 2 pm, check-out noon. Fitness room. **$**
🏃

★ ★ **HOLIDAY INN.** *101 East Blvd, Williamston (27892).* Phone 252/792-3184; toll-free 800/792-3101; fax 252/792-9003. *www.holiday-inn.com.* 100 rooms, 2 story. Pets accepted. Check-in 3 pm, check-out 11 am. Restaurant, bar. Outdoor pool. **$**
🐾 🛏

Wilmington (D-7)

See also Southport, Wrightsville Beach

Settled 1732
Population 75,838
Elevation 25 ft
Area Code 910
Information Cape Fear Coast Convention and Visitors Bureau, 24 N 3rd St, 28401; phone 910/341-4030 or toll-free 800/222-4757
Web Site www.cape-fear.nc.us

Chief port of North Carolina, Wilmington is the region's major trade and retail center. Manufacturing, tourism, and port-oriented business lead the area's growth.

Patriots who defied the Crown in the Revolution were led by William Hooper, a signer of the Declaration of Independence. In 1765, eight years before the Boston Tea Party, the citizens of Wilmington kept the British from unloading their stamps for the Stamp Act. In 1781, Cornwallis held the town as his main base of operation for almost a year. After the battle of Guilford Courthouse, the Lord General came back to Wilmington before heading for Yorktown and defeat.

During the Civil War, blockade runners brought fortunes in goods past Federal ships lying off Cape Fear, making Wilmington the Confederacy's chief port until January 1865, when it fell. Wilmington was North Carolina's biggest town until 1910, when railroad-fed industries of the inland Piedmont area outgrew the limited facilities of the harbor. The channel, harbor, and expanded port facilities bring goods from throughout the world to the area.

What to See and Do

Battleship *North Carolina*. *Battleship Rd, Wilmington (28401). Jct of Hwy 74/76, 17 and 421.* Phone 910/251-5797. World War II vessel moored on west bank of Cape Fear River. Tour of museum, gun turrets, galley, bridge, sick bay, engine room, wheelhouse. (Daily) **$$**

Bellamy Mansion Museum of History and Design Arts. *503 Market St, Wilmington.* Phone 910/251-3700. Restored 1859 landmark home has exhibits featuring history, restoration, Southern architecture, and regional design arts. Tours. (Tues-Sun) **$$**

Burgwin-Wright House. *224 Market St, Wilmington . At 3rd St.* Phone 910/762-0570. (1770) Restored colonial town house built on foundation of abandoned town jail. British General Cornwallis had his headquarters here during April 1781. Eighteenth-century furnishings and garden. Tours. (Tues-Sat; closed holidays; also Jan and week of Dec 25) **$$**

Captain J. N. Maffitt **River Cruises.** *Located at the foot of Market St.* Phone 910/343-1611; toll-free 800/676-0162.Five-mile narrated sightseeing cruise covering Wilmington's harbor life and points of interest. Also "river taxi" service (additional fee) from Battleship *North Carolina.* (May-Sept, daily)

Carolina Beach State Park. *1010 Masion Borro State Park Rd, Wilmington. 15 miles S off Hwy 421.* Phone 910/458-8206.This 700-acre park is a naturalist's delight; the rare Venus's flytrap, as well as five other species of insect-eating plants, grow here. Fishing, boating (ramps, marina). Picnicking, concession. Nature, hiking trails. Camping (dump station). Naturalist program.

Cotton Exchange. *321 N Front St, Wilmington.* Phone 910/343-9896. Specialty shops and restaurants in historic buildings on Cape Fear River. (Daily; closed holidays, some stores closed Sun)

Greenfield Gardens. *302 Willard St, Wilmington (28401). 2 1/2 miles S on Hwy 421.* Phone 910/341-7855. A 150-acre municipal park with 180-acre lake, 5-mile scenic drive; canoe and paddleboat rentals (Apr-Oct); bike path; fragrance garden; amphitheater; picnicking; nature trail. (Daily) **FREE**

Henrietta III **Riverboat Cruises.** *Downtown. At riverfront.* Phone 910/343-1611; toll-free 800/676-0162. Narrated sightseeing cruise (1 1/2 hours) down Cape Fear River to North Carolina State Port. (June-Aug, one cruise Tues-Sun; Apr-May, Sept-Oct, two cruises Tues-Sun) Dinner cruises (Apr-Dec, Fri-Sat).

Louise Wells Cameron Art Museum. *3201 S 17th St, Wilmington.* Phone 910/395-5999. Collection of Mary Cassatt prints; paintings and works on paper, Jugtown Pottery, sculpture. Changing exhibits; lectures; educational programs. (Tues-Sun; closed holidays) **$$**

Moores Creek National Battlefield. *40 Patriot Paul Dr, Currie. 17 miles N on Hwy 421, then 3 miles W on Hwy 210.* Phone 910/283-5591. In 1776, the loosely knit colonists took sides against each other—patriots versus loyalists. Colonels Moore, Lillington, and Caswell, with the blessing of the Continental Congress, broke up the loyalist forces, captured the leaders, and seized gold and quantities of weapons. The action defeated British hopes of an early invasion through the South and encouraged North Carolina to be the first colony to instruct its delegates to

vote for independence in Philadelphia. The 86-acre park has a visitor center near its entrance to explain the battle. Picnic area. (Daily; closed Jan 1, Dec 25) **FREE**

North Carolina Aquarium/Fort Fisher. *900 Loggerhead Rd, Kure Beach. 21 miles S on Hwy 421.* Phone 910/458-8257. Fifteen aquariums of North Carolina native sea life; marine exhibits, films, workshops, programs; nature trails. (Daily; closed Jan 1, Thanksgiving, Dec 25) **$$**

Orton Plantation Gardens. *9149 Orton Rd SE, Wilmington (28479). 18 miles S on Hwy 133.* Phone 910/371-6851. Formerly a rice plantation, now beautiful gardens (20 acres) with ancient oaks, magnolias, ornamental plants and lawn and water scenes; rice fields now a waterfowl refuge. Antebellum Orton House (not open), begun in 1730, can be seen from garden paths. Overlooks Cape Fear River. (Mar-Nov, daily) **$$**

Poplar Grove Plantation. *10200 Hwy 17, Wilmington (28411). 8 miles NE on Hwy 17.* Phone 910/686-9989. (Circa 1850) Restored Greek Revival plantation; manor house, smokehouse, tenant house, blacksmith, loom weaver, basket weaver. Guided tours (Daily; closed Easter, Thanksgiving, Dec 25; also first Mon in Feb). **$$**

Wilmington Railroad Museum. *501 Nutt St, Wilmington.* Phone 910/763-2634. Exhibits on railroading past and present, centering on the Atlantic Coast Line and other Southeastern rail lines. HO scale regional history exhibit on first and second floor; outside are ACL steam locomotive and caboose for on-board viewing. (Mid-Mar-Oct, daily; Nov-Feb, Mon-Sat; closed holidays) **$**

Special Events

North Carolina Azalea Festival. Phone 910/794-4650. Garden and home tours, horse show, celebrity entertainers, pageants, parade, street fair. Early Apr.

Riverfest. Phone 910/452-6862. Arts and crafts, music, dancing, and entertainment; boat rides, raft regatta; street fair. Late Sept-early Oct.

Limited-Service Hotels

★ ★ **COURTYARD BY MARRIOTT.** *151 Van Campen Blvd, Wilmington (28403).* Phone 910/395-8224; toll-free 800/321-2211; fax 910/452-5569. *www.marriott.com/ilmcy.* 128 rooms, 2 story. Check-in 3 pm, check-out 11 am. High-speed Internet access, wireless Internet access. Fitness room. Outdoor pool, whirlpool. Business center. **$**

★ **HAMPTON INN.** *1989 Eastwood Rd, Wilmington (28403). Phone 910/256-9600; toll-free 877/256-9600; fax 910/256-1996. www.landfallparkhotel.com.* 120 rooms, 4 story. Complimentary continental breakfast. Check-in 3 pm, check-out 11 am. High-speed Internet access. Bar. Fitness room. Outdoor pool. **$**
🏃 ⛱

★ ★ **HOLIDAY INN.** *5032 Market St, Wilmington (28405). Phone 910/392-1101; toll-free 800/833-4721; fax 910/397-0698. www.holiday-inn.com.* Perfect for either a business trip or a family stay, this Holiday Inn is near the campus of the University of North Carolina-Wilmington, the Cape Fear Coast Convention Center, and the historic downtown area. 124 rooms, 5 story. Complimentary continental breakfast. Check-in 3 pm, check-out noon. Restaurant. Fitness room. Indoor pool, whirlpool. **$**
🏃 ⛱

Full-Service Hotels

★ ★ ★ **HILTON WILMINGTON RIVERSIDE.**
301 N Water St, Wilmington (28401). Phone 910/763-5900; toll-free 800/445-8667; fax 910/763-0038. www.wilmingtonhilton.com. This hotel is a short walk from shops, restaurants, cultural attractions, and the city's riverwalk. Guest rooms are comfortable and attractively decorated and offer magnificent views of Cape Fear River. 274 rooms, 9 story. Pets accepted, some restrictions; fee. Check-in 4 pm, check-out 11 am. High-speed Internet access, wireless Internet access. Restaurant, bar. Fitness room. Outdoor pool. Business center. **$**
🐾 🏃 ⛱ 🎿

★ ★ ★ **THE WILMINGTONIAN.** *101 S 2nd St, Wilmington (28401). Phone 910/343-1800; toll-free 800/525-0909; fax 910/251-1149. www.thewilmingtonian. com.* Located in downtown Wilmington, just two blocks from Cape Fear River and a 40-minute drive to the beaches on the Atlantic Coast, this renovated inn caters to both leisure and business travelers. 40 rooms, 3 story, all suites. Pets accepted; fee. Complimentary continental breakfast. Check-in 3 pm, check-out 11 am. High-speed Internet access, wireless Internet access. Restaurant, bar. **$**
🐾

Specialty Lodgings

C. W. WORTH HOUSE. *412 S 3rd St, Wilmington (28401). Phone 910/762-8562; toll-free 800/340-8559; fax 910/763-2173. www.worthhouse.com.* 7 rooms, 3 story. Children over 12 years only. Complimentary full breakfast. Check-in 4 pm, check-out 11 am. High-

speed Internet access, wireless Internet access. **$**
🖥

DARLINGS BY THE SEA - OCEANFRONT WHIRLPOOL SUITES. *329 Atlantic Ave, Kure Beach (28449). Phone 910/458-8887; toll-free 800/383-8111; fax 910/458-6468. www.darlingsbythesea.com.* Best described as a quaint honeymooners cottage. Each whirlpool suite has a wonderful terrace overlooking the ocean. 5 rooms, 3 story, all suites. No children allowed. Complimentary continental breakfast. Check-in 2 pm, check-out 11 am. Fitness room. Beach. **$$**
🏃

FRONT STREET INN. *215 S Front St, Wilmington (28401). Phone 910/762-6442; toll-free 800/336-8184; fax 910/762-8991. www.frontstreetinn.com.* 12 rooms, 2 story, all suites. Pets accepted, some restrictions. Complimentary continental breakfast. Check-in 4 pm, check-out 11 am. High-speed Internet access, wireless Internet access. Bar. Fitness room. **$$**
🖥 🐾 🏃

THE GRAYSTONE INN. *100 S Third St, Wilmington (28401). Phone 910/763-2000; toll-free 888/763-4773; fax 910/763-5555. www.graystoneinn.com.* Experience true turn-of-the-century style in this historic, landmark bed-and-breakfast. The spacious, antique-filled public rooms include a music room with a grand piano, a mahogany-paneled library, and a chandelier-lit dining room. Rooms are decorated in period furnishingssome with claw-foot tubs. 9 rooms, 3 story. Children over 12 years only. Complimentary full breakfast. Check-in 4 pm, check-out 11 am. High-speed Internet access, wireless Internet access. Fitness room. **$$**
🖥 🏃

ROSEHILL INN. *114 S 3rd St, Wilmington (28401). Phone 910/815-0250; toll-free 800/815-0250; fax 910/815-0350. www.rosehill.com.* This elegant Victorian home was built in 1848 in the heart of the historic district in Wilmington. Enjoy the city's finest dining, shopping, and entertainment located only three blocks away. Each of the large, luxurious guest rooms has its own individual charm and is perfect for a romantic retreat. 6 rooms, 2 story. Children over 14 years only. Complimentary full breakfast. Check-in 3:30 pm, check-out 11 am. High-speed Internet access, wireless Internet access. **$$**
🖥

THE VERANDAS. *202 Nun St, Wilmington (28401). Phone 910/251-2212; fax 910/251-8932. www.verandas. com.* This 8,500-square-foot, Victorian-Italianate

mansion sits two blocks from Cape Fear River. The 1853 structure was almost entirely rebuilt and refurbished in 1996. Climb the spiral staircase to the enclosed cupola for a spectacular sunset view. 8 rooms, 3 story. Children over 12 years only. Complimentary full breakfast. Check-in 4 pm, check-out 11 am. **$$**
🅱

Restaurants

★ **CAFE PHOENIX.** *9 S Front St, Wilmington (28401). Phone 910/343-1395; fax 910/251-8596.* Mediterranean menu. Lunch, dinner. Closed holidays. Bar. Children's menu. Casual attire. Reservations recommended. Outdoor seating. **$$**

★ ★ **COTTAGE.** *1 N Lake Park Blvd, Carolina Beach (28428). Phone 910/458-4383; fax 910/458-6906.* Seafood menu. Lunch, dinner. Closed Sun; holidays; also Dec 26. Bar. Children's menu. Business casual attire. Reservations recommended. Outdoor seating. **$$**

★ **DRAGON GARDEN.** *341-52 S College Rd, Wilmington (28403). Phone 910/452-0708.* Chinese, sushi, Thai menu. Lunch, dinner. Closed Thanksgiving, Dec 24-25. Casual attire. Reservations recommended. **$**

★ ★ **EDDIE ROMANELLI'S.** *5400 Oleander Dr, Wilmington (28403). Phone 910/799-7000; fax 910/350-7862. www.romanellisrestaurant.com.* Italian, American menu. Lunch, dinner, late-night. Closed Thanksgiving, Dec 25. Bar. Children's menu. Casual attire. **$$**

★ ★ **ELIJAH'S.** *2 Ann St, Wilmington (28401). Phone 910/343-1448; fax 910/251-7628. www.elijahs. com.* American menu. Lunch, dinner, Sun brunch. Closed Jan 1, Thanksgiving, Dec 25. Bar. Children's menu. Casual attire. Reservations recommended. Outdoor seating. **$$**

★ **HIERONYMUS SEAFOOD.** *5035 Market St, Wilmington (28405). Phone 910/392-6313; fax 910/392-6328. www.hieronymusseafood.com.* Seafood menu. Dinner. Closed Jan 1, Thanksgiving, Dec 24-25. Bar. Children's menu. Casual attire. Reservations recommended. Outdoor seating. **$$$**

★ ★ **FREDDIE'S.** *111 K Ave, Kure Beach (28449). Phone 910/458-5979; fax 910/458-7988.* Italian, American menu. Dinner. Closed Mon; Jan 1, Thanksgiving, Dec 25. Bar. Children's menu. **$$**
🅱

★ ★ **PILOT HOUSE.** *2 Ann St, Wilmington (28401). Phone 910/343-0200; fax 910/343-0441. www.*

pilothouserest.com. American menu. Lunch, dinner, Sun brunch. Closed Jan 1, Dec 24-25. Bar. Children's menu. Casual attire. Outdoor seating. **$$$**

★ ★ **PORT CITY CHOP HOUSE.** *1981 Eastwood Rd, Wilmington (28405). Phone 910/256-4955; fax 910/256-4926. chophousesofnc.com.* Seafood, steak menu. Lunch, dinner. Closed Sun; Thanksgiving, Dec 25. Bar. Children's menu. Business casual attire. Reservations recommended. Outdoor seating. **$$$**

★ ★ **ROY'S RIVERBOAT LANDING.** *2 Market Street, Wilmington (28401). Phone 910/763-7227; fax 910/343-1038. www.riverboatlanding.com.* International/Fusion menu. Lunch, dinner, Sun brunch. Closed four days in Dec. Bar. Casual attire. Reservations recommended. Outdoor seating. **$$$**

★ **WATER STREET.** *5 S Water St, Wilmington (28401). Phone 910/343-0042; fax 910/343-0004. www.5southwaterstreet.com.* American. Lunch, dinner. Closed Thanksgiving, Dec 25. Bar. Children's menu. Casual attire. Outdoor seating. Riverfront dining in old warehouse. **$$**

Wilson (B-7)

See also Rocky Mount

Population 44,405
Elevation 145 ft
Area Code 252
Web Site www.wilson-nc.com

Located just off Interstate 95, midway between New York and Florida, Wilson is a convenient rest stop for road-weary travelers. It is one of the Southeast's leading antique markets and is said to have one of the nation's largest tobacco markets.

Limited-Service Hotels

★ **BEST WESTERN LA SAMMANA.** *817-A Ward Blvd, Wilson (27893). Phone 252/237-8700; toll-free 800/937-8376; fax 252/237-8092. www.bestwestern.com.* 83 rooms, 2 story. Pets accepted; fee. Complimentary continental breakfast. Check-in 2 pm, check-out 11 am. Outdoor pool. **$**
🐾 🏊

★ **COMFORT INN.** *4941 Hwy 264 W, Wilson (27893). Phone 252/291-6400; toll-free 800/424-6423; fax 252/291-7744. www.choicehotels.com.* 76 rooms, 2 story. Complimentary continental breakfast. Check-in 2 pm, check-out 11 am. Outdoor pool. **$**

★ **HAMPTON INN.** *1801 S Tarboro St, Wilson (27895). Phone 252/291-2323; fax 252/291-7696. www. hamptoninn.com.* 100 rooms, 2 story. Complimentary continental breakfast. Check-out 11 am. Outdoor pool. Business center. **$**

Winston-Salem (A-5)

See also Greensboro, High Point, Lexington

Founded Salem: 1766; Winston: 1849; combined as Winston-Salem: 1913
Population 185,776
Elevation 912 ft
Area Code 336
Information Convention and Visitors Bureau, 601 W 4th St, 27101; phone 336/728-4200 or toll-free 800/331-7018
Web Site www.wscvb.com

First in industry in the Carolinas and one of the South's chief cities, Winston-Salem is a combination of two communities. Salem, with the traditions of its Moravian founders, and Winston, an industrial center, matured together. Tobacco markets, large banks, and arts and crafts galleries contribute to this thriving community.

What to See and Do

Bowman Gray Stadium. *1250 S Martin Luther King Jr. Dr, Winston-Salem (27107). Phone 336/727-2900. www.bowmangrayracing.com.* Bowman Gray Stadium is a multi-use public arena that hosts Winston-Salem State Rams college football games, and features a 1/4-mile asphalt oval. Part of the city's Lawrence Joel Veterans Memorial Coliseum Complex, Bowman Gray has been hosting races for more than 50 years, making it the longest operating NASCAR short track in the country. The stadium is about an hour away from Lowe's Motor Speedway and seats 17,000. **$$**

Hanging Rock State Park. *State Rd 1001, Danbury. 32 miles N, between Hwy 66 and 89 near Danbury. Phone 336/593-8480.* Approximately 6,200 acres in Sauratown Mountains. Lake swimming, bathhouse, fishing, boating (rentals). Nature trails. Picnicking, conces-

sion. Tent and trailer sites, six family cabins (Mar-Nov, by reservations only). Observation tower.

Historic Bethabara Park. *2147 Bethabara Rd, Winston-Salem . Phone 336/924-8191.* Site of first Moravian settlement in North Carolina (1753); restored buildings include Gemeinhaus (1788), Potter's House (1782), and Buttner House (1803); reconstructed palisade fort (1756-1763); stabilized archaeological foundations of original settlement and God's Acre (graveyard); reconstructed community gardens (1759). Visitor center, exhibits, slide show. Nature trails, 175-acre wildlife preserve with walking trails. Picnicking. (Apr-Nov, Tues-Sun; walking tour all year) **$**

Historic Old Salem. *900 Old Salem Rd, Winston-Salem (27101). S of business district on Old Salem Rd. Phone 336/721-7300; toll-free 888/348-5420.* (1766) Restoration of a planned community that Moravians, with their old-world skills, made the 18th-century trade and cultural center of North Carolina's Piedmont. Many of the sturdy structures built for practical living have been restored and furnished with original or period pieces. Early crafts are demonstrated throughout the town. Here also is an original Tannenberg organ in working condition. A number of houses are privately occupied. Nine houses plus outbuildings are open to the public. Tours (self-guided) start at the visitor center on Old Salem Rd. Special events are held during the year. (Tues-Sun; no tours Easter, Thanksgiving, Dec 24-25) **$$$$** In the old village are

Museum of Early Southern Decorative Arts. *924 S Main St, Winston-Salem. Phone 336/721-7300.* Twenty-one period rooms and six galleries (16901820), with decorative arts of Maryland, Virginia, Georgia, Kentucky, Tennessee, and the Carolinas. (Tues-Sun; closed Thanksgiving, Dec 24-25) **$$$$**

Salem Academy and College. *601 S Church St, Winston-Salem (27101). Phone 336/721-2600.* (1772) (1,100 women) When founded by the Moravians, it was the only school of its kind for women in the South. The Fine Arts Center offers art exhibits, lectures, films, concerts, and plays (mid-Sep-mid-May, daily; evenings during special events; some fees). Campus tours on request.

Reynolda House, Museum of American Art. *2250 Reynolda Rd, Winston-Salem . Approximately 2 miles N on University Pkwy, then 1/2 miles E on Coliseum Dr then N on Reynolda Rd. Phone 336/758-5150. www.reynoldahouse.org.* On estate of the late R. J. Reynolds of the tobacco dynasty. American paintings, original furniture, art objects, costume collection. Adjacent is Reynolda Gardens, 125 acres of open fields and naturalized woodlands; formal gardens, greenhouse. (Tues-Sat, also Sun afternoons; closed Jan 1, Thanksgiving, Dec 25) **$$**

SciWorks. *400 W Hanes Mill R,Winston-Salem . At Hwy 52 N. Phone 336/767-6730. www.sciworks.org.* Hands-on exhibits of physical and natural sciences; planetarium; 31-acre outdoor environmental park and nature trails. (Memorial Day-Labor Day, Mon-Sat; closed holidays) **$$**

Southeastern Center for Contemporary Art. *750 Marguerite Dr, Winston-Salem. Phone 336/725-1904.* Exhibits by contemporary artists from across the country with accompanying educational programs. (Wed-Sun; closed holidays) **$**

Tanglewood Park. *4061 Clemmons Rd, Clemmons (27012). 12 miles SW off I-40 (exit 182). Phone 336/778-6300.* Fishing, boating (paddleboats, canoes); horseback riding; golf, tennis; nature trail. Picnicking, playgrounds. Steeplechase (seasonal). (Daily) **$**

Wake Forest University. *1834 Wake Forest Rd, Winston-Salem. Phone 336/758-5000.* (1834) (5,600 students) On campus are Fine Arts Center, Museum of Anthropology; also Reynolda Village, a complex of shops, offices, and restaurants. Bowman Gray School of Medicine is on Medical Center Blvd.

Limited-Service Hotels

★ ★ **HOLIDAY INN.** *5790 University Pkwy, Winston-Salem (27105). Phone 336/767-9595; toll-free 800/553-9595; fax 336/744-1888.* 150 rooms, 6 story. Check-in 3 pm, check-out noon. Restaurant, bar. Fitness room. Outdoor pool. Business center. **$**

★ **QUALITY INN.** *5719 University Pkwy, Winston-Salem (27105). Phone 336/767-9009; toll-free 800/426-7866; fax 336/661-0448. www.qualitywinstonsalem. com.* 115 rooms, 2 story. Pets accepted; fee. Complimentary continental breakfast. Check-in 3 pm, check-out noon. Fitness room. Outdoor pool. **$**

Specialty Lodging

AUGUSTUS T ZEVELY. *803 S Main St, Winston Salem (27101). Phone 336/748-9299; toll-free 800/928-9299; fax 336/721-2211.* 12 rooms, 3 story. Pets accepted, some restrictions; fee. Children over 12 years

only. Complimentary continental breakfast. Check-in 3 pm, check-out 11 am. Built in 1844; restored to its mid-19th century appearance. Moravian ambience. **$**

BROOKSTOWN INN. *200 Brookstown Ave, Winston-Salem (27101). Phone 336/725-1120; toll-free 800/845-4262; fax 336/773-0147. www.brookstowninn. com.* This historic inn was built in 1837 as a textile mill. The conversion preserved the original handmade brick and exposed beam construction. The romantic rooms include European-style breakfast. 71 rooms, 4 story. Complimentary continental breakfast. Check-in 3 pm, check-out noon. Fitness room. **$$**

TANGLEWOOD PARK. *4061 Clemmons Rd, Clemmons (27012). Phone 336/778-6370; fax 336/778-6379. www.tanglewoodpark.org.* 28 rooms, 2 story. Complimentary continental breakfast. Check-in 2 pm, check-out noon. Golf. Tennis. Facilities of Tanglewood Park available. **$**

Restaurants

★ ★ ★ **RYAN'S RESTAURANT.** *719 Coliseum Dr, Winston-Salem (27106). Phone 336/724-6132; fax 336/724-5761. www.ryansrestaurant.com.* American menu. Dinner. Closed Sun; Jan 1, Thanksgiving, Dec 24-25. Bar. Business casual attire. Reservations recommended. Outdoor seating. Wooded setting. **$$**

★ ★ **VINEYARD.** *120 Reynolda Village, Winston-Salem (27106). Phone 336/748-0269; fax 336/723-5980.* American menu. Lunch, dinner. Closed Sun; week of July 4; holidays. Bar. Casual attire. Reservations recommended. Outdoor seating. **$$**

★ ★ **ZEVELY HOUSE.** *901 W 4th St, Winston-Salem (27101). Phone 336/725-6666. www.zevelyhouse. com.* American, French menu. Dinner, Sun brunch. Closed Mon; holidays. Bar. Casual attire. Reservations recommended. Outdoor seating. **$$**

Wrightsville Beach (D-8)

See also Wilmington

Population 2,593
Elevation 7 ft
Area Code 910
Zip 28480
Web Site www.wrightsville.com

A very pleasant family-oriented resort town, Wrightsville Beach offers swimming, surfing, fishing, and boating. The public park has facilities for tennis, basketball, soccer, softball, volleyball, shuffleboard, and other sports.

Limited-Service Hotel

★ ★ **HOLIDAY INN SUNSPREE RESORT.**
1706 N Lumina Ave, Wrightsville Beach (28480). Phone 910/256-2231; toll-free 877/330-5050; fax 910/256-9208. www.holiday-inn.com. 184 rooms. Check-in 3 pm, check-out 11 am. Three restaurants, bar. Indoor pool, outdoor pool. **$**

Restaurants

★ ★ **BRIDGE TENDER.** *1414 Airle Rd, Wrightsville Beach (28480). Phone 910/256-4519; fax 910/256-0380.* Seafood, steak menu. Lunch, dinner. Closed Jan 1, Thanksgiving, Dec 25. Bar. Casual attire. Reservations recommended. Outdoor seating. **$$$**

★ **DOCKSIDE.** *1308 Airlie Rd, Wrightsville Beach (28403). Phone 910/256-2752; fax 910/256-5397. www.docksidewb.com.* American menu. Lunch, dinner. Closed Thanksgiving, Dec 24-25. Bar. Children's menu. Casual attire. Outdoor seating. **$$**

★ ★ **KING NEPTUNE.** *11 N Lumina Ave, Wrightsville Beach (28480). Phone 910/256-2525.* Seafood, steak menu. Dinner. Closed Thanksgiving, Dec 25. Bar. Children's menu. Casual attire. **$$**

★ ★ **OCEANIC.** *703 S Lumina Ave, Wrightsville Beach (28480). Phone 910/256-5551; fax 910/256-4527. www.oceanicrestaurant.com.* Seafood, steak menu. Lunch, dinner, Sun brunch. Closed Jan 1, Thanksgiving, Dec 25. Bar. Children's menu. Casual attire. Outdoor seating. **$$**

South Carolina

In South Carolina, the modern age has neither masked the romance of the Old South nor overshadowed the powerful events of colonial and Confederate times. This state's turbulent and romantic history tells a story that remains deeply ingrained in the history of the US.

Spanish explorers made the first attempt to settle in present-day South Carolina in 1526, less than 35 years after the Europeans discovered America. A severe winter, hostile natives, and disease proved too much for the Spanish to overcome, and the settlement was abandoned. In 1562, a group of French Huguenots, led by Jean Ribaut, landed near the site of present-day Parris Island Marine Corps Base. The French colony might have been a success, had Ribaut's return to the colony from business in France not been delayed. The remaining colonists, fearing they had been abandoned, built a craft and sailed for home. Light winds stranded their boat at sea, and they faced the danger of starvation until a passing English ship rescued them.

The task of settlement fell to the English, whose challenge to Spanish control of the New World eventually met with success. A land grant from England's King Charles II gave the Carolinas to eight English noblemen (still known today as the "Lords Proprietors"). In 1670, the English arrived at Albemarle Point and established Charles Towne, the first successful European settlement in the Carolinas.

During the American Revolution, almost 200 battles and skirmishes were fought in South Carolina. The first overt act of revolution occurred at Fort Charlotte on July 12, 1775; this was the first British property seized by American Revolutionary forces. On December 20, 1860, South Carolina became the first state to secede from the Union. The initial clash of the Civil War also occurred on South Carolina soil; the bombardment of Fort Sumter in 1861 resulted in its seizure by Confederate forces, who maintained possession until the evacuation of Charleston in 1865. Bloodied, impoverished, and blackened by the fires of General Sherman's "March to the Sea," South Carolina emerged from the difficult Reconstruction days and was readmitted to the Union in 1868.

For most of the period since the Civil War, South Carolina has had economic problems, but in recent years these difficulties have eased as industry has been attracted by hospitable communities and favorable tax rates. From town to town throughout the state, diversified industries have brought greater prosperity with them. South Carolina is a major producer of tobacco, cotton, pine lumber, corn, oats, sweet potatoes, soybeans, peanuts, peaches, melons, beef cattle, and hogs. Power projects have been created by damming the Santee, Saluda, Savannah, and other rivers. Four atomic energy plants provide commercial energy. Tourism, the state's second-largest industry, continues to grow.

Population: 3,497,800

Area: 30,207 square miles

Elevation: 0-3,560 feet

Peak: Sassafras Mountain (Pickens County)

Entered Union: Eighth of original 13 states (May 23, 1788)

Capital: Columbia

Motto: Prepared in mind and resources; While I breathe, I hope

Nickname: Palmetto State

Flower: Carolina Yellow Jessamine

Bird: Carolina Wren

Tree: Palmetto

Fair: October in Columbia

Time Zone: Eastern

Web Site: www.travelsc.com

Calendar Highlights

MARCH

Triple Crown *(Aiken). For more information, contact the Aiken Chamber of Commerce, phone 803/641-1111. Three events: trials (Aiken Training Track), steeple-chase (Clark Field), harness race (Aiken Mile Track).*

APRIL

Family Circle Magazine Cup Tennis Tournament *(Hilton Head Island). Sea Pines Racquet Club. Phone toll-free or 800/677-2293.*

MAY

Freedom Weekend Aloft *(Greenville). Phone 864/232-3700.* More than 200 balloonists compete.

Spoleto Festival USA *(Charleston). Phone 843/722-2764.* Internationally acclaimed counterpart to the arts festival in Spoleto, Italy, founded by Gian Carlo Menotti; includes opera, ballet, dance, visual arts, theater, chamber music, jazz, symphonic, and choral performances and much more. Piccolo Spoleto, running concurrent with the main festival, has performances by local and regional artists.

JUNE

Sun Fun Festival *(Myrtle Beach). Contact the Chamber of Commerce, phone 843/626-7444 or toll-free 800/356-3016.* More than 60 seaside entertainment events, including parades.

SEPTEMBER

Hilton Head Island Celebrity Golf Tournament *(Hilton Head Island). Indigo Run, and Sea Pines Plantation. Phone 843/842-7711.*

OCTOBER

Fall Tour of Homes and Gardens *(Beaufort). Contact the Historic Beaufort Foundation, phone 843/524-3163 or toll-free 800/638-3525.*

South Carolina State Fair *(Columbia). Fairgrounds. Phone 803/799-3387.* Agricultural, floral, home, craft, livestock, and commercial exhibits. Entertainment, shows, carnival.

NOVEMBER

Colonial Cup International Steeplechase *(Camden). Springdale Race Course. Phone 803/432-6513.*

When to Go/Climate

South Carolina enjoys a moderate climate, making it an attractive all-year resort. The cool upland western area merges into a subtropical seacoast. Summers, however, especially in the low country and along the coast, can be uncomfortably hot and humid. The barrier islands and up-country elevations provide summer havens from the blistering heat. Early spring and late fall are good times to visit, with comfortable temperatures and moderate rainfall.

AVERAGE HIGH/LOW TEMPERATURES (°F)

Charleston

Jan 56/41	**May** 80/66	**Sep** 83/71
Feb 59/43	**Jun** 85/72	**Oct** 75/61
Mar 65/50	**Jul** 88/75	**Nov** 67/52
Apr 73/58	**Aug** 87/75	**Dec** 60/45

Greenville

Jan 50/30	**May** 80/56	**Sep** 81/61
Feb 54/32	**Jun** 86/64	**Oct** 72/49
Mar 64/40	**Jul** 88/68	**Nov** 63/41
Apr 72/48	**Aug** 87/67	**Dec** 53/33

Parks and Recreation

Water-related activities, hiking, various other sports, picnicking, and visitor centers, as well as camping, are available in many of South Carolina's state parks. Cabins are located at Barnwell, Cheraw, Devils Fork, Dreher Island, Edisto Beach, Givhans Ferry, Hickory Knob Resort, Hunting Island, Keowee-Toxaway, Myrtle Beach, Oconee, Poinsett, Santee, and Table Rock. No pets are allowed in cabins. Cabin reservations can be made at individual parks. Camping: 14-day maximum; reservations accepted only at Calhoun Falls, Devils Fork, Dreher Island, Edisto Beach, Hunting Island, Huntington Beach, Lake Hartwell, Myrtle Beach, Oconee, Santee, and Table Rock; $12-$25/night; pets on leash

TRAVELING THE LOW COUNTRY

South Carolina's Atlantic coastline stretches from developed beaches at the North Carolina border to the "low country" at the Georgia border, a region of remote marshlands and subtropical barrier islands of palmetto, live oak, and Spanish moss. The 100 miles between Charleston and Savannah form the heart of the low country.

Head west from Charleston along Highway 17 south, the old Atlantic Coast Highway, a well-used local route. Take every opportunity to detour east to remote islands for a close look at the distinct coastal ecology. The first side trip takes you 24 miles south from Highway 17 along Highway 174 to Edisto Beach. This island is developed as a low-key beach town with vacation homes, restaurants, and lodgings. Stay at the beach-front campground or at cozy state park cabins a short drive from the wide white-sand beach. Return to Highway 17 and continue south 22 miles to the Highway 21 turnoff to Beaufort, 18 miles east. A modest, quiet village, Beaufort serves as the unofficial capital of the low country. Downtown, tidy Victorian homes and a small set of storefronts overlook a beautiful marshland landscape. Several restaurants and a shoreline path give visitors a chance to enjoy the view.

Cross the marsh on the Highway 21 bridge east to St. Helena Island. Less than 10 miles in, a central village of sorts holds a restaurant, gas station, and the Penn Center, which tells the story of the island's history. In 1861, federal troops took St. Helena Island, freeing the 10,000 slaves who worked local cotton plantations. The next year, women religious leaders from Philadelphia started the Penn Center as one of the first schools for African Americans in the nation. The museum contains exhibits about the teachers, students, and the Sea Islander community.

Continue beyond St. Helena Island to Hunting Island. Stop at the impeccable white-sand beaches of Hunting Island State Park to swim, sunbathe, fish, or go crabbing. The beachfront campground is a great place to spend the night.

Retrace your path to return to Beaufort, but instead of heading back to Highway 17, take Highway 170 southeast from Beaufort through Chelsea to Highway 278 south. This route juts east to Hilton Head Island, named after English sea captain William Hilton, who explored the island in 1664. Before the Civil War, the island was rich in Sea Island cotton, rice, and indigo. Now it's rich with vacationers looking for recreation for the whole family: not only sand and surf, but also two dozen golf courses, hundreds of tennis courts, horseback riding, and all kinds of water sports.From the southern tip of Hilton Head Island, a passenger ferry makes the trip over to neighboring Daufuskie Island, accessible only by boat. Daufuskie is the home of Gullah community, descended from African Americans so isolated on these islands that they were able to maintain many more African traditions than more assimilated mainlanders.

Return west on Highway 278 to Highway 170 to connect back up with Highway 17, the old Atlantic Coast Highway, which crosses the state line at the Savannah River. Proceed into Savannah to visit a historic district that rivals Charleston's. You'll have a wonderful selection of places to eat and stay over-night. When you're ready to return to Charleston, you may prefer to head up I-95 north as a speedy alternative, or you can retrace your steps through the low country. **(Approximately 100 miles)**

---

only. Not all state parks are open every day; hours of operation also vary. Contact the Columbia office or the individual park before making your final trip plans. Fees subject to change. For cabin rates and further information, contact the Department of Parks, Recreation, and Tourism, Edgar A. Brown Building, 1205 Pendleton St, Columbia 29201; phone 803/734-0156 or toll-free 888/88-PARKS; www.southcarolinaparks.com.

FISHING AND HUNTING

There is no closed fishing season; well-stocked lakes and rivers are close at hand in all parts of the state. Surf casting and deep-sea fishing can be enjoyed all along the Atlantic shore. Mountain streams offer trout fishing. Nonresident freshwater license: $35; seven-day nonresident license: $11. Saltwater stamp: $5.50. No license or permit is required for children under 16. Fees are subject to change. Quail, dove, wild turkey, white-tailed deer, rabbit, squirrel, and fox are all legal quarry. Nonresident annual license: $125; 10-day (consecutive) license: $75; three-day (consecutive) license: $40; wildlife management area permit: $76. Nonresident big game permit for deer, turkey, and bear: $100. State duck stamp: $5.50. Fees are subject to change. For further hunting and fishing information, contact the South Carolina Department of Natural Resources, PO Box 167, Columbia 29202; phone 803/734-3888 (general information) or 803/734-3886 (wildlife and freshwater fisheries).

Driving Information

Safety belts are mandatory for all persons anywhere in a vehicle. Children must be in approved safety seats or wear safety belts. For more information phone 803/737-8340.

INTERSTATE HIGHWAY SYSTEM

The following alphabetical listing of South Carolina towns listed in this book shows that these cities are within 10 miles of the indicated interstate highways. Check a highway map for the nearest exit.

Highway Number	Cities/Towns within 10 Miles
Interstate 20	Aiken, Camden, Columbia, Darlington, Florence.
Interstate 26	Charleston, Clinton, Columbia, Newberry, Orangeburg, Spartanburg.
Interstate 77	Columbia, Rock Hill.
Interstate 85	Anderson, Clemson, Gaffney, Greenville, Spartanburg.
Interstate 95	Darlington, Dillon, Florence, Hardeeville, Santee, Walterboro.

Additional Visitor Information

For additional information about South Carolina, contact the Department of Parks, Recreation, and Tourism, 1205 Pendleton St, Columbia 29201; phone 803/734-0122 or toll-free 888/SC-SMILE.

There are 10 travel information centers in South Carolina; visitors will find the information provided at these stops useful for planning travel and making lodging reservations in the state. Their locations are at the eastern end of the state, on I-95 on the SC/NC border; in the eastern coastal region on Hwy 17 on the SC/NC border; in the southern section on Hwy 301 on the SC/GA border and on I-95 on the SC/GA border; midstate on the southbound side of I-95 near Santee; on the southwestern side on I-20 on the SC/GA border; in the western part of the state on I-85 on the SC/GA border; in the northwestern part of the state, centers are located on I-85 on the SC/NC border and on I-26 on the SC/NC border; in the northern part of the state on I-77 on the SC/NC border and at the State House Tour and Information Center located in Columbia.

Aiken (D-3)

See also Allendale, Orangeburg

Founded 1834
Population 25,337
Elevation 476 ft
Area Code 803
Information Chamber of Commerce, 121 Richland Ave E, PO Box 892, 29802; phone 803/641-1111
Web Site www.goaiken.com

Aiken is a popular social and sports center in the winter months, providing flat-racing training, steeplechase and harness racing, polo, fox hunts, drag hunts, tennis, and golf. The University of South Carolina-Aiken is located here.

What to See and Do

Aiken County Historical Museum. *433 Newberry St SW, Aiken (29801). Phone 803/642-2015. www.aikencounty. net/tourism/aikencountymuseum.html.* Period room settings and displays in late-1800s home. Log cabin (1808) and one-room schoolhouse (1890) on grounds. Special features include an archaeology exhibit and a 1950s drug store. Museum store. (Tues-Fri 9:30 am-4:30 pm, Sat-Sun 2-5 pm; closed holidays) **DONATION**

Aiken State Park. *1145 State Park Rd, Aiken (29856). 16 miles E on unnumbered road between Hwy 78 and Hwy 4. Phone 803/649-2857.* Approximately 1,000 acres on the South Edisto River. Swimming, fishing, boating (rentals). Nature trail. Picnicking (shelters), playground. Camping (hookups, dump station).

Hopeland Gardens. *Whiskey Rd and Dupree Pl, Aiken. Phone 803/642-7630.* A 14-acre public garden on a former estate; terraces, reflecting pools, continuous blooms; sculptures. Garden trail for the visually impaired. Summer concert series (Mon evenings). (Daily 10 am-sunset) **FREE** Also here is

Thoroughbred Racing Hall of Fame. *135 Dupree Pl, Aiken (29803). Phone 803/642-7631.* Enshrinement of champion horses trained and wintered in Aiken. (Sept-May, Tues-Sun 2-5 pm; June-Aug, Sat-Sun 2-5 pm) **FREE**

Redcliffe. *181 Redcliffe Rd, Beech Island (29842). 15 miles SE off Hwy 278, near Beech Island. Phone 803/827-1473.* On 350 acres. Built in a 1850s by James Henry Hammond. Greek Revival mansion furnished with family pieces, Southern antiques, art collection, historic documents, and books. Picnic area. (Thurs-Mon 9 am-6 pm; house noon-4 pm) **FREE**

Special Events

Lobster Race. *Phone 803/648-4981.* Aiken restaurants provide seafood fare. Festivities include lobster races, beach music, and other activities. May.

Polo games. *Whitney Field,* Aiken. *Phone 803/643-3611. www.aikenpolo.net.* Guest are invited to the wide-open spaces (10-football fields worth), fresh air, and the beauty and excitement of a polo match; and they mingle in the clubhouse while stomping divots at halftime. Sun afternoons. Feb-July and Sept-Nov.

Triple Crown. *Phone 803/648-8955. www.aiken. augusta.com/info/triplecrown.shtml.* Three events: trials (Aiken Training Track), steeplechase (Clark Field), polo (Aiken Mile Track). Three consecutive Sat in Mar.

Full-Service Hotel

★ ★ ★ **THE WILLCOX.** *100 Colleton Ave S, Aiken (29801). Phone 803/648-1898; toll-free 877/648-2200; fax 803/648-6664. www.thewillcox.com.* The Willcox perfectly captures the romance and refinement of the South. This distinguished mansion set on 2,000 acres of the Hitchcock Woods shares the best of South Carolina's horse country with lucky guests. From the rocking chairs on the large porch to the afternoon tea, everything about The Willcox oozes laid-back sophistication. Warm and welcoming, the guest rooms and suites are gloriously decorated with antiques, Oriental rugs, and four-poster beds, and most accommodations have working fireplaces. Dining is equally exceptional here, where great Southern breakfasts signal the arrival of morning and evenings are spent savoring the elegant riffs on Southern favorites. If the gentle pace and small-town charm haven't calmed frayed nerves, the European-style spa certainly will. 22

rooms, 3 story. Pets accepted, some restrictions; fee. Complimentary full breakfast. Check-in 3 pm, check-out noon. Restaurant. Fitness room, spa. **$$$**

Allendale (E-4)

See also Aiken, Orangeburg, Walterboro

Population 4,052
Elevation 191 ft
Area Code 803
Zip 29810
Information Chamber of Commerce, PO Box 517; phone 803/584-0082
Web Site www.allendalecountychamber.org

Having moved 6 miles in 1872 to its present site to be on the old Port Royal Railroad line, Allendale is an agricultural town with access to the lush hunting and fishing areas of the Savannah River Valley. More than 130 commercial farms with an average size in excess of 1,000 acres—the largest in the state—surround the town.

What to See and Do

Barnwell State Park. *223 State Park Rd, Blackville. 17 miles N on Hwy 278 to Barnwell, then 7 miles N on Hwy 3. Phone 803/284-2212.* Approximately 300 acres preserved in their natural state with an abundance of trees and flowers. Boating (rentals); fishing. Nature trails. Picnicking (shelters), barbecue pit, playground. Camping, cabins.

Rivers Bridge State Historic Site. *325 State Park Rd, Allendale (29081). 15 miles E off Hwy 641. Phone 803/267-3675. www.discoversouthcarolina.com.* Approximately 400 acres on the site of a Civil War skirmish. River fishing. Nature trails. Picnicking (shelter), recreation building (rentals). **$**

Anderson (C-2)

See also Clemson, Greenville, Greenwood

Founded 1826
Population 25,514
Elevation 770 ft
Area Code 864
Information Anderson Area Chamber of Commerce, 907 N Main St, PO Box 1568, 29621; phone 864/226-3454
Web Site www.andersonscchamber.com

Textile mills and fiberglass plants lead an array of diversified industries that team with the products of the surrounding farmland to make Anderson a lively business center. The town was created as the seat of Anderson County; both were named for General Robert Anderson, who fought in the Revolutionary War.

What to See and Do

Agricultural Museum. *History Ln and Hwy 76, Anderson (29670). Phone 864/646-3782. www.pendleton-district.org/museums.htm.* Antique farming equipment, tools, pre-Eli Whitney cotton gin. (By appointment) **FREE**

Hartwell Dam and Lake. *5625 Anderson Hwy, Hartwell (30643). W and S of town via Hwy 29. Phone 706/376-4788; toll-free 888/893-0678.* This 56,000-acre reservoir with a 962-mile shoreline was created by a dam on the Savannah River. Swimming, water-skiing, boating (81 ramps, five marinas), fishing. Picnicking (shelters). Camping (Mar-Nov; some all year; hook-ups, dump station). Fee for some activities. On the lake are

> **Lake Hartwell State Park.** *19138 A S Hwy 11, Anderson (29643). S on I-85 exit 1. Phone 864/972-3352.* Located on 680 acres along Lake Hartwell. Swimming, fishing, boating (ramps). Nature trail. Picnicking (shelter), playground, store. Camping (hook-ups, dump station), laundry. (Daily)

> **Sadlers Creek State Park.** *940 Sadlers Creek Park Rd, Anderson (29626). 13 miles SW off I-85 and Hwy 187. Phone 864/226-8950.* On 395 acres. Lake fishing, boating (ramps). Nature trails. Picnicking (shelters), playground. Camping (hook-ups, dump station). (Daily)

"The Old Reformer." *Main and Whitner sts, Anderson. In front of courthouse.* Cannon used by both British and Americans during the Revolution; was fired in 1860, when the Ordinance of Secession was signed.

Pendleton Historic District and Tourism. *7 miles NW of I-85 off Hwy 76. Phone toll-free 800/862-1795. www.pendleton-district.org.* Settled in 1790, this town was the seat of what is now Anderson, Oconee, and Pickens counties. There are self-guided tours (free), 2 1/2-hour guided group tours (by appointment, fee) or auto/walking tape tours (cassette, also in French; fee) of 45 historic homes and buildings. For information, contact the Pendleton District Historical and Recreational Commission, 125 E Queen St, PO Box 565. (Mon-Fri; closed holidays). Research library, Hunter's Store (circa 1850) across from village green; arts and crafts shop; visitor center (Mon-Fri; closed holidays). On Pendleton Town Square are

> **Historic homes.** *Phone 864/646-7249.* Two of the many beautiful homes in the area are Ashtabula and Woodburn. (Apr-Nov, Sat/Sun; also by appointment) **$$**

> **Pendleton Farmers' Society Building.** *105 Exchange St, Anderson (29670).* (1826) Begun as the courthouse, bought and completed by the Farmers' Society. Believed to be the oldest Farmers' Society building in America in continuous use.

Special Events

Anderson County Fair. *431 Williamston Rd, Anderson (29621). www.andersoncountyfair.com.* Circus, car derby, entertainment, and carnival rides are some of the activities found at this county fair. Mid-Oct. **$$**

Freedom Weekend Aloft. *Anderson Sports and Entertainment Center, 3027 Mall Rd, Anderson (29625). Phone 864/232-3700; fax 864/271-9339. www.freedomwkend.org.* More than 100 balloonists compete. Memorial Day weekend. Also concerts, amusement rides (fee). **FREE**

Beaufort (F-4)

See also Charleston, Hardeeville, Hilton Head Island, Kiawah Island, Walterboro

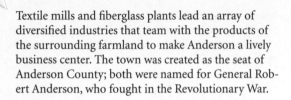

Founded 1710
Population 12,950
Elevation 11 ft
Area Code 843
Zip 29902
Information Greater Beaufort Chamber of Commerce, 1106 Carteret St, PO Box 910, 29901-0910; 843/524-3163
Web Site www.beaufortsc.org

The atmosphere of antebellum days is preserved in this old town's gracious houses and churches. Second oldest town in the state, Beaufort (BEW-fort) looks to the sea from Port Royal Island, one of 64 islands that comprise the county. Tourism and the military are major sources of income in this community.

Spanish explorers first noted the harbor in 1514-1515. In 1526, colonists from Spain made an unsuccessful attempt to settle the area. In 1562, a group of Frenchmen established the first Protestant colony on the continent, which also failed. English and Scottish attempts followed, with success finally coming when the present city was laid out and named for the Duke of Beaufort. The town was almost completely destroyed by Native Americans in 1715, captured by the British in the Revolution, and menaced by British cannons in 1812. Nearly the entire population evacuated Beaufort when it was captured by Northern troops during the Civil War.

What to See and Do

Hunting Island State Park. *2555 Sea Island Pkwy, Beaufort (29920). 16 miles SE on Hwy 21. Phone 843/838-2011. www.southcarolinaparks.com.* A 5,000-acre barrier island in a semitropical setting; beaches, forest, marshes; lighthouse. Swimming, ocean fishing. Nature trails. Picnicking (shelters), playground, boardwalk; concession. Camping (hookups, dump station), cabins. Recreation and nature programs. **$**

John Mark Verdier House Museum. *801 Bay St, Beaufort (29902). www.historic-beaufort.org.* (Circa 1790) Federal period house once known as the Lafayette Building; the Marquis de Lafayette is said to have spoken here from the piazza in 1825.

Marine Corps Air Station. *Boundary St, Beaufort (29904). Phone 843/522-1663. www.beaufort.usmc.mil.* Home of Marine Aircraft Groups MACS-5, MWSS-273, MALS-31, and CSSD-23. Windshield tours available.

National Cemetery. *1601 Boundary St, Beaufort (29902). Phone 843/524-3925; fax 843/524-8538. www. cem.va.gov/nchp/beaufort.htm.* (1863) More than 11,000 interments, including Confederate and Union soldiers. **FREE**

Parris Island. *10 miles S. Phone 843/228-3650. www. mcrdpi.usmc.mil.* Famous US Marine Corps Recruit Depot. Visitor center in Building 283; museum in War Memorial Building. Ribaut Monument is a memorial to Jean Ribaut, French Huguenot founder of Charlesfort (1562); Iwo Jima monument; monument to Spanish settlement of Santa Elena (1521).

St. Helena's Episcopal Church. *505 Church St, Beaufort (29901). At North St. Phone 843/522-1712. www. sthelenas1712.org.* (1712) Still in use; tombstones from surrounding burial ground became operating tables when the church was used as a hospital during the Civil War. Silver Communion set in church was donated in 1734 by Captain John Bull in memory of his wife, who was captured by Native Americans. (Tues-Fri 10 am-4 pm, Sat 10 am-1 pm, Mon by appointment) **FREE**

US Naval Hospital. *4 miles S on Hwy 802, between Beaufort and Port Royal, an early French settlement. Phone 843/524-1851; fax 843/524-1902.* On the grounds are ruins of Fort Frederick (1731), one of the largest "tabby" (cement and oyster shell) forts in the US.

Special Events

Beaufort Shrimp Festival. *Waterfront Park, 1106 Carteret St, Beaufort. Phone 843/986-5400. www.beaufortsc. org.* Waterfront. Bridge Run, shrimp recipe tastings, frogmore stew contest, Bless'en de Fleet. Mid-Oct.

Beaufort Water Festival. *912 8TH ST, Beaufort. Along the waterfront at the harbor. Phone 843/524-0600. www.bftwaterfestival.com.* Parade, water show, boat races, concerts, dance. Mid-July.

Limited-Service Hotel

★ **BEST WESTERN SEA ISLAND INN.** *1015 Bay St, Beaufort (29902). Phone 843/522-2090; toll-free 800/780-7234; fax 843/521-4858. www.bestwestern. com.* 43 rooms, 2 story. Complimentary continental breakfast. Check-in 3 pm, check-out 11 am. Fitness room. Outdoor pool. **$**

Full-Service Inns

★ ★ ★ **BEAUFORT INN.** *809 Port Republic St, Beaufort (29902). Phone 843/521-9000; fax 843/521-9500. www.beaufortinn.com.* Built in 1897, this romantic low country inn offers rooms; suites; and a private, two-bedroom cottage, all including a full breakfast and afternoon tea. The dining room offers seasonal, plantation-style cuisine and an extensive wine list. 21 rooms, 3 story. Children over 8 years in inn only. Complimentary full breakfast. Check-in 3 pm. Check-out 11 am. Restaurant. **$$$**

★ ★ ★ **THE RHETT HOUSE INN.** *1009 Craven St, Beaufort (29902). Phone 843/524-9030; toll-free 888/480-9530; fax 843/524-1310. www.rhetthouseinn. com.* Travelers take a step back in time while visiting Beaufort, where stately homes and massive oaks draped in Spanish moss capture the essence of the Old South. One block from the Intracoastal Waterway, The Rhett House Inn is Beaufort's best lodging. With its gracious manner and country charm, this plantation home, which dates back to 1820, opens its arms to visitors. The guest rooms have a distinctive allure, with floral fabrics, fireplaces, four-poster beds, and antiques. Oriental rugs grace the hardwood floors in this quintessentially low country home. Breakfast convinces guests to rise early for pancakes, French toast, and traditional Southern grits. Visitors succumb to the region's unhurried rhythms on the verandah, where afternoons are spent sipping tea and nibbling freshly baked cookies or brownies, and cool evenings are spent relaxing in the wicker chairs and enjoying cocktails and hors doeuvres. 17 rooms, 3 story. Complimentary continental breakfast. Check-in 3 pm, check-out 11 am. **$$**

Restaurants

★ ★ **BEAUFORT INN.** *809 Port Republic St, Beaufort (29902). Phone 843/379-; fax 843/521-9500. www. beaufortinn.com.* The elegant décor of this restaurant makes for a wonderful dining experience. American menu. Breakfast, lunch, dinner, Sun brunch. Closed Dec 25. Bar. Casual attire. Outdoor seating. **$$$**

★ ★ **BREAKWATER RESTAURANT & BAR.** *205 W St, Beaufort (29902). Phone 843/524-4994.* French menu. Dinner. Closed Sun; Memorial Day, Labor Day, Dec 24-25. Bar. Casual attire. Outdoor seating. **$$**

★ ★ **BRITISH OPEN PUB OF BEAUFORT.** *8 Waveland Cat Island, Beaufort (29920). Phone 843/524-4653.* American menu. Lunch, dinner, Sun brunch. Closed Dec 25. Bar. Casual attire. Outdoor seating. **$$**

★ ★ **PLUMS.** *904 1/2 Bay St, Beaufort (29402). Phone 843/525-1946.* American menu. Lunch, dinner. Closed Jan 1, Thanksgiving, Dec 25. Bar. Children's menu. Casual attire. Outdoor seating. **$$**
🅳

Bennettsville (C-6)

See also Cheraw, Darlington, Dillon, Florence, Hartsville

Founded 1819
Population 9,425
Elevation 150 ft
Area Code 803
Zip 29512
Information Marlboro County Chamber of Commerce, 300 W Main St, PO Box 458
Web Site www.marlborocountysc.org

Near the geographic center of the Carolinas, Bennettsville radiates highway spokes in every direc-

tion. Founded by Welsh settlers, and now the seat of Marlboro County, it has diversified industry including paper and electrical products, textiles, and farm equipment. Agriculture is still important; cotton is the leading crop.

What to See and Do

Jennings-Brown House Restoration. *119 S Marlboro St, Bennettsville. Phone 843/479-5624.* (1826) Served as headquarters for Union troops when Bennettsville was captured in 1865. The restored house is furnished with antiques predating 1860. (Mon, Wed, Fri 10 am-1 pm; Tues, Thurs 2-5 pm; also by appointment; closed holidays) **$**

Lake Wallace. *At N edge of city, off Country Club Dr.* A 500-acre lake with separate sections for swimming (June-Labor Day), water-skiing, fishing, and boating. Waterfowl refuge.

Camden (D-5)

See also Cheraw, Columbia, Hartsville, Sumter

Settled 1732
Population 6,682
Elevation 213 ft
Area Code 803
Zip 29020
Information Kershaw County Chamber of Commerce and Visitor Center, 724 S Broad St, PO Box 605; phone 803/432-2525 or toll-free 800/968-4037
Web Site www.camden-sc.org

The oldest inland town in the state, Camden was named after Lord Camden, defender of colonial rights. During the Revolution, General Cornwallis occupied Camden and made it the principal British garrison in the state and the interior command post for the South. Although several battles were fought in and near the town, including the Battle of Camden, the town was never recaptured by the Americans. Instead, it was evacuated and burned by the British in 1781. Camden contributed six generals to the Confederate cause and served as a storehouse, a hospital for the wounded, and a haven of refuge until captured by General Sherman in 1865.

Today, Camden is famous for its history and equestrian sports—horseback riding, horse shows, hunt meets, polo, and steeplechase races. There are 200 miles of bridle paths in the area and three race tracks; Springdale Course is an extremely difficult and exciting steeplechase run.

What to See and Do

Bethesda Presbyterian Church. *502 DeKalb St, Camden (29020). On Hwy 1. Phone 803/432-4593; fax 803/432-3585. www.bethesdapresbyterianchurch.org.* (1820) Called House of Five Porches; steeple in rear. Designed by the architect of the Washington Monument, Robert Mills; the church is considered a masterpiece. (Mon-Fri 9 am-4 pm) In front of the church is

> **DeKalb Monument.** German-born hero of Battle of Camden is buried here; the monument consists of modest shaft with a base of 24 granite blocks, one for each state in the Union at that time. General Lafayette laid the cornerstone on Mar 9, 1825.

Camden Antique District. *King, DeKalb, Campbell, and Fair sts, 724 Broad St, Camden. Phone 803/432-2525. www.camden-sc.org/Antiques.asp.* Offers all varieties of antiques in 13 stores, some housing over 35 dealers. (Daily; closed holidays)

Hampton Park. *1117 Brandon Ave, Columbia (29209). Lyttleton St near Hwy 1. Phone 803/776-9082. www.columbiasc.net.* Named for a Confederate general who later became governor. Flagstones used in crosswalks were once part of the sidewalks of old Camden and are said to have been brought over as ballast in British ships.

Historic Camden Revolutionary War Site. *(Hwy 521 S),222 S Broad St, Camden (29020). Phone 803/432-9841; fax 803/432-3815. www.historic-camden.net.* Archaeological site of South Carolina's oldest inland town. Visitor area includes two early 19th-century log cabins and a restored 18th-century townhouse. Trails lead to the reconstructed foundation of a pre-Revolutionary War powder magazine, Kershaw-Cornwallis House, and two reconstructed British fortifications. Picnicking, nature trail, historical film. The site of the Battle of Camden, a National Historic Landmark, lies 5 miles north of town. Self-guided and guided tours (Tues-Sun). (See SPECIAL EVENTS) (Daily; closed holidays) **$**

Lake Wateree State Recreation Area. *881 State Park Rd, Camden (29810). S on Hwy 1, E on Hwy 34, then N on Hwy 21 to Hwy 41, continue W. Phone 803/482-6401.* Approximately 200 acres. Fishing, boating (ramp), bait shop. Nature trail. Picnicking, store. Camping (hookups, dump station).

N. R. Goodale State Park. *650 Park Rd, Camden (29020). 2 miles NW off Hwy 1 on Old Wire Rd. Phone 803/432-2772. www.southcarolinaparks.com.* Approximately 763 acres. Lake swimming, boating (rentals), fishing. Nine-hole golf course. Picnicking (shelters), recreation building.

Quaker Cemetery. *713 Meeting St, Camden (29020). Broad and Meeting sts, SW edge of town. Phone 803/432-4356.* Buried here are Richard Kirkland, who gained fame in the Battle of Marye's Hill by risking death to take water to dying Union troops; two of the three residents of the county who won Congressional Medals of Honor prior to World War II; and Dr. George Todd, brother-in-law of Abraham Lincoln.

Rectory Square. *Chesnut and Lyttleton sts, Camden.* Pantheon; six columns serve as a memorial to Camden's six generals of the Confederacy.

Special Events

Carolina Cup Steeplechase. *Springdale Race Course, 200 Knights Hill Rd, Camden. Phone 803/432-6513; toll-free 800/780-8117. www.carolina-cup.org.* The annual 'rites of spring' draws over 70,000 fans to enjoy the sport of steeplechase horse racing amid a flurry of spring fashions and elaborate tailgate parties. Early Apr. **$$$$**

Carolina Downhome Blues Festival and Fine Arts Center. *Fine Arts Center of Kershaw County, 810 Lyttleton St, Camden. Phone 803/425-7676. www.camden. bluesbash.com.* The annual Carolina Downhome Blues Festival is a blues 'club crawl' with performances in the cozy theatre of the Fine Arts Center of Kershaw County. Most venues are in walking distance of each other. Early Oct. **$$$**

Colonial Cup International Steeplechase. *Springdale Race Course, 200 Knights Hill Rd, Camden. Phone 803/432-6513; toll-free 800/780-8117. www.carolina-cup.org.* Known as 'Where Champions are Crowned' the Colonial Cup draws over 15,000 fans and horsemen from around the world. The Colonial Cup provides the seasons grand finale—often deciding all the national titles including jockey of the year, trainer of the year, and horse of the year. Mid-Nov.

Revolutionary War Field Days. *Historic Camden Revolutionary War Site, 222 Broad St, Camden. Phone 803/432-9841; fax 803/432-3815. www. historic-camden.net.* Two-day American Revolution encampment, festivities, battle reenactments. First full weekend in Nov. **$$**

Specialty Lodging

GREENLEAF INN. *1308 Broad St, Camden (29020). Phone 803/425-1806; toll-free 800/437-5874; fax 803/425-5853. www.greenleafinnofcamden.com.* The Greenleaf Inn is located in the historic district. Its guesthouses were built in 1805 and 1890 and are decorated in Victorian style. 10 rooms, 2 story. Complimentary full breakfast. Check-in 3 pm, check-out 11 am. Wireless Internet access. **$**

Charleston (E-5)

See also Beaufort, Kiawah Island, Summerville, Walterboro

Founded 1670
Population 96,650
Elevation 9 ft
Area Code 843
Information Visitor Reception and Transportation Center, 375 Meeting St, PO Box 975, 29402; phone 843/853-8000 or toll-free 800/868-8118
Web Site www.charlestoncvb.com

This aristocratic and storied American city lives up to its reputation for cultivated manners. Charleston's homes, historic shrines, old churches, lovely gardens, winding streets, and intricate iron-laced gateways exude charm and dignity.

Charleston enjoys international and coastal commerce in the fine harbor formed, according to local opinion, where the "Ashley and Cooper rivers unite to form the Atlantic Ocean." The strategic harbor, inlets, and sea islands provide recreational retreats.

The Charleston of today is the survivor of siege, flood, hurricane, and epidemic. Capital of the province until 1786, its history and that of South Carolina are almost the same. Charleston received colonists from the Old World and sent them into the wilderness. The city served as the personification of Europe's luxury and culture in the New World.

The first permanent settlement in the Carolinas, Charles Towne, as it was first called, was established as a tiny colony, westward across the Ashley River, by Anthony Ashley Cooper, Earl of Shaftesbury. At the same time, he established the only American nobility in history, with barons, landgraves (dukes), and caciques (earls), each owning great plantations.

This nobility lasted less than 50 years, but it was the foundation for an aristocratic tradition that still exists, even though the rice and indigo that made the early Charleston people rich are gone. Colonists from Barbados, England, and Ireland came to enlarge the settlement in 1670, and by 1680, the colony moved across the river to become a city-state. Although many of the colonists went on to the Carolina low country and established grand plantations, every year on the traditional date of May 10, the planters and their families moved back to Charleston to escape the mosquitoes and malarial heat. From spring to frost, these planters created a season of dancing, sport, musicales, theater, and socials. Commerce and plantations provided the prosperity on which the city's cosmopolitan graces were based. Charleston founded the first playhouse designed solely for presentation of drama, the first museum, the first public school in the colony, the first municipal college in America, and the first fire insurance company on the continent. (It was a victim the next year of a fire that destroyed half the city.) The city became famous throughout the world as "a flourishing capital of wealth and ease."

The First Provincial Congress of South Carolina met in Charleston in 1775 and prepared the city to repulse a British attack on June 28, 1776. But in 1780, the city was captured and occupied by the enemy for two and a half years. Charleston was almost the last point in the state to be cleared of British troops. With peace came great prosperity, but rivalry between the small farmers of the interior and the merchants and plantation owners of the lowlands resulted in removal of the capital to Columbia.

The convention that authored the Ordinance of Secession came to Charleston to pass that declaration; the Civil War then began with the bombardment of Fort Sumter by Fort Johnson. A long siege followed, including the gallant defense of Fort Sumter (1863-1865), blockade running, the first submarine warfare, evacuation after Sherman had demolished Columbia, and, finally, bombardment of the city by the Union Army.

Additional Visitor Information

Forever Charleston, a multimedia presentation about the city, is shown every half hour at the visitor center.

The Charleston Visitor Reception and Transportation Center, 375 Meeting Street, has information on other points of interest, tours, campsites, fishing trips, cultural events, special

Exploring the Historic District

Named for King Charles II, Charles Towne was founded by British settlers in 1670. Today, the beautiful city retains outstanding architecture in its large historic district downtown, with a rich mix of styles from early Colonial, Georgian, Federal, Greek Revival, and Italianate to Victorian. It is a wonderful place to explore on foot.

The Old City Market, (Market Street at Church), is the classic starting point. Here, on a site where vendors have swapped their wares for centuries, such favorite Charleston souvenirs as handmade sweetgrass baskets and fresh pralines can be found. Horse-drawn carriage tours depart from here.

A walk 3 blocks down Church Street from the Old City Market passes the old power magazine built in 1713, the oldest building in the city, which now houses exhibits from 18th-century Charleston. The 1772 Heyward-Washington House (87 Church Street at Broad), where George Washington slept during a 1791 visit, is now a house museum. Jog west 1 block to Meeting Street and proceed south to the Nathaniel Russell House (51 Meeting Street at Water). Built in 1808, the house is considered one of the finest examples of Federal-style architecture and is also the home of the Historic Charleston

Foundation. Continue south through the stunning residential district here to White Point Gardens, a wide shady park of tall oaks and palmettos at the waterfront with a panoramic view of Charleston Harbor. Lining the shore is the Battery, where cannons remain posed to protect the harbor. When the first shots of the Civil War were fired at Fort Sumter in the center of the harbor, Charlestonians gathered here to watch.

Follow the Battery north around to East Bay Street. Here the cobblestone lanes hold many shops, cafés, and restaurants, such as Magnolia's (185 East Bay Street), which serves nouveau Southern cuisine. On the water side, a walk-through fountain attracts children—and some adults—to jump in and cool off. Behind the fountain, a wide pier has swinging benches that are ideal spots for unwinding after a long day of sightseeing.

East Bay Street leads back to the Old City Market where you started. But part of the greatest fun of a visit to Charleston is simply to wander the streets at random for a glimpse of a back garden through a set of ornamental gates that may be as lovely an image to take home with you as that of the most revered restoration.

events, maps, and self-guided walking tour of the city. (Daily; closed Jan 1, Thanksgiving, Dec 25) Contact PO Box 975, 29402; phone 843/853-8000. For city bus service information, phone SCE & G at 843/747-0922; for DASH, Downtown Area Shuttle, phone 803/577-6970, ext 500.

What to See and Do

Aiken-Rhett House. *48 Elizabeth St, Charleston (29403). Corner of Judith St. Phone 843/723-1159. www.historiccharleston.org.* Built around 1818, this palatial residence was enlarged and redecorated by Governor and Mrs. William Aiken Jr. in the mid-1800s. After traveling in Europe, they returned home with crystal and bronze chandeliers, paintings, and classical sculptures. Many treasures are still in the rooms for which they were purchased. This home, which remained in the family until 1975, is on the National Register of Historic Places. (Daily; closed Thanksgiving, Dec 24-25) **$$**

Beth Elohim Synagogue. *90 Hasell St, Charleston (29401). Between King and Meeting sts. Phone 843/723-1090; fax 843/723-0537. www.kkbe.org.* Attracted by civil and religious freedoms and economic opportunities, the first Jews came to the Charleston area shortly after 1670. By 1749, enough Jewish settlers were present to organize a congregation. The current synagogue, a Greek Revival structure dating to 1840, is the second oldest in the United States and the oldest in continuous use. A previous synagogue was built in 1794 but was destroyed by fire in 1838. In 1824, the first Reform Jewish congregation in the US was born here. Guided tours (Mon-Fri, Sun 10 am-noon) **FREE**

⭐ **Boone Hall Plantation.** *1235 Long Point Rd,* Mount Pleasant (29464). *Phone 843/884-4371; fax 843/884-0475. www.boonehallplantation.com.* This 738-acre estate encompasses a 1935 Georgian-style house similar to the original plantation house that fell into ruin, as well as an avenue of Spanish moss-draped oak trees, a cotton gin house, a pecan grove, and gardens of antique roses. Several rooms on the first floor of the house may be visited. Nine original slave cabins, haunting in their emptiness, were constructed of brick made on-site. If the property, originally a cotton plantation, somehow seems familiar to visitors, it's probably because *The North and the South*, a TV miniseries, and other productions were filmed here. Battle reenactments are held during the summer and draw Civil War buffs. (Apr-Labor Day: Mon-Sat 8:30 am-6:30 pm, Sun 1-5 pm; Labor Day-Mar: Mon-Sat 9 am-5 pm, Sun 1-4 pm; closed Thanksgiving, Dec 25) **$$$**

Chamber of Commerce. *2750 Speisseggar Dr, North Charleston (29405). Phone 843/577-2510. www. charlestonchamber.net.* (Organized in 1773) This is one of the oldest city commercial organizations in the country.

Charles Towne Landing. *1500 Old Town Rd, Charleston (29407). On Hwy 171, W of the Ashley River. Phone 843/852-4200; fax 843/852-4205. www. discoversouthcarolina.com/stateparks.* It's back to the beginning at this 664-acre park. In 1670, colonists established the first permanent English settlement in the Carolinas in this location. Today, visitors find archaeological investigations, reconstructed fortifications, an experimental garden of 1670s crops, and formal gardens, as well as nature trails, a colonial village, and a replica of *Adventure*, a 17th-century trading ketch. Tram tours are available, and there also is a natural habitat zoo of indigenous animals on-site. (Daily 8:30 am-5 pm) **$**

⭐ **Charleston Museum.** *360 Meeting St, Charleston (29403). Across the street from the Charleston Visitor Center. Phone 843/722-2996. www.ego.net/us/sc/chs/ cmuseum.* Founded in 1773 and first opened to the public in 1824, the Charleston Museum claims status as Americas oldest museum. The institution has a rich and eclectic collection of all things Charlestonian but interprets them in such a way as to make visitors— even Yankees—feel engaged and interested. Key components in the natural and cultural history of Charleston and the South Carolina low country include an impressive early silver display (George Washington's christening cup is among the pieces), an Egyptian mummy, South Carolina ceramics, a skeleton of a primitive toothed whale, South Carolina ornithology, the chairs that delegates sat in to sign South Carolina's Ordinance of Secession, and firearms used in the ensuing Civil War (or, as Southerners prefer to say, the War between the States). Children will especially enjoy the museums hands-on exhibits. (Mon-Sat 9 am-5 pm, Sun 1-5 pm; closed holidays) **$$**

Charleston Water Tours. *10 Wharfside St, Charleston (29401). Foot of Market St. Phone 843/722-1112; toll-free 800/344-4483. www.charlestonharbortours. com.* Tours (approximately two hours) leaving from Charleston Maritime Center of harbor, US Naval Base, view of forts, other points of interest. Contact 800/344-4483. **$$$$**

The Citadel, Military College of South Carolina. *171 Moultrie St, Charleston (29409). Phone 843/953-5000; fax 843/953-6767. www.citadel.edu.* The Citadel is one of those storied institutions that inspires pride in the hearts of South Carolinians, especially those who live in Charleston. Established in 1842 by an act of the South Carolina General Assembly, the Citadel originally was located on Marion Square in downtown Charleston near the Revolutionary War rampart. In 1922, the college was moved to a picturesque setting on the bank of the Ashley River. Nearly 2,000 students are enrolled in 19 degree programs. The site is home to 24 major buildings, including Sumerall Chapel, a shrine of patriotism and remembrance, as well as a popular place for weddings. A full athletic schedule includes football, baseball, basketball, and other events. Citadel parades on Friday afternoons are said to be "the best free show in Charleston." Visitors may take self-guided campus tours. Cadet-led tours for groups of eight or more areavailable through the Public Affairs Office, at phone 843/953-6779. (Mon-Fri; closed Sat-Sun) On campus is

Citadel Archives Museum. *171 Moultrie St, Charleston (29409). Phone 843/953-6846; fax 843/953-6956.*In a city (and region) that reveres the past, it would be hard to over-exaggerate the importance of the history of the Citadel. The Museum presents the history of the Military College of South Carolina from its beginning to the present day, with exhibits featuring military, academic, athletic, and social aspects of cadet life. Here are photographs, memorabilia from special events, biographical sketches of college presidents, cadet uniforms and arms. Citadel rings from 1895 to the present are displayed in the museums foyer. Self-guided and group tours of the museum are available. The Archives contain more than 300 collections that relate to the history of the Citadel itself or have military significance. Among the noteworthy documents are military papers and photographs of World War II General Mark W. Clark. Guided tours available by appointment (Museum Sun-Fri 2-5 pm, Sat noon-5 pm; archives Mon-Fri 8:30 am-5 pm; closed holidays) **FREE**

City Hall Art Gallery. *80 Broad St, Charleston (29401). At Meeting St. Phone 843/724-3799; fax 843/724-3732. www.ci.charleston.sc.us.* On the site of a colonial marketplace, this handsomely proportioned 1801 building first housed the Bank of the United States and then became Charleston's City Hall in 1818. A gallery in the Council Chamber on the second floor grew out of a custom of commissioning artists to paint famous visitors. The gallery includes a portrait of George Washington by John Trumbull (considered one of the best of the general in his later years) and also a portrait of President James Monroe by Samuel F. B. Morse. A guide is available to answer questions. (Mon-Fri) **FREE**

Cypress Gardens. *3030 Cypress Garden Rd, Moncks Corner (29461). 24 miles N off Hwy 52, between Goose Creek and Moncks Corner. Phone 843/553-0515; fax 843/569-0644. www.cypressgardens.org.* Giant cypresses, a blackwater swamp, and a butterfly house share 163 acres with luxuriant dogwoods, azaleas, camellias, and daffodils. Visitors can wander along 4 miles of walking trails, paddle a flat-bottomed boat through a cypress swamp, and explore a freshwater aquarium and reptile house, whose residents include crocodiles, snakes, and turtles. (Daily 9 am-5 pm; closed Thanksgiving, Dec 25) **$$**

Dock Street Theatre. *135 Church St, Charleston (29401). SW corner of Church and Queen sts. Phone 843/577-7183; toll-free 800/454-7093. www.charlestonstage.com.* In 1736, a building on this site opened as the very first in America constructed specifically for theatrical productions. Later, the street name changed to Queen, but the Dock Street Theatre name stuck. Today's theater is on the site of the original and presents numerous productions of the Charleston Stage Company during the spring and fall. Dock Street Theatre also is a performance venue for Charlestons Spoleto Festival USA. (Daily 9 am-5 pm) **FREE**

Drayton Hall. *3380 Ashley River Rd, Charleston (29414). 9 miles NW via Hwy 6. Phone 843/769-2600. www.draytonhall.org.* One of the oldest surviving pre-American Revolution plantation houses (1738) in the area, this Georgian Palladian house is surrounded by live oaks and is located on the Ashley River. Held in the Drayton family for seven generations, the mansion has been maintained in virtually its original condition. A National Trust for Historic Preservation property. Tours (hourly). (Daily; closed Jan 1, Thanksgiving, Dec 25) **$$$**

Edisto Beach State Park. *8377 State Cabin Rd, Edisto Island (29438). 21 miles W on Hwy 17, then 29 miles S on Hwy174. Phone 843/869-2756.* The 1,255-acre park on this remote sea island makes for a nice day trip out of Charleston. Fortunately, vacation cabins and a campground are available for those who cant bear to leave the live oak forest, extensive sea marsh, and towering palmetto trees so soon. A 4-mile nature trail winds along, with views to write home about. Surf and marsh fishing, boating, swimming, picnicking, and searching the beach for shells are among the options here. Rich in Native American history, this beachfront park was initially developed by the Civilian Conservation Corps in the 1930s. (Standard time, daily 8 am-6 pm; daylight savings time, daily 6 am-10 pm) **$**

Edmondston-Alston House. *21 E Battery St, Charleston (29401). Phone 843/722-7171. www.middletonplace.org.* (Circa 1825) Built by a wealthy merchant and wharf owner, remodeled by the next owner, an important rice planter, beginning in 1838; Greek Revival style. Uninterrupted view across the harbor. Documents, engravings, portraits, original furnishings, elaborate woodwork. Guided tours (daily; closed first full week in Jan, Thanksgiving, Dec 25). **$$**

Folly Beach County Park. *1010 W Ashley Ave, Charleston (29439). S via Hwy 171 on W end of Folly Island. Phone 843/588-2426. www.beachparks.com/follybeach.htm.* Located on the 6-mile-long barrier island of the same name, this is the beach that's closest to the historic heart of Charleston. With some 4,000 feet of ocean frontage, 2,000 feet of river frontage, a 600-foot swimming beach, and a 1,045-foot fishing pier, it is an easy-to-get-to place to get away from it all. (May-Labor Day, daily 9 am-7 pm; Apr, Sept-Oct daily 10 am-6 pm; Nov-Mar daily 10 am-5 pm) **$**

Fort Sumter Tours. *Liberty Square at Aquarium Wharf, Charleston. Phone 843/881-7337; toll-free 800/789-3678; fax 843/881-2960. www.spiritlinecruises.com.* A trip to Fort Sumter National Monument (see also), located on a small manmade island in Charleston Harbor, is a unique opportunity to cruise back in time to the morning hours of April 12, 1861, when South Carolina troops of the Confederacy fired upon the Union-occupied fort in what became the opening engagement of the Civil War. Visitors can learn more about the fort and the war at a museum and from National Park service rangers on site. The tour also includes narration describing Charleston Harbor and a good look at many of the historic homes nestled among the trees that line the Battery (the tip of the peninsula) and other points of interest. The tour takes about two hours and 15 minutes. In addition to Liberty Square, you can purchase tickets on the Cooper River in downtown Charleston, in Mount Pleasant, and at Patriots Point Maritime Museum (40 Patriot Point Dr, Mount Pleasant). **$$$**

Francis Marion National Forest. *2421 Witherbee Rd, Cordesville (29434). NE via Hwy 17 and 17 A, Hwy 41.* Francis Marion grew up in the wilds of South Carolinas backcountry, and became well-versed in unconventional warfare at an early age. He put these skills to good use during the Revolutionary War and frustrated the British by slipping away into the backwoods swamps, where tracking was impossible. This magnificent 250,000-acre forest, named for the "Swamp Fox", lies along the Intracoastal Waterway some 40 miles north of Charleston. Camping, hiking, fishing, hunting, horseback riding, biking, boating, canoeing, nature study, bird watching, photography, and picnicking are excellent reasons for coming here. Bald eagles are among the 250 species of birds in the forest. Other residents include beavers, bobcats, black bears, and otters. The best time to visit is from late fall through early spring. Summers can be very hot and humid.

French Huguenot Church. *44 Queen St, Charleston (29401). Phone 843/722-4385; fax 843/722-4388. www. frenchhuguenotchurch.org.* As early as 1687, French Huguenots were worshipping in a church on this site, having fled France to avoid religious persecution. The current church, the third, is a National Historic Landmark. Completed in 1845, it was the first Gothic Revival building in Charleston. Constructed of brick covered with stucco, the church features distinctive windows, buttresses, and unusual ironwork. Even the clear glass windows are original. The first church, while not destroyed *by* fire, was destroyed *because* of fire. In 1796, the building was detonated to create a fire break for a fire that raced through the neighborhood. A second church was completed in 1800, but was torn down to make way for the current building. In early days, services were timed with the tides. Over the years, the church has been closed at times because of declining membership. Re-established most recently in 1983, this is the only French Calvinist congregation in the US. Sunday services are held at 10:30 am, with a French liturgy service held every spring. **FREE**

⭐ **Gibbes Museum of Art.** *135 Meeting St, Charleston (29401). Phone 843/722-2706; fax 843/720-1682. www. gibbesmuseum.org.* This museum, which will be 100 years old in 2005, has an eclectic collection that includes Japanese woodblock prints, as well as miniature rooms depicting traditional American and French architecture,

decorative arts, and design. This museum is also known for its portraits of notable South Carolinians by notable artists, including Thomas Sully, Benjamin West, and Rembrandt Peale, and one of the oldest and finest miniature portrait collections in the country. Don't miss the Charleston Renaissance Gallery, which showcases works by Charleston artists who were responsible for the city's cultural renaissance in the 1920s and 1930s. Special exhibitions and other events are scheduled throughout the year. Docents give an overview of the museum's exhibitions at 2:30 pm every Tues and Sat. Tours at 5 pm on the second Tues of every month are part of the museum's Art After Dark program. (Tues-Sat 10 am-5 pm, Sun 1-5 pm) **$$**

Gray Line bus tours. *375 Meeting St, Charleston (29402). Phone 843/722-4444; fax 843/722-0173. www. graylineofcharleston.com.* For information or reservations, contact PO Box 219, 29402-0219 or 843/722-4444 **$$$$**

Hampton Park. *Rutledge Ave and Cleveland St, Charleston. Phone 843/724-7470; fax 843/720-3943.* Historic park with camellias and azaleas in spring, roses in summer; 1-mile nature trail; Charleston's mounted horse patrol stables. **FREE**

⭐ **Heyward-Washington House.** *87 Church St, Charleston (29401). Phone 843/722-0354. www. charlestonmuseum.org.* Located in the heart of Charleston's historic district, within the area of the original city walls, this brick double house was built in 1772 during the Revolutionary era. Rice planter Daniel Heyward gave the house, which is noteworthy for its handsome collection of Charleston-made furniture, to his son Thomas Heyward Jr., a signer of the Declaration of Independence. George Washington stayed here during his weeklong visit to the city in 1791. Outdoors are a carriage shed, a 1740s kitchen building, and a formal garden with plants that would have been familiar to late-18th-century Charlestonians. Years later, Dubose Heyward used the evocative neighborhood in which the house stands as the setting for *Porgy and Bess.* (Mon-Sat 10 am-5 pm, Sun 1-5 pm; closed holidays) **$$**

Joseph Manigault House. *350 Meeting St, Charleston (29403). Across from the Charleston Museum. Phone 843/722-2996. www.charlestonmuseum.org.* Another house that rice built, this home was designed by Gabriel Manigault for his brother, Joseph. The brothers were descendants of a French Huguenot family who left Europe and came to the US to avoid persecution. (Gabriel also is said to have designed the Charleston

City Hall and the South Carolina Society Hall.) This elegant neoclassical three-story brick town house, a National Historic Landmark, reflects the wealthy lifestyle of the Manigault family, as well as living conditions of the slaves who worked there. A dramatic, sweeping staircase connects restored rooms on the first and second floors. The home has been furnished with outstanding examples of early 19th-century American, English, and French pieces. Outdoors are the kitchen, slave quarters, stable, and privy. (Daily; closed holidays) **$$**

⭐ **Magnolia Plantation and Gardens.** *3550 Ashley River Rd, Charleston (29414). 10 miles NW on Hwy 61. Phone 843/571-1266; toll-free 800/367-3517; fax 843/571-5346. www.magnoliaplantation.com.* These internationally famous gardens are America's oldest (circa 1676); they now cover 50 acres with camellias, azaleas, magnolias, and hundreds of other flowering species. Azaleas are best from mid-Mar-Apr; camellias put on their best show from mid-Nov-Mar. Also on the grounds are a 125-acre waterfowl refuge, a trilevel observation tower, a 16th-century maze, an 18th-century herb garden, biblical gardens, a topiary garden, nature trails, and a petting zoo. Canoe and bicycle rentals are available, and there are designated areas for picnicking. Gift shop, snack shop; orientation theater. Plantation home and local art gallery (additional fee). (Mar-Oct: 8 am-dusk; Nov-Feb: call for hours) **$$$** Through Magnolia Plantation, enter

Audubon Swamp Garden. *3550 Ashley River Rd, Charleston (29414). Phone 843/571-1266; toll-free 800/367-3517; fax 843/571-5346.* Boardwalks, bridges, and dikes make this 60-acre blackwater cypress and tupelo swamp accessible to visitors. Home to all local species of wildlife, including alligators, this colorful area is planted with hundreds of varieties of local and exotic flowering shrubs. (Mar-Oct: daily 8 am-dusk; Nov-Feb: call for hours) **$$**

Medical University of South Carolina. *171 Ashley Ave, Charleston (29425). Phone 843/792-2300. www.musc. edu.*(1824) (2,200 students) The oldest medical school in the South. A self-guided tour brochure is available on campus at 41 Bee Street. On campus is

Waring Historical Medical Library & Macaulay Museum of Dental History. *175 Ashley Ave, Charleston (29425). Phone 843/792-2288.* (Mon-Fri 8:30 am-5 pm; closed holidays; museum open by request) **FREE**

Middleton Place Plantation. *4300 Ashley River Rd, Charleston (29414). 14 miles NW on Hwy 61. Phone 843/556-6020; toll-free 800/782-3608. www. middletonplace.org.* Once the home of Arthur Middleton, a signer of the Declaration of Independence, Middleton Place encompasses America's oldest landscaped gardens, the Plantation Stableyards, and the restored House Museum. The gardens, laid out in 1741, highlight ornamental butterfly lakes, sweeping terraces, and a wide variety of flora and fauna. The Stableyards feature numerous craftspeople demonstrating skills necessary for a self-sufficient 18th-century plantation. House (additional fee). Guided tours (additional fee). Special events include Starlight Pops (May), Spoleto Finale (mid-June), Plantation Days (Nov), and Plantation Christmas (Dec). (Daily from 9 am) **$$$$**

Moo Roo Handbags. *316 King St, Charleston (29401). Phone 843/724-1081; toll-free 866/666-7661; fax 843/534-0508. www.mooroo.com.* For the woman who has everything and needs a chic bag to carry it around in, this Charleston upstart on busy King Street may be just the place to look. Sharon Stone, Andie MacDowell, and other glitterati are fans and customers. Locals like the creatively fashioned bags, too--think satin, leather, and wool tweed, with semi-precious stones, flowers, or other embellishments. (Mon-Sat) **FREE**

⭐ **Nathaniel Russell House.** *51 Meeting St, Charleston (29401). Phone 843/724-8481. www.historiccharleston. org.* Regarded as Charleston's grandest neoclassical house museum, this beauty (circa 1808) features graceful interiors, lavish plasterwork, oval drawing rooms, and a magnificent "free-flying" staircase. Period antiques and works of art furnish the home, set among formal gardens. This mansion interprets the lives of both the Russells and their slaves. (Daily; closed Thanksgiving, Dec 24-25) **$$**

⭐ **Old Exchange and Provost Dungeon.** *122 E Bay St, Charleston (29401). Phone 843/727-2165; toll-free 888/763-0448. www.oldexchange.com.* The history of the Royal Exchange and Custom House is more colorful and turbulent than the stately Georgian-style building would suggest. Completed by in 1771, this structure is one of the most historically significant buildings of Colonial and Revolutionary America. Designed primarily to accommodate heavy export-import trade and as a place to conduct business on upper levels, the lower level confined common prisoners, pirates, and suspected rebels, also known as American Patriots. Among the latter were three signers of the Declaration of Independence (Arthur Middleton,

Thomas Heyward Jr., and Edward Rutledge). In 1776, South Carolina declared independence from Great Britain on the Exchange steps, and in 1788, South Carolina delegates gathered in the building to ratify the US Constitution. George Washington was a guest of honor here at a grand ball in 1791. Nearly 200 years later, restored and remodeled, the Old Exchange was reopened to the public. (Daily 9 am-5 pm) **$$**

Old Powder Magazine. *79 Cumberland St, Charleston (29401). Phone 843/722-9350. www.powdermag. org.* The oldest public building in the Carolinas, the Powder Magazine dates back to the Lords Proprietors, a group of English nobles who owned and ruled the joint province. The building was authorized in 1703 and constructed about ten years later. Crucial for the storage of powder in defense of the city, the magazine was still in use during the Revolutionary era, although a "new" powder magazine had been built in 1748. Now a National Historic Landmark, this gabled brick structure houses an exhibit on colonial Charleston. (Mid-Mar-Labor Day, daily) **FREE**

Old South Carriage Company. *14 Anson St, Charleston (29401). Phone 843/723-9712; fax 843/722-2553. www. oldsouthcarriagetours.com.* Offers narrated, horse-drawn carriage tours of Old Charleston (One hour). Summer evening tours (Half-hour). Free shuttle service from visitor center. (Daily; closed Thanksgiving, Dec 25) **$$$$**

Palmetto Carriage Tours. *40 N Market St, Charleston (29401). Phone 843/723-8145. www.carriagetour.com.* One-hour tour through Old Charleston by horse- and mule-drawn carriages. Tours originate at Red Barn. (Daily 9 am-5 pm; closed Dec 25). **$$$$**

Palmetto Islands County Park. *444 Needlerush Pkwy, Mt. Pleasant (29464). N on Hwy 17, 1/2 mile past Snee Farm, then left on Long Point Rd. Phone 843/884-0832. www.ccprc.com/palmetto.htm.* Nature-oriented park in tropical setting. Bicycle paths, marsh boardwalks, picnicking, and grills throughout park. Pond. Canoe trails. Pedal boat and bicycle rentals. BigToy Playground. 50-foot observation tower with play area. Interpretive trails. Splash Island Water Park. Fishing supplies; concession. (Daily; closed Jan 1, Thanksgiving, Dec 24-25) **$**

Rainbow Row. *79-107 E Bay St, Charleston (29401).* Many of Charleston's sights are simply free for the looking. One of the most delightful spots to take a look at the city's past is Rainbow Row, a series of private homes numbering from 79 to 107 on East Bay Street. These town houses, constructed in the mid-1700s, are painted whatever color—pink, pale blue, yellow—that the current owners favor. Originally, these buildings were owned by merchants who lived on the upper floors and used the ground floors for counting rooms and shops.

★ **South Carolina Aquarium.** *100 Aquarium Wharf, Charleston (29401). On Charleston Harbor at the end of Calhoun St. Phone 843/720-1990. www.scaquarium. org.* Charleston's most-visited attraction is making a big splash, with more than 10,000 fish, river otters, snakes, loggerhead turtles, sharks, jellyfish, alligators, birds, and other animals. Since the aquarium's opening in 2002, exhibits have focused on the Appalachian Watershed—the mountains, piedmont, coastal plain, coast, and ocean. Interpretive programs encourage interaction and enhance the aquarium experience for all ages. Expansive views of Charleston Harbor and refreshing breezes are an added bonus. (Apr-mid-Aug: Mon-Sat 9 am-6 pm, Sun noon-6 pm; rest of the year: Mon-Sat 9 am-5 pm, Sun noon-5 pm; closed Thanksgiving, Dec 25) **$$$**

St. John's Lutheran Church. *5 Clifford St, Charleston (29401). Archdale and Clifford sts. Phone 843/723-2426; fax 843/577-2543. www.stjohnscharleston.org.* Completed in 1818, this church displays both Federal and Baroque elements and is home to Charleston's oldest Lutheran congregation. The Italianate steeple, added in 1859, was built by David Lopez, who was the contractor for Kadal Kadosh Beth Elohim Synagogue. The first Lutheran congregation was organized by 1752, and dedicated a wooden church located behind the site of the current building. Two pastors stand out: Rev. John Nicholas Martin was expelled from the city by the British during the American Revolution because he refused to pray for the king of England, and Dr. John Bachman, pastor during the Civil War, collaborated with John James Audubon on the famous books *Birds of America* and *The Quadrupeds of North America.* (By appointment; also Sun worship)

★ **St. Mary's Church.** *89 Hassell St, Charleston (29401). Phone 843/722-7696; fax 843/577-5036. www. catholic-doc.org/saintmarys.* This is the mother church for the Catholic diocese of the Carolinas and Georgia. The congregation was organized in 1789 and first worshipped in a rundown Methodist meeting house on the present site. A new church built in 1801 was destroyed by fire in 1838. The present building, completed in 1839, is a wonderful example of the Classical Revival style, featuring galleries on three sides of the sanctuary. Among the paintings in the church is an 1814 work that was salvaged from the 1838 fire and restored by the original artist, John S. Cogdell. Other paintings, copies of Old Masters, were done in Rome and installed in St. Marys in 1896. Newer elements include a series of stained-glass windows. In the churchyard, many of the tombstones are in French. Parish records were kept in that language until 1822. (Mon-Fri 10 am-2 pm, after Sun mass)

⭐ **St. Michael's Episcopal Church.** *71 Broad St, Charleston (29401). SE corner of Meeting and Broad sts. Phone 843/723-0603; fax 843/724-7578. www.stmichael-schurch.net.* On Sunday mornings in Charleston, church bells ring in loud and joyful cacophony to awaken residents and visitors alike. Among the citys handsome and historic houses of worship, St. Michaels, with its 186-foot-tall white steeple, stands out. Completed in 1761, with bells dating to 1764, the building of St. Michaels Church is the oldest in the city. Many other houses of worship were destroyed by fire, which periodically ravaged Charleston. George Washington worshipped here when he visited Charleston in 1791, and Robert E. Lees name also is on a pew. (Mon-Fri) **FREE**

St. Philip's Episcopal Church. *142 Church St, Charleston (29401). Phone 843/722-7734; fax 843/722-6978. www.stphilipschurchsc.org.* Established in 1670, this is the oldest congregation in Charleston and the first Episcopal church in the Carolinas. The first church building stood at the corner of Meeting and Broad sts, where St. Michaels Church now stands. Fire destroyed earlier buildings on the present site. Todays building was completed in 1838. During the Civil War, its bells were removed and converted into cannons for the Confederacy. New bells were placed in the steeple on July 4, 1976. Among the notables buried in the churchyard are John C. Calhoun, Charles Pinckney, John Rutledge, and Dubose Heyward. (Mon-Fri) **FREE**

⭐ **Sword Gates.** *32 Legare St, Charleston (29402)* Practical, graceful, durable, and sometimes downright fanciful, wrought iron was, and still is, a highly prized art form in Charleston. One of handsomest examples around is a set of gates that features two horizontal swords joining at the center of a broadsword to form a cross. Beyond the gates stands a masonry and frame home, which date to the early 1800s. The famed gates were forged around 1838 by Christopher Werner, an important Charleston ironsmith. They were designed for the City Guard House, which explains the design, and placed here about 10 years later. Wrought-iron fences and gates served as more than mere decoration.

Although they ensured a certain degree of privacy for owners, they also hindered escape by slaves.

⭐ **Unitarian Church.** *4 Archdale St, Charleston (29401). Phone 843/723-4617; fax 843/723-0120. www.charlestonuu.org.* A National Historic Landmark, this is the oldest Unitarian church in the South and the second oldest church in Charleston. Its history threads back to 1772, when the Independent Church on Meeting Street was growing so rapidly that it needed to construct a second church building on Archdale Street. Construction was interrupted by British occupation during the Revolutionary War. The building was completed in 1787 and chartered as the Second Independent Church, with a Unitarian minister presiding. As the American Unitarian Association was not organized until 1825, it was 1839 by the time this congregation was recharted as Unitarian. The building was remodeled in the mid-1800s with a crenelated tower, arched windows, pseudo-buttresses, and Tudor arch entrance. The interior vaulting was modeled on that of the Henry VII chapel at Westminster Abbey in London. Repairs were made after the church suffered damage in the earthquake of 1886 and Hurricane Hugo in 1989. (Fri-Sat 10 am-1 pm)

White Point Gardens. *Murray Blvd and E Bay St, Charleston (29401).* After a day of traipsing through historic homes, museums, and shops, visitors tend to drift toward the tip of the peninsula that the city of Charleston graces. They come here to admire the gardens, rest under the live oaks and palmettos, and marvel at the magnificent antebellum homes. They also come to take in the refreshing ocean breezes. This is, after all, where the Ashley and Coopers rivers come together to form the Atlantic Ocean. Old cannons are mounted here, too, as a reminder of battles past and of strong-willed Charlestonians. Out in the harbor lie Fort Moultrie and Fort Sumter. This park was an excellent vantage point for the opening chapter of the Civil War as Confederate forces at Fort Moultrie fired upon Fort Sumter. Early settlers named this area White Pointe because of the discarded oyster shells left here by Indians. The area was first used as a public garden in 1837. **FREE**

Special Events

Fall House and Garden Candlelight Tours. *147 King St, Charleston (29401). Phone 843/722-4630; toll-free 800/968-8175; fax 843/723-4381. www.preservationsociety.org.* The traditional allure of Charleston presents itself during the annual Candlelight Tours of Homes and Gardens. Visitors are welcomed into significant residential architecture of the 18th, 19th, and 20th centuries in historic districts that are listed on the National Register of Historic Places. Tours are self-paced and self-guided (although there are volunteer guides at each site) and include eight to ten stops per tour, rain or shine. For comfort and safety, wear walking shoes—no high-heeled shoes allowed—and bring a flashlight. The Preservation Society of Charleston sponsors these tours, in keeping with its goal "to transmit the city not less, but greater and more beautiful than it was." Founded in 1920, the Society is the oldest community-based organization of its kind in the country. Late Sept-late Oct. **$$$$**

Festival of Houses and Gardens. *40 E Bay St, Charleston (29402). Phone 843/722-3405. www.historic-charleston.org.* Sponsored by the Historic Charleston Foundation, this award-winning series of tours and special events enables visitors to experience the real Charleston—past and present—as they explore the interiors and stroll through the private gardens of some of Charleston's grandest homes. The welcome mats are out at 150 historic private homes in 11 colonial and antebellum neighborhoods, and spring blossoms are at their peak. Also available are additional excursions, lectures, luncheons featuring low country foods and beverages, afternoon teas, wine tastings, and book signings. Charleston's homes and gardens are widely admired, so early reservations are an absolute must. Most events sell out well in advance. Mid-Mar-Mid-Apr. **$$$$**

Piccolo Spoleto Festival. *Phone 843/724-7305. www.piccolospoleto.com.* This 17-day arts event in late May and early June is a companion piece to the larger Spoleto Festival USA, reaching out to children as well as adults. Events are held in 40 various venues throughout the city, including the Customs House, theaters, churches, parks, storefronts, and on the streets—wherever people might gather to watch, listen, sing, and dance. Performances showcase young artists and performers from South Carolina and elsewhere in the Southeast. Late May-early June.

Southeastern Wildlife Exposition. *211 Meeting St, Charleston (29401). Phone 843/723-1748; fax 843/723-4729. www.sewe.com.* The largest event of its kind in the nation, this 3-day celebration kicks off the spring season in Charleston, attracting more than 500 exhibitors (including some 150 artists), plus some 40,000 visitors interested in wildlife art, environmental education, and conservation. Paintings, sculptures, crafts,

and outdoor sporting goods are for sale, and a variety of demonstrations are held. The exposition takes place at various locations in and around Charleston and includes grand parties and oyster roasts. Mid-Feb. **$$$**

Spoleto Festival USA. *Gaillard Municipal Auditorium, 77 Calhoun St, Charleston. Phone 843/722-2764. www.spoletousa.org.* One of the best, and best-known, arts festivals in the country, Spoleto USA is a counterpart to the arts festival held in Spoleto, Italy, that was founded by composer Gian Carlo Menotti. The Charleston festival encompasses a cornucopia of offerings in opera, dance, chamber music, theater, symphonic music, jazz, solo voice, choral performance, visual arts, and varied special events, including conversations with various artists—more than 120 offerings in total. Venues include the Gaillard Auditorium and historic Dock Street Theatre in Charleston, as well as less-conventional locales such as Middleton Place and Mapkin Abbey Monastery. Late May-early June. **$$$$**

Limited-Service Hotels

★ **BEST WESTERN KING CHARLES INN.** *237 Meeting St, Charleston (29401). Phone 843/723-7451; toll-free 866/546-4700; fax 843/723-2041.www.kingcharlesinn.com.* 93 rooms, 4 story. Check-in 4 pm, check-out noon. Restaurant. Outdoor pool. **$**

★ **BEST WESTERN SWEETGRASS INN.** *1540 Savannah Hwy, Charleston (29407). Phone 843/571-6100; toll-free 800/937-8376; fax 843/766-6261. www.bestwestern.com.* 87 rooms. Pets accepted, some restrictions; fee. Complimentary continental breakfast. Check-in 2 pm, check-out noon. Fitness room. Outdoor pool. **$**

★ **HAMPTON INN.** *11 Ashley Pointe Dr, Charleston (29407). Phone 843/556-2000; fax 843/571-5499.* 175 rooms, 4 story. Complimentary continental breakfast. Check-in 4 pm, check-out noon. Outdoor pool. **$**

★ **THE INN AT MIDDLETON PLACE.** *4290 Ashley River Rd, Charleston (29414). Phone 843/556-0500; toll-free 800/543-4774; fax 843/556-5673. www.theinnatmiddletonplace.com.* 52 rooms, 3 story. Complimentary full breakfast. Check-in 4 pm, check-out noon. Restaurant, bar. Children's activity center. Outdoor pool. Business center. **$$**

★ **LA QUINTA INN RIVERVIEW.** *345 Meeting St, Charleston (29403). Phone 843/723-4000; toll-free 888/759-4001; fax 843/722-3725.www. laquintainnriverview.com.* 171 rooms, 5 stor y. Complimentary continental breakfast. Check-in 4 pm, check-out noon. Outdoor pool. **$**

Full-Service Hotels

★ ★ ★ ★ **CHARLESTON PLACE.** *205 Meeting St, Charleston (29401). Phone 843/722-4900; toll-free 800/611-5545; fax 843/722-0728. www.charleston-place.com.* A sweeping staircase topped off by a huge Venetian glass chandelier sets the tone at Charleston Place, where luxury and Southern hospitality blend to create a memorable experience. Located on Meeting Street in the heart of the historic district, the hotel puts antebellum mansions, luscious gardens, shopping temptations, and colonial markets within an easy stroll. The guest rooms are traditional and attractively appointed with Early American-style furnishings. A fitness center, pool with retractable roof, and shops such as Godiva and Gucci make this a perfect base for travelers who relish modern comforts. This well-rounded hotel features three restaurants with varied settings. Lazy afternoons are best spent at Palmetto Grill, and the Lobby Lounge is a local favorite for its afternoon tea. Charleston Grill, acclaimed for its sassy interpretation of Southern classics, is a surefire hit, especially when accompanied by the mellow sounds of the Frank Duvall Jazz Trio. 441 rooms, 8 story. Pets accepted, some restrictions; fee. Check-in 4 pm, check-out noon. High-speed Internet access. Two restaurants, two bars. Fitness room, fitness classes available, spa. Indoor pool, outdoor pool, children's pool, whirlpool. Business center. **$$$**

★ ★ ★ **FRANCIS MARION HOTEL.**
387 King St, Charleston (29403). Phone 843/722-0600; toll-free 877/756-2121; fax 843/723-4633. www. francismarioncharleston.com. Originally opened in 1924, as the largest and grandest hotel in the Carolinas, this European-style hotel was named for the "Swamp Fox" of the American Revolution. This property, with its expansive lobby, has been carefully restored. It now boasts over 14,000 square feet of meeting and banquet space and offers all the traditional services of a grand hotel and an excellent restaurant. While the rooms are cozy and even cramped, the amenities of this hotel and its prompt, courteous

service make for a comfortable stay. 227 rooms, 12 story. Check-in 4 pm, check-out noon. Restaurant, two bars. Fitness room. Business center. **$$**

★ ★ ★ **MARKET PAVILION HOTEL.** *225 E Bay St, Charleston (29401). Phone 843/723-0500; toll-free 877/440-2250; fax 843/723-4320. www.marketpavilion. com.* 66 rooms. Complimentary continental breakfast. Check-in 3 pm, check-out noon. High-speed Internet access. Two restaurants, two bars. Fitness room. Outdoor pool. **$$$**

★ ★ ★ **RENAISSANCE CHARLESTON HOTEL HISTORIC DISTRICT.** *68 Wentworth St, Charleston (29401). Phone 843/534-0300; fax 843/534-0700. www.renaissancehotels.com.* 166 rooms, 4 story. Check-in 3 pm, check-out noon. High-speed Internet access, wireless Internet access. Restaurant, bar. Fitness room. Outdoor pool. Business center. **$$**

Full-Service Resorts

★ ★ ★ **BOARDWALK INN AT WILD DUNES RESORT.** *5757 Palm Blvd, Isle of Palms (29451). Phone 843/886-6000; toll-free 888/778-1876; fax 843/886-2916. www.wilddunesresort.com.* Only 20 minutes from downtown, Isle of Palms is where Charlestonians have been coming to relax for decades. This breezy barrier island blends sophistication with seaside ease, especially at its top resort, Wild Dunes. The Boardwalk Inn, in the heart of the resorts old-fashioned walking village, is the shining star of this resort complex. Beachy elegance defines the atmosphere at this top-notch property. Two 18-hole Tom Fazio-designed golf courses, a 17-court tennis center, a marina, and a fitness center are among the many recreational opportunities available here, and the resorts plentiful restaurants make dining a memorable event. The resort's signature friendly spirit makes it a perfect choice for families, while its cosmopolitan attitude appeals to couples. 93 rooms, 5 story. Check-in 4 pm, check-out 11 am. High-speed Internet access. Two restaurants, two bars. Children's activity center. Fitness room, fitness classes available. Outdoor pool, children's pool. Golf, 36 holes. Tennis. **$$**

★ ★ ★ **HILTON CHARLESTON HARBOR RESORT AND MARINA.** *20 Patriot Pt, Charleston (29464). Phone 843/856-0028; toll-free 888/485-0136;*

fax 843/856-8333. www.charlestonharborresort.com. This luxurious resort sits on an 18-hole private championship golf course, private beach, and 450-slip marina. Spectacular sunsets across the Charleston Harbor and historic skyline, with many antebellum buildings and churches, are visible from most rooms. All types of water sports are available, from charter fishing to parasailing. 129 rooms, 4 story. Pets accepted; fee. Check-in 4 pm, check-out noon. High-speed Internet access. Two restaurants, bar. Outdoor pool, whirlpool. Business center. **$$**

Full-Service Inns

★ ★ ★ **ANCHORAGE INN.** *26 Vendue Range, Charleston (29401). Phone 843/723-8300; toll-free 800/421-2952; fax 843/723-9543. www. anchoragencharleston.com.* Afternoon tea, English toiletries, and period furnishings make for a sophisticated stay at this inn in the downtown historic district. 21 rooms, 2 story. Complimentary continental breakfast. Check-in 3 pm. Check-out 11 am. **$**

★ ★ ★ **CHARLESTON'S VENDUE INN.** *19 Vendue Range, Charleston (29401). Phone 800/845-7900; toll-free 800/845-7900; fax 843/577-2913. www. vendueinn.com.* With its polished pine floors, Oriental rugs, period furniture, and other historic accents, this romantic inn affords a perfect Charleston stay. Many of the individually decorated rooms overlook the Charleston Harbor and Waterfront Park. 69 rooms, 3 story. Complimentary full breakfast. Check-in 3-11 pm. Check-out 11 am. Restaurant, bar. Fitness room. **$**

★ ★ ★ **HARBOUR VIEW INN.** *2 Vendue Range, Charleston (29401). Phone 843/853-8439; toll-free 888/853-8439; fax 843/853-4034. www. harbourviewcharleston.com.* Spectacular vistas of Charleston's East Harbor, opposite beautiful Waterfront Park, await the discerning traveler who demands both a choice location and luxurious accommodations. This modern, architectural award-winning inn sits amid some of the city's best restaurants, placing Charleston's renowned cuisine within easy walking distance. Complimentary wine and cheese and late-night snack. Comfortable rooms and suites, many with great views from large windows. 57 rooms, 4 story. Check-in 3 pm. Check-out noon. **$$**

★ ★ ★ **PLANTERS INN.** *112 N Market St, Charleston (29401). Phone 843/722-2345; toll-free 800/845-7082; fax 843/577-2125. www.plantersinn. com.* Historic Charleston is at the doorstep of the Planters Inn. This delightful inn, located right on the Market, carefully blends historic references with modern amenities. Grace and charm are the hallmark of this special place. White glove service cossets guests who luxuriate in the spacious and elegant rooms and suites. Period furnishings reflect the city's signature style, while whirlpool baths, fireplaces, or piazzas overlooking the courtyard add to the modern-day traveler's experience. This hotel's dedication to excellence extends to its award-winning restaurant, the Peninsula Grill, where the chef wins kudos from locals and guests alike for his artfully presented and palate-pleasing culinary creations. 68 rooms, 4 story. Pets accepted, some restrictions; fee. Complimentary continental breakfast. Check-in 4 pm, check-out noon. Restaurant. **$$**

★ ★ ★ **WENTWORTH MANSION.** *149 Wentworth St, Charleston (29401). Phone 843/853-1886; toll-free 888/466-1886; fax 843/720-5290. www. wentworthmansion.com.* Steeped in tradition, the Wentworth Mansion offers guests a glimpse of Charleston's Gilded Age. Once a private home, this stunning mansion in the city's historic center has visitors swooning over its exquisite details. Hand-carved marble fireplaces, ornate plasterwork, Tiffany stained-glass windows, and tile floors reflect the elegance of a bygone era. The guest rooms offer a taste of the good life, with patrician furnishings, gas fireplaces, and charming views. The public rooms are glorious, and guests often roam from room to room enjoying the resplendent settings. The sun porch hosts a bountiful European breakfast each morning, and the Rodgers Library calls for a good read or a snifter of brandy. Visitors in the know are sure to book a table at the inn's restaurant (circa 1886). Nestled in the gardens behind the mansion, this white glove establishment tantalizes the palate with its sensational creations and dazzles the eye with its refined setting. 21 rooms, 4 story. Pets accepted. Complimentary full breakfast. Check-in 4 pm, check-out noon. Restaurant. Business center. **$$$**

Specialty Lodgings

ANSONBOROUGH INN. *21 Hasell St, Charleston (29401). Phone 843/723-1655; toll-free 800/522-2073; fax 843/577-6888. www.ansonboroughinn.com.* 37 rooms, all suites. Complimentary continental breakfast. Check-in 3 pm, check-out noon. Bar. Business center. **$$**

BARKSDALE HOUSE INN. *27 George St, Charleston (29401). Phone 843/577-4800; toll-free 888/577-4980; fax 843/853-0482. www.barksdalehouse.com.* Built as a town home in 1778 by a wealthy Charlestonian, George Barksdale, this stately bed-and-breakfast is filled with period furnishings and modern conveniences. It is located in the historic district. 14 rooms, 3 story. Children over 10 years only. Complimentary continental breakfast. Check-in 3 pm, check-out 11 am. **$**

BATTERY CARRIAGE HOUSE INN. *20 S Battery St, Charleston (29401). Phone 843/727-3100; toll-free 800/775-5575; fax 843/727-3130. www.batterycarriagehouse.com.* Hidden within the flowering gardens of the Steven-Lathers Mansion, an exquisite private home, this 1843 bed and breakfast offers private entrances and romantic décor. The location overlooking Charleston Harbor can't be beat. 12 rooms, 2 story. Children over 12 years only. Complimentary continental breakfast. Check-in 3 pm, check-out noon. **$**
🐾

THE GOVERNOR'S HOUSE INN. *117 Broad St, Charleston (29401). Phone 843/720-2070; toll-free 800/720-9812. www.governorshouse.com.* 11 rooms. Check-in 2:30 pm, check-out 11 am. **$$$**

INDIGO INN. *1 Maiden Ln, Charleston (29401). Phone 843/577-5900; toll-free 800/845-7639; fax 843/577-0378. www.indigoinn.com.* Housed in an 1850 warehouse once used to store indigo for dying textiles, this colorful inn is located in the middle of the historic district, just one block from City Market. Each of the rooms is color coordinated.40 rooms, 3 story. Pets accepted, some restrictions; fee. Complimentary continental breakfast. Check-in 3 pm. Check-out noon. **$**
🐾

JOHN RUTLEDGE HOUSE INN. *116 Broad St, Charleston (29401). Phone 843/723-7999; toll-free 866/720-2609; fax 843/720-2615.www. johnrutledgehouseinn.com.* This genteel inn not only sends you back to an earlier era, but puts you in the midst of historic living. Arrive late in the afternoon and take tea in the salon. Enjoy the luxuriously appointed rooms with great views of the city's spires. 19 rooms, 1 story. Complimentary continental breakfast. Check-in 4 pm. Check-out noon. **$$**
🔲

KINGS COURTYARD INN. *198 King St, Charleston (29401). Phone 843/723-7000; toll-free 866/720-2949; fax 843/720-2608. www.kingscourtyardinn.com.* This three-story, antebellum, Greek Revival structure was built in 1854 and remains one of the gems of Charleston's historic district. 44 rooms, 3 story. Complimentary continental breakfast. Check-in 3 pm. Check-out noon. **$**

MAISON DU PRE. *317 E Bay St, Charleston (29401). Phone 843/723-8691; toll-free 800/844-4667; fax 843/723-3722. www.maisondupre.com.* The main house dates from 1804, as does the charm of the welcome. Located in historic downtown, adjacent to the Gaillard Auditorium, this inn is decorated in period furniture and art made by the family that runs it. 15 rooms, 3 story. Complimentary continental breakfast. Check-in 2 pm. Check-out noon. **$**

MEETING STREET INN. *173 Meeting St, Charleston (29401). Phone 843/723-1882; toll-free 800/842-8022; fax 843/577-0851. www.meetingstreetinn.com.* Each room in this classic, Charleston-style single-house inn opens onto the piazza and courtyard. The rooms are individually decorated with period furniture. The inn is conveniently located opposite the City Market in historic downtown. 56 rooms, 4 story. Complimentary continental breakfast. Check-in 3 pm, check-out noon. **$**

VICTORIA HOUSE INN. *208 King St, Charleston (29401). Phone 843/720-2944; toll-free 866/720-2946; fax 843/720-2930. www.thevictoriahouseinn.com.* Built in the late 1880s, this Romanesque-style Victorian house now serves as a lovely inn. Located in the downtown historic district, the inn offers genteel amenities, such as a bedside champagne breakfast. 22 rooms, 3 story. Complimentary continental breakfast. Check-in 3 pm. Check-out noon. **$**
🔲

Restaurants

★ ★ **82 QUEEN.** *82 Queen St, Charleston (29401). Phone 843/723-7591; toll-free 800/849-0082; fax 843/577-7463. www.82queen.com.* Southern menu. Lunch, dinner, Sun brunch. Bar. Children's menu. Business casual attire. Reservations recommended. Outdoor seating. **$$$**

★ ★ **ANSON.** *12 Anson St, Charleston (29401). Phone 843/577-0551; fax 843/720-1955. www.ansonrestaurant.com.* Southern menu. Dinner. Bar. Children's menu. Business casual attire. Reservations recommended. **$$$**

★ ★ **CAROLINA'S.** *10 Exchange St, Charleston (29401). Phone 843/724-3800; toll-free 888/486-7673; fax 843/722-9493. www.carolinasrestaurant.com.* American menu. Dinner. Closed Dec 25. Bar. Business casual attire. Reservations recommended. Valet parking. **$$$**

★ ★ ★ **CHARLESTON GRILL.** *224 King St, Charleston (29401). Phone 843/577-4522; fax 843/724-8405. www.charlestongrill.com.* The Charleston Grill is a posh, clubby spot located in the Charleston Place hotel. Stained-glass French doors, dark wood-paneled walls, marble floors, and vases filled with impressive floral arrangements come together to create a classy, old-world atmosphere. Menu appearances by such dishes as Maine lobster tempura with lemon grits and fried mini green tomatoes and baked country crepinette of local rabbit loin with seared foie gras and Vidalia onions in a sausage sawmill gravy should give you a good idea of the delicious sort of low-country fare served at this sophisticated, ever-popular destination restaurant. Live jazz and terrific classic cocktails make this a hotspot for a young crowd of music lovers as well as a mature audience of discerning foodies. American menu. Dinner. Bar. Children's menu. Business casual attire. Reservations recommended. Valet parking. Outdoor seating. **$$$$**

★ ★ ★ **CIRCA 1886.** *149 Wentworth St, Charleston (29412). Phone 843/853-7828; fax 843/720-5292. www.circa1886.com.* American menu. Dinner. Closed Sun. Bar. Business casual attire. Reservations recommended. **$$$**

★ ★ ★ **CYPRESS A LOWCOUNTRY GRILLE.** *167 E Bay Street, Charleston (29401). Phone 843/727-0111; fax 843/937-4027. www.magnolias-blossoms-cypress.com.* Low-country menu. Dinner. Bar. Business casual attire. Reservations recommended. **$$$**

★ ★ **FULTON FIVE.** *5 Fulton St, Charleston (29401). Phone 843/853-5555; fax 843/853-6212.* Located in the historic district, this restaurant features European décor with an intimate atmosphere. The baking is all done on-site. Italian menu. Dinner. Closed Sun; holidays; also week before Labor Day. Bar. Business casual attire. Reservations recommended. Outdoor seating. **$$**

★ ★ **GAULART & MALICLET FRENCH CAFE.** *98 Broad St, Charleston (29401). Phone 843/577-9797. www.fastandfrench.org.* French menu. Breakfast, lunch, dinner Tues-Sat. Closed Sun. Casual attire. **$$**

★ ★ **HANK'S SEAFOOD RESTAURANT.** *10 Hayne St, Charleston (29401). Phone 843/723-3474. www.hanksseafoodrestaurant.com.* Seafood menu. Dinner. Bar. Children's menu. Casual attire. **$$**

★ ★ ★ **HIGH COTTON.** *199 E Bay St, Charleston (29401). Phone 843/724-3815; fax 843/724-3616. www.high-cotton.net.* American menu. Lunch, dinner, Sun brunch. Closed Dec 25; Super Bowl Sun. Bar. Children's menu. Business casual attire. **$$**

★ ★ **HOMINY GRILL.** *207 Rutledge Ave, Charleston (29403). Phone 843/937-0930. www.hominygrill.com.* Low country Southern menu. Breakfast, lunch, dinner, brunch. Closed Thanksgiving; late Dec. Casual attire. Outdoor seating. **$$**

★ ★ ★ **MAGNOLIAS.** *185 E Bay St, Charleston (29401). Phone 843/577-7771; fax 843/722-0035. www.magnolias-blossom-cypress.com.* This smart, uptown restaurant specializes in updated Southern food. Chef Barickman uses Southern ingredients in mouth-watering combinations. He constantly focuses on the quality of prime ingredients, freshness, and the use of local products. American menu. Lunch, dinner, Sun brunch. Closed Dec 25. Bar. **$$**

★ ★ ★ **MCCRADY'S.** *2 Unity Alley, Charleston (29401). Phone 843/577-0025; fax 843/577-3681. www.mccradysrestaurant.com.* Housed in a beautifully restored former tavern that was built in 1778, McCrady's is a one-of-a-kind restaurant. As you enter the long, sexy, dark-wood bar and take a seat amid the swanky cocktail crowd, you know you are somewhere special. The experience gets even better when you move to the clubby dining room, with original hardwood floors and brickwork, vaulted wood-beamed ceilings, soaring skylights, magnificent floor-to-ceiling windows, and lavish tufted leather seating. The service is warm and knowledgeable and specializes in little details like offering black linen napkins to guests who don't wish to leave with white lint coating their dark trousers. But the food really takes the cake. Chef-partner Michael Kramer wows his savvy guests with his bold brand of flashy, progressive American fare. Plates arrive in a hush of envy from other tables and return to the kitchen empty, making easy work for the dishwashers. Coffee-rubbed filet mignon is a signature and will have you saving coffee grinds to reinvent this dish at home. International menu. Dinner. Closed Jan 1, Thanksgiving, Dec 25. Bar. Business casual attire. Reservations recommended. **$$$**

★ ★ **MERITAGE.** *235 E Bay St, Charleston (29401). Phone 843/723-8181; fax 843/723-8138.* International menu. Dinner. Closed Dec 24-25; second Sun in June. Bar. Casual attire. Outdoor seating. **$**

★ ★ ★ **PENINSULA GRILL.** *112 N Market St, Charleston (29401). Phone 843/723-0700; fax 843/577-2125. www.peninsulagrill.com.* Located in the Planter's Inn, Peninsula Grill is a place where the words *fun* and *Four-Star dining* can easily be used in the same sentence. The comfortably elegant restaurant is richly styled with crushed velvet walls, polished dark woods, and local cypress crown moldings. It has the sophisticated feel of an urban eatery without losing sight of its Southern charm and hospitality. The menu is inventive and exciting, offering boldly flavored dishes spiced up with low-country accents like collards, hushpuppies, grits, and black-eyed peas. A perfect way to start any meal is with a glass of champagne, and at Peninsula Grill, you have five champagnes and sparkling wines by the glass to choose from. There's also a fun "Champagne Bar Menu" of decadent little treats like oysters, lobster, foie gras, caviar, and duck pâté to match up with your glass(es) of bubbly. Prepare your toasts in advance. The staff at Peninsula Grill will guide you effortlessly through an evening that is both delicious and entertaining. Before you know it, many hours and many glasses of wine will have passed, and you'll want to do it all over again. American menu. Dinner. Bar. Business casual attire. Reservations recommended. Outdoor seating. **$$$**

★ ★ **SERMET'S CORNER.** *276 King St, Charleston (29401). Phone 843/853-7775; fax 843/853-7770.* Mediterranean menu. Lunch, dinner. Closed Thanksgiving, Dec 25. Bar. Children's menu. **$$**

★ ★ **SLIGHTLY NORTH OF BROAD.** *192 E Bay St, Charleston (29401). Phone 843/723-3424; fax 843/724-3811. www.slightlynorthofbroad.net.* Lowcountry menu. Lunch, dinner. Closed July 4, Dec 25. Bar. Children's menu. Casual attire. **$$**

Cheraw (C-5)

See also Bennettsville, Camden, Darlington, Florence, Hartsville

Settled 1740
Population 5,524
Elevation 150 ft
Area Code 843
Zip 29520
Information Chamber of Commerce, 221 Market St; phone 843/537-8425 or 843/537-7681
Web Site www.cheraw.com

Profiting in commerce from both Carolinas, Cheraw grew rapidly when the Pee Dee River was opened for traffic. It is said that the town owes its many trees to an ordinance that required every person seen intoxicated in public to go out into the woods and fetch a tree for planting within the town.

What to See and Do

Carolina Sandhills National Wildlife Refuge. *23734 Hwy 1, Mc Bee (29101). On Hwy 1, 4 miles NE of McBee; approximately 20 miles SW on Hwy 1. Phone 843/335-8401; fax 843/335-8406. www.fws.gov/carolinasandhills.* Approximately 46,000 acres house almost 300 species of birds, mammals, reptiles, and amphibians. Auto tour route, hiking trails, and observation towers available. Fishing, hunting permitted. Interpretive displays available at headquarters. (Daily, dawn-dusk) **FREE**

★ **Cheraw Historical District.** *221 N Market St, Cheraw (29520). Phone 843/537-8425; toll-free 888/537-0014. www.cheraw.com.* Cheraw showcases a 213-acre historic district with several recommended walking routes. The town's roots date back to before the Revolutionary War, and Cheraw has a deep Civil War history as well. The town green (circa 1768) is the site of the small Cheraw Lyceum Museum (circa 1820). Other notable buildings are Town Hall (circa 1858), Market Hall (circa 1837), and the Inglis-McIver Law Office (circa 1830). Victorian and Revival homes dot the walking trail through the heavily wooded town. Limit your drinking: local lore has it that in the past, anyone found drunk in public in Cheraw had to plant a tree in the town limits. **FREE**

Cheraw State Park. *100 State Park Rd, Cheraw (29520). 4 miles SW on Hwy 52. Phone 843/537-9656; toll-free 800/868-9630.* Located on 7,361 acres of gently rolling green sandhills, the park offers lake swimming, boat rentals, fishing, nature trails, an 18-hole golf course, picnic shelters, a playground, and a recreation building. You'll also find camping and cabins. Unusually cool in hot-weather periods. **$**

Cheraw State Park Camping. *100 State Park Rd, Cheraw (29520). Phone 843/537-9656. www.discoversouthcarolina.com/stateparks.* There are 17 campsites on packed gravel that accommodate RVs up to either 40 feet or 34 feet. Six of the sites are along Lake Juniper, the parks 360-acre lake. They have water and electrical hook-ups. Boaters may set up camp at the old boat landing on the north side of the lake. Equestrian camping, which includes central water, is also available near the lake. Reserved sites are $1 extra per night, while most sites rent on a first-come, first-served basis. Cheraw State Park also has furnished one-bedroom cabins with living supplies such as bed and bath linens, kitchen utensils and appliances, and outside grills. Dump station, restrooms, showers.

Old St. David's Episcopal Church. *100 Church St, Cheraw. Phone 843/537-7681.* (1768) Restored to the 1820s period; last Anglican parish established in the state prior to the American Revolution. Used as a hospital by British during Revolution, later by Union Army during Civil War; about 50 British soldiers are buried in the churchyard. Tours (by appointment); for self-tours, pick up keys at Chamber of Commerce.

Special Event

Spring Festival. *Cheraw Community Center, 200 Powe St, Cheraw (29520). Phone 843/537-8420. www.cheraw. com.* Family Fun Run; tours; arts and crafts shows; Confederate reenactments; entertainment, trolley rides, car show. Early Apr.

Chester (C-4)

See also Rock Hill

Settled 1755
Population 6,476
Elevation 485 ft
Area Code 803
Zip 29706
Information Chester County Chamber of Commerce, 109 Gadsden St, PO Box 489; phone 803/581-4142
Web Site www.chestersc.org

Seat of Chester County, this town was named by settlers from Pennsylvania. Aaron Burr, guarded here in 1807 while under arrest for treason, broke away and climbed a high rock. After haranguing a surprised crowd, he was recaptured.

What to See and Do

Chester State Park. *759 State Park Dr, Chester (29706). 3 miles SW on Hwy 72. Phone 803/385-2680.* Approximately 500 acres. Lake fishing, boating. Nature trail. Picnicking (shelters), recreation building. Camping (hookups, dump station). Equestrian show ring. **$**

Clemson (C-2)

See also Anderson, Greenville

Founded 1889
Population 11,939
Elevation 850 ft
Area Code 864
Zip 29631
Information Clemson Area Chamber of Commerce, PO Box 1622, 29633; phone 864/654-1200 or toll-free 800/542-0746
Web Site www.clemsonchamber.org

Home of Clemson University, this community also hosts vacationers attracted to the huge lake that the Hartwell Dam has formed on the Savannah River.

What to See and Do

Clemson University. *109 Daniel Dr, Clemson (29631). 11 miles NW of I-85 at jct Hwy 76, Hwy 93. Phone 864/656-3311. www.clemson.edu.* (1889) (17,000 students) Named for Thomas G. Clemson, son-in-law of John C. Calhoun, who bequeathed the bulk of his estate, Fort Hill, for establishment of a scientific college. Guided tours (daily; closed school holidays and exam week). On this 1,400-acre campus are

Fort Hill. *Clemson University, Fort Hill St & Calhoun Dr, Clemson (29634). Phone 864/656-2475; fax 864/656-1026.* (1803) Mansion on 1,100 acres acquired by Calhoun during his first term as vice president. House has many original furnishings belonging to Calhoun, Clemson. (Daily; closed holidays)

Hanover House. *South Carolina Botanical Garden, Clemson University, 102 Garden Trail, Clemson (29634). Phone 864/656-2475; fax 864/656-1026.* (1716) This French Huguenot house was moved here from its original site in Berkeley County to prevent submersion by Lake Moultrie. (Sat-Sun by appointment only). **$**

South Carolina Botanical Garden. *Clemson University, 102 Garden Trail, Clemson (29634). E side of campus. Phone 864/656-3405.* This 250-acre area includes azalea and camelia trails, ornamental plantings, large collection of shrubs; dwarf conifer flower and turf display gardens; wildflower pioneer and bog garden labeled in Braille. (Daily) **FREE**

Oconee State Park. *624 State Park Rd, Mountain Rest (29664). 20 miles NW of town, 12 miles NW of Walhalla on Hwy 107. Phone 864/638-5353.* Approximately 1,100 acres of park nestled in the foothills of the Blue Ridge and surrounded by Sumter National Forest (see GREENWOOD). Lake swimming, lifeguard (summer), boating (rentals), fishing. Nature, hiking trails; recreation building; recreation and nature programs (summer); carpet golf. Picnicking (shelters), playground, concession, restaurant. Camping (hookups, dump station), cabins. **$**

Raft trips. *1251 Academy Rd, Long Creek (29658). 34 miles NW on Hwy 76. Phone toll-free 800/451-9972. www.wildwaterrafting.com.* Guided whitewater rafting trips on the Chattooga National Wild and Scenic River. Reservations required. Also canoe and kayak clinics and overnight trips. (Daily, Mar-Oct) **$$$$**

World of Energy. *7812 Rochester Hwy, Seneca (29672). 12 miles NW on Hwys 130, 123. Phone 864/885-4600; toll-free 800/777-1004. www.dukepower.com.* Three-dimensional displays on the "Story of Energy," with exhibits on hydro, coal, and nuclear production of electricity; also displays on radiation and supplemental energy sources. Computer games; films. Overlooks Lake Keowee and one of the world's largest nuclear generating plants. Picnic area and boat dock adjacent. (Mon-Fri 9 am-5 pm, Sat-Sun noon-5 pm; closed Jan 1, Thanksgiving, Dec 24-25) **FREE**

Special Event

Clemson Fest. *Foothills Area Family YMCA, 275 YMCA Cle, Clemson (29678). Phone 864/654-1200. www.clemsonchamber.org.* Entertainment, arts and crafts, children's activities. Boat parade and contest precedes fireworks display. July 4th weekend. **$**

Limited-Service Hotel

★ **COMFORT INN.** *1305 Tiger Blvd, Clemson (29631). Phone 864/653-3600; toll-free 877/424-6423; fax 864/654-3123. www.comfortinn.com.* 122 rooms, 4 story. Pets accepted, some restrictions. Complimentary continental breakfast. Check-in 4 pm, check-out noon. Outdoor pool, whirlpool. **$**

Specialty Lodging

SUNRISE FARM BED & BREAKFAST INN. *325 Sunrise Dr, Salem (29676). Phone 864/944-0121; toll-free 888/991-0121; fax 864/944-6195. www.bbonline.*

com/sc/sunrisefarm. 8 rooms, 2 story. Pets accepted, some restrictions; fee. Complimentary full breakfast. Check-in 3-6 pm, check-out 11 am. Built in 1890; Victorian country farmhouse. **$**

Clinton (C-3)

See also Greenville, Greenwood, Newberry, Spartanburg

Population 8,091
Elevation 680 ft
Area Code 864
Zip 29325
Information Laurens County Chamber of Commerce, PO Box 248, Laurens 29360; phone 864/833-2716
Web Site www.laurenscounty.org

In 1865, Clinton was "a mudhole surrounded by barrooms," according to the young Rev William Jacobs, who not only rid the town of barrooms, but founded a library, orphanage, high school, and Presbyterian College (1880). A young attorney by the name of Henry Clinton Young was hired by the townspeople to help lay out the streets, hence the town came to be named for his middle name.

What to See and Do

Rose Hill Plantation State Historic Site. *2677 Sardis Rd, Union (29379). 15 miles E on Hwy 72, 2 miles N on Hwy 176, then W on Sardis Rd. Phone 864/427-5966. www.discoversouthcarolina.com.* (Circa 1825) Forty-four acres. Located in Rose Hill State Park, this restored cotton plantation was the home of William H. Gist, known as South Carolina's secession governor. The Federal-style house with 1860 furnishings sits on a gently rising knoll amid boxwoods and roses. House (Thurs-Mon 1-4 pm; tour **$**). Grounds (Thurs-Mon 9 am-6 pm). Picnic area, nature trail. **FREE**

Columbia (D-4)

See also Camden, Newberry, Orangeburg, Sumter

Founded 1786
Population 116,278
Elevation 213 ft
Area Code 803
Information Columbia Metropolitan Visitors Center, PO Box 15, 29202; phone toll-free 800/264-4884
Web Site www.columbiacvb.com

The broad-boulevarded capital of South Carolina is not only the state's political and governmental capital, but also its wholesale and retail trade center. Located within 3 miles of the geographic center of the state, Columbia was laid out as the capital as a compromise between the contending up-country and low-country farmers. The city rarely departs from a checkerboard pattern; the streets are sometimes 150 feet wide, planned that way originally to discourage malaria.

The General Assembly met for the first time in the State House in Columbia on January 4, 1790. George Washington was a guest here during his Southern tour the next year. On December 17, 1860, a convention assembled in Columbia's First Baptist Church and drew up the Ordinance of Secession, setting off a chain of events that terminated, for the city, on February 17, 1865, when General William T. Sherman's troops occupied Columbia and reduced it to ashes. An area of 84 blocks and 1,386 buildings was destroyed; on Main Street only the unfinished new statehouse and the home of the French consul were spared. From these ashes, a city of stately buildings has risen.

The economy of the city is based on trade, industry, finance, and government.

Since 1801, when the South Carolina College, now the University of South Carolina, was established here, the city has been an educational center; today it is the site of nine schools of higher education.

Columbia is the headquarters for the Francis Marion National Forest (see CHARLESTON) and the Sumter National Forest (see GREENWOOD).

What to See and Do

Columbia Museum of Art. *Main and Hampton sts, Columbia (29202). Phone 803/799-2810. www.colmusart. org* .Galleries house Renaissance paintings from the collection of Samuel H. Kress; 19th- and 20th-century American, emphasizing the Southeast, and European paintings; changing exhibitions drawn from permanent collection and objects on loan. Concerts, films, lectures, and special events accenting exhibitions. (Wed-Thurs, Sat 10 am-5 pm; Fri to 9 pm, to 5 pm in Dec; Sun 1-5 pm; closed holidays) **$**

Confederate Relic Room and Museum. *Columbia Mills Building, 301 Gervais St, Columbia (29201). Phone 803/737-8095. www.state.sc.us/crr.* Relic collection from the Colonial period through the space age with

special emphasis on South Carolina's Confederate period. (Tues-Sat 10 am-5 pm) **$**

Congaree National Park. *100 National Park Rd, Hopkins (29061). 20 miles SE off Hwy 48. Phone 803/776-4396; fax 803/783-4241. www.nps.gov/cosw.* Congaree is South Carolina's only and the nation's newest national park. The lush enclave has a Jurassic-era feel. Roughly 22,000 acres of old-growth forest spill across wetlands rich with wildlife. There are 20 miles of hiking trails, fishing, canoeing, and boardwalks. Primitive camping is allowed by permit. (Daily; closed Dec 25) **FREE**

First Baptist Church. *1306 Hampton St, Columbia (29201). Phone 803/256-4251; fax 803/343-8584. www. fbccola.com.* (1859) First Secession Convention, which marked the beginning of the Civil War, met here on Dec 17, 1860. (Mon-Fri, Sun; closed holidays)

First Presbyterian Church. *1420 Lady St, Columbia (29201). At Lady St. Phone 803/799-9062. www. firstprescola.com.* (1853) First congregation organized in Columbia (1795); President Woodrow Wilson's parents are buried in churchyard. (Daily)

Fort Jackson. *Fort Jackson,4442 Jackson Blvd, Columbia (29207). E edge of city, between I-20 and Hwy 76. Phone 803/751-7419. www.jackson.army.mil.* The most active initial entry training center for the US Army, with 16,000 soldiers assigned. Museum on Jackson Blvd has displays on the history of the fort and today's army. (Mon-Fri 9 am-4 pm; closed holidays) **FREE**

Governor's Mansion. *800 Richland St, Columbia (29201). Phone 803/737-1710. www.scgovernorsmansion. org.* (1855) Built as officers' quarters for Arsenal Academy. Tours every half-hour (Tues-Wed 10-11 am). Reservations required. **FREE**

Hampton-Preston Mansion. *1615 Blanding St, Columbia (29201). Phone 803/252-1770. www. historiccolumbia.org/history/hampton_preston.html.* (1818) Purchased by Wade Hampton I; occupied by the Hamptons and the family of his daughter, Mrs. John Preston. In Feb 1865, it served as headquarters for Union General J. A. Logan. Many Hampton family furnishings and decorative arts of the antebellum period. Tours on the hour(Tues-Sun; closed holidays).**$**

Lake Murray. *2184 N Lake Dr, Columbia. 15 miles NW via I-26, Irmo exit. Phone 803/749-1554.* The lake is 41 miles long, with a 520-mile shoreline; it's impounded by the Saluda Dam for hydroelectric purposes. Swimming, water-skiing, boating, fishing; picnicking, camping (fee). Lighthouse Marina is 17 miles NW.

Lexington County Museum Complex. *231 Fox St, Lexington (29072). 10 miles W via Hwy 378 at Fox St. Phone 803/359-8369.www.discoversouthcarolina.com.* A historic restoration from the mid-1700s; depicts the life of area farmers. Period country furnishings, textiles, decorative arts. Spinning and weaving tours. (Tues-Sat 10 am-4 pm, Sun 1-4 pm; closed holidays) **$**

Riverbanks Zoo and Garden. *500 Wildlife Pkwy, Columbia (29210). Phone 803/779-8717. www.riverbanks.org.* Exhibits of animals in nonrestrictive natural habitat areas; aquarium-reptile complex with diving demonstrations; demonstrations at Riverbanks Farm; penguin and sea lion feedings. (Daily 9 am-5 pm, Apr-Sept Sat-Sun to 6 pm; closed Thanksgiving, Dec 25) **$$**

Robert Mills Historic House and Park. *1616 Blanding St, Columbia (29201). Phone 803/252-1770. www. historiccolumbia.org/history/mills.html.* (1823) One of a few residences designed by Robert Mills, Federal architect and designer of the Washington Monument; mantels, art, furnishings of Regency period. Tours on the hour (Tues-Sun; closed holidays). **$**

Sesquicentennial State Park. *9564 Two Notch Rd Columbia (29223). 13 miles NE on Hwy 1. Phone 803/788-2706.* On 1,445 acres. Log house (1756). Interpretive center. Lake swimming, bathhouse, boating (rentals), fishing. Nature, biking, exercise trails. Picnicking (five shelters), playground. Recreation building. Camping (hookups, dump station). Swimming and boating (Memorial Day-Labor Day). (Daily 8 am-6 pm) **$**

South Carolina Archives Building. *8301 Parklane Rd, Columbia (29223). Phone 803/896-6100; fax 803/896-6198. www.state.sc.us/scdah.* Historical and genealogical research facility with documents dating from 1671; changing exhibits. Research room (Mon-Fri 8:45 am-4:45 pm; closed holidays). Tours (by appointment). **FREE**

South Carolina State Museum. *301 Gervais St, Columbia (29201). Phone 803/898-4921. www.museum.state. sc.us.* Located in the world's first fully electric textile mill (1894); exhibits on art, natural history, cultural history, and science and technology with an emphasis on contributions by South Carolinians; numerous hands-on exhibits; dioramas. Included is a center dedicated to Nobel Prize winner Charles Townes, who helped develop the laser. Gift shop. (Tues-Sat 10 am-5 pm, Sun 1-5 pm; also Mon in June-early Sept; closed holidays) **$**

Town Theatre. *1012 Sumter St, Columbia (29201). Phone 803/799-2510; fax 803/799-6463. www.*

towntheatre.com. One of the oldest (since 1919) community theater groups in the US. Broadway plays and musicals. Tours (by appointment). Performances (late Sept-late May; also summer show).

Trinity Cathedral. *1100 Sumter St, Columbia (29201). At Senate St, opposite Statehouse. Phone 803/771-7300; fax 803/254-4885. www.trinityepiscopalcathedral.org.* (1846) Reproduction of Yorkminster, England; the oldest church building in Columbia and one of the largest Episcopal congregations in the US. Hiram Powers baptismal font, box pews, English stained glass. Three Wade Hamptons (a politically prominent South Carolina family) are buried in the churchyard; graves of seven governors and six bishops are also here. In 1977, it became the Cathedral Parish of the Episcopal Diocese of Upper South Carolina. (Daily) **FREE**

University of South Carolina. *McKissick Visitor Center, 816 Bull St, Columbia (29208). Phone 803/777-0169; toll-free 800/922-9755. www.sc.edu.* (1801) (26,000 students) Located downtown. For campus tour information, stop at the University of South Carolina Visitor Center. (Mon-Fri, select weekends) Points of interest include

> **Carolina Coliseum.** *701 Assembly St, Columbia (29201). Phone 803/777-5113; fax 803/777-5114.* Houses Gamecock basketball games and other sports events, concerts, exhibitions, trade shows, circuses, and other entertainment.

> **The Horseshoe.** *University of South Carolina, 816 Bull St, Columbia (29208). Off Sumter St. Original campus area. Phone 803/777-0169; toll-free 800/922-9755; fax 803/777-0687.* Ten of the 11 buildings on the quadrangle date back to the 19th century and are listed in the National Register of Historic Places. Monument erected in 1827 was designed by Robert Mills.

> **Koger Center for the Arts.** *University of South Carolina, 1051 Greene St, Columbia (29201). Phone 803/777-7500.* Contemporary structure houses center for the performing arts. Diverse musical, theatrical, and dance programs.

> **McKissick Museum.** *University of South Carolina, 816 Bull St, Columbia (29208). At the head of the Horseshoe. Phone 803/777-7251; fax 803/777-2829.* Houses Bernard M. Baruch Silver Gallery with antique European silver, J. Harry Howard gemstone collection, Laurence L. Smith Mineral Library, Catawba Native American pottery collection, Southern folk art, historical collections, art gallery, education museum, broadcasting archives.

(Mon-Fri 8:30 am-5 pm, Sun 11 am-3 pm; closed university and state holidays) **FREE**

Woodrow Wilson Boyhood Home. *1705 Hampton St, Columbia (29201). Phone 803/252-1770. www. historiccolumbia.org.* (1872) The house was built by Wilson's father and contains items associated with Wilson's family and career. Guided tours on the hour (Tues-Sat 10 am-4 pm, Sun 1-5 pm; closed holidays) **$**

Special Event

South Carolina State Fair. *Fairgrounds, 1200 Rosewood Dr, Columbia (29201). Phone 803/799-3387; fax 803/799-1760. www.scstatefair.org.* Agricultural, floral, home, craft, livestock, and commercial exhibits. Entertainment, shows, carnival. Mid-Oct. **$$**

Limited-Service Hotels

★ ★ **COLUMBIA PLAZA.** *8105 Two Notch Rd, Columbia (29223). Phone 803/736-5600; toll-free 800/272-6232; fax 803/736-1241. www.columbiaramadaplaza. com.* 186 rooms, 6 story. Pets accepted; fee. Check-in 3 pm, check-out noon. Restaurant, bar. Fitness room. Outdoor pool. **$**
🐾 🏃 🏊

★ ★ **EMBASSY SUITES HOTEL COLUMBIA-GREYSTONE.** *200 Stoneridge Dr, Columbia (29210). Phone 803/252-8700; toll-free 800/362-2779; fax 803/256-8749. www.embassysuites.com.* This hotel is situated near the city's main attractions, including the state capitol, the University of South Carolina, shopping malls, and the airport. The lobby features a seven-story atrium with lush tropical plants and waterfalls, and the spacious suites are decorated with gold walls and accents of terra-cotta, gold, beige, and green. 214 rooms, 7 story, all suites. Complimentary full breakfast. Check-in 3 pm, check-out noon. High-speed Internet access. Restaurant, bar. Fitness room. Indoor pool, whirlpool. Airport transportation available. Business center. **$$**
🏃 🏊 🏃

★ **HAMPTON INN-DOWNTOWN HISTORIC DISTRICT.** *822 Gervais St, Columbia (29201). Phone 803/231-2000; toll-free 800/426-7866; fax 803/231-2868. www.hamptoninncolumbia.com.* With a location in the heart of historic downtown Columbia, this Hampton Inn is within walking distance to boutique and antique shops, concerts, and many dining options. The exterior of the hotel is faced in brick, keeping up with the appearance of the town, and the guest rooms are

decorated with beige and terra-cotta accents and feature two-poster beds with white bedding. A manager's reception is offered Monday through Thursday, from 5:30 to 7 pm. 122 rooms. Complimentary continental breakfast. Check-in 3 pm, check-out noon. High-speed Internet access, wireless Internet access. Fitness room. Outdoor pool. Business center. **$**
🏃 🏊 🏃

★ ★ **RAMADA.** *7510 Two Notch Rd, Columbia (29223). Phone 803/736-3000; toll-free 877/308-4986; fax 803/736-6399. www.hotelcarolinian.com.* 251 rooms, 2 story. Pets accepted, some restrictions; fee. Check-in 3 pm, check-out noon. High-speed Internet access, wireless Internet access. Restaurant, bar. Fitness room. Indoor pool, outdoor pool, whirlpool. **$**
🐾 🏃 🏊

Restaurants

★ ★ **HAMPTON STREET VINEYARD.** *1201 Hampton St, Columbia (29202). Phone 803/252-0850; fax 803/931-0193. www.hamptonstreetvineyard.com.* The Hampton Street Vineyard is located in the heart of downtown, within walking distance to the sidewalk shops of the historic section of town. Housed in the Sylvan Building (1871), the restaurant features some areas with original flooring. The walls are brick with accents of gold and red. Black high-polished tables are set with oil lamps and flowers. The private wine room is set for ten and features floor-to-ceiling wine bottles, gold-colored walls, and a painted red floor. American menu. Lunch, dinner. Closed Sun. Bar. Casual attire. Reservations recommended. Outdoor seating. **$$$**
🅿

★ ★ **HENNESSY'S.** *1649 Main St, Columbia (29201). Phone 803/799-8280; fax 803/256-3147. www. hennessyssc.com.* Housed in a converted hardware store that dates to 1881, Hennessy's is located in the heart of the downtown historic section of Columbia, within walking distance of many shops and lodging opportunities. The décor has a European feel, with dark wooden pillars; a wood-accented balcony over the main dining room; and tall, dark wood and leather chairs that grace the tables. The artwork adorning the walls is supplied by a local artist and is changed frequently. The bar is located upstairs, offering more dining options. *Note:* children under the age of 6 years are not allowed. American menu. Lunch, dinner. Closed Sun. Bar. Business casual attire. Reservations recommended. **$$**

★ ★ ★ **RISTORANTE DIVINO.** *803 Gervais St, Columbia (29201). Phone 803/799-4550; fax 803/695-4393. www.ristorantedivino.com.* Ristorante Divino is located in the heart of the downtown historic district of Columbia, within walking distance to a variety of boutique shops. The décor is inviting—the bar is in the entrance lobby, opening up to the stylish dining room, which is decorated with sheer curtains, a brick wall, wooden pillars, and tables set with crisp white tablecloths. The wine cellar features more than 3,000 bottles of wine and includes 400 varieties. Northern Italian menu. Dinner. Closed Sun; Memorial day, July 4, Labor Day. Bar. Business casual attire. Reservations recommended. Valet parking. **$$$**

Darlington (D-5)

See also Bennettsville, Cheraw, Dillon, Florence, Hartsville

Founded 1798
Population 6,720
Elevation 157 ft
Area Code 843
Zip 29532
Information Greater Darlington Chamber of Commerce, 38 Public Sq; phone 843/393-2641
Web Site www.visitdarlingtoncounty.org

Darlington is situated in one of the most fertile sections of the state. Along with its agricultural economy, the area has diversified industry. Darlington was a pioneer in the culture and marketing of tobacco as a cash crop and has a large tobacco market. It is the home of what is said to be the nation's largest automobile auction market and is a stock car racing center.

What to See and Do

Joe Weatherly Stock Car Museum and National Motorsports Press Association Stock Car Hall of Fame. *1301 Harry Byrd Hwy, Darlington (29532). 1 mile W on Hwy 34 at Darlington Raceway, the oldest superspeedway in the country. Phone 843/395-8499. www.darlingtonraceway.com.* Explore Darlington's storied history with NASCAR. The Hall of Fame features everyone from David Pearson and Dale Earnhardt to NASCAR's first champion, Red Byron. Several rooms are filled with stock cars that once sped across the raceway, including the blue Plymouth that Richard Petty drove to victory in ten races back in 1967; a 1991 Chevy driven by Darrell Waltrip that rolled eight

times during a race; and a 1971 Mercury driven by Pearson, the all-time winner at Darlington. It adjoins a small gift shop. (Daily 9 am-5 pm; closed Thanksgiving, Dec 25) **$**

Liberty Lane Walk of Fame. *100 Pearl St, Darlington (29532). 100 block of Pearl St. Phone toll-free 888/427-8720.* Stroll down the Walk of Fame, which honors NASCAR stock car drivers who have won at Darlington Raceway. Compare your hands with the cement prints of NASCAR greats like Neil Bonnett, Dale Earnhardt, Bill Elliott, Harry Gant, and Richard Petty. **FREE**

Special Events

Mountain Dew Southern 500 Race Weekend. *Darlington Raceway, 1301 Harry Byrd Hwy, Darlington (29532). Phone 843/395-8499.* 500-mile stock car classic; beauty pageant; "Southern 500" Festival parade; golf tournament. Preceded by two days of trials. Labor Day weekend.

Sweet Potato Festival. *505 Anderson Dr, Darlington (29532). Phone 843/395-2940. www.visitdarlingtoncounty.org.* Entertainment, food, clowns and the famous spud are just some of the activities found at this event. Early Oct.

TranSouth Financial 400. *Darlington Raceway, 1301 Harry Byrd Hwy, Darlington (29532). Phone 866/459-7223.* Late-model stock car race. Late Mar.

Dillon (C-6)

See also Bennettsville, Darlington, Florence

Settled 1887
Population 6,316
Elevation 115 ft
Area Code 843
Zip 29536

Industrial growth and diversification characterize this town, which is the county seat. Dillon also serves as a shipping center for farm produce.

What to See and Do

Little Pee Dee State Park. *1298 State Park Rd (Hwy 22), Dillon (29536). 11 miles SE between Hwys 9 and 57, near I-95. Phone 843/774-8872. www.discoversouthcarolina.com/stateparks.* Along the Little Pee Dee River and convenient to Interstate 95, this

835-acre park offers a tranquil setting for picnicking, fishing in the 54-acre Lake Norton, camping, or just relaxing. Roam through the small river swamp and dry sandy areas and explore the variety of flora and fauna. (Daily 9 am-6 pm) **$**

Little Pee Dee State Park Camping. *1298 State Park Rd (Hwy 22), Dillon (29536). Phone 843/774-8872. www.discoversouthcarolina.com/stateparks.* Within the state park, youll find 32 sites with water and electrical hook-ups, and 18 tent sites with only water hook-ups. Dump station, restroom, showers. Reserved sites are $1 extra per night, while most sites rent on a first-come, first-served basis.

Full-Service Inn

★ ★ ★ **ABINGDON MANOR.** *307 Church St, Latta (29565). Phone 843/752-5090; toll-free 888/752-5090; fax 843/752-6034. www.abingdonmanor.com.* Located in the center of the Grand Strand, right on the Atlantic Ocean, the Beach Cove Resort is just minutes from theaters, shopping at Broadway at the Beach, and dining on Restaurant Row. Enjoy breakfast, lunch, and dinner at the on-site restaurant, or prepare your own meals in your guest room, which come equipped with either efficiency kitchens or full kitchens. 7 rooms, 2 story. Children over 10 years only. Complimentary full breakfast. Check-in 3 pm, check-out 11 am. High-speed Internet access, wireless Internet access. Restaurant, bar. **$$**
🅳

Restaurant

★ ★ ★ **ABINGDON MANOR RESTAURANT.** *307 Church St, Latta (29365). Phone 843/752-5090; toll-free 888/752-5090. www.abingdonmanor.com.* The elegant Abingdon Manor restaurant, located inside the charming inn of the same name, offers a creative menu of American fare using fresh ingredients, including herbs and vegetables from their own garden. American menu. Dinner. Closed sun. Bar. Business casual attire. Reservations recommended. **$$$**

Florence (D-5)

See also Bennettsville, Cheraw, Darlington, Dillon, Hartsville

Settled 1890

Population 30,248
Elevation 149 ft
Area Code 843
Information Greater Florence Chamber of Commerce, 610 W Palmetto St, PO Box 948, 29503; phone 843/665-0515
Web Site www.florencesccvb.com

Since extensive railroad shops and yards were established here by the Atlantic coastline, this community has grown from a sparsely settled crossroads into a major retail and wholesale distribution center. The economy is no longer dependent on agriculture; a balance of farm and industry has been attained. Florence is also the home of Francis Marion College and Florence-Darlington Technical College.

What to See and Do

Beauty Trail. 12-mile trail within city featuring beautiful gardens (usually best in Apr). **FREE**

Florence Museum of Art, Science and History. *558 Spruce St, Florence (29501). At Graham St. Phone 843/662-3351. www.florenceweb.com/museum.htm.* This interesting local museum showcases rotating art exhibits; historic objects from the Florence and Pee Dee area; Southwestern pueblo pottery; African and Asian artifacts; and a Civil War collection donated by Francis A. Lord, the author of a five-volume encyclopedia about Civil War collectibles. The museum also has an outpost Railroad Museum nearby, which allows visitors to stroll through a vintage caboose and box car filled with railroad memorabilia from Florence's days as a railroad town (June-Aug: Sat-Sun 3-5 pm). (Tues-Sat 10 am5 pm, Sun 2-5 pm; closed holidays) **$**

Florence National Cemetery. *803 E National Cemetery Rd, Florence (29506). S on Hwy 52/301 to Cherokee Rd. Phone 843/669-8783; fax 843/662-8318. www.cem.va.gov/nchp/florence.htm.* This is the smaller of South Carolina's Civil War cemeteries, after the better-known Beaufort Union captives who died at the neighboring stockade are buried here. Researchers have identified many of the dead, who were originally buried as unknown soldiers. Lists are available from the cemetery. **FREE**

Florence Stockade. *Stockade and National Cemetery rds, Florence (29506). Off National Cemetery Rd, near Hwy 95.* The stockade was a Civil War prison that housed Union soldiers transferred from the notorious Andersonville prison. Roughly 2,800 soldiers died there over about six months of operation, including

Florena Budwin, who Friends of the Florence Stockade say is the only female Civil War prisoner to die in captivity. She is buried in the adjoining cemetery. The site is a Civil War Heritage Site, and the society has put a marker along the south wall to commemorate the soldiers who died. A 1947 marker put up by the United Daughters of the Confederacy of Florence memorializes "the Confederate soldiers and the citizens of the community who in the line of duty guarded these prisoners." **FREE**

Jeffries Creek Nature Park. *1501 Hillside Dr, Florence. www.florenceweb.com/parks.htm.* Fishing. Nature trails. Picnicking, playground. **FREE**

Lucas Park. *501 Azalea Lane, Florence. www.florenceweb.com/parks.htm.* Picnicking, playground; tennis courts. Rose gardens, camellias, azaleas, rhododendrons; lighted fountain. **FREE**

Lynches River State Park. *902 Spine Rd, Florence (29530). 15 miles S off Hwy 52.* Phone 843/389-2785. Approximately 650 acres. Located on old stagecoach route. Swimming pool (fee), fishing. Nature trail, bird-watching. Picnicking, playground, community building. Primitive camping.

McLeod Park. *Santiago Dr, Florence. www.florenceweb.com/parks.htm.* Swimming pool (fee), fishing pond. Lighted tennis; basketball courts, ball fields. Picnicking, playground.

Mister Mark's Fun Park. *1331 N Cashua Dr, Florence (29501). Phone 843/669-7373. www.mistermarksfunpark.com.* This entertainment complex has a restaurant, an 18-hole miniature golf course ($), an oval sprint car track and go-cart road course ($$$$), and a 10,000-square-foot arcade. (Hours vary by season)

Pee Dee Golfing. *3290 W Radio Dr, Florence (29501). Phone 843/669-0950; toll-free 800/325-9005.* Pee Dee Golfing arranges packages including accommodations, breakfast, 18-hole greens fees, and cart fees. It can book times at a variety of local courses.

Pee Dee State Farmers' Market. *2513 W Lucas St (Hwy 52), Florence (29501). Between Florence and Darlington. Phone 843/665-5154; fax 843/665-5263. www.pdfarmersmarket.com.* The Pee Dee State Farmers' Market draws farmers from around the state and fills table after table with fresh produce and local cheese and honey. This is a great place for campers to find fresh food, or for racegoers to catch a break from restaurants. It's also the first stop for picnickers or hikers on their way to the region's parks. Open year-round. (Mon-Sat 8 am-6 pm)

Timrod Park. *400 Timrod Park Dr, Florence. Phone 843/665-3253.* One-room schoolhouse in which Henry Timrod, Poet Laureate of the Confederacy, taught. Playgrounds, picnic areas, barbecue pits; lighted tennis courts. Azalea display in spring. Test rose gardens. Nature trails; fitness station, jogging trail. Special fitness court for the disabled. (Daily) **FREE**

War Between the States Museum. *107 S Guerry St, Florence (29501). Phone 843/669-1266. www.florenceweb.com/warmuseum.htm.* Explore artifacts, pictures, and stories that bring you back to the Civil War. (Wed, Sat 10 am-5 pm) **$**

Woods Bay State Natural Area. *24 miles SW, off Hwy 301 and I-95. Phone 843/659-4445.* Approximately 1,500 acres of unique natural area with an abundance of wildlife, including alligators and more than 150 species of birds, in a "Carolina Bay" (an elliptical, swampy depression mostly underwater). Lake fishing, canoe trail (rentals). Picnic area (shelter). Boardwalk for nature and wildlife observation. (Thurs-Mon 9 am-6 pm) **$**

Special Event

Arts Alive. *Francis Marion University, Florence. Phone 843/661-1225.* Arts, crafts, music, dance, theater, demonstrations, exhibits. Apr.

Fort Sumter National Monument (E-5)

See also Charleston, Kiawah Island

Web Site www.nps.gov/fosu

On an island in Charleston Harbor. Accessible by private boat or by Fort Sumter tour boat, leaving from the City Marina, Lockwood Dr, Charleston; and from Patriots Point Naval Museum, Mount Pleasant.

The national monument includes Fort Sumter, located 3 miles southeast of Charleston at the harbor entrance, and Fort Moultrie, located 1 mile east of Fort Sumter on Sullivan's Island. Fort Moultrie is reached via Hwy 17 to Hwy 703; turn right and follow the signs. Fort Moultrie was originally built in 1776, of sand and palmetto logs. Colonel William Moultrie's forces drove British ships from Charleston Harbor at Fort Moultrie in June 1776. The present Fort Moultrie was completed in 1809 and was garrisoned by Union forces in late 1860, when these forces were moved to Fort Sumter.

South Carolina, the first state to secede, passed its Ordinance of Secession on December 20, 1860. Surrender of Fort Sumter was demanded on April 11, 1861. This demand was refused by Major Robert Anderson, in command of Union forces at the fort. At 4:30 am on April 12, Confederate firing began, and the fort was surrendered after 34 hours of intense bombardment. This attack compelled President Lincoln to call for 75,000 volunteers to put down the rebellion, thus beginning the Civil War. Fort Sumter and Fort Moultrie have been modified through the years. Both were active through World War II.

Fort Moultrie has been restored by the National Park Service; visitor center has an audiovisual program depicting the evolution of seacoast defense. Self-guided tour. (Daily; closed Dec 25) **$**

Fort Sumter's ruins have been partially excavated, and a museum has been established. (Daily; closed Dec 25) Contact the Superintendent, 1214 Middle St, Sullivan's Island 29482; phone 843/883-3123 or 843/883-3124. Daily tour boat (fee). **$**

Gaffney (C-3)

See also Charlotte, Rock Hill, Spartanburg

Settled 1803
Population 12,968
Elevation 779 ft
Area Code 864
Zip 29340
Information Cherokee County Chamber of Commerce, 225 S Limestone St; phone 864/489-5721
Web Site www.cherokeechamber.org

Once a prosperous resort town where plantation owners sought to cure malaria attacks with the supposedly therapeutic waters of the limestone springs, Gaffney is now a textile and metalworking center and the home of a variety of other industries and agricultural products, particularly peaches. On I-85, just outside of town, stands the Gaffney Peachoid (1981), an elevated tank that resembles a gigantic peach and holds a million-gallon water supply.

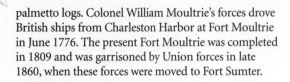

Gaffney Fun Fact

The Peachoid water tank in Gaffney is the only water tank of its kind in the world; it holds 1 million gallons of water.

What to See and Do

Cowpens National Battlefield. *4001 Chesnee Hwy, Gaffney (29341). 11 miles NW on Hwy 11, 1/2 mile from jct Hwy 110. Phone 864/461-2828; fax 864/461-7795. www.nps.gov/cowp.* This was the scene of the victory of General Daniel Morgan's American Army over superior British forces on Jan 17, 1781. The British suffered 110 men killed, 200 wounded, and 550 captured, while American losses were minimal. This victory was followed by the Battle of Guilford Courthouse, and then the forces moved on to Yorktown, where Cornwallis was forced to surrender. An 843-acre tract with exhibits, an information and visitor center, a self-guided tour road, and a walking trail with audio stations and a restored 1830 historic house. Slide program (fee). Picnicking (shelters). (Daily 9 am-5 pm; closed Jan 1, Thanksgiving, Dec 25) **FREE**

Kings Mountain National Military Park. *20 miles NE of Gaffney off I-85, near Grover, NC.* On these 3,950 rugged acres, a fierce attack by Carolina, Georgia, and Virginia frontiersmen in October 1780 broke up Britain's southern campaign. The mountain men and other patriots were faced with the invasion of their homes by advancing Tories. After traveling more than 200 miles, the Americans surrounded and attacked Cornwallis's left wing, which was encamped atop Kings Mountain spur and under the command of Major Patrick Ferguson. Although untrained in formal warfare, American patriots killed, wounded, or captured Ferguson's entire force of 1,104 Tories. Twenty-eight patriots were killed, and 62 were wounded. The battle led to renewed American resistance and American victory at Yorktown. Near the center of the park is the battlefield ridge, with several monuments, including the Centennial Monument, dedicated in 1880, and the US Monument, erected in 1909. The visitor center has exhibits and a film. Self-guided trail leads to main features of battlefield. (Daily; closed Jan 1, Thanksgiving, Dec 25) Contact Superintendent, PO Box 40, Kings Mountain, NC 28086. Phone 864/936-7921. **FREE**

Prime Outlets Gaffney. *625 Factory Shops Blvd, Gaffney (29341). At exit 90 off I-85. Phone 864/902-*

9911; toll-free 888/545-7194; fax 864/902-0096. www. primeoutlets.com. An open-air, village-style manufacturers' outlet. Contains 235,000 square feet of space, featuring 65 outlet shops. (Daily)

Special Event

South Carolina Peach Festival. *225 South Limestone St, Gaffney (29340). Phone 864/489-5716. www. scpeachfestival.org.* Arts and crafts, sports events, entertainment. Throughout July.

Georgetown (E-6)

See also Myrtle Beach

Founded 1729
Population 8,950
Area Code 843
Zip 29440
Information Georgetown County Chamber of Commerce, 531 Front St, PO Box 1776, 29442; phone 843/546-8436 or toll-free 800/777-7705
Web Site www.georgetownchamber.com

A seaport throughout its long history, Georgetown enjoyed a resurgence of ship traffic following the deepening of the channel and the building of a new cargo dock. The shore of Winyah Bay, on which Georgetown is situated, was the site of the first European settlement on the North American mainland outside of Mexico. In 1526, a group of Spaniards settled here, only to be driven out within a year by disease and Native American attacks. Rice and indigo plantations were established along nearby rivers around 1700. Georgetown was founded by Rev Elisha Screven, son of the first Baptists in the South; the city was finally laid out to honor King George II of England. It became increasingly important as an export center with quantities of lumber and naval stores, rice, and indigo. Lafayette landed near here to join the American cause in the Revolution. The city was later occupied by British troops. Known as a sawmill city during the first three decades of this century, Georgetown currently boasts several manufacturing industries as well as a thriving tourist economy.

What to See and Do

Brookgreen Gardens. *1931 Brookgreen Dr, Murrells Inlet (29576). 18 miles N on Hwy 17, 3 miles S of Murrells Inlet. Phone 843/235-6000; toll-free 800/849-1931;* fax 843/235-6039. www.brookgreen.org. On the site of former rice and indigo plantations, these gardens contain more than 500 pieces of American sculpture; boxwood, massive moss-hung oaks, and native plants; and a wildlife park with native animals. Creek and all-terrain vehicle excursions take visitors through forests, creeks, old plantation homes, and old rice fields that are now inhabited by alligators, snakes, and other creatures. Picnicking. (Daily 9:30 am-5 pm, until 9 pm Wed-Fri in summer; closed Mon in Dec; also closed Dec 25) **$$$**

Captain Sandy's Plantation Tours. *343 Ida Dr, Georgetown (29440). Phone 843/527-4106.* Leaves from Harborwalk Seaport. Three-hour plantation tours and five-hour Shell Island tours. **$$$$**

Fishing. Charter boats from docks. Channel fishing for bass or deep-sea fishing for barracuda, amberjack, albacore, bonito, mackerel. (Apr-Nov)

Hampton Plantation State Park. *1950 Rutledge Rd, McClellanville (29458). 20 miles S off Hwy 17. Phone 843/546-9361; fax 843/527-4995. www. discoversouthcarolina.com.* Restored 18th-century mansion was centerpiece of large rice plantation; ancestral home of Rutledge family. Guided tours on the hour, special programs. (Grounds: Memorial Day-Labor Day, daily 9 am-6 pm; rest of the year, Thurs-Mon 9 am-6 pm; mansion: Memorial Day-Labor Day, daily 11 am-4 pm; rest of the year, Thurs-Mon 1-4 pm) **$**

Harold Kaminski House. *1003 Front St, Georgetown (29440). Phone 843/546-7706; toll-free 888/233-0383; fax 843/545-4062. www.cityofgeorgetownsc.com/ kaminski.aspx.* (Circa 1760) Pre-Revolutionary house furnished with antiques. Hourly tours. (Daily; closed holidays) **$**

Hopsewee Plantation. *494 Hopsewee Rd, Georgetown (29440). 12 miles S on Hwy 17. Phone 843/546-7891. www.hopsewee.com.* (Circa 1740) Preserved rice plantation house on the North Santee River. Birthplace of Thomas Lynch, Jr., a signer of the Declaration of Independence. (Mar-Oct, Mon-Fri 10 am-4 pm; rest of year, Thurs-Fri 10 am-4 pm and by appointment). **$$**

Huntington Beach State Park. *16148 Ocean Hwy, Georgetown (29576). 17 miles N on Hwy 17, 3 miles S of Murrells Inlet. Phone 843/237-4440.* Approximately 2,500 acres. Ocean swimming, surf fishing. Hiking, nature trails; marsh boardwalk. Picnicking (shelters); playground; concession. Camping. **$$** Also here is

Atalaya. *Huntington Beach State Park, 16148 Ocean Hwy, Murrells Inlet (29576). Phone 843/237-4440; fax 843/237-3387.* Former home and studio of the sculptor Anna Hyatt Huntington. (daily 9 am-5 pm) Art festival (Mid-late Sept). **$**

Prince George Winyah Church. *300 Broad St, Georgetown (29442). Phone 843/546-4358. www.pgwinyah. org.* (Circa 1750) The English stained-glass window behind the altar was originally a part of St. Mary's Chapel for Negroes at Hagley Plantation on Waccamaw. The church has been in continuous use since its founding, except during the American Revolution and the Civil War. Tours are available. (Memorial Day-Oct, Mon-Fri 11:30 am-4:30 pm) **DONATION**

Town Clock Building. *633 Front St, Georgetown (29440).* (Rebuilt 1842) Tablet marks landing of Lafayette at North Island in 1777; Federal troops came ashore on the dock, at the rear of building, in an attempt to capture the town. Inside is

> **Rice Museum.** *Front and Screven Sts, Georgetown (29442). Phone 843/546-7423.* Maps, dioramas, film, artifacts, and exhibits depict development and production of crop that was once the basis of Georgetown's economy. (Mon-Sat 10 am-4:30 pm; closed holidays) **$**

Limited-Service Hotel

★ **CAROLINIAN INN.** *706 Church St, Georgetown (29440). Phone 843/546-5191; toll-free 800/722-4667; fax 843/546-1514. www.carolinianinn.com.* 89 rooms, 2 story. Pets accepted. Complimentary continental breakfast. Check-in 2 pm, check-out 11 am. Outdoor pool. **$**
🔃 🏊

Specialty Lodging

SEAVIEW INN. *414 Myrtle Ave, Pawleys Island (29585). Phone 843/237-4253; fax 843/237-7909. www. seaviewinn.net.* 20 rooms, 2 story. Closed Nov-mid-Apr. Pets accepted, some restrictions; fee, Children over 3 years only. Check-in noon, check-out 10 am. Beach. **$**
🔃

Restaurants

★ ★ **RICE PADDY.** *732 Front St, Georgetown (29440). Phone 843/546-2021; fax 843/546-0211.* American menu. Lunch, dinner. Closed Sun; holidays. Bar. Children's menu. Casual attire. **$$**

★ ★ **RIVER ROOM.** *801 Front St, Georgetown (29440). Phone 843/527-4110; fax 843/546-0706.* Seafood menu. Lunch, dinner. Closed Sun; Thanksgiving, Dec 24-25. Bar. Children's menu. **$$**

Greenville (C-3)

See also Anderson, Clemson, Clinton, Spartanburg,; also see Washington, NC

Founded 1797
Population 56,002
Elevation 966 ft
Area Code 864
Information Convention and Visitors Bureau, 206 S Main St, City Hall Building, PO Box 10527, 29603; phone 864/233-0461 or toll-free 800/717-0023
Web Site www.greenvillecvb.com

Greenville has several hundred manufacturing plants producing clothing, nylon, chemicals, plastic film, and machinery. It is best known for its numerous textile plants. Yet the town is also well named—beautiful trees line the streets, and there are many forested parks in the area. The Reedy River, passing over falls in the heart of Greenville, originally provided the city's power. Pleasant streets now border the twisting Sylvan Stream.

What to See and Do

Bob Jones University. *1700 Wade Hampton Blvd, Greenville (29614). At jct Hwys 29, 291. Phone 864/242-5100.www.bju.edu.* (1927) (5,000 students) During the academic year, the university offers vesper concerts (twice/month, Sun). Multimedia presentation (daily; closed holidays). Tours. On campus are

> **Bob Jones University Collection of Religious Art.** *1700 Wade Hampton Blvd, Greenville (29609). Phone 864/770-1331; fax 864/770-1306.* Houses collection of rare biblical material and collection of sacred art, including works by Botticelli, Veronese, Rembrandt, Rubens. Children under 6 years not permitted. (Tues-Sun; closed holidays) **$**

> **J.S. Mack Library.** *Bob Jones University, 1700 Wade Hampton Blvd, Greenville (29614). Phone 864/242-5100; fax 864/232-1729.* Contains Archives Room and Jerusalem Chamber, display area for the university's collection of rare Bibles. **FREE**

Caesars Head State Park. *8155 Geer Hwy, Cleveland (29635). 30 miles NW via Hwy 276. Phone 864/836-6115.* Approximately 7,000 acres. At 3,208 feet above sea level, the park overlooks a valley of almost impenetrable brush and dense forest. One side of the mountain resembles Caesar's head. Raven Cliff Falls. Scenic overlook. Hiking trails. Picnicking (shelter). Trailside camping, store, special programs. **$**

Greenville County Museum. *420 College St, Greenville (29601). Phone 864/271-7570; fax 864/271-7579. www.greenvillemuseum.org.* Permanent collection of American art, featuring historical and contemporary works. Changing exhibits include painting, sculpture, photography. Lectures, tours. (Tues-Sun; closed holidays) **FREE**

Greenville Zoo. *150 Cleveland Park Dr, Greenville (29601). Phone 864/467-4300. www.greenvillezoo.com.* Wildlife from around the world are displayed in natural, open-air exhibits. Picnicking, concessions. Lighted tennis courts, ball field; nature, jogging, hiking, and bicycle trails; park. (Daily; closed Jan 1, Thanksgiving, Dec 25) Children under 13 must be accompanied by an adult. **$**

Paris Mountain State Park. *2401 State Park Rd, Greenville (29609). 6 miles N off Hwys 276 and 253.Phone 864/244-5565.* Approximately 1,300 acres with three lakes. Thick forest setting with swiftly flowing streams. Lake swimming, fishing, pedal boats (rentals); nature, hiking trail, picnicking, playground, camping (hookups, dump station). (Daily 9 am-6 pm) **$**

Table Rock State Park. *158 E Ellison Ln, Pickens (29671). 16 miles N on Hwy 25, then 15 miles W on Hwy 11. Phone 864/878-9813.* Approximately 3,000 acres. Extends over Table Rock Mountain (elevation 3,124 feet) and valleys. Lake swimming; fishing; boating, canoeing (rentals). Hiking trail; carpet golf. Picnicking, restaurant, store. Camping (hookups, dump station), cabins; recreation building. Nature center; nature and recreation programs. (Daily 7 am-9 pm) **$**

Special Event

Freedom Weekend Aloft. *Anderson Sports and Entertainment Center, 3027 Mall Rd, Anderson (29625). Phone 864/232-3700; fax 864/271-9339. www.freedomwkend.org.* More than 100 balloonists compete. Memorial Day weekend. Also concerts, amusement rides (fee). **FREE**

Limited-Service Hotels

★ ★ **COURTYARD BY MARRIOTT.** *70 Orchard Park Dr, Greenville (29615). Phone 864/234-0300; toll-free 800/321-2211; fax 864/234-0296. www.courtyard.com.* This Courtyard property is located right off Interstate 385 (exit 39) and adjacent to the Haywood Shopping Mall. Downtown Greenville and Bi-Lo Center are just 3 miles away, and the Bob Jones and Furman universities are nearby. Guest laundry is offered, and a snack market is available in the lobby. 146 rooms, 3 story. Check-in 3 pm, check-out noon. High-speed Internet access. Restaurant. Fitness room. Outdoor pool, whirlpool. Business center. **$**
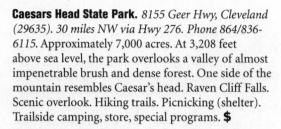

★ **DAYS INN.** *60 Roper Mountain Rd, Greenville (29607). Phone 864/297-9996; toll-free 800/329-7466; fax 864/297-9965. www.daysinn.com.* Guests looking for a good value will find it at this Days Inn property located just off Interstate 385 at exit 37. Less than a mile from the Haywood and Greenville malls, it is also 2 1/2 miles from the Palmetto Exposition Center and 9 miles from the GSI Airport and downtown. 121 rooms, 3 story. Complimentary continental breakfast. Check-in 3 pm, check-out noon. High-speed Internet access, wireless Internet access. Outdoor pool. **$**

★ ★ **EMBASSY SUITES HOTEL GREENVILLE GOLF RESORT AND CONFERENCE CENTER.** *670 Verdae Blvd, Greenville (29607). Phone 864/676-9090; toll-free 800/362-2779; fax 864/676-0669. www.embassysuites.com.* Located in the foothills of the Blue Ridge Mountains, this golf resort/conference center is also within minutes of the airport, Palmetto Exhibition Center, the Bi-Lo Center, and BMW and Michelin headquarters. Many lakes, whitewater rivers and other attractions, including shopping and dining locations are nearby. The lobby features a large atrium, lush plants, and waterfalls, and each guest room has a private bedroom, two televisions, a microwave, and refrigerator. 268 rooms, 9 story, all suites. Complimentary full breakfast. Check-in 3 pm, check-out noon. High-speed Internet access. Restaurant, bar. Fitness room. Indoor pool, outdoor pool, whirlpool. Golf, 18 holes. Tennis. Airport transportation available. Business center. **$**

★ **HAMPTON INN.** *246 Congaree Rd, Greenville (29607). Phone 864/288-1200; toll-free 800/426-7866; fax 864/288-5667. www.hamptoninn.com.* Located

across the street from the Haywood Shopping Mall, this Hampton Inn property is off Interstate 385 at exit 39. It is situated 1 mile from the Palmetto Exposition Center and 10 miles from the Greenville Spartanburg Airport. 123 rooms, 4 story. Complimentary continental breakfast. Check-in 3 pm, check-out noon. High-speed Internet access, wireless Internet access. Outdoor pool. Business center. **$**
🏊🚶

Full-Service Hotels

★ ★ ★ **GREENVILLE MARRIOTT.** *115 Parkway E, Greenville (29615). Phone 864/213-9009; toll-free 800/833-2221; fax 864/281-0801. www.marriott.com.* Conveniently located, this Marriott property is right off Interstate 85 (exit 54), minutes to downtown Greenville, adjacent to Michelin headquarters, and approximately 3 miles to the Greenville-Spartanburg Airport. The hotel has a contemporary theme, with marble floors and leather chairs in the lobby and yellow-striped wall coverings and light wood furniture in the guest rooms. A large plasma TV is set in the high-tech theater-style meeting room, where every seat is wired for the Internet. 204 rooms, 7 story. Check-in 3 pm, check-out 11 am. High-speed Internet access, wireless Internet access. Restaurant, bar. Fitness room, spa. Indoor pool, outdoor pool, whirlpool. Airport transportation available. Business center. **$$**
🚶🏊🚶

★ ★ ★ **HILTON GREENVILLE AND TOWERS.** *45 W Orchard Park Dr, Greenville (29615). Phone 864/232-4747; toll-free 800/445-8667; fax 864/235-6248. www.greenvillesc.hilton.com.* This hotel, located in Greenville's business district, is surrounded by landscaped gardens. Located off Interstate 385 (exit 39), it is just 3 miles to downtown Greenville and the Bi-Lo Center and 9 miles to the Greenville Spartanburg Airport. Also nearby are Bob Jones and Furman universities. The lobby is decorated in neutral beige tones and has an Asian feel. The ambience is calm and relaxed in the guest rooms, which are also decorated in beige tones. A snack shop is provided in the lobby. 256 rooms, 9 story. Check-in 3 pm, check-out noon. High-speed Internet access, wireless Internet access. Restaurant, bar. Fitness room. Indoor pool, whirlpool. Airport transportation available. Business center. Credit cards accepted. **$$**
🚶🏊🚶

★ ★ ★ **HYATT REGENCY GREENVILLE.** *220 N Main St, Greenville (29601). Phone 864/235-1234;* toll-free 800/233-1234; fax 864/232-7584. www.hyatt.com. Situated in the heart of downtown Greenville, this Hyatt property is only blocks away from Interstate 385 and within walking distance of the Bi-Lo Center. Also nearby are the Peace Center for the Performing Arts and Bob Jones and Furman universities. The ultramodern lobby features high-polished brick floors, an atrium ceiling, and an entire wall of glass, offering views of lush tropical plants and waterfalls. Guest rooms are decorated in aqua and terra-cotta hues. 328 rooms, 8 story. Check-in 3 pm, check-out noon. High-speed Internet access, wireless Internet access. Restaurant, bar. Fitness room. Outdoor pool. Airport transportation available. Business center. **$$**
🚶🏊🚶

★ ★ ★ **THE WESTIN POINSETT.** *120 Main St, Greenville (29601). Phone 864/421-9700; toll-free 800/937-8461; fax 864/421-0460. www.westin.com.* This historic hotel, built in 1925, is located in the heart of Greenville, amongst boutique shops and dining spots and near the Bi-Lo Center and Bob Jones and Furman universities. The lobby features plaster ceilings, crystal chandeliers, and terrazzo floors. Sitting areas and a balcony with wrought-iron railings look down upon the lobby. Guest rooms are decorated in warm beige hues and feature Heavenly Bedding. 200 rooms, 11 story. Check-in 3 pm, check-out noon. High-speed Internet access, wireless Internet access. Restaurant, bar. Fitness room. Airport transportation available. Business center. **$**
🚶🚶

Restaurant

★ ★ ★ **STAX'S PEPPERMILL.** *30 Orchard Park Dr, Greenville (29615). Phone 864/288-9320; fax 864/288-7202. www.staxs.com.* Guests can choose from several different dining rooms at this restaurant located in the Haywood Shopping Center. Situated approximately 3 miles north of downtown, it is right off Interstate 385 at exit 39. A wine room dining area, where guests can view many signed bottles, seats 24. Another dining room is set in an enclosed porch with window views. Walls are colored in slate blue and pottery tan and are contemporary in design. Tables are set with tan or blue tablecloths, have small lamps hanging overhead, and oil lamps set on top. The lounge features inviting sofas and soft upholstered booths for a more relaxed ambience. American, Greek menu. Dinner. Closed Sun; holidays. Bar. Children's menu. Business casual attire. Reservations recommended. **$$$**

Greenwood (D-3)

See also Anderson, Clinton, Newberry

Settled 1830
Population 22,071
Elevation 665 ft
Area Code 864
Information Chamber of Commerce, 110 Phoenix St, 29648; phone 864/223-8431
Web Site www.greenwoodscchamber.org

At the junction of highways and railways, Greenwood was originally the plantation of Green Wood; it later became known as the community of Woodville and finally adopted its present name. Greenwood's Main Street is one of the widest (316 feet) in the nation. The town enjoys diversified industry.

Greenwood Fun Fact

Greenwood, South Carolina, has the widest Main Street in the world.

What to See and Do

Baker Creek State Park. *Hwy 3, McCormick (29835). 28 miles SW via Hwy 221, Hwy 378 W. Phone 864/443-2457. www.discoversouthcarolina.com.* Approximately 1,300 acres. Lake swimming, bathhouse; lake fishing; boating (ramps). Nature, bridle trails; carpet golf. Picnicking, playground. Camping (dump station). (Daily 6 am-6 pm, to 9 pm during Daylight Savings Time) **$**

Hickory Knob Resort. *Hwy 4, McCormick (29835). 32 miles SW via Hwy 221, Hwy 378 W. Phone 864/391-2450; toll-free 800/491-1764; fax 864/391-5390. www.discoversouthcarolina.com.* On 1,091 acres. Water-skiing; lake fishing, supplies, boating (ramps, rentals). Nature trails; 18-hole golf course, putting green, field archery course, skeet range, field trial area. Playground, restaurant. Camping (hookups, dump station), lodge, cabins. Recreation and nature programs. Convention facilities.

J. Strom Thurmond Lake. *Clarks Hill,Hwy 1, McCormick (29821). 30 miles SW via Hwy 221, 378. Phone 864/333-1100; toll-free 800/533-3478. www.sas.usace.army.mil/lakes/thurmond.* Formed by the damming of the Savannah River. Fishing, boating (ramps). Picnicking (shelters). Campgrounds (fees). (Daily) **FREE**

Lake Greenwood. *302 State Park Rd, Greenwood (29666). 13 miles E on Hwy 34, then N on Hwy 702. Phone 864/543-3535.* On 914 acres bordering Greenwood Lake, which is 20 miles long and 2 miles wide. Water-skiing, fishing, bait shop, boating (ramps). Nature trails. Picnicking (shelters), store. Camping (hookups, dump station). Recreation building.

The Museum. *106 Main St, Greenwood (29646). Phone 864/229-7093. www.themuseum-greenwood.org.* Features a nostalgic "street" lined with houses, shops. Displays of minerals, mounted animal heads, Native American artifacts, ethnographic materials. Art gallery with regional art, traveling exhibits. (Wed-Fri 10 am-5 pm, Sat 2-5 pm; closed holidays) **$**

Ninety Six National Historic Site. *1103 Hwy 248 S, Ninety Six (29666). 9 miles E on Hwy 34 to present town of Ninety Six, then 2 miles S on Hwy 248. Phone 864/543-4068. www.nps.gov/nisi.* Site of old Ninety Six, an early village in South Carolina backcountry, so named because of its distance of 96 miles from the Cherokee Village of Keowee on the Cherokee Path. Site of the South's first land battle of the American Revolution in 1775 and of the 28-day siege of Ninety Six in 1781. The earthworks of the British-built Star Fort remain, along with reconstructed siegeworks and other fortifications of the period. Visitor center; museum, video presentation. Also here are subsurface remains of two village complexes, a trading post/plantation complex, and a network of 18th-century roads. (Daily 8 am-5 pm; closed Jan 1, Dec 25) **FREE**

Sumter National Forest. *In three sections: SW via Hwy 221; NW via Hwy 28; and NE via Hwy 72. Phone 864/561-4000.* Approximately 353,000 acres in the Piedmont Plateau and the Blue Ridge Mountains. Miles of trails through pine and hardwood forest; canoeing, whitewater trips, swimming, trout fishing; hunting for deer, turkey, quail; picnicking, camping. Fees may be charged at recreation sites.

Special Event

South Carolina Festival of Flowers. *Phone 864/223-8411. www.scfestivalofflowers.org.* Arts and crafts, photography display, musical groups, golf and tennis tournaments, theater, water show, Railroad Historical Exhibit, flower shows, Park Seed Flower Day. Third weekend in June.

Specialty Lodging

BELMONT INN. *104 E Pickens St, Abbeville (29620).*

Phone 864/459-9625; toll-free 877/459-8118; fax 864/459-9625. www.belmontinn.net. 25 rooms, 3 story. Complimentary continental breakfast. Check-in 3 pm. Check-out noon. Restaurant, bar. Historic building (1903); restored. Period reproduction; antique furnishings. **$**

Hardeeville (F-4)

See also Beaufort, Hilton Head Island

Population 1,793
Elevation 80 ft
Area Code 843
Zip 29927
Web Site www.cityofhardeeville.com

What to See and Do

Savannah National Wildlife Refuge. *1000 Business Center Dr, Suite 10, Hardeeville (31405). 17 miles S via Hwy 17. Phone 912/652-4415. www.fws.gov/savannah.* Approximately 25,600 acres. More than half the acreage consists of bottomland hardwoods reminiscent of the great cypress/tupelo swamps that once extended along the Carolina and Georgia low country. Argent Swamp can only be reached by boat; wild azaleas, iris, spider lilies, and other flowers bloom in succession, beginning in spring. Laurel Hill Wildlife Dr, open to cars, allows viewing of wildlife, especially waterfowl (Dec-Feb). Migrating songbirds are abundant in spring and fall. Tupelo-Swamp Walk (mid-Mar-Sept) is best for bird-watchers and photographers. (Daily; some areas closed Oct-Nov for hunting; impoundments N of Hwy 17 closed Nov-mid-Mar; Laurel Hill Dr hours posted at gate) **FREE**

Limited-Service Hotel

★ **ECONO LODGE AND SUITES.** *Hwy 17 and I-95, Hardeeville (29927). Phone 843/784-2221; toll-free 877/424-6423; fax 843/784-6102. www.econolodge.com.* 100 rooms, 2 story. Pets accepted, some restrictions; fee. Check-in 3 pm, check-out 11 am. Outdoor pool. **$**
🐾 ➳

Hartsville (C-5)

See also Bennettsville, Camden, Cheraw, Darlington, Florence

Settled 1760
Population 7,556

Elevation 200 ft
Area Code 843
Zip 29550
Information Chamber of Commerce, 214 N 5th St, PO Box 578, 29551; phone 843/332-6401
Web Site www.hartsvillesc.com

From a crossroads store, Hartsville has become a vigorous trading center, raising crops of cotton, soybeans, tobacco, and oats, and boasts 15 major manufacturers—including makers of consumer packaging, plastic bags, fertilizer, roller bearings, boats, brass, textiles, and paper. The town developed from what was once the Hart plantation and the pioneer store established by Major James Lide Coker, a Harvard graduate who founded a series of businesses here and built a railroad to the town.

What to See and Do

Hartsville Museum. *222 N Fifth St, Hartsville (29550). Phone 843/383-3005; fax 843/383-2477. www.hartsvillemuseum.org.* Founded in 1980, this local history museum is housed in a 1930s post office building. The galleries depict history, arts, and present-day events, and include Native American art and an ancient spinning wheel. After perusing the museum, head outside to wander through the sculpture courtyard. (Mon-Fri 10 am-5 pm, Sat 10 am-2 pm) **FREE**

Kalmia Gardens of Coker College. *1624 W Carolina Ave, Hartsville (29550). Approximately 2 1/2 miles W on Carolina Ave. Phone 843/383-8145. www.coker.edu/kalmia.* A 30-acre botanical garden with walking trails through blackwater swamp; mountain laurel thickets; uplands of pine, oak, and holly; and a beech bluff. Plantings of azaleas, camellias, and other ornamentals complement the native plants. (Daily, dawn-dusk) **FREE**

Lee State Natural Area. *487 Loop Rd, Bishopville (29010). Phone 803/428-5307. www.discoversouthcarolina.com/stateparks.* There are 25 sites for family camping and 23 designated for equestrian campers. A primitive equestrian camping area near the stable is available as well. Sites accommodate RVs up to either 30 feet or 36 feet. Water, electrical hook-ups. Restrooms, showers. Reserved sites are $1 extra per night, while most sites rent on a first-come, first-served basis.

Lee State Natural Area Camping. *487 Loop Rd, Bishopville (29010). 16 miles SW via Hwy 15, 3 miles S on Hwy 341, then 2 miles E off I-20, exit 123. Phone 803/428-3833.* Approximately 2,500 acres on Lynches River. Lake swimming; river fishing, boating (pedal boat rentals). Nature trails; horse trails, show ring, stable (no rentals).

Picnicking (shelters), playground. Camping (hookups, dump station). Recreation building. **$**

Hilton Head Island (F-4)

See also Beaufort, Hardeeville

Population 33,862
Elevation 15 ft
Area Code 843
Information Chamber of Commerce, PO Box 5647, 29938; phone 843/785-3673
Web Site www.hiltonheadisland.org

This year-round resort island, the development of which began in 1956, is reached by a bridge on Hwy 278. The island is bordered by one of the few remaining unpolluted marine estuaries on the East Coast and is the largest sea island between New Jersey and Florida. Its growth was rapid; there are 12 miles of beaches, and the climate is delightful. Activities include numerous golf courses and tennis courts; swimming; miles of bicycle paths; horseback riding; four nature preserves; and deep-sea, sound, and dockside fishing. The facilities also include nine marinas and a paved 3,700-foot airstrip with parallel taxiway. There are more than 3,000 hotel and motel rooms, more than 6,000 homes/villas/condos on the rental market, more than 200 restaurants, and 28 shopping centers. For the less athletic, there are many art galleries and numerous sporting and cultural events.

What to See and Do

Daufuskie Island Resort golf. *421 Squire Pope Rd, Hilton Head (29926). Phone 843/842-2000. www. daufuskieresort.com.* In terms of getting more golf for your money, Daufuskie is a good bet. Rates for both resort guests and day players are relatively low for the great course they get to play on in return for their greens fee. There are two 18-hole courses on the property, the Melrose (designed by Jack Nicklaus) and the Bloody Point (designed by Tom Weiskopf and Jay Morrish), both of which offer challenging holes and great views of the Atlantic Ocean, which abuts the courses at several points. **$$$$**

Harbour Town Golf Links. *Sea Pines Resort, 32 Greenwood Dr, Hilton Head Island (29928). Phone toll-free 888/807-6873. www.seapines.com.* Perhaps the most famous course in South Carolina, Pete Dye-designed

Harbour Town features its signature red-and-white-striped lighthouse, which serves as a backgroup for the course's 18th hole. The par-71 layout is less than 7,000 yards from the back tees, but the fairways can be narrow and the greens small, making for a good target golf experience. There are plenty of deep bunkers to make you think twice about challenging the greens, which can play fast and unaccepting to approach shots that are not hit well. Two other courses at the resort, Ocean and Sea Pines, add 36 more holes to the offerings. **$$$$**

Special Events

Hilton Head Island Celebrity Golf Tournament. *Phone 843/842-7711; fax 843/785-2163. www.hhcelebritygolf. com.* This golf event matches amateurs and celebrities to raise funds for 19 children's charities on 3 of the world's finest courses: The Golf Club at Indigo Run, The Robert Trent Jones Course in Palmetto Dunes, & The Harbour Town Golf Links in Sea Pines. Labor Day weekend. **FREE**

MCI Heritage Classic. *71 Lighthouse Rd #100, Hilton Head Island (29928). Phone 843/671-2448; toll-free 800/234-1107; fax 843/671-6738. www.mciheritage. com.* Harbour Town Golf Links. Top PGA golfers. Mid-Apr. **$$$$**

Springfest. *Phone 843/686-4944; toll-free 800/424-3387; fax 843/686-4169. www.hiltonheadhospitalityassociation. com/springfest.htm.* Food, wine, and seafood festivals. Sports events. Concerts, shows, and house tours. Mar.

St. Luke's Tour of Homes. *Phone 843/301-1568.* Tour of distinctive contemporary houses. Oct.

Limited-Service Hotels

★ **DAYS INN.** *9 Marina Side Dr, Hilton Head Island (29928). Phone 843/842-4800; fax 843/842-5388.* 119 rooms, 3 story. Complimentary continental breakfast. Check-in 3 pm, check-out 11 am. Outdoor pool. **$**
🏊

★ **HAMPTON INN.** *1 Dillon Rd, Hilton Head Island (29926). Phone 843/681-7900; toll-free 800/426-7866; fax 843/681-4330. www.hamptoninn.com.* 125 rooms, 2 story. Complimentary continental breakfast. Check-in 4 pm, check-out noon. Outdoor pool. **$**
🏊

★ ★ **QUALITY INN & SUITES.** *200 Museum St, Hilton Head Island (29926). Phone 843/681-3655; toll-free 800/784-1180; fax 843/681-5698. www.*

qualityinnsuiteshiltonhead.com. 127 rooms. Pets accepted; fee. Check-in 4 pm, check-out 11 am. Restaurant, bar. **$**

Full-Service Hotel

★ ★ ★ **CROWNE PLAZA.** *130 Shipyard Dr, Hilton Head Island (29928). Phone 843/842-2400; toll-free 800/334-1881; fax 843/785-8463. www.cphiltonhead. com.* Located in Shipyard Plantation, this 11-acre resort is paradise for golfers and tennis players. Of course, there are also miles of sandy oceanfront. 340 rooms, 5 story. Check-in 4 pm, check-out noon. Three restaurants, one bar. Children's activity center. Fitness room. Beach. Indoor pool, outdoor pool, children's pool, whirlpool. Tennis. Business center. **$$**

Full-Service Resorts

★ ★ ★ **DAUFUSKIE ISLAND RESORT AND BREATHE SPA.** *421 Squire Pope Rd, Hilton Head Island (29926). Phone 843/842-2000; toll-free 800/648-6778; fax 843/341-8524. www.daufuskieresort.com.* Part of the Daufuskie Island Resort, which also includes vacation cottages and villas.192 rooms. Pets accepted, some restrictions; fee. Check-in 4 pm, check-out noon. Three restaurants, four bars. Children's activity center. Fitness room, spa. Beach. Outdoor pool, children's pool, whirlpool. Golf, 36 holes. Tennis. Business center. **$$**

★ ★ ★ **HILTON HEAD MARRIOTT BEACH AND GOLF RESORT.** *1 Hotel Cir at Palmetto Dunes, Hilton Head Island (29928). Phone 843/686-8400; toll-free 800/228-9290; fax 843/686-8450. www. hiltonheadmarriott.com.* The hotel is located at Palmetto Dunes, within walking distance from the Shelter Cove Marina shops and attractions. 512 rooms, 10 story. Check-in 4 pm, check-out 11 am. Three restaurants, two bars. Children's activity center. Fitness room, fitness classes available. Beach. One indoor pool, two outdoor pools, three whirlpools, children's pool. Business center. **$**

★ ★ ★ **HILTON OCEANFRONT RESORT HILTON HEAD ISLAND.** *23 Ocean Ln, Hilton Head Island (29928). Phone 843/842-8000; toll-free 800/845-8001. www.hiltonheadhilton.com.* Enjoy the widest beach on the island at this lush, self-contained resort. Manicured gardens and lagoons adorn the property,

part of the 2,000-acre private Palmetto Dunes development. 324 rooms, 5 story. Check-in 4 pm, check-out 11 am. Three restaurants, two bars. Children's activity center. Fitness room, fitness classes available. Beach. Two outdoor pools, children's pool, two whirlpools. Golf. Tennis. Business center. **$$$**

★ ★ ★ ★ **THE INN AT PALMETTO BLUFF.** *476 Mount Pilla Rd, Bluffton (29910). Phone 843/706-6500; toll-free 866/706-6565; fax 843/706-6550. www. palmettobluffresort.com.* The Inn is surrounded by 20,000-acres of the natural beauty of Palmetto Bluff, affording spectacular views of the May River and surrounding islands. The spacious, well-appointed cottages feature such amenities as separate steam showers and bathtubs, plasma TVs, fireplaces, vaulted ceilings, and screened-in porches. Activities abound at Palmetto Bluff, from golf at the Inn's Jack Nickalus-designed, 18-hole course to boating and kayaking, fishing, beach excursions, history tours, and art classes. For guests wishing to indulge in total relaxation, the world-class Spa at Palmetto Bluff offers an extensive number of services, including manicures, pedicures, and facials as well as massages, body wraps, and aromatic baths on private outdoor verandas. When hunger pangs strike, The Inn is ready and waiting to provide both casual and fine dining experiences at Buffalo's, Golf Club Grill, and River House. Or, if you prefer something more intimate, enjoy dining in your room or on your private porch with the in-room dining service, available 24 hours a day. 50 rooms, all suites. Check-in 3 pm, check-out 11 am. Restaurant, bar. Fitness Room. Golf. **$$$$**

★ ★ ★ **THE WESTIN RESORT, HILTON HEAD ISLAND.** *2 A Grasslawn Ave, Hilton Head Island (29928). Phone 843/681-4000; fax 843/681-1096. www.westin.com/hiltonhead.* Situated on 24 acres of oceanfront property, this self-contained resort boasts everything from golf and water recreation to state-of-the-art business to first-rate dining facilities. Rooms have balconies overlooking either the ocean or the island. 412 rooms, 5 story. Pets accepted, some restrictions; fee. Check-in 4pm, check-out noon. High-speed Internet access. Three restaurants, bar. Children's activity center. Fitness room, fitness classes available. Beach. Indoor pool, two outdoor pools, whirlpool. Airport transportation available. Business center. **$$**

Full-Service Inn

★ ★ ★ **MAIN STREET INN.** *2200 Main St, Hilton Head Island (29926). Phone 843/681-3001; toll-free 800/471-3001; fax 843/681-5541. www.mainstreetinn. com.* The Main Street Inn is a beacon of sophistication on South Carolinas renowned Hilton Head Island. The heady scents of jasmine and gardenia fill the air and invite repose in the lovely Charleston-style gardens at this endearing hotel. The inn, with its sumptuous décor and personalized service, is the antithesis of the impersonal mega-resort. The 32 rooms are individually designed, yet all feature luxurious velvet and silk linens, unique artwork, and distinctive furnishings. A bountiful breakfast buffet is served daily in the elegant breakfast room, and afternoon tea is a daily tradition here, making it a challenge to venture beyond the inn's doors to explore the islands celebrated golf courses and beaches. 32 rooms, 3 story. Pets accepted, some restrictions; fee. Children over 12 years only. Complimentary full breakfast. Check-in 3 pm, check-out noon. Outdoor pool, whirlpool. **$**

Restaurants

★ ★ **ALEXANDER'S.** *76 Queens Folly Rd, Hilton Head Island (29926). Phone 843/785-4999; fax 843/785-2117. www.alexandersrestaurant.com.* American, seafood menu. Dinner. Closed Thanksgiving, Dec 24-25. Bar. Children's menu. Casual attire. **$$**

★ **AUNT CHILADAS EASY STREET CAFE.** *69 Pope Ave, Hilton Head (29928). Phone 843/785-7700.* Mexican, seafood, steak menu. Lunch, dinner, late-night, brunch. Closed Thanksgiving, Dec 24-25. Bar. Children's menu. Casual attire. **$**

★ ★ **CAFE EUROPA.** *160 Lighthouse Rd, Hilton Head Island (29928). Phone 843/671-3399; fax 843/671-6655.* Seafood menu. Breakfast, lunch, dinner. Closed Nov-mid-Feb. Children's menu. **$$**

★ ★ **CHARLIE'S L'ETOILE VERTE.** *8 New Orleans Rd, Hilton Head Island (29928). Phone 843/785-9277. www.charliesofhiltonhead.com.* Eclectic décor with French artwork and fresh flowers give this restaurant a feel of France. French menu. Lunch Tues-Sat, dinner. Closed Sun; holidays. Bar. Casual attire. Reservations recommended. **$$**

★ ★ ★ **HARBOURMASTER'S OCEAN GRILL.** *1 Shelter Cove Ln, Hilton Head Island (29928). Phone 843/785-3030; fax 843/842-2252. www.*oceangrillrestaurant.com. This is waterfront dining at its finest. Located on the waterway entrance to Shelter Cove Harbour, it offers the finest in creative cuisine. Exceptional service, unmatched ambience, and dramatic views offer the dining guest the finest the island has to offer. Seafood menu. Dinner. Closed Thanksgiving, Dec 25; also Jan. Bar. Children's menu. Casual attire. Reservations recommended. Outdoor seating. **$$$**

★ ★ **HOFBRAUHAUS.** *Pope Ave and Executive Park Rd, Hilton Head Island (29928). Phone 843/785-3663; fax 843/785-3663. www.hofbrauhausofhiltonhead. com.* Festive German décor; stained-glass windows, stein and mug collection. German menu. Dinner. Closed Sun after Thanksgiving to the week before Dec 25. Bar. Children's menu. Casual attire. **$$**

★ ★ **IRON WOLF CHOP HOUSE.** *Building B-6, Hilton Head Island (29928). Phone 843/341-2467; fax 843/341-6775. www.villageatwexford.com/IronWolf. htm.* Steak menu. Dinner. Bar. Children's menu. Casual attire. Reservations recommended. **$$**

★ ★ **JAXX.** *105 Festival Center, Hilton Head Island (29928). Phone 843/342-2400; fax 843/342-2871. www. jaxxofhiltonhead.com.* International menu. Dinner. Closed Sun; holidays. Bar. Business casual attire. Reservations recommended. **$$$**

★ ★ **LITTLE VENICE.** *Shelter Cove, Hilton Head Island (29928). Phone 843/785-3300.* Italian menu. Dinner. Bar. Casual attire. Reservations recommended. Outdoor seating. **$$**

★ ★ **OLD OYSTER FACTORY.** *101 Marshland Rd, Hilton Head Island (29928). Phone 843/681-6040. www.oldoysterfactory.com.* Seafood menu. Dinner. Closed Thanksgiving, Dec 25. Bar. Children's menu. Outdoor seating. **$$**

★ ★ ★ **RED FISH.** *8 Archer Rd, Hilton Head Island (29928). Phone 843/686-3388; fax 843/686-4628. www. redfishofhiltonhead.com.* Caribbean menu. Lunch, dinner. Closed Thanksgiving, Dec 25. Bar. Children's menu. Business casual attire. Reservations recommended. Outdoor seating. **$$**

★ **SCOTT'S FISH MARKET.** *Shelter Cove Harbour, Hilton Head Island (29938). Phone 843/785-7575; fax 843/785-6658.* Seafood menu. Dinner. Closed Jan. Bar. Children's menu. Casual attire. Outdoor seating. **$$**

★ **STEAMERS SEAFOOD COMPANY.** *28 Coligny Plz, Hilton Head (29928). Phone 843/785-2070; fax 843/785-8007.* Seafood menu. Lunch, dinner.

Closed Dec 24-25. Bar. Children's menu. Casual attire. Outdoor seating. **$$**

Isle of Palms (E-5)

Population 4,583
Area Code 843
Web Site www.isle-of-palms.sc.us

Full-Service Resort

★ ★ ★ BOARDWALK INN AT WILD DUNES RESORT. *5757 Palm Blvd, Isle of Palms (29451). Phone 843/886-6000; toll-free 888/778-1876; fax 843/886-2916. www.wilddunesresort.com.* Only 20 minutes from downtown, Isle of Palms is where Charlestonians have been coming to relax for decades. This breezy barrier island blends sophistication with seaside ease, especially at its top resort, Wild Dunes. The Boardwalk Inn, in the heart of the resort's old-fashioned walking village, is the shining star of this resort complex. Beachy elegance defines the atmosphere at this top-notch property. Two 18-hole Tom Fazio-designed golf courses, a 17-court tennis center, a marina, and a fitness center are among the many recreational opportunities available here, and the resort's plentiful restaurants make dining a memorable event. The resort's signature friendly spirit makes it a perfect choice for families, while its cosmopolitan attitude appeals to couples. 93 rooms, 5 story. Check-in 4 pm, check-out 11 am. High-speed Internet access. Two restaurants, two bars. Children's activity center. Fitness room, fitness classes available. Outdoor pool, children's pool. Golf, 36 holes. Tennis. **$$**

Restaurant

★ ★ THE BOATHOUSE RESTAURANT. *101 Palm Blvd, Isle of Palms (29451). Phone 843/886-8000; fax 843/886-0555. www.boathouserestaurants. com.* Seafood menu. Dinner, Sun brunch. Closed Dec 24-25. Bar. Children's menu. Casual attire. Outdoor seating. **$$$**

Kiawah Island (F-5)

See also Beaufort, Charleston, Fort Sumter National Monument

Population 1,163
Area Code 843
Information Visitor Center, 22 Beachwalker Dr, 29455; phone 843/768-5116 or 843/768-5117
Web Site www.charlestoncvb.com

Kiawah Island (pronounced KEE-a-wah) is one of the richest natural environments in the Middle Atlantic states. The island is a model for maintaining the ecological balance while allowing human habitation. Named for the Native Americans who once hunted and fished here, the island is separated from the mainland by the Kiawah River and a mile-wide salt marsh.

Extensive environmental study has helped preserve nature while also providing for human needs. Separate resort areas and private residential neighborhoods have been planned to provide a minimum of automobile traffic and leave much of the island untouched. The Kiawah Island Resort offers activities like golf, tennis, and nature programs that take advantage of the island's natural beauty.

Full-Service Resort

★ ★ ★ ★ THE SANCTUARY AT KIAWAH ISLAND. *1 Sanctuary Beach Dr, Kiawah Island (29455). Phone 843/768-6000; toll-free 877/683-1234; fax 843/768-5150. www.thesanctuary.com.* With five championship courses just outside its door, The Sanctuary at Kiawah Island is a natural choice for golfers, yet this serenely elegant resort appeals to a wide range of travelers with its fine dining, first-class spa, and beautiful setting. Just 30 minutes from downtown Charleston, this resort retains the sophistication and Southern hospitality associated with that city while celebrating its slow pace and rugged natural beauty. The accommodations blend traditional Early American-style furnishings with a crisp coastal ambience, and all rooms showcase ocean views from spacious balconies. Inspired by the beachfront setting, the nature-themed spa entices guests with its luscious treatments incorporating mineral-rich mud, seaweed, and botanical extracts, while the three restaurants also borrow from the locale with seafood-heavy menus and striking views of the water. 255 rooms. Check-in 4 pm, check-out noon. High-speed Internet access, wireless Internet access. Three restaurants, three bars. Children's activity center. Fitness room, fitness classes available, spa. Beach. Indoor pool, two outdoor pools, children's pool, whirlpool. Golf, 90 holes. Tennis. Airport transportation available. Business center. **$$$$**

Spa

★ ★ ★ ★ **SPA AT THE SANCTUARY.** *1 Sanctuary Beach Dr, Kiawah Island (29455). Phone 843/768-6000; toll-free 877/683-1234; fax 843/768-5150. www.thesanctuary.com.* With its serene, picture-perfect location off South Carolina's coast, the Spa at the Sanctuary is the ideal destination for relaxing the body and soothing the spirit. Taking its inspiration from nature and the charm of the South, The Spa gives luxury a new twist. Tucked inside The Sanctuary at Kiawah Island, The Spa is reminiscent of the back porch of a grand Southern seaside mansion. Outside, there are no sounds of urban life—just the gentle waves of the Atlantic Ocean and the jingle of the garden's delicate chimes. Inside, the hospitable staff greets guests with herbal tea and fresh fruit before guiding them to one of 12 rooms for magnificent nature-based treatments, which feature botanical extracts, natural enzymes, and a signature Southern touch. From facials and massages to customized spa experiences, the choices for relaxation are endless at The Spa. Try a Mint Julep...facial, that is. In this exfoliating treatment, invigorating mint is combined with equalizing minerals to gently clean, detoxify, and energize the skin. Or re-energize your entire body with the Lowcountry Verbena Body Polish. With fresh lemon verbena and mild buffing grains of ruby grapefruit and blood orange extracts, dry skin is massaged back into hydration. For the ultimate in indulgent experiences, The Spa offers "Spa Medleys," which last from two to four hours and include "The Fairway," ideal after a long day of golf; and "The Fit Retreat," a personalized training session combined with muscle relaxation therapy. If exercise in on your mind, head downstairs to the impressive fitness center. This ultra-modern facility features the latest cardiovascular and resistance equipment, a 65-foot-long indoor pool, and Pilates and yoga studios. But your experience at The Spa won't be complete until you have a chance to take it all in with a visit to the mineral whirlpool, steam room, or sauna. Isn't Southern hospitality wonderful?

Restaurants

★ ★ ★ ★ **OCEAN ROOM.** *1 Sanctuary Beach Dr, Kiawah Island (29455). Phone 843/768-6253; toll-free 877/683-1234. www.thesanctuary.com.* The Ocean Room is everything you would expect from a restaurant located within The Sanctuary at Kiawah Island (see), the sumptuous seaside mansion resort on Kiawah Island. The elegant dining space is warmed by mahogany tones and brightened by large windows with breathtaking second-floor views of the South Carolina coastline. The staff charms its guests with southern hospitality and caters to their every culinary whim with friendly yet unobtrusive service. Plates sparkle with selections from the menu of New American fare with a seafood focus. The culinary adventure may begin with an appetizer of seared Hudson Valley foie gras with sauted snow peas, sweet soy, and a snow pea sorbet; or a deconstructed shrimp BLT with heirloom tomato, baby organic arugula, and bacon aioli. That may be followed with seared rare Ahi tuna with crispy shrimp dumplings, wilted wasabi leaves, and lavender-scented jasmine rice; or strawberry and Serrano pepper glazed salmon with arugula, toasted pine nuts, jicima, and lime vinaigrette. If you're feeling especially indulgent, you can order a side of the Iranian ossetra caviar, priced at $220 per ounce. Seafood menu. Dinner. Bar. Business casual attire. Reservations recommended. **$$$**

★ **OLD POST OFFICE RESTAURANT.** *1442 Hwy 174, Edisto Island (29438). Phone 843/869-2339; fax 843/869-2372.* Childhood friends Philip Bardin and David Gressette revamped this community building into a Southern low-country restaurant in 1988. Guests will enjoy dining at this charming white-clapboard cottage. American menu. Dinner. Closed Sun; holidays; also one week in Jan. Bar. Casual attire. **$$**

Mount Pleasant

Founded 1680
Population 47,609
Information Mount Pleasant/Isle of Palms Visitor Center, 100 Ann Edwards Ln, 29464 (Bridge Way Village); phone 843/884-8517
Web Site www.townofmountpleasant.com

What to See and Do

Patriots Point Naval and Maritime Museum. *40 Patriots Point Rd, Mount Pleasant (29464). Phone 843/884-2727. www.state.sc.us/patpt.* This is an amazing assemblage of naval equipment and lore, appropriately located in Charleston Harbor. There's plenty of detail for adult visitors and ample space for kids to roam. The undisputed star of the show is the famed World War II aircraft carrier, the USS *Yorktown*. A film, *The Fighting Lady,* depicts life aboard the carrier. Onboard the *Yorktown* are numerous displays, including the Congressional Medal of Honor Societys museum and headquarters, the World War II Fast Carrier exhibit, the Battle of Midway Torpedo Squadrons memorial, and a World War II cruiser room. Other vessels include the *Savannah,* the worlds first nuclear-powered merchant ship; the *Laffey,* a World War II destroyer; the *Clamagore,* a World War II submarine; and the *Ingham,* a Coast Guard cutter. (Apr-Sept: 9 am-7:30 pm; Oct-Mar: 9 am-6:30 pm; closed Dec 25) **$$$**

Restaurant

★ **THE WRECK.** *106 Haddrell St, Mount Pleasant (29464). Phone 843/884-0052.* Seafood menu. Dinner. Jacket required. Outdoor seating. **$**
🄳

Myrtle Beach (D-6)

See also Georgetown

Population 22,759
Elevation 30 ft
Area Code 843
Information Myrtle Beach Area Chamber of Commerce, 1200 N Oak St, PO Box 2115, 29578; phone 843/626-7444 or toll-free 800/356-3016
Web Site www.myrtlebeachlive.com

With the Gulf Stream only a few miles offshore and dunes to shelter miles of white sand, Myrtle Beach is one of the most popular seaside resorts on the Atlantic Coast. Swimming, fishing, golf, tennis, and boardwalk amusements combine to lure millions of vacationers each summer. The many myrtle trees in the area give this resort its name.

What to See and Do

Barefoot Landing. *4898 Hwy 17 S, Myrtle Beach (29582). Phone 843/272-8349; toll-free 800/272-2320. www.bflanding.com.* With a mixture of specialty shops and factory stores, Barefoot Landing appeals to a variety of shoppers, from Birkenstock wearers to beer enthusiasts. There are also more than a dozen eateries and a variety of entertainment options, including the House of Blues for live music and a video arcade. (Daily, hours vary by season; closed Dec 25, Dec 31)

Barefoot Resort. *4980 Barefoot Resort Bridge Rd, North Myrtle Beach (29582). Phone 843/390-3200; toll-free 800/320-6536. www.bfresort.com.* Maybe the best place in Myrtle Beach to play golf, Barefoot Resort features four stunning courses designed by some of the sport's biggest names. Davis Love III, Tom Fazio, Greg Norman, and Pete Dye all took a piece of the land and crafted courses boasting their signature touches. The courses take the best of both British and American golf and bring them together in one spectacular place. **$$$$**

Broadway at the Beach. *1325 Celebrity Cir, Myrtle Beach (29577). Phone 843/444-3200; toll-free 800/386-4662. www.broadwayatthebeach.com.* This sprawling 350-acre complex, billed as the largest venue of its kind in South Carolina, brings together shops, dining, nightclubs, and a wide variety of entertainment. Shops run the gamut from Build-A-Bear Workshop to Gap to Harley Davidson, with many options for picking up souvenirs and beach items. When you get hungry, stop in at one of the center's many restaurants, which include standards like Joe's Crab Shack, Hard Rock Cafe, and NASCAR Cafe. Several of them stay open late, joining several nightclubs to offer dancing and libations. Also on-site are a 16-screen movie theater, an IMAX theater, a NASCAR SpeedPark, a miniature golf course, a water park, and an aquarium. Broadway at the Beach is home to the Myrtle Beach Pelicans, a Class A affiliate of the Atlanta Braves, too. (Daily, hours vary by season; closed Dec 25)

⭐ **"The Grand Strand."** Sixty miles of beach from the North Carolina border south to Georgetown. Camping, fishing, golf, tennis, amusement parks.

Myrtle Beach State Park. *4401 S Kings Hwy, Myrtle Beach (29575). 3 miles S on Hwy 17 Business. Phone 843/238-5325.* Approximately 300 acres. Ocean and pool swimming; surf fishing (supplies available). Nature trail. Picnicking (shelters), playground, stores. Camping, cabins. Interpretive center. **$**

NASCAR Speedpark. *1820 21st Ave N, Myrtle Beach (29577). Phone 843/918-8725. www.nascarspeedpark.com.* Enjoy racing fun with tracks you can drive, miniature golf courses, kiddie rides, an indoor climbing wall, bumper boats, an arcade, and NASCAR souvenirs. **$$$$**

Special Event

Sun Fun Festival. *800 N Ocean Blvd, Myrtle Beach (29577). Phone 843/916-7239. www.sunfunfestival.com.* More than 60 seaside entertainment events, including parades and pageants. First weekend in June.

Limited-Service Hotels

★ ★ **BEACH COVE RESORT.** *4800 S Ocean Blvd, North Myrtle Beach (29582). Phone 843/918-9000; toll-free 800/369-7043; fax 843/918-8399. www.beachcove. com.* Located in the center of the Grand Strand, right on the Atlantic Ocean, the Beach Cove Resort is just minutes from theaters, shopping at Broadway at the Beach, and dining on Restaurant Row. Enjoy breakfast, lunch, and dinner at the on-site restaurant, or prepare your own meals in your guest room, which come equipped with either efficiency kitchens or full kitchens. 320 rooms, 16 story, all suites. Check-in 4 pm, check-out 11 am. Restaurant, two bars. Children's activity center. Fitness room. Beach. Indoor pool, outdoor pool, children's pool, whirlpool. **$$**

★ ★ **THE BREAKERS RESORT.** *2006 N Ocean Blvd, Myrtle Beach (29578). Phone 843/444-4444; toll-free 800/952-4507; fax 843/626-5001. www.breakers.com.* 550 rooms, 18 story. Check-in 3 pm, check-out 11 am. Restaurant, bar. Children's activity center. Fitness room. Beach. Indoor pool, outdoor pool, children's pool, whirlpool. Airport transportation available. **$**

★ ★ **COURTYARD BY MARRIOTT MYRTLE BEACH-BAREFOOT LANDING.** *1000 Commons Blvd (Hwy 17), Myrtle Beach (29572). Phone 843/361-1730; toll-free 877/502-4653; fax 843/361-1729. www. courtyard.com.* Basic and reliable accommodations are found at this Courtyard by Marriott located in the middle of the Grand Strand. 157 rooms. Check-in 3 pm, check-out noon. High-speed Internet access, wireless Internet access. Restaurant. Fitness room. Indoor pool, whirlpool. **$**

★ **FAIRFIELD INN.** *1350 Paradise Cir, Myrtle Beach (29577). Phone 843/444-8097; toll-free 800/217-1511; fax 843/444-8394. www.fairfieldinn.com/myrfb.* Just 5 miles from Myrtle Beach International Airport and across the street from Broadway at the Beach, The Fairfield Inn offers vacationers location, location, location. Guest room are comfortable with basic conveniences, and an Information Center provides information on an array of area attractions. 111 rooms, 4 story. Complimentary continental breakfast. Check-in 3 pm, check-out noon. High-speed Internet access, wireless Internet access. Outdoor pool, whirlpool. Business center. **$**

★ **HAMPTON INN.** *1140 Celebrity Cir, Myrtle Beach (29577). Phone 843/916-0600; fax 843/946-6308. www. hamptoninn.com.* With its location in the 350-acre Broadway at the Beach complex, shopping and dining are right outside the Hampton's doorstep. The NASCAR Speed Park, Ripley's Aquarium, and the Palace Theater are also nearby, and the beach is just a few short blocks away. 141 rooms, 8 story. Complimentary continental breakfast. Check-in 3 pm, check-out 11 am. High-speed Internet access. Children's activity center. Fitness room. Indoor pool, outdoor pool, whirlpool. Airport transportation available. Business center. **$**

★ **HAMPTON INN & SUITES OCEANFRONT.** *1803 S Ocean Blvd, Myrtle Beach (29577). Phone 843/946-6400; toll-free 877/946-6400; fax 843/946-0031. www.hamptoninnoceanfront.com.* Shopping, golf, dining, and entertainment are all just a few short miles from the Hampton Inn, making its location ideal for a Myrtle Beach getaway. Guest rooms are nicely decorated in tones of blue and white and feature conveniences like irons, coffee makers, and high-speed Internet access. 116 rooms. Complimentary continental breakfast. Check-in 3 pm, check-out 11 am. High-speed Internet access. Fitness room. Beach. Indoor pool, outdoor pool, children's pool, whirlpool. Airport transportation available. Business center. **$$**

★ **LA QUINTA INN.** *1561 21st Ave N, Myrtle Beach (29577). Phone 843/916-8801; toll-free 800/687-6667; fax 843/916-8701. www.laquinta.com.* 128 rooms, 4 story. Pets accepted, some restrictions. Complimentary continental breakfast. Check-in 3 pm, check-out noon. High-speed Internet access. Fitness room. Outdoor pool, whirlpool. Airport transportation available. **$**

★ ★ **SHERATON MYRTLE BEACH CONVENTION CENTER HOTEL.** *2101 N Oak St, Myrtle Beach (29577). Phone 843/918-5000; toll-free 800/325-3535; fax 843/918-5004.* Situated in the center of Myrtle Beach, within walking distance to the Broadway at the Beach shopping Mecca, the Sheraton offers guests an ideal location in addition to comfortable accommodations. Guest rooms feature signature Sweet Sleeper Bed and soothing tones of beiges and greens. 402 rooms. Check-in 3 pm, check-out noon. High-speed Internet access. Restaurant, bar. Fitness room. Indoor pool, whirlpool. Airport transportation available. Business center. **$$**

Full-Service Hotel

★ ★ ★ **HILTON MYRTLE BEACH RESORT.**
10000 Beach Club Dr, Myrtle Beach (29572). Phone 843/449-5000; toll-free 877/887-9549; fax 843/497-0168. www.hilton.com. This beautiful oceanfront property offers magnificent views of the Atlantic Ocean as well as inviting accommodations. The atrium entrance features oversized white gazebos with comfortable sofas and chairs, while guest rooms are decorated in bright but soothing hues of gold, blue, green and terra-cotta. Nearby activities include shops at Broadway at the Beach, the NASCAR Speedway, the Palace Theater, as well as many dining options. 383 rooms, 15 story. Check-in 4 pm, check-out noon. High-speed Internet access, wireless Internet access. Restaurant, bar. Fitness room. Beach. Indoor pool, children's pool, whirlpool. Golf, 18 holes. Tennis. Business center. **$$$**

Full-Service Resorts

★ ★ **COMPASS COVE OCEANFRONT RESORT.** *2311 S Ocean Blvd, Myrtle Beach (29577). Phone 843/448-8373; toll-free 800/331-0934; fax 843/448-5444. www.compasscove.com.* Shopping, dining, and entertainment are all just minutes away from the Compass Cove, a sprawling resort in southern Myrtle Beach. Well-appointed guest suites feature all the comforts of home, including kitchens with ovens, microwaves, and refrigerators. 532 rooms, 16 story, all suites. Pets accepted, some restrictions; fee. Check-in 3 pm, check-out 11 am. Restaurant, bar. Children's activity center. Fitness room. Beach. Three indoor pools, outdoor pool, children's pool, whirlpool. Airport transportation available. **$$**

★ ★ ★ **EMBASSY SUITES.** *9800 Queensway Blvd, Myrtle Beach (29572). Phone 843/449-0006; toll-free 800/876-0010; fax 843/497-7910. www.kingstonplantation.com.* Modern and inviting, the Embassy Suites offers a perfect location for experiencing all that Myrtle Beach has to offer; theatres, restaurants, water parks, and shopping near Barefoot Landing are all nearby, as are the soothing sounds of the Atlantic Ocean. 255 rooms, 20 story. Complimentary full breakfast. Check-in 4 pm, check-out noon. High-speed Internet access, wireless Internet access. Restaurant, bar. Children's activity center. Fitness room. Beach. Indoor pool, three outdoor pools, children's pool, whirlpool. Golf, 18 holes. Tennis. Business center. **$$**

★ ★ ★ **LITCHFIELD PLANTATION.** *King's River Rd, Pawleys Island (29585). Phone 843/237-9121; toll-free 800/869-1410; fax 843/237-1041. www.litchfieldplantation.com.* 35 rooms, 2 story. Complimentary full breakfast. Check-in 3 pm, check-out 11 am. Restaurant, bar. Outdoor pool. Tennis. Business center. **$$**

★ ★ **OCEAN CREEK RESORT.** *10600 N Kings Hwy, Myrtle Beach (29572). Phone 843/272-7724; toll-free 877/844-3800; fax 843/272-9621. www.oceancreek.com.* Villas, garden homes, suites, and condos comprise this 57-acre resort located in the center of Myrtle Beach's Grand Strand. With outlet shopping, theatres, golfing, and dining on the famed Restaurant Row are all a short distance away, you'll never be at a loss for things to do. 400 rooms, all suites. Check-in 4 pm, check-out 11 am. Restaurant, bar. Children's activity center. Fitness room. Beach. Two indoor pools, seven outdoor pools, children's pool, two whirlpools. Tennis. **$**

Full-Service Inn

★ ★ ★ **THE CYPRESS INN.** *16 Elm St, Conway (29528). Phone 843/248-8199; toll-free 800/575-5307; fax 843/248-0329. www.acypressinn.com.* Relax in this graceful 12-room bed-and-breakfast located in the quiet town of Conway. Guests can enjoy bicycle riding or surrender their worries to a massage therapist. Tucked away in a quaint marina, guests have the options to take on deep-sea fishing or simply walk the beautiful stretches of South Carolina beaches, located only 15 minutes away. 12 rooms, 3 story. Complimentary full breakfast. Check-in 3-8 pm, check-out 11 am. **$**

Specialty Lodging

SEAVIEW INN. *414 Myrtle Ave, Pawleys Island (29585). Phone 843/237-4253; fax 843/237-7909. www.seaviewinn.net.* 20 rooms, 2 story. Closed Nov-mid-Apr. Pets accepted, some restrictions; fee, Children over 3 years only. Check-in noon, check-out 10 am. Beach. **$$**

SERENDIPITY, AN INN. *407 71st Avenue N, Myrtle Beach (29572). Phone 843/449-5268; toll-free 800/762-3229; fax 843/449-3998. www.serendipityinn.*

com. A quaint and casual inn, the Serendipity's lobby is furnished with a piano, wicker furniture, antiques, and fireplaces, while guest accommodations offer comfortable standard rooms with queen four-poster beds, queen suites with stoves; refrigerators; and microwaves, and king suites complete with full kitchens. 15 rooms, 2 story. Complimentary full breakfast. Check-in 3-7 pm, check-out 11 am. Outdoor pool, whirlpool. **$**

Restaurants

★ ★ **CAGNEY'S OLD PLACE.** *9911 N Kings Hwy, Myrtle Beach (29572). Phone 843/449-3824; fax 843/449-0288. www.cagneysoldplace.com.* Model airplanes hanging from the ceiling and antique memorabilia decorate the main dining room of this unique and casual restaurant located on Myrtle Beach's "Restaurant Row." American menu. Dinner. Closed Sun; also Jan and Dec. Bar. Children's menu. Casual attire. Reservations recommended. **$$**

★ ★ **CAPTAIN DAVE'S DOCKSIDE.** *4037A Hwy 17 Business, Murrell's Inlet (29576). Phone 843/651-5850; fax 843/651-8915. www.captdavesdockside.com.* Seafood menu. Lunch, dinner. Closed Jan 1, Thanksgiving; also week of Dec 25. Bar. Children's menu. Casual attire. Reservations recommended. Outdoor seating. **$$**

★ **CAPTAIN GEORGE'S SEAFOOD.** *1401 29th Ave Ext, Myrtle Beach (29577). Phone 843/916-2278. www.captaingeorges.com.* Fresh seafood takes center stage at this nautical-themed restaurant, known for its legendary buffet. Seafood menu. Dinner. Closed Dec 25. Bar. Children's menu. Casual attire. **$$**

★ ★ **CHESTNUT HILL RESTAURANT.** *9922 Hwy 17 N, Myrtle Beach (29572). Phone 843/449-3984; fax 843/449-7308. www.chestnuthilldining.com.* You'll find fresh, homemade American bistro fare and Southern hospitality at this casual Myrtle Beach restaurant. American menu. Dinner. Brunch. Closed Thanksgiving, Dec 24-25; also Super Bowl Sun. Bar. Children's menu. Casual attire. Reservations recommended. **$$$**

★ ★ **COLLECTORS CAFE.** *7726 N Kings Hwy, Myrtle Beach (29572). Phone 843/449-9370; fax 843/449-6129. www.collectorscafeandgallery.com.* It's a 2-for-1 deal at Collectors Café. Not only will your taste buds dance with delight from the Mediterranean-influenced fare at this upscale Myrtle Beach

spot, but your eyes will be treated to a feast as well. The dining room also serves as an art gallery, with an array of original artwork from 40 local artists adorning the brown and gold walls. The cafe's lounge area, a coffee house-like setting with more art pieces and colorful modern sofas and chairs, is a great spot to enjoy dessert and coffee, offered from noon to midnight. Mediterranean menu. Dinner. Closed Sun; also two weeks in Jan. Bar. Children's menu. Business casual attire. Reservations recommended. **$$$**

★ **DIRTY DON'S OYSTER BAR & GRILL.** *408 21st Ave N, Myrtle Beach (29577). Phone 843/448-4881; fax 843/626-2894. www.dirtydonsoysterbar.com.* A casual eatery just a half-block from the beach, Dirty Don's put out plates of wonderfully fresh seafood in a rustic, nautical setting. American, seafood menu. Lunch, dinner. Closed closed one week in mid-Dec. Bar. Children's menu. Casual attire. Outdoor seating. **$$**

★ ★ **JOE'S BAR AND GRILL.** *810 Conway Ave, North Myrtle Beach (29582). Phone 843/272-4666; fax 843/272-3691. www.dinejoes.com.* Whether you enjoy Joe's fresh continental cuisine inside the casually elegant dining room or outside on the deck near the wood burning fireplace, you'll be treated to lovely views of the marsh lands. Continental menu. Dinner. Closed Dec 25; first week in Jan. Bar. Children's menu. Casual attire. Reservations recommended. Outdoor seating. **$$**

★ ★ ★ **LOUIS'S AT PAWLEYS & THE FISH CAMP BAR.** *10880 Ocean Hwy, Pawleys Island (29585). Phone 843/237-8757. www.louisatpawleys.com.* Low country menu. Lunch, dinner. Closed Dec 25; also Super Bowl Sun. Bar. Children's menu. Casual attire. Reservations recommended. Outdoor seating. **$$**

★ **MARINA RAW BAR.** *1407 13th Ave N, North Myrtle Beach (29582). Phone 843/249-3972. www.marinarawbar.com.* Nautical memorabilia and mounted fish decorate this casual seafood restaurant, which offers beautiful views of the marina. Seafood menu. Lunch, dinner. Closed Thanksgiving, Dec 25. Bar. Children's menu. Casual attire. Outdoor seating. **$$**

★ ★ **SEA CAPTAIN'S HOUSE.** *3002 N Ocean Blvd, Myrtle Beach (29577). Phone 843/448-8082; fax 843/626-6960. www.seacaptains.com.* Fresh seafood is the star at the Sea Captain's House, where favorites like oysters, scallops, lobster, and crab are creatively prepared and served in a picturesque oceanfront setting. Six different dining areas with fireplaces and comfortable sofas and chairs add to the cozy atmosphere during dinner, while the screened patio is perfect for enjoying the beautiful ocean views during lunch. Seafood menu. Breakfast, lunch, dinner. Closed Dec 24-27; also one week in Jan. Bar. Children's menu. Casual attire. Outdoor seating. **$$**

★ **SHUCKERS RAW BAR.** *300 N Kings Hwy, Myrtle Beach (29577). Phone 843/448-6162.* Seafood menu. Lunch, dinner, late-night. Bar. Casual attire. Outdoor seating. **$$**

★ ★ **SUGAMI.** *9711 N Kings Hwy, Myrtle Beach (29572). Phone 843/449-7271.* Japanese, sushi menu. Dinner. Closed Memorial Day weekend. Bar. Casual attire. Reservations recommended. Outdoor seating. **$$**

★ ★ **TONY'S.** *1407 US 17 N, North Myrtle Beach (29582). Phone 843/249-1314; fax 843/280-9081. www. tonysitalianrestaurant.com.* The oldest Italian restaurant on the Grand Strand, this family-owned eatery has been going strong since 1953. Italian menu. Dinner. Closed Sun; early Dec-early Feb. Bar. Children's menu. Casual attire. **$$**

Newberry (D-3)

See also Clinton, Columbia, Greenwood

Population 10,580
Elevation 500 ft
Area Code 803
Zip 29108
Web Site www.cityofnewberry.com

What to See and Do

Dreher Island State Park. *3677 State Park Rd, Newberry (29127). 20 miles SE via Hwy 76 to Chapin, then 9 miles SW via unnumbered road. Phone 803/364-4152.* Approximately 340 acres. Three islands with 12-mile shoreline. Lake swimming, fishing (supplies), boating (ramps, rental slips). Nature trail. Picnicking (shelters), playground, recreation building, store. Camping (hookups, dump station; higher fees for lakefront campsites in summer).

Sumter National Forest. *4931 Broad River Rd, Columbia (29212). N via Hwy 121, Hwy 176. Phone 803/561-4000. www.fs.fed.us/r8/fms.* (See GREENWOOD.)

Orangeburg (E-4)

See also Aiken, Allendale, Columbia, Santee

Settled 1730s
Population 12,765
Elevation 245 ft
Area Code 803
Zip 29115
Information Orangeburg County Chamber of Commerce, 155 Riverside, Box 328, 29116-0328; phone 803/534-6821
Web Site www.orangeburgsc.net

Named for the Prince of Orange, this community is the seat of Orangeburg County, one of the most prosperous farm areas in the state. Manufacturing plants for wood products, ball bearings, textiles, textile equipment, chemicals, hand tools, and lawn mowers are all located within the county.

What to See and Do

Edisto Memorial Gardens. *367 Green St, Orangeburg (29115). S on Hwy 301, within city limits, alongside N Edisto River. Phone 803/533-6020; toll-free 800/545-6153. www.orangeburg.sc.us/gardens/edisto.htm.* City-owned 110-acre site. Seasonal flowers bloom all year; more than 3,200 rose bushes, camellias, azaleas; also many flowering trees. Gardens (daily, dawn-dusk). Wetlands boardwalk park. Tennis courts, disc-golf, mountain brook, picnic areas, shelters nearby, playground. **FREE**

South Carolina State University. *300 College St NE, Orangeburg (29117). Phone 803/536-7000; toll-free 800/260-5956. www.scsu.edu.* (1896) (5,000 students). Tours by appointment only. On campus is

   I. P. Stanback Museum and Planetarium. *300 College St NE, Orangeburg (29115). Phone 803/536-8710.* Museum has changing exhibits (Sept-May, Mon-Fri; closed holidays). Planetarium Christmas shows (First and second Sun in Dec, by reservation). **FREE**

Special Event

Orangeburg County Fair. *Orangeburg County Fairgrounds, 350 Magnolia St, Orangeburg. Phone 803/534-0358.* 4-H shows, tractor pulls, entertainment, and carnival rides are some of the activities found at this county fair. Mid-Oct.

Pawleys Island

See also Aiken, Allendale, Columbia, Santee

Full-Service Resort

★ ★ ★ **LITCHFIELD PLANTATION.** *King's River Rd, Pawleys Island (29585). Phone 843/237-9121; toll-free 800/869-1410; fax 843/237-1041. www. litchfieldplantation.com.* 35 rooms, 2 story. Complimentary full breakfast. Check-in 3 pm, check-out 11 am. Restaurant, bar. Outdoor pool. Tennis. Business center. **$$**

Specialty Lodging

SEAVIEW INN. *414 Myrtle Ave, Pawleys Island (29585). Phone 843/237-4253; fax 843/237-7909. www.seaviewinn. net.* 20 rooms, 2 story. Closed Nov-mid-Apr. Pets accepted, some restrictions; fee, Children over 3 years only. Check-in noon, check-out 10 am. Beach. **$$**

Restaurant

★ ★ ★ **LOUIS'S AT PAWLEYS & THE FISH CAMP BAR.** *10880 Ocean Hwy, Pawleys Island (29585). Phone 843/237-8757. www.louisatpawleys.com.* Low country menu. Lunch, dinner. Closed Dec 25; also Super Bowl Sun. Bar. Children's menu. Casual attire. Reservations recommended. Outdoor seating. **$$**

Rock Hill (C-4)

See also Chester, Gaffney

Founded 1852
Population 49,765
Elevation 667 ft
Area Code 803
Information York County Convention & Visitors Bureau, 452 S Anderson Rd, PO Box 11377, 29730; phone 803/329-5200 or toll-free 800/866-5200
Web Site www.visityorkcounty.com

Both a college and an industrial town, Rock Hill takes its name from the flint rock that had to be cut through when a railroad was being built through town.

What to See and Do

Andrew Jackson State Park. *196 Andrew Jackson Park Rd, Lancaster (29720). 9 miles N on Hwy 521. Phone* 803/285-3344. Approximately 360 acres. Lake fishing, boating (rentals). Nature trail. Picnicking (shelters). Camping. Recreation building, outdoor amphitheater. Log house museum contains documents, exhibits of Jackson lore. One-room school with exhibits. **$**

Catawba Cultural Center. *1536 Tom Steven Rd, Rock Hill. Phone 803/328-2427; fax 803/328-5791. www. ccppcrafts.com.* Located on the Catawba Indian Reservation, this center strives to preserve the heritage of the Catawba's culture. Tours and programs demonstrating the Catawba's culture and heritage are available (by appointment; fee). Gift shop. (Mon-Sat 9 am-5 pm; closed holidays) **FREE**

Glencairn Garden. *Edgemont and Charlotte Ave, Rock Hill. Phone 803/329-5620; fax 803/329-8786. www. rockhillrocks.com.* Municipally owned 8 acres of colorful azaleas, dogwood, redbud, crepe myrtle, boxwood; pool, fountain. (Daily, dawn-dusk) **FREE**

Historic Brattonsville. *1444 Brattonsville Rd, McConnells (29726). SW via Hwy 322, near McConnells. Phone 803/684-2327. www.chmuseums.org/ Brattonsville.htm.* Learn about local history in this restored village of over two dozen structures, including Backwoodsman Cabin, Colonel Bratton Home (circa 1780), Homestead House (circa 1823), and Brick Kitchen. Gift shop. Guided tours (by appointment). Self-guided audio tour. (Mon-Sat 10 am-5 pm, Sun 1-5 pm; closed holidays) **$$**

Lake Wylie. *N on Hwy 274. Phone 704/382-8587.* Created by Duke Power Company Dam on the Catawba River. 12,455 acres. Freshwater fishing, boating, waterskiing, swimming.

Landsford Canal State Park. *2051 Park Dr, Catawba. 15 miles S off Hwy 21. Phone 803/789-5800.* Approximately 250 acres. Site of a canal built in the 1820s; locks, stone bridges. Trail parallels canals. Picnicking (shelter), community building. (Thurs-Mon) **$**

Museum of York County. *4621 Mount Gallant Rd, Rock Hill (29732). 7 miles NW, off I-77 exit 82 A. Phone 803/329-2121. www.yorkcounty.org.* Contains a large collection of mounted African hoofed mammals; large African artifacts collection. Hall of Western Hemisphere contains mounted animals from North and South America. Art galleries and planetarium. Catawba pottery sold here. Nature trail, picnic area. (Mon-Sat 10 am-5 pm, Sun 1-5 pm; closed Jan 1, Thanksgiving, Dec 24-25) **$**

Winthrop University. *701 Oakland Ave, Rock Hill (29733). Phone 803/323-2236. www.winthrop.edu.* (1886) (5,000 students) Coeducational; 100 undergraduate and graduate programs. Concerts, lectures, sports, plays, art galleries. Large lake and recreational area.

Special Event

"Come-See-Me". *725 Crest St, Rock Hill (29732). Phone 803/329-7625; toll-free 800/681-7635; fax 803/329-7761. www.comeseeme.rockhill.net.* Art shows, tour of houses, entertainment, road race, concerts. 10 days early Apr.

Limited-Service Hotels

★ **HAMPTON INN.** *2111 Tabor Dr, Rock Hill (29730). Phone 803/325-1100; toll-free 800/426-7866; fax 803/325-7814. www.hamptoninn.com.* This Hampton Inn is located off exit 79 of Interstate 77, near Winthrop University, and approximately 25 miles south of Charlotte. Features here include three meeting rooms, a double setup in the business center, guest laundry, and a Tuesday and Thursday wine and cheese reception. 162 rooms, 5 story. Complimentary continental breakfast. Check-in 2 pm, check-out 11 am. Wireless Internet access. Fitness room. Outdoor pool. Business center. **$**
🕐 ➤ 🏃

★ **MICROTEL INN & SUITES CHARLOTTE/ ROCK HILL.** *1047 Riverview Rd, Rock Hill (29730). Phone 803/817-7700; fax 803/817-7700.* 77 rooms. Check-in 3 pm, check-out 11 am. **$**

Specialty Lodging

EAST MAIN GUEST HOUSE. *600 E Main St, Rock Hill (29730). Phone 803/366-1161; fax 803/366-1210. www.eastmainsc.com.* With a convenient location, East Main Guest House is just minutes from downtown Rock Hill, Winthrop University, Manchester Village shopping complex, and Interstate 77. Built in 1916, this gray brick Cape Cod features tastefully decorated rooms and a common area, equipped with a TV, refrigerator, snacks, and games. The garden area, to the rear of the inn, is a relaxing spot where guests can unwind. 3 rooms, 2 story. Children over 12 years only. Complimentary full breakfast. Check-in 3 pm, check-out 11 am. Built in 1910. **$**
🅓

Restaurant

★ **TAM'S TAVERN.** *1027 Oakland Ave, Rock Hill (29732). Phone 803/329-2226. www.tamstavern.com.* Tam's Tavern is near Winthrop University, Interstate 77, and within minutes of lodging. The dining room tables are covered with laminated Waverly floral prints, and a sitting area offers intimate booths. The artwork consists of the largest animated picture collection on the East Coast. Cajun, seafood menu. Lunch, dinner. Closed Sun; also week of July 4. Bar. Business casual attire. Reservations recommended. **$$**

Santee (E-5)

See also Orangeburg

Population 740
Elevation 250 ft
Area Code 803
Zip 29142
Information Santee-Cooper Country, 9302 Old Hwy 6, PO Drawer 40; phone 803/854-2131 or toll-free 800/227-8510 outside SC
Web Site www.santeecoopercountry.org

This community serves as the gateway to the Santee-Cooper lakes recreation area, created by the Pinopolis and Santee dams on the Santee and Cooper rivers. There are numerous marinas and campgrounds on the Santee-Cooper lakes.

What to See and Do

Eutaw Springs Battlefield Site. *12 miles SE off Hwy 6.* Site where ragged colonials fought the British on Sept 8, 1781, in what is considered to be the last major engagement in South Carolina; both sides claimed victory. Three acres maintained by state. No facilities. **FREE**

Fort Watson Battle Site and Indian Mound. *4 miles N, 1 mile off Hwy 15/301. On Lake Marion.* A 48-foot-high mound; site of American Revolution battle April 15-23, 1781, during which General Francis Marion attacked and captured a British fortification, its garrison, supplies, and ammunition. Three acres maintained by state. No facilities. Observation point has view of Santee-Cooper waters. **FREE**

Santee National Wildlife Refuge. *Secondary State Rd 803 and Hwy 301/15, Summerton (29148). 4 miles N on Hwy 15/301 or exit 102 from I-95. Phone 803/478-2217.* Attracts many geese and ducks during winter. Observation tower, self-guided nature trail; visitor information center with exhibits (Tues-Sun 8 am-4 pm; closed holidays). Seasonal hunting and fishing, wildlife observation, and photography. **FREE**

Santee State Park. *251 State Park Rd, Santee (29152). 3 miles NW off Hwy 6. On shores of Lake Marion.* Phone 803/854-2408. Approximately 2,500 acres. Lake swimming, fishing (supplies available), boating (ramp, rentals, dock). Scenic lake tours. Nature trails; tennis. Picnicking (shelters), playground, restaurant, groceries. Camping, cabins (higher fees for lakefront sites), primitive camping. Interpretive center, recreation building. **$**

Limited-Service Hotel

★ ★ **BEST WESTERN.** *Hwy 95 exit 98, Santee (29142). Phone 803/854-3089; fax 803/854-3093. www. bestwestern.com.* 108 rooms. Complimentary continental breakfast. Check-in 1 pm, check-out 11 am. Restaurant. Outdoor pool, whirlpool. **$**
🌊

Spartanburg (C-3)

See also Clinton, Gaffney, Greenville

Founded 1785
Population 39,673
Elevation 816 ft
Area Code 864
Information Convention and Visitors Bureau, 298 Magnolia St, PO Box 1636, 29306; phone 864/594-5050
Web Site www.visitspartanburg.com

An array of highways and railroads feeds agricultural products into, and moves manufactured products out of, heavily industrialized Spartanburg. Textiles and peaches are the leading products. The Spartan Regiment of South Carolina militia, heroes of the Battle at Cowpens, gave both the county and its seat their names.

What to See and Do

Croft State Park. *450 Croft State Park Rd, Spartanburg (29302). 3 miles SE on Hwy 56. Phone 864/585-1283.* On part of old Camp Croft military area. Approximately 7,000 acres. Swimming pool (fee), lake fishing. Nature, exercise trails, bridle trail (no rentals); stable, show ring; tennis. Picnicking (shelters), playground. Camping (hookups, dump station). **$**

Regional Museum. *100 E Main St, Spartanburg (29306). Phone 864/596-3501. www.spartanarts.org/ history/Regional_Museum/Museum_text.htm.* Exhibits depict up-country history of state; Pardo Stone (1567), doll collections, Native American artifacts. (Tues-Sat 10 am-5 pm; closed holidays) **$**

The Spartanburg County Museum of Art. *385 S Spring St, Spartanburg (29306). Phone 864/582-7616; fax 864/948-5353. www.spartanburgartmuseum.org.* Permanent and changing exhibits; classes in visual and performing arts. (Mon-Fri 9 am-5 pm, Sat 10 am-2 pm, Sun 2-5 pm; closed holidays) **FREE**

Walnut Grove Plantation. *1200 Otts Shoals Rd, Roebuck (29376). 8 miles SE near jct I-26, Hwy 221. Phone 864/576-6546. www.spartanarts.org.* (1765). Restored girlhood home of Kate Moore Barry, Revolutionary heroine; period furniture; schoolhouse, kitchen, doctor's office, other buildings; family cemetery; herb gardens with "dipping well." Tours on the hour (Apr-Oct: Tues-Sat 11 am-5 pm, Sun 2-5 pm; rest of year, Sat 11 am-5 pm, Sun 2-5 pm; closed holidays) **$$**

Special Event

Piedmont Interstate Fair. *575 Fairgrounds Rd, Spartanburg (29305). Phone 864/582-7042. www. piedmontinterstatefair.com.* Art exhibit, livestock and flower shows, needlecraft and food displays; auto race. Second full week in Oct.

Summerville (E-5)

See also Charleston

Population 27,752
Information Summerville-Dorchester County Chamber of Commerce and Visitor Center, 402 N Main St, 29483; phone 843/873-2931
Web Site www.summervilletourism.com

What to See and Do

✪ **Francis Beidler Forest.** *336 Sanctuary Rd, Summerville (29483). From Charleston, 40 miles NW via I-26 W to exit 187, then S on Hwy 27 to Hwy 78, then W to Hwy 178 and follow the signs. Phone 843/462-2150. www.audubon.org/local/sanctuary/beidler.* Located in the heart of the low country, this 11,000-acre site in Four Holes Swamp encompasses the largest remaining virgin stand of bald cypress and tupelo gum trees in the world. Oak, ash, and blackgum also grow here, as do

300 varieties of wildlife and numerous flowers, ferns, vines, and other plants. The swamp is fed by springs and runoff from surrounding areas (probably carved by tides and wind when the Atlantic Ocean covered more of the coastal plain than it does now) and joins the Edisto River, from which it exits into the ocean. A National Audubon Society sanctuary, the forest is named for a lumberman who championed conservation on both public and private lands. A 6,500-foot boardwalk into the swamp leads out from and back to the visitor center. Guided walks and canoe trips are available. (Tues-Sun 9 am-5 pm; closed holidays) **$$**

Old Dorchester State Historic Site. *300 State Park Rd, Summerville (29485). 19 miles NW on Hwy 642. Phone 843/873-1740.* This 325-acre park is on the site of a colonial village founded in 1697 by a group representing the Congregational Church of Dorchester, Massachusetts. The town prospered, but it was seized by the British during the American Revolution. By the time the war was over, the town had been abandoned. Overlooking the Ashley River, the site today includes remnants of a fort, a cemetery, and the bell tower of St. Georges Parish Church. Archaeological excavations are ongoing. Kiosks describe the history of the area and what life was like on the upper Ashley River. Fishing, hiking, boating, and picnic areas are available. (Thurs-Mon 9 am-6 pm) **$**

Full-Service Resort

★ ★ ★ ★ **WOODLANDS RESORT & INN.** *125 Parsons Rd, Summerville (29483). Phone 843/875-2600; toll-free 800/774-9999; fax 843/875-2603. www.woodlandsinn.com.* The Woodlands Resort & Inn expertly blends the essence of the English countryside with the inimitable flavor of the South. This country estate, set on 42 acres, is a lovely retreat just down the road from some of the low country's most famous plantations. The 1906 Greek Revival Main House has casual, refined, and lavishly appointed guest rooms designed by interior decorator David Eskell-Briggs. Individually characterized, the accommodations share a common theme of English floral patterns and Early American reproductions. Guests dip their toes in the pool, volley on the two clay tennis courts, play croquet matches on the lawn, and ride bikes to the nearby town of Summerville. Sandalwoods Day Spa features Aveda products in all of its treatments. The Dining Room (see) turns out delicious meals and is a sight to be seen with its 14-foot coffered ceilings of blue sky and white clouds. 19 rooms, 3 story. Pets accepted. Check-in 3 pm, check-out noon. Restaurant, bar. Chil-

dren's activity center. Outdoor pool. Tennis. Airport transportation available. Business center. **$$$**

Restaurant

★ ★ ★ ★ **THE DINING ROOM AT THE WOODLANDS.** *125 Parsons Rd, Summerville (29483). Phone 843/308-2115; toll-free 800/774-9999; fax 843/875-2603. www.woodlandsinn.com.* Inside the Woodlands Resort & Inn (see), a charming 1906 country home turned resort just a short distance from Charleston, you'll discover The Dining Room, an elegant European-styled restaurant that is accented with fresh roses, cherry wood furnishings, cream-colored walls, a marble fireplace, and white linen tables topped with fine crystal and floral-print china. Perfecting the atmosphere of Southern charm in a post-plantation setting, The Dining Room offers gracious service and a daily changing menu of flavorful, regional American dishes that play with colorful accents from the Mediterranean, Asia, and the American South. The kitchen showers loving attention on ingredients from the region, often mentioning local farmers by name. This practice adds a nice sense of place to the menu and enhances your experience on an educational level. The trouble with an evening at The Dining room at the Woodlands is that, as with most good things, it must come to an end. But with desserts like white chocolate beignets, it is a sweet ending indeed. American menu. Breakfast, lunch, dinner, Sun brunch. Bar. Jacket required (dinner). Reservations recommended. Valet parking. Outdoor seating. **$$$$**

Sumter (D-5)

See also Camden, Columbia

Settled 1785
Population 39,643
Elevation 173 ft
Area Code 803
Information Convention and Visitors Bureau, 32 E Calhoun St, PO Box 1449, 29150; phone 803/778-5434 or toll-free 800/688-4748
Web Site www.sumter-sc-tourism.com

Long the center of a prosperous agricultural area, Sumter has, in recent years, become an industrial center. Both the city and county are named for General Thomas Sumter, the "fighting gamecock" of the American Revolution. As a tourism spot, Sumter offers a unique contrast of antebellum mansions and modern facilities. Shaw Air Force Base, headquarters of the 9th Air Force and the 363rd Tactical Fighter Wing, is nearby.

What to See and Do

Church of the Holy Cross. *335 N Kings Hwy, State-burg (29154). 10 miles W via Hwy 76, exit at Hwy 261. Phone 803/494-8101; toll-free 800/688-4748; fax 803/775-0915. www.dioceseofsc.org/churches/hcs.htm.* (1850) Built of *pise de terre* (rammed earth); unusual architectural design and construction. Also noted for stained-glass windows set to catch the rays of the rising sun. Many notable South Carolinians from the 1700s are buried in the old church cemetery, including Joel R. Poinsett. **FREE**

Opera House. *21 N Main St, Sumter (29150). Phone 803/436-2616; toll-free 888/688-4748. www.sumter-sc.com.* Today the 1893 Opera House stands not only as a symbol of the past but also as an active sign of the ongoing progressive spirit of the people of Sumter. The 600-seat auditorium is used for concerts, school events, and other local happenings. Fees vary for booked activities; many performances are free. (By appointment only; closed holidays) **FREE**

Poinsett State Park. *6660 Poinsett Park Rd, Wedge-field (29168). 18 miles SW via Hwy 763, 261. Phone 803/494-8177.* Approximately 1,000 acres of mountains, swamps. Named for Joel R. Poinsett, who introduced the poinsettia (which originated in Mexico) to the US. Spanish moss, mountain laurel, rhododendron. Fishing, boating (rentals). Hiking, nature trails;. Picnicking (shelters). Primitive and improved camping (dump station), cabins. Nature center. **$**

Sumter County Museum. *122 N Washington St, Sumter (29151). Phone 803/775-0908; fax 803/436-5820. www.sumtercountymuseum.org.* Two-story Edwardian house depicting Victorian lifestyle; period rooms, historical exhibits, war memorabilia, economic and cultural artifacts, artwork, and archives (genealogical research). Museum is surrounded by formal gardens designed by Robert Marvin; several outdoor exhibits of farm implements, rural life; carriage house. (Tues-Sat 10 am-5 pm, Sun 2-5 pm; closed holidays) **DONATION**

Sumter Gallery of Art. *200 Hasel St, Sumter (29151). Phone 803/775-0543. www.sumtercountymuseum.org.* Located in the new 24,000 square foot facility at the Sumter County Cultural Center, regional artwork features paintings, drawings, sculpture, photography, and pottery; permanent collection of touchable works for the blind and changing exhibits. (Tues-Sat 11 am-5 pm, Sun 1:30-5 pm) **FREE**

Swan Lake Iris Gardens. *822 W Liberty St, Sumter. Phone 803/436-2640. www.sumter-sc.com/VisitingUs/SwanLake.aspx.* Covers 150 acres. Kaemp-feri and Japanese iris; seasonal plantings, nature trails; ancient cypress, oak, and pine trees; 45-acre lake with all eight species of swan. Picnicking, playground. (Daily 7:30 am-dusk) Home to the Iris Festival held every May. (See SPECIAL EVENTS) **FREE**

Special Events

Sumter Iris Festival. *Swan Lake Iris Gardens, 822 West Liberty St, Sumter. Phone 803/436-2640; toll-free 800/688-4748; fax 803/436-2652. www.sumtersc.gov/VisitingUs/Festivals_Iris.aspx.* Fireworks display, parade, art show, golf and tennis tournaments, barbecue cook-off, local talent exhibition, square dance, iris gardens display. Late May.

Visual and Performing Arts Festival. *Central Carolina Technical College, 506 N Guignard Dr, Sumter (29150). Phone 803/778-6653.* Features visual and performing arts, concerts, and choral groups. Third weekend in Oct.

Limited-Service Hotel

★ **FAIRFIELD INN.** *2390 Broad St, Sumter (29150). Phone 803/469-9001; toll-free 800/228-2800; fax 803/469-9070. www.fairfieldinn.com.* Close to a number of area universities and colleges, as well as the Swan Lake Iris Gardens and the Sumter Opera House, this well-appointed hotel is sure to please guests. 124 rooms, 2 story. Complimentary continental breakfast. Check-in 3 pm, check-out noon. Fitness room. Outdoor pool. Business center. **$**

Walterboro (E-4)

See also Allendale, Beaufort, Charleston

Settled 1784
Population 5,153
Area Code 843
Zip 29488
Information Walterboro-Colleton Chamber of Commerce, 109 Benson St, PO Box 426; phone 843/549-9595
Web Site www.walterboro.org

Settled in 1784 by Charleston plantation owners as a summer resort area, Walterboro has retained its charm of yesterday despite its growth. The town boasts a casual pace and rural lifestyle where people can enjoy fishing and hunting, early-19th-century architectural designs, plantations, and beach and recreational facilities.

What to See and Do

Colleton County Courthouse. *101 Hampton St, Walterboro. Hampton St and Jefferies Blvd.* Building designed by Robert Mills; the first public nullification meeting in the state was held in 1828.

Colleton State Park. *147 Way 5 Ln, Canadys (29433). 11 miles N on Hwy 15. Phone 843/538-8206.* On 35 acres; tree-shaded area on banks of Edisto River. Canoeing (dock), river fishing. Nature trails. Picnicking (shelters). Camping (hookups, dump station). **$**

Old Colleton County Jail. *239 N Jefferies Blvd, Walterboro (29488). Phone 843/549-2303. www. southcarolinamuseums.org/colleton/colleton.htm.* (1855) Neo-Gothic structure resembles a castle and is home to the Colleton Museum and the Chamber of Commerce. Served as Walterboro jail until 1937. **FREE**

South Carolina Artisans Center. *334 Wichman St, Walterboro (29488). In Hickory Valley Historic District. Phone 843/549-0011; fax 843/549-7433. www. southcarolinaartisanscenter.org.* Features handcrafted art and gifts by regional artists. Craftspeople demonstrate their skills. Educational programs and special events also offered. (Mon-Sat 9 am-6 pm, Sun 1-6 pm; closed holidays) **FREE**

Special Events

Edisto Riverfest. *Colleton State Park, 1205 Pendleton St, Canadys. Phone 803/734-0156. www.edistoriver. org/edisto_riverfest.html.* Canoe and kayak trips, river rafting, music, displays, and workshops. June.

Rice Festival. *239 N Jefferies Blvd, Walterboro (29488). Phone 843/549-1079; fax 843/549-5232.www. ricefestival.org.* Entertainment, parade, arts and crafts, street dances, soapbox derby. Last full weekend in Apr.

Limited-Service Hotel

★ ★ **COMFORT INN & SUITES.** *97 Downs Ln, Walterboro (29488). Phone 843/538-5911; toll-free 877/424-6423; fax 843/538-3673. www.comfortinn.com.* 96 rooms, 2 story. Complimentary continental breakfast. Check-in 2 pm, check-out 11 am. High-speed Internet access. Restaurant. Fitness room. Outdoor pool. Business center. **$**

Index

C

C. W. Worth House (Wilmington, NC), 162

Caesars Head State Park (Cleveland, SC), 200

Cafe (Atlanta, GA), 22

Cafe Europa (Hilton Head Island, SC), 207

Cafè Napoli (Clayton, GA), 41

Cafe Phoenix (Wilmington, NC), 163

Cagney's Old Place (Myrtle Beach, SC), 213

Callaway Plantation (Washington, GA), 82

Calverts (Augusta, GA), 33

Camden Antique District (Camden, SC), 175

Candlewood Suites (Raleigh, NC), 149

Candlewood Suites (Raleigh, NC), 150

Canoe (Atlanta, GA), 22

Canton Station (Fayetteville, NC), 122

Cape Fear Botanical Garden (Fayetteville, NC), 121

Cape Hatteras National Seashore (Cape Hatteras National Seashore, NC), 101

Cape Lookout National Seashore (Harkers Island, NC), 95

Capital Area Visitor Center (Raleigh, NC), 148

Capitoline Wolf Statue (Rome, GA), 68

Captain Bill's Waterfront (Morehead City, NC), 141

Captain Dave's Dockside (Myrtle Beach, SC), 213

Captain George's Seafood Rest (Myrtle Beach, SC), 213

Captain J. N. Maffitt River Cruises (Wilmington, NC), 161

Captain Joe's (Brunswick, GA), 36

Captain Sandy's Plantation Tours (Georgetown, SC), 199

Captain's Quarters Inn (Edenton, NC), 119

Carbo's Cafe (Atlanta, GA), 23

Carl Sandburg Home National Historic Site (Flat Rock, NC), 129

Carolina Beach State Park (Wilmington, NC), 161

Carolina Coliseum (Columbia, SC), 193

Carolina Crossroads (Chapel Hill, NC), 105

Carolina Cup Steeplechase (Camden, SC), 175

Carolina Dogwood Festival (Statesville, NC), 157

Carolina Downhome Blues Festival and Fine Arts Center (Camden, SC), 175

Carolina Hotel (Pinehurst, NC), 145

Carolina Hurricanes (NHL) (Raleigh, NC), 148

Carolina Inn (Chapel Hill, NC), 104

Carolina Panthers (NFL) (Charlotte, NC), 106

Carolina Sandhills National Wildlife Refuge (Mc Bee, SC), 189

Carolina's (Charleston, SC), 187

Carolinian Inn (Georgetown, SC), 200

Carter Display (Americus, GA), 7

Carteret County Museum of History and Art (Morehead City, NC), 140

Carters Lake (Chatsworth, GA), 40

Carvers Creek (Raleigh, NC), 151

Casa Carbone Ristorante (Raleigh, NC), 151

Castle Inn (Helen, GA), 54

Cataloochee Ski Area (Maggie Valley, NC), 138

Cataloochee Ski Area (Maggie Valley, NC), 138

Catawba County Museum of History (Newton, NC), 130

Catawba Cultural Center (Rock Hill, SC), 215

Catawba Science Center (Hickory, NC), 130

Cecil B. Day Butterfly Center (Pine Mountain, GA), 67

Cedar Crest Victorian Inn (Asheville, NC), 94

Cedar Island to Ocracoke Ferry Service (Ocracoke, NC), 144

Cedars Inn (Beaufort, NC), 96

Centennial Olympic Park (Atlanta, GA), 13

Center City Fest (Charlotte, NC), 107

CenterFest (Durham, NC), 116

Central Shelby Historic District Walking Tour (Shelby, NC), 154

Chalet Inn (Whittier, NC), 100

Chalet Switzerland Inn (Little Switzerland Inn, NC), 137

Chamber of Commerce (Charleston, SC), 178

Chanticleer Inn (Lookout Mountain, GA), 58

Chapel of the Cross (Chapel Hill, NC), 103

Charles Seafood Restaurant (Tifton, GA), 80

Charles Towne Landing (Charleston, SC), 178

Charleston Grill (Charleston, SC), 188

Charleston Museum (Charleston, SC), 178

Charleston Place (Charleston, SC), 185

Charleston Water Tours (Charleston, SC), 178

Charleston's Vendue Inn (Charleston, SC), 186

Charlie Tripper's (Valdosta, GA), 82

Charlie's L'Etoile Verte (Hilton Head Island, SC), 207

Charlotte Bobcats (NBA) (Charlotte, NC), 106

Charlotte Coliseum (Charlotte, NC), 106

Charlotte Hawkins Brown Memorial State Historic Site (Sedalia, NC), 126

Charlotte JW Marriott Southpark (Charlotte, NC), 108

Charlotte Museum of History and Hezekiah Alexander Homesite (Charlotte, NC), 106

Charlotte Sting (WNBA) (Charlotte, NC), 106

Chart House (Savannah, GA), 75

Charter House Inn (Bainbridge, GA), 34

Chastain Memorial Park (Atlanta, GA), 14

Chateau Elan Winery (Braselton, GA), 36

Chateau Elan Winery and Resort (Braselton, GA), 36

Chateau Elan's Le Clos (Braselton, GA), 35

Chattahoochee National Forest (Dahlonega, GA), 45

Chattahoochee Valley Art Museum (La Grange, GA), 58

Chattooga Wild and Scenic River (Clayton, GA), 41

Checkered Flag Lightening (Concord, NC), 113

Chelsea (St. Simons Island, GA), 78

Cheraw Historical District (Cheraw, SC), 189

Cheraw State Park (Cheraw, SC), 189

Cheraw State Park Camping (Cheraw, SC), 189

Cherokee Heritage Museum and Gallery (Cherokee, NC), 112

Cherry Blossom Festival (Macon, GA), 60

Chester State Park (Chester, SC), 190

Chestnut Hill Restaurant (Myrtle Beach, SC), 213

Chetola Resort At Blowing Rock (Blowing Rock, NC), 97

Chickamauga and Chattanooga National Military Park (Chickamauga and Chattanooga National Military Park, GA), 40

Chieftains Museum (Rome, GA), 68

Children's Museum (Rocky Mount, NC), 152

Chimney Rock Park (Asheville, NC), 91

Chops (Atlanta, GA), 23

Chowan County Courthouse (Edenton, NC), 119

Christ Episcopal Church (Savannah, GA), 70

Church of the Holy Cross (Stateburg, SC), 219

Church-Waddel-Brumby House (Athens, GA), 9

Circa 1886 (Charleston, SC), 188

Citadel Archives Museum (Charleston, SC), 178

Citadel, Military College of South Carolina (Charleston, SC), 178

City Grill (Atlanta, GA), 23

City Hall (Macon, GA), 59

City Hall (Savannah, GA), 71

City Hall Art Gallery (Charleston, SC), 179

Civil War Village of Andersonville (Andersonville, GA), 8

King-Bazemore House (Williamston, NC), *160*

King-Keith House Bed & Breakfast (Atlanta, GA), *20*

Kings Courtyard Inn (Charleston, SC), *187*

Kings Mountain National Military Park (Grover, NC), *198*

Kiwanis Ogeechee Fair (Statesboro, GA), *78*

Knife & Fork (Charlotte, NC), *110*

Kobe Japanese House of Steak & Seafood (Cornelius, NC), *115*

Koger Center for the Arts (Columbia, SC), *193*

Kolomoki Mounds State Historic Park (Blakely, GA), *34*

Kyma (Atlanta, GA), *25*

L

La Bibliotheque (Charlotte, NC), *111*

La Grotta (Atlanta, GA), *25*

La Maison Restaurant & Veritas Wine &Tapas (Augusta, GA), *33*

La Paz (Asheville, NC), *94*

La Quinta Atlanta Marietta (Marietta, GA), *62*

La Quinta Inn (Myrtle Beach, SC), *211*

La Quinta Inn (Norcross, GA), *64*

La Quinta Inn (Columbus, GA), *43*

La Quinta Inn And Suites (Valdosta, GA), *82*

La Quinta Inn And Suites Charlotte Coliseum (Charlotte, NC), *108*

La Quinta Inn Riverview (Charleston, SC), *185*

La Residence (Chapel Hill, NC), *105*

La Strada (Marietta, GA), *63*

La Terrace (Southern Pines, NC), *156*

Lake Cammack Park and Marina (Burlington, NC), *100*

Lake Chatuge (Hiawassee, GA), *55*

Lake Chehaw (Albany, GA), *5*

Lake Gaston (Roanoke Rapids, NC), *152*

Lake Greenwood (Greenwood, SC), *203*

Lake Hartwell State Park (Anderson, SC), *172*

Lake Hickory (Hickory, NC), *131*

Lake James (Morganton, NC), *141*

Lake Lanier Islands (Buford, GA), *36*

Lake Lanier Islands (Gainesville, GA), *51*

Lake Lure Inn (Lake Lure, NC), *130*

Lake Murray (Columbia, SC), *192*

Lake Norman (Cornelius, NC), *114*

Lake Norman State Park (Troutman, NC), *157*

Lake Oconee (Eatonton, GA), *48*

Lake Oconee (Madison, GA), *61*

Lake Sinclair (Milledgeville, GA), *63*

Lake Thorpe (Cashiers, NC), *102*

Lake Tobesofkee (Macon, GA), *59*

Lake Wallace (Bennettsville, SC), *174*

Lake Walter F. George (Lumpkin, GA), *58*

Lake Wateree State Recreation Area (Camden, SC), *175*

Lake Winfield Scott (Dahlonega, GA), *45*

Lake Wylie (Lake Wylie, NC), *124*

Lake Wylie (Rock Hill, SC), *215*

Landsford Canal State Park (Catawba, SC), *215*

Lapham-Patterson House State Historic Site (Thomasville, GA), *79*

Las Margaritas (Garner, NC), *151*

Latitude 31 (Jekyll Island, GA), *57*

Latta Plantation Center and Nature Preserve (Huntersville, NC), *106*

Laura S. Walker State Park (Waycross, GA), *83*

Laurel Grove Cemetery (South) (Savannah, GA), *71*

Laurel Hill Bed & Breakfast (Atlanta, GA), *20*

LaVecchia's Seafood Grille (Charlotte, NC), *111*

Lee State Natural Area Camping (Bishopville, SC), *204*

Lee State Park (Bishopville, SC), *204*

Lenoir-Rhyne College (Hickory, NC), *131*

Levine Museum of the New South (Charlotte, NC), *106*

Lexington County Museum Complex (Lexington, SC), *193*

Liberty Lane Walk of Fame (Darlington, SC), *195*

Linville Caverns (Marion, NC), *140*

Lion And The Rose (Asheville, NC), *94*

Litchfield Plantation (Pawleys Island, SC), *212*

Litchfield Plantation (Pawleys Island, SC), *215*

Little Pee Dee State Park (Dillon, SC), *195*

Little Pee Dee State Park Camping (Dillon, SC), *196*

Little Venice (Hilton Head Island, SC), *207*

Little White House Historic Site (Warm Springs, GA), *67*

Lobster Race (Aiken, SC), *171*

Lodge at Sea Island Golf Club (St. Simons Island, GA), *75*

Lodge on Lake Lure Bed & Breakfast (Lake Lure, NC), *130*

Lodge on Little St. Simons Island (St. Simons Island, GA), *77*

Lois Jane's Riverview Inn (Southport, NC), *156*

Lombardi's (Atlanta, GA), *25*

Long Beach Scenic Walkway (Long Beach, NC), *156*

Lords Proprietors Inn (Edenton, NC), *119*

Lost Colony Outdoor Drama (Manteo, NC), *122*

Lost Colony Outdoor Drama (Manteo, NC), *139*

Louise Wells Cameron Art Museum (Wilmington, NC), *161*

Louis's At Pawleys & The Fish Camp Bar (Pawleys Island, SC), *215*

Louis's at Pawleys & the Fish Camp Bar (Pawleys Island, SC), *213*

Lover's Oak (Brunswick, GA), *35*

Lovill House Inn (Boone, NC), *98*

Lowndes County Historical Society Museum (Valdosta, GA), *81*

Lucas Park (Florence, SC), *197*

Lupie's CafÈ (Charlotte, NC), *111*

Lynches River State Park (Florence, SC), *197*

M

Macon County Fair (Franklin, NC), *123*

Macon County Gemboree (Franklin, NC), *123*

Macon County Historical Museum (Franklin, NC), *123*

Macon Historic District (Macon, GA), *60*

Macon Museum of Arts and Sciences & Mark Smith Planetarium (Macon, GA), *60*

Madison-Morgan Cultural Center (Madison, GA), *61*

Madison's Restaurant and Wine Garden (Highlands, NC), *133*

Magnolia (Pinehurst, NC), *146*

Magnolia Grill (Durham, NC), *118*

Magnolia Plantation and Gardens (Charleston, SC), *181*

Magnolias (Charleston, SC), *188*

Main Street Inn (Hilton Head Island, SC), *207*

Main Theater (Savannah, GA), *72*

Maison Du Pre (Charleston, SC), *187*

Makoto (Boone, NC), *99*

Mama Fu's Asian House (Charlotte, NC), *111*

Maple Lodge (Blowing Rock, NC), *97*

Maple Street Mansion (Carrollton, GA), *39*

Margaret Mitchell House (Atlanta, GA), *14*

Marietta Conference Center And Resort (Marietta, GA), *62*

Marina (Elizabeth City, NC), *120*

Marina Raw Bar (North Myrtle Beach, SC), *213*

Marine Corps Air Station (Beaufort, SC), *173*

Maritime Museum (Southport, NC), *156*

Market CafÈ (Pittsboro, NC), *147*

Market Pavilion Hotel (Charleston, SC), *185*

Market Place Restaurant & Wine Bar (Asheville, NC), *94*

Marriott (Columbus, GA), *43*

Marriott Alpharetta (Alpharetta, GA), *6*

Marriott Atlanta Gwinnett Place (Duluth, GA), *64*

Marriott Atlanta Norcross-Peachtree Corners (Norcross, GA), *64*

Chain Restaurants

Georgia

Acworth

O'Charley's, 285 Cobb Pkwy NW, Acworth, GA, (678) 574-7378, 11 am-10 pm

Longhorn Steakhouse, 3366 Cobb Pky, NW, Acworth, GA, 30101, (770) 975-8703, 11 am-10 pm

Beef O'Brady's, 3344 Cobb Pkwy #600, Acworth, GA, 30102, (678) 574-0049, 11 am-11 pm

Albany

Cracker Barrel, 114 Westover Blvd, Albany, GA, 31707, (229) 420-0058, 6 am-10 pm

Golden Corral, 2524 Archwood Dr, Albany, GA, 31707, (229) 446-0101, 11 am-9 pm

Hooters, 2817 Old Dawson Rd, Albany, GA, 31707, (229) 435-2556, 11 am-midnight

Logan's Roadhouse, 1230 N Westover Blvd, Albany, GA, 31707, (229) 434-0491, 11 am-10 pm

Longhorn Steakhouse, 2733 Dawson Rd, Albany, GA, 31707, (229) 889-1866, 11 am-10 pm

Ryan's Grill Buffet Bakery, 1228 N Westover Blvd, Albany, GA, 31707, (229) 446-4340, 10:45 am-9 pm

CiCi's Pizza, 2800 Old Dawson Rd, Ste 17, Albany, GA, 31707, (229) 439-0063, 11 am-9 pm

Alpharetta

Chili's, 5035 Windward Pkwy, Alpharetta, GA, 30004, (770) 619-1818, 11 am-10 pm

Romano's Macaroni Grill, 5045 Windward Pkwy, Alpharetta, GA, 30004, (770) 360-6302, 11 am-10 pm

P.F. Changs, 7925 N Point Pkwy, Alpharetta, GA, 30022, (770) 992-3070, 11 am-10 pm

On the Border, 10575 Davis Dr, Alpharetta, GA, 30004, (770) 998-3335, 11 am-10 pm

Golden Corral, 915 N Pt Dr, Alpharetta, GA, 30022, (678) 867-2881, 11 am-9 pm

Copeland's, 970 N Point Dr, Alpharetta, GA, 30022, (678) 297-2000, 11 am-10 pm

Chili's, 7800 N Point Pkwy, Alpharetta, GA, 30022, (770) 594-9063, 11 am-10 pm

Cheesecake Factory, 2075 N Point Circle, Alpharetta, GA, 30022, (770) 751-7011, 11 am-11 pm

Benihana, 2365 Mansell Rd, Alpharetta, GA, 30022, (678) 461-8440, 11:30 am-10 pm

Fuddruckers, 6360 Northpoint Pkwy, Alpharetta, GA, 30201, 11 am-9 pm

Americus

Ryan's Grill Buffet Bakery, 1712 E Lamar St, Americus, GA, 31709, (229) 924-4088, 10:45 am-9 pm

Athens

Longhorn Steakhouse, 196 Alps Rd, Ste 42, Athens, GA, 30606, (706) 548-1341, 11 am-10 pm

CiCi's Pizza, 3190 Atlanta Hwy Stes 5 / 6, Athens, GA, 30606, (706) 613-2424, 11 am-9 pm

On the Border, 3640 Atlanta Hwy, Athens, GA, 30606, (706) 543-2299, 11 am-10 pm

McAlister's Deli, 2440 W BRd St, Athens, GA, (706) 369-6700, 10:30 am-10 pm

Ryan's Grill Buffet Bakery, 2020 Barnett Shoals Rd, Athens, GA, 30605, (706) 549-0186, 10:45 am-9 pm

Cracker Barrel, 1913 Epps Bridge Pkwy, Athens, GA, 30606, (706) 208-0304, 6 am-10 pm

Chili's, 183 Alps Rd, Athens, GA, 30606, (706) 613-5405, 11 am-10 pm

Logan's Roadhouse, 3668 Atlanta Hwy, Athens, GA, 30606, (706) 227-9890, 11 am-10 pm

Fire Mountain, 1021 Dowdy Rd, Athens, GA, 30606, (706) 543-8203, 10:45 am-9:30 pm

Atlanta

Maggiano's, 4400 Ashford Dunwoody Rd, Space #3035, Atlanta, GA, 30346, (770) 804-3313, 11 am-10 pm

Hometown Buffet, NorthE Plz, 3371 Buford Hwy NE, Atlanta, GA, 30329, (404) 321-6107, 11 am-8:30 pm

Hooters, 209 Peachtree St, Atlanta, GA, 30303, (404) 522-9464, 11 am-midnight

Hooters, 2977 Cobb Pkwy SE, Atlanta, GA, 30339, (770) 984-0287, 11 am-midnight

Longhorn Steakhouse, 2973 Cobb Pky, Atlanta, GA, 30339, (770) 859-0341, 11 am-10 pm

Longhorn Steakhouse, 6390 Roswell Rd, Atlanta, GA, 30328, (404) 843-1215, 11 am-10 pm

Longhorn Steakhouse, 2892 N Druid Hills Rd, Atlanta, GA, 30329, (404) 636-3817, 11 am-10 pm

Maggiano's, 3368 Peachtree Rd, Atlanta, GA, 30326, (404) 816-9650, 11 am-10 pm

Maggiano's, 1601 Cumberland Mall SE, Ste 200, Atlanta, GA, 30339, 11 am-10 pm

On the Border, #1 Buckhead Loop NE, Ste# 130, Atlanta, GA, 30326, (404) 816-3171, 11 am-10 pm

P.F. Changs, Cumberland Mall, Atlanta, GA, 11 am-10 pm

P.F. Changs, 500 Ashwood Pkwy, Atlanta, GA, 30338, (770) 352-0500, 11 am-10 pm

Eatzi's, 3221 Peachtree Rd NE, Atlanta, GA, 30305, (404) 237-2266, 8 am-10 pm

Longhorn Steakhouse, 2430 Piedmont Rd, Atlanta, GA, 30324, (404) 816-6338, 11 am-10 pm

Benihana, 229 Peachtree St NE Level A, Atlanta, GA, 30303, (404) 522-9629, 11:30 am-10 pm

Fuddruckers, 815 Buckhead Sydney Marcus Blvd NE, Atlanta, GA, 30324, 11 am-9 pm

Benihana, 2143 Peachtree Rd NE, Atlanta, GA, 30309, (404) 355-8565, 11:30 am-10 pm

Cheesecake Factory, 3024 Peachtree Rd NW, Atlanta, GA, 30305, (404) 816-2555, 11 am-11 pm

Cheesecake Factory, 4400 Ashford-Dunwoody Rd Ste 3005, Atlanta, GA, 30346, (678) 320-0201, 11 am-11 pm

Chili's, 2133 Lavista Rd NE, Atlanta, GA, 30329, (404) 325-8680, 11 am-10 pm

Chili's, 2420 Piedmont Rd, NE, Atlanta, GA, 30324, (404) 848-7979, 11 am-10 pm

Copeland's, 3365 Piedmont Rd, Atlanta, GA, 30305, (404) 475-1000, 11 am-10 pm

Copeland's, 3131 Cobb Pkwy SE, Ste 200, Atlanta, GA, 30339, (770) 612-3311, 11 am-10 pm

Dave and Buster's, I-75 Delk Rd, Atlanta, GA, (770) 951-5554, 11:30 am-midnight

Don Pablo's, 3131 Cobb Pkwy SE Ste 100, Atlanta, GA, 30339, (770) 955-5929, 11 am-10 pm

Eatzi's, 4505 Ashford-Dunwoody Rd, Atlanta, GA, 30346, (678) 634-0000, 8 am-9 pm

Fuddruckers, 240 Perimeter Center Pkwy, Atlanta, GA, 30346, 11 am-9 pm

CiCi's Pizza, 6690 Roswell Rd, Ste 410, Atlanta, GA, 30328, (404) 257-9944, 11 am-9 pm

Augusta

Golden Corral, 227 Bobby Jones Exwy, Augusta, GA, 30907, (706) 863-9292, 11 am-9 pm

Tony Roma's, 203 Robert C Daniel Pkwy, Augusta, GA, 30909, (706) 733-9497, 11 am-10 pm

Ryan's Grill Buffet Bakery, 3034 Peach Orchard Blvd, Augusta, GA, 30906, (706) 796-8717, 10:45 am-9 pm

Romano's Macaroni Grill, 275 Robert C Daniels Jr Pkwy, Augusta, GA, 30909, (706) 736-3029, 11 am-10 pm

O'Charley's, 276 Robert C Daniel Jr Pkwy, Augusta, GA, (706) 739-0855, 11 am-10 pm

Longhorn Steakhouse, 3241 Washington Rd, Augusta, GA, 30907, (706) 650-6600, 11 am-10 pm

Logan's Roadhouse, 269 Robert C Daniel Pkwy, Augusta, GA, 30909, (706) 738-8088, 11 am-10 pm

CiCi's Pizza, 3206 Peach Orchard Rd, Unit 10, Augusta, GA, 30906, (706) 771-0160, 11 am-9 pm

Golden Corral, 3010 Peach Orchard Rd, Augusta, GA, 30906, (706) 796-1807, 11 am-9 pm

Hooters, 2834 Washington Rd, Augusta, GA, 30909, (706) 736-8454, 11 am-midnight

Austell

O'Charley's, 4130 Austell Rd, Austell, GA, (770) 941-0253, 11 am-10 pm

Longhorn Steakhouse, 1355 East-West Connector, Ste B-1, Austell, GA, 30106, (770) 941-4816, 11 am-10 pm

Chili's, 4145 Austell Rd, Austell, GA, 30106, (770) 941-7279, 11 am-10 pm

CiCi's Pizza, 3999 Austell Rd, Ste 802, Austell, GA, 30106, (770) 745-9779, 11 am-9 pm

Golden Corral, 3845 Austell Rd, Austell, GA, 30106, (770) 732-8014, 11 am-9 pm

Bainbridge

Golden Corral, 1302 E Shotwell St, Bainbridge, GA, 39819, (229) 246-6011, 11 am-9 pm

Braselton

Cracker Barrel, 301 Exchange Way, Braselton, GA, 30517, (706) 658-0009, 6 am-10 pm

Brunswick

Beef O'Brady's, 5314 New Jesup Hwy, Brunswick, GA, 31520, (912) 264-8404, 11 am-11 pm

Cracker Barrel, 109 Tourist Dr, Brunswick, GA, 31520, (912) 267-7905, 6 am-10 pm

Golden Corral, 114 Golden Isles Plz, Brunswick, GA, 31520, (912) 262-1945, 11 am-9 pm

Ryan's Grill Buffet Bakery, 665 Scranton Rd, Brunswick, GA, 31520, (912) 261-2022, 10:45 am-9 pm

Buford

P.F. Changs, 3333 Buford Dr, Mall of Georgia, Buford, GA, 30519, (678) 546-9005, 11 am-10 pm

Romano's Macaroni Grill, 3207 Buford Dr, Buford, GA, 30519, (678) 714-0049, 11 am-10 pm

On the Border, 3206 Buford Dr, Buford, GA, 30519, (678) 546-4595, 11 am-10 pm

Longhorn Steakhouse, 1800 Mall of Georgia Blvd, Buford, GA, 30519, (678) 482-7750, 11 am-10 pm

Golden Corral, 4020 Hwy 20, Buford, GA, 30518, (770) 831-3500, 11 am-9 pm

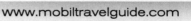

Chili's, 3215 Buford Dr, Buford, GA, 30519, (770) 945-7667, 11 am-10 pm

O'Charley's, 3217 Buford Dr, Buford, GA,(770) 271-0534, 11 am-10 pm

Ryan's Grill Buffet Bakery, 3843 Buford Dr, Buford, GA, 30519, (770) 831-1066, 10:45 am-9 pm

Calhoun

Cracker Barrel, 100 Cracker Barrel Dr, Calhoun, GA, 30701, (706) 624-1661, 6 am-10 pm

Fire Mountain, 422 W Belmont Dr, Calhoun, GA, 30701, (706) 625-3619, 10:45 am-9:30 pm

Canton

Beef O'Brady's, 6199 Hickory Flat Hwy, #114, Canton, GA, 30115, (678) 493-1843, 11 am-11 pm

Ryan's Grill Buffet Bakery, 150 Keith Dr, Canton, GA, 30114, (770) 704-0556, 10:45 am-9 pm

O'Charley's, 1409 Riverstone Pkwy, Canton, GA,(770) 720-6161, 11 am-10 pm

Longhorn Steakhouse, 1375 Riverstone Pkwy, Canton, GA, 30114, (770) 345-4511, 11 am-10 pm

Cracker Barrel, 715 Transit Ave, Canton, GA, 30114, (770) 479-2336, 6 am-10 pm

Beef O'Brady's, 110 Prominence Pt Blvd, #116, Canton, GA, 30114, (770) 345-9464, 11 am-11 pm

Hooters, 100 River Pointe Pkwy, Canton, GA, 30114, (678) 493-0369, 11 am-midnight

Carrollton

Longhorn Steakhouse, 1155 Bankhead Hwy, Carrollton, GA, 30117, (770) 838-5886, 11 am-10 pm

Ryan's Grill Buffet Bakery, 1156 Bankhead Hwy, Carrollton, GA, 30116, (770) 836-8887, 10:45 am-9 pm

Cartersville

Longhorn Steakhouse, 463 E Main St, Cartersville, GA, 30120, (770) 607-0280, 11 am-10 pm

Beef O'Brady's, 700 Douthit Ferry Rd, Ste 750, Cartersville, GA, 30120, (770) 607-9494, 11 am-11 pm

Ryan's Grill Buffet Bakery, 823 Joe Frank Harris Pkwy, Cartersville, GA, 30120, (770) 606-1500, 10:45 am-9 pm

Cracker Barrel, 5631 SR 20 Northeast, Cartersville, GA, 30120, (770) 386-6973, 6 am-10 pm

CiCi's Pizza, 240 Cherokee Pl, Cartersville, GA, 30121, (770) 387-9797, 11 am-9 pm

Hooters, 887 Joe Frank Harris Pkwy, Cartersville, GA, 30120, (770) 607-9474, 11 am-midnight

Centerville

O'Charley's, 2990 Watson Blvd, Centerville, GA,(478) 971-1145, 11 am-10 pm

College Park

Longhorn Steakhouse, 5403 Old National Hwy, College Park, GA, 30337, (404) 761-8018, 11 am-10 pm

Columbus

Hooters, 2650 Adams Farm Rd, Columbus, GA, 31909, (706) 596-4668, 11 am-midnight

Ryan's Grill Buffet Bakery, 1900 Manchester Expressway, Columbus, GA, 31904, (706) 322-0445, 10:45 am-9 pm

O'Charley's, 1528 Bradley Park Dr, Columbus, GA,(706) 324-2929, 11 am-10 pm

McAlister's Deli, 6755 Veterans Pkwy, Columbus, GA,(706) 323-4456, 10:30 am-10 pm

Logan's Roadhouse, 2643 Manchester, Columbus, GA, 31904, (706) 653-0111, 11 am-10 pm

Golden Corral, 1505 Manchester Exwy, Columbus, GA, 31904, (706) 320-0300, 11 am-9 pm

Cracker Barrel, 1500 Bradley Park Dr, Columbus, GA, 31904, (706) 317-3460, 6 am-10 pm

CiCi's Pizza, 1931 Auburn Ave, Columbus, GA, 31906, (706) 569-9096, 11 am-9 pm

CiCi's Pizza, 1660 Whittlesey Rd, Ste 300, Columbus, GA, 31904, (706) 317-3332, 11 am-9 pm

Chili's, 5555 Whittlesey Blvd, Columbus, GA, 31909, (706) 641-9990, 11 am-10 pm

Longhorn Steakhouse, 3201 Macon Rd, Columbus, GA, 31906, (706) 563-2221, 11 am-10 pm

Commerce

Cracker Barrel, 138 Eisenhower Dr, Commerce, GA, 30529, (706) 335-3788, 6 am-10 pm

Longhorn Steakhouse, 30769 Hwy 441 S, Commerce, GA, 30529, (706) 336-6632, 11 am-10 pm

Ryan's Grill Buffet Bakery, 243 Steven B Tanger Blvd, Commerce, GA, 30529, (706) 335-3213, 10:45 am-9 pm

Conyers

Longhorn Steakhouse, 1300 Iris Dr, Conyers, GA, 30013, (770) 760-8070, 11 am-10 pm

Golden Corral, 1350 Georgia Hwy 138, Conyers, GA, 30013, (770) 761-5555, 11 am-9 pm

O'Charley's, 1289 Dogwood Dr SW, Conyers, GA,(770) 922-2280, 11 am-10 pm

Hooters, 1099 Iris Dr, Conyers, GA, 30207, (770) 483-5010, 11 am-midnight

CiCi's Pizza, 1485-1527 Hwy 138, B-102 & B-104, Conyers, GA, 30013, (770) 929-3350, 11 am-9 pm

Chili's, 1570 Dogwood Dr SE, Conyers, GA, 30012, (770) 602-1301, 11 am-10 pm

Chili's, 1161 SE Old Salem Rd, Conyers, GA, 30094, (770) 388-7500, 11 am-10 pm

Cracker Barrel, 1182 Dogwood Dr, Conyers, GA, 30094, (770) 785-7600, 6 am-10 pm

Cordele

Golden Corral, 2110 16th Ave E, Cordele, GA, 31015, (229) 273-7820, 11 am-9 pm

Cracker Barrel, 1905 Central Ave, Cordele, GA, 31015, (229) 271-0331, 6 am-10 pm

Covington

Longhorn Steakhouse, 6112 Pavilion Way NW, Covington, GA, 30014, (678) 625-4320, 11 am-10 pm

Cumming

Beef O'Brady's, 2619 Freedom Pkwy, Cumming, GA, 30041, (770) 781-8803, 11 am-11 pm

O'Charley's, 920 Buford Rd, Cumming, GA,(770) 888-3880, 11 am-10 pm

Longhorn Steakhouse, 925 Market Pl Blvd, Cumming, GA, 30041, (678) 947-4228, 11 am-10 pm

Chili's, 874 Buford Rd, Cumming, GA, 30041, (678) 947-3165, 11 am-10 pm

CiCi's Pizza, 655 Atlanta Rd, Ste 606/607, Cumming, GA, 30040, (770) 886-0055, 11 am-9 pm

Dallas

Beef O'Brady's, 55 E Paulding Dr, Dallas, GA, 30157, (678) 383-8247, 11 am-11 pm

Dalton

CiCi's Pizza, 1345 W Walnut Ave, Dalton, GA, 30720, (706) 278-2424, 11 am-9 pm

O'Charley's, 1520 W Walnut Ave, Dalton, GA,(706) 226-5057, 11 am-10 pm

Ryan's Grill Buffet Bakery, 2144 E Walnut, Dalton, GA, 30721, (706) 277-4190, 10:45 am-9 pm

Longhorn Steakhouse, 1315 W Walnut Ave, Dalton, GA, 30720, (706) 281-1568, 11 am-10 pm

Logan's Roadhouse, 2140 E Walnut Ave, Dalton, GA, 30721, (706) 259-3220, 11 am-10 pm

Cracker Barrel, 938 Market St, Dalton, GA, 30720, (706) 226-5231, 6 am-10 pm

Chili's, 881 College Dr, Dalton, GA, 30720, (706) 226-1011, 11 am-10 pm

Fuddruckers, 1515 Walnut Ave, Dalton, GA, 30720, 11 am-9 pm

Dawsonville

Beef O'Brady's, 837 Hwy 400 S, Ste #180, Dawsonville, GA, 30534, (706) 216-0900, 11 am-11 pm

Fire Mountain, 126 Hwy 400 North, Dawsonville, GA, 30534, (706) 265-1565, 10:45 am-9:30 pm

Longhorn Steakhouse, 795 Hwy 400 S, Dawsonville, GA, 30534, (706) 265-2007, 11 am-10 pm

Decatur

CiCi's Pizza, 3912 N Druid Hills Rd, Decatur, GA, 30033, (404) 329-1535, 11 am-9 pm

Douglas

Golden Corral, 1208 S Madison Ave, Douglas, GA, 31533, (912) 384-5370, 11 am-9 pm

Douglasville

Logan's Roadhouse, 9380 The Landing Dr, Douglasville, GA, 30135, (770) 942-0181, 11 am-10 pm

Smokey Bones, 6855 Douglas Blvd, Douglasville, GA, 30135, (678) 838-7779, 11 am-10 pm

O'Charley's, 9320 The Landing Dr, Douglasville, GA,(770) 920-4646, 11 am-10 pm

Longhorn Steakhouse, 8471 Hospital Dr, Douglasville, GA, 30134, (770) 942-7795, 11 am-10 pm

Golden Corral, 6975 Doublas Blvd, Douglasville, GA, 30135, (678) 838-4376, 11 am-9 pm

Fire Mountain, 7090 Concourse Pkwy, Douglasville, GA, 30134, (770) 947-1116, 10:45 am-9:30 pm

Cracker Barrel, 5483 Westmoreland Plz, Douglasville, GA, 30134, (770) 949-0999, 6 am-10 pm

Hooters, 7010 Concourse Pkwy, Douglasville, GA, 30134, (770) 947-8009, 11 am-midnight

Dublin

Cracker Barrel, 104 Tr Avel Center Blvd, Dublin, GA, 31021, (478) 275-4220, 6 am-10 pm

Golden Corral, 2113 Veterans Blvd, Dublin, GA, 31021, (478) 272-6463, 11 am-9 pm

Duluth

Golden Corral, 3270 Satellite Blvd, Duluth, GA, 30096, (770) 495-7999, 11 am-9 pm

Smokey Bones, 1555 Pleasant Hill Rd, Duluth, GA, 30096, (678) 380-9002, 11 am-10 pm

Ryan's Grill Buffet Bakery, 3370 Venture Pkwy, Duluth, GA, 30096, (770) 497-1854, 10:45 am-9 pm

Romano's Macaroni Grill, 9700 Medlock Bridge Rd S112, Duluth, GA, 30097, (770) 495-7855, 11 am-10 pm

Romano's Macaroni Grill, 1565 Pleasant Hill Rd, Duluth, GA, 30096, (770) 564-0094, 11 am-10 pm

On the Border, 2275 Pleasant Hill Rd, Duluth, GA, 30096, (770) 232-9169, 11 am-10 pm

Melting Pot, 3610 Satellite Blvd NW , Duluth, GA, 30095, (770) 623-1290, 5 pm-10:30 pm

McAlister's Deli, 10900 Medlock Bridge Rd, Ste 201, Duluth, GA,(770) 495-8809, 10:30 am-10 pm

Longhorn Steakhouse, 10845 Medlock Bridge Rd, Duluth, GA, 30155, (770) 622-7087, 11 am-10 pm

Hooters, 3550 Gwinnett Pl Rd, Duluth, GA, 30136, (770) 497-0880, 11 am-midnight

Fuddruckers, 2180 Merchants Way, Duluth, GA, 30136, 11 am-9 pm

Dave and Buster's, 4000 Venture Dr I-85 Steve Reynolds Blvd /Exit 103, Duluth, GA,(770) 497-1152, 11:30 am-midnight

Chili's, 11720 Medlock Bridge Rd, Duluth, GA, 30097, (770) 814-2377, 11 am-10 pm

Chili's, 3520 Gwinnett Pl Dr, Duluth, GA, 30096, (770) 497-1536, 11 am-10 pm

Longhorn Steakhouse, 3525 Mall Blvd, Duluth, GA, 30096, (770) 476-9026, 11 am-10 pm

Dunwoody

Smokey Bones, 4764 Ashford Dunwoody Rd, Dunwoody, GA, 30338, (678) 587-9084, 11 am-10 pm

Romano's Macaroni Grill, 4788 Ashford Dunwoody Rd, Dunwoody, GA, 30338, (770) 394-6676, 11 am-10 pm

Max & Ermas, 1155 Mt Vernon Hwy, Dunwoody, GA,(770) 551-0055, 11 am-11 pm

Chili's, 4784 Ashford Dunwoody Rd, Dunwoody, GA, 30338, (770) 394-6175, 11 am-10 pm

East Point

Longhorn Steakhouse, 3480 Camp Creek Pkwy, East Point, GA, 30344, (404) 346-4110, 11 am-10 pm

Ellijay

Longhorn Steakhouse, 30 Highland Crossing S, Ellijay, GA, 30539, (706) 515-0050, 11 am-10 pm

Fayetteville

McAlister's Deli, 180 Hwy 314, Fayetteville, GA,(678) 817-4924, 10:30 am-10 pm

O'Charley's, 1350 Hwy 85 N, Fayetteville, GA,(770) 716-3731, 11 am-10 pm

Flowery Branch

Beef O'Brady's, 7380 Spout Springs Rd, #170, Flowery Branch, GA, 30542, (770) 967-3077, 11 am-11 pm

Fort Gordon

Godfather's Pizza, Building 29722, Fort Gordon, GA, 30905, (706) 790-8646,

Freehome

Beef O'Brady's, 12418 Cumming Hwy, Ste 406, Freehome, GA, 30115, (678) 513-8800, 11 am-11 pm

Ft. Oglethorpe

Golden Corral, 760 Battlefield Pkwy, 2-A, Ft. Oglethorpe, GA, 30742, (706) 866-7514, 11 am-9 pm

CiCi's Pizza, 723 Battlefield Pkwy, Ft. Oglethorpe, GA, 30742, (706) 858-7401, 11 am-9 pm

Logan's Roadhouse, 2584 Battlefield Pkwy, Ft. Oglethorpe, GA, 30742, (706) 858-8482, 11 am-10 pm

O'Charley's, 2542 Battlefield Pkwy, Ft. Oglethorpe, GA,(706) 861-5520, 11 am-10 pm

Gainesville

Longhorn Steakhouse, 1709 Browns Bridge Rd, Gainesville, GA, 30501, (770) 538-0400, 11 am-10 pm

Smokey Bones, 1701 Browns Bridge Rd, Gainesville, GA, 30501, (770) 534-8400, 11 am-10 pm

O'Charley's, 1711 Brown's Bridge, Gainesville, GA,(770) 534-2455, 11 am-10 pm

Fire Mountain, 2415 Browns Bridge Rd, Gainesville, GA, 30504, (770) 531-7926, 10:45 am-9:30 pm

Chili's, 669 Dawsonville Hwy, Gainesville, GA, 30501, (770) 532-9844, 11 am-10 pm

CiCi's Pizza, 250 John W Morrow Jr Pkwy, Gainesville, GA, 30501, (770) 534-9400, 11 am-9 pm

Griffin

CiCi's Pizza, 1424 N Expressway, Ste 114, Griffin, GA, 30223, (770) 228-5900, 11 am-9 pm

Fire Mountain, 1323 N Express Way, Griffin, GA, 30223, (770) 233-3326, 10:45 am-9:30 pm

O'Charley's, 1512 W McIntosh Rd, Griffin, GA,(770) 233-8156, 11 am-10 pm

Grovetown

Cracker Barrel, 460 Parkwest Dr, Grovetown, GA, 30813, (706) 650-2414, 6 am-10 pm

Hinesville

CiCi's Pizza, 230 General Screven Way, Ste 100, Hinesville, GA, 31313, (912) 448-2777, 11 am-9 pm

Hiram

O'Charley's, 4790 Jimmy Lee Smith Pkwy, Hiram, GA,(770) 222-0822, 11 am-10 pm

Ryan's Grill Buffet Bakery, 55 Pace Court, Hiram, GA, 30141, (770) 439-6004, 10:45 am-9 pm

Hooters, 5464 Wendy Bagwell Pkwy, Hiram, GA, 30141, (770) 943-8896, 11 am-midnight

Chili's, 5100 Jimmy Lee Smith Pkwy, Hiram, GA, 30141, (770) 943-6965, 11 am-10 pm

Longhorn Steakhouse, 4800 Jimmy Lee Smith Pkwy, Hiram, GA, 30141, (770) 222-2298, 11 am-10 pm

Jonesboro

Hooters, 6785 Tara Blvd, Jonesboro, GA, 30236, (770) 478-2262, 11 am-midnight

Longhorn Steakhouse, 7882 Tara Blvd, Jonesboro, GA, 30236, (770) 477-5365, 11 am-10 pm

Golden Corral, 8465 Tara Blvd, Jonesboro, GA, 30236, (770) 477-0036, 11 am-9 pm

Kennesaw

Longhorn Steakhouse, 2700 Town Center Dr, Kennesaw, GA, 30144, (770) 421-1101, 11 am-10 pm

Smokey Bones, 2475 George Busbee Pkwy, Kennesaw, GA, 30144, (678) 290-7771, 11 am-10 pm

Romano's Macaroni Grill, 780 Cobb Pl Blvd, Kennesaw, GA, 30144, (770) 590-7774, 11 am-10 pm

On the Border, 790 Cobb Pl Blvd, Kennesaw, GA, 30144, (678) 797-9670, 11 am-10 pm

O'Charley's, 705 Town Park Ln, Kennesaw, GA,(770) 792-7866, 11 am-10 pm

McAlister's Deli, 2950 Busbee Pkwy, Ste 102, Kennesaw, GA,(770) 499-1581, 10:30 am-10 pm

Chili's, 851 Cobb Pl Blvd, Kennesaw, GA, 30144, (770) 419-8809, 11 am-10 pm

Melting Pot, 2500 Cobb Pl Ln, Ste 800 , Kennesaw, GA, 30144, (770) 425-1411, 5 pm-10:30 pm

Golden Corral, 700 Barrett Pkwy, Kennesaw, GA, 30144, (770) 428-6770, 11 am-9 pm

Fuddruckers, 2708 Town Center Dr, Kennesaw, GA, 30144, 11 am-9 pm

Cracker Barrel, 3389 George Busbee Pkwy, Kennesaw, GA, 30144, (770) 429-1524, 6 am-10 pm

Copeland's, 1142 Barrett Pkwy NW , Kennesaw, GA, 30144, (770) 919-9612, 11 am-10 pm

CiCi's Pizza, 3160 Cobb Pkwy NW, Ste 490, Kennesaw, GA, 30152, (770) 529-0900, 11 am-9 pm

Hooters, 2102 Old Hwy 41, Kennesaw, GA, 30144, (770) 590-8820, 11 am-midnight

Kingsland

Cracker Barrel, 1200 Boone Ave Ext, Kingsland, GA, 31548, (912) 576-1991, 6 am-10 pm

LaGrange

Cracker Barrel, 105 Hoffman Dr, LaGrange, GA, 30241, (706) 884-0159, 6 am-10 pm

Ryan's Grill Buffet Bakery, 1509 Lafayette Pkwy, LaGrange, GA, 30241, (706) 845-7004, 10:45 am-9 pm

Golden Corral, 100 Corporate Plz, LaGrange, GA, 30241, (706) 882-7555, 11 am-9 pm

Lake Park

Cracker Barrel, 4914 Timber Dr, Lake Park, GA, 31636, (229) 559-0864, 6 am-10 pm

Lawrenceville

Golden Corral, 2155 Riverside Pkwy, Lawrenceville, GA, 30043, (678) 442-8677, 11 am-9 pm

O'Charley's, 830 Lawrenceville-Suwanee Rd, Lawrenceville, GA, (770) 237-3788, 11 am-10 pm

On the Border, 1250 Scenic Hwy, Ste 1300, Lawrenceville, GA, 30045, 11 am-10 pm

Chili's, 947 Lawrenceville Suwanee Rd, Lawrenceville, GA, 30043, (770) 513-0970, 11 am-10 pm

Longhorn Steakhouse, 800 Lawrenceville-Suwanee Rd, Lawrenceville, GA, 30243, (770) 338-0646, 11 am-10 pm

McAlister's Deli, 1030 Old Peachtree Rd NW, Ste 106, Lawrenceville, GA, (678) 407-0818, 10:30 am-10 pm

Lilburn

Chili's, 4031 Hwy 78, Lilburn, GA, 30047, (770) 978-6568, 11 am-10 pm

Lithia Springs

Cracker Barrel, 970 W Point Ct, Lithia Springs, GA, 30122, (678) 398-8568, 6 am-10 pm

Lithonia

Chili's, 2920 Stonecrest Cir, Lithonia, GA, 30038, (770) 482-5944, 11 am-10 pm

Smokey Bones, 2930 Stonecrest Circle, Lithonia, GA, 30038, (770) 484-0020, 11 am-10 pm

Loganville

Beef O'Brady's, 2715 Loganville Hwy, Ste 7-C&D, Loganville, GA, 30052, (770) 682-5224, 11 am-11 pm

Lovejoy

Fire Mountain, 11440 Tara Blvd, Lovejoy, GA, 30250, (770) 477-5688, 10:45 am-9:30 pm

Macon

Cracker Barrel, 3950 Riverside Dr, Macon, GA, 31210, (478) 474-7029, 6 am-10 pm

Ryan's Grill Buffet Bakery, 4690 Presidential Pkwy, Macon, GA, 31206, (478) 405-6800, 10:45 am-9 pm

O'Charley's, 3740 Bloomfield Rd, Macon, GA, (478) 477-2050, 11 am-10 pm

McAlister's Deli, 6255 Zebulon Rd, Ste 370, Macon, GA, (478) 405-6825, 10:30 am-10 pm

McAlister's Deli, 4641 Presidential Pkwy, Macon, GA, (478) 474-7783, 10:30 am-10 pm

Longhorn Steakhouse, 3072 Riverside Dr, Macon, GA, 31210, (478) 471-7844, 11 am-10 pm

Logan's Roadhouse, 3933 Arkwright Rd, Macon, GA, 31210, (478) 477-8806, 11 am-10 pm

Fuddruckers, 5981 Zebulon Rd, Macon, GA, 31220, 11 am-9 pm

Cracker Barrel, 4905 Brookh Aven Rd, Macon, GA, 31206, (478) 477-4848, 6 am-10 pm

CiCi's Pizza, 4640 Presidential Pkwy, Macon, GA, 31206, (478) 477-9700, 11 am-9 pm

Chili's, 3704 Northside Dr, Macon, GA, 31210, (478) 477-7576, 11 am-10 pm

Hooters, 112 Riverside Pkwy, Macon, GA, 31210, (478) 471-7675, 11 am-midnight

Madison

Cracker Barrel, 2003 Eatonton Rd, Madison, GA, 30650, (706) 343-9963, 6 am-10 pm

Marietta

Fuddruckers, 3000 Windy Hill Rd, Marietta, GA, 30067, 11 am-9 pm

O'Charley's, 3550 Sandy Plains Rd, Marietta, GA, (770) 579-2690, 11 am-10 pm

Longhorn Steakhouse, 2636 Dallas Hwy, SW, Marietta, GA, 30064, (770) 514-0245, 11 am-10 pm

Longhorn Steakhouse, 4721 Lower Roswell Rd, Marietta, GA, 30067, (770) 977-3045, 11 am-10 pm

Chili's, 3625 Dallas Hwy, Ste 100, Marietta, GA, 30064, (678) 354-7550, 11 am-10 pm

Chili's, 4111 Roswell Rd NE, Marietta, GA, 30062, (770) 973-9419, 11 am-10 pm

Beef O'Brady's, 3718 Dallas Hwy SW, Marietta, GA, 30064, (770) 424-3001, 11 am-11 pm

Romano's Macaroni Grill, 3625 Dallas Hwy SW, Marietta, GA, 30064, (678) 581-5624, 11 am-10 pm

Cracker Barrel, 2150 Delk Rd, Marietta, GA, 30067, (770) 951-2602, 6 am-10 pm

Martinez

CiCi's Pizza, 4020 Washington Rd, Ste D/E/F, Martinez, GA, 30907, (706) 869-0400, 11 am-9 pm

Ryan's Grill Buffet Bakery, 208 Bobby Jones Expressway, Martinez, GA, 30907, (706) 860-2668, 10:45 am-9 pm

McDonough

Logan's Roadhouse, 20 Mill Rd, McDonough, GA, 30223, (770) 957-6030, 11 am-10 pm

Ryan's Grill Buffet Bakery, 1001 Regency Plz Blvd, McDonough, GA, 30253, (678) 432-7155, 10:45 am-9 pm

Longhorn Steakhouse, 1856 Jonesboro Rd, McDonough, GA, 30253, (678) 583-6970, 11 am-10 pm

Hooters, 1858 Jonesboro Rd, McDonough, GA, 30253, (678) 583-9003, 11 am-midnight

Golden Corral, 1755 Jonesboro Rd, McDonough, GA, 30253, (678) 432-4554, 11 am-9 pm

Cracker Barrel, 1124 Hwy 20/81, McDonough, GA, 30253, (678) 583-9931, 6 am-10 pm

CiCi's Pizza, 1876 Jonesboro Rd, McDonough, GA, 30253, (678) 432-5757, 11 am-9 pm

Chili's, 1740 Jonesboro Rd, McDonough, GA, 30253, (770) 898-5774, 11 am-10 pm

O'Charley's, 1842 Jonesboro Rd, McDonough, GA, (770) 954-9871, 11 am-10 pm

Milledgeville

Golden Corral, 1913 N Columbia St, Milledgeville, GA, 31061, (478) 414-1344, 11 am-9 pm

Morrow

Chili's, 2230 Mt Zion Pkwy, Morrow, GA, 30260, (770) 603-9900, 11 am-10 pm

Cracker Barrel, 1458 Southlake Plz Dr, Morrow, GA, 30260, (770) 961-4533, 6 am-10 pm

Longhorn Steakhouse, 2256 Mt Zion Pkwy, Morrow, GA, 30260, (770) 210-3200, 11 am-10 pm

On the Border, 2330 Mt Zion Pkwy, Morrow, GA, 30260, (770) 210-2929, 11 am-10 pm

Smokey Bones, 1971 Mt Zion Rd, Morrow, GA, 30260, (678) 479-9909, 11 am-10 pm

Newnan

Golden Corral, 605 Bullsoboro Dr, Newnan, GA, 30265, (770) 253-9992, 11 am-9 pm

Fire Mountain, 941 Bullsboro Dr, Newnan, GA, 30264, (770) 253-7880, 10:45 am-9:30 pm

O'Charley's, 545 Bullsboro Dr, Newnan, GA, (770) 252-8584, 11 am-10 pm

Hooters, 1001 Bullsboro Dr, Newnan, GA, 30264, (770) 254-1687, 11 am-midnight

Beef O'Brady's, 141 Newnan Station Dr, Newnan, GA, 30265, (770) 683-3866, 11 am-11 pm

CiCi's Pizza, 1094 Bullsboro Dr, Ste D, Newnan, GA, 30265, (678) 423-7870, 11 am-9 pm

Longhorn Steakhouse, 1112 Bullsboro Dr, Newnan, GA, 30264, (770) 252-5300, 11 am-10 pm

Chili's, 321 Bullsboro Dr, Newnan, GA, 30263, (770) 254-1838, 11 am-10 pm

Cracker Barrel, 527 Bullsboro Dr, Newnan, GA, 30265, (770) 252-1055, 6 am-10 pm

Norcross

Chili's, 3446 Holcomb Bridge Rd, Norcross, GA, 30092, (770) 448-7566, 11 am-10 pm

CiCi's Pizza, 6050 Peachtree Pkwy, Ste 220, Norcross, GA, 30092, (770) 300-0535, 11 am-9 pm

Cracker Barrel, 6175 McDonough Dr, Norcross, GA, 30093, (770) 446-1313, 6 am-10 pm

Fire Mountain, 7045 Jimmy Carter Blvd, Norcross, GA, 30092, (770) 840-9096, 10:45 am-9:30 pm

Hooters, 5929 Jimmy Carter Blvd, Norcross, GA, 30071, (770) 729-8449, 11 am-midnight

J. Alexander's, 5245 Peachtree Pkwy, Norcross, GA, 30092, (770) 263-9755, 11 am-10 pm

Peachtree City

Romano's Macaroni Grill, 200 Market Pl Connector, Peachtree City, GA, 30269, (770) 487-0379, 11 am-10 pm

Smokey Bones, 100 Market Pl Blvd, Peachtree City, GA, 30269, (678) 364-8460, 11 am-10 pm

Chili's, 250 Market Pl Connector, Peachtree City, GA, 30269, (770) 487-9828, 11 am-10 pm

Beef O'Brady's, 100 Peachtree Pkwy N, Ste 18, Peachtree City, GA, 30269, (770) 486-1860, 11 am-11 pm

Longhorn Steakhouse, 2633 Floy Farr Pkwy, Peachtree City, GA, 30269, (770) 486-8791, 11 am-10 pm

Perry

Cracker Barrel, 101 Lect Dr, Perry, GA, 31069, (478) 987-2242, 6 am-10 pm

Pooler

Cracker Barrel, 1000 E US 80, Pooler, GA, 31322, (912) 748-7411, 6 am-10 pm

Powder Springs

Beef O'Brady's, 4400 Brownsville Rd, #205, Powder Springs, GA, 30127, (770) 439-3135, 11 am-11 pm

Ringgold

Cracker Barrel, 50 Biscuit Way, Ringgold, GA, 30736, (706) 937-2785, 6 am-10 pm

Riverdale

Ryan's Grill Buffet Bakery, 7643 Hwy 85, Riverdale, GA, 30274, (770) 477-0150, 10:45 am-9 pm

CiCi's Pizza, 7523 Hwy 85, Riverdale, GA, 30274, (770) 997-3303, 11 am-9 pm

Rome

Ryan's Grill Buffet Bakery, 2305 Shorter Ave SW, Rome, GA, 30165, (706) 234-7973, 10:45 am-9 pm

Longhorn Steakhouse, 144 Shorter Ave, Rome, GA, 30165, (706) 235-4232, 11 am-10 pm

Hooters, 104 Hicks Dr, Rome, GA, 30162, (706) 292-0209, 11 am-midnight

Fuddruckers, 509 Riverside Pkwy, Rome, GA, 30165, 11 am-9 pm

Chili's, 1310 Turner McCall Blvd, Rome, GA, 30161, (706) 232-7000, 11 am-10 pm

CiCi's Pizza, 2519 Redmond Circle, Rome, GA, 30165, (706) 235-8800, 11 am-9 pm

Roswell

Melting Pot, 1055 Mansell Rd, Roswell, GA, 30076, (770) 518-4100, 5 pm-10:30 pm

McAlister's Deli, 1425 Market Blvd, Ste 1370, Roswell, GA, (770) 594-3220, 10:30 am-10 pm

Longhorn Steakhouse, 900 Mansel Rd, Roswell, GA, 30076, (770) 642-8588, 11 am-10 pm

Fuddruckers, 11000 Alpharetta Hwy, Roswell, GA, 30076, 11 am-9 pm

Beef O'Brady's, 910 Woodstock Rd, #120, Roswell, GA, 30075, (678) 352-0307, 11 am-11 pm

CiCi's Pizza, 10516 Alpharetta Hwy, Roswell, GA, 30076, (770) 645-1550, 11 am-9 pm

Hooters, 795 Holcomb Bridge Rd, Roswell, GA, 30076, (770) 992-4540, 11 am-midnight

Savannah

Hooters, 4 Gateway Blvd W, Savannah, GA, 31405, (912) 925-2536, 11 am-midnight

Tony Roma's, 7 E Bay St, Savannah, GA, 31401, (912) 341-7427, 11 am-10 pm

Romano's Macaroni Grill, 7804 Abercorn St #70A, Savannah, GA, 31406, (912) 692-1488, 11 am-10 pm

Logan's Roadhouse, 11301 Abercom St, Savannah, GA, 31419, (912) 921-1510, 11 am-10 pm

Golden Corral, 7822 Abercorn St Ext, Savannah, GA, 31406, (912) 925-1274, 11 am-9 pm

Fire Mountain, 209 Stephenson Ave, Savannah, GA, 31405, (912) 354-5595, 10:45 am-9:30 pm

Cracker Barrel, 17017 Abercorn St, Savannah, GA, 31419, (912) 927-6559, 6 am-10 pm

CiCi's Pizza, 7400 Abercorn St, Ste 801, Savannah, GA, 31406, (912) 691-2777, 11 am-9 pm

Chili's, 7805 Abercorn St Ste 26, Savannah, GA, 31406, (912) 352-3636, 11 am-10 pm

Beef O'Brady's, 461 Johnny Mercer Blvd, Ste #11, Savannah, GA, 31410, (912) 897-8277, 11 am-11 pm

Godfather's Pizza, 8303 White Bluff Rd, Savannah, GA, 31406, (912) 925-9303,

Longhorn Steakhouse, 7825 Abercorn Expy, Savannah, GA, 31406, (912) 352-4784, 11 am-10 pm

Snellville

Chili's, 1350 Scenic Hwy, Ste 1000, Snellville, GA, 30078, (770) 982-4727, 11 am-10 pm

Ryan's Grill Buffet Bakery, 2380 Wisteria Dr, Snellville, GA, 30078, (770) 979-2434, 10:45 am-9 pm

Romano's Macaroni Grill, 1350 Scenic Hwy, Ste 900, Snellville, GA, 30078, (678) 639-3412, 11 am-10 pm

O'Charley's, 2049 Scenic Hwy N, Snellville, GA, (770) 736-3231, 11 am-10 pm

Longhorn Steakhouse, 2120 Killian Hill Rd, Snellville, GA, 30278, (770) 972-4188, 11 am-10 pm

Golden Corral, 3888 Stone Mtn Hwy, Snellville, GA, 30078, (770) 985-9700, 11 am-9 pm

CiCi's Pizza, 2420 Wisteria Dr, Ste 12, Snellville, GA, 30078, (770) 736-7777, 11 am-9 pm

The Ground Round, 2302 Main St E, Snellville, GA, 30078, (770) 972-3188, 11 am-11 pm

Fuddruckers, 1915 Scenic Hwy North, Snellville, GA, 30078, 11 am-9 pm

Statesboro

Ryan's Grill Buffet Bakery, 806 Hwy 80 East, Statesboro, GA, 30458, (912) 489-9481, 10:45 am-9 pm

Longhorn Steakhouse, 719 Northside Dr E, Statesboro, GA, 30458, (912) 489-5369, 11 am-10 pm

Stockbridge

CiCi's Pizza, 3542 Hwy 138, Ste 214, Stockbridge, GA, 30281, (770) 389-0234, 11 am-9 pm

Golden Corral, 7291 Davidson Pkwy, Stockbridge, GA, 30281, (770) 389-4830, 11 am-9 pm

O'Charley's, 3511 Hwy 138 SE, Stockbridge, GA, (770) 389-4095, 11 am-10 pm

Ryan's Grill Buffet Bakery, 5425 N Henry Blvd, Stockbridge, GA, 30281, (770) 389-9598, 10:45 am-9 pm

Stone Mountain

CiCi's Pizza, 1825 Rockbridge Rd, Stone Mountain, GA, 30087, (678) 476-9399, 11 am-9 pm

Suwanee

Beef O'Brady's, 3590 Old Atlanta Rd, #210, Suwanee, GA, 30024, (770) 886-8221, 11 am-11 pm

Beef O'Brady's, 3463-A Lawrenceville Suwanee Rd, Ste 100, Suwanee, GA, 30024, (678) 546-5644, 11 am-11 pm

CiCi's Pizza, 3255 Lawrenceville-Suwanee Rd, Ste M, Suwanee, GA, 30024, (678) 482-9117, 11 am-9 pm

Cracker Barrel, 75 Gwinco Blvd, Suwanee, GA, 30024, (770) 932-5692, 6 am-10 pm

Thomaston

Chili's, 947 N Church St, Thomaston, GA, 30286, (706) 646-4100, 11 am-10 pm

Thomasville

Beef O'Brady's, 1508 E Jackson St, Thomasville, GA, 31792, (229) 551-9464, 11 am-11 pm

Ryan's Grill Buffet Bakery, 15370 US Hwy 19 S, Thomasville, GA, 31757, (229) 226-5870, 10:45 am-9 pm

Thomson

Ryan's Grill Buffet Bakery, 2217 Harrison Rd, Thomson, GA, 30824, (706) 597-1020, 10:45 am-9 pm

Tifton

CiCi's Pizza, 1909 Hwy 82 W, Ste 4, Tifton, GA, 31794, (229) 556-9873, 11 am-9 pm

Cracker Barrel, 708 US 319 South, Tifton, GA, 31794, (229) 386-4412, 6 am-10 pm

Golden Corral, 190 S Virginia Ave, Tifton, GA, 31794, (229) 382-4121, 11 am-9 pm

Longhorn Steakhouse, 1314 Hwy 82 W, Tifton, GA, 31794, (229) 386-8870, 11 am-10 pm

Tucker

Chili's, 2075 Cooledge Rd, Tucker, GA, 30084, (770) 493-1779, 11 am-10 pm

Fuddruckers, 3953 La Vista Rd, Tucker, GA, 30084, 11 am-9 pm

Longhorn Steakhouse, 4315 Hugh Howell Rd, Tucker, GA, 30084, (770) 939-9842, 11 am-10 pm

O'Charley's, 2039 Crescent Centre Blvd, Tucker, GA, (770) 491-6245, 11 am-10 pm

Union City

Cracker Barrel, 4540 Jonesboro Rd, Union City, GA, 30291, (770) 964-9996, 6 am-10 pm

Valdosta

Hooters, 1854 Clubhouse Dr, Valdosta, GA, 31602, (229) 241-9377, 11 am-midnight

Longhorn Steakhouse, 1110 N St Augustine Rd, Valdosta, GA, 31601, (229) 333-0100, 11 am-10 pm

CiCi's Pizza, 1717 Norman Dr, Valdosta, GA, 31601, (229) 244-2464, 11 am-9 pm

Beef O'Brady's, 3200 N Ashley St, Ste G, Valdosta, GA, 31602, (229) 241-9464, 11 am-11 pm

Ryan's Grill Buffet Bakery, 3286 Inner Perimeter Rd, Valdosta, GA, 31602, (229) 244-4957, 10:45 am-9 pm

Cracker Barrel, 1195 St Augustine Rd, Valdosta, GA, 31601, (229) 244-5258, 6 am-10 pm

Villa Rica

Godfather's Pizza, 95 Liberty Rd, Villa Rica, GA, 30180, (770) 459-1518,

Warner Robins

Cracker Barrel, 2700 Watson Blvd, Warner Robins, GA, 31093, (478) 953-1818, 6 am-10 pm

Fuddruckers, 133 Margie Dr, Warner Robins, GA, 11 am-9 pm

Logan's Roadhouse, 2701 Watson Blvd, Warner Robbins, GA, 31093, (478) 929-0252, 11 am-10 pm

Hooters, 210 Margie Dr, Warner Robins, GA, 31088, (478) 953-7200, 11 am-midnight

Longhorn Steakhouse, 2901 Watson Blvd, Warner Robins, GA, 31093, (478) 971-1203, 11 am-10 pm

Ryan's Grill Buffet Bakery, 1992 Watson Blvd, Warner Robins, GA, 31093, (478) 922-9716, 10:45 am-9 pm

Waycross

Ryan's Grill Buffet Bakery, 2330 Memorial Dr, Waycross, GA, 31501, (912) 338-9562, 10:45 am-9 pm

Winder

Beef O'Brady's, 17 Monroe Hwy, Ste W, Winder, GA, 30680, (770) 867-2890, 11 am-11 pm

Golden Corral, 163 E May St, Winder, GA, 30680, (770) 867-7111, 11 am-9 pm

Woodstock

Chili's, 1460 Towne Lake Pkwy, Woodstock, GA, 30189, (770) 592-7676, 11 am-10 pm

CiCi's Pizza, 12186 Hwy 92, Ste 110, Woodstock, GA, 30188, (770) 592-6885, 11 am-9 pm

Longhorn Steakhouse, 1420 Towne Lake Pkwy, Woodstock, GA, 30189, (770) 924-5494, 11 am-10 pm

O'Charley's, 10009 Hwy 92, Woodstock, GA, (770) 592-7501, 11 am-10 pm

Beef O'Brady's, 4427 Towne Lake Pkwy #200, Woodstock, GA, 30189, (770) 928-2338, 11 am-11 pm

North Carolina

Aberdeen

Golden Corral, 265 Turner St, Aberdeen, NC, 28315, (910) 695-9023, 11 am-9 pm

Albemarle

CiCi's Pizza, 636 NC 24 27 Byp E, Ste 14, Albemarle, NC, 28001, (704) 982-2424, 11 am-9 pm

Fire Mountain, 625 Hwy 24-27 Bypass East, Albemarle, NC, 28001, (704) 983-3395, 10:45 am-9:30 pm

Apex

Chili's, 1120 Be Aver Creek Commons Dr, Apex, NC, 27502, (919) 387-7701, 11 am-10 pm

Arden

Beef O'Brady's, 2625 Hendersonville Rd, Arden, NC, 28704, (828) 684-2295, 11 am-11 pm

Asheboro

CiCi's Pizza, 1337 E Dixie Dr, Asheboro, NC, 27203, (336) 636-5666, 11 am-9 pm

Fire Mountain, 1415 E Dixie Dr, Asheboro, NC, 27203, (336) 625-2441, 10:45 am-9:30 pm

Golden Corral, 1070 E Dixie Dr, Asheboro, NC, 27203, (336) 625-6734, 11 am-9 pm

Asheville

Longhorn Steakhouse, 3 Restaurant Ct, Asheville, NC, 28805, (828) 225-2838, 11 am-10 pm

O'Charley's, 2 Kenilworth Knoll, Asheville, NC,(828) 281-0540, 11 am-10 pm

Ryan's Grill Buffet Bakery, 1000 Brevard Rd, Asheville, NC, 28806, (828) 665-9963, 10:45 am-9 pm

Cracker Barrel, 5 Crowell Rd, Asheville, NC, 28806, (828) 665-2221, 6 am-10 pm

Ryan's Grill Buffet Bakery, 1053 Patton Ave, Asheville, NC, 28806, (828) 258-3761, 10:45 am-9 pm

Cracker Barrel, 34 Tunnel Rd, Asheville, NC, 28805, (828) 350-7531, 6 am-10 pm

Hooters, 518 Kenilworth Dr, Asheville, NC, 28805, (828) 253-4660, 11 am-midnight

Don Pablo's, 4 Tunnel Rd, Asheville, NC, 28805, (828) 252-3900, 11 am-10 pm

CiCi's Pizza, 80 S Tunnel Rd, Ste 40, Asheville, NC, 28805, (828) 298-0010, 11 am-9 pm

Chili's, 253 Tunnel Rd, Asheville, NC, 28805, (828) 252-4999, 11 am-10 pm

Fuddruckers, 130 Charlotte St, Asheville, NC, 28801, 11 am-9 pm

Boone

CiCi's Pizza, 139 New Market Center, Boone, NC, 28607, (828) 266-9688, 11 am-9 pm

Golden Corral, 187 Watauga Village Dr, Boone, NC, 28607, (828) 264-9909, 11 am-9 pm

McAlister's Deli, Trivette Hall/170 Stadium Dr, Boone, NC,(828) 262-2213, 10:30 am-10 pm

Burlington

CiCi's Pizza, 3356 S Church Rd, Burlington, NC, 27215, (336) 584-9596, 11 am-9 pm

O'Charley's, 521 Huffman Mill Rd, Burlington, NC,(336) 584-5652, 11 am-10 pm

Longhorn Steakhouse, 153 Huffman Mill Rd, Burlington, NC, 27215, (336) 586-0082, 11 am-10 pm

Hooters, 3122 Garden Rd, Burlington, NC, 27216, (336) 538-9688, 11 am-midnight

Cracker Barrel, 850 Huffman Mill Rd, Burlington, NC, 27215, (336) 584-3833, 6 am-10 pm

Chili's, 1445 University Dr, Burlington, NC, 27215, (336) 538-2531, 11 am-10 pm

Golden Corral, 3108 Garden Loop, Burlington, NC, 27215, (336) 584-3890, 11 am-9 pm

Cary

Romano's Macaroni Grill, 740 SE Maynard Rd, Cary, NC, 27511, (919) 467-7727, 11 am-10 pm

On the Border, 1102 Walnut St, Cary, NC, 27511, (919) 460-0880, 11 am-10 pm

O'Charley's, 101 Ashville Ave, Cary, NC,(919) 851-9777, 11 am-10 pm

McAlister's Deli, 1361 Kildaire Farm Rd, Cary, NC,(919) 466-8040, 10:30 am-10 pm

Golden Corral, 5707 Dillard Dr, Cary, NC, 27511, (919) 816-0352, 11 am-9 pm

CiCi's Pizza, 683-F Cary Towne Blvd, Ste F, Cary, NC, 27511, (919) 469-9988, 11 am-9 pm

Chili's, 1388 Kildaire Farm Rd, Cary, NC, 27511, (919) 460-7075, 11 am-10 pm

Beef O'Brady's, 1275 NW Maynard Rd, Cary, NC, 27513, (919) 468-9494, 11 am-11 pm

Chapel Hill

McAlister's Deli, 205 E Franklin St, Chapel Hill, NC,(919) 969-1102, 10:30 am-10 pm

Charlotte

Texas Land & Cattle, 517 University Center Blvd, Charlotte, NC, 28262, (704) 503-3830, 11 am-10 pm

O'Charley's, 1920 Sardis Rd N, Charlotte, NC,(704) 841-1656, 11 am-10 pm

McAlister's Deli, 15201 John J DeLny Dr, Charlotte, NC,(704) 542-0727, 10:30 am-10 pm

McAlister's Deli, 4130 Carmel Rd, Charlotte, NC,(704) 540-7199, 10:30 am-10 pm

McAlister's Deli, 9601-A N Tryon St, Charlotte, NC,(704) 595-9993, 10:30 am-10 pm

McAlister's Deli, 8943 S Tryon St, Ste A, Charlotte, NC,(704) 714-5300, 10:30 am-10 pm

Melting Pot, 901 S Kings Dr, Ste 140B, Charlotte, NC, 28204, (704) 334-4400, 5 pm-10:30 pm

O'Charley's, 8140 S Tryon St, Charlotte, NC,(704) 588-2737, 11 am-10 pm

O'Charley's, 8420 University City Blvd, Charlotte, NC,(704) 593-0106, 11 am-10 pm

On the Border, 10710 Providence Rd, Charlotte, NC, 28277, (704) 847-4080, 11 am-10 pm

On the Border, 8315 Northlake Commons Blvd, Charlotte, NC, 28216, (704) 921-1166, 11 am-10 pm

P.F. Changs, 6809-F Phillips Pl Court, Phillips Pl, Charlotte, NC, 28210, (704) 552-6644, 11 am-10 pm

Romano's Macaroni Grill, 8620 Research Dr, Charlotte, NC, 28262, (704) 595-9696, 11 am-10 pm

Romano's Macaroni Grill, 10706 Providence Rd, Charlotte, NC, 28277, (704) 841-2511, 11 am-10 pm

McAlister's Deli, 8046-D Providence Rd, Charlotte, NC,(704) 752-9665, 10:30 am-10 pm

Sullivan's Steakhouse, 1928 S Blvd, Ste 200, Charlotte, NC, 28203, (704) 335-8228, 11 am-11 pm

Golden Corral, 9430 S Blvd, Charlotte, NC, 28273, (704) 643-2345, 11 am-9 pm

Uno Chicago Grill, 401 S Tryon St St 130 First Union Center, Charlotte, NC, 28202, (704) 373-0085, 11 am-12:30 am

R.J Gator's, Chancellor's Park, 8225 University City Blvd, Charlotte, NC, 28213, (704) 599-2808, 11 am-10 pm

Smokey Bones, 8760 Jm Keynes Dr, Charlotte, NC, 28262, (704) 549-8282, 11 am-10 pm

CiCi's Pizza, 3635 Mt Holly-Huntersville Rd, Ste 506, Charlotte, NC, 28216, (704) 971-0411, 11 am-9 pm

Cheesecake Factory, 4400 Sharon Rd Space A, Charlotte, NC, 28211, (704) 770-0076, 11 am-11 pm

Chili's, 5521 Westpark Dr, Charlotte, NC, 28217, (704) 522-1036, 11 am-10 pm

Chili's, 2521 N Sardis Rd, Charlotte, NC, 28227, (704) 847-7849, 11 am-10 pm

Chili's, 8302 Pineville-Matthews Rd, Charlotte, NC, 28226, (704) 543-6265, 11 am-10 pm

Chili's, 500 University Center Blvd, Charlotte, NC, 28262, (704) 510-0626, 11 am-10 pm

Chili's, 8164 S Tryon St, Charlotte, NC, 28273, (704) 583-5490, 11 am-10 pm

Chili's, 8325 Northlake Commons Blvd, Charlotte, NC, 28216, (704) 494-8403, 11 am-10 pm

Chili's, 9730 Rea Rd, Charlotte, NC, 28277, (704) 543-5353, 11 am-10 pm

Logan's Roadhouse, 630 University Center Blvd, Charlotte, NC, 28262, (704) 510-0553, 11 am-10 pm

CiCi's Pizza, 10900 University City Blvd, Ste 13-15, Charlotte, NC, 28213, (704) 510-5595, 11 am-9 pm

Max & Ermas, 8619 JW Clay Blvd, Charlotte, NC,(704) 510-1025, 11 am-11 pm

CiCi's Pizza, 10720 S Tryon St, Ste 1, Charlotte, NC, 28273, (704) 504-0004, 11 am-9 pm

Copeland's, 8630 University Executive Park Dr, Charlotte, NC, 28262, (704) 503-6003, 11 am-10 pm

Cracker Barrel, 3203 S I-85 Service Rd, Charlotte, NC, 28208, (704) 393-2670, 6 am-10 pm

Damon's Grill, 13230 Carowinds Blvd, Charlotte, NC, 28278, (704) 504-1991, 11 am-11 pm

Hooters, 9807 S Blvd, Charlotte, NC, 28273, (704) 643-2044, 11 am-midnight

Longhorn Steakhouse, 700 E Morehead St, Charlotte, NC, 28202, (704) 332-2300, 11 am-10 pm

Longhorn Steakhouse, 8115 Old Mallard Creek Rd, Charlotte, NC, 28262, (704) 921-5971, 11 am-10 pm

Maggiano's, 4400 Sharon Rd #R02, Charlotte, NC, 28211, (704) 916-2300, 11 am-10 pm

CiCi's Pizza, 10707 Park Rd, Ste R, Charlotte, NC, 28210, (704) 341-9303, 11 am-9 pm

Charlotte University

Melting Pot, 230 E WT Harris Blvd, Ste C1, Charlotte University, NC, 28262, (704) 548-2432, 5 pm-10:30 pm

Cherokee

Big Boy, 34 Hwy 441 N, Cherokee, NC, 28719, (828) 497-4590, 6:30 am-10 pm

Clayton

CiCi's Pizza, 905 Town Centre Blvd, Clayton, NC, 27520, (919) 359-0175, 11 am-9 pm

Clemmons

Cracker Barrel, 6420 Sessions Court, Clemmons, NC, 27012, (336) 712-9880, 6 am-10 pm

Clinton

Golden Corral, 206 SE Blvd, Clinton, NC, 28328, (910) 596-0141, 11 am-9 pm

Concord

O'Charley's, 1389 Concord Pkwy, Concord, NC,(704) 785-9864, 11 am-10 pm

On the Border, 8001 Concord Mills Blvd, Concord, NC, 28027, (704) 979-9029, 11 am-10 pm

McAlister's Deli, 8657 Concord Mills Blvd, Concord, NC,(704) 979-0600, 10:30 am-10 pm

Longhorn Steakhouse, 351 Copperfield Blvd, Concord, NC, 28025, (704) 795-1030, 11 am-10 pm

Hooters, 7702 Gateway Ln, Concord, NC, 28027, (704) 979-0130, 11 am-midnight

Fire Mountain, 8601 Concord Mills Blvd, Concord, NC, 28027, (704) 979-1055, 10:45 am-9:30 pm

Dave and Buster's, 8361 Concord Mills Blvd, Concord, NC, 28027, (704) 979-1700, 11 am-midnight

Chili's, 1365 Concord Pkwy N, Concord, NC, 28025, (704) 721-3859, 11 am-10 pm

Cracker Barrel, 7809 Lyles Ln NW, Concord, NC, 28027, (704) 979-0404, 6 am-10 pm

Cracker Barrel, 1175 Copperfield Blvd, NE, Concord, NC, 28025, (704) 792-0277, 6 am-10 pm

Golden Corral, 1540 US Hwy 29 N, Concord, NC, 28025, (704) 782-0044, 11 am-9 pm

Uno Chicago Grill, 8021 Concord Mills Blvd, Concord, NC, 28027, (704) 979-0140, 11 am-12:30 am

Conover

Godfather's Pizza, 1343 Rock Barn Rd, Conover, NC, 28613, (828) 465-5256,

Cornelius

McAlister's Deli, 19930 W Catawba Ave, #150, Cornelius, NC,(704) 896-3354, 10:30 am-10 pm

R.J Gator's, 19707 Liverpool Pkwy, Cornelius, NC, 28031, (704) 892-9600, 11 am-10 pm

Dunn

Cracker Barrel, 1102 E Cumberland St, Dunn, NC, 28334, (910) 892-7814, 6 am-10 pm

Durham

Romano's Macaroni Grill, 4020 Chapel Hill Blvd, Durham, NC, 27707, (919) 489-0313, 11 am-10 pm

Golden Corral, 3800 N Roxboro Rd, Durham, NC, 27704, (919) 477-1226, 11 am-9 pm

On the Border, 4600 Chapel Hill Blvd, Durham, NC, 27707, (919) 493-5092, 11 am-10 pm

Maggiano's, 8030 Renaissance Pkwy, Ste 890, Durham, NC, 27713, (919) 572-0070, 11 am-10 pm

Golden Corral, 5006 Apex Hwy 55, Durham, NC, 27713, (919) 544-2275, 11 am-9 pm

Cracker Barrel, 3703 Hillsborough Rd, Durham, NC, 27705, (919) 309-2888, 6 am-10 pm

CiCi's Pizza, 4600 Chapel Hill Blvd, Durham, NC, 27707, (919) 403-2424, 11 am-9 pm

Chili's, 6917 Fayetteville Rd, Durham, NC, 27713, (919) 572-7878, 11 am-10 pm

Chili's, 4600 Chapel Hill Blvd, Durham, NC, 27707, (919) 489-6699, 11 am-10 pm

Cheesecake Factory, 8030 Renaissance Pkwy, Ste 950, Durham, NC, 27713, (919) 206-4082, 11 am-11 pm

Fuddruckers, 1809 Martin Luther King Pkwy, Durham, NC, 27707, 11 am-9 pm

P.F. Changs, 6801Fayetteville Rd, Renaissance Center at Southpoint, Durham, NC, 27713, (919) 294-3131, 11 am-10 pm

Eden

Golden Corral, 110 N Van Buren Rd, Eden, NC, 27288, (336) 627-0911, 11 am-9 pm

Edenton

Golden Corral, 318 Virginia Rd, Edenton, NC, 27932, (252) 482-4955, 11 am-9 pm

Elizabeth City

Golden Corral, 406 Halstead Blvd, Elizabeth City, NC, 27909, (252) 338-6651, 11 am-9 pm

Fayetteville

Smokey Bones, 1891 Skibo Rd, Fayetteville, NC, 28303, (910) 864-1068, 11 am-10 pm

On the Border, 115 Glensford Dr, Fayetteville, NC, 28314, (910) 487-6690, 11 am-10 pm

O'Charley's, 1498 Skibo Rd, Fayetteville, NC,(910) 826-1583, 11 am-10 pm

Logan's Roadhouse, 1490 Skibo Rd, Fayetteville, NC, 28303, (910) 864-5176, 11 am-10 pm

Fire Mountain, 1470 Skibo Rd, Fayetteville, NC, 28314, (910) 864-0727, 10:45 am-9:30 pm

Hooters, 516 N Mcpherson Church Rd, Fayetteville, NC, 28303, (910) 868-0700, 11 am-midnight

Tony Roma's, 161 Glensford Dr, Fayetteville, NC, 28314, (910) 864-4090, 11 am-10 pm

Golden Corral, 1806 Skibo Rd, Fayetteville, NC, 28303, (910) 868-5868, 11 am-9 pm

Cracker Barrel, 1625 Jim Johnson Rd, Fayetteville, NC, 28301, (910) 323-2025, 6 am-10 pm

CiCi's Pizza, 229 Wwood Shopping Center, Fayetteville, NC, 28314, (910) 868-7333, 11 am-9 pm

CiCi's Pizza, 3811 Ramsey St, Fayetteville, NC, 28311, (910) 323-4000, 11 am-9 pm

Chili's, 635 Cross Creek, Fayetteville, NC, 28303, (910) 864-4363, 11 am-10 pm

Beef O'Brady's, 5540 Camden Rd, Fayetteville, NC, 28306, (910) 860-8000, 11 am-11 pm

Golden Corral, 3901 Ramsey St, Fayetteville, NC, 28311, (910) 482-3800, 11 am-9 pm

Flat Rock

Cracker Barrel, 105 Commercial Blvd, Flat Rock, NC, 28731, (828) 692-5560, 6 am-10 pm

Forest City

Chili's, 128 Sparks Crossing, Forest City, NC, 28043, (828) 286-0008, 11 am-10 pm

Ryan's Grill Buffet Bakery, 115 Ryans Dr, Forest City, NC, 28043, (828) 286-8022, 10:45 am-9 pm

Fort Bragg

Godfather's Pizza, 4802 Reilly Rd, Bldg H, Fort Bragg, NC, 28307, (910) 497-0419,

Fuquay Varina

CiCi's Pizza, 1029 E BRd St, Fuquay Varina, NC, 27526, (919) 557-4929, 11 am-9 pm

Garner

Cracker Barrel, 5199 SR 42 West, Garner, NC, 27529, (919) 661-4044, 6 am-10 pm

Logan's Roadhouse, 1000 Timber Dr E, Garner, NC, 27529, (919) 329-9340, 11 am-10 pm

Chili's, 115 Carillon Dr, Garner, NC, 27529, (919) 771-1700, 11 am-10 pm

Golden Corral, 1504 US Hwy 70 E, Garner, NC, 27529, (919) 772-6603, 11 am-9 pm

Golden Corral, 60 Son-Lan Pkwy, Garner, NC, 27529, (919) 661-1111, 11 am-9 pm

Gastonia

Ryan's Grill Buffet Bakery, 2900 E Franklin Blvd, Gastonia, NC, 28056, (704) 868-8314, 10:45 am-9 pm

R.J Gator's, 3638 E Franklin Blvd, Gastonia, NC, 28054, (704) 823-8400, 11 am-10 pm

On the Border, 2409 E Franklin Blvd, Gastonia, NC, 28054, (704) 866-9601, 11 am-10 pm

O'Charley's, 1601 E Franklin Blvd, Gastonia, NC, (704) 865-6633, 11 am-10 pm

Longhorn Steakhouse, 405 Cox Rd, Gastonia, NC, 28054, (704) 868-3300, 11 am-10 pm

CiCi's Pizza, 3746 E Franklin Blvd, Gastonia, NC, 28056, (704) 823-8636, 11 am-9 pm

Hooters, 3725 E Franklin Blvd, Gastonia, NC, 28054, (704) 823-0025, 11 am-midnight

Golden Corral, 2300 E Franklin Blvd, Gastonia, NC, 28054, (704) 868-7118, 11 am-9 pm

Godfather's Pizza, 3318 S Union Rd, Gastonia, NC, 28056, (704) 867-3508,

Chili's, 3086 E Franklin Blvd, Gastonia, NC, 28056, (704) 867-0276, 11 am-10 pm

Cracker Barrel, 1821 Remount Rd, Gastonia, NC, 28054, (704) 866-7069, 6 am-10 pm

Logan's Roadhouse, 2840 E Franklin Blvd, Gastonia, NC, 28054, (704) 869-9288, 11 am-10 pm

Goldsboro

Chili's, 1013 Sunburst Dr, Goldsboro, NC, 27534, (919) 759-2214, 11 am-10 pm

Logan's Roadhouse, 1011 Sunburst Dr, Goldsboro, NC, 27534, (919) 751-1700, 11 am-10 pm

CiCi's Pizza, 413 N Berkeley Blvd, Goldsboro, NC, 27534, (919) 778-8899, 11 am-9 pm

Ryan's Grill Buffet Bakery, 600 N Berkeley Blvd, Goldsboro, NC, 27534, (919) 778-7773, 10:45 am-9 pm

Greensboro

Logan's Roadhouse, 1300 Bridford Pkwy, Greensboro, NC, 27407, (336) 292-4950, 11 am-10 pm

Hooters, 3030 High Point Rd, Greensboro, NC, 27403, (336) 852-4600, 11 am-midnight

Smokey Bones, 3302 High Pt Rd, Greensboro, NC, 27407, (336) 315-8755, 11 am-10 pm

Romano's Macaroni Grill, 3120 Northline Ave, Greensboro, NC, 27408, (336) 855-0676, 11 am-10 pm

P.F. Changs, 3338 W Friendly Ave, Greensboro, NC, 27410, (336) 291-1302, 11 am-10 pm

O'Charley's, 4505 Landover Rd, Greensboro, NC, (336) 852-5758, 11 am-10 pm

Melting Pot, 2924 Battleground Ave, Ste A, Greensboro, NC, 27408, (336) 545-6233, 5 pm-10:30 pm

Longhorn Steakhouse, 2925 Battleground Ave, Ste A, Greensboro, NC, 27408, (336) 545-3200, 11 am-10 pm

Golden Corral, 2419 Lawndale Dr, Greensboro, NC, 27408, (336) 545-5808, 11 am-9 pm

Chili's, 3024 High Point Rd, Greensboro, NC, 27403, (336) 852-0100, 11 am-10 pm

Golden Corral, 4404 Landview Dr, Greensboro, NC, 27407, (336) 294-8443, 11 am-9 pm

Fuddruckers, 4411 W Wendover Ave, Greensboro, NC, 27407, 11 am-9 pm

Cracker Barrel, 3701 Elmsley Court, Greensboro, NC, 27406, (336) 274-1853, 6 am-10 pm

Cracker Barrel, 4402 Landview Dr, Greensboro, NC, 27407, (336) 294-0911, 6 am-10 pm

CiCi's Pizza, 3379 Battleground Ave, Greensboro, NC, 27410, (336) 545-6440, 11 am-9 pm

CiCi's Pizza, 4648 W Market St, Greensboro, NC, 27407, (336) 297-4008, 11 am-9 pm

Chili's, 1599 New Garden Rd, Greensboro, NC, 27410, (336) 632-1097, 11 am-10 pm

Longhorn Steakhouse, 6012 Landmark Center Blvd, Greensboro, NC, 27407, (336) 855-5300, 11 am-10 pm

Greenville

Golden Corral, 504 SW Greenville Blvd, Greenville, NC, 27834, (252) 756-4412, 11 am-9 pm

Ryan's Grill Buffet Bakery, 3437 S Memorial Dr, Greenville, NC, 27834, (252) 355-3111, 10:45 am-9 pm

O'Charley's, 610 SE Greenville Blvd, Greenville, NC, (252) 756-8570, 11 am-10 pm

McAlister's Deli, 740 SouthE Greenville Blvd, Ste 600, Greenville, NC, (252) 353-8000, 10:30 am-10 pm

Longhorn Steakhouse, 520 SE Greenville Blvd, Greenville, NC, 27858, (252) 830-6100, 11 am-10 pm

Hooters, 316 SW Greenville Blvd, Greenville, NC, 27834, (252) 353-5995, 11 am-midnight

Fuddruckers, 1605 E Firetower Rd, Greenville, NC, 27858, 11 am-9 pm

Cracker Barrel, 710 SW Greenville Blvd, Greenville, NC, 27834, (252) 355-1662, 6 am-10 pm

CiCi's Pizza, 425-D Greenville Blvd SE, Greenville, NC, 27858, (252) 756-4333, 11 am-9 pm

Chili's, 3050 S Evans St, Greenville, NC, 27834, (252) 355-7449, 11 am-10 pm

Logan's Roadhouse, 603 SE Greenville Blvd, Greenville, NC, 27858, (252) 439-4313, 11 am-10 pm

Henderson

Cracker Barrel, 1002 Ruin Creek Rd, Henderson, NC, 27536, (252) 431-9111, 6 am-10 pm

Golden Corral, 103 N Cooper Dr, Henderson, NC, 27536, (252) 438-9500, 11 am-9 pm

Hendersonville

Beef O'Brady's, 825 Spartanburg Hwy #12, Hendersonville, NC, 28792, (828) 694-1110, 11 am-11 pm

O'Charley's, 65 Highland Sq Dr, Hendersonville, NC, (828) 692-4224, 11 am-10 pm

Hickory

Fuddruckers, 1510 8th St Dr Southwest, Hickory, NC, 28602, 11 am-9 pm

O'Charley's, 2360 Hwy 70 SE, Hickory, NC, (828) 431-4777, 11 am-10 pm

Longhorn Steakhouse, 1332 Hwy 70 SE, Hickory, NC, 28602, (828) 322-2944, 11 am-10 pm

Golden Corral, 1053 Lenoir Rhyne Blvd, Hickory, NC, 28602, (828) 324-2122, 11 am-9 pm

Fire Mountain, 2664 Hwy 70 SE, Hickory, NC, 28602, (828) 322-9877, 10:45 am-9:30 pm

Cracker Barrel, 1250 11th St Court SE, Hickory, NC, 28602, (828) 261-0508, 6 am-10 pm

CiCi's Pizza, 2025 US Hwy 70 SE, Hickory, NC, 28602, (828) 345-1444, 11 am-9 pm

Beef O'Brady's, 1423 29th Ave Dr NE, Hickory, NC, 28601, (828) 256-2333, 11 am-11 pm

Hooters, 1211 13th Ave Dr, SE, Hickory, NC, 28602, (828) 324-5700, 11 am-midnight

High Point

Chili's, 920 Mall Loop, High Point, NC, 27262, (336) 889-2505, 11 am-10 pm

CiCi's Pizza, 2705 N Main St, Ste 112, High Point, NC, 27265, (336) 885-3333, 11 am-9 pm

Golden Corral, 1080 Mall Loop Rd, High Point, NC, 27265, (336) 884-1655, 11 am-9 pm

Longhorn Steakhouse, 1540 N Main St, High Point, NC, 27262, (336) 883-7373, 11 am-10 pm

McAlister's Deli, 5870 Samet Dr Ste 119, High Point, NC, (336) 887-1300, 10:30 am-10 pm

Uno Chicago Grill, 3800 Sutton Way, High Point, NC, 27265, (336) 884-4400, 11 am-12:30 am

Huntersville

Longhorn Steakhouse, 16641 Statesville Rd, Huntersville, NC, 28078, (704) 895-3488, 11 am-10 pm

Max & Ermas, 8700 Sam Furr Rd, Huntersville, NC, (704) 895-9994, 11 am-11 pm

Fuddruckers, 16625 Statesville Rd, Huntersville, NC, 28078, 11 am-9 pm

CiCi's Pizza, 14205 Reese Blvd W, Ste E2, Huntersville, NC, 28078, (704) 992-1661, 11 am-9 pm

Chili's, 16632 Stateville Rd, Huntersville, NC, 28078, (704) 895-0133, 11 am-10 pm

O'Charley's, 16609 Statesville Rd, Huntersville, NC, (704) 987-1160, 11 am-10 pm

Jacksonville

Chili's, 1301 Western Blvd, Jacksonville, NC, 28546, (910) 938-4400, 11 am-10 pm

CiCi's Pizza, 1315 A Wern Blvd, Jacksonville, NC, 28546, (910) 478-0606, 11 am-9 pm

Cracker Barrel, 1260 Western Blvd, Jacksonville, NC, 28541, (910) 989-2625, 6 am-10 pm

Fire Mountain, 1345 Western Blvd, Jacksonville, NC, 28546, (910) 347-9555, 10:45 am-9:30 pm

Fuddruckers, 253 Western Ave, Jacksonville, NC, 28546, 11 am-9 pm

Golden Corral, 2055 N Marine Blvd, Jacksonville, NC, 28546, (910) 455-3773, 11 am-9 pm

Hooters, 463 Western Blvd, Jacksonville, NC, 28546, (910) 346-9464, 11 am-midnight

Logan's Roadhouse, 1177 Western Blvd, Jacksonville, NC, 28546, (910) 938-0905, 11 am-10 pm

O'Charley's, 1270 Western Blvd, Jacksonville, NC, (910) 455-8407, 11 am-10 pm

Jonesville

Cracker Barrel, 1717 SR 67 , Jonesville, NC, 28642, (336) 835-6011, 6 am-10 pm

Kannapolis

Logan's Roadhouse, 2431 Wonder Dr, Kannapolis, NC, 28083, (704) 721-0100, 11 am-10 pm

CiCi's Pizza, 1000 Cloverleaf Plz, Kannapolis, NC, 28083, (704) 795-7400, 11 am-9 pm

Ryan's Grill Buffet Bakery, 3000 Cloverleaf Pkwy, Kannapolis, NC, 28083, (704) 784-2105, 10:45 am-9 pm

Kernersville

Fire Mountain, 1180 S Main St, Kernersville, NC, 27284, (336) 996-0456, 10:45 am-9:30 pm

Kinston

Golden Corral, 4468 US 70 W, Kinston, NC, 28504, (252) 523-7585, 11 am-9 pm

Kitty Hawk

Hooters, 4020 N Croatan Hwy, Kitty Hawk, NC, 27949, (252) 255-1808, 11 am-midnight

Knightdale

CiCi's Pizza, 4001 Wide Waters Pkwy, Ste G, Knightdale, NC, 27545, (919) 861-2442, 11 am-9 pm

Laurinburg

Golden Corral, 904 US 401 Bypass N, Laurinburg, NC, 28352, (910) 277-1620, 11 am-9 pm

Lexington

Golden Corral, 1507 cCotton Grove Rd, Lexington, NC, 27292, (336) 357-3383, 11 am-9 pm

Cracker Barrel, 12 Plz Pkwy, Lexington, NC, 27292, (336) 242-1212, 6 am-10 pm

Lincolnton

Ryan's Grill Buffet Bakery, 357 N Generals Blvd, Lincolnton, NC, 28092, (704) 732-8009, 10:45 am-9 pm

Lumberton

Cracker Barrel, 3375 Lackey St, Lumberton, NC, 28360, (910) 738-1481, 6 am-10 pm

Ryan's Grill Buffet Bakery, 220 Jackson Court, Lumberton, NC, 28358, (910) 738-1228, 10:45 am-9 pm

CiCi's Pizza, 3221 Fayetteville Rd, Lumberton, NC, 28358, (910) 608-6400, 11 am-9 pm

Marion

Godfather's Pizza, 3308 Hwy 226 S, Marion, NC, 28752, (828) 652-3422,

Matthews

CiCi's Pizza, 1804 Windsor Square Rd, Ste U-V, Matthews, NC, 28105, (704) 845-5002, 11 am-9 pm

McAlister's Deli, 2217-A Matthew Township Pkwy, Matthews, NC,(704) 846-1711, 10:30 am-10 pm

Fuddruckers, 1643 Matthews-Township Pkwy, Matthews, NC, 28105, 11 am-9 pm

Hooters, 9201 E Independence Blvd, Matthews, NC, 28105, (704) 849-8322, 11 am-midnight

Mebane

Cracker Barrel, 135 Spring Forrest Dr, Mebane, NC, 27302, (919) 304-9932, 6 am-10 pm

Monroe

Chili's, 2861 W Hwy 74, Monroe, NC, 28110, (704) 225-8499, 11 am-10 pm

CiCi's Pizza, 1226 W Roosevelt Blvd, Monroe, NC, 28110, (704) 225-0829, 11 am-9 pm

Logan's Roadhouse, 2336 W Roosevelt Blvd, Monroe, NC, 28110, (704) 225-7240, 11 am-10 pm

McAlister's Deli, 2803 W Hwy 74, Monroe, NC,(704) 283-4700, 10:30 am-10 pm

O'Charley's, 2412 W Roosevelt Blvd, Monroe, NC,(704) 238-8554, 11 am-10 pm

Mooresville

CiCi's Pizza, 168-Z Norman Station Blvd, Mooresville, NC, 28117, (704) 799-8789, 11 am-9 pm

Cracker Barrel, 123 Regency Center Dr, Mooresville, NC, 28117, (704) 660-6314, 6 am-10 pm

Golden Corral, 120 gallery Center Dr, Mooresville, NC, 28117, (704) 660-6622, 11 am-9 pm

Hooters, 132 Gallery Center Dr, Mooresville, NC, 28117, (704) 663-5398, 11 am-midnight

O'Charley's, 604 River Hwy, Mooresville, NC,(704) 799-8571, 11 am-10 pm

Morehead City

Golden Corral, 4060 Arendell St, Morehead City, NC, 28557, (252) 726-1609, 11 am-9 pm

Hooters, 5050 Hwy 70 W, Morehead City, NC, 28557, (252) 727-1803, 11 am-midnight

Morrisville

Cracker Barrel, 955 Airport Blvd, Morrisville, NC, 27560, (919) 463-9222, 6 am-10 pm

Golden Corral, 9601 Chapel Hill Rd, Morrisville, NC, 27560, (919) 481-9037, 11 am-9 pm

Hooters, 1001 Claren Circle, Morrisville, NC, 27560, (919) 469-2900, 11 am-midnight

Mt Airy

Golden Corral, 2226 Rockford St, Mt Airy, NC, 27030, (336) 786-1400, 11 am-9 pm

New Bern

CiCi's Pizza, 3015 Martin Luther King Jr Blvd, New Bern, NC, 28562, (252) 633-4500, 11 am-9 pm

Golden Corral, 400 Hotel Dr, New Bern, NC, 28562, (252) 638-4010, 11 am-9 pm

McAlister's Deli, 2037 S Glenbernie Rd, New Bern, NC,(252) 638-9010, 10:30 am-10 pm

Pineville

Tony Roma's, 9920 Leitner Dr, Pineville, NC, 28134, (704) 544-3302, 11 am-10 pm

Longhorn Steakhouse, 10605 Centrum Pkwy, Pineville, NC, 28134, (704) 543-0484, 11 am-10 pm

Raleigh

O'Charley's, 4380 Fayetteville Rd, Raleigh, NC,(919) 771-0411, 11 am-10 pm

Golden Corral, PO Box 91663, Raleigh, NC, 27675, (919) 840-9691, 11 am-9 pm

Sullivan's Steakhouse, 414 Glenwood Ave, Raleigh, NC, 27603, (919) 833-2888, 11 am-11 pm

Romano's Macaroni Grill, 3421 Sumner Blvd, Raleigh, NC, 27616, (919) 792-2515, 11 am-10 pm

O'Charley's, 8115 Brier Creek Pkwy, Raleigh, NC,(919) 484-4038, 11 am-10 pm

Melting Pot, 3100 Wake Forest Rd, Raleigh, NC, 27609, (919) 878-0477, 5 pm-10:30 pm

McAlister's Deli, 4361 Lassiter at N Hills Ave, Raleigh, NC,(919) 787-9543, 10:30 am-10 pm

Longhorn Steakhouse, 8121 Brier Creek Pkwy, Raleigh, NC, 27617, (919) 484-7669, 11 am-10 pm

Hooters, 4206 Wake Forest Rd, Raleigh, NC, 27609, (919) 850-9882, 11 am-midnight

Uno Chicago Grill, 8401 Brier Creek Pkwy, Raleigh, NC, 27617, (919) 544-6700, 11 am-12:30 am

CiCi's Pizza, 3501 Capital Blvd, Ste 132, Raleigh, NC, 27604, (919) 863-2424, 11 am-9 pm

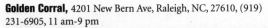

Golden Corral, 4201 New Bern Ave, Raleigh, NC, 27610, (919) 231-6905, 11 am-9 pm

Chili's, 6324 Glenwood Ave, Raleigh, NC, 27612, (919) 571-3600, 11 am-10 pm

P.F. Changs, 4325 Glenwood Ave, Crabtree Valley Mall, Raleigh, NC, 27612, (919) 787-7754, 11 am-10 pm

Chili's, 8341 Brier Creek Pkwy, Raleigh, NC, 27617, (919) 405-7100, 11 am-10 pm

CiCi's Pizza, 7901 Falls of Neuse Rd, Ste 133, Raleigh, NC, 27615, (919) 861-2424, 11 am-9 pm

Cheesecake Factory, 4325 Glenwood Ave, Raleigh, NC, 27612, (919) 781-0050, 11 am-11 pm

Damon's Grill, 1235 Hurricane Alley Way, Raleigh, NC, 27607, (919) 277-7000,

Fuddruckers, 4800 Signet Dr, Raleigh, NC, 27616, 11 am-9 pm

Godfather's Pizza, Term A, 3rd Floor, Airport, Raleigh, NC, 27623, (919) 840-0506,

Golden Corral, 2909 Millbrook Rd, Raleigh, NC, 27604, (919) 872-0500, 11 am-9 pm

Golden Corral, 6129 Glenwood Ave, Raleigh, NC, 27612, (919) 782-4880, 11 am-9 pm

Chili's, 3411 Sumner Blvd, Raleigh, NC, 27616, (919) 792-2545, 11 am-10 pm

Reidsville

Golden Corral, 1566 Freeway Dr, Reidsville, NC, 27320, (336) 616-1960, 11 am-9 pm

Roanoke Rapids

Ryan's Grill Buffet Bakery, 1500 Julian Allsbrook Hwy, Roanoke Rapids, NC, 27870, (252) 535-4266, 10:45 am-9 pm

CiCi's Pizza, 180 Premier Blvd, Roanoke Rapids, NC, 27870, (252) 410-0010, 11 am-9 pm

Cracker Barrel, 1918 Julian RAllsbrook Hwy, Roanoke Rapids, NC, 27870, (252) 535-1747, 6 am-10 pm

Logan's Roadhouse, 200 Premier Blvd, Roanoke Rapids, NC, 27870, (252) 537-1414, 11 am-10 pm

Rocky Mount

Ryan's Grill Buffet Bakery, 1450 Benvenue Rd, Rocky Mount, NC, 27804, (252) 212-1720, 10:45 am-9 pm

Chili's, 1276 Home Depot Plz, Rocky Mount, NC, 27804, 11 am-10 pm

Golden Corral, 921 N Wesleyan Blvd, Rocky Mount, NC, 27804, (252) 972-2043, 11 am-9 pm

CiCi's Pizza, 3022 Sunset Ave, Rocky Mount, NC, 27804, (252) 443-4643, 11 am-9 pm

Roxboro

Golden Corral, 40 Weeks Dr, Roxboro, NC, 27573, (336) 599-1780, 11 am-9 pm

Salisbury

Fire Mountain, 730 S Jake Alexander Blvd, Salisbury, NC, 28147, (704) 639-1811, 10:45 am-9:30 pm

O'Charley's, 123 N Arlington St, Salisbury, NC, (704) 636-9445, 11 am-10 pm

Sanford

Golden Corral, 2618 S Horner Blvd, Sanford, NC, 27330, (919) 775-3295, 11 am-9 pm

Shallotte

Chili's, 104 Shallotte Pkwy, Shallotte, NC, 28470, (910) 755-5033, 11 am-10 pm

Shelby

Golden Corral, 1108 E Dixon Blvd, Shelby, NC, 28152, (704) 481-8283, 11 am-9 pm

Ryan's Grill Buffet Bakery, 1712 E Dixon Blvd, Shelby, NC, 28152, (704) 480-8488, 10:45 am-9 pm

Smithfield

Cracker Barrel, 1109 Industrial Park Dr, Smithfield, NC, 27577, (919) 989-2140, 6 am-10 pm

Golden Corral, 1319 N brightleaf Blvd, Smithfield, NC, 27577, (919) 989-1125, 11 am-9 pm

Ryan's Grill Buffet Bakery, 1273 N Brightleaf Blvd, Smithfield, NC, 27577, (919) 938-3541, 10:45 am-9 pm

CiCi's Pizza, 161 Industrial Park Dr, Smithfield, NC, 27577, (919) 938-2424, 11 am-9 pm

Southern Pines

Chili's, 170 Partner Circle, Southern Pines, NC, 28387, (910) 693-3302, 11 am-10 pm

Southport

Golden Corral, 5059 Southport Supply Rd, Southport, NC, 28461, (910) 457-9425, 11 am-9 pm

Spring Lake

CiCi's Pizza, 237 Skyland Plz, Ste 100, Spring Lake, NC, 28390, (910) 436-2000, 11 am-9 pm

Statesville

Cracker Barrel, 1043 Glenway Dr, Statesville, NC, 28625, (704) 878-0366, 6 am-10 pm

Golden Corral, 195 Turnersburg Hwy, Statesville, NC, 28625, (704) 838-1686, 11 am-9 pm

Hooters, 1026 Glenway Dr, Statesville, NC, 28625, (704) 873-9464, 11 am-midnight

Logan's Roadhouse, 1071 Glenway Dr, Statesville, NC, 28625, (704) 873-3122, 11 am-10 pm

CiCi's Pizza, 1929 E BRd St, Statesville, NC, 28625, (704) 883-9988, 11 am-9 pm

Sylva

Ryan's Grill Buffet Bakery, 374 Walmart Plz, Sylva, NC, 28779, (828) 631-2520, 10:45 am-9 pm

Wake Forest

O'Charley's, 11206 Capital Blvd, Wake Forest, NC,(919) 554-1131, 11 am-10 pm

CiCi's Pizza, 12516-101 Capital Blvd, Wake Forest, NC, 27587, (919) 556-1911, 11 am-9 pm

Washington

Golden Corral, 1424 Carolina Ave, Washington, NC, 27889, (252) 948-0570, 11 am-9 pm

Wilkesboro

Ryan's Grill Buffet Bakery, 1917 US Hwy 421 Business, Wilkesboro, NC, 28697, (336) 838-7926, 10:45 am-9 pm

Wilmington

O'Charley's, 5104 S College Rd, Wilmington, NC,(910) 791-6570, 11 am-10 pm

Golden Corral, 5211 S College Blvd, Wilmington, NC, 28412, (910) 392-7777, 11 am-9 pm

Smokey Bones, 1055 International Dr, Wilmington, NC, 28405, (910) 256-9801, 11 am-10 pm

Romano's Macaroni Grill, 1035 International Dr, Wilmington, NC, 28405, (910) 256-4550, 11 am-10 pm

On the Border, 1128 Military Cutoff Rd, Wilmington, NC, 28405, (910) 509-3065, 11 am-10 pm

O'Charley's, 6 Van Campen Blvd, Wilmington, NC,(910) 796-8110, 11 am-10 pm

McAlister's Deli, 740 S College Rd, Wilmington, NC,(910) 799-1229, 10:30 am-10 pm

Hooters, 5112 Market St, Wilmington, NC, 28405, (910) 791-0799, 11 am-midnight

Golden Corral, 5130 New Centre Dr, Wilmington, NC, 28403, (910) 392-1984, 11 am-9 pm

Cracker Barrel, 21 Van Campen Blvd, Wilmington, NC, 28403, (910) 794-1162, 6 am-10 pm

CiCi's Pizza, 341 S College Rd (NC Hwy 132), Ste 8A, Wilmington, NC, 28403, (910) 332-0281, 11 am-9 pm

Chili's, 819 S College Rd, Wilmington, NC, 28403, (910) 313-1477, 11 am-10 pm

Longhorn Steakhouse, 925 International Dr, Wilmington, NC, 28405, (910) 509-1550, 11 am-10 pm

Wilson

Golden Corral, 1711 Raleigh Rd Pkwy W, Wilson, NC, 27893, (252) 291-1887, 11 am-9 pm

Chili's, 2823 Raleigh Rd W, Wilson, NC, 27896, (252) 246-0069, 11 am-10 pm

CiCi's Pizza, 175 Raleigh Rd W, Wilson, NC, 27893, (252) 291-5836, 11 am-9 pm

Cracker Barrel, 5006 Hayes Pl West, Wilson, NC, 27896, (252) 234-7600, 6 am-10 pm

Winston-Salem

McAlister's Deli, 4926 Old Country Club Rd, Winston-Salem, NC,(336) 765-1121, 10:30 am-10 pm

Romano's Macaroni Grill, 1915 Hampton Inn Ct, Winston-Salem, NC, 27103, (336) 765-6676, 11 am-10 pm

Fuddruckers, 100 Haynes Square Circle, Winston-Salem, NC, 27106, 11 am-9 pm

CiCi's Pizza, 2857 Reynolda Rd, Winston-Salem, NC, 27106, (336) 723-7273, 11 am-9 pm

McAlister's Deli, 368 E Hanes Mill Rd, Winston-Salem, NC,(336) 377-3005, 10:30 am-10 pm

Fire Mountain, 333 Summit Square, Winston-Salem, NC, 27105, (336) 377-2533, 10:45 am-9:30 pm

Chili's, 100 Stratford Commons Ct, Winston-Salem, NC, 27103, (336) 760-1500, 11 am-10 pm

Chili's, 348 E Hanes Mill Rd, Winston-Salem, NC, 27105, (336) 377-2310, 11 am-10 pm

Golden Corral, 4965 University Pkwy, Winston-Salem, NC, 27106, (336) 767-3505, 11 am-9 pm

Golden Corral, 180 hanes mall Circle, Winston-Salem, NC, 27103, (336) 760-8040, 11 am-9 pm

Hooters, 120 Hanes Sq Circle, Winston-Salem, NC, 27103, (336) 760-4300, 11 am-midnight

Longhorn Steakhouse, 955 Hanes Mall Blvd, Winston-Salem, NC, 27103, (336) 760-1700, 11 am-10 pm

O'Charley's, 300 E Hanes Mill Rd, Winston-Salem, NC,(336) 377-2350, 11 am-10 pm

O'Charley's, 150 Hanes Mall Circle, Winston-Salem, NC,(336) 765-9960, 11 am-10 pm

South Carolina

Aiken

O'Charley's, 168 S Aiken Ln, Aiken, SC,(803) 644-8874, 11 am-10 pm

Ryan's Grill Buffet Bakery, 1953 Whiskey Rd, Aiken, SC, 29803, (803) 648-2460, 10:45 am-9 pm

Anderson

O'Charley's, 3723 Clemson Blvd, Anderson, SC,(864) 224-1417, 11 am-10 pm

Hooters, 112 Interstate Blvd, Anderson, SC, 29621, (864) 332-0400, 11 am-midnight

Ryan's Grill Buffet Bakery, 3517 Clemson Blvd, Anderson, SC, 29621, (864) 226-7335, 10:45 am-9 pm

Longhorn Steakhouse, 3730 Clemson Blvd, Anderson, SC, 29621, (864) 224-2100, 11 am-10 pm

Logan's Roadhouse, 3402 Clemson Blvd, Anderson, SC, 29621, (864) 261-7366, 11 am-10 pm

Fuddruckers, 100 Destination Blvd, Anderson, SC, 29621, 11 am-9 pm

Cracker Barrel, 126 Interstate Blvd, Anderson, SC, 29621, (864) 225-4566, 6 am-10 pm

CiCi's Pizza, 3128 N Main St, Anderson, SC, 29621, (864) 222-2595, 11 am-9 pm

Chili's, 3801 Clemson Blvd, Anderson, SC, 29621, (864) 231-9082, 11 am-10 pm

Ryan's Grill Buffet Bakery, 203 28 By-Pass, Anderson, SC, 29624, (864) 225-7723, 10:45 am-9 pm

Golden Corral, 3546 Clemson Blvd, Anderson, SC, 29621, (864) 332-8032, 11 am-9 pm

Beaufort

Beef O'Brady's, 41-B Robert Smalls Pkwy, Beaufort, SC, 29902, (843) 379-8333, 11 am-11 pm

Golden Corral, 122 Robert Small Pkwy, Beaufort, SC, 29906, (843) 525-9896, 11 am-9 pm

Bluffton

Golden Corral, 1196 Fording Island Rd, Bluffton, SC, 29910, (843) 836-1905, 11 am-9 pm

Charleston

O'Charley's, 2126 Henry Tecklenburg Dr, Charleston, SC, (843) 763-9568, 11 am-10 pm

Bubba Gump Shrimp, 99 S Market St, Charleston, SC, 29401, (843) 723-5665, 11 am-10 pm

Ryan's Grill Buffet Bakery, 829 St Andrews Blvd, Charleston, SC, 29407, (843) 571-5685, 10:45 am-9 pm

CiCi's Pizza, 630 Skylark Rd, Ste N, Charleston, SC, 29407, (843) 556-2500, 11 am-9 pm

Columbia

McAlister's Deli, 4710-A Forest Dr, Columbia, SC, (803) 790-5995, 10:30 am-10 pm

Longhorn Steakhouse, 2760 Decker Blvd, Columbia, SC, 29206, (803) 736-7464, 11 am-10 pm

Longhorn Steakhouse, 171 Harbison Blvd, Columbia, SC, 29212, (803) 732-2482, 11 am-10 pm

Fire Mountain, 1304 Bower Pkwy, Columbia, SC, 29212, (803) 732-3603, 10:45 am-9:30 pm

Longhorn Steakhouse, 902-A Gervais St, Columbia, SC, 29201, (803) 254-5100, 11 am-10 pm

McAlister's Deli, 300 Columbiana Dr, Columbia, SC, (803) 781-4550, 10:30 am-10 pm

McAlister's Deli, 119 Sparkleberry Ln, Columbia, SC, (803) 788-7600, 10:30 am-10 pm

Melting Pot, 1410 Colonial Life Blvd, Columbia, SC, 29210, (803) 731-8500, 5 pm-10:30 pm

O'Charley's, 1000 Bower Pkwy, Columbia, SC, (803) 407-7190, 11 am-10 pm

O'Charley's, 10136 Two Notch Rd, Unit 105, Columbia, SC, (803) 699-1192, 11 am-10 pm

Romano's Macaroni Grill, 148 Harbison Blvd, Columbia, SC, 29212, (803) 781-2313, 11 am-10 pm

Smokey Bones, 410 Columbiana Dr, Columbia, SC, 29212, (803) 749-6760, 11 am-10 pm

Hooters, 7711 Two Notch Rd, Columbia, SC, 29223, (803) 419-3456, 11 am-midnight

Ryan's Grill Buffet Bakery, 10052 Two Notch Rd, Columbia, SC, 29223, (803) 462-0247, 10:45 am-9 pm

Cracker Barrel, 2300 Legrand Rd, Columbia, SC, 29223, (803) 699-5389, 6 am-10 pm

Fuddruckers, 1801 Bush River Rd, Columbia, SC, 29210, 11 am-9 pm

Beef O'Brady's, 2742 N Lake Dr, #104, Columbia, SC, 29212, (803) 781-5656, 11 am-11 pm

Beef O'Brady's, 4561 Hard Scrabble Rd, Columbia, SC, 29229, (803) 699-9687, 11 am-11 pm

CiCi's Pizza, 141-A Pelham Dr, Columbia, SC, 29209, (803) 776-8900, 11 am-9 pm

Cracker Barrel, 2208 Bush River Rd, Columbia, SC, 29210, (803) 731-0672, 6 am-10 pm

Damon's Grill, 900 Senate St, Columbia, SC, 29201, (803) 758-5880, 11 am-11 pm

El Chico Café, 1728 Bush River Rd, Columbia, SC, 29210, (803) 772-0770, 11 am-10 pm

Hooters, 5195 Fernandina Rd, Columbia, SC, 29212, (803) 407-9464, 11 am-midnight

Fire Mountain, 7550 Garner's Ferry Rd, Columbia, SC, 29209, (803) 695-5359, 10:45 am-9:30 pm

Godfather's Pizza, 1714 BRd River Rd, Columbia, SC, 29210, (803) 731-5350,

Golden Corral, 5300 Forest Dr, Columbia, SC, 29206, (803) 787-4446, 11 am-9 pm

CiCi's Pizza, 6120 St Andrews Rd, Columbia, SC, 29212, (803) 750-5900, 11 am-9 pm

Conway

Ryan's Grill Buffet Bakery, 2904 Church St, Conway, SC, 29526, (843) 365-4664, 10:45 am-9 pm

Easley

Ryan's Grill Buffet Bakery, 6410 Calhoun Memorial Hwy, Easley, SC, 29640, (864) 859-0627, 10:45 am-9 pm

Florence

Golden Corral, 880 S Irby St, Florence, SC, 29501, (843) 676-9545, 11 am-9 pm

Ryan's Grill Buffet Bakery, 1622 W Palmetto St, Florence, SC, 29501, (843) 667-8471, 10:45 am-9 pm

Cracker Barrel, 1824 W Lucas St, Florence, SC, 29501, (843) 662-9023, 6 am-10 pm

CiCi's Pizza, 1945 W Palmetto St, Florence, SC, 29501, (843) 413-0600, 11 am-9 pm

Ft. Mill

Cracker Barrel, 295 Carowinds Blvd, Ft. Mill, SC, 29708, (803) 802-7477, 6 am-10 pm

Beef O'Brady's, 940 Market St, #110, Ft. Mill, SC, 29708, (803) 548-7878, 11 am-11 pm

Godfather's Pizza, 135 Sutton Ridge Ln, Ft. Mill, SC, 29708, (803) 802-7340,

Gaffney

Cracker Barrel, 8 Factory Shops Blvd, Gaffney, SC, 29341, (864) 489-3350, 6 am-10 pm

Ryan's Grill Buffet Bakery, 1521 W Floyd Baker Blvd, Gaffney, SC, 29341, (864) 206-0062, 10:45 am-9 pm

Georgetown

Ryan's Grill Buffet Bakery, 1120 N Fraser, Georgetown, SC, 29440, (843) 527-1423, 10:45 am-9 pm

Goose Creek

Godfather's Pizza, 429 St James Ave, Goose Creek, SC, 29445, (843) 797-8393,

Greenville

McAlister's Deli, 1401-A Woodruff Rd, Greenville, SC, (864) 286-8680, 10:30 am-10 pm

McAlister's Deli, 535-A Congaree Rd, Greenville, SC, (864) 679-3354, 10:30 am-10 pm

Ryan's Grill Buffet Bakery, 1255 Woodruff Rd, Greenville, SC, 29607, (864) 329-9280, 10:45 am-9 pm

O'Charley's, 775 Haywood Rd, Greenville, SC, (864) 297-6267, 11 am-10 pm

P.F. Changs, 1127 Woodruff Rd, Greenville, SC, 29607, (864) 297-0589, 11 am-10 pm

Romano's Macaroni Grill, 105 E Beacon Dr, Greenville, SC, 29615, (864) 675-6676, 11 am-10 pm

Ryan's Grill Buffet Bakery, 6124 White Horse Rd, Greenville, SC, 29611, (864) 269-3711, 10:45 am-9 pm

Melting Pot, 475-5 Haywood Rd, Greenville, SC, 29607, (864) 297-5035, 5 pm-10:30 pm

McAlister's Deli, 1708 B Augusta St, Greenville, SC, (864) 232-8933, 10:30 am-10 pm

Ryan's Grill Buffet Bakery, 2426 Laurens Rd, Greenville, SC, 29607, (864) 288-0841, 10:45 am-9 pm

On the Border, 74 Beacon Dr, Greenville, SC, 29615, (864) 234-0012, 11 am-10 pm

Logan's Roadhouse, 53 Beacon Dr, Greenville, SC, 29615, (864) 213-9444, 11 am-10 pm

Hooters, 2401 Laurens, Greenville, SC, 29607, (864) 987-9464, 11 am-midnight

Fuddruckers, 1147 Woodruff Rd, Greenville, SC, 29607, 11 am-9 pm

Don Pablo's, 741 Haywood Rd, Greenville, SC, 29607, (864) 627-8550, 11 am-10 pm

Cracker Barrel, 21 Old Country Rd, Greenville, SC, 29607, (864) 297-3847, 6 am-10 pm

CiCi's Pizza, 3216 W Blue Ridge Dr, Greenville, SC, 29611, (864) 220-1919, 11 am-9 pm

CiCi's Pizza, 583 Haywood Rd, Ste 503, Greenville, SC, 29607, (864) 675-9277, 11 am-9 pm

Chili's, 1209 Woodruff Rd, Greenville, SC, 29607, (864) 297-0263, 11 am-10 pm

Chili's, 490 Haywood Rd, Greenville, SC, 29607, (864) 281-0547, 11 am-10 pm

Longhorn Steakhouse, 30 Orchard Park Dr, Ste E, Greenville, SC, 29615, (864) 297-7600, 11 am-10 pm

Greenwood

Ryan's Grill Buffet Bakery, 1703 By-Pass NE, Greenwood, SC, 29646, (864) 229-1145, 10:45 am-9 pm

O'Charley's, 452 Bypass 72 NW, Greenwood, SC, (864) 227-0272, 11 am-10 pm

McAlister's Deli, 529 Bypass 72 NW, Greenwood, SC, (864) 943-3354, 10:30 am-10 pm

Cracker Barrel, 101 Commons Dr, Greenwood, SC, 29649, (864) 229-9026, 6 am-10 pm

Beef O'Brady's, 521-1 A Bypass 72 NW, Greenwood, SC, 29649, (864) 227-2333, 11 am-11 pm

Chili's, 501 Bypass 72 NW, Greenwood, SC, 29649, (864) 229-4052, 11 am-10 pm

Greer

Ryan's Grill Buffet Bakery, 1501 W Poinsett, Greer, SC, 29650, (864) 877-1869, 10:45 am-9 pm

Hilton Head

Fuddruckers, 32 Shelter Cove Center Bldg A, Hilton Head, SC, 29938, 11 am-9 pm

Longhorn Steakhouse, 841 Hwy 278, Hilton Head, SC, 29928, (843) 686-4056, 11 am-10 pm

Tony Roma's, 840 William Hilton Pkwy, Hilton Head, SC, 29928, (843) 842-4825, 11 am-10 pm

Johns Island

Godfather's Pizza, 3622 Savannah Hwy, Johns Island, SC, 29414, (843) 556-4207,

Lancaster

Ryan's Grill Buffet Bakery, 1502 SC Hwy 9 Bypass West, Lancaster, SC, 29720, (803) 285-7926, 10:45 am-9 pm

Laurens

Ryan's Grill Buffet Bakery, 904 E Main St, Laurens, SC, 29360, (864) 984-8088, 10:45 am-9 pm

Lexington

Godfather's Pizza, 815 N Lake Dr, Lexington, SC, 29072, (803) 808-9750,

McAlister's Deli, 5175 Sunset Blvd, Lexington, SC, (803) 951-3332, 10:30 am-10 pm

O'Charley's, 5595 Sunset Blvd, Lexington, SC, (803) 356-4220, 11 am-10 pm

Ryan's Grill Buffet Bakery, 5579 Sunset Blvd, Lexington, SC, 29072, (803) 996-1442, 10:45 am-9 pm

Uno Chicago Grill, 5304 Sunset Blvd Hwy 378, Lexington, SC, 29072, (803) 359-3888, 11 am-12:30 am

Mt. Pleasant

On the Border, 1875 Hwy 17 North, Mt. Pleasant, SC, 29464, (843) 881-7944, 11 am-10 pm

CiCi's Pizza, 1501 N Hwy 17, Ste J, Mt. Pleasant, SC, 29464, (843) 216-2122, 11 am-9 pm

Longhorn Steakhouse, 1845 Hwy 17 N, Mt. Pleasant, SC, 29464, (843) 881-7231, 11 am-10 pm

McAlister's Deli, 644-A Long Point Rd, Mt. Pleasant, SC,(843) 284-2288, 10:30 am-10 pm

Murrells Inlet

Cracker Barrel, 1303 Tadlock Dr, Murrells Inlet, SC, 29576, (843) 357-4372, 6 am-10 pm

Hooters, 852 Mall Dr, Murrells Inlet, SC, 29576, (843) 357-9666, 11 am-midnight

Myrtle Beach

Golden Corral, 868 Oak Forest Ln, Myrtle Beach, SC, 29577, (843) 626-2300, 11 am-9 pm

McAlister's Deli, 1760 Pine Island Rd Ste 105, Myrtle Beach, SC,(843) 286-1400, 10:30 am-10 pm

Uno Chicago Grill, 1202 Celebrity Circle, BRdway at the Beach, Myrtle Beach, SC, 29577, (843) 626-8665, 11 am-12:30 am

Tony Roma's, 1317 Celebrity Circle, Myrtle Beach, SC, 29577, (843) 448-7427, 11 am-10 pm

Smokey Bones, 1218 N Retail Ct, Myrtle Beach, SC, 29577, (843) 448-1080, 11 am-10 pm

Melting Pot, 5001 N Kings Hwy #104, Myrtle Beach, SC, 29577, (843) 692-9003, 5 pm-10:30 pm

McAlister's Deli, 1000 S Commons Blvd, Ste 5, Myrtle Beach, SC,(843) 286-2222, 10:30 am-10 pm

Longhorn Steakhouse, 1180 Oak Forrest Ln, Myrtle Beach, SC, 29577, (843) 839-3310, 11 am-10 pm

Logan's Roadhouse, 1136 Oak Forest Dr, Myrtle Beach, SC, 29577, (843) 839-4666, 11 am-10 pm

Hooters, 3901 N Kings Hwy, Myrtle Beach, SC, 29577, (843) 626-3467, 11 am-midnight

Hooters, 10133 N Kings Hwy, Myrtle Beach, SC, 29572, (843) 272-3739, 11 am-midnight

Godfather's Pizza, 608 S Kings Hwy, Myrtle Beach, SC, 29577, (843) 626-3300,

Fuddruckers, 10435 N King's Hwy, Myrtle Beach, SC, 29572, 11 am-9 pm

Fuddruckers, 2101 N King's Hwy, Myrtle Beach, SC, 29577, 11 am-9 pm

Damon's Grill, 2985 S Ocean Blvd, Myrtle Beach, SC, 29577, (843) 626-8000, 11 am-10 pm

Cracker Barrel, 1208 N Retail Court, Myrtle Beach, SC, 29577, (843) 916-8241, 6 am-10 pm

CiCi's Pizza, 3553 Ngate Rd, Myrtle Beach, SC, 29577, (843) 294-2121, 11 am-9 pm

Beef O'Brady's, 3689 Renee Dr, Myrtle Beach, SC, 29579, (843) 236-7761, 11 am-11 pm

Beef O'Brady's, 8703 Hwy 17 Byp S, #B-2 & 3, Myrtle Beach, SC, 29575, (843) 215-6523, 11 am-11 pm

Golden Corral, 10600 Kings Rd, Myrtle Beach, SC, 29572, (843) 449-0300, 11 am-9 pm

North Augusta

Fire Mountain, 1275 Knox Ave, North Augusta, SC, 29841, (803) 510-0140, 10:45 am-9:30 pm

North Charleston

Cracker Barrel, 7351 Mazyck Rd, North Charleston, SC, 29406, (843) 553-4232, 6 am-10 pm

Godfather's Pizza, 8976 University Blvd, North Charleston, SC, 29405, (843) 797-8568,

Ryan's Grill Buffet Bakery, 7321 Rivers Ave, North Charleston, SC, 29406, (843) 553-9693, 10:45 am-9 pm

Hooters, 2171 Northwoods Blvd, North Charleston, SC, 29406, (843) 824-8661, 11 am-midnight

Longhorn Steakhouse, 7258 Rivers Ave, North Charleston, SC, 29406, (843) 863-0310, 11 am-10 pm

O'Charley's, 2150 Northwoods Blvd, North Charleston, SC,(843) 824-2365, 11 am-10 pm

Smokey Bones, 7250 Rivers Ave, North Charleston, SC, 29405, (843) 572-3420, 11 am-10 pm

North Myrtle Beach

Hooters, 1211 Hwy 17 No, North Myrtle Beach, SC, 29582, (843) 280-9850, 11 am-midnight

Logan's Roadhouse, 4511 Hwy 17 S, North Myrtle Beach, SC, 29582, (843) 272-3435, 11 am-10 pm

Ryan's Grill Buffet Bakery, 3607 Hwy 17, North Myrtle Beach, SC, 29582, (843) 272-1051, 10:45 am-9 pm

Damon's Grill, 4810 Hwy 17 South, North Myrtle Beach, SC, 29582, (843) 272-5107, 11 am-9 pm

Cracker Barrel, 4835 Hwy 17 South, North Myrtle Beach, SC, 29582, (843) 361-2221, 6 am-10 pm

Orangeburg

Ryan's Grill Buffet Bakery, 2580 N Rd, Orangeburg, SC, 29118, (803) 534-6605, 10:45 am-9 pm

Cracker Barrel, 699 Citadel Rd, Orangeburg, SC, 29118, (803) 536-4773, 6 am-10 pm

Piedmont

Cracker Barrel, 591 Hwy 183, Piedmont, SC, 29673, (864) 220-9232, 6 am-10 pm

Rock Hill

McAlister's Deli, 335 Herlong Ave, Ste 20, Rock Hill, SC,(803) 980-1717, 10:30 am-10 pm

O'Charley's, 2265 Cross Pointe Dr, Rock Hill, SC,(803) 329-4530, 11 am-10 pm

McAlister's Deli, 735 Addison Ave, Rock Hill, SC, (803) 329-0042, 10:30 am-10 pm

Longhorn Steakhouse, 2255 Cross Pointe Dr, Rock Hill, SC, 29730, (803) 980-6255, 11 am-10 pm

Hooters, 1423 Riverchase Blvd, Rock Hill, SC, 29732, (803) 980-4300, 11 am-midnight

Cracker Barrel, 2140 Manna Court, Rock Hill, SC, 29730, (803) 327-6141, 6 am-10 pm

CiCi's Pizza, 1807 Cherry Rd, #163-165, Rock Hill, SC, 29732, (803) 324-3433, 11 am-9 pm

Chili's, 630 Tinsley Way, Rock Hill, SC, 29730, (803) 980-8334, 11 am-10 pm

Beef O'Brady's, 1807 Cherry Rd, Rock Hill, SC, 29732, (803) 980-2627, 11 am-11 pm

Golden Corral, 1031 N Anderson Rd, Rock Hill, SC, 29730, (803) 328-0327, 11 am-9 pm

Ryan's Grill Buffet Bakery, 2367 D Ave Lyle Blvd, Rock Hill, SC, 29731, (803) 327-3200, 10:45 am-9 pm

Santee

Cracker Barrel, 250 Britain St, Santee, SC, 29142, (803) 854-3020, 6 am-10 pm

Seneca

Ryan's Grill Buffet Bakery, 1616 Sandifer Rd, Seneca, SC, 29678, (864) 888-4204, 10:45 am-9 pm

Simpsonville

Ryan's Grill Buffet Bakery, 3940 Grandview Dr, Simpsonville, SC, 29680, (864) 963-1290, 10:45 am-9 pm

O'Charley's, 671 Fairview Rd, Simpsonville, SC, (864) 228-3681, 11 am-10 pm

Beef O'Brady's, 404 Harrison Bridge Rd, #A, Simpsonville, SC, 29680, (864) 967-8394, 11 am-11 pm

Cracker Barrel, 3954 Grandview Dr, Simpsonville, SC, 29680, (864) 967-4881, 6 am-10 pm

Spartanburg

Fuddruckers, 1509 Reidville Rd, Spartanburg, SC, 29301, 11 am-9 pm

O'Charley's, 106 Blackstock Rd, Spartanburg, SC, (864) 595-4011, 11 am-10 pm

McAlister's Deli, 150 Dorman Centre Rd, Ste B, Spartanburg, SC, (864) 595-0550, 10:30 am-10 pm

Golden Corral, 1492 W O Ezell Blvd, Spartanburg, SC, 29301, (864) 595-7011, 11 am-9 pm

Fire Mountain, 151 Dorman Center Dr, Spartanburg, SC, 29301, (864) 576-7398, 10:45 am-9:30 pm

Cracker Barrel, 9021 Fairforest Rd, Spartanburg, SC, 29301, (864) 576-6949, 6 am-10 pm

CiCi's Pizza, 150 E Blackstock Rd, Ste D, Spartanburg, SC, 29301, (864) 576-2277, 11 am-9 pm

Fire Mountain, 2255 E Main St, Spartanburg, SC, 29307, (864) 579-7401, 10:45 am-9:30 pm

Summerville

Ryan's Grill Buffet Bakery, 1314 N Main St, Summerville, SC, 29483, (843) 871-7600, 10:45 am-9 pm

Beef O'Brady's, 975 Bacons Bridge Rd, Ste 148, Summerville, SC, 29485, (843) 875-2233, 11 am-11 pm

CiCi's Pizza, 10150 Dorchester Rd, Unit 10/20, Summerville, SC, 29485, (843) 871-2499, 11 am-9 pm

Godfather's Pizza, 2908 W 5th N St, Summerville, SC, 29483, (843) 873-0286,

Logan's Roadhouse, 211 Azalea Square Blvd, Summerville, SC, 29483, (843) 851-8666, 11 am-10 pm

McAlister's Deli, 400-A Azalea Square Blvd, Summerville, SC, (843) 376-0116, 10:30 am-10 pm

Sumter

Golden Corral, 2385 Walmart Blvd, Sumter, SC, 29150, (803) 905-3190, 11 am-9 pm

CiCi's Pizza, 1338 BRd St, Ste 160, Sumter, SC, 29150, (803) 905-5080, 11 am-9 pm

Fire Mountain, 1390 BRd St, Sumter, SC, 29150, (803) 469-6000, 10:45 am-9:30 pm

Surfside Beach

Ryan's Grill Buffet Bakery, 8671 Hwy17 Bypass, Surfside Beach, SC, 29575, (843) 215-0878, 10:45 am-9 pm

Taylors

Fuddruckers, 6100 Wade Hampton Blvd, Taylors, SC, 29687, 11 am-9 pm

Walterboro

Cracker Barrel, 59 Cane Branch Rd, Walterboro, SC, 29488, (843) 538-7800, 6 am-10 pm

West Columbia

Ryan's Grill Buffet Bakery, 1707 Charleston Hwy, West Columbia, SC, 29169, (803) 796-2728, 10:45 am-9 pm